U.S. Foreign Policy

Steven W. Hook
Kent State University

THE PARADOX OF WORLD POWER

CQ PRESS

A Division of Congressional Quarterly Inc.
Washington, D.C.

CQ Press
1255 22nd Street, N.W., Suite 400
Washington, D.C. 20037

202-729-1900; toll-free: 1-866-4CQ-PRESS (1-866-427-7737)

www.cqpress.com

Cover design by Archeographics
Color maps by International Mapping Associates

Printed and bound in the United States of America

08 07 06 05 04   5 4 3 2 1

♾ The paper used in this publication exceeds the requirements of the American National
Standard for Information Sciences—Permanence of Paper for Printed Library Materials,
ANSI Z39.48-1992.

Library of Congress Cataloging-in-Publication Data

Hook, Steven W.
    U.S. foreign policy : the paradox of world power / Steven W. Hook.
        p. cm.
    Includes bibliographical references and index.
    ISBN 1-56802-330-8 (pbk. : alk. paper)
    1. United States—Foreign relations. 2. United States—Foreign relations—2001-
3. United States—Foreign relations—Decision making. 4. Balance of power. I. Title.

E183.7.H66 2005
327.73—dc22

                                                                2004020094

*To my family, students, and those on
the front lines of U.S. foreign policy*

Brief Contents

Contents

PART I   The Setting of U.S. Foreign Policy

PART II   Inside-Out: Governmental Sources of Foreign Policy

PART IV Policy Domains

10 National Security and Defense Policy 293

11 Economic Statecraft 329

Figures and Tables

Figures

Tables

Boxes

Maps

(See color map insert following the Preface.)

Preface

There has never been a more crucial time than today to study the formulation and conduct of U.S. foreign policy. The United States stands at the start of the twenty-first century as the world's most powerful and most embattled country, with mounting challenges on several fronts. How American foreign-policy makers respond to these issues and problems will dictate the course of the rest of the century for the United States and world politics as a whole. The outcome is anything but certain.

The challenges facing the United States will not be easy to resolve. The nation currently struggles to maintain its competitive edge in the world economy: it produces more goods and services than any other country, but it is at the same time accumulating trade deficits and a national debt of unprecedented scale. Several years after the attacks of September 11, 2001, U.S. military forces remain engaged in an open-ended "war on terrorism" that has produced more casualties and physical destruction than the attacks that led the George W. Bush administration to declare such a war. Although the international community offered its support to the United States following September 11, the preventive invasion of Iraq in 2003, the failure of U.S. forces to find weapons of mass destruction in that country, and the human rights abuses committed by U.S. troops at the Abu Ghraib prison and other Iraqi jails led many foreign leaders to question U.S. motives and policies. Surveys find the United States to be widely distrusted and feared overseas, even by the citizens of its closest allies.

This estrangement did not begin with Bush's arrival in the White House in January 2001 nor with the al Qaeda attacks nine months later. Rather, it began a decade earlier, with the collapse of the Soviet Union. After the United States became the world's lone superpower, its leaders could not agree on the purpose the nation's hard-won primacy should serve. While President Bill Clinton adopted global engagement as a grand strategy, the Republican-controlled Congress slashed international programs and rejected a variety of treaties and commitments. This impasse prevented the restructuring of U.S. foreign-policy institutions to reflect the changes of the post–cold war era. Liberals and conservatives, despite their ideological differences, had one thing in common: a growing reliance on financial contributions from political action committees to fund their perpetual reelection campaigns. Such considerations further clouded their judgment regarding the nation's future role in world politics.

In the polarized political climate of the 1990s, many Americans felt alienated and cynical toward their own government and were uninterested in world affairs. They registered little concern as ethnic conflicts erupted around the world, scientific evidence revealed the worrisome extent of global warming, and the AIDS epidemic swept across developing nations. Media coverage and the public's attention were fixed not on the upheavals overseas, but on the O. J. Simpson murder trial. Meanwhile, Congress wrestled with a shutdown of the federal government after failing to resolve a budget standoff with the White House and later consumed itself with the impeachment of Clinton over issues resulting from his affair with a White House intern.

The United States, in short, seemed to lose its way at the very time that its self-proclaimed mission to re-create the global order appeared within reach. Amid the domestic discord noted above, the forces of democratization, intergovernmental cooperation, and economic globalization—so vigorously promoted by U.S. leaders in the "American century"—suddenly seemed threatening to the nation's sovereignty and freedom of action. Government officials felt trapped by UN peacekeeping missions, a proposed international criminal court, and global treaties to restrict fossil-fuel emissions and ban the testing of nuclear weapons. The government's antipathy extended to the growing array of nongovernmental organizations overseas, many of them empowered by U.S.-style political reforms and mobilized through the Internet. To many foreign-policy makers, the endurance of *pax Americana* appeared to be at risk—as did the Westphalian nation-state system that had come to be dominated by the United States.

These developments reveal a paradox in the U.S. experience as a world power: the very sources of strength for the United States during its steady growth—a deeply ingrained sense of national exceptionalism, the diffusion of foreign-policy powers, the free rein granted to civil society—have increasingly become sources of vulnerability as well. The decentralized and highly constrained federal government, largely unchanged since its creation more than two centuries ago, cannot effectively manage the dynamic world order that, to a considerable extent, is of its own making. In this sense, the United States is a victim as well as beneficiary of its own success.

Despite the United States' problems, the country today continues to inspire many governments and citizens. Indeed, the freedoms American citizens enjoy—even in the more restrictive environment prompted by the war on terrorism—are widely envied abroad. The same can be said for the living standards, educational opportunities, scientific advances, cultural outlets, and other by-products of the U.S. political and economic system. These sources of "soft power" remain vital to the United States. Further, in the current power structure, no individual country or bloc of states appears capable of supplanting U.S. primacy. This does not mean, however, that the United States is immune from antagonistic forces overseas nor that it can maintain its primacy by resisting the international community it once championed.

My primary objective in writing this book was to explore this paradox of U.S. world power, to identify its key sources and manifestations, and to consider its future implications. The sheer magnitude of U.S. military might, economic wealth, and political and cultural influence makes the choices of U.S. foreign-policy makers resonate in all corners of the world. Those choices, however, are made in a domestic institutional setting that is purposefully fragmented and conflicted. The coherence of U.S. policy choices is further impaired by the equally fractious array of transnational institutions—including corporations, nonprofit interest groups, the news media, and global public opinion—that are part of the U.S. foreign-policy process as never before.

Because the contradictions and dilemmas inherent to U.S. foreign policy are woven into the nation's institutional structure, they are unlikely to be overcome in the foreseeable future. The stakes in the policy process will, however, remain high. The developments of the past several years have for obvious reasons lent a particular urgency to the study of foreign-policy making. The attacks of September 11, the military response against Afghanistan, the promulgation of the Bush Doctrine, and the U.S.-led invasion of Iraq all cry out for scrutiny and analytic clarity. If this book helps its readers make sense of these cascading developments, and if readers are better able to grasp the link between the process and the conduct of U.S. foreign policy, then the book will have achieved its main purpose.

My secondary goal for this book was to present a clear and concise, yet comprehensive, overview of the U.S. foreign-policy process to students at all levels. Readers seeking a stronger grasp of this subject deserve a text that is straightforward, limited in its use of jargon, and visually appealing. No account of this subject will have its intended effect if its readers are lost in translation.

To this end, the twelve chapters that follow are organized into four parts—each with three chapters and each of roughly equal length—that cover distinct aspects of U.S. foreign policy. Part I introduces the book's theme, briefly reviews key historical developments and milestones, and identifies theories of international relations and foreign policy that offer contending explanations of the decision-making process. Parts II and III identify the roles played in this process by state and transnational actors, respectively. Particular emphasis is given to the governmental and societal *institutions* that shape policy choices and define the possibilities and limitations of U.S. actions. These sections also highlight the interplay of internal and external forces and the growing tensions that exist between the U.S. government's need for autonomy and its adaptation to societal and market forces increasingly beyond its control. Part IV highlights the three primary domains of foreign policy: national security and defense, economic relations, and the management of transnational problems. The final chapters also evaluate the dilemmas currently facing U.S. foreign-policy makers in these areas.

This analytic framework was designed to facilitate instruction in several ways. The symmetrical structure of the volume lends itself to break points and examinations at regular intervals. Visual aids—full-color maps, photographs, figures, and tables—enliven the text and reinforce its key lessons. The boxed features—Point/Counterpoint and In Their Own Words—summarize ongoing debates and provide insightful perspectives on the policy process. Parenthetical citations and a detailed bibliography identify scholarly references while directing readers' attention to a vast supporting literature on U.S. foreign policy useful in informing research papers and subsequent study. Internet references, highlighted at the end of each chapter, provide additional guidance to students. A glossary at the end of the book defines the key concepts introduced in bold type throughout the text.

Students and instructors also benefit from a variety of ancillary resources. A companion Web site, available at **college.cqpress.com/hook,** provides chapter summaries, interactive practice quizzes, exercises to promote active learning, and annotated hyperlinks to a wealth of online resources. I invite instructors to use the PowerPoint slides, the electronic versions of the graphics appearing in the book, and the test banks covering each of the chapters, along with the *CQP Test Writer* software for generating tests. All of these are included on a CD-ROM available free to adopters.

This book is intended not simply to inform its readers, but to provoke them and force them to grapple with the many puzzles that are daily parts of the U.S. foreign-policy process. As noted earlier, the paradox outlined in this book is ultimately based upon the strengths that enabled the United States to achieve its success in world politics and to serve so often as a catalyst for democratic reforms and improved living standards beyond its shores. The management of this success, however, imposes a different set of demands on the makers of U.S. foreign policy. Reconciling these strengths and limitations is the primary task facing foreign-policy making in the years ahead. Understanding them is the challenge posed to the readers of this book.

Acknowledgments

The chapters that follow are products of a collective effort that was required to realize the ambitious goals of this project. Although my name appears alone on the cover of the book, this designation does not do justice to the large supporting cast that made this volume possible.

I am especially grateful to the editors at CQ Press who provided the substantial resources—and patience—necessary to produce this volume. Their personal attention to the project, increasingly rare in the publishing industry, made the writing process not only manageable, but highly enjoyable. Brenda Carter and Charisse Kiino oversaw the project from the start, tolerating the occasional delays and inevitable frustrations that attended the preparation of a manuscript during the turbulent circumstances in the United States and the world today. Michael Kerns provided invaluable guidance and support on a day-to-day basis. His constructive advice on editorial decisions and receptiveness to my nearly constant queries were greatly appreciated. Jarelle Stein skillfully fine-tuned the completed manuscript, and Gwenda Larsen ensured that the book would be visually attractive and reader friendly from start to finish.

I also thank my colleagues at Kent State University, who provided me the necessary time and space to see this project through. The quality of the volume would not have been possible without the help of several research assistants, including Jeremy Lesh, Guang Zhang, Jim Bralski, Christine Mutuku, and Xiaoyu Pu. In particular, David Rothstein combined a strong grasp of the subject with high-caliber technical skills to strengthen the volume and the ancillary materials. Many reviewers provided much-needed criticism at various stages of the project. They include Darlene Budd, Central Missouri State University; Robert J. Lieber, Georgetown University; Witold J. Lukaszewski, Sam Houston State University; James A. Mitchell, California State University, Northridge; Richard Nolan, University of Florida; Karen Rasler, Indiana University; and Barry Steiner, California State University, Long Beach. Their suggestions, some of which called for substantial restructuring and streamlining, were consistently on target. Any deficiencies in the volume are due to my own inability to heed their collective guidance.

I also owe a debt of gratitude to John Spanier, my coauthor on another CQ Press book, *American Foreign Policy Since World War II.* I continue to try, with only mixed success, to emulate Professor Spanier's analytic skill and narrative style. Given that the two books are intended to complement each another—this new book focuses on the formulation of U.S. foreign policy, whereas the ongoing book with Professor Spanier focuses on its conduct—I have endeavored to make both books live up to the standards set by Professor Spanier many years ago.

The quality of this book is also due to the assistance I received from researchers in a variety of foreign-policy nongovernmental organizations, including Rachel Stohl at the Center for Defense Information and Chris Hellman at the Center for Arms Control and Non-Proliferation. These and other researchers seem to labor tirelessly with limited rewards beyond contributing to the public interest. They filled many "cracks" in the text by providing critical information unavailable from other sources. In addition, I am indebted to my fellow travelers in the Foreign Policy Analysis Section of the International Studies Association. Together, we have found a hospitable "epistemic community" and an invaluable arena for field-testing our ideas and various writing projects, including several parts of this volume.

Finally, I offer my enduring thanks to my wife, Debra-Lynn, and to my children, Benjamin, Emily, and Christopher, for tolerating my preoccupation with a writing project that became a virtual, if at times unwelcome, part of the family.

Map 1 Nineteenth-Century European Empires and U.S. Continental Expansion

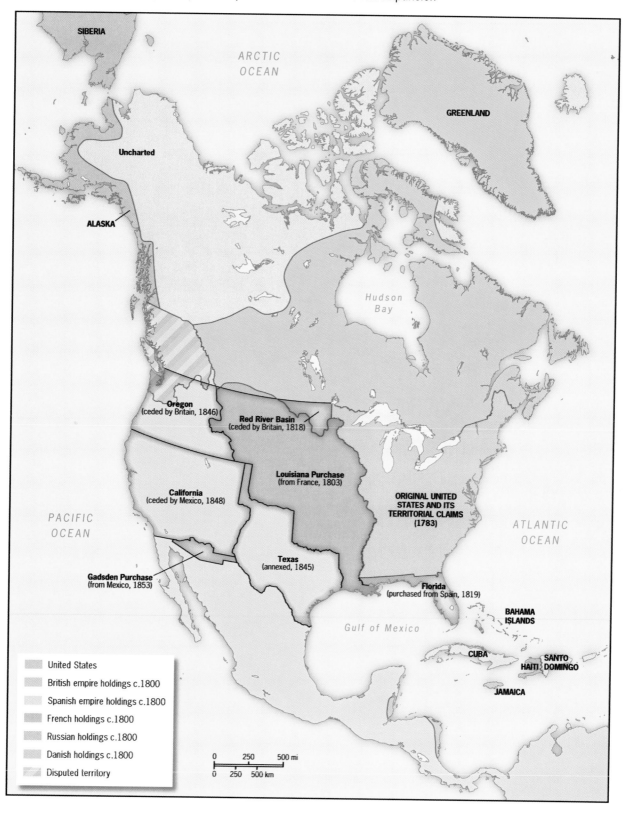

SIBERIA

ARCTIC
OCEAN

GREENLAND

Uncharted

ALASKA

Hudson
Bay

Oregon
(ceded by Britain, 1846)

Red River Basin
(ceded by Britain, 1818)

Louisiana Purchase
(from France, 1803)

California
(ceded by Mexico, 1848)

ORIGINAL UNITED
STATES AND ITS
TERRITORIAL CLAIMS
(1783)

PACIFIC
OCEAN

ATLANTIC
OCEAN

Gadsden Purchase
(from Mexico, 1853)

Texas
(annexed, 1845)

Florida
(purchased from Spain, 1819)

BAHAMA
ISLANDS

Gulf of Mexico

CUBA

SANTO
DOMINGO

HAITI

JAMAICA

United States

British empire holdings c.1800

Spanish empire holdings c.1800

French holdings c.1800

Russian holdings c.1800

Danish holdings c.1800

Disputed territory

0   250   500 mi

0   250   500 km

Map 2 Cold War Division of Europe

Map 3 Cold War Alliances with the United States

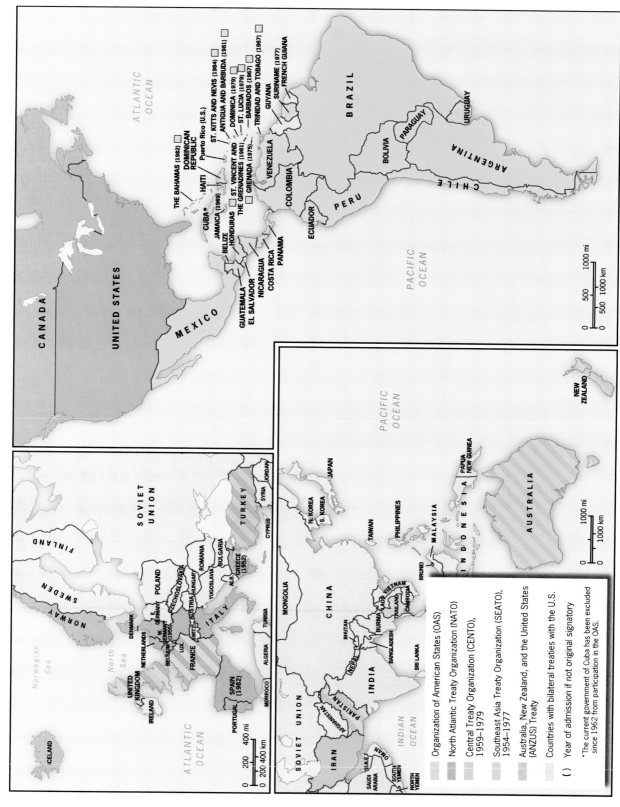

Organization of American States (OAS)

North Atlantic Treaty Organization (NATO)

Central Treaty Organization (CENTO), 1959–1979

Southeast Asia Treaty Organization (SEATO), 1954–1977

Australia, New Zealand, and the United States (ANZUS) Treaty

Countries with bilateral treaties with the U.S.

( ) Year of admission if not original signatory

*The current government of Cuba has been excluded since 1962 from participation in the OAS.

Map 4 Post–Cold War U.S. Military Operations

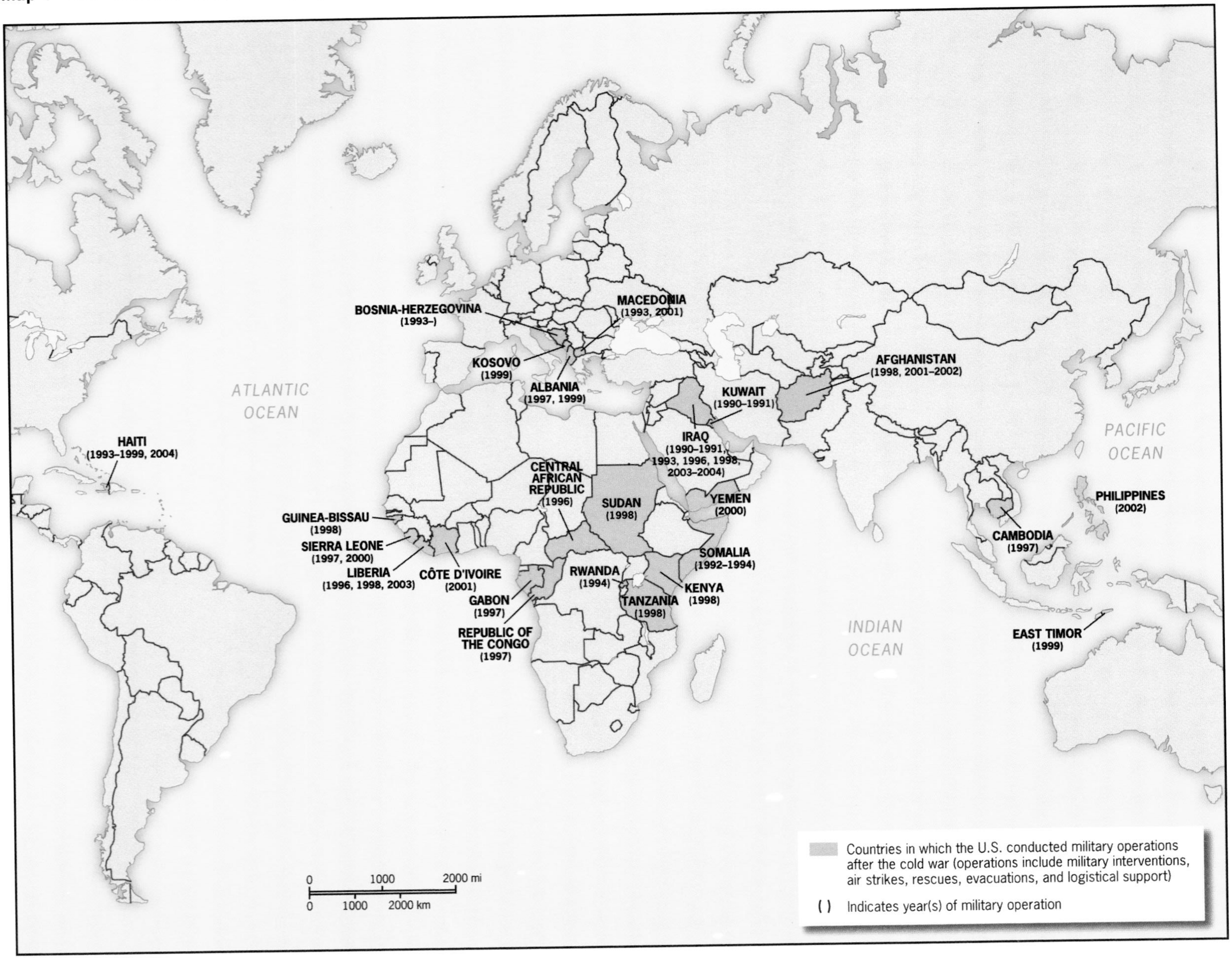

HAITI
(1993–1999, 2004)

BOSNIA-HERZEGOVINA
(1993–)

GUINEA-BISSAU
(1998)

SIERRA LEONE
(1997, 2000)

LIBERIA
(1996, 1998, 2003)

KOSOVO
(1999)

ALBANIA
(1997, 1999)

MACEDONIA
(1993, 2001)

CENTRAL
AFRICAN
REPUBLIC
(1996)

CÔTE D'IVOIRE
(2001)

GABON
(1997)

REPUBLIC OF
THE CONGO
(1997)

RWANDA
(1994)

SUDAN
(1998)

TANZANIA
(1998)

KENYA
(1998)

SOMALIA
(1992–1994)

YEMEN
(2000)

IRAQ
(1990–1991,
1993, 1996, 1998,
2003–2004)

KUWAIT
(1990–1991)

AFGHANISTAN
(1998, 2001–2002)

CAMBODIA
(1997)

PHILIPPINES
(2002)

EAST TIMOR
(1999)

ATLANTIC
OCEAN

PACIFIC
OCEAN

INDIAN
OCEAN

Countries in which the U.S. conducted military operations
after the cold war (operations include military interventions,
air strikes, rescues, evacuations, and logistical support)

( ) Indicates year(s) of military operation

0   1000   2000 mi

0   1000   2000 km

Map 5 Major Ongoing Conflicts in the Middle East and South Asia

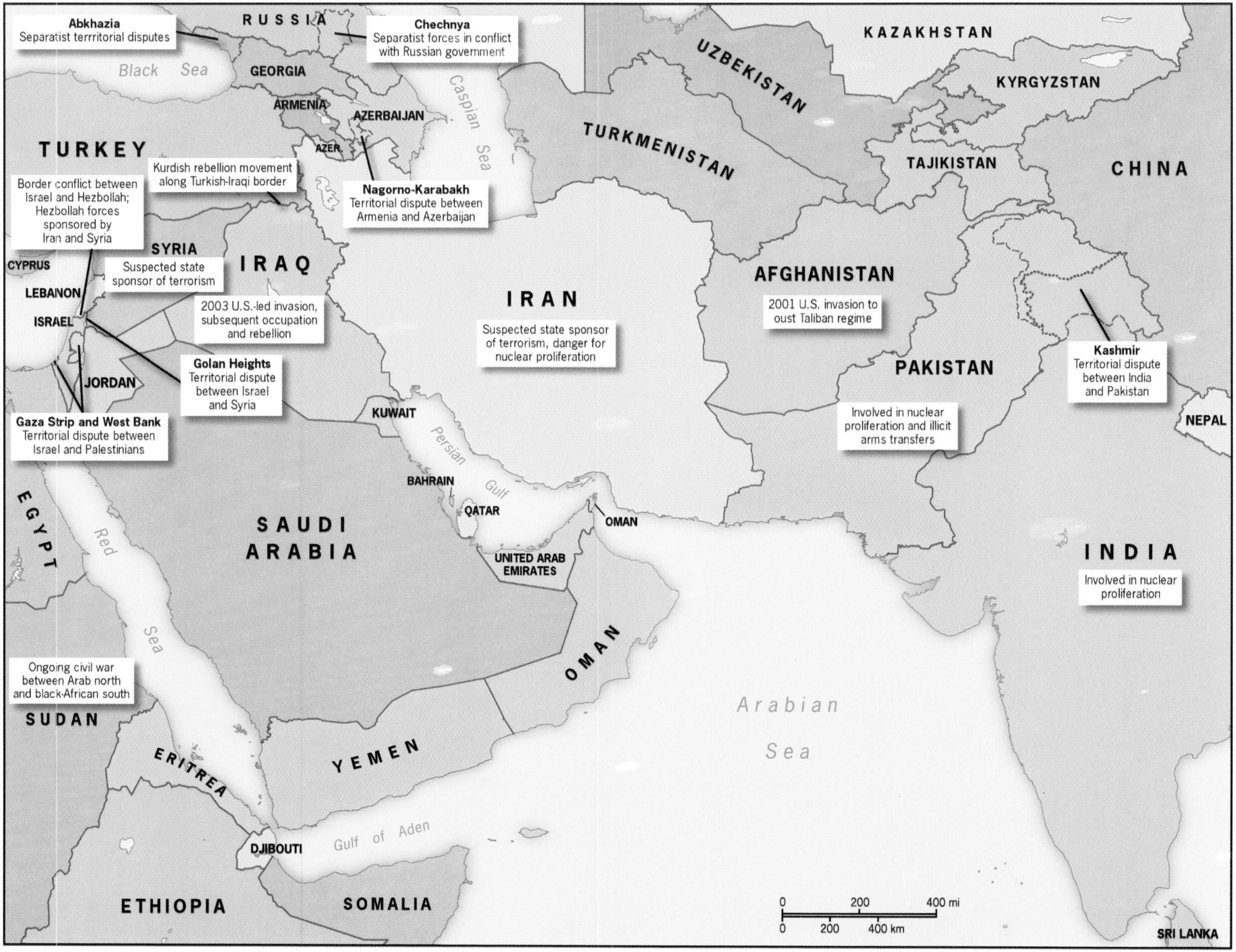

RUSSIA

Abkhazia
Separatist terrritorial disputes

Chechnya
Separatist forces in conflict with Russian government

GEORGIA

Black Sea

ARMENIA

AZERBAIJAN

AZER.

Nagorno-Karabakh
Territorial dispute between Armenia and Azerbaijan

Caspian Sea

TURKEY

Kurdish rebellion movement along Turkish-Iraqi border

CYPRUS

LEBANON

Border conflict between Israel and Hezbollah; Hezbollah forces sponsored by Iran and Syria

ISRAEL

SYRIA

Suspected state sponsor of terrorism

IRAQ

2003 U.S.-led invasion, subsequent occupation and rebellion

JORDAN

Golan Heights
Territorial dispute between Israel and Syria

Gaza Strip and West Bank
Territorial dispute between Israel and Palestinians

EGYPT

KAZAKHSTAN

KYRGYZSTAN

UZBEKISTAN

TAJIKISTAN

CHINA

TURKMENISTAN

NEPAL

Kashmir
Territorial dispute between India and Pakistan

AFGHANISTAN

2001 U.S. invasion to oust Taliban regime

PAKISTAN

Involved in nuclear proliferation and illicit arms transfers

INDIA

Involved in nuclear proliferation

IRAN

Suspected state sponsor of terrorism, danger for nuclear proliferation

KUWAIT

Persian Gulf

BAHRAIN

QATAR

UNITED ARAB EMIRATES

OMAN

OMAN

Arabian Sea

SRI LANKA

SAUDI ARABIA

YEMEN

Gulf of Aden

Red Sea

SUDAN

Ongoing civil war between Arab north and black-African south

ERITREA

DJIBOUTI

ETHIOPIA

SOMALIA

0   200   400 km

0   200   400 mi

Map 6 The World

ARCTIC OCEAN

GREENLAND
(DENMARK)

Beaufort Sea

Baffin
Bay

RUSSIA

UNITED STATES

CANADA

Hudson Bay

Labrador Sea

Bering
Sea

Gulf of Alaska

ST. PIERRE-MQ. (FR)

NORTH
PACIFIC
OCEAN

NORTH
ATLANTIC
OCEAN

BERMUDA
(UK)

UNITED STATES

PUERTO RICO (US)
BRITISH VIRGIN ISLANDS
U.S. VIRGIN ISLANDS
ANGUILLA (UK)
ST. KITTS-NEVIS
ANTIGUA & BARBUDA
MONTSERRAT (UK)
GUADELOUPE (FR)
DOMINICA
MARTINIQUE (FR)
ST. LUCIA
BARBADOS
ST. VINCENT
TRINIDAD & TOBAGO
GUYANA
SURINAME
FRENCH GUIANA

THE BAHAMAS

CUBA

MEXICO

Gulf of Mexico

DOM. REP.

JAMAICA

HAITI

BELIZE

HONDURAS

NE. ANTILLES (NE)

GUATEMALA

NICARAGUA

ARUBA

GRENADA

EL SALVADOR

COSTA RICA

VENEZUELA

PANAMA

COLOMBIA

NAURU

KIRIBATI

ECUADOR

SOLOMON
ISLANDS

TOKELAU (NZ)

AMERICAN
SAMOA
(US)

PERU

BRAZIL

TUVALU

WALLIS & FUTUNA
ISLANDS (FR)

SAMOA

BOLIVIA

Coral Sea

VANUATU

FIJI

FRENCH
POLYNESIA
(FR)

PARAGUAY

NEW CALEDONIA (FR)

TONGA

COOK ISLANDS (NZ)

NORFOLK ISLAND
(AUSTRALIA)

PITCAIRN ISLANDS (UK)

RAPANUI / EASTER ISLAND
(CHILE)

CHILE

SOUTH
PACIFIC
OCEAN

URUGUAY

ARGENTINA

Tasman Sea

SOUTH
ATLANTIC
OCEAN

NEW ZEALAND

FALKLAND ISLANDS
(UK)

SOUTH GEORGIA ISL.

Map 7 Department of Defense Regional Commands

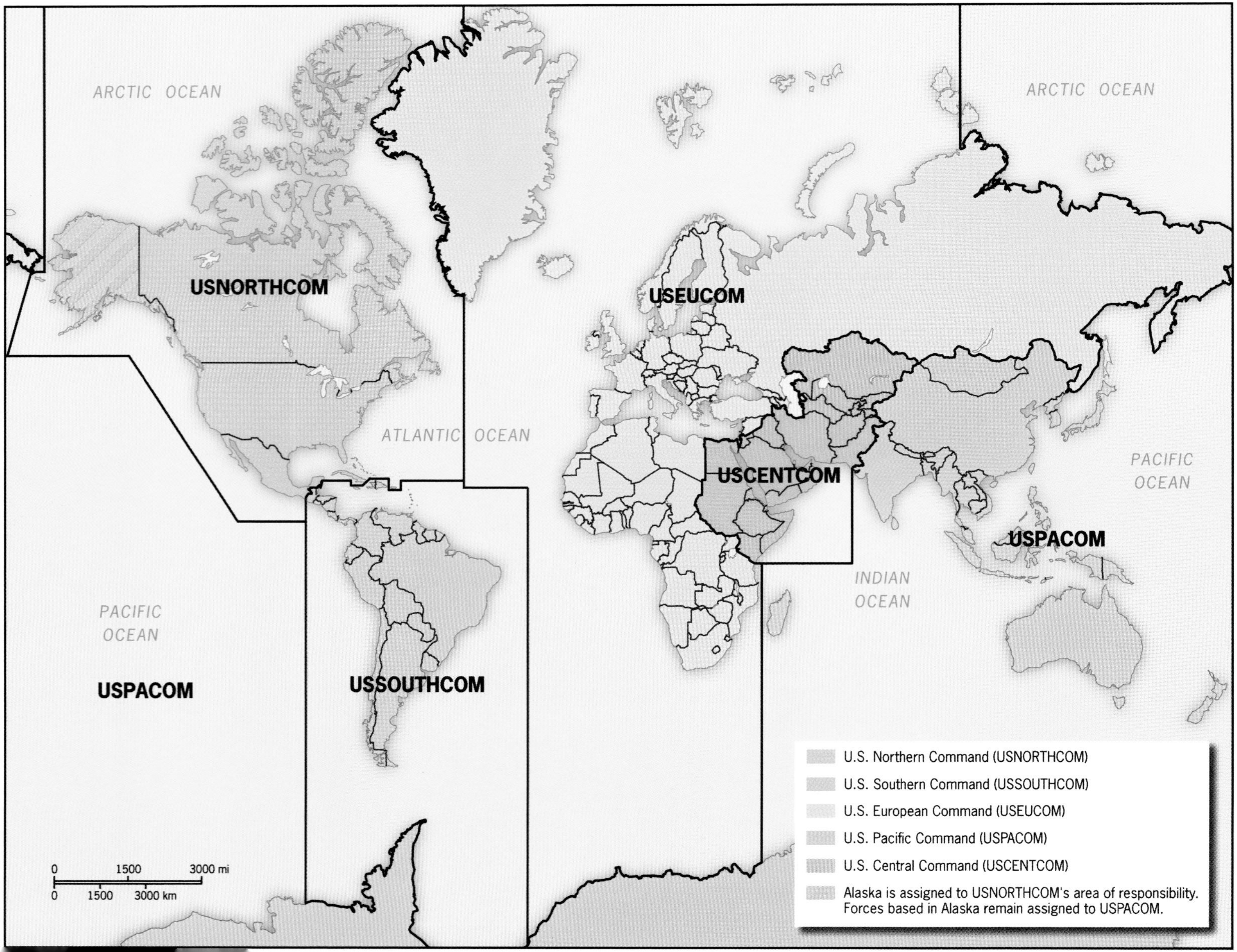
ARCTIC OCEAN
ARCTIC OCEAN
USNORTHCOM
USEUCOM
ATLANTIC OCEAN
USCENTCOM
PACIFIC OCEAN
USPACOM
INDIAN OCEAN
PACIFIC OCEAN
USPACOM
USSOUTHCOM
0 1500 3000 mi
0 1500 3000 km
U.S. Northern Command (USNORTHCOM)
U.S. Southern Command (USSOUTHCOM)
U.S. European Command (USEUCOM)
U.S. Pacific Command (USPACOM)
U.S. Central Command (USCENTCOM)
Alaska is assigned to USNORTHCOM's area of responsibility. Forces based in Alaska remain assigned to USPACOM.

Map 8 NATO Expansion

Legend:

- Original signatories, 1949 (includes U.S. and Canada, not pictured)
- Joined in 1952
- Joined in 1955 (unified Germany in 1990)
- Joined in 1982
- Joined in 1999
- Joined in 2004
- Application to join pending

Map labels:

Greenland (DENMARK)

ARCTIC OCEAN

ICELAND

Norwegian Sea

ATLANTIC OCEAN

N O R W A Y
S W E D E N
F I N L A N D

RUSSIA

ESTONIA
LATVIA
LITHUANIA
RUSSIA

North Sea
Baltic Sea

IRELAND
UNITED KINGDOM

DENMARK

NETHERLANDS
BELGIUM
LUXEMBOURG

GERMANY

POLAND

BELARUS

UKRAINE

CZECH REPUBLIC
SLOVAKIA

MOLDOVA

FRANCE

LIECHTENSTEIN
SWITZ.
AUSTRIA
HUNGARY

SLOVENIA
CROATIA

ROMANIA

ANDORRA

ITALY

BOSNIA
SERBIA AND MONTENEGRO

BULGARIA

Black Sea

GEORGIA
ARMENIA

PORTUGAL

SPAIN

Corsica

Sardinia

Adriatic Sea

MACEDONIA
ALBANIA

GREECE

TURKEY

Mediterranean

Sicily

SYRIA
IRAQ

MOROCCO
ALGERIA
TUNISIA

MALTA

CYPRUS
LEBANON

ISRAEL
JORDAN

Sea

LIBYA

EGYPT

SAUDI ARABIA

0   200   400 mi
0   200   400 km

Map 9 Nuclear Threats and U.S. Defense Installations

ARCTIC OCEAN

PACIFIC OCEAN

NEW ZEALAND

Kwajalein Atoll
(MARSHALL ISLANDS)

JAPAN

N. KOREA
S. KOREA

Hong Kong

AUSTRALIA

CHINA

SINGAPORE

INDONESIA

RUSSIA

INDIAN OCEAN

INDIA

PAKISTAN

British Indian
Ocean Territories
(UK)

OMAN

IRAN

U.A.E.

BAHRAIN

KENYA

TURKEY

ISRAEL

EGYPT

SOUTH
AFRICA

GREECE

LIBYA

ITALY

NORWAY

DEN.

GER.

AUST.

NETH.

UNITED
KINGDOM

FRANCE

BELG.

LUX.

SPAIN

PORTUGAL

ICELAND

St. Helena
(UK)

ANTIGUA AND BARBUDA

Greenland
(DENMARK)

ATLANTIC OCEAN

THE BAHAMAS

CUBA

HONDURAS

VENEZUELA

COLOMBIA

PERU

BRAZIL

ARGENTINA

CANADA

UNITED STATES

Alaska
(US)

ARCTIC OCEAN

PACIFIC OCEAN

ANTARCTICA

3000 mi

0   1500   3000 km

0   1500   3000 mi

Countries with nuclear weapons capabilities

Countries with unacknowledged nuclear weapons capabilities

Countries with U.S. Department of Defense installations

Countries with active nuclear proliferation programs

Countries with abandoned nuclear weapons programs

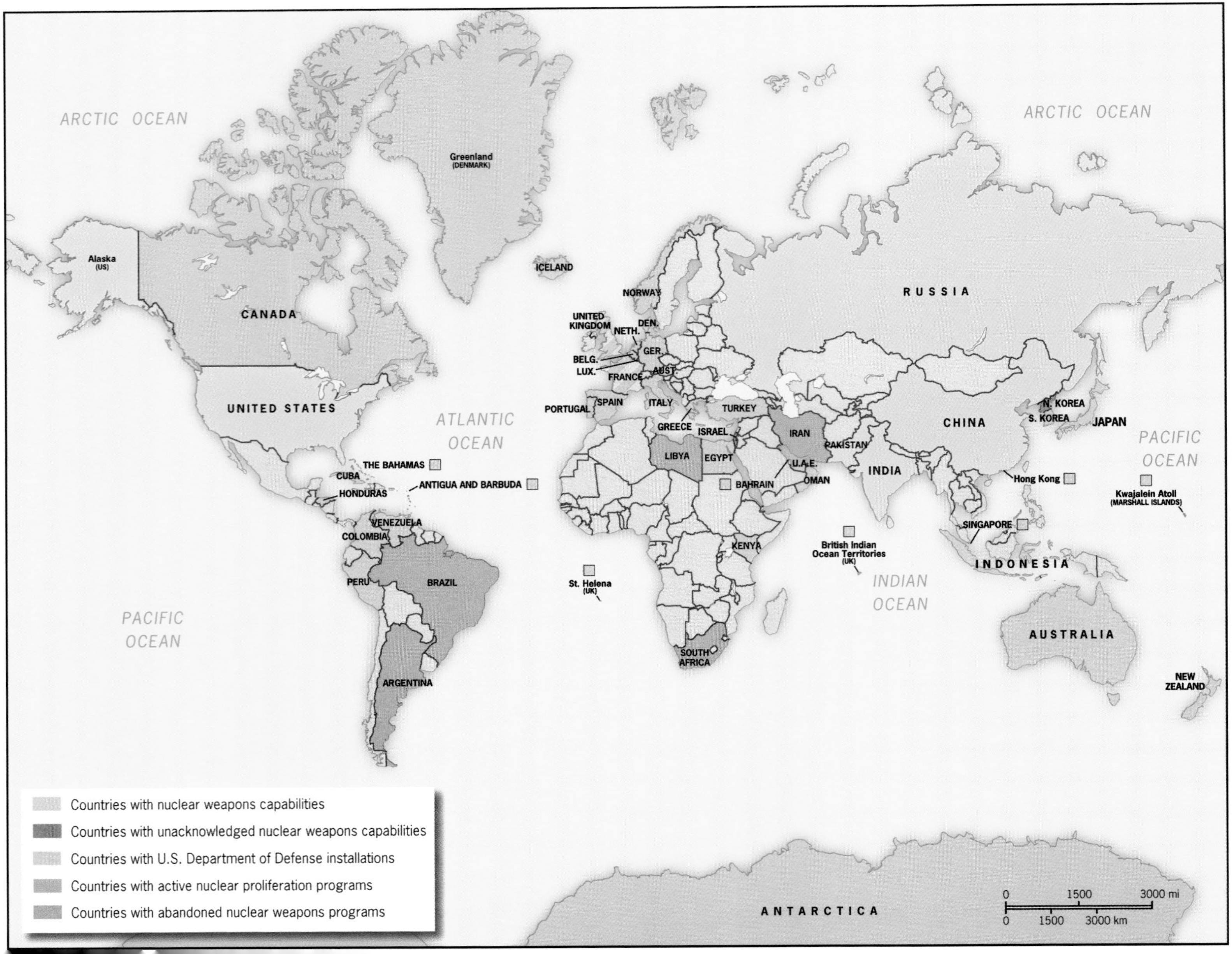

Map 10 U.S. Foreign Economic Relations

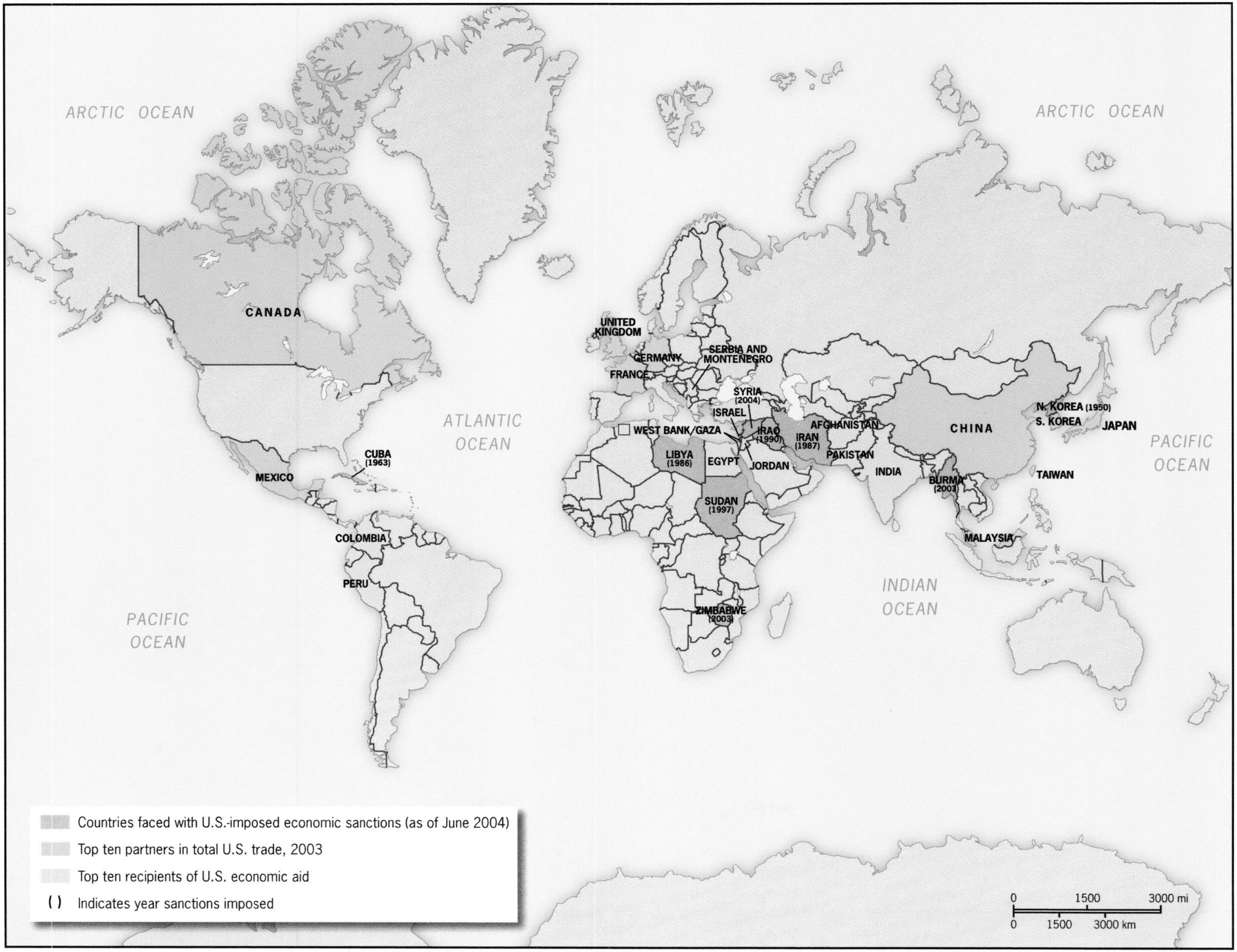

ARCTIC OCEAN

ARCTIC OCEAN

PACIFIC OCEAN

PACIFIC OCEAN

ATLANTIC OCEAN

INDIAN OCEAN

CANADA

MEXICO

CUBA (1963)

COLOMBIA

PERU

UNITED KINGDOM

FRANCE

GERMANY

SERBIA AND MONTENEGRO

SYRIA (2004)

ISRAEL

WEST BANK/GAZA

LIBYA (1986)

EGYPT

SUDAN (1997)

ZIMBABWE (2003)

IRAQ (1990)

JORDAN

IRAN (1987)

AFGHANISTAN

PAKISTAN

INDIA

CHINA

N. KOREA (1950)

S. KOREA

JAPAN

TAIWAN

BURMA (2003)

MALAYSIA

Countries faced with U.S.-imposed economic sanctions (as of June 2004)

Top ten partners in total U.S. trade, 2003

Top ten recipients of U.S. economic aid

( ) Indicates year sanctions imposed

0   1500   3000 mi

0   1500   3000 km

Map 11 Freedom in the World, 2004

Free

Partly free

Not free

ARCTIC OCEAN

ARCTIC OCEAN

PACIFIC OCEAN

PACIFIC OCEAN

ATLANTIC OCEAN

INDIAN OCEAN

0   1500   3000 mi

0   1500   3000 km

1

The United States in a Turbulent World

American troops take positions in the Iraqi city of Fallujah in October 2003, the site of some of the most intense fighting since the U.S.-led invasion of the country began in March. The bloodletting included the deaths of Western contractors whose bodies were mutilated in March 2004 and dragged through city streets. The United States tried to stop the violence by creating a "Fallujah Brigade" comprising Iraqi paramilitary forces, but the insurgency continued into the summer.

The United States today stands alone as the most powerful country in world history. Having emerged victorious from two world wars in the twentieth century, then a protracted cold war, the nation maintains unrivaled military strength and the world's most productive economy. American leaders have enormous clout in global diplomacy, and U.S. political institutions are widely emulated by foreign governments undertaking democratic reforms. Moreover, the global reach of U.S. "soft power"—its cultural influence—has no historical precedent.

Yet, at the same time, the United States is beset by problems at home and abroad. Its urban centers continue to suffer from poverty, despite the prosperity of the 1990s, and racial tensions. Sluggish economic growth and heightened foreign competition have produced widespread layoffs and cutbacks in government spending on education and other vital social services. A series of political scandals and disabling partisan struggles have boosted cynicism about government, a significant feat given the public's historic distaste for politics.

Overseas, the United States remains mired in a war on terrorism that began on September 11, 2001, when Islamic terrorists struck the country's economic and political centers. The attacks initially produced an outpouring of sympathy and support from abroad, but this sentiment proved short-lived. As they carried their counterterrorism campaign to Iraq without the blessing of the

United Nations, the United States and its president, George W. Bush, saw global public opinion turn against them. Critics charged that Bush sought above all to seize Iraqi oil supplies, or worse, to use Iraq as a stepping-stone to the creation of a U.S. world empire. Prominent surveys conducted in 2003 and 2004 found the United States to be widely considered a global threat rather than an agent of peace.

Ill will toward the United States, however, did not originate with Bush's response to September 11. To the contrary, a series of earlier developments left the country isolated within the international community. Four prominent examples highlight this rise in tensions.

First, in the late 1990s, the United States refused to pay its past United Nations dues, which had grown to more than $1 billion. Cutbacks in U.S. foreign-aid programs, meanwhile, left the United States, among all donors, with the lowest aid contributions as a percentage of its economic output.

Second, the U.S. Senate in October 1999 rejected the Comprehensive Test Ban Treaty, which more than 150 foreign governments supported. The Senate's action marked its first repudiation of a major treaty in eighty years and its first-ever rejection of a nuclear treaty. The United States rejected several other arms control treaties widely adopted elsewhere, including bans on antipersonnel land mines, small arms trafficking, and weapons in space.

Third, shortly after taking office in 2001, President Bush rejected the Kyoto Protocol, a global environmental treaty designed to curb emissions of greenhouse gases that contribute to global warming. The United States was also one of the few industrialized countries that refused to ratify the Convention on Biological Diversity.

Finally, evidence became public in 2004 that U.S. occupation forces had repeatedly abused Iraqi detainees at the Abu Ghraib prison, the same facility in which Saddam Hussein had tortured his enemies. Photographs of the abuses appeared worldwide in newspapers and on televised newscasts and Internet sites. It was later revealed that high-level U.S. officials knew about the abuses for months yet neither informed Congress nor took action at Abu Ghraib and other detention centers.

These events tarnished the image of the United States at the very time the nation seemed to have fulfilled its historic ambition of assuming global leadership. In many respects, including its democratic political system and the vitality of its economy, the United States remains widely admired overseas. However, in many other areas the nation has incited anger and resentment. Such challenges to U.S. **primacy**, the nation's predominant stature in the hierarchy of global power, took their most violent form with the terrorist attacks of September 2001. These challenges, along with the global responsibilities that naturally descend upon the world's most powerful country, are inescapable. How U.S. leaders manage the challenges and responsibilities will profoundly affect the course of the twenty-first century for American citizens and those beyond their shores. For this reason, a thorough understanding of U.S. foreign policy is more vital than ever.

Point/Counterpoint
UNILATERALISM VS. MULTILATERALISM

A central point of contention in recent U.S. foreign policy involves the degree to which the United States works with other governments or "goes it alone" in pursuing its perceived national interests. Upon taking office in 2001, President George W. Bush embraced widespread public and congressional concerns that the *multilateral* foreign policy adopted by his predecessors since World War II was threatening the country's sovereignty and weakening its capacity to use its vast power and influence abroad. His shift toward a more *unilateral* foreign policy predictably angered foreign leaders, particularly those with whom the U.S. government had previously established close alliance relationships and other means of collaboration.

Among Bush's primary critics was Jacques Chirac, the president of France, who openly complained about the U.S. government's turn away from multilateral engagement. "Any community with only one dominant power is always a dangerous one and provokes reactions," Chirac told *Time* magazine. "That's why I favor a multipolar world in which Europe obviously has its place." He was especially upset with the Bush decision to launch a preventive invasion of Iraq in 2003 without support from the United Nations, an action he claimed was "a violation of international law and a threat to the current global balance of power."

Snapshot: The United States in the World

It is helpful to begin this inquiry by reviewing some basic indicators of the global balance of power.[1] Taken together, these figures indicate a **unipolar** balance, in which one country—at present the United States—maintains a predominant share of the economic, military, and other resources needed to advance its interests in the interstate system. This concentration of power resources is particularly notable given that the United States contains fewer than 300 million citizens, less than 5 percent of the world's population.

Much of the nation's power advantage derives from the vast size and global scale of its economy. The United States produces more than $10 trillion in national income, or nearly one-third of the world's total (see Figure 1.1). The second largest national economy, that of Japan, is less than one-half the size of the U.S. economy.[2] The nation's output currently exceeds that of the total produced

---

1. Unless otherwise noted, the figures in this section are drawn from the World Bank's *World Development Indicators* (2004).

2. Gross national income refers to the sum value of goods and services produced in a given year plus the income derived from foreign aid and remittances from foreign workers. Gross national product (GNP), which had been commonly used, does not include these latter sources of revenue.

Figure 1.1 World Economic Output, Seven Largest Producers, 2002

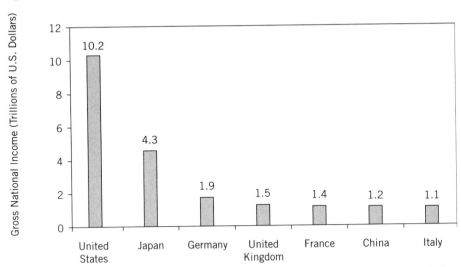

SOURCE: World Bank, *World Development Indicators* (2004), "World View," table 1.1, www.worldbank.org/data/wdi2004.

by all the members of Europe's monetary union. China's economy, which has grown rapidly in recent years, represents about 12 percent of U.S. output. And Russia's economy, having experienced more than a decade of postcommunist "shock therapy," has shrunk to less than 4 percent of the size of the U.S. economy.

The United States holds the additional distinction of being the world's foremost trading state, exporting more than all other nations during the past decade while displaying a voracious appetite for overseas goods and services (WTO 2004). American firms recorded about $1 trillion in annual exports in 2003, nearly 15 percent of the global total. The nation's imports were even larger in absolute terms ($1.5 trillion in 2003) and as a share of world imports (about 20 percent). Germany, the second largest world trader, still records only about 60 percent of the U.S. trade volume.

Other areas reveal the dynamism of the American economy. More foreign direct investment (FDI) has traveled across the nation's borders than anywhere else since the boom in FDI flows began in the 1990s, although the pace of foreign investments has slowed in recent years (OECD 2003). The amount of money invested in U.S. stock markets—nearly $14 trillion in 2001—matches that invested in all other stock markets combined. The nation also ranks first in the number of radios, television sets, and personal computers owned by its citizens. At the turn of the new century, more than one-third of global Internet communications originated or terminated in the United States, and more than 90 percent of the most visited Internet Web sites were based there (Dizard 2001, 4). These instruments provide vital outlets for the **soft power** of the United States—the expression of its political and cultural values that other societies and governments may find appealing (see Nye 2004).

The degree of U.S. predominance is even greater in the military realm (see Figure 1.2). The United States spends more than $400 billion on national defense, nearly one-half of the global total (Center for Defense Information 2003). Having grown considerably since the war on terrorism began, the U.S. defense budget is larger than the *combined* budgets of the next twenty military spenders. Since nearly all of these countries are U.S. allies and maintain close security ties to Washington, D.C., their military spending effectively *strengthens,* rather than weakens, American military strength and security.

In addition to its unrivaled defense forces, the United States leads in global arms exports (Hook and Rothstein 2005). The nation approved more than $13 billion in government-to-government sales in 2002, nearly half of the world's arms trade, while providing another $4 billion worth of security assistance (Grimmett 2003).[3] Government officials approved more than 250 licenses for commercial weapons sales in 2002 and 2003 and conducted military-training programs in more than 130 countries. As with the defense budget, the volume of arms exports increased sharply after the September 11 terrorist attacks.

Figure 1.2 U.S. Military and World Military Spending (as Percentage of World Total)

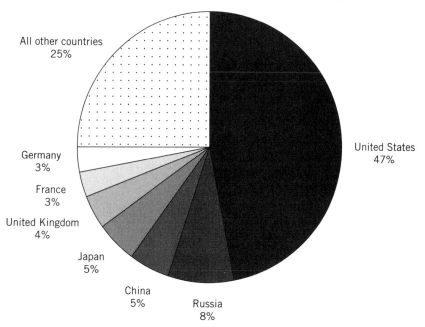

SOURCE: Center for Defense Information, "Last of the Big Time Spenders: U.S. Military Budget Still the World's Largest, and Growing" (March 19, 2003), www.cdi.org/program/issue/index.cfm?ProgramID=15&issueid=34.

---

3. See the U.S. Defense Security Cooperation Agency (2004) for more timely data regarding the country's arms transfers, along with information provided by the Federation of American Scientists (2004) and the Center for Defense Information (2004).

Energy and environmental statistics also reveal the long shadow cast by the United States (see Figure 1.3). Americans consume approximately one-third of the electricity used worldwide and about one-quarter of the global output of oil, coal, and natural gas. Among other environmental impacts, this energy consumption annually produces more than 20 billion metric tons of carbon dioxide emissions—a major source of air pollution and global warming—nearly one-quarter of the total worldwide. In addition, the United States serves as the world's primary source of nuclear and hazardous wastes.

This high-profile position of the United States is not unique to the current period. Indeed, the U.S. government assumed a leading international role after World War II and quickly sought to maintain its "predominance of power" (Leffler 1992, 19). The cold war strategy of "containing" communism was designed to accomplish the broader objective of sustaining U.S. primacy (see Chapter 10). After the Soviet Union's collapse in 1991, the first Bush administration devised a grand strategy to "establish and protect a new order that holds the promise of convincing potential competitors that they need not aspire to a greater role" (*New York Times* 1992, A14). A central objective of this doctrine was to extend the reach of U.S. **hegemony,** or controlling influence over other countries and societies that falls short of formal political authority.

The election of George W. Bush, followed by the terrorist attacks in September 2001, elevated the doctrine of U.S. primacy to a new level. "America has, and intends to keep, military strengths beyond challenge, thereby making the destabilizing arms races of other eras pointless, and limiting rivalries to trade and other pursuits of peace," Bush told army cadets at West Point (White House 2002a). Later in 2002, the president's *National Security Strategy of the United States of*

Figure 1.3 The World's Six Largest Energy Consumers, 2002

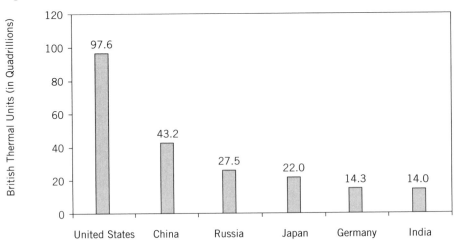

SOURCE: U.S. Department of Energy, "International Total Primary Energy and Related Information" (2004), www.eia.doe.gov/emeu/international/total.html.

America explicitly established U.S. primacy as a pillar of the nation's foreign policy. As the document stated, American military forces "will be strong enough to dissuade potential adversaries from pursuing a military build-up in hopes of surpassing, or equaling, the power of the United States" (White House 2002b, 30).

Challenges to U.S. Primacy

Despite its many strengths, the United States today confronts a variety of challenges to its global primacy. These challenges fall into three general categories. The first of these relates to the difficulties faced by past world powers in preserving their advantages. The second challenge concerns the process of economic globalization and its close association with the United States. Finally, the United States faces the more immediate threat posed by international terrorism, which has preoccupied foreign-policy makers since September 2001.

Cycles in the Balance of Power

Some political analysts see a U.S.-dominated world order as advantageous not only for the United States but also for global stability, economic growth, and political freedoms. A preponderant yet benign world power, they argue, maintains stability in the international system, discouraging conflicts among regional powers and reassuring them that a peaceful and prosperous global order can be achieved and preserved. Under these circumstances, less powerful states will "bandwagon" with the dominant power rather than challenge it by forming rival blocs. The United States can serve this constructive role given its stated goals of promoting democracy and economic prosperity instead of its own selfish interests.

This optimistic view is hardly universal. Other analysts express doubts about the concentration of power in one country, no matter how noble its intentions may be. Among political scientists, structural realists such as Kenneth Waltz (1997, 915) believe that "unbalanced power, whoever wields it, is a potential danger to others." To Robert Gilpin (1981), world history reveals the "increasing costs of dominance" that come with global supremacy and the cataclysmic wars that inevitably result when rising challengers seek the upper hand. Historian Paul Kennedy traced *The Rise and Fall of the Great Powers* (1987) to a recurring pattern of "imperial overstretch." The Roman, Dutch, Ottoman, Spanish, British, and Russian empires ultimately bit off more than they could chew, then succumbed to uprisings in their far-flung provinces and to political infighting at home.

Such lessons are relevant today for the United States, whose global reach exceeds that of any previous world power. Rising defense costs, long-term foreign occupations, and chronic budget and trade deficits have proven the undoing of past empires. The same can be said for the tendency of political leaders in dominant states to exaggerate the threats posed by foreign adversaries, largely for domestic purposes. All these problems have become evident in the United States since it assumed the pivotal position in a unipolar world. The nation's chronic trade deficits have reached record levels in recent years, as have its budget deficits and imbalances of foreign payments (see Chapter 11). Moreover, recent actions by American leaders have alarmed, rather than reassured, foreign leaders, who have vowed to restrain the U.S. "hyperpower."

Resistance to Globalization

A second challenge to the United States stems from the process of economic **globalization,** the linking of national and regional markets into a single world economy (see Stiglitz 2002). Advances in transportation and communication technology, intellectual developments, and public-policy shifts in the eighteenth century first spurred this historic trend. The communications revolution late in the twentieth century accelerated the pace of globalization. In today's world economy, goods, services, and financial investments travel across national borders at a record pace. This commerce is increasingly conducted by multinational corporations (MNCs) with headquarters, research centers, production facilities, stockholders, and customers in many countries.

Throughout much of its history, the United States has been among the nations in the forefront of the globalization wave. While Great Britain was at the vanguard through the nineteenth century, the primary catalyst since then has been

An unidentified textile worker toils in a *maquila,* or sweatshop, in Guatemala City late in 2001. Critics of economic globalization worry that such sweatshop labor will become more common as factories in the United States and other industrialized nations move their production lines to the developing world, where labor costs are lower. While many corporations have adopted their own codes of conduct, the United States opposes mandatory standards that may discourage corporations from expanding into poor countries.

the United States. Globalization conforms to a national consensus that private enterprise, unfettered by government interference, provides the surest path to prosperity as well as individual liberty. According to this consensus, a prosperous world economy would resemble that of the United States, with few internal barriers to the movement of goods, services, labor, and capital. Trade, not political or military competition, would be the primary arena of foreign policy. Furthermore, "trading states" would have strong interests in a stable international system and would be reluctant to wage wars against each other. Globalization, then, would be a harbinger of world peace.

When the cold war ended in 1991, it appeared that this market-based model of political economy had triumphed and would become truly global. Governments rushed to reform their economies along U.S. lines, hoping to reap the benefits of the rapidly integrating world economy. The United States supported these reforms and provided financial aid to former communist countries that shut down government enterprises, created private companies, reduced regulations, and opened their markets to foreign competition. Through the World Bank and the International Monetary Fund, both based in Washington, D.C., the United States and other wealthy nations also assisted poor countries that agreed to follow the market-friendly script.

While the quickening pace of economic globalization brought improved living standards to many nations, others fell behind, unable to attract foreign investment or find new markets for their goods. The growing gaps between the world's rich and poor created new strains in the international system. To critics, globalization produced a variety of other problems: the triumph of consumerism over cultural diversity, heightened pollution and deforestation, and the exploitation of "sweatshop" laborers by multinational corporations. Since the largest share of these corporations were based in the United States and its government had played such a vital role in the globalization boom, these protests were directed toward that country. The most dramatic example of this backlash occurred at the 1999 annual meeting of the World Trade Organization in Seattle, when antiglobalization protesters blocked streets, smashed storefronts, and otherwise prevented the delegates from achieving their goal of furthering free trade.

Terrorism and Asymmetric Warfare

The challenge posed by antiglobalization protesters is directly linked to another threat to the United States—global terrorism. Among other motives for the September 11 attacks, a primary grievance of al Qaeda terrorists was the country's pervasive influence in the Middle East. The region and its vast oil fields have long been considered a vital interest of the U.S. government, which has used whatever means necessary to gain and retain access to them. Since the Middle East lies in the heart of Islam, many Muslims view encroachments by the United States and its Western allies as desecrations of holy lands. These dissidents, who also condemn the U.S. government's support for Israel, generally lack political power as well as substantial economic resources. As a result, they frequently turn to terrorism to force political change.

Terrorism, with a history that long precedes the rise of militant Islam, seeks to gain the upper hand in a political struggle through psychological means (see Pillar 2001). Terrorists seek not to overpower the enemy in one swift blow—impossible given their small numbers and lack of resources—but to gain attention and political concessions by instilling mass fear in the population that their enemy controls. In this regard, terrorism is a form of **asymmetric warfare,** which "exploits vulnerabilities . . . by using weapons and tactics that are unplanned or unexpected" (de Wijk 2002, 79). Terrorists choose the time and place of their attacks, leaving an adversary perpetually on the defensive. They operate in the shadows, beyond enemy reach, and they meld into the civilian communities from which they receive moral and material support. Terrorists' use of unconventional tactics—car bombings, kidnappings, the hijacking of airlines—further confounds their enemies.

The United States faces three problems in confronting terrorism, which was deemed the primary threat to its national security after the September 11 attacks. First, the United States is widely seen as the primary enemy of global terrorists due to its visible role in the Middle East and its more general association with economic globalization. Secondly, U.S. military strategy has historically been based on fighting conventional wars. Defeating foreign enemies with overwhelming forces has always been the nation's way of war. Finally, the United States has traditionally viewed warfare as an exception to the general rule of peaceful coexistence among countries. Fighting terrorism, however, is an ongoing struggle with no clear end. Furthermore, the enemy is not a nation-state, such as Nazi Germany or even Saddam Hussein's Iraq, but an invisible foe impossible to engage through the standard channels of statecraft.

The United States faces other challenges as it seeks to consolidate its preeminent position in the global hierarchy. Efforts to promote democracy overseas, a consistent foreign-policy goal throughout U.S. history, meet numerous obstacles: the practical limits of "exporting" democracy, tensions between U.S. security interests and the repressive rule of strategically vital allies, and fundamental differences regarding the very meaning of democracy (see Hook 1997).[4] Other foreign-policy issues such as illegal immigration and drug smuggling prove equally difficult to resolve. Finally, U.S. bilateral relations with many countries—Cuba, for example—have been hardened by decades of mutual suspicion and hostility, hindering the chances for diplomatic breakthroughs that would be in the mutual interests of both parties.

The Paradox of America's World Power

These challenges to the United States raise profound questions about the nation's capacity to sustain its dominant position in the unipolar world. As noted above,

---

4. A central point of contention regarding the nature of democracy is whether it extends beyond political liberty to include economic equality. While most countries support the broader definition, the U.S. government traditionally favors the more restrictive one (see Chapter 12).

this objective has long been pursued by the U.S. government but recently has been explicitly embraced as the top national-security priority. Achieving this goal would appear well within reach considering the vast and unprecedented lead the country maintains in the essential categories of national power.

Such an outcome, however, will not be as easy to bring about as the hard numbers suggest. It is a central paradox of America's world power that, in seeking to sustain its global primacy, the United States is increasingly constrained by the very forces that propelled its rise to global predominance. These strengths—a culturally embedded sense of national exceptionalism, the diffusion of domestic foreign-policy powers, and the free reign granted to civil society in the policy process—also create vulnerabilities for the U.S. government. Derived from an eighteenth-century model, the nation's governing structures remain remarkably unchanged in the twenty-first century. Yet the world order that the United States played a lead role in creating has changed in profound ways, along with the country's role in that order.

This book explores this paradox by examining its impact on the process of making U.S. foreign policy. Of particular interest are the institutions of power inside and outside the U.S. government that define the roles of public and private actors; create and reinforce common values, norms, and codes of conduct; and define what is possible among contending foreign-policy choices. These institutions of power become more complex as the scope of U.S. foreign policy broadens, as the lines between domestic- and foreign-policy concerns are increasingly blurred, as the number and magnitude of problems crossing national borders increases, and as more individuals and groups become stakeholders and participants in the foreign-policy process.

This paradox, and the damaging consequences that result for the United States, can be seen in several recent examples:

- Domestic divisions over U.S. grand strategy in the 1990s prevented the United States from adopting a coherent world role despite its resounding victory in the cold war and unprecedented global power. Instead, the Clinton administration pursued four contradictory strategies, often at once: retrenchment, primacy, liberal internationalism, and selective engagement (Posen and Ross 1996–1997).

- A 1995 stalemate over foreign aid in the Senate Foreign Relations Committee prompted Chairman Jesse Helms, R-N.C., to recess the committee indefinitely. "The day-to-day foreign policy business on Capitol Hill has ground to a halt," the *New York Times* reported (Sciolino 1995, 1A). The ongoing stalemate prevented Congress from authorizing new foreign-aid bills for the rest of the decade.

- Several members of Congress sued President Clinton in 1999, without success, to force a withdrawal of U.S. forces from Kosovo. Legislators later charged that Clinton intervened in the renegade Yugoslav province to divert the public's attention from his impeachment by the House of

Representatives for lying about an affair with a White House intern. Well aware of domestic opposition to the intervention, Clinton limited U.S. military action in Kosovo to high-altitude bombing raids, many of which missed their targets and produced large civilian casualties.

- President George W. Bush's decision in 2002 to increase tariffs on imports of foreign steel prompted the World Trade Organization (WTO) to threaten economic sanctions against the United States, which had long regarded itself as the world's foremost champion of free trade. With the imposition of WTO sanctions as well as the threat of retaliation by the European Union just days away, Bush rescinded the steel tariffs in late 2003. Bush's reversal angered the same interest group—the domestic steel industry—he had aimed to please with his initial trade action.

- The U.S. government failed to approve a new energy policy in 2003 despite widespread concern about the nation's dependence on foreign oil, global warming, and power blackouts. Bitter partisan disputes quickly erupted over Vice President Dick Cheney's refusal to identify members of his Energy Task Force and over Republican legislators' refusal to include Democrats in drafting the bill. The United States remained without an approved energy policy as gasoline prices topped two dollars a gallon in 2004.

In each of these examples, tensions among the presidency, the foreign-policy bureaucracy, Congress, public opinion, the news media, interest groups, and intergovernmental organizations produced negative consequences for U.S. foreign policy. The failure of the United States to steer a coherent course in these and many other cases, clearly visible to a global audience, reinforced the nation's image as a potent, but dysfunctional superpower.

Cultural Roots of the Paradox

The roots of this paradox can be found in the United States' **national style,** the cultural influences that have historically shaped the country's approach to international relations. Although national style is an ambiguous concept and cultural influences are difficult to identify with precision, the conduct of every country's foreign policy reflects its distinctive sense of place within the international system. This sense of place, in turn, is shaped by tangible factors such as geographic location, the availability of natural resources, and the size and characteristics of the population. Other factors, such as a country's historical experience, also influence its national style.

When it became the first independent country in the Western Hemisphere, the United States was geographically far removed from the great powers of the time. This distance, combined with the ample territory and natural resources available within the thirteen original states, enabled the new nation to develop its political and economic systems with little outside assistance. The United States was distinctive in that its civil society, compared with those of most other countries, did not feature sharp divisions between a small but powerful aristocracy and a large but powerless feudal peasantry. As Alexis de Tocqueville ([1835] 1988, 56) observed after his tour of the young United States, "One finds a vast multitude of people with roughly the same ideas about religion, history, science, political economy, legislation, and government." The absence of deep social and economic gaps produced a relatively narrow spectrum in which debates over domestic and foreign policies would take place.

This consensus encouraged a sense of national **exceptionalism,** by which citizens felt the United States was destined not simply to survive as a nation-state but to achieve the status of a superior world power. Long before the nation's independence, the first European settlers to North America proclaimed the founding of a "city upon a hill" that would inspire societies far from its shores. Colonial leaders later believed that independence from Great Britain would create "a more perfect union" based upon limited and representative government. To Thomas Jefferson (quoted in Tucker and Hendrickson 1992, 30), Americans had proven themselves to be "the chosen people of God, if ever he had a chosen people, whose breasts he has made his peculiar deposit for substantial and genuine virtue."

How did these historical and cultural factors influence the conduct of U.S. foreign policy? First, the values underlying the nation's political system were widely considered by Americans to be universal in scope. To Abraham Lincoln (quoted in Rose 2000–2001, 186), the Declaration of Independence promised democracy "not alone to the people of this country, but hope to the world for all future time." As an "exceptional" nation, the United States would pursue the interests of the international system in general as well as its own. President Woodrow Wilson (quoted in Rose 2000–2001, 187) captured this sentiment in arguing that the United States should enter the First World War "for the ultimate peace of the world and for the liberation of its peoples."

This sense of moral righteousness, reducing world politics to a contest between good and evil, continued into the cold war and persists today. In the early 1980s, President Ronald Reagan condemned the Soviet Union as an "evil empire." Bill Clinton adapted this view to the post–cold war world by identifying "rogue states" as the principal threat to the United States. Nine days after the terrorist attacks of September 2001, George W. Bush described the struggle in starkly biblical terms: "Freedom and fear, justice and cruelty, have always been at war, and we know that God is not neutral between them." A year later, Bush declared the nation's enemies to be part of an "axis of evil," led by Iran, Iraq, and North Korea, that must be destroyed for the United States, and world order in general, to be truly secure.

This moralistic view has profound, but contradictory, implications for the conduct of U.S. foreign policy. To some, the United States should primarily lead by example; an activist foreign policy would only dirty the hands of U.S. leaders in power politics. The physical distance of Americans from the "outside world" permitted them to focus their attention on domestic concerns and allow problems overseas to run their course. Splendid isolation encouraged American schools to neglect world history and geography, leaving the public lacking in basic knowledge about international affairs. This posed no problem for U.S. foreign policy, however, since the United States was largely self-sufficient and looked westward, *away* from the forever warring powers of Europe.

To others, the United States should harness its virtues to save the war-prone international system from itself. This same self-sufficiency gave the United States immense strength and vitality, along with a lack of historic commitments to other countries that would tie its hands in foreign interventions. The spiritual enlightenment of the new republic would inspire its people to engage in a global crusade against injustice, aggression, and war itself. Lacking consensus in times of peace, the United States has pursued both strategies, detaching itself from the outside world during certain periods and immersing itself in foreign affairs during others. Most often, U.S. foreign policy exhibits the two tendencies at once, confounding observers at home and overseas (see Hook and Spanier 2004).

The public's ambivalent approach to foreign affairs is most acute when the United States is at peace. In 1999, when participants in a national survey were asked to identify the biggest foreign-policy problem facing the United States, they most often replied, "Don't know" (Rielly 1999, 11). Americans tend to focus on more immediate domestic concerns during these times, and elected officials respond in kind. Only when foreign problems reach crisis proportions do they spark the public's interest. As a result, the public makes a hasty demand for action by the U.S. government, which responds impulsively, frequently with little knowledge of the underlying problems that provoked the crisis. George Kennan (1951, 59), the architect of U.S. cold war strategy, found this aspect of democratic foreign-policy making particularly troublesome:

> I sometimes wonder whether in this respect a democracy is not uncomfortably similar to one of those prehistoric monsters with a body as long as this room and a brain the size of a pin. He lies there in his comfortable primeval mud and pays little attention to his environment; he is slow to wrath—in fact, you practically have to whack his tail off to make him aware that his interests are being disturbed. But, once he grasps this, he lays about with such blind determination that he not only destroys his adversary but largely wrecks his native habitat.

Such internal contradictions related to the "democratic" conduct of its foreign policy did not prevent the United States from steadily increasing its global influence. The domestic institutions of foreign policy expanded after World War II, while the general public and transnational interest groups became more involved in the foreign-policy process. This did not pose a serious problem during the cold war as long as national consensus regarding the strategy of communist "containment" persisted. This consensus fell apart, however, during the Vietnam War, after which there was little agreement regarding the ends and means of U.S. foreign policy. In place of consensus, public attitudes splintered along ideological fault lines. Policy makers and legislators followed this trend, becoming more polarized and concerned with serving narrow interests.

By committing itself to such lofty moral standards and then often failing to live up to them, the United States has exposed itself to charges of hypocrisy. Critics view the U.S. role during the cold war in toppling elected governments—as in Guatemala in 1954 and Chile in 1973—as departures from the country's stated principles. The disastrous U.S. involvement in Vietnam raised the most serious questions about American moral limitations. Of more recent concern are the U.S. government's close economic ties to the People's Republic of China despite that government's repressive treatment of its own citizens. In the war on terrorism, the U.S. government has created informal alliances with "front-line" states such as Indonesia, Pakistan, and Tajikistan that are known violators of human rights.

Institutional Branches

Every nation's political culture has a direct impact on the structures of governance that regulate public affairs, define the relationships between rulers and ruled, and carry out public policies. Prevalent ideas regarding the proper role of the government at home and abroad express themselves in the creation of legislatures, courts, and government agencies. These institutional "branches" of a nation's political culture determine what is possible in the policy-making process, constraining the options of policy makers. In addition, political institutions commonly multiply and produce new agencies and governing structures that further shape the policy process.

The links among prevalent cultural norms, political institutions, and government behavior can be clearly seen in the United States. Under the prevailing theory of the Enlightenment era, in which the United States came into being, governments often do not simply regulate society but also deny or suppress basic freedoms and, in the economic sphere, threaten private property and the profitability of firms through excessive taxes and regulations. Thus for individual liberties to be secure, governments, to be truly democratic, must be actively restrained.

The architects of the U.S. government restrained its power in several ways. First, they established political liberties in the Bill of Rights, such as freedoms of speech and religion, that limited the sphere of governmental authority. Second, they disbursed power among the federal, state, and local governments. Finally, they provided for the sharing of federal powers between Congress and the president. Under the system of "checks and balances," neither branch would dominate national affairs nor violate individual rights. This institutional blueprint, devised more than two centuries ago, endures today. "The central feature of American politics is the fragmentation and dispersion of power and authority. It is not clear in the United States where sovereignty rests, if indeed it rests anywhere at all" (Krasner 1978, 61–62).

Yet for all its virtues in restraining centralized power, this fragmentation creates problems in the conduct of U.S. foreign policy, which requires a unified statement of national purpose, clear chains of command, consistency, and timely action taken by the head of state. Democratic norms "undermine and weaken the power and authority of government and detract, at times seriously, from its ability to compete internationally" (Huntington 1982, 18). Foreign powers can exploit internal divisions and try to divide and conquer its more fragmented rival. At home, a weak state is likely to be dominated, or "captured," by powerful interest groups, catering to their own needs rather than national interests. In this respect, de Tocqueville considered democracies "decidedly inferior" to other governments (see In Their Own Words box).

In disbursing foreign-policy powers across the legislative and executive branches, the architects of the U.S. government extended an "invitation to struggle for the privilege of directing American foreign policy" (Corwin 1957, 171). The institutional reality of divided powers leads to chronic friction between Congress and the White House over the ends and means of foreign policy. Unless the nation faces an unambiguous foreign challenge, the federal government rarely speaks with one voice. As a result, much of U.S. foreign policy is made, in the words of former Supreme Court Justice Robert Jackson (quoted in Henkin 1987–1988, 285), in a "zone of twilight in which [the president] and Congress may have concurrent authority, or in which its distribution is uncertain."

Institutional struggles within the U.S. government are not limited to legislative-executive relations. The executive branch itself is highly fragmented and prone to fierce internal competition over foreign policy. The Departments of

---

•))) IN THEIR OWN WORDS: ALEXIS DE TOCQUEVILLE (((•

Alexis de Tocqueville, an aristocratic Frenchman, traveled through the United States in 1831–1832 to chronicle the social, political, public, religious, and intellectual life of the emerging democratic nation. His account of these travels, Democracy in America, *long considered one of the most astute observations of American life ever written, is still widely read and studied by historians and political scientists alike.*

I have no hesitation in saying that in the control of society's foreign affairs democratic governments do appear decidedly inferior to others. . . . Foreign policy does not require the use of any of the good qualities peculiar to democracy but does demand the cultivation of almost all those which it lacks. . . .

Democracy favors the growth of the state's internal resources; it extends comfort and develops public spirit, strengthens respect for law in the various classes of society, all of which things have no more than an indirect influence on the standing of one nation in respect to another. But a democracy finds it difficult to coordinate the details of a great undertaking and to fix on some plan and carry it through with determination in spite of obstacles. It has little capacity for combining measures in secret and waiting patiently for the result.

Source: Alexis de Tocqueville, Democracy in America, *ed. J. P. Mayer (New York: Perennial Library, [1835] 1988), 228–230.*

State and Defense routinely disagree over policy issues and compete for White House attention, larger budgets, and greater authority. In this process, they must also contend with other departments, such as Commerce, Treasury, Energy, and the newly established Homeland Security. In the fray as well can be found more than a dozen intelligence agencies seeking to influence foreign policy. The National Security Council, created after World War II to coordinate this vast array of government institutions from inside the White House, has itself become an independent power center.

Presidents are often frustrated by their inability to reign in the bureaucratic actors presumably under their control. President Harry Truman (quoted in Neustadt 1960, 9) famously expressed this frustration in 1952 when he warned his successor, Dwight Eisenhower, not to expect the kind of military discipline he enjoyed as commander of U.S. armed forces during World War II. "He'll sit here and he'll say 'Do this! Do that!' And nothing will happen. Poor Ike—it won't be a bit like the Army. He'll find it very frustrating."

Pervasive Civil Society

In addition to these domestic political institutions, forces outside the government, and increasingly beyond the United States altogether, further complicate the American foreign-policy process. These external forces, which include public opinion, the news media, interest groups, and intergovernmental organizations, collectively form a **transnational civil society** that also constrains policy makers. In this context, the term *transnational* denotes societal forces extending beyond the political boundaries of the United States, including intergovernmental organizations and a growing number of private interest groups, corporate and nonprofit. As U.S. elected officials must be concerned with domestic public opinion for electoral reasons, so must they be sensitive to public opinion overseas, particularly in democratic countries whose support for American foreign policy is needed. Additionally, the financial ownership and coverage of major news outlets has become increasingly transnational. One of the most popular cable news networks, Fox, is based in Australia.

Although states remain the ultimate arbiters of policy, "transnational actors crucially affect state interests, policies, and inter-state relations" (Risse-Kappen 1995, 15). Churches, organized ethnic groups, multinational corporations, and other groups have influenced foreign policy throughout U.S. history, but never before have they been so well organized, visible, and connected with their counterparts overseas. This "power shift," Jessica Mathews (1997, 50) observed, affects all countries today:

> Increasingly, resources and threats that matter, including money, information, pollution, and popular culture, circulate and shape lives and economics with little regard for political boundaries. International standards of conduct are gradually beginning to override claims of national or regional singularity. Even the most powerful states find the marketplace and international public opinion compelling them more often to follow a particular course.

After World War II, the United States promoted such activism as part of a "constitutional" world order (Ikenberry 2001) that would project U.S. democratic principles and institutions on a global level. In this sense, transnational civil society serves as an extension of the nation's own civil society, which values public opinion and a free press while providing interest groups access to the government through many channels—congressional committees, executive agencies, the White House, and political campaigns. "Such organized groups," political theorist David Truman (1951, 502) observed more than half a century ago, "are as clearly a part of the government institution as are the political parties or the branches of government formally established by law or constitution." These forces exert enormous influence on political leaders, influence unseen in more insulated polities.

Each day, hundreds of intergovernmental organizations (IGOs) and thousands of nongovernmental organizations (NGOs) actively engage in foreign-policy issues of concern to the United States. These organizations, with membership increasingly drawn from multiple countries, pursue their policy preferences in many areas, including economic development, environmental protection, arms control, immigration, public health, and human rights (see Keck and Sikkink 1998). While serving as agents of U.S. foreign policy, however, they frequently challenge U.S. positions and preferences. Indeed, the constraints on U.S. sovereignty posed by these organizations, particularly IGOs associated with the United Nations, prompted the Bush administration's turn away from the international community when it came to power in 2001.

Each presidential administration in the United States selectively chooses which groups it will invite into the foreign-policy process. To the Bush administration, a primary source of input has been multinational corporations (MNCs) that share close connections with many top foreign-policy officials (see Table 1.1). The firms, which contributed large amounts of money to the Bush 2000 and 2004 presidential campaigns, naturally seek benefits from the U.S. government in the form of subsidies, public contracts, tax breaks, favorable regulations, or access to foreign markets.[5]

The prevalence of MNCs over nonprofit groups such as Amnesty International and Greenpeace, a consistent pattern that preceded Bush's election, makes it clear that not all interest groups are created equal. The Bush administration was commonly criticized for Vice President Dick Cheney's connection to Halliburton, a global energy company he headed before taking office. The Army Corps of Engineers disclosed in April 2003 that a Halliburton subsidiary received a noncompetitive contract in December 2001, worth up to $7 billion, to restore Iraqi oil wells in the aftermath of a possible war with the United States. Citing national-security concerns, U.S. officials did not solicit competitive bids for this and other contracts. Later in 2003, Defense Department investigators accused Halliburton of overcharging U.S. taxpayers for oil imports into Iraq and other services. Federal auditors in June 2004 told Congress they "saw very little con-

---

5. A useful guide to these corporate contacts is provided by the Center for Responsive Politics, a nonprofit NGO, via its Internet Web site, www.opensecrets.org.

cern for cost considerations" in Halliburton's management of these military contracts (Eckholm 2004).

Critics of the **pluralist theory** of democracy—the view that key groups compete for political influence on a level playing field—have long warned of undue corporate influence (see Chapter 3). "If there is government intervention in the corporate economy, so there is corporate intervention in the government process," C. Wright Mills observed in *The Power Elite* (1956, 8). This pattern, to be expected in any society that encourages a robust civil society, raises questions about a "democratic" foreign-policy process. To E. E. Schattschneider, "The flaw in the pluralist heaven is that the heavenly chorus sings with a strong upper-class accent" (1960, 35). Of central concern is how free U.S. leaders can be to make policy choices in the national interest when these leaders are so closely tied to corporations and their policy preferences. Constrained freedom of action, or autonomy, is the central feature of a "weak" state.

Other key elements of transnational civil society include public opinion and the news media, which further shape the external institutional environment surrounding U.S. foreign policy. Public opinion plays an important role in

Table 1.1 President Bush's Corporate Cabinet Connections

Cabinet Official (Position)	Corporate Connection
Richard Cheney (Vice President)	EDS Halliburton Procter & Gamble Union Pacific
Donald Rumsfeld (Secretary of Defense)	Allstate Amylin Pharmaceuticals Asea Brown Boveri G. D. Searle/Pharmacia General Dynamics General Instrument/Motorola Gilead Sciences Gulfstream Aerospace Kellogg Sears, Roebuck & Co. Tribune Company
Spencer Abraham (Secretary of Energy)	DaimlerChrysler Ford Motor Company General Motors Lear Corp.
Colin Powell (Secretary of State)	America Online/Time Warner General Dynamics Gulfstream Aerospace
Senior Staff (Position)	**Corporate Connection**
Condoleezza Rice (National Security Advisor)	Charles Schwab Chevron Transamerica Corp.

SOURCE: Center for Responsive Politics, "The Bush Administration Corporate Connections" (2004), www.opensecrets.org/bush/cabinet.asp.

the policy process of any democratic nation. Early studies in the United States found Americans to be largely ignorant of events taking place overseas and undependable as a source of guidance regarding U.S. foreign policy (Almond 1950; Bailey 1948; and Lippmann 1922). More recent surveys suggest greater coherence in public preferences (Jentleson 1992; Holsti 1992; and Wittkopf 1990). Nonetheless, surveys and nationwide tests of U.S. school students reveal a lack of in-depth knowledge of world history, geography, and international problems. Given the preeminent world role of the United States, these patterns are peculiar. They do, however, reflect the nation's physical distance from other power centers.

Trends in public opinion are closely related to coverage of international affairs by the news media. Such coverage decreased dramatically after the cold war as news organizations shut down overseas bureaus and reduced the percentage of international news to about 10 percent of total news coverage in the print and broadcast media (Graber 2002). National surveys (see, for example, Rielly 2003, 1999) consistently reveal that foreign news least concerns U.S. newspaper readers. All this changes when the United States faces an international crisis—media outlets then provide saturation coverage, "parachuting" into war zones correspondents who have little knowledge of the regions or conflicts they will be covering. Nonetheless, ratings for U.S. news networks skyrocketed during the 2003 invasion of Iraq, where news reporters "embedded" in U.S. battalions provided instant and dramatic images of Operation Iraqi Freedom.

Conclusion

A central question this book examines is how well the United States can provide the international leadership it espouses given the domestic and global constraints that are essential features of its political and social system. Of particular concern is whether a political culture alternately indifferent to foreign affairs and obsessed with events overseas is compatible with this type of dominant world role. The institutions of power raise further concerns about the U.S. government's ability to overcome domestic divisions as well as pressures from transnational civil society, particularly economic pressures. How the government manages the paradox of its world power will determine how long U.S. primacy endures in the turbulent new millennium.

This chapter began by noting the many ways the United States has not only inspired other countries but also provoked resentment from them. The mutual love-hate relationship between the United States and the world beyond its borders may be inevitable given the nation's unprecedented primacy. There is little doubt, however, that the country's successes and failures are also due to the peculiarities of the U.S. political system and social structures, the growing pressures imposed by transnational civil society, and their collective impact on the policy-making process.

All of these issues make the study of U.S. foreign policy a challenging, yet rewarding, enterprise at this critical period in the history of the nation and the world. The chapters ahead examine more closely the impact of domestic and transnational institutions on the process of U.S. foreign-policy making. The book's second and third sections analyze the structure of these institutions, and the final section illustrates their role in the primary domains of foreign policy: security and defense, economic affairs, and global problems such as environmental decay and weapons proliferation. First, we will review the origins and evolution of U.S. foreign policy in Chapter 2 and introduce the contending theories of foreign-policy decision making in Chapter 3.

Key Terms

asymmetric warfare, p. 10

exceptionalism, p. 13

globalization, p. 8

hegemony, p. 6

national style, p. 12

pluralist theory, p. 19

primacy, p. 2

soft power, p. 4

terrorism, p. 10

transnational civil society, p. 17

unipolar balance, p. 3

Internet References

The **American Foreign Policy Council** (www.afpc.org) is a nonprofit organization that focuses on democratization and bilateral and regional relationships between the United States and other countries. The organization has programs in Russia, China, and Asia to produce research regarding trade, defense, and other policy issues.

The **Brookings Institution** (www.brook.edu) is a nonprofit and nonpartisan think tank located in Washington, D.C. Brookings has a number of scholars, fellows, and academics who produce policy reports, briefs, and books related to U.S. foreign policy. Specific areas of interest are trade, defense, diplomacy, international institutions, and bilateral relations with foreign countries.

The **Carnegie Council on Ethics and International Affairs** (www.carnegiecouncil.org) focuses on human rights, conflict, environmental issues, economic disparities, and political reconciliation in the world. Scholars produce research briefs and books regarding current topics that analyze the ethics of international relations with a specific focus on the U.S. role in these policy issues. The Carnegie Council puts out a number of publications, including the journal *Ethics and International Affairs,* much of which is available online through the "publications" link on their home page.

The **Carnegie Endowment for International Peace** (www.ceip.org) is a private, nonprofit, and nonpartisan organization that focuses on global change by examining international organizations, bilateral relations, and political-economic forces in the world. Special focus is devoted to United States–Russia relationships as well as geopolitics involving the United States and other countries. The Carnegie Endowment for International Peace is also responsible for publishing *Foreign Policy,* one of the leading magazines for discussing world politics and foreign policy with a specific emphasis on the United States. *Foreign Policy* is available online at www.foreignpolicy.com.

The **Center for Strategic and International Studies** (www.csis.org) is a nonprofit and nonpartisan organization focusing on international defense and security issues. There is an emphasis on policy analysis, policy recommendations, and geographic analysis. The center publishes the *Washington Quarterly* (online at www.twq.com), which analyzes global changes and foreign policies with an emphasis on the U.S. role in the world, defense procurement, terrorism and counterterrorism, and regional issues.

The **Council on Foreign Relations** (www.cfr.org) studies international affairs, foreign policy, and the role of the United States in the world. The council covers an array of issues focusing on the United States, such as trade, defense, security, globalization, terrorism, specific regions, energy resources and the environment, and political systems. The council also publishes *Foreign Affairs* (online at www.foreignaffairs.org), which is a leading journal featuring scholarly analysis of these issues.

The **Department of State** (www.state.gov) manages many aspects of diplomacy, including foreign aid, peace building, democratization, disease and poverty prevention, and many other facets of the U.S. foreign-policy process. The Web site provides speeches, policy descriptions, and issue explanations for those studying American foreign policy.

continues

Internet References *(continued)*

The **Foreign Policy Association** (www.fpa.org) is a nonprofit organization with the mission of educating legislators and the American public on U.S. foreign-policy issues. It focuses on all aspects of U.S. foreign policy, with an emphasis on current events and global issues. The association provides reports, videos, and books on regional and specific policy issues.

Foreign Policy in Focus (www.fpif.org) is a think tank that writes policy reports focusing on the United States and its role in the world. Specific policy briefs and reports include, but are not limited to, human rights, regional relationships, bilateral relationships, defense funding and procurement, terrorism, trade, energy, and environmental issues.

Part of Johns Hopkins University, the **Foreign Policy Institute** (www.sais-jhu.edu/centers/fpi) provides training and research on the global role of the United States. The institute brings all disciplines interested in U.S. foreign policy together. It also publishes the *SAIS Review* (online at www.saisreview.org), which analyzes current international policies.

The **Foreign Policy Research Institute** (www.fpri.org) is a research-based organization that focuses on studying U.S. national interests, the war on terrorism, security relationships, and long-term policy planning. The research is based on a multidisciplinary approach including scholars and advisers from economics, politics, law, the media, and history. *ORBIS,* a quarterly journal published by FPRI (online at www.fpri.org/orbis), consists of reports from conferences and scholars regarding U.S. and world national interests.

The **Hoover Institution on War, Revolution, and Peace** (www-hoover.stanford.edu) is a center devoted to policy analysis and both domestic and international affairs research within the ideological framework of an emphasis on free society. The Hoover Institution researches trade, markets, postcommunist transition, international law, and democratic growth. Fellows at the Hoover Institution produce policy briefs, the *Hoover Digest*, and books through the Hoover Press.

The **Institute for Foreign Policy Analysis** (www.ifpa.org) provides briefings for foreign-policy students who are interested in costs, benefits, and planning of U.S. foreign policy. The institute covers a variety of issues but focuses on globalization, missile defense, international institutions, and grand strategies.

The **RAND Corporation** (www.rand.org) is a private research group focusing on international affairs, homeland security, terrorism, and U.S. national security issues. It also produces reports on individual countries that have close ties to the United States. RAND produces the *RAND Review* (online at www.rand.org/publications/randreview), a magazine about current security and defense issues.

2

The Expansion of U.S. Power

U.S. President Theodore Roosevelt tests a steam shovel during construction of the Panama Canal in November 1906. Roosevelt had supported earlier efforts by Panamanian rebels to seize control of the future canal zone, declare independence from Colombia, and seek diplomatic recognition by the United States. Congress promptly approved a treaty with the new government that granted the United States "power and authority" over the canal "in perpetuity." Under President Jimmy Carter, the U.S. government agreed in 1977 to turn control of the canal over to Panama in 2000.

The central goal of this book is to help readers understand U.S. foreign policy today. Such an understanding is impossible, however, without reference to the nation's past experience, first as a regional power and then as the predominant world power. In this chapter, we review these developments and consider their relevance to the current policy process. We cannot provide an exhaustive survey of U.S. diplomatic history in a single chapter, but we can highlight the pivotal events that shaped the nation's relations with the world beyond its shores.[1]

Two major themes of U.S. foreign policy are discussed in this historical review. The first involves the expansion of American territory and wealth during a period, stretching from the Revolutionary War to the First World War, when the United States remained aloof from the diplomacy of the European powers. The second theme involves the management of U.S. global commitments once the country became a great power. Of particular concern are the institutional arrangements, domestic and transnational, created during the U.S. government's "rise to globalism" (Ambrose 1988) and persisting today under very different and rapidly changing circumstances.

---

1. There are many sources available for more extensive information on this subject. See, for example, Hook and Spanier (2004) for a detailed review of U.S. foreign policy after World War II. A more critical view of the cold war is provided by LaFeber (2004) and McCormick (1995), among others. H. Jones (2002) and Paterson, Clifford, and Hagan (2000) offer informative histories of the nation's early foreign policy.

Economic and Territorial Expansion

Constructing political institutions that could preserve the nation's independence was a primary concern of early American leaders. The Articles of Confederation, which in 1781 established the framework of the first American political system, featured a very weak central government. Under the Articles, the original thirteen states conducted their own trade policies while the cash-starved Congress largely dismantled the nation's military forces, actions that made the United States vulnerable to intimidation from the more unified powers overseas. The country cried out for a stronger national government.

Under the U.S. Constitution, devised in 1787 and ratified in 1788, states maintained primary control over their internal affairs while ceding sovereignty to the federal government. The president and Congress shared responsibilities for American foreign policy (see Chapters 4 and 5). To James Madison, the primary architect of the Constitution, such power sharing was crucial to the democratic control of government. On the one hand, the president, who would serve as commander in chief of U.S. armed forces while conducting the day-to-day business of foreign policy, would be able to act more quickly and decisively than Congress. On the other, Congress, with its powers to declare war and control spending, among other powers, would restrain the president. Together they would provide a unified front for the advancement of the nation's foreign-policy goals.

The new framework was not meant to encourage U.S. activism in diplomacy, which many Americans saw as an artifact of the Old World, long dominated by monarchs, priests, and feudal despots. Thomas Jefferson (quoted in Rubin 1985, 3), the first secretary of state and third president, dismissed diplomacy as "the pest of the peace of the world, as the workshop in which nearly all the wars of Europe are manufactured." Although the State Department was the first federal agency created under the Constitution, it received few resources and, for more than a century, maintained only a tiny staff.[2]

Architects of U.S. foreign-policy institutions made an exception for foreign *economic* relations, which they considered more suitable than diplomacy in advancing the nation's interests. Early in the nineteenth century, the government hired hundreds of consular officers to secure markets overseas and ensure the protection of U.S. merchant ships and crews. By 1820, the United States had become the fourth richest country in the world as measured by per capita income (Prestowitz 2003, 84). A leading exporter of agriculture, primarily cotton and tobacco, the nation would soon become a major producer of industrial goods as well.

Although early American leaders disagreed about the means of attaining foreign-policy goals, they shared an expansive view of the nation's future. Alexander Hamilton (quoted in Earle 1937, 69), the first treasury secretary, believed the

---

2. The State Department had just eight employees in 1790, twenty-three in 1830, and forty-two in 1860. The U.S. government did not create a full-scale foreign service until 1924, long after the United States had emerged as a major world power. (See www.state.gov for a chronology of the department's budget and personnel.)

Point/Counterpoint
HAMILTON VS. JEFFERSON

Differences over the direction U.S. foreign policy should take were epitomized in the nation's early years by Alexander Hamilton and Thomas Jefferson. Although both political leaders believed the United States was destined to join the ranks of the great powers, they disagreed about how this feat should be accomplished.

An admirer of Great Britain's political and economic system, Hamilton thought the United States should establish itself as a major industrial power with a strong navy and close financial ties to foreign capitals, including London. Jefferson believed the United States should adopt a more modest course, refining its democracy at home and creating a nation of small farmers rather than industrialists. He worried that building the stronger national government favored by Hamilton would inevitably lead to a standing military force and a tyrannical head of state.

The two men never resolved their ideological differences. However, after taking office in 1801, Jefferson, in the types of actions he undertook, displayed much of Hamilton's penchant for wielding power. The new president moderated his staunch support for France, where he had previously served as ambassador. As France descended into the Napoleonic Wars, Jefferson proclaimed that U.S. security should be maintained by "peace, commerce, and honest friendship with all nations—entangling alliances with none." Jefferson also exploited his presidential powers in negotiating the Louisiana Purchase and undertaking other measures that enhanced the nation's territorial and military strength.

country should "erect one great American system, superior to the control of all trans-Atlantic force or influence, and able to dictate the terms of the connection between the old and the new world." Jefferson, too, envisioned U.S. dominance extending beyond the nation's borders. He foresaw an "empire of liberty" in which "our rapid multiplication will . . . cover the whole northern if not southern continent, with people speaking the same language, governed by similar forms, and by similar laws" (quoted in McDougall 1997, 78).

Contrary to conventional wisdom, the United States was hardly an isolationist country during this period (see Table 2.1). The government pursued an expansionist foreign policy, westward and *away* from the great powers of Europe, while also becoming immersed in foreign trade. This period was one of **unilateralism.** Rather than collaborating and pooling resources with allies, leaders pursuing a unilateral foreign policy seek to be self-sufficient. To President George Washington, who severed an alliance with France in 1793 despite that nation's earlier role in securing American independence, the benefits of going it alone

Table 2.1 U.S. Foreign-Policy Chronology, 1783–1945

1783	United States gains independence from Great Britain.
1788	Constitution establishes stronger American government.
1793	United States proclaims neutrality in European wars.
1803	France sells Louisiana territory to United States.
1812	Territorial and trade disputes provoke U.S. war with Great Britain.
1823	Monroe Doctrine proclaims U.S. sphere of influence throughout Western Hemisphere.
1845	United States annexes Texas.
1846–1848	Mexican-American War.
1853	United States forcefully "opens" Japan to American trade.
1867	Russia sells Alaska to the United States.
1898	United States annexes Hawaii.
1898	Spanish-American War.
1899	United States calls for "open-door policy" toward China.
1902	U.S. troops overcome insurrection in the Philippines.
1903	United States signs treaty to build Panama Canal.
1904	Roosevelt Corollary to Monroe Doctrine proclaims United States "international police power."
1914	World War I begins in Europe.
1917	United States declares war against Germany.
1918	German surrender ends World War I.
1919	U.S. Senate rejects Treaty of Versailles and League of Nations.
1928	Kellogg-Briand Pact renounces war as "instrument of national policy."
1935, 1936	Congress passes neutrality acts barring American intervention in Europe.
1939	German territorial conquests lead to World War II.
1941	Japanese attack on Hawaii provokes U.S. entry into World War II.
1944	Bretton Woods system, including World Bank and International Monetary Fund, created to manage world economy.
1945	Defeat of Axis powers ends World War II. Creation of United Nations.

outweighed those of alliance.[3] Alliances, in fact, had significant costs in expanding the nation's overseas commitments. Upon leaving office three years later, Washington summarized his view (quoted in Merrill and Paterson 2000, 75–76):

> The great rule of conduct for us in regard to foreign nations is, in extending our commercial relations to have with them as little political connection as possible. . . . Europe has a set of primary interests which to us have none or a very remote relation. Hence she must be engaged in frequent controversies, the causes of which are essentially foreign to our concerns. . . . Our detached and distant situation invites and enables us to pursue a different course. . . . It is our true policy to steer clear of permanent alliances with any portion of the foreign world.

---

3. The ill-fated pact between the United States and France was the last peacetime alliance signed by the U.S. government until the mid-twentieth century.

Manifest Destiny on the Western Frontier

The United States, driven by a "cult of nationalism" (Van Alstyne 1965) that provided a moral basis for expansion, came to dominate the Western Hemisphere by default. The nation's emergence as a regional power coincided with the demise of the British, French, Russian, and Spanish outposts in North America. The United States filled this geopolitical vacuum in a variety of ways: by buying vast territories at bargain prices, negotiating settlements, and forcefully seizing territories when other measures failed. Through these actions, the United States became the hemisphere's economic and military giant, and a global superpower in the making.

In expanding westward, settlers and government forces violently subdued the American Indian population, whose relatively small numbers, internal divisions, and lack of modern weaponry left them incapable of successfully resisting encroachments on their lands. Early government leaders sought to assimilate the American Indians into the general population and society (Steele 1994). But their successors abandoned such notions and made the displacement or elimination of Native Americans an object of government policy. Though this aspect of U.S. expansion falls outside the conventional bounds of foreign policy, it is nevertheless "a central theme of American diplomatic history" (LaFeber 1989, 10).

The first major territorial gain occurred in 1803, when Jefferson acquired the vast Louisiana territory, which stretched westward from the Mississippi River to the Rocky Mountains and northward from the Gulf of Mexico to the Oregon Territory. Napoleon Bonaparte, who had regained the territory from Spain two years earlier, was unable to govern, let alone defend, such a massive amount of land in North America while pursuing his ambitions in Europe. He made the most of his plight by offering Louisiana to the United States for $15 million. Jefferson, though suspecting that his role in the Louisiana Purchase was "an act beyond the Constitution," eagerly accepted the offer (see Kukla 2003).

The acquisition of the Louisiana territory, followed by the displacement of Spain from Florida, left the United States free to focus on state building, economic development, and further continental expansion. (See Map 1, Nineteenth-Century European Empires and U.S. Continental Expansion, in the map section at the front of the book.) After the War of 1812, in which they struggled over unresolved trade and territorial differences, the United States and Great Britain established close economic ties. The Spanish empire's demise in Latin America, which led to the liberation of its Latin American colonies, paved the way for U.S. regional hegemony, external dominance without formal political authority. In 1823, President James Monroe, seeking to discourage renewed European intrusions in Latin America as well as Russian ambitions along the Pacific coast, proclaimed the **Monroe Doctrine** (quoted in Merrill and Paterson 2000, 171), which further separated the United States from the European powers:

> In the wars of the European powers in matters relating to themselves we have never taken any part, nor does it comport with our policy to do so. . . . With the movements in this hemisphere we are of necessity more immediately connected. . . . The political system of the [European] powers is essentially different in this respect from

that of America. . . . [W]e should consider any attempt on their part to extend their system to any portion of this hemisphere as dangerous to our peace and safety.

Mexico's independence from Spain in 1821 paved the way for the next significant act of U.S. expansion. With an impotent government and a citizenry impoverished by Spanish exploitation, the new nation proved weak and vulnerable. Over the years, many Americans purchased land in the northern Mexican province of Texas, and in 1835, this growing population launched an independence movement of their own. Within a year, Texan rebels had defeated the Mexican army and declared Texas an independent country.

The U.S. government's annexation of Texas in 1845 was widely viewed not simply as another territorial gain but as further evidence that the United States had God's blessing to continue its westward expansion. In the *Democratic Review,* editor John O'Sullivan (quoted in Pratt 1927, 797–798) proclaimed the **manifest destiny** of the United States "to overspread the continent allotted by Providence for the free development of our yearly multiplying millions." Such popular claims were applied to the weakly defended Mexican territories west and north of Texas, for which President James Polk initiated a series of border skirmishes that escalated into a full-scale war. The United States quickly defeated the Mexican army, then signed a peace treaty in 1848 requiring Mexico to cede nearly 1 million square miles of land.

This period of continental expansion coincided with the rapid growth of the U.S. economy. Another myth about this period (in addition to the one of U.S. isolationism) holds that the United States served as a champion and exemplar of free trade. To the contrary, the U.S. government protected domestic firms through an aggressive industrial policy that maintained high tariffs, or taxes, on imports while subsidizing domestic firms with grants and low-interest government loans. In this respect early U.S. leaders adopted the same policies of economic nationalism that the Japanese government pursued during its industrial boom in the twentieth century (see Chapter 11).

Domestic business and trade groups, seen by government leaders as de facto ambassadors of U.S. diplomatic policy, assumed a vital role in shaping the nation's foreign policy. Long before interest-group lobbying became a booming industry in Washington, D.C., business leaders had close ties to their representatives in Congress, which under the Constitution was granted the power to "regulate commerce." These leaders, almost exclusively white and male, formed a powerful voting bloc at a time when women, blacks, and other minority groups were disenfranchised. As a result, Congress was "little more than an instrument for negotiating, reconciling, and accommodating the demands of American businessmen for higher tariffs" (Dahl 1967, 404).

Opening the Door to Asia

The conquest of northern Mexico, along with the acquisition of the Oregon Territory from Great Britain in 1846, effectively closed the western frontier, which had been a symbol of virtually endless opportunity for American expansion. Advocates of continued expansion turned to the Pacific Ocean as the new frontier. "He would be a rash prophet who should assert that the expansive character of America has now entirely ceased," wrote historian Frederick Jackson Turner in 1920 (37). "Movement has been its dominant fact, and, unless this training has no effect upon a people, the American energy will continually demand a wider field for its exercise."

The United States had much to gain economically by tapping into the enormous markets of East Asia. Expansionists downplayed this economic rationale, however, emphasizing nobler motivations instead. An appeal to economic interests would cast the country in the same light as the traditional great powers, which supposedly lacked the "manifest destiny" uniquely bestowed upon the Americans. Even as it fought the Mexican army for control of the western frontier, the United States was making overtures to Japan for commercial relations. When these efforts failed, President Millard Fillmore, in 1853, deployed naval vessels to Tokyo. Faced with this early example of **gunboat diplomacy,** Japan's emperor accepted a "treaty of friendship" in 1854 that provided for U.S. access to the Japanese market.

American interests on the Pacific Ocean extended well beyond Japan. The United States occupied several islands that served as coaling stations for U.S. ships; and such occupation also prevented other countries from taking the islands. The United States was especially interested in the Hawaiian Islands, located midway between North America and Asia. American officials first sought favorable commercial treatment from the Hawaiian monarchy. Unable to achieve a treaty on its own terms, the U.S. government, in 1893, recruited a rebel army that staged a successful coup against the monarchy. Within days, the new government of Hawaii had signed a treaty of annexation with the United States. The United States also gained control of Alaska during this period, purchasing the remote territory from Russia's czar for $7 million.[4]

Critics accused the United States of behaving like the European empires it had long condemned. Such protests proved futile as illustrated by the Spanish-American War, in which the United States clashed with Spain over its colony in Cuba. As American forces were ousting Spain from Cuba, a U.S. fleet on the other side of the world was defeating Spanish forces in the Philippines, another Spanish colony. The United States gained control of the Philippines only after waging a lengthy war that left thousands of casualties, largely Filipino, in its wake. President William McKinley chose not to annex Cuba, preferring to control the island indirectly, but adopted a different approach to the Philippines. The United States recognized the Southeast Asian islands' commercial potential, particularly when linked to the rapidly expanding markets of China. Advocates of American occupation seized upon the prospect of bringing Christianity and "civilization" to the Philippines. These factors contributed to McKinley's decision to rule the Philip-

---

4. Alaska and Hawaii remained U.S. territories until 1959, when they became the forty-ninth and fiftieth states of the union, respectively.

pines as a U.S. colony, marking an exception to the U.S. government's general rule of opposing colonization.

The United States entered the twentieth century as the only major regional superpower, a hegemon, with foreign-policy interests of global proportions. The nation's territorial reach extended across North America and the Pacific Ocean. Its population had doubled to 71 million between 1865 and 1900, due in large part to European immigration. Meanwhile, U.S. economic output matched, then exceeded, that of the major European powers. More Americans lived in cities than in rural areas, and industrial production contributed more than agriculture to national output. As an increasing number of American corporations became multinational, conditions overseas became all the more vital at home. In 1899, the United States had proclaimed an **open-door policy** toward China, which reaffirmed the equal access of all nations to Chinese ports. Designed to prevent the nation from being carved up among European trading interests, the policy also firmly established the American presence on the Asian mainland. To the critical historian William Appleman Williams (1959, 43), the open-door policy "was derived from the proposition that America's overwhelming economic power would cast the economy and the politics of the weaker, under-developed countries in a pro-American mold."

A Big Stick in Latin America

President Theodore Roosevelt, a former naval commander, a veteran of the Spanish-American War, and a strong advocate of U.S. expansion (see Morris 2001), proved to be the key American figure in foreign policy as the new century began. He eagerly sought to become a world leader. In 1905, he received the Nobel Peace Prize for negotiating the end of the Russo-Japanese War. Two years later, Roosevelt deployed a U.S. naval armada around the world, a symbol of the nation's arrival as a global power. The president believed in a version of social Darwinism that viewed wars as both inevitable and noble, with the victors assigned a "mandate from civilization" to look after less-powerful nations. Citing a favorite aphorism from his safaris in Africa, Roosevelt pledged that the United States would "speak softly, but carry a big stick."

The Roosevelt administration concerned itself in particular with Latin America, a U.S. sphere of influence since the proclamation of the Monroe Doctrine. The president engineered a domestic uprising in northern Colombia in 1903, after which the United States recognized the new Republic of Panama and signed a treaty to build and lease the Panama Canal. Concerned now not only with European meddling in the region, but also with internal power struggles that threatened friendly governments, the president issued the **Roosevelt Corollary** to the Monroe Doctrine. Such unrest, it stated, "may ultimately require intervention by some civilized nation" and "may force the United States, however reluctantly . . . to the exercise of an international police power." In the years to follow, the United States would intervene militarily in the Dominican Republic, Haiti, Honduras, Nicaragua, and other countries where internal unrest threatened foreign investments and produced large debts for the United States and other nations.

Fighting Two World Wars

While the Roosevelt Corollary affirmed U.S. dominance of the Western Hemisphere, developments elsewhere created new challenges for the United States. In Europe, a century of relative calm was quickly coming to an end. The creation of a unified German state in 1871 started this downward spiral. Germany's rise coincided with the decline of the Ottoman, Russian, and Austro-Hungarian empires, all of which had contributed to a crude, but durable, balance of power in Europe. These major shifts in the global balance of power, with the United States and Japan rising in stature beyond Europe, would lead to two world wars in the first half of the twentieth century.

The First World War

For Americans, Europe's plunge into war in 1914 affirmed the prudence of their country's historic aversion to foreign entanglements (see Tuchman 1962). Austria-Hungary's war declaration against Serbia, for example, had been made possible by Germany's support for the empire. Alliance commitments also came into play as Germany went to war against Russia, an ally of Serbia, and against France, an ally of Russia. Great Britain justified its entry into the war with its security guarantees to Belgium, through which German troops passed on their way to France.

As order unraveled in Europe, President Woodrow Wilson sought to keep the United States "neutral in fact as well as name." But the country could not maintain its detached posture once the conflict in Europe extended into the Atlantic Ocean. The German navy began attacking merchant ships, many of them owned and operated by Americans. Any hopes for U.S. noninvolvement ended in May 1915, when a German submarine destroyed the British ocean liner *Lusitania,* whose passengers had included 128 American citizens. Although the United States managed to stay out of combat for another two years, Germany's prosecution of submarine warfare had angered the American public, inclining it toward war. Russia's withdrawal from the conflict in November 1917 secured Germany's position in the east and allowed its forces to concentrate along the western front. The prospect of German control over all Europe, and the implications this would have for U.S. security, prompted Wilson to declare war against Germany.

The United States contributed to the war effort in two ways. First, Wilson drew upon the nation's immense industrial capacity by shipping massive volumes of weapons, munitions, and medical supplies to its allies, who were mired in a defensive stalemate against Germany. Troops on both sides were dug into long lines of mud-filled trenches, unable to advance against the new generation of armored tanks, long-range artillery, and automatic weapons. Second, Wilson deployed U.S. troops to the western front to reinforce the exhausted French and British forces and begin the slow counteroffensive. The arrival and strength of the U.S. forces ultimately tipped the balance in the First World War, leading to Germany's surrender in November 1918.

Failed Efforts to Keep the Peace

As noted earlier, neither the U.S. government nor the general public was eager for the United States to become engaged in the First World War. The "entangling alliances" of the European powers, which transformed a regional crisis into a world war, were precisely what U.S. diplomats had long avoided. However, Germany's early success in the war raised the prospect of an even greater threat: the emergence of a single European state that would overturn the balance of power. Such a scenario had struck fear into American leaders since the day Thomas Jefferson (quoted in Graebner 1964, 122) declared, "It cannot be to our interest that all Europe should be reduced to a single monarchy."

The U.S. government, however, was also uncomfortable with a security policy based entirely upon **geopolitics,** the distribution of global power. For Wilson, who was the son of a Presbyterian minister and had a strong sense of moral mission (see George and George 1956), the nation had to have a moral rationale for intervention. In his view, the United States should not fight simply for its survival or that of its allies. The nation should defend a more general principle: the right of citizens of any country to determine their own destinies. World War I, then, became a war to "make the world safe for democracy." When the war ended, Wilson felt duty bound to seek a world order that would put these principles into practice and ensure that the recent conflict had been "the war to end wars." To the president, the United States was uniquely able, and divinely ordained, to lead this effort: "America has said to mankind at her birth: 'We have come to redeem the world by giving it liberty and justice.' Now we are called upon before the tribunal of mankind to redeem that immortal pledge" (Wilson 1927, 645).

Wilson believed that a long-term solution was needed to overcome the anarchic world order, whose lack of global governance allowed such horrific wars to take place. His proposed solution was a new system based on the concept of **collective security.** In such a system, leaders would renounce war as an instrument of statecraft, then pledge to defend each other in the case of outside aggression. If every government agreed to such a scheme and backed up their words with concrete action, any aggression would be doomed. Expansionist states would be deterred, and world peace would be assured. Wilson outlined his plan to Congress early in 1918, when he identified "fourteen points" that all countries should respect. Among them were worldwide disarmament, decolonization, freedom of the seas, open markets, and the prohibition of secret diplomacy. Most importantly, the president proposed the formation of the League of Nations, which would provide the institutional foundation for collective security. In the League, conflicting states would have a forum to discuss and resolve their differences peacefully. If any government violated the rules and invaded another country, League members would collectively repel the aggression.

Wilson's design, which would presumably deter nations from foreign aggression in the first place, was generally well received by other governments. In seeking to transform world politics, however, Wilson forgot about U.S. politics. Specifically, he neglected the separation of powers that provided Congress with a vital role in foreign, as well as domestic, policy. Legislators resented their exclusion from the peace conference and complained that the Treaty of Versailles, in requiring military interventions when necessary to uphold collective security, deprived Congress of its constitutional power to declare war. This combination of animosity toward Wilson and constitutional concerns led Congress to exercise another of its foreign-policy powers by voting down the treaty. Thus the United States, whose leader had been the primary architect of the organization, never joined the League of Nations.

Wilson also underestimated the powerful grip held by national sovereignty on the calculations of political leaders. In seeking to remake the interstate system, the League sought to weaken national sovereignty in its most vital area: military self-defense. The enduring hold of sovereignty over collective security was revealed in 1931, when Japanese troops invaded the province of Manchuria in northern China. This clear case of aggression presumably should have triggered the League's collective-security mechanism. Yet most members displayed no interest in deploying their troops to a remote region of little concern to them. League members denounced the Japanese invasion and voted to impose economic sanctions but took no military action. Italy's 1935 invasion of Ethiopia, in the horn of Africa, brought the same responses. In both instances, the League revealed itself as a paper tiger that, far from rendering war obsolete, seemed to encourage and reward aggression by creating a false sense of security among nations that did not have aggressive designs.

Its absence from the League of Nations did not keep the United States from seeking ways to prevent another world war. To the contrary, during the 1920s, the government actively engaged in efforts to rebuild trust among the European powers and to achieve stability at the global level. Two of these efforts are particularly noteworthy.

First, the U.S. government sought disarmament among the major powers. At the time, most people believed that the arms buildups that began just after the turn of the century fueled distrust among the major powers, encouraged expansionism, and once fighting broke out, produced a more destructive and protracted war than would otherwise have been possible. With these presumptions in mind, President Warren Harding convened the Washington Naval Conference in 1921 and 1922, which the foreign ministers of Great Britain, France, Italy, and Japan attended. The participating governments agreed to suspend construction of large naval vessels and to limit the size of aircraft carriers. In addition, they agreed on a complex balance of naval power by which the size of the five navies would be fixed and strictly regulated.

Second, the United States favored an international treaty to "outlaw" war. Two assumptions underlay the treaty: military force was wrongly considered an acceptable tool of statecraft, and the destructive power of modern military weapons, clearly demonstrated in the First World War, made the future use of such weapons suicidal to all parties. While critics considered these assumptions naive in the extreme, leading intellectuals and popular figures in the United States and Europe embraced a global ban on war. In 1928, representatives from fifteen countries signed the Kellogg-Briand Pact, which condemned "recourse to war for the solution of international controversies (and) as an instrument of national policy." Eventually, sixty-two governments, including Germany, Italy, Japan, and the Soviet Union, signed the agreement.

These heralded reforms, however, did not prevent the major powers from playing the same old game of power politics. After Japan seized control of Manchuria in 1931, Prime Minister Hideki Tojo ordered his forces to gain control of the entire Chinese coastline. Two years later, Adolph Hitler became chancellor of Germany, repudiated the Treaty of Versailles, and vowed to obtain the *lebensraum* (living space) required by the German people. Taking its cue from Hitler, Italy's fascist government, led by Benito Mussolini, launched its invasion of Ethiopia in 1935.

In the United States, foreign-policy makers reverted to their traditional posture of detachment. President Franklin Roosevelt, elected in 1932, was most concerned with rescuing the American economy from the Great Depression. The crash of the U.S. stock market in 1929 had sent unemployment soaring. A global trade war, which had culminated in the Smoot-Hawley Tariff Act of 1930, boosting U.S. tariffs to their highest levels ever, had greatly worsened the economic slump.

The State Department suffered deep cuts in the ensuing budget crisis and remained "unhonored, underpaid, and understaffed" (Rubin 1985, 20–21). "Ambassadors received little guidance. Americans were bystanders to the tragic march of events that led to World War II." Roosevelt initially sought to aid the victims of Italy's aggression. But Congress rejected his efforts and instead passed Neutrality Acts in 1935 and 1936 that barred the United States from aiding any of the belligerents.[5]

The Second World War

Once again, however, events in Europe made the U.S. hands-off policy impossible to maintain. After repudiating the Versailles treaty and rebuilding his armed forces, Hitler annexed Austria and eastern Czechoslovakia. He assured other European leaders afterward that these actions satisfied his territorial needs, but his pledges soon proved empty. In 1939, Germany invaded Poland and then divided the defeated country with the Soviet Union, with whom Hitler earlier had signed a nonaggression pact. That pact proved just as worthless as the German's leader's earlier promises. In 1941, Hitler launched a massive blitzkrieg against the Soviet Union. Having "neutralized" the eastern front, German forces then overran most of western Europe. Only Great Britain remained free of German domination.

By this time, American political leaders generally favored U.S. intervention, but the public remained unconvinced that the escalating conflict in Europe threatened the United States. Publicly, Roosevelt bowed to the public view. With his eye on the November 1940 elections, he (quoted in Schulzinger 1994, 172) declared, "I have said this before and I shall say it again and again and again: Your boys are

---

5. Isolationist sentiment was fueled by the publication of a best-selling book, *Merchants of Death* (Engelbrecht 1934), which charged that the U.S. entry into World War I had been the result of political pressure imposed by profit-hungry arms manufacturers.

not going to be sent into any foreign wars." Nonetheless, Roosevelt brought the nation's considerable resources to bear in support of its allies. As Germany advanced toward the English Channel, the president, through the lend-lease program, provided Great Britain with U.S. military hardware and ships in exchange for American access to British bases in the Caribbean.

The first direct assault on the United States occurred half a world away. With French and Dutch colonies in East Asia up for grabs, Japanese leaders knew that only the United States stood in the way of their plan to create a Japanese-led "co-prosperity sphere" throughout the region. On December 7, 1941, Japanese warplanes attacked the large American naval base at Pearl Harbor, Hawaii. The raid killed some 2,500 Americans and devastated the U.S. fleet. Roosevelt declared December 7 a "day of infamy." Three days later, Germany, which had formed an "axis" with Japan and Italy, declared war against the United States. Domestic debates on American intervention ended.

Roosevelt chose to avoid the moralistic rationales for U.S. involvement that Wilson had employed in World War I. Instead, he identified clear threats to national security and focused on military measures to overcome them. The United States would be engaged militarily on two fronts, thousands of miles apart. In the Pacific, the United States would restore its naval forces and reverse Japan's advances, which by 1943 included the Philippines (still a U.S. colony) as well as Malaya, Singapore, and Vietnam. In the European struggle, U.S. and British forces would first expel the Axis powers from North Africa, then direct their counteroffensive into Europe from the south. Allied forces would then land on the west coast of France and begin their eastward push against German troops.

Despite staggering death tolls, the Allies slowly achieved their goals. After landing on the coast of Normandy, France, on June 6, 1944, the U.S.-led forces steadily pushed the German army back to Berlin. Here the Allied forces joined Soviet troops that had been equally successful on the eastern front. Germany's surrender, along with Hitler's suicide, came in May 1945. The Japanese emperor, however, remained defiant, despite the retreat of his forces to the mainland.

A month before the surrender, Roosevelt had suffered a fatal stroke and was replaced by Harry Truman. The new president would face the most fateful decision of the war, possibly the most ominous decision in human history. Unbeknown to Truman, U.S. military scientists had been experimenting with nuclear energy, which if ignited through atomic fusion could yield an explosive force of unprecedented magnitude. The scientists involved in the secret Manhattan Project, based in Los Alamos, New Mexico, detonated the first nuclear bomb there on July 16, 1945. Only then did government officials notify Truman of this awesome new weapon, which could soon be made available for use against Japan. The president understood that defeating Japan through conventional means would require a massive assault on the Japanese mainland, leading to an incalculable loss of life on both sides. With this in mind, he approved the August 6 nuclear bombing of Hiroshima and the August 9 bombing of Nagasaki, which together killed nearly 150,000 Japanese citizens. Faced with the prospect of additional U.S. nuclear attacks, Japan surrendered to the United States and brought World War II to a merciful close.

Global Primacy and the Cold War

Immediately after World War II, the United States entered the third global conflict of the twentieth century. This conflict was named the cold war because it never led to direct military combat between its principal antagonists, the United States and the Soviet Union. The basis of this conflict was ideological, pitting the capitalist countries, led by the United States, against the communist countries, primarily the Soviet Union. Whereas capitalism respected private property and glorified free enterprise, communism sought to improve living standards by erecting a powerful state that owned and operated the means of economic production. A military showdown between the two superpowers would have produced death and destruction of unknowable proportions. The cold war, while it avoided such an outcome, produced an endless series of "hot" wars in other parts of the world, mainly among developing countries caught in the crossfire (see Table 2.2).

The United States emerged from World War II as the predominant world power, maintaining a nuclear monopoly and producing as much economic output as the rest of the world combined. However, the Soviet Union, exploiting its con-

Table 2.2 U.S. Foreign-Policy Chronology: The Cold War

1945	Yalta Conference of victorious powers seeks to organize postwar world.
1946	George Kennan devises containment strategy as cold war sets in.
1947	Marshall Plan and Truman Doctrine call for U.S. aid to allies; National Security Act creates new structures of U.S. foreign policy.
1949	NATO is formed by United States and 11 other nations.
1950	North Korea attacks South Korea, prompting UN military intervention.
1953	End of Korean War; CIA aids overthrow of Iran's government.
1954	CIA aids overthrow of Guatemala's government.
1959	Cuban rebels overthrow U.S.-backed Batista regime.
1962	Cuban missile crisis forces military and diplomatic showdown between USSR and United States.
1964	Congress authorizes U.S. military intervention in Vietnam.
1968	Tet offensive in Vietnam prompts antiwar movement in United States.
1970	Nixon orders bombing and invasion of Cambodia; four students killed at Kent State University, Ohio.
1972	Nixon launches détente strategy, visits Soviet Union and China, signs antiballistic missile (ABM) treaty with USSR.
1979	Iranian militants seize U.S. embassy in Teheran, leading to 444-day hostage crisis; Sandinista revolution in Nicaragua; Soviet Union invades Afghanistan.
1981	Reagan begins major military buildup as cold war heats up.
1986	Reagan and Gorbachev approve Strategic Arms Reduction Treaty (START); U.S. covert support for Nicaraguan contras leads to Iran-contra scandal.
1989	Hungary opens borders with Austria, signaling the beginning of the end of the cold war.
1990	Russia and Ukraine declare independence from Soviet Union; Germany reunified.
1991	Soviet Union dissolves, ending the cold war.

siderable resources, both real and potential, soon shifted the global balance of power to a **bipolar** one, with the United States and Soviet Union representing the contesting "poles." (See Figure 2.1.) With a sphere of influence that spanned from East Germany to the Alaskan border, the Soviet Union possessed the world's largest conventional forces and gradually caught up with the United States in the nuclear arms race. In addition to the arms race, the worldwide competition for allies became a defining element of the cold war. Each superpower hoped to tip the balance in its favor by recruiting allies beyond its borders.

Strains between the United States and Soviet Union, allies against the Axis powers in World War II, became insurmountable shortly after the war. Joseph Stalin, the Soviet leader, imposed firm control over the countries of Eastern Europe that his armies had liberated from Nazi Germany. Stalin had no interest in withdrawing from the region that twice in his lifetime had served as a staging base for German invasions. In February 1946, he predicted an inevitable clash between the communist and capitalist countries and the eventual triumph of communism. A month later, Winston Churchill, the former British prime minister who had left office just before the war ended, announced the division of Europe that would last throughout the cold war. He declared, "[A]n **iron curtain** has descended across the Continent." (See Map 2, Cold War Division of Europe, in the map section at the front of the book.)

The task of formulating a cold war strategy was assigned to George Kennan, a Soviet specialist in the State Department. Kennan first laid out his plan in a February 1946 "long telegram" that circulated within the government; it was reprinted a year later in the journal *Foreign Affairs*. (See In Their Own Words box.) Kennan's call for the **containment** of communism struck a middle ground between two alternatives: U.S. detachment from the emerging conflict and an all-out invasion and "liberation" of the Soviet Union. Under the containment strategy, the United States would accept the existing sphere of Soviet influence but prevent further Soviet expansion by any means, including military force. In so doing, the United States would wait out the Soviet Union, looking forward to the day when its internal flaws—the denial of individual rights, the lack of a market economy, the high costs of foreign occupation—would cause the communist system to collapse from within.

Figure 2.1 Bipolar Balance of Power in Early Cold War

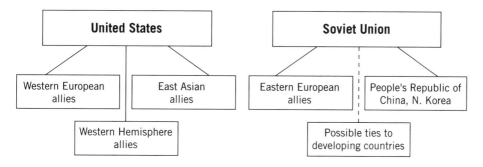

IN THEIR OWN WORDS: GEORGE KENNAN

George Kennan spent years studying the Soviet Union before devising the containment policy that became a pillar of U.S. foreign policy during the cold war. Kennan's knowledge of Russian history and his contact with Soviet leaders during World War II reinforced his sense that though the coming struggle would be long, the United States would ultimately win it.

The political personality of Soviet power as we know it today is the product of ideology and circumstances: ideology inherited by the present Soviet leaders from the movement in which they had their political origin, and circumstances of the power which they now have exercised for nearly three decades. . . .

The maintenance of this pattern of Soviet power, namely, the pursuit of unlimited authority domestically, accompanied by the cultivation of the semi-myth of implacable foreign hostility, has gone far to shape the actual machinery of Soviet power as we know it today. . . . This means that we are going to continue for a long time to find the Russians difficult to deal with. It does not mean that they should be considered as embarked upon a do-or-die program to overthrow our society by a given date. The theory of the inevitability of the eventual fall of capitalism has the fortunate connotation that there is no hurry about it. . . .

In these circumstances it is clear that the main element of any United States policy toward the Soviet Union must be that of a long-term, patient but firm and vigilant containment of Russian expansive tendencies. . . . Soviet pressure against the free institutions of the Western world is something that can be contained by the adroit and vigilant application of counter-force at a series of constantly shifting geographical and political points, corresponding to the shifts and maneuvers of Soviet policy. . . .

The future of Soviet power may not be by any means as secure as Russian capacity for self-delusion would make it appear. . . . The possibility remains (and in the opinion of this writer it is a strong one) that Soviet power, like the capitalist world of its conception, bears within it the seeds of its own decay, and that the sprouting of these seeds is well advanced.

Source: George F. Kennan, "The Sources of Soviet Conduct," Foreign Affairs 25, no. 4 (July 1947): 566–582. © by the Council on Foreign Relations, Inc. Reprinted by permission.

Beyond waging the cold war, the United States sought to create a stable world order that reflected its own political and economic principles. The behavior of the fascist governments had provided a strong case for democratic rule, as a means of organizing political life at home and managing foreign relations. Economic prosperity based upon private property and free markets, meanwhile, would do more than simply prevent communist movements from forming and gaining political power. The U.S. economy would naturally thrive in a market-friendly global trading system that provided outlets for American goods and services. In addition, U.S. banks, multinational corporations, and private investors would benefit enormously if they had free access to foreign markets. In this respect, the American grand strategy during the cold war pursued objectives that extended well beyond the East-West struggle (see Chapter 12).

Institutional Reforms and Restructuring

The challenges and opportunities facing the United States after World War II, combined with the lessons of the interwar years, stopped U.S. foreign-policy makers from retreating again into their hemispheric shell. It was clear that the country had to engage in world politics. Less clear, however, was *how* the United States would engage in them. Would the U.S. government pursue its own interests or those of the international community? Would it choose military or nonmilitary instruments to achieve its goals? Would it act alone or in collaboration with other governments? The answers came in the late 1940s. U.S. leaders found the nation's interests intimately tied to global stability, political reform, and economic growth. A world of governments and economies resembling those of the United States, they believed, would be more peaceful, democratic, and prosperous.

The United States would promote such a world order through a variety of means, working, when possible, with other governments. To historian Daniel Yergin (1977, 196), the new strategy left nowhere in the world outside the U.S. sphere of influence:

> It postulates the interrelatedness of so many different political, economic, and military factors that developments halfway around the globe are seen to have automatic and direct impact on America's core interests. Virtually every development in the world is perceived to be potentially crucial. An adverse turn of events anywhere endangers the United States. Problems in foreign relations are viewed as urgent and immediate threats. Thus, desirable foreign-policy goals are translated into issues of national survival, and the range of threats becomes limitless.

A common element found in all postwar American foreign policies was the creation of new institutions to convert the nation's principles into practice. The institutions of the **national security state** overshadowed the nonmilitary agencies of the government and rendered the foreign-policy process far more complex than at any other time in the nation's history. Enlarged domestic institutions demanded huge budget allocations, competed with one another for influence, and frequently engaged in activities overseas that exceeded their mandates or even their legal authority. Newly formed intergovernmental organizations (IGOs) such as the United Nations, meanwhile, adopted policy preferences that clashed with those of the U.S. government. As more countries established open civil societies with mobilized and empowered interest groups, a vast array of nongovernmental organizations (NGOs) became active players in the foreign-policy process.

Global pressures compelled the United States to centralize national-security structures and increase the president's direct control over military policy, steps viewed as vital in the nuclear age. The National Security Act of 1947, the most sweeping reorganization of U.S. foreign policy in the nation's history, had three primary components.

First, the U.S. armed services—the army, navy, and air force—came together within a single department, the Department of Defense (DOD).[6] In replacing the Department of War, U.S. leaders chose the word *defense* to signify that military affairs were now a permanent concern, not one reserved for wartime. To James For-restal (quoted in Yergin 1977, 299), the first secretary of defense, the United States had to "maintain such overwhelming military power as to make it abundantly clear that future aggressors will eventually suffer the ruinous fate of Germany."

Second, the National Security Council (NSC) was created to coordinate the foreign-policy process. The president's national-security adviser, with an office close to the Oval Office, became a primary source of guidance and a gatekeeper controlling the flow of foreign-policy advice from other government officials. A small NSC staff would specialize in various areas of foreign policy, and the most crucial decisions would be made at NSC meetings (see Chapter 6).

Third, the act also created the Central Intelligence Agency (CIA) to oversee the collection, analysis, and distribution of information regarding other countries and world developments of concern to the United States. Analysts widely agreed that intelligence failures virtually invited the Pearl Harbor attacks in 1941 and that the Office of Strategic Services, hastily established early in World War II, was not up to the task of global intelligence gathering on a permanent basis.

As noted previously, the creation of these agencies produced new tensions within the U.S. government and foreign-policy process. Rivalries between the armed services, primarily the navy and air force, turned the DOD into its own kind of battle zone. Struggles over budget resources and, more importantly, missions in the emerging cold war led the service chiefs to place their organizational self-interests above those of the nation. The NSC, meanwhile, soon found itself competing against the State Department for control of the foreign-policy agenda, and the huge budget outlays required by the DOD left the foreign service chronically short-changed (see Hook 2003). The CIA proved incapable of serving as a "central" source of intelligence; more than a dozen other intelligence agencies came into being within various federal departments. In preserving and even encouraging internal power struggles, the new system was "flawed by design" (Zegart 1999).

Transnational institutions also took shape during these hectic transition years from World War II to the cold war. The United States led the way in creating a worldwide IGO that adopted many goals sought by the League of Nations while recognizing that organization's limitations. Toward this end, officials from fifty governments came to San Francisco early in 1945 to create the United Nations (UN). Under the approved plan, the UN would be open to all countries and pro-

---

6. *National Security Act of 1947,* Public Laws, 80th Congress, 1st sess., 495.

vide a forum for resolving conflicts among them, solving problems that crossed national borders, and proclaiming shared principles regarding human rights and other issues. The last of these UN roles particularly interested the United States, which expected the world body to serve as an extension of its own values and principles. Maintaining collective security, the primary objective of the League of Nations, was conspicuously absent from the UN's mandate.

Along with the other great powers—China, France, Great Britain, and the Soviet Union—the United States protected its interests by having a permanent seat and veto power on the UN Security Council. Key votes in the UN General Assembly, in which all countries had one vote, could also be nullified by the Security Council's permanent members. Under Article 51 of the UN Charter, the United States and other countries kept their military options open by reserving "the inherent right of individual or collective self-defense" if they were attacked.[7] Finally, the newly created International Court of Justice was granted power to resolve interstate disputes, but only if the governments involved accepted the court's jurisdiction on specific cases brought before it.

The U.S. government, meanwhile, departed from its traditional practice of avoiding peacetime military alliances. The creation of the North Atlantic Treaty Organization (NATO) in 1949 resulted from several troubling developments in Europe. In 1947, Great Britain withdrew its military support for Greece and Turkey, whose governments faced internal revolts by communists and other groups. Under the **Truman Doctrine,** the United States provided military aid to both states and, more broadly, pledged support for "free peoples who are resisting attempted subjugation by armed minorities or by outside pressures." In February 1948, the Soviet Union gained control of Czechoslovakia by supporting a coup against its elected leader and imposing a communist regime in its place. Several months later, Stalin erected a blockade around the German city of Berlin, which was split into two zones by then, one open to the Western powers (West Berlin), the other controlled by the Soviets (East Berlin). Truman responded with a massive airlift to support the citizens of West Berlin with food, coal, and other necessities. After nearly a year, Stalin finally gave up the blockade and reopened the Western zones of occupation.

These developments led to the formation of NATO, which comprised the United States, nine Western European countries, Canada, and Iceland. Under the terms of the North Atlantic Treaty, signed in April 1949, an armed attack against one or more of the members "shall be considered an attack against them all." By assuming the lead role in NATO, the United States committed itself to the security of Western Europe for the duration of the cold war and long after its conclusion.

On the economic front, the U.S. government also engaged in a flurry of institution building. The nation's economy had grown rapidly in the years before and during the war (see Figure 2.2), and by 1945, U.S. output matched the rest of the

---

7. This provision allowed the United States and other governments in the Western Hemisphere to form the Organization of American States in 1947, based in Washington, D.C., whose primary mission was to preserve regional security.

Figure 2.2 U.S. Economic Growth, 1885–1945

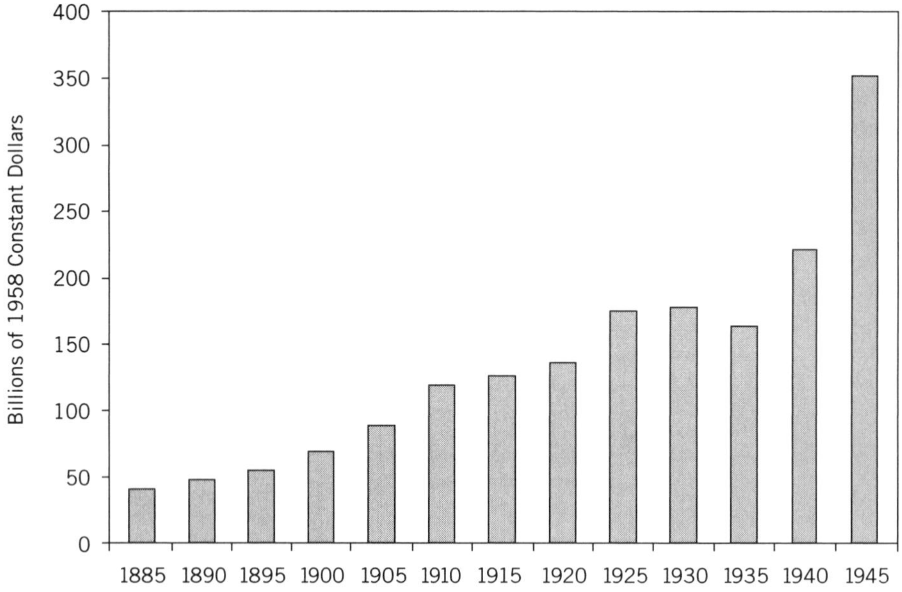

SOURCE: U.S. Bureau of the Census, *The Statistical History of the United States: From Colonial Times to the Present* (New York: Basic Books, 1976).

world's combined production. In the summer of 1944, officials from forty-four governments met in Bretton Woods, New Hampshire, to discuss postwar financial arrangements. The **Bretton Woods agreements** created a system of fixed currency exchange rates based on the U.S. dollar, which because of American economic clout would be considered "good as gold." The Bretton Woods system included two international financial institutions designed to stabilize the world economy further (see Chapter 9). The World Bank would lend money to member states to rebuild their industries. The International Monetary Fund (IMF), meanwhile, would manage currency exchanges and provide relief to member states facing short-term currency crises. Another multilateral pact, the General Agreement on Tariffs and Trade (GATT), was signed in 1947 to create rules for keeping national markets open to global commerce.

The **Marshall Plan,** named after Secretary of State George Marshall, paved the way for Western Europe's economic recovery and its eventual political alignment within the European Union (EU). Truman agreed with Marshall that Europe urgently needed U.S. help to revive its slumping economies. Congress authorized the transfer of $13 billion (approximately $50 billion in current dollars) in low-interest loans to these countries, which were required to coordinate their plans for recovery. They did so in 1948 by creating the Organization for European Economic Cooperation (OEEC). By 1950, with political stability returning to the region, the Europeans had regained their prewar economic growth. The success of the OEEC led to the creation in 1957 of the European Economic Community (EEC), which later became the European Community (EC) and is now the EU. In this respect, the Soviet Union was instrumental not simply in rallying a unified Western response to a perceived external threat, but also in forcing the Western European states to overcome their deep historical animosities toward each other.

Regional Conflicts and the Vietnam Syndrome

These measures laid the institutional foundations for postwar U.S. foreign policy. Such wide-ranging initiatives seemed essential given the opportunities available to the United States (the only major power to emerge *stronger* from the war) for achieving its historic mission of creating a world order in its own image. The new architecture also countered the threat posed by the Soviet Union, which detonated a nuclear device in September 1949 and neutralized the U.S. advantage in this area of military power. Of concern to U.S. leaders as well was the victory of communist forces in China after more than three decades of civil war. The People's Republic of China (PRC) came into being in October 1949 under the leadership of Mao Zedong. Among its first actions, the PRC, in 1950, signed a treaty of cooperation with the Soviet Union, which deepened fears in Washington that the balance of global power was shifting against the United States and toward communism.

The PRC was particularly troubling because, unlike the Soviet Union, China represented a potential role model for other developing countries, largely located in the Southern Hemisphere, whose populations greatly outnumbered those in the industrialized nations. Colonial rule was yielding to the creation of new Asian and African countries, which quickly gained a voting majority in the UN General Assembly. The crushing poverty in these new states, and the lack of political institutions in place to satisfy their citizens' rising expectations, raised additional U.S. fears that these countries would turn to communism. The *third world,* a term used to distinguish the region from the *first world* (the capitalist bloc) and the *second world* (the communist bloc), figured prominently in U.S. foreign policy.

Amid these changes in the interstate system, key figures in the Truman administration argued that an even greater military buildup was required. They insisted that the perils facing the United States must be proclaimed in stark, dramatic terms to jolt the public and large segments of Congress out of their complacency at a time when the country was, at least on the surface, at peace. Toward that end, Truman commissioned a secret study by the National Security Council. Delivered on April 14, 1950, the study, known as **NSC-68,** became a blueprint for the globalization of containment. "The issues that face us are momentous," wrote Paul Nitze (quoted in May 1993, 26), the primary author of the study, "involving the fulfillment or destruction not only of the Republic but of civilization itself." According to NSC-68, the Soviet Union would soon be capable of paralyzing the United States in a surprise nuclear attack. With its preponderant conventional forces, the Soviet Union would then be able to overrun and control Western Europe, Japan, and the Middle East. Only through a massive U.S. military buildup would the United States be able to avoid such a calamity.

Hot spots in the early cold war. The dire warnings of NSC-68 seemed to be affirmed as the cold war first became "hot" in East Asia. On June 25, 1950, North Korean forces attacked their counterparts in South Korea, violating a postwar agreement that divided the country along the thirty-eighth parallel until the creation of a unified national government. The communist-backed North Korean forces quickly overran the opposition, prompting Truman to seek relief from the UN Security Council. A multinational force led by the United States pushed North Korean troops back across the thirty-eighth parallel.[8] Then North Korea struck again and seized Seoul, the South Korean capital, and the conflict dragged on. Truman failed to negotiate an end to the war in 1951 and 1952. His successor, Dwight Eisenhower, threatened North Korea with a new offensive if a peace treaty could not be signed. The two sides finally reached an agreement in July 1953 that effectively restored the prewar status quo. With no clear victor, North Korea and South Korea remained divided for the rest of the cold war and into the twenty-first century, a large contingent of U.S. troops still deployed along the border to keep the peace.

The Korean War demonstrated developing countries' importance to U.S. foreign policy in the cold war. Recognizing this, Eisenhower turned to the CIA as a tool for influencing weaker governments and, occasionally, toppling regimes not favored in Washington. In Iran, the CIA backed the 1953 overthrow of Prime Minister Mohammed Mossedegh after he nationalized the country's oil fields. Returned to power, Shah (King) Mohammed Riza Pahlevi reopened the oil fields to British and U.S. oil companies. In 1954, the CIA staged another coup in Guatemala, whose elected president, Jacobo Arbenz Guzmán, had launched a sweeping land reform.[9] Eisenhower declared the impoverished Central American country a potential communist stronghold and authorized the president's overthrow. Arbenz was replaced by a military general who promptly reversed the land reforms.

In addition to covert CIA operations, nuclear weapons played a key role in Eisenhower's foreign policy, which he labeled the **New Look.** To the president, nuclear weapons provided more "bang for the buck" than did conventional forces. The New Look also featured new military alliances that created a "containment belt" around the Soviet Union and China. Before the formation of NATO, the United States had pledged, under the 1947 Rio treaty, to protect the Western Hemisphere. The alliance wave accelerated with the creation of the ANZUS alliance (with Australia and New Zealand) in 1951, the Southeast Asia Treaty Organization (SEATO) in 1954, and the Central Treaty Organization (CENTO) in 1959. In addition to these multilateral alliances, the United States created bilateral pacts with Japan, the Philippines, South Korea, and Taiwan. (See Map 3, Cold War Alliances with the United States, in the map section at the front

---

8. The Soviet Union, which would have vetoed the resolution, was boycotting the UN at the time to protest its refusal to recognize the new communist regime in China.

9. At the time, the richest 2 percent of Guatemala's population owned nearly three-fourths of the land. The U.S.-based United Fruit Company was the largest landholder in the country.

of the book.) Each ally found a place under the U.S. "nuclear umbrella," and each became eligible for large volumes of U.S. foreign aid.

Cuba. The gravest challenge to U.S. foreign policy during the cold war came from the island of Cuba, less than a hundred miles from Florida. In 1959, the American-backed military regime of Fulgencio Batista was overthrown and replaced by a Marxist regime led by Fidel Castro, who openly declared the United States an enemy of the Cuban people. Eisenhower's successor, John F. Kennedy, turned to the CIA in 1961 to get rid of Castro. But the agency's covert operation failed as the invading force of Cuban exiles was repelled on the Bay of Pigs. Later efforts by the CIA to assassinate Castro, through the use of exploding cigars and other bizarre tactics, served only to elevate the Cuban leader's stature among other developing nations.

The standoff between the United States and Cuba took a perilous turn in November 1962. During routine aerial reconnaissance overflights, American officials discovered that the Cuban government, at the behest of the Soviet Union, had begun installing medium-range nuclear missiles on the island. The missiles had been secretly shipped to Cuba from the Soviet Union, and U.S. cities were their intended targets. Kennedy, well aware of the source of the nuclear missiles, insisted that Castro remove the missiles or face swift military action. After nearly two weeks of tense negotiations between the U.S. and Soviet governments, Soviet leader Nikita Khrushchev ordered the missiles removed. A direct, and possibly apocalyptic, clash between the superpowers was narrowly averted.

Vietnam War. As the events in Cuba unfolded, the United States also was becoming more deeply immersed in a more distant conflict. Its outcome would reveal the limits of U.S. military power, raise doubts about the country's moral posture in the cold war, and shatter the domestic consensus favoring the containment strategy. The conflict had erupted after World War II in Indochina, a tropical region in Southeast Asia long dominated by foreign powers. After Japan's defeat in 1945, France had insisted on reclaiming its colony in Vietnam rather than granting independence to the people. But the French could not subdue an independence movement in Vietnam and withdrew in 1954. The U.S. government, which feared the rise to power of a communist regime, stepped into the quagmire. Eisenhower had viewed Vietnam through the lens of a **domino theory,** which held that a communist victory in one country would lead to a succession of additional victories in neighboring states (see Kattenburg 1980, Chap. 2).

The U.S. military presence in Vietnam grew slowly in the early 1960s, then soared to half a million by 1968. Like Korea, Vietnam was split into northern and southern regions, with the north allied with communism and the south receiving support from the United States and its allies. Despite the superior firepower of the United States, Kennedy and his successor, Lyndon Johnson, could not defeat the Vietminh forces, led by Ho Chi Minh. Back in the United States, growing U.S. deployments, followed by continued defeats and casualties, prompted an antiwar movement there. As television networks broadcast graphic images of the carnage on a daily basis, the Vietnam War came home to President Richard Nixon when he took office in January 1969. Despite Nixon's promises to end the war, the conflict continued into the mid-1970s, when Vietnam at last gained its independence under a communist government. Nearly 59,000 U.S. troops had died in the conflict, and another 153,000 had been wounded. More than 1 million Vietnamese had been killed or wounded.

The Vietnam War proved disastrous for the United States in several ways. First, U.S. leaders had wrongly viewed it as an ideological struggle rather than a war of independence and self-determination. As a result, their goal of winning the hearts and minds of the Vietnamese people had been doomed from the start. Militarily, the United States failed to adapt to the demands of guerilla war, ground forces had been left without clear orders, and the daily aerial assaults by American bombers had merely strengthened the will of the Vietnamese.[10] All of this offended the moral sensibilities of many Americans, who had long believed in the righteousness of their country's actions overseas. As the national soul-searching associated with the **Vietnam Syndrome** took hold across the country after the war, the moral superiority of the United States could no longer be taken for granted. Nor could the virtues and open-ended military commitments of the containment doctrine.

The End of the Cold War

By the early 1970s, the Soviet Union had caught up with the United States in the most potent category of military power, nuclear weapons. At the same time, the U.S. economy was showing serious signs of distress. The costs of the Vietnam War and other burdens had prevented the country from maintaining its role as the "lender of last resort." Domestic unrest and new regional crises, particularly in the Middle East, forced Nixon to change the course of U.S. foreign policy.

Nixon assigned his national security adviser, Henry Kissinger, the task of designing a strategy that recognized these new realities. Kissinger, a Jewish refugee from Nazi Germany and a political scientist, soon settled upon **détente,** a French term meaning an easing of tensions. Under the détente policy, U.S. and Soviet leaders established a closer working relationship so that regional crises could be resolved without threatening a direct confrontation. In addition, in return for Soviet restraint the United States offered the Soviet Union material benefits, including American agricultural exports badly needed in Moscow. The two governments also negotiated a series of arms control treaties that first limited, and later reduced, the stockpiles of nuclear weapons on both sides.

Nixon also sought improved relations with the People's Republic of China, whose communist government the United States had not yet recognized. The PRC, still ruled by Mao Zedong, was struggling; it stood to benefit greatly from the economic opportunities U.S. recognition would bring. The breakthrough between the countries came in a May 1972 visit by Nixon to China, during which the United

---

10. For a reassessment of the Vietnam ordeal by the secretary of defense under Kennedy and Johnson, see McNamara (1995).

States officially recognized the PRC as the legitimate government of China. In return, Mao agreed to cooperate with the United States rather than the Soviet Union. By attaining this commitment, Nixon and Kissinger achieved the upper hand in the now triangular superpower rivalry.

Despite these gains, memories of Vietnam and the Watergate scandal that drove Nixon from office in 1974 compelled Americans to seek yet another shift in U.S. foreign policy. Jimmy Carter, a former peanut farmer and born-again Christian from Georgia, made much of his stature as a Washington outsider during the 1976 presidential election. Once elected, Carter turned the nation's attention away from the confrontation of the cold war and toward a more cooperative posture emphasizing human rights, improved living conditions in the developing world, and a stronger role for the United Nations. Carter vowed that above all, the United States would live up to its principles as a democratic nation and use its power not simply for the promotion of American self-interests but for the betterment of people throughout the world. Carter's policy of **liberal internationalism** achieved many of its goals, including the 1978 Camp David accord between Israel and Egypt.

In his final years in office, however, Carter suffered a series of setbacks. First, a 1979 revolution in Nicaragua brought a Marxist regime to power. Second, Iranian militants stormed the U.S. embassy in Teheran and held fifty-two Americans hostage for the remainder of Carter's presidency. The U.S.-backed shah was replaced by a new government based on Islamic law and harshly critical of the United States. The final blow came in December 1979, when the Soviet Union sent 80,000 troops into Afghanistan to bolster a new puppet government. Carter, who declared the Soviet action the greatest threat to world peace since World War II, could not overcome these challenges to U.S. foreign policy. He lost his bid for reelection to Ronald Reagan, a Republican "hawk" who vowed to overpower, not accommodate, U.S. adversaries abroad.

Upon taking office in January 1981, Reagan called the Soviet Union "the focus of evil in the modern world." His rhetorical offensive was accompanied by an expansion of U.S. armed forces, which the president believed had been neglected during the détente and Carter years. Reagan also raised the stakes of the arms race by proposing a U.S. "missile shield" in outer space that would shoot down Soviet missiles headed for the United States. Congress supported Reagan's proposals and, by the mid-1980s, had allowed annual defense spending to nearly double. As the buildup continued, many Americans became anxious about an impending nuclear war. Their fears were strengthened by scientific evidence suggesting that even a "limited" nuclear war would produce a "nuclear winter," leading to the extinction of most plant and animal life (Sagan 1983–1984). Reagan dismissed these fears, insisting that the greater threat to U.S. security lay in the Soviet nuclear arsenal and tyrannical regime.

Amid these fears, prospects for improved superpower relations appeared. The deaths of three aged leaders (Leonid Brezhnev, Yuri Andropov, and Konstantin Chernenko) between 1982 and 1985 brought to power a new generation of Soviet leaders, most notably Mikhail Gorbachev, who openly acknowledged his nation's problems. The economy had succumbed to centralized control, a demoralized labor force, and a crumbling infrastructure, while the rigid political system had discouraged public participation and new ideas. Gorbachev proposed two reforms to rectify these problems: **perestroika,** or the restructuring of the Soviet economy to spur innovation and efficiency; and **glasnost,** or greater openness in the political system. Soviet citizens and foreign leaders, including Reagan, welcomed both reforms.

By the time George H. W. Bush took office in January 1989, the only question remaining about the Soviet Union was whether its decay was irreversible. Efforts by Gorbachev to salvage his nation merely compounded the problem. The Soviet leader first sought to ease the strains on the Soviet periphery in Eastern Europe by permitting client states to launch their own reforms. Citizens seized on the opportunity, not to restructure their communist systems, but to get rid of them altogether. The critical turning point came in September 1989, when Hungary's government opened its borders with Austria, permitting thousands of East Europeans to cross the iron curtain. The Berlin Wall fell two months later, and in quick succession democratic regimes were established across the region. Their leaders rushed to create market economies and attract foreign investment.

As the Soviet bloc crumbled around him, Gorbachev confronted an uprising among the fifteen republics that composed the Soviet Union. In Russia, by far the largest republic, Boris Yeltsin won free elections held in May 1990. Yeltsin, whose election as president provided him with the legitimacy the communist leaders had never had, moved quickly to assert authority over Russia's government, economy, and foreign relations. His actions prompted a similar independence movement in neighboring Ukraine, the second largest Soviet republic. Belarus and the other twelve republics then issued their own declarations of independence. In the United States, the Bush administration adopted a cautious strategy of supporting Gorbachev and a "soft landing" for the Soviet Union. The president was criticized in some quarters for propping up the Soviet leader for too long. Ultimately, though, his strategy proved successful. In the end, the United States won the cold war in the most favorable manner possible—through the peaceful and orderly dismantling of its longtime rival in Moscow.

New Challenges after the Cold War

The end of the cold war caught the world by surprise. The East-West conflict had become a deeply entrenched fact of life on both sides of the iron curtain. The ideological competition between communism and capitalism seemed to defy resolution. The nuclear doctrine of "mutual assured destruction" locked the Soviet Union and United States into a strategic stalemate, and the logic of bipolarity established a manageable framework for superpower relations while constraining the ambitions of regional powers.

Largely unexpected in the 1980s was the demise and peaceful disappearance of one of the superpowers. Few analysts anticipated the dissolution of the Soviet bloc and the subsequent collapse of the Soviet Union itself. Such an outcome seemed beyond the realm of possibility given the firm grip in which the Kremlin held the Warsaw Pact states. Domestically, Soviet leaders had demonstrated an almost limitless capacity to retain control even in the face of mounting economic and social distress. The Kremlin's massive nuclear stockpile appeared to provide the Soviet Union indefinite status as a military superpower.

In Washington, CIA estimates of Soviet invulnerability, particularly in the area of conventional and nuclear weaponry, fueled expectations regarding a virtually endless cold war. These reports emphasized the formidable scale of Soviet forces in *quantitative* terms. What they neglected to take into account, however, were the *qualitative* shortcomings of the Soviet military, especially its technological decay and the worsening morale among Soviet troops. U.S. intelligence also failed to consider the growing discontent among Soviet citizens. Shortages of consumer goods, dilapidated housing, and poor medical services were slowly, but surely, undermining public confidence. The denial of citizens' spiritual aspirations and political rights further sapped their loyalty to the communist regime.

In the past, Soviet leaders had overcome these problems by exploiting their monopoly on information. But this monopoly could not be sustained amid the communications revolution, which broke down the walls between the Soviet bloc and the outside world—indeed, hurtling over barriers across the globe. Advances in satellite technology extended the reach of televised coverage into areas previously isolated by government restrictions on the news media. The arrival of personal computers into the Soviet bloc, including Internet access and e-mail capabilities, permitted contacts across national borders that could not be controlled by government officials. As a result, citizens gained new exposure to the world around them. The new information not only contradicted the images and messages they had been receiving from the government but also revealed the profound gaps between their living standards and those of their Western neighbors.

Elements of the New World Order

The victory of the United States in the cold war represented more than the defeat of one international coalition by another. The Soviet Union's collapse marked the triumph of liberalism over the two competing ideologies of the twentieth century: fascism and communism. The challenge of fascism was subdued with the military defeat of Germany, Italy, and Japan during World War II. Communism died a slower death with the demise of the Soviet bloc and the transition of Chinese communism into an economic system based largely on market forces. In his 1989 article "The End of History," Francis Fukuyama captured the exuberant spirit of the time: "What we may be witnessing is not just the end of the cold war, or the passing of a particular period of history, but the end of history as such, that is, the end point of mankind's ideological evolution and the universalization of Western liberal democracy as the final form of government" (4).

Nine months before the Soviet Union's collapse, President Bush (quoted in Sloan 1991, 19) had expressed this sense of triumphalism in an address to a joint session of Congress: "We can see a new world coming into view, a world in which

President George H. W. Bush shares a Thanksgiving dinner with U.S. troops in Saudi Arabia during the 1990 buildup of forces associated with Operation Desert Shield. The balance of world power was shifting rapidly at this time, as the Soviet Union was on the verge of collapse and newly independent countries were taking over in Eastern Europe. Saddam Hussein's invasion of Kuwait threatened the "new world order" envisioned by Bush, prompting him to lead a UN coalition to liberate Kuwait.

there is the very real prospect of a **new world order,** a world where the United States—freed from cold war stalemate—is poised to fulfill the historic vision of its founders; a world in which freedom and respect for human rights finds a home among all nations." The president did not fully detail what this order would look like, but in his public statements he repeatedly emphasized three overlapping elements: democratization, economic globalization, and multilateral cooperation.

Democratization. The dismantling of communist regimes advanced the trend toward global democratization underway since the 1970s. During that decade, many Latin American countries overcame long histories of military rule and installed new political systems based upon constitutionalism, free multiparty elections, and the protection of basic civil and political rights. Many African and Asian countries adopted similar reforms in the 1980s, as did the postcommunist countries in Europe in the early 1990s. As noted previously, democratization overseas had long been a central goal of the United States. Democratic freedoms and human rights, Americans widely believed, should be adopted and protected on a universal basis According to the theory of **democratic peace,** a world of democracies would be more cooperative and less prone to civil and interstate violence (see Russett 1993).[11]

Economic globalization. A second key aspect of the new world order involved the trend toward market-based economic commerce both within and among states, a trend that also had gained momentum in the latter stages of the cold war. A fully globalized economy would allow people, capital, goods, and services to travel freely across national boundaries. In short, international commerce in the world economy would resemble interstate commerce within the U.S. economy, which occurs with limited government intervention. This model had long been attractive to members of the European Union, who gradually moved toward a single market in the 1990s by eliminating internal trade barriers, creating a central bank and a single currency (the euro), and adopting a unified position in global trade negotiations.[12]

Multilateral cooperation. A third feature of the new world order involved enhanced interstate cooperation in a variety of areas. Economic globalization was fueled not simply by the widespread adoption of free-market principles but also by multilateral institutions such as the World Bank and the IMF. Following the cold war, these Bretton Woods institutions undertook new missions, providing funds for economic reforms in postcommunist states and preventing currency shortfalls from sparking crises in Mexico in 1994 and across East Asia in the late 1990s. Meanwhile, the World Trade Organization (WTO), created in 1995, enforced the market-friendly trade reforms written into the most recent global trade pact. The U.S. government also welcomed greater security cooperation and expected the UN to assume a strong peacekeeping role unattainable during the cold war. The United States led the effort to maintain, and expand, NATO even though its adversary, the Soviet Union, had disappeared.

President Bill Clinton embraced all three elements when he took office in January 1993. Clinton, whose primary interest was in domestic rather than foreign policy, believed the United States would be more secure and prosperous in a more tightly knit world whose nations shared common values, interests, and political institutions. His national-security policy of **engagement and enlargement** presumed that closer interactions between countries, primarily on economic matters, would provide collective benefits to them while discouraging defections or challenges to the status quo. The rewards of engagement, in sum, would outweigh its costs. To Anthony Lake (1993, 659), Clinton's national security adviser, "The successor to a doctrine of containment must be a strategy of enlargement of the world's free community."

---

11. This connection between democracy and world peace was made two centuries earlier by Enlightenment theorists Immanuel Kant and Jeremy Bentham, who anticipated a "pacific federation" of democratic states (see Doyle 1986).

12. Eleven of the fifteen members of the EU adopted the common currency in 1999. Denmark, Great Britain, and Sweden maintained their own currencies while Greece's economic problems prevented its government from joining the euro bloc.

Overseas Unrest and Domestic Unease

Despite their great expectations for the new world order, U.S. leaders confronted a variety of armed conflicts overseas, which revealed that history had not "ended" with the demise of the Soviet Union. Instead, regional conflicts and internal power struggles suppressed during the cold war resurfaced, producing large-scale violence and attracting the attention and military intervention of outside forces, including the United States. Conflicts in three regions—the Persian Gulf, Northeast Africa, and Yugoslavia—dampened the enthusiasm of American leaders for "engagement" and provoked a turn away from multilateral cooperation, which would intensify in the new millennium under Clinton's successor, George W. Bush (see Table 2.3).

The first regional conflict erupted in the Persian Gulf before the Soviet Union collapsed. Iraq's invasion of neighboring Kuwait on August 2, 1990, directly challenged the new world order and prompted the United States to deploy a military force to protect Saudi Arabia. The UN played a key role in this response, which included a series of UN resolutions demanding Iraq's withdrawal. When the Iraqi leader, Saddam Hussein, ignored these resolutions, the UN authorized a military assault on Iraqi troops in the Kuwaiti desert, known as **Operation Desert Storm.** This U.S.-led assault quickly crushed the Iraqi troops. Saddam remained in power, however, and he defied resolutions that he comply with UN inspectors in ridding his country of weapons of mass destruction. The imposition of economic sanctions and a "no-fly zone" across much of the country did not produce compliance

Table 2.3 U.S. Foreign-Policy Chronology: Post–Cold War

1991	Iraq is forced out of Kuwait by a UN coalition led by the United States.
1992	Civil war escalates across former Yugoslavia.
1993	U.S. forces killed in Somalia, forcing U.S. withdrawal; Congress ratifies North American Free Trade Agreement (NAFTA).
1994	Plan for World Trade Organization approved.
1995	United States brokers Dayton Peace Accords, ending ethnic warfare in Bosnia-Herzegovina.
1996	Clinton signs Comprehensive Test Ban Treaty (CTBT).
1997	Czech Republic, Hungary, and Poland are invited to join NATO.
1998	Al Qaeda terrorists bomb U.S. embassies in Kenya and Tanzania; global economic crisis spreads from East Asia to Russia and Latin America.
1999	NATO forces intervene in Kosovo to stop ethnic cleansing by Yugoslav government; Congress rejects CTBT.
2000	Terrorist bombing of USS *Cole* kills seventeen and injures thirty-seven Americans.
2001	George W. Bush renounces Kyoto Protocol on global warming; Islamic terrorists crash jets into World Trade Center and Pentagon; United States invades Afghanistan and overthrows Taliban regime linked to September 11 attacks; United States withdraws from 1972 ABM treaty with Russia.
2002	Bush declares Iran, Iraq, and North Korea an "axis of evil" that encourages terrorism; "Bush doctrine" threatens preemptive strikes against U.S. adversaries.
2003	A "coalition of the willing" led by the United States invades Iraq and overthrows Hussein regime; U.S. occupation fails to uncover weapons of mass destruction that prompted invasion.

from Saddam, who became a primary target for the American counterterrorism offensive that followed the September 11, 2001, attacks.

The UN also struggled to resolve upheavals in **failed states,** those countries incapable of maintaining order or providing even minimal services to their citizens. (See Map 4, Post–Cold War U.S. Military Operations, in the map section at the front of the book.) Primary among these failed states was Somalia, where nearly 50,000 citizens died in a civil war before a UN-sponsored ceasefire could be arranged in March 1992. By this time, a drought had led to widespread famine, and there was no government in place to provide relief to the starving population. The humanitarian crisis compelled the United States to intervene militarily and provide relief to the Somalis. A more ambitious UN effort to find a long-term solution failed, leading to more unrest and American casualties, which prompted Clinton to withdraw from Somalia. When a much bloodier ethnic conflict broke out in nearby Rwanda and Burundi, leaving nearly 1 million dead, the United States, fearing a repeat of the Somalia disaster, let the carnage run its course. With no other major powers willing to step in, the UN, too, stood by as the genocide unfolded.

The end of the cold war also revived hostilities in the crumbling European state of Yugoslavia. Religious differences among Catholics, Orthodox Christians, and Muslims had been suppressed for decades by a communist government led by Marshal Josip Tito. The cold war's end quickly unearthed these differences, producing a new cycle of violence, territorial conquest, and foreign intervention. Neither the UN nor the European Union could organize an effective response to the "ethnic cleansing" in Yugoslavia. In 1995 and 1999, respectively, the United States finally ended the bloodshed in the provinces of Bosnia-Herzegovina and Kosovo. Clinton overrode domestic opposition to both interventions, limited the exposure of U.S. troops to enemy fire, and once the fighting stop, turned over the reconstruction efforts to multilateral institutions. By the end of the decade, Yugoslavia had broken up into several republics.

These foreign entanglements occurred at a time in which the United States was experiencing a period of unprecedented economic growth and prosperity. As stock markets reached record highs, inflation and unemployment fell to negligible levels. Americans were enjoying a heyday in the first post–cold war decade and had little patience for conflicts overseas. This turn inward, historically common when the United States is at peace, was stimulated in large measure by the failure of the U.S. and UN missions in Somalia. Clinton responded by restricting U.S. involvement in future peacekeeping missions and by refusing to intervene in other failed states. The shift in U.S. foreign policy gained further momentum in November 1994, when the Republican Party seized control of both houses of Congress for the first time in four decades. Republican legislators opposed the latest round of liberal internationalism and used their "power of the purse" (see Chapter 5) to reduce U.S. foreign-aid commitments and other international operations.

The Senate's refusal to sign the Comprehensive Test Ban Treaty (CTBT) in October 1999 epitomized the **new unilateralism** in U.S. foreign policy. As during the Reagan administration, the United States adopted a hostile stance toward the

UN and its agencies, refusing to pay past dues owed them. The nation that only recently had fulfilled its ambition to lead the interstate system found itself trapped by the commitments, sacrifices, and compromises such leadership required. Clinton, despite his support for global engagement, succumbed to the political realities at home. Vice President Al Gore's subsequent 2000 electoral failure and the presidency of George W. Bush guaranteed that the new unilateralism would endure.

Still, the new president surprised most observers, including foreign leaders, in departing so starkly from the course U.S. foreign policy had steered since World War II. Bush followed his renunciation of the Kyoto Protocol by abrogating the antiballistic missile (ABM) treaty Nixon had signed with the Soviet Union. The shock of September 11, 2001, compelled Bush to make U.S. primacy the basis of

IN THEIR OWN WORDS: GEORGE W. BUSH'S NATIONAL SECURITY STRATEGY

Each presidential administration is required by law to outline its national-security strategy in a report to Congress and the public. The terrorist attacks of September 11, 2001, prompted President George W. Bush to focus his strategy, highlighted below, on fighting terrorism and striking preemptively, where and when necessary, against U.S. enemies abroad.

The United States possesses unprecedented—and unequaled—strength and influence in the world. Sustained by faith in the principles of liberty, and the value of a free society, this position comes with unparalleled responsibilities, obligations, and opportunity. The great strength of this nation must be used to promote a balance of power that favors freedom. . . .

The United States of America is fighting a war against terrorists of global reach. The enemy is not a single political regime or person or religion or ideology. The enemy is terrorism—premeditated, politically motivated violence perpetrated against innocents. . . . The United States will make no concessions to terrorist demands and strike no deals with them. We make no distinction between terrorists

and those who knowingly harbor or provide aid to them. . . . In the war against global terrorism, we will never forget that we are ultimately fighting for our democratic values and way of life. Freedom and fear are at war, and there will be no quick or easy end to this conflict. . . .

The United States has long maintained the option of preemptive actions to counter a sufficient threat to our national security. The greater the threat, the greater is the risk of inaction—and the more compelling the case for taking anticipatory action to defend ourselves, even if uncertainty remains as to the time and place of the enemy's attack.

Source: The White House, "The National Security Strategy of the United States of America" (September 2002), www.whitehouse.gov/nsc/nss.pdf.

his national-security strategy and to justify preemptive wars against other countries that appeared to threaten the United States. (See In Their Own Words box).

The president's decision to launch such a war against Iraq early in 2003, despite the opposition of the UN Security Council, further isolated the United States in the international community. Bush, whose political support was derived in large part from multinational corporations, pledged his allegiances elsewhere. Yet even those allegiances were closely tied to events overseas and to foreign entanglements that beckoned the United States on a daily basis. As the journalist Michael Hirsh (2003, 25) observed, "We are in this world with both feet now. We have achieved our Founding Fathers' fondest dream, and, at the same time, their worst nightmare. We are a shining success, the supreme power on earth. And we are entangled everywhere."

Conclusion

As we have seen, U.S. foreign policy today is a product of the nation's history of global expansion, measured by territorial control as well as economic wealth, military might, and political and cultural influence. With these strengths have come equally formidable commitments overseas and a vast array of stakeholders in the foreign-policy process. Each branch of government, federal agency, and intergovernmental organization stands to win or lose in this process, along with individual citizens, interest groups, corporations, the news media, and other agents of civil society.

In short, the United States must make the most of a world order it had a large hand in making. Its success in balancing its commitments and capabilities, overcoming threats, and reconciling U.S. power and principles depends largely upon its ability to manage these far-flung, and often conflicting, actors in the policy process. The role of these actors, and their impact on American behavior beyond U.S. borders, is the primary concern of the chapters that follow.

Key Terms

bipolar balance of power, p. 37

Bretton Woods agreements, p. 42

collective security, p. 32

containment, p. 37

democratic peace, p. 50

détente, p. 46

domino theory, p. 45

engagement and enlargement, p. 51

failed states, p. 53

geopolitics, p. 32

glasnost, p. 48

gunboat diplomacy, p. 29

iron curtain, p. 37

liberal internationalism, p. 47

manifest destiny, p. 28

Marshall Plan, p. 42

Monroe Doctrine, p. 27

national security state, p. 39

New Look, p. 44

new unilateralism, p. 53

new world order, p. 50

NSC-68, p. 43

open-door policy, p. 30

Operation Desert Storm, p. 52

perestroika, p. 48

Roosevelt Corollary, p. 30

Truman Doctrine, p. 41

unilateralism, p. 25

Vietnam Syndrome, p. 46

Internet References

This site containing a **chronology of U.S. historical documents** (www.law.ou.edu/hist) is maintained and updated by the University of Oklahoma College of Law. The college provides links to the full text and printable versions of U.S. historical documents from the pre-colonial era through the twenty-first century, such as speeches, charters, major laws, and agreements.

The **CNN Archives** (www.cnn.com/SPECIALS) provide in-depth articles, reports, maps, and interviews regarding U.S. current events and foreign relations from 1995 to 2004. "Special Reports" such as "Kosovo Conflict" and "Yugoslavia in Transition," are archived by year and date. Interactive media features include moving maps, live coverage of the events, and photographs. In addition, the site has a detailed series dedicated to the cold war between the United States and the Soviet Union along with relations of other countries (www.cnn.com/SPECIALS/cold.war).

In conjunction with the Smithsonian Institution, the **Cold War Museum** (www.cold-war.org) focuses on the half-century struggle between the United States and the Soviet Union from early developments in the 1940s to the end of the Soviet Union in the early 1990s. Links to specific texts, chronologies, videos, congressional testimony, and relevant books and Web sites for specific aspects of the cold war are included. Presidential doctrines, strategies, and cold war military conflicts are a focus of this site.

The Government Printing Office's **Core Documents of U.S. Democracy** site (www.gpoaccess.gov/coredocs.html) provides full-text links to documents considered most relevant to educating citizens on U.S. democracy. Categories range from early historical addresses to bills and laws from all congressional sessions. In addition to these documents, this site provides access to demographic and economic indicators and statistics relevant to the United States.

Developed and maintained by the University of Houston, the **Digital History** project (www.digitalhistory.uh.edu) utilizes Web technology to present chronologies, images, and sound bites from U.S. history. A full U.S. history and development textbook is included on the site, as well as suggested readings on specific time periods relevant to U.S. foreign relations, such as colonial expansion, military history, and relations with Europe.

Organized, researched, and published by the U.S. Department of State, the **Foreign Relations Series** (www.state.gov/www/about_state/history/frus.html) covers U.S. diplomacy and foreign-policy decisions since the early 1800s. Included are presidential documents, treaties, intelligence reports, government conversations, and other relevant activity. The series has more than 350 individual volumes, including most-recent additions on the Kennedy and Johnson presidential administrations.

History Matters (historymatters.gmu.edu) is developed and maintained by George Mason University. This site provides links and sources to help students and researchers understand crucial events of U.S. history. The site also provides advice and methods for analyzing historical works.

Internet References

The **History News Network** (hnn.us) is a nonprofit and independent group of historians and journalists who post articles and editorial writings regarding U.S. foreign relations. Critical reactions to historical events, quotes, polls, and multimedia links for understanding history are included on this site.

The **Library of Congress** (lcweb.loc.gov) provides up-to-date access to legislation, historical documents, memorials, maps, and virtual and digital collections of historic time periods. For researchers with a specific focus, the library provides bibliographic and citation lists for topics such as the Cuban missile crisis or the war on terrorism. The library also has an interactive feature of communicating with a researcher and librarian for in-depth questioning and help on research activities.

PBS (www.pbs.org) provides detailed access to historical events and biographies of leaders relevant to U.S. foreign relations. In addition to original Web text, PBS incorporates its television programs by posting interviews and full text of their programs (with sound bites) on this site. Photos, maps, chronologies, and links to relevant sources are part of each series. *American Experience, Frontline,* and *People's Century* are the three primary programs relevant to U.S. foreign relations. *Frontline* features in-depth coverage of the Bush Doctrine and the ongoing war on terrorism.

The **Smithsonian Institution** (www.si.edu) is committed to helping researchers and citizens understand American identity, history, and culture. Exhibitions such as "American Expansion" as well as bibliographies of key leaders are useful for those wishing to understand the development of American history and politics.

The World Wide Web Virtual Library's **History of the United States** site (www.ukans.edu/history/VL/USA), hosted by the University of Kansas, presents useful chronologies, timelines, biographies, maps, and links to journals and other databases regarding the history of the United States. Topics of interest include the colonial era, the revolutionary era, the expansionary era, and the cold war era.

3

Members of President George W. Bush's foreign-policy team meet in the White House to discuss strategy in the war on terrorism. While tensions existed within the group, notably between Secretary of State Colin Powell and Donald Rumsfeld, the defense secretary, Bush's team remained unified as the war plan unfolded following the attacks of September 11, 2001. Presidential advisers play a crucial role in the U.S. foreign-policy process, which has become increasingly concentrated within the White House since World War II.

Dynamics of Decision Making

The paradox of world power outlined in Chapter 1 became increasingly evident as the United States prevailed over the Soviet Union in the cold war and assumed an unprecedented measure of global primacy in the 1990s. Even before this seismic shift in world politics, the U.S. foreign-policy process had grown steadily more crowded and complex since the end of World War II. This growth was driven by transnational forces, including economic globalization, technological advances, and the adoption of democratic reforms by many foreign governments, all actively encouraged by the United States.

The same trends, however, imposed constraints on the U.S. government's effective use of its power, adding to the constraints already built into the Constitution. The creation of new centers of power in the executive branch invited bureaucratic rivalries and the sending of mixed messages to allies and adversaries abroad. The proliferation of congressional committees slowed the pace of legislation. And technological advances produced a powerful electronic news media that could cover U.S. foreign policy instantaneously, often in graphic detail. Domestic upheavals during and after the Vietnam War reached such an extent that "not only our government but our whole society has been undergoing a systematic breakdown when attempting to fashion a coherent and consistent approach to the world" (Destler, Gelb, and Lake 1984, 11).

This chapter explores these challenges to the United States' exercise of world power by considering theories of foreign-policy decision making. Theories help us identify the causes of foreign-policy behavior so we can anticipate, explain, and possibly influence government action. A theoretical perspective goes beyond questions of what happens in the foreign-policy process, who makes key decisions, and when or where decisions are made. It also helps us to understand *why* policy makers act the way they do. According to the authors of a classic study of foreign policy, "We would go so far as to say *that the 'why' questions cannot be answered without analysis of decision-making*" (Snyder, Bruck, and Sapin 2002, 35, emphasis in original).

Theories serve as prisms through which we view and make sense of the world around us. Generally adopted at a young age, our distinctive worldviews reflect our normative values regarding right and wrong, the possibilities and limitations of human nature, and the need for social and political reform. The perspectives we adopt provide a consistent basis for making judgments across foreign and domestic policy issues, from human rights and UN peacekeeping to the death penalty and gun control. The worldviews of political leaders are driven by the same normative principles, and the tradeoffs among them—economic liberty versus equality, for example, or national versus transnational interests—compel leaders to favor some policies over others. In this respect, debates over foreign policy reflect fundamental differences over human behavior, social values, and the appropriate role of governments at home and overseas.

Contending Worldviews

We first turn our attention to the differing worldviews that shape the formulation and conduct of U.S. foreign policy, particularly the predominant theories of realism and liberalism. The **realist theory** envisions a dark world of irreconcilable differences and recurring conflicts among states. A brighter view is presented by proponents of **liberal theory,** who believe these conflicts can be overcome by the learning of past lessons, political reforms that empower more people and groups, and foreign policies that favor cooperation over competition. Realism and liberalism, along with three critical theories briefly described below, illuminate distinctive, but vital, aspects of U.S. foreign policy (Betts 2002). The nation's behavior cannot be adequately grasped without reference to each theoretical tradition.

Realism

Realist theory has long dominated the study of world politics (see Haslam 2002; and Gilpin 1986). To traditional realists, irreversible flaws in human nature produce destructive behavior at all levels of social interaction, including foreign affairs. One must, therefore, accept the world as it is; attempts to change the violent course of human history are exercises in futility.

The contemporary variant of this theory, **neorealism,** focuses on the anarchic nature of the international system, that is, the lack of a world government (see Mearsheimer 2001; and Waltz 1979). The Treaty of Westphalia of 1648, which ended the Thirty Years' War in Europe, created the modern nation-state system that exists today. This treaty granted secular governments, not religious leaders, **sovereignty** over their territories and populations. In this regard, sovereignty is both *internal,* relating to domestic control, and *external,* relating to the right of all states to be free from attack.

While it created a more orderly system for domestic governance as well as interstate relations, the Treaty of Westphalia left the anarchic world order intact. In this void, the primary objective of foreign policy must be self-preservation. To Niccolò Machiavelli ([1532] 1985, 71), an adviser to an Italian prince, state survival is itself a moral end, justifying actions that may be considered cruel or immoral: "So let a prince win and maintain his state; the means will always be judged honorable, and will be praised by everyone." This self-justifying rationale of *raison d'état* (reason of state) commonly appears today in the identification of **national interest** as a grounds for foreign-policy decisions.

Under these anarchic circumstances, the interstate system operates not by morality or law, but by the coercive logic of power, whether implied, threatened, or actually employed. "We assume that statesmen think and act in terms of interest defined as power, and the evidence of history bears that assumption out," observed Hans Morgenthau (1967, 5), a well-known American realist of the cold war. Peace can only be maintained by a **balance of power** among the strongest nation-states. Power must counteract power and create the global stability that would otherwise be provided by a world government.

In making these claims about world politics, neorealism greatly simplifies the analysis of foreign policy. Neorealists consider political leaders to be **rational actors,** who weigh their options based upon common understandings of national interest and tangible measures of national power. In this view, foreign-policy goals are self-evident, or "given," as are the relative merits of alternative means to achieve those goals (see Verba 1961). Neorealists also see governments as **unitary actors,** speaking with one voice. While all modern governments have multiple bureaucratic agencies involved in foreign policy, the most crucial decisions are made by top government officials in the name of the "national interest." These officials can override the institutional self-interests of their subordinates and fend off pressure from individuals and interest groups outside the government. Based on these assumptions, neorealists believe it is possible to understand foreign policy without reference to the internal debates or tradeoffs that led to those policies.

The realist concept of geopolitics, or the impact of a nation's geographic position and resources relative to other powers, is useful in understanding the historic conduct of U.S. foreign policy (see S. Cohen 2003; Turchin 2003; and Brzezinski 1997).[1] The territorial expansion of the United States was due in large part to the nation's advantageous position in North America and the fading presence of other great powers in the Western Hemisphere (Sicker 2002). In keeping with geopolitics as well, U.S. security policy historically presumed that the nation

---

1. See Spykman (1942) and Mackinder (1942) for earlier analyses of geopolitics that emphasized the importance of Europe to the global balance of power—and to U.S. security.

would be threatened if either Europe or Asia became controlled by a single state. The United States applied this concern, and the call to action it implied, to Germany and Japan in the Second World War and to the Soviet Union in the cold war.

In confronting the world as a great power, American leaders have consistently preached the "gospel of national security" (Yergin 1977, Chap. 8; see also Wolfers 1962) while turning to standard instruments of realism, such as arms buildups and military alliances, to maintain this security. The Bush administration explicitly based its emphasis on U.S. primacy in its *National Security Strategy* (White House 2002b) on neorealist assumptions. In particular, the strategy claimed that a unipolar balance of power led by the United States could enhance global stability by discouraging challenges from weaker states. Realism, therefore, helps us understand key aspects of U.S. grand strategy over time while shedding less light on the day-to-day process by which policy is made. This process, which is equally vital to the conduct of U.S. foreign policy, draws our attention to liberal theories of world politics and foreign policy.

Liberalism

In contrast to realists, liberals maintain a more positive view of human nature and the prospects for cooperation at all levels of governance (see Table 3.1). Liberals acknowledge the anarchic structure of the interstate system but believe the absence of a world government does not inevitably lead to conflict. The historical record speaks for itself, liberals point out: most countries have been at peace most of the time. Human beings have further demonstrated a capacity to *learn* from their past mistakes, including such discredited practices as dueling, slavery, and perhaps, the recourse to world war (Mueller 1989).

According to liberalism, global cooperation reflects and strengthens informal **norms** of behavior (see Kratochwil 1989). Such norms—that countries should not invade other countries, for example, or that treaties and alliance obligations should be honored—have been widely observed over time. Liberal norms are

Table 3.1 Key Assumptions of Realism and Liberalism

	Realism	Liberalism
Pioneers	Machiavelli, Hobbes	Kant, Locke
Exemplars in U.S. history	Henry Kissinger	Woodrow Wilson
Human nature	Irrational, selfish	Rational, cooperative
Nature of the state	Unitary	Fragmented
Essence of interstate system	Anarchy	Interdependence
Key global actors	States	States, IGOs, NGOs
State motives	Power, national interests	Transnational concerns
Path to peace	Balance of power	International laws and organizations
Outlook	Pessimistic	Optimistic

rooted in a concern for individual liberty in the face of potential government tyranny. In the political sphere, the state may deny the individual basic freedoms and civil rights; in the economic sphere, the state may threaten private property rights or the profitability of firms through excessive taxes and regulations. Liberals thus favor the *liberation* of citizens from government abuse or, more generally, from social persecution and economic distress.

In considering world politics, liberal theorists emphasize the type of governments that engage in foreign policy. Of particular interest in this regard is the historic lack of war between democracies, a significant pattern given the proliferation of democratic regimes since the 1980s (Freedom House 2004). Many reasons are offered for the democratic peace, including the spread of democratic norms, the greater activism of private citizens, the openness of democratic states to outside scrutiny, and the influence of private firms that benefit by a stable and peaceful international system (see Rosato 2003; Ray 1995; and Russett 1993). Whatever the cause, this connection between democracy and peace is hardly new. To Immanual Kant ([1795] 1914), an Enlightenment philosopher, only democracies joining together in a pacific federation could maintain a "perpetual peace." This concept was refined during the cold war with the emergence of a **security community** (Deutsch et al. 1957) in North America and Western Europe that rendered war among these democratic states largely unthinkable.

Just as realism spawned its modern variant neorealism (focusing on the interstate system), so liberal theory produced **neoliberal institutionalism,** which extends beyond assumptions of human nature (see Oye 1986). Whether they like it or not, political leaders must repeatedly interact with their counterparts in other governments. According to this view, the lesson of these repeated interactions is that cooperative gestures are returned by reciprocal gestures of trust and goodwill. Such a pattern rewards both sides while discouraging future acts of coercion or aggression.

From this perspective, greater cooperation can be expected in the future given the growing sense of **transnational interdependence,** a result of closer economic ties and greater recognition of borderless problems, including pollution, poverty, and epidemics such as AIDS (see Keohane and Nye 2001). These problems do not respect state sovereignty; thus solving them must occur beyond the narrow bounds of the Westphalian interstate system. The United Nations, the World Trade Organization, and other intergovernmental organizations (IGOs) are needed to confront collective problems that individual countries cannot resolve on their own. Nongovernmental organizations (NGOs) such as Greenpeace play a vital role as well, mobilizing private citizens around these causes, pressuring governments to cooperate with each other, and in some cases, lending their own resources and expertise to the resolution of transnational problems.

Liberal theory further departs from realism by refuting the claim that states are rational and unitary actors. Analysts must open the "black box" of the foreign-policy process and observe the unfolding of domestic politics, the internal competition and bargaining among government and external actors with a stake in policy outcomes (see Gourevitch 2002). Opening this box reveals fragmented centers of decision making that contradict the image of unitary action and calls into

Point/Counterpoint
REALISTS VS. LIBERALS ON CAUSES OF WAR

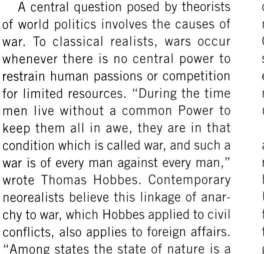

A central question posed by theorists of world politics involves the causes of war. To classical realists, wars occur whenever there is no central power to restrain human passions or competition for limited resources. "During the time men live without a common Power to keep them all in awe, they are in that condition which is called war, and such a war is of every man against every man," wrote Thomas Hobbes. Contemporary neorealists believe this linkage of anarchy to war, which Hobbes applied to civil conflicts, also applies to foreign affairs. "Among states the state of nature is a state of war," wrote Kenneth Waltz. "Among men as among states, anarchy, or the absence of government, is associated with the occurrence of violence."

President Theodore Roosevelt adopted another realist rationale for war: the advancement of national character. "There are higher things in life than the soft and easy enjoyment of material comfort," he observed. "A rich nation which is slothful, timid, or unwieldy is an easy prey for any people which still retain those valuable qualities, the martial virtues." As a senior naval officer and later as president, Roosevelt pursued this vision by advocating U.S. military expansion in Asia and Latin America.

Liberals reject these rationales for war. To John Locke, an English theorist of the Enlightenment era, state tyranny over individual freedoms is a more common cause of war than anarchy in a "state of nature." Immanuel Kant, a like-minded German philosopher, argued that wars squander private liberty as well as public energies. As a result, "the full development of the capacities of mankind are undoubtedly retarded in their progress."

The U.S. leader most closely associated with liberal theory, Woodrow Wilson, rejected the "martial virtues" highlighted by Roosevelt and sought instead to direct U.S. foreign policy toward the transnational cause of peace. "I am proposing that all nations henceforth avoid entangling alliances which would draw them into competitions of power; catch them in a net of intrigue and selfish rivalry, and disturb their own affairs with influences intruded from without. There is no entangling alliance in a concert of power." Wilson's failure to achieve his goals through the League of Nations has not prevented contemporary liberals from promoting world peace through the Wilsonian means of international law, cooperation through the United Nations, and democratic governments that protect individual rights.

Sources: Thomas Hobbes, Leviathan *(Indianapolis: Bobbs-Merrill, [1651] 1983), 64; Kenneth N. Waltz,* Theory of International Relations *(Reading, Mass.: Addison-Wesley, 1989), 83; Keith L. Nelson and Spencer C. Olin Jr.,* Why War? Ideology, Theory, and History *(Berkeley: University of California Press, 1979), 27, 40.*

question the notion of a unified national interest. In this view, foreign policy represents a **two-level game** (Putnam 1988) in which government officials simultaneously negotiate with their counterparts overseas and domestic actors who have stakes in the policy process. The tradeoffs resulting from these two-level games, which may lead to less-than-optimal outcomes on either level, are unavoidable in democratic governments that welcome private interests in the process. Thus while outcomes may not be ideal, the more democratic means by which they are achieved enhance the policy process and prospects for success.

The diffusion of foreign-policy influence complicates the already daunting task of decision makers, whose judgments are shaped by preexisting beliefs, cognitive limitations, and widely varying personality traits and management styles. No single person can possibly comprehend all the information that may prove useful in solving a particular foreign-policy problem, and human passions inevitably obstruct rational action. In short, individuals matter. One must, therefore, pay close attention to the people involved in the foreign-policy process and avoid viewing the state as "an object or system having an existence of its own apart from the real persons and their behaviors" (Snyder, Bruck, and Sapin 2002, 39, 50).

Much of the U.S. foreign-policy process corresponds to the liberal model. The conflicting demands of civil society, decentralized government, and unpredictable human behavior make this process anything but strictly rational. While liberalism emphasizes *process*, it can also be used to explain aspects of the nation's *conduct* of foreign policy. In particular, the moralistic tone of U.S. foreign policy, among its most distinctive qualities as seen from overseas, reflects deeply held normative principles arising from the country's origins in the Enlightenment era (see Hook and Spanier 2004). In proposing a system of collective security and calling for "not a balance of power, but a community of power," Woodrow Wilson epitomized the nation's liberal ideals. His effort to rise above *raison d'état* could be seen later in John F. Kennedy's Peace Corps and Jimmy Carter's promotion of human rights. Liberalism also provides a better explanation than realism for the failed U.S. mission in Somalia, which sought to end a humanitarian crisis and had no clear relationship to U.S. national interests.

Considering realism and liberalism to be mutually exclusive, however, creates a false dichotomy, one that ignores the melding of these approaches in the policy process. "International relations," Arthur A. Stein (1990, 12) observed, "involve both cooperation and conflict, evincing more cooperation than realists admit and more conflict than liberals recognize." The same fusion of realism and liberalism can be observed within the U.S. government, as foreign-policy decisions result from the competition and frequent compromises among various centers of power (see Kaarbo 1998). *Power politics*, a term most often associated with realism, can be clearly observed in the presumably liberal arena of domestic politics. Similarly, nation-states routinely impose their will on the UN, the World Bank, and other agents of the neoliberal world order. The pressure from governments varies widely, depending on their degrees of national power, which further suggests that power always lies close to the surface in foreign policy, no matter which theoretical world one inhabits.

Critical Perspectives

Other theories take a more critical look at U.S. foreign policy than do the two discussed above. While these perspectives differ from each other in important ways, they share a concern for underlying societal forces that deter U.S. foreign policy from representing common interests of the public as a whole or even those of the majority population. Three critical theories may be considered in this context: Marxism, elitism, and constructivism.

Marxism. The first critique is based upon the insights of Karl Marx (1818–1883), a Prussian theorist who condemned the wide gaps between Europe's rich and poor populations. Such inequality, he believed, stemmed from factors of economic production that allowed wealthy property owners (the *bourgeoisie*) to exploit workers (the *proletariat*). Marx focused his criticism on capitalism, the economic system widely adopted during this period by many industrialized countries, including the United States. He predicted that the proletariat's living conditions would become so miserable, and the lifestyles of the bourgeoisie so luxurious, that the workers would revolt against the system and create a more equitable alternative.

Marxism, whose scope was initially limited to domestic markets, became a major theory of world politics in the twentieth century. Vladimir Lenin (1870–1924), the first leader of the Soviet Union, charged that global imperialism was "the highest stage of capitalism" and had to be destroyed by a transnational alliance of exploited workers. After World War II, the hybrid theory of Marxism-Leninism became attractive to the leaders of developing countries, many of them newly freed from colonial rule or other forms of domination. In China, the communist regime created in 1949 by Mao Zedong vowed to lift the world's largest population from poverty and foreign manipulation. A decade later, Fidel Castro created a communist state in Cuba and portrayed himself as a role model for other revolutionaries in the Western Hemisphere. (See In Their Own Words box.)

The Marxist critique did not die with the Soviet Union in 1991. Indeed, persistent gaps between the world's richest and poorest peoples since the cold war, combined with the expanding presence of multinational corporations in the developing world, have sustained the Marxist critique into the new millennium. While the demise of Soviet communism revealed the defects of the model of "command economics," one need not embrace this alternative to capitalism to fault the social inequities and corruption stemming from the concentration of wealth in a relatively few hands. The theory continues to offer both an explanation for the plight of these countries and an ideal model for a new political and economic order that removes the uncertainties of market economics.

Marxism offers a model of domestic decision making in capitalist states as well, one that presumes government officials have little freedom of action, or autonomy, in their decisions. Instead, economic elites outside the government dictate government policy, foreign and domestic, by imposing economic and political pressure on the leaders. Money, in short, buys power in the United States and other capitalist nations. As Marx and his collaborator, Frederick Engels, wrote in

IN THEIR OWN WORDS: FIDEL CASTRO

Theories of world politics are not simply academic exercises; they have real consequences for global alignments and foreign policies. In this respect, Marxist theories have inspired many revolutionary leaders to overthrow existing governments and create their own. Cuban president Fidel Castro accomplished both goals in 1959 by leading a revolution against the U.S.-backed government of Fulgencio Batista. A year later, Castro addressed the United Nations, describing the principles that guided his revolution.

We proclaim the right of peoples to nationalism. Nationalism means a desire to recover resources. We are with all noble aspirations of peoples. We are with everything that is right; we are against exploitation, militarism, the arms race, playing with war, and colonialism. . . .

We bring before this assembly the main part of the Havana Declaration. . . . It proclaims the rights to land, to jobs, to medical care, free education, the right of nations to enjoy full sovereignty, the right of nations to reinforce their people to defend against imperialist attacks.

It is necessary to arm the workers, students, the Negro, the Indian, the young and old, to defend their rights and future. Some have wondered what is the stand of the Cuban Government. Well, this is our stand.

Source: Fidel Castro, "Speech to the United Nations on September 26, 1960," lanic.utexas.edu/project/castro/1960.

The Communist Manifesto ([1848] 2002, 82), "The executive of the modern state is but a committee for managing the common affairs of the whole bourgeoisie."

Elitism. A closely related critical theory is **elitism,** whose scope extends beyond economic leaders to include the news media, universities, foundations, and "policy-discussion groups" (see Domhoff 2002, 72). Like Marxism, this view challenges the theory of pluralism. A prominent variation of democratic theory in the mid-twentieth century, pluralism envisions evenly matched interest groups competing on a "level playing field" over government policy in democratic states, including the United States (see, for example, Dahl 1967; and Truman 1951). "We must recognize this description as a set of images out of a fairly tale," observed C. Wright Mills, a critic of the pluralist view (1956, 300; see also McConnell 1966). Mills believed that a **power elite,** composed of a small number of government and business leaders, controlled the United States.[2] The capture by powerful interest

---

2. See Parenti (2002) and Kolko (1962) for other major critiques of elitism in the United States. This theme, with particular emphasis on government propaganda in the news media, has been central to dozens of books by the critical theorist Noam Chomsky (2002; 2003).

groups of major sectors of the American political process in the 1960s and 1970s marked "the end of liberalism" (Lowi 1979).

Elite theory has been readily applied to U.S. foreign policy and the influence of interest groups, particularly corporations, in many areas of policy.[3] Survey results in the United States consistently demonstrate a lack of concern among the general public for foreign-policy issues unless the United States directly faces an international threat (see Chapter 7). This lack of public interest and scrutiny, due in part to the complexity of many foreign-policy issues and their apparent lack of connection to the daily lives of the mass public, leaves the policy process open to special interests, particularly large corporations. Their expertise on foreign-policy issues, combined with their strong self-interests and the considerable resources they commit to advancing those interests in the policy process, create a skewed foreign policy that favors a powerful minority of the American population.

The fragmentation of the U.S. political system further allows for a closed network of actors to shape policy with a high degree of autonomy from the public or even the president, who cannot possibly reign in the far-flung societal forces that find niches in the policy system. These actors are seen as rational, in search of self-serving payoffs and benefits. They succeed by forming alliances with government officials who share the groups' preferences. Many aspects of the foreign-policy process can thus be viewed as an **iron triangle**, linking influential interest groups, congressional committees, and the corresponding executive branch agencies that carry out policies of mutual concern. At the same time, an iron triangle can effectively exclude other members of Congress, the White House, and the general public from making decisions on key foreign-policy matters (see Figure 3.1).

A commonly cited example of an iron triangle is the U.S. defense industry, identified by President Eisenhower in his 1961 Farewell Address as the "military-industrial complex." Defense contractors such as General Dynamics and Lockheed exert strong influence over congressional members, who control defense funding and the fate of individual weapons programs. These legislators, primarily within the armed services committees, have strong incentives to satisfy the contractors, who represent many jobs (and possible votes) in their districts and provide large campaign contributions. The Department of Defense (DOD), meanwhile, wishes to maintain its funding, which translates into political influence over the direction of U.S. foreign policy, so it places constant pressure on congressional committees to increase military spending. Other iron triangles in the foreign-policy process involve energy policies, foreign investment, veterans' affairs, and arms transfers (see Hook and Rothstein 2005).

The Marxist and elitist critiques cannot be ignored in the United States at a time when elected officials routinely exchange preferential treatment for campaign contributions, which flow in record volumes primarily from the most affluent Americans, corporations, and trade groups. While their influence is most often directed toward domestic policy, it commonly involves such "intermestic" areas

---

3. Among other "revisionists" in the field of diplomatic history, William Appleman Williams most powerfully expressed this critique in *The Tragedy of American Diplomacy* (1959).

Figure 3.1 The Iron Triangle

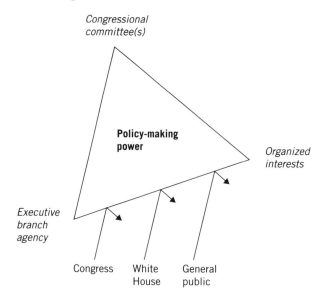

SOURCE: William T. Gormley Jr. and Steven J. Balla, *Bureaucracy and Democracy* (Washington, D.C.: CQ Press, 2004). Reprinted by permission.

(where international and domestic concerns merge) of foreign policy as trade, foreign investment, energy policy, and weapons procurement. Even in such vital matters of national security as the U.S. invasion of Iraq, one must consider the close economic connections between senior American decision makers and private firms, primarily the oil industry and companies such as Halliburton that specialize in reconstructing oil fields along with logistical support for U.S. military forces (see Mayer 2004).

Still, public engagement in the foreign-policy process comes from many sources, including nonprofit NGOs (Edwards and Gaventa 2001), "ethnic identity groups" (Ambrosio 2002), and state and local governments (Hobbs 1994). The electoral clout of well-organized groups may in some cases offset the financial clout of wealthy elites, who cannot deliver the voting majorities needed by presidents and legislators. Policy "intellectuals," in government as well as private think tanks, foundations, and universities, often influence U.S. foreign policy as well. And bureaucratic actors, as we will see below, also play a crucial role in shaping foreign policies to their liking even though they operate outside the circles of the "power elite."

Constructivism. A third critical theory with applications to U.S. foreign policy is **constructivism** (see Onuf 1989 for an early and definitive explanation). Advocates of this approach argue that world politics, along with domestic politics and other aspects of public life, do not have fixed properties—they are "socially constructed," primarily through public discourse. The global balance of power, therefore, is only threatening if political leaders *create* threats by making distinctions between "friends" and "enemies." From this perspective, interstate anarchy is not necessarily a recipe for conflict but is instead "what states make of it" (Wendt 1992; 1999). There are no inherent national interests, only interests constructed by political leaders and then transformed into public policy through the creative use of language and images of domestic ideals and global threats.

A central aspect of constructivist theory relates to **identity,** or the definition of an individual or group as considered apart from others. Political identities, which are socially constructed (they have no objective material basis), define relations among governments and stipulate whether they will be allies or adversaries. From this perspective, the shared identities of the United States and Western Europe after World War II had more to do with NATO's creation than the threat posed by the Soviet Union. "If material capabilities are all that count in world politics, one would have expected Western Europe to align with the Soviet Union rather than with the United States" (Risse-Kappen 1996, 359). Those same identities kept the NATO members within the alliance after the cold war, despite the absence of their stated enemy in Moscow, an outcome that also contradicts realist theory.

Once constructed, national identities are reinforced by the deliberate promotion of adversarial relationships with other states and peoples. These rivalries, including the U.S.-Soviet struggle during the cold war, are purposefully fueled by governments on both sides, which benefit from the exaggeration of foreign threats and dismiss opportunities for cooperation. "The boundaries of a state's identity are secured by the representation of danger integral to foreign policy," David Campbell (1992, 3, 69) observed. "Foreign policy creates the very dangers to which we are supposed to accommodate ourselves." After being conveyed repeatedly in the news media and popular culture, these messages become ingrained in public opinion.

Constructivists view the nineteenth-century discourse of "manifest destiny" in the United States as a moral justification for westward expansion and territorial conquests. In rallying the public during World War II, the U.S. government and major media outlets bolstered national morale by spreading stereotyped images of German soldiers as monsters and Japanese soldiers as rats (Hunt 1987). In vilifying and threatening such nations as Fidel Castro's Cuba during the cold war, American leaders fomented global tensions, including the Cuban missile crisis that brought the world close to nuclear holocaust (Weldes 1999). More recently, Bill Clinton's concerns about "rogue states" and George W. Bush's statements about an "axis of evil" further served the purpose of constructing a perilous world of U.S. foreign policy that requires aggressive action by the government to maintain primacy.

The Role of Ideas in Policy Formulation

A common point of contention among all these theories is the role of *ideas* in foreign policy. For all of their differences, realists, Marxists, and elite theorists identify material resources—capital, property, the means of economic production—as the primary source of state action. Liberals and constructivists, by contrast, believe subjective factors such as norms, values, principles and beliefs motivate decision makers (see Drezner 2000; and Finnemore 1996). Once expressed as ideas in policy discussions, they serve as road maps that give direction to foreign policy (Goldstein and Keohane 1993, 12). As in the case of realism and liberalism, a full understanding of U.S. foreign policy captures the impact of both forces (see Figure 3.2). Physical capabilities and financial wealth, when combined with the nation's cultural values and ideals, shape the formulation and conduct of foreign policy. The U.S. invasion of Iraq in 2003, for example, required a convergence of economic motivations and the ideas put forth by defense intellectuals regarding the doctrines of primacy and preventive war the U.S. government used to support the overthrow of Saddam Hussein.

In seeking to *explain* government actions and *predict* future behavior, political theories also *prescribe* solutions to problems and, in the case of foreign policy, offer strategies for managing global relations. Realists, for example, urge leaders to focus on national interests, build adequate military defenses, and maintain a balance of world power. Realists tend to be pessimists, however, making them skeptical that even these measures will keep the peace indefinitely. Indeed, they fear that leaders will try in vain to transform the anarchic world order through collective-security measures, a utopian exercise that would merely reward predators clinging to the status quo, such as Adolph Hitler in the 1930s (Carr 1939). The prescriptions of critical theorists—that economic liberty give way to social equality, or that political discourse be overhauled—may be even further beyond reach in practice.

Liberal theories generally produce the most pragmatic and tangible policy prescriptions. The separation of powers, constitutionalism, and the rational organization of bureaucracies are common remedies advanced by liberal theorists, who see institutional reform as the key to enlightened policy. In this respect, liberal theory represents the closest fit with the U.S. foreign-policy process, which has sought historically to overcome the twin perils of domestic tyranny and systemic anarchy by devising institutional mechanisms to counteract both. These institutions play vital roles inside and outside the government, but as we will discuss in the next section, they assume a life of their own that also hinders coherent foreign-policy making.

Figure 3.2 Sources of U.S. Foreign Policy

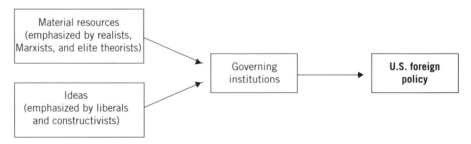

Institutional Momentum

The debates highlighted above draw our attention to the role of institutions in channeling preferences into policy outcomes. Institutional analysis focuses on formal government bodies as well as on nonstate actors such as interest groups and the news media. This approach, though most commonly used to explain U.S. domestic policy (see Kernell and Jacobson 2003), has also proven fruitful in understanding foreign policy. As this section will discuss, the U.S. experience since World War II reveals a consistent pattern of **institutional momentum,** or the proliferation and deepening roles of organized political actors in the foreign-policy process at home and abroad.

This pattern can be found on two levels, governmental and nongovernmental. In the first case, the concept refers to the expansion of domestic governing institutions—the presidency, Congress, and agencies of the executive branch (examined in detail in part 2 of this volume). The decisions of these "inside-out" institutions, while presumably made on behalf of national interests, also reflect the institutional biases and self-interests of these bureaucratic actors. On the second level, institutional momentum refers to the agents of transnational civil society—public opinion, the news media, private interest groups, and intergovernmental organizations (the subjects of part 3) based in the United States and abroad. These "outside-in" institutions play a critical role in shaping U.S. foreign policy given the democratic nature of the government, which opens much of the policy process to external pressure and welcomes the interplay of public and private interests.

The scale and vitality of these bi-level pressures make the foreign-policy process highly complex. This complexity reflects the fact that U.S. foreign policy is made at the convergence of three spheres of political activity: domestic governing institutions, the interstate system, and transnational civil society (see Figure 3.3). The degree to which different actors engage in the foreign-policy process varies across issue areas, as will be demonstrated below. Nonetheless, the effective man-

Figure 3.3 The Matrix of U.S. Foreign Policy

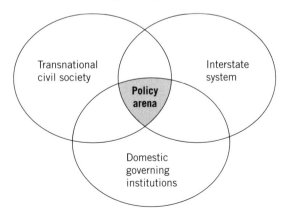

agement of foreign policy requires that the needs and policy preferences of actors in all three spheres be taken into account, if not ultimately reconciled.

Beyond complicating the policy process, institutional pressures restrict the government's freedom of action by narrowing the range of options available to the president and other top decision makers, whose goals cannot be achieved without the support of legislative leaders and key bureaucratic actors. The government, meanwhile, is "constantly subject to capture and recapture" by well-organized private groups that are able to dictate policy outcomes (Moravcsik 1997, 518). At the same time, pressure from the UN, international financial institutions, and other intergovernmental organizations has intensified to the point that it is regularly seen as threatening U.S. sovereignty. This perception, which grew steadily in the late 1990s, led directly to George W. Bush's turn away from the international community and his later defiance of the UN in the Iraq crisis.

Taken together, these cross-pressures fuel and reinforce the paradox of world power (outlined in Chapter 1) that confronts the United States today. These institutions are to varying degrees creations of the U.S. government, which long ago sought to constrain its own ability to act efficiently by empowering civil society as a hedge against state tyranny. But the "constitutional" world order (Ikenberry 2001) created after World War II under U.S. leadership, which sought to implant this model at the global level, became so dynamic and empowered such an array of transnational actors that support for the U.S. government could no longer be taken for granted. To the contrary, the widening base and growing clout of transnational civil society made challenges to the United States inevitable.

Inside-Out Pressures

As detailed in Chapter 2, the United States experienced a flurry of institution building after World War II. These cold war structural arrangements proved resilient after the Soviet Union's collapse and continue to shape the decision-making environment today. Though attempts to modify these structures have led to modest adjustments, none has produced fundamental changes in the institutional framework.

The Department of Defense provides a case in point. Although the army, navy, and air force accepted deep cutbacks in the 1990s, they blocked attempts to transform their core missions and organizational structures. "The house may be smaller, but it still has three rooms all the same size, and furnished the same way" (C. Williams 2001, 8). Several efforts, from Secretary of Defense Les Aspin's "bottom-up review" in 1993 through Secretary of Defense Donald Rumsfeld's *Quadrennial Defense Review* in 2001, have done little to alter the department's institutional architecture. The same problem hampers progress toward military unification, a goal of presidents since World War II. Resistance to unifying the armed forces "can only be understood as proof of the institutionalized clout that the separate services had acquired over the previous five decades" (Stuart 2002, 14).

Similarly, the National Security Council (NSC) has retained its cold-war organizational form and function in the post–cold war. Contrary to expectations during the Iran-contra scandal that its role would be scaled back, the NSC has continued to serve as a "second" State Department, with its own team of policy analysts and advisers to the president. The Central Intelligence Agency (CIA) adopted new missions after the cold war but with a structural framework largely unchanged from its founding (Lowenthal 2003). Early developments in the war on terrorism suggested that the CIA's covert-operational role would be *broadened* considerably, a move that provoked little opposition from Congress despite its misgivings and restrictive measures put into place late in the cold war. The chronic problems related to the CIA also have persisted, particularly the inability of the director of central intelligence to coordinate the federal government's far-flung intelligence-gathering units.

The heightened importance of geoeconomics (economic and geographic factors related to international trade) after the cold war brought such federal agencies as the Commerce Department and the Office of the U.S. Trade Representative into the heart of the foreign-policy process. The terrorist attacks of September 2001 provided the government with the most recent impetus for institutional momentum. The creation of the Department of Homeland Security (DHS) represented the largest structural change to domestic institutions since World War II. The internal functions of the DHS have proved highly complex, as have the department's relationship with other federal, state, and local agencies (see Chapter 10).

Importantly, during the cold war, societal pressures prevented the U.S. government from creating a "garrison state." These antistatist pressures, not present in the Soviet Union, left the United States with a robust private sector and a supportive public that contributed significantly to the nation's victory (Friedberg 2000). The sluggish adaptation of these domestic institutions to the post–cold war, however, hindered the U.S. government's ability to respond to emerging global problems and anticipate emerging threats. Furthermore, the heightened influence of private groups, particularly corporate interests in the administration of George W. Bush, raised troubling questions about the government's ability to chart its own, independent course in foreign affairs.

Outside-In Pressures

This pattern of institutional momentum and its impact on U.S. foreign policy extend well beyond the domestic realm (Keohane 2002; and Martin 1999). The global network of IGOs, created after World War II, has endured and grown denser; by the end of 2003, the United States was participating in seventy-eight such organizations. The United Nations remains the world's only multipurpose, universal-membership IGO. Despite the high-profile dispute in 2003 between the UN and the U.S. government over Iraq, more than 45,000 UN-sponsored forces, including U.S. personnel, from ninety-four countries were conducting peacekeeping operations in thirteen countries at the end of 2003.[4]

---

4. See the UN's Department of Peacekeeping Operations Web site for the most recent statistics regarding UN peacekeeping missions (www.un.org/Depts/Dpko/home.shtml).

Members of the UN Security Council approve a measure in June 2004 calling for the transfer of sovereignty back to Iraq after more than a year of occupation by U.S.-led forces. The Security Council had earlier opposed the U.S. government's call to use force against Saddam Hussein after UN inspectors failed to uncover weapons of mass destruction in the country late in 2002. The lack of support by the Security Council did not stop George W. Bush from ordering Saddam's overthrow in March 2003.

The Bretton Woods institutions, too, remain firmly in place. As noted in Chapter 2, the mission of the World Bank, originally limited to the reconstruction of Western Europe, expanded to include developing countries and, after the cold war, political and economic reforms in the former Soviet bloc. The International Monetary Fund, meanwhile, assumed greater authority than its founders had envisioned by providing emergency aid to entire regions, such as South America and East Asia. In promoting world trade, the General Agreement on Tariffs and Trade, signed in 1947, gave way in 1995 to the World Trade Organization, which was granted broad powers to enforce standards of free trade and punish violators.

The global network of U.S. military alliances provides yet another example of institutional momentum. Created in 1949 as a united front against the Soviet Union, the North Atlantic Treaty Organization (NATO) not only outlasted the Soviet Union but also added new members and missions after the cold war. The alliance played a key role in ending the violent conflicts in Bosnia-Herzegovina and Kosovo in the 1990s; in 2003, NATO forces launched their first "out-of-area" mission in Afghanistan. The United States continues as well to manage its bilateral alliances with Japan, the Philippines, and South Korea, all created as agents of anticommunist containment in East Asia.

Finally, the number of NGOs engaged in the U.S. foreign-policy process has grown steadily in recent years (see Chapter 8). Multinational corporations and other for-profit NGOs have a visible presence in Washington, D.C., where they seek favorable treatment from the government in overseas trade and investment, regulation, and potential subsidies. Nonprofit NGOs and "advocacy coalitions," too, have become more active in recent years, making use of the Internet to unite members from many countries in an attempt to influence U.S. foreign policy.

These groups serve as an extension of the domestic interest-group environment that has always been a central feature of U.S. domestic politics. Managing the vast array of private groups is a difficult, but inescapable, part of the foreign-policy process in all democracies. "Since democratic systems are based on the separation of state and society, their governments are less able to control the transnational activities of their citizens than authoritarian political systems," observed Thomas Risse-Kappen (1995a, 38–39). "Transnational and transgovernmental coalitions are then likely to become legitimate participants of the domestic political processes."

The Governmental Process

Opening the black box of U.S. foreign policy is a daunting task. Press reports that the United States "made" a particular decision may be technically accurate and easy to digest, but lurking behind such a decision is a struggle for power and influence among competing government agencies, intergovernmental organizations, and private interest groups. Decisions regarding each foreign-policy issue produce winners and losers in the policy process; the success or failure of the United States in world politics follows directly from the compromises and bargains the government made at home.

Bureaucratic Politics and Organizational Behavior

The decentralized structure of the U.S. government produces a high level of tension within the executive branch. As a result, the process of bureaucratic politics plays a crucial, though often dysfunctional, role in shaping the formulation and conduct of U.S. foreign policy. As societies modernized throughout nineteenth century Europe, bureaucrats took on an ever-widening array of tasks and became powerful political actors as well, their greater expertise, longevity in government, and direct access to the instruments of policy giving them significant advantages over elected leaders.

Contemporary scholars have applied these facets of bureaucratic politics in their analyses of the U.S. federal government, whose immense size, spending power, structural complexity, and global reach have no historical precedents and are unequaled by any other government today. As a result of their studies, scholars have questioned the presumed role of bureaucracies in promoting *rational* government. "American public bureaucracy is not designed to be effective," Terry Moe (1989, 267) observed. "The bureaucracy arises out of politics, and its design reflects the interests, strategies, and compromises of those who exercise political power." To Graham Allison (1971, 144), who first applied bureaucratic politics systematically to the U.S. foreign policy, the "name of the game is politics."

> The Governmental (or Bureaucratic) Politics Model sees no unitary actor but rather many actors as players—players who focus not on a single strategic issue but on many diverse intra-national problems as well; players who act in terms of no consistent set of strategic objectives but rather according to various conceptions of national, organizational, and personal goals; players who make government decisions not by a single, rational choice but by the pulling and hauling that is politics.

From this perspective, bureaucracies in the United States and other industrialized societies exhibit similar characteristics. Among the most important of these characteristics for our understanding of U.S. foreign policy are resilience, autonomy, self-interest, conservatism, and inefficiency.

Resilience. "Once it is fully established," German sociologist Max Weber (1946, 228) observed, "bureaucracy is among those social structures which are the hardest to destroy." The creation of U.S. federal agencies is a difficult and time-consuming task requiring public support, consensus within Congress, and presidential approval. Once formed, an agency becomes part of the institutional landscape, welcoming new missions and clients that have a stake in its future activities. Often an agency is "captured" by clients whose preferences for continuity, if not expansion, of its mission are embraced by the agency's managers. As described above, this pattern can be clearly seen in the institutional momentum of American foreign-policy agencies.

Autonomy. Bureaucracies enjoy a high level of freedom from outside interference. Agency managers have more expertise in their domains than elected leaders, giving the managers an upper hand in shaping and implementing policy. They also tend to last longer in their jobs, where they accumulate still greater expertise along with on-the-job training in mastering the political system. Finally, although agencies in the executive branch fall under the president's authority, they can elude presidential oversight even when monitoring measures exist. "Agencies can ignore presidential directives, delay implementation of presidential programs, and limit presidential options when it suits their needs to do so because presidents do not have the time or resources to watch them" (Zegart 1999, 47). The most troublesome aspects of bureaucratic autonomy led to the 1986 Iran-contra scandal, in which the NSC conducted "off-the-shelf" military operations in Central America without the knowledge of President Reagan.

Self-interest. Thrust into a competitive relationship with other agencies, agency managers are often more concerned with their own preferences and needs than with what would best serve the national interest. Bureaucratic rivalries extend beyond competition for material resources to competition for intangible assets. Of particular importance among the latter are greater *influence* over policy and the enhanced *prestige* within the policy community that comes with such influence. During the Cuban missile crisis, for example, the advice of senior military leaders reflected their parochial concerns rather than an objective determination of the most effective means for defusing the conflict and preventing a nuclear war between the United States and the Soviet Union (see Allison and Zelikow 1999). More recently, in George W. Bush's administration, tensions between Secretary of State Colin Powell and Secretary of Defense Donald Rumsfeld over Iraq had as much to do with built-in bureaucratic rivalries than with substantive policy differences.

Conservatism. Agencies put into place **standard operating procedures (SOPs)**, or consistent measures for addressing commonly encountered situations, as a matter of routine. These SOPs stress continuity over change, the execution of specialized roles, and a high level of internal order. Within bureaucracies, an organizational culture develops that further encourages business as usual and discourages innovation or changes of course (see Drezner 2000; and Brehm and Gates 1997). These problems plagued Donald Rumsfeld in 2003 as he sought to "transform" the U.S. military. Rumsfeld's frustration became so great that he fired Tom White, the army secretary. Rumsfeld did so in part because of White's refusal to support the cancellation of a pet project, the $11-billion Crusader artillery system, which Rumsfeld considered obsolete. Attempts to reform agencies, though occasionally successful (Abramson and Lawrence 2001), generally lead to frustration and failure.

Inefficiency. The fragmentation of bureaucracies leads to breakdowns in communication and coordination. This problem was illustrated during the 1983 U.S. invasion of the tiny Caribbean island of Grenada, launched by the Reagan administration to prevent a pro-Soviet regime from taking power. Despite their overwhelming force, the 6,000 U.S. troops needed three days to subdue a small brigade of enemy fighters, many of them construction workers from Cuba. Eighteen Americans died in battle, partly as a result of a battle plan guaranteeing each of the armed services a role in the invasion. There were also severe problems with communications. One marine, unable to contact his superiors by radio, simply used a pay telephone to contact the Pentagon and provide the location of enemy forces.

These aspects of bureaucratic behavior suggest to many observers a U.S. government on automatic pilot, controlled by bureaucrats who are driven by institutional self-interests. It is important to note, however, that this **bureaucratic-politics model** is hardly universal and is challenged by two other models of decision making. The **presidential-control model** views presidents as "caretakers of the national interest" (Bendor and Hammond 1992) who can rise above domestic politics, particularly in cases in which U.S. security interests are at stake (see also Art 1973; and Krasner 1972). The **congressional-dominance model** holds that legislators make their preferences clear to agency managers, who then have a material incentive—in the form of future budget support—to ensure those preferences are realized (see Weingast 1984; and Shepsle 1979). Once again, students can find evidence supporting both models in different areas of U.S. foreign policy, as we will see in the next two chapters.

Other critics of the bureaucratic-politics model argue that it is too *deterministic,* falsely identifying agencies with singular and predictable interests and policy positions (Welch 1992). The State Department, for example, was deeply divided over U.S. involvement in the Vietnam War; similar strains could be seen in more recent interventions in Somalia, Kosovo, and Iraq. These divisions, as well as those between agencies, may be constructive and serve the function of checks and balances central to the U.S. political system. Pointing to a silver lining of bureaucratic inefficiency, Paul 't Hart and Uriel Rosenthal (1998, 234) remind us, "Most of the tragic excesses that have marred the twentieth century have been caused by bureaucracy's ruthless efficiency in the name of extremist political masters."

State and Local Governments

The pluralistic nature of U.S. foreign policy extends to the state and local levels as well. As the previous chapter described, the original blueprint for American government—the Articles of Confederation—granted state governments control over most aspects of foreign policy. Placed in a system of domestic anarchy, the thirteen states engaged in trade wars against each other, pursued separate relations with foreign governments, and conducted their own military expeditions on the western frontier. As a result, the Founders designed the Constitution, in part, to shift key foreign-policy powers to the federal government, a system that remains in place today.

Under this system, however, state and local governments can still pass resolutions on foreign-policy issues, pursue foreign investments, organize cultural exchanges, and manage intermestic problems, such as pollution, affecting them. "As decisions are made and events transpire outside the boundaries of the nation-state that may have an immediate and profound effect on citizens at the grassroots level, these citizens demand that their interests be protected not only by their national governments but also by the subnational governments closest to where they live" (Fry 1998, 15). Furthermore, Jessica Mathews (1997, 65–66), president of the Carnegie Endowment, observed, nation-states "may simply no longer be the natural problem-solving unit."

Public activism in U.S. foreign policy frequently takes place on the state and local levels. It is there that Americans learn about problems overseas, discuss possible solutions to these problems, and take action to influence national policy makers. With more direct access to the political process at these levels, citizens frequently mobilize around the slogan "Think globally, act locally." Such activism in the 1980s was intended to moderate the bellicose rhetoric and nuclear strategies of the Reagan administration (Shuman 1992). Nearly 1,000 localities had called for a nuclear freeze by the time the cold war ended; nearly 200 had demanded a halt to nuclear testing, and 120 had refused to comply with federal civil-defense guidelines in the event of nuclear war. Reagan's early talk of defeating the "evil empire" in Moscow compelled millions of Americans to join peace groups, conduct public-information campaigns, and lobby local and state governments to speak out on their behalf.

To an extent previously unseen, the war on terrorism declared in 2001 brought local governments directly into the foreign-policy process. These governments serve on the front lines of the homeland-security effort in three primary ways. First, they must protect their citizens with enhanced police forces. Second, they must be prepared to immediately and effectively respond to terrorist attacks, a task managed with such courage on September 11 by the New York City Fire Department and other first responders. Third, local governments and agencies must play an intelligence-gathering role in looking out for possible terrorist "cells" or suspicious activities in their jurisdictions. In all three areas, local governments must work closely with federal officials and, when necessary, gain additional resources from Washington, D.C.

In the economic realm, the annual output of many states exceeds that of most foreign countries (see Table 3.2). The overseas exports of U.S. manufacturing firms have grown tremendously in the past decades. As a result, most states now operate overseas offices in foreign countries, while promoting joint ventures, sponsoring trade conferences, and subsidizing export promotion at home. Governors compete intensely for foreign industries to locate within their borders, offering a variety of economic incentives, such as tax breaks, highway improvements, and regulatory relief, to make this happen. Members of Congress commonly support these efforts and provide federal resources where possible to attract industries. In addition, military bases provide a substantial boost to employment, tax revenue, and spin-off economic activity at the state and local levels.

Local governments are more likely than states to voice their opinions on general foreign-policy issues, attracting attention by approving resolutions on

Table 3.2 Economies of U.S. States and Other Countries, 2002

	Nation or U.S. State	Billions of U.S. Dollars
1.	United States	$10,417
2.	Japan	3,979
3.	Germany	1,976
4.	United Kingdom	1,552
5.	France	1,410
6.	*California*	*1,359*
7.	China	1,237
8.	Italy	1,181
9.	*New York*	*826*
10.	*Texas*	*764*
11.	Canada	716
12.	Spain	650
13.	Mexico	637
14.	India	515
15.	*Florida*	*491*
16.	Korea, Rep.	477
17.	*Illinois*	*476*
18.	Brazil	452
19.	Netherlands	414
20.	*Pennsylvania*	*408*
21.	*Ohio*	*374*
22.	*New Jersey*	*365*
23.	Russia	347
24.	*Michigan*	*320*
25.	*Georgia*	*300*
26.	*Massachusetts*	*288*
27.	*North Carolina*	*276*
28.	*Virginia*	*273*
29.	Switzerland	268
30.	Belgium	248

SOURCES: World Bank, *World Development Indicators* (2003), www.worldbank.org/data/wdi2003; and U.S. Department of Commerce, *Statistical Abstract of the United States* (2004), www.census.gov/statab/www.

NOTES: Figures for U.S. states, in italics, represent gross state product; figures for countries represent gross domestic product.

Table 3.3 Selected Cities, Counties, and States with Resolutions Opposing the Iraq War

Akron, Ohio	Hawaii, State House of Representatives	Oakland, Calif.
Ann Arbor, Mich.	Ithaca, N.Y.	Orange County, N.C.
Atlanta, Ga.	Kalamazoo, Mich.	Philadelphia, Pa.
Baltimore, Md.	Kauai County, Hawaii	Pittsburgh, Pa.
Berkeley, Calif.	Key West, Fla.	Portland, Maine
Blaine County, Idaho	Lansing, Mich.	Providence, R.I.
Bloomington, Ind.	Lorain County, Ohio	Rochester, N.Y.
Boston, Mass.	Los Angeles, Calif.	Rockland County, N.Y.
Boulder, Colo.	Madison, Wis.	San Francisco, Calif.
Buffalo, N.Y.	Maine, State House of Representatives	San Jose, Calif.
Cambridge, Mass.	Maine, State Senate	San Miguel County, Colo.
Chapel Hill, N.C.	Manistee County, Mich.	Santa Clara County, Calif.
Chicago, Ill.	Mansfield, Conn.	Santa Cruz, Calif.
Cleveland, Ohio	Mendocino County, Calif.	Santa Fe, N. Mex.
Corvallis, Ore.	Milwaukee, Wis.	Santa Monica, Calif.
Denver, Colo.	Multnomah County, Ore.	Syracuse, N.Y.
Detroit, Mich.	New Haven, Conn.	West Hollywood, Calif.
Gary, Ind.	New York City, N.Y.	

SOURCE: Cities for Peace Campaign, "City and County Council and Related Resolutions Opposing Preemptive/Unilateral War in Iraq" (2004), www.ips-dc.org/citiesforpeace/resolutions.htm.

these matters. More than 160 cities and counties approved resolutions opposing President Bush's preventive invasion of Iraq early in 2003 (see Table 3.3). "Military action in Iraq will divert attention from economic issues and challenges confronting the American people and American cities," the city of Cleveland's resolution stated. "This resolution constitutes an emergency measure for the immediate preservation of public peace, property, health, or safety" (see Cities for Peace Campaign 2004). While this plea went unheeded by national policy makers—as such resolutions often do—the opposition of Cleveland, along with that of Chicago, Philadelphia, San Francisco, and other major cities was made clear to a global audience, signaling the limits of domestic support for the invasion and subsequent occupation of Iraq.

To critics of local activism, foreign policy should be left to the experts in Washington, D.C., and city councils should stick to their core responsibilities. "Local officials are elected because of their competency to manage local concerns, not because of their personal beliefs on national and international affairs," policy analyst Beth Waldron (2003) argued. "Hijacking local-government meetings for the debate of federal policy accomplishes painfully little and costs plenty. Municipalities should keep the 'local' in local government and leave national policy up to the appropriate duly elected federal officials."

Issue Networks and
Transnational Coalitions

The complex, highly fragmented nature of the U.S. foreign-policy system suggests that the process of decision making is highly idiosyncratic and variable. This observation directs our attention to the specific *issue areas* in which policy is made. Each issue area, from military procurement and NATO expansion to AIDS and family planning, contains its own cast of characters with particular interests and expertise. Coalitions within the government also form around these issues, and their ability to prevail over societal groups varies across issues. The U.S. government has historically been most insulated from group pressure on issues of national security (high politics) and most susceptible to pressure on economic issues (low politics). These differences have eroded, however, as American trade, energy policy, technology transfers, and other issues are increasingly considered matters of national security.

While iron triangles explain certain issue areas, decision making in others involves more actors and is more open to competing viewpoints than that model suggests. A more accurate model to describe the policy process is **issue networks** (Heclo 1978). These networks bring together interested government and private actors with shared knowledge and expertise, if not similar policy preferences. Indeed, the groups that come together in ad hoc issue networks often bitterly oppose one another, leading to a process of *contestation* rather than *collusion,* the essence of iron triangles. The growth of issue networks in the 1970s followed structural reforms by Congress, which created more subcommittees and expanded the federal bureaucracy in response to public demands for more services and access to the decision-making process.

"Politics makes strange bedfellows" has repeatedly been proven to be true. The antiglobalization protests during the 1999 WTO conference in Seattle, Washington, for example, involved anarchists, trade unions, environmentalists, feminists, and human rights activists. Proponents of the WTO's proglobalization agenda, meanwhile, included most governments and major corporations, as well as some liberal activists who viewed closer integration of the world economy as a step toward political cooperation and peace. Although these groups came from different backgrounds and pursued widely varying agendas, all were attempting to influence the same broad policy area. (The protesters succeeded in disrupting the conference and calling attention to their needs but ultimately failed to stop the WTO from furthering the cause of free trade.)

During this same period, a similar issue network formed around the issue of China's trading status with the U.S. government (see Figure 3.4). In this case, the Clinton administration strongly favored granting China most-favored-nation (MFN) status, a step that would lead directly to China's entry into the WTO. Clinton, who defended his initiative on behalf of "engaging" repressive governments, was supported by large corporations based in the United States that hoped to profit from heightened commercial relations between Washington, D.C., and Beijing. The government of China, of course, favored the move, as did the World

Figure 3.4 China MFN Issue Network

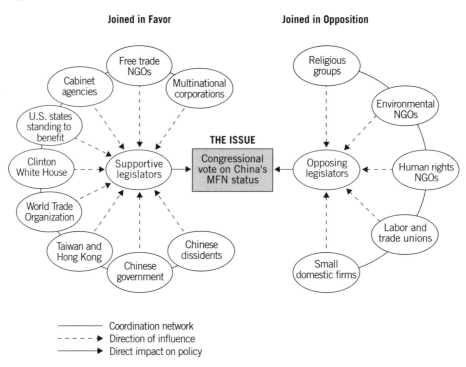

SOURCES: Steven W. Hook, "Sino-American Trade Relations: Privatizing Foreign Policy," in *Contemporary Cases in U.S. Foreign Policy: From Terrorism to Trade,* 2d ed., ed. Ralph G. Carter (Washington, D.C.: CQ Press, 2005); Mary H. Cooper, "U.S.-China Trade," *CQ Researcher Online* (April 15, 1994), library.cqpress.com/cqresearcher; David Masci, "China after Deng," *CQ Researcher Online* (June 13, 1997), library.cqpress.com/cqresearcher; Washington Council on International Trade, "Issue Brief: China's MFN Status" (April 11, 1997), www.wcit.org/resources/publications/issue_briefs/ib_china_mfn_status.htm.

Trade Organization, recently created as the institutional locomotive of free trade. Opposing the president were conservative members of Congress and a variety of private groups that protested the move because it rewarded a Chinese Communist Party that had committed atrocities against its own people. A variety of labor and trade unions as well as many small manufacturers opposed the measure too. Clinton ultimately won this policy debate, gaining Senate ratification of the trade measure and ensuring China's entry into the WTO (Hook 2005).

Due to the expansion of interest group activism and increased fragmentation in the federal government, decision making on domestic policies generally corresponds to the issue-network model. While iron triangles endure in many foreign-policy areas, issue networks appear more commonly in the process today as boundaries between foreign and domestic policy erode and intermestic issues demand a greater share of the government's attention. Thus understanding issue networks is crucial to our understanding of how domestic politics and U.S. foreign policy converge.

Issue networks increasingly extend across national borders, imposing demands on multiple national governments at once. The work of **transnational advocacy networks** further complicates the U.S. foreign-policy process as coalitions of environmentalists, human rights activists, and other groups organize in the name of deeply held principles. These networks—which may include religious institutions, trade unions, universities and research foundations, the news media, and intergovernmental organizations—"participate in domestic and international politics simultaneously" (Keck and Sikkink 1998, 15). In making transnational links, these coalitions gain the support of some national governments, then use that support to generate cooperation from other, more reluctant, governments. Such a "boomerang pattern" has affected U.S. foreign policy in many issue areas, including ending apartheid in South Africa and greater World Bank support for environmental protection.

The Human Factor

We now turn to the individual dimension of foreign-policy making. We must always remember that *people* make foreign policy, not inanimate objects such as nation-states or bureaucratic organizations. Despite our efforts to understand world politics by focusing on such abstractions, the simple fact remains that individuals respond in different ways to similar problems. The human factor, therefore, can never be eliminated from the equation (see Hill 2003, chaps. 4–5; and De Rivera 1968).

As with bureaucratic politics, studies of human behavior challenge the model of rational decision making presumed by neorealists. In the real world, top decision makers routinely disagree over the content of national interests, over the severity of threats to those interests, and over the implications of both for the day-to-day conduct of foreign policy. Their differences matter for policy outcomes, particularly in democratic political systems with multiple power centers and openings to external pressure. Even should all decision makers agree about the nature of a problem, information regarding the problem is likely to be incomplete or inaccurate. The other extreme exists as well, however, when information pours in at such high volumes that decision makers cannot hope to manage it. Making sound policy choices proves even more difficult in this case because the costs and benefits of each option cannot be calculated with precision.

In this world of **bounded rationality** (Simon 1957), foreign-policy makers cope as best they can with the personal as well as institutional limitations facing them. In this decision-making environment, the characteristics of individual actors are vital. This link between psychology and political behavior, as demonstrated in recent studies of American presidents (see Table 3.4), shapes the U.S. foreign-policy process in important ways. It is therefore critical that we examine the political psychology of foreign policy in three areas: perceptions and beliefs of key decision makers, their personalities and styles of leadership, and the dynamics of decision making in groups.

Table 3.4 The Political Psychology of Presidents Bill Clinton and George W. Bush

Bill Clinton	George W. Bush
• Favorable view of policy-making environment	• Outgoing and gregarious personality
• Optimism regarding political goals	• Need to control or dominate others
• Cooperative approach to problem solving	• Sensitivity to criticism
• Reliance on rewards rather than punishments	• Tendency to take impulsive action
• Aversion to taking risks	• Willingness to take risks

SOURCES: Stephen G. Walker, Mark Schafer, and Michael Young, "William Jefferson Clinton: Operational Code Beliefs and Object Appraisal," in *The Psychological Assessment of Political Leaders,* ed. Jerrold M. Post (Ann Arbor: University of Michigan Press, 2003), 324–328; and Aubrey Immelman, "The Political Personality of U.S. President George W. Bush," in *Political Leadership for the New Century: Personality and Behavior Among American Leaders,* ed. Linda O. Valenty and Ofer Feldman (Westport, Conn.: Praeger, 2002), 81–103.

Beliefs and Perceptions

According to political psychologists, decision makers come to their positions of authority with distinctive **belief systems** (Holsti 1962), which directly influence their foreign-policy goals and strategies as well as their responses to specific problems. Belief systems, which are formed early in life and are stubbornly resistant to change, link the fragmented impressions people have of the outside world to form a coherent whole (see Mowle 2003).

Two factors infuse beliefs with structure and coherence: philosophical and instrumental judgments. Every individual makes philosophical judgments regarding the virtues and limitations of human nature, the proper relationship of citizens to states, and the responsibilities of states to their citizens and to the larger world around them. Each person also makes instrumental judgments regarding the most pressing problems facing her or him on any given day and the best means available for solving these problems (Renshon and Larson 2003). Philosophical and instrumental beliefs combine in the policy-making world to create an **operational code,** that is, "a political leader's beliefs about the nature of politics and political conflict, his views regarding the extent to which historical developments can be shaped, and his notions of correct strategy and tactics" (George 1989, 486).

In managing foreign policy, decision makers are unconsciously guided by both sets of judgments. His childhood experience as the son of a Presbyterian minister, for example, profoundly shaped Woodrow Wilson's moralistic approach to world politics (George and George 1956). Early in the cold war, Christian beliefs led Secretary of State John Foster Dulles to assume the worst about the "atheistic" regime of the Soviet Union (Holsti 1962). For Henry Kissinger, his conception of world politics as an arena of great-power manipulation dictated his approach to the Vietnam War (Walker 1977), as the "black-and-white" thinking of Ronald Reagan shaped that president's confrontational approach toward the Soviet Union (Glad 1983). Such links between operational codes and foreign-policy behavior continued to shape the course of U.S. foreign policy during the Clinton years (Walker, Schafer, and Young 1998) and during the war on terrorism (Renshon and Larson 2003).

Perceptions are critical to the way decision makers define and respond to foreign-policy problems (see Sylvan and Voss 1998). This assertion, borne out by historical research, draws our attention to **cognitive psychology,** the process by which individuals obtain and process information about the world around them (see Vertzberger 1990; and Jervis 1976). The sheer enormity of information available makes it impossible for individuals to absorb even a tiny fraction. They must, therefore, constantly make choices regarding what information they will expose themselves to and how they will act upon what they have learned.

Although psychologists have identified dozens of ways individuals absorb and manage information, three cognitive patterns in particular are relevant to our understanding of U.S. foreign policy. First, in their attempts to make sense of a complex world, people strive for **cognitive consistency.** "We tend to believe that people we like act in ways we approve of, have values similar to ours, and oppose people and institutions we dislike," Lebow (1981, 103) observed. "People we dislike, we expect to act in ways repugnant to us, have values totally dissimilar to ours, and to support people we disapprove of." In this respect, foreign-policy makers tend to exaggerate the extent to which their interests converge with those of their allies and the depth of hostility adversaries have to those same interests. In distorting the true nature of friends and foes, both tendencies hinder the process of reconciling differences among states.

A second and related tendency concerns individuals engagement in **selective perception** as they collect and process information about the outside world. Once their belief systems have formed in the socialization process, people tend to seek out information that reinforces their worldviews while ignoring or dismissing information that contradicts them. In the process of making foreign policy, this hardening of belief systems discourages presidents from weighing information evenly or considering evidence that a chosen policy may be flawed. Senior officials in the Bush administration appear to have engaged in such selective perception as they prepared for the invasion of Iraq early in 2003, relying only upon intelligence reports that claimed Saddam Hussein had weapons of mass destruction and posed an imminent danger to the United States (Rieff 2003a).

Third, presidents often find the process of decision making a stressful one, particularly when the information they receive proves fragmented or contradictory. Their desire to make a decision quickly leads to **cognitive closure,** the adoption of a given solution to a problem before the available information has been fully examined and alternative strategies considered. A primary example of this involves Lyndon B. Johnson, whose chosen strategy in the Vietnam War only became ever more rigid despite increasing problems on the battlefield and the intensification of domestic opposition to the war. The setbacks in the war effort did ultimately force Johnson's successors to adapt their belief systems, and U.S. foreign-policy strategies, to the realities of world politics in the final years of Vietnam and after the war ended (see Holsti and Rosenau 1979).

Another example of cognitive closure involves President Truman in the early stages of the cold war, when U.S. containment policy led policy makers in Washington to interpret Soviet actions in ways that "rationalized" the policy. As

Deborah Larson (1985) discovered, Truman's anti-Soviet beliefs became more pronounced *after* he had settled on containment and was compelled to sell the strategy to Congress and the public. Evidence for this can be found in the announcement of the Truman Doctrine, which called for U.S. military aid to Greece and Turkey as a means of preventing Soviet expansion to the Mediterranean Sea:

> Having embarked on a course of action that divided the world into two rival blocs and increased the risk of war with the Soviet Union, the Truman administration had to find some compelling explanation of why containment of Soviet expansion into Greece and Turkey was necessary and legitimate. . . . The action context compelled [Truman] to reach cognitive closure, to settle on an interpretation of Soviet policy that supported the containment strategy (Larson 1985, 342–343).

In sum, how government leaders see the world has an important impact on how they are likely to conduct foreign policy. Their perceptions of the external environment, along with their sense of cultural differences and relative balances of power, relate directly to how they will interpret and respond to individual problems (Herrmann 1984). Psychological limitations cause leaders to ignore foreign-policy problems until they reach crisis proportions; at that point, presidents "*must* act, whether knowledge is plentiful or, as is more usually the case, uncertain, incomplete, and insufficient" (Larson 1985, 352, emphasis in original). For all these reasons, students of foreign policy should "characterize the political situation, not as it appears 'objectively' to the analyst, but as it appears subjectively to the actor" (Simon 1985, 297).

Personality and Crisis Behavior

A second general area of political psychology involves the outward, observable behavior of policy makers, which serves as an expression of their beliefs and perceptions of the outside world. In this section, we first consider the personality of presidents, particularly as it relates to the conduct of U.S. foreign policy. We then turn our attention to crisis behavior, another aspect of foreign policy that stems more directly from personal factors than institutional structures or legal designs.

Personality. Most analysts assume that the personality of presidents, or that of organizational leaders in any setting, plays an important role in the decision-making process (Hermann 1984). In short, it matters whether a leader is aggressive or passive, gregarious or withdrawn, competitive or cooperative, or emotionally stable or temperamental. These and other personality traits directly, if subtly, shape the *social* environment in which decisions are made. More specifically, the personality traits and behavioral styles of leaders often determine the roles played by secondary members of the decision-making team in policy discussions and debates (see Warshaw 1996).

One prominent study (Barber 1992) divided U.S. presidents into four categories based on where they fit along two dimensions. The first dimension involves whether presidents take an "active" or "passive" approach to their jobs. Of particular interest here is how much energy presidents invest in their work and how strongly they assert themselves in decision making. The second dimension considers whether presidents maintain a "positive" or "negative" view of their working environment. Is their work "a burden to be endured or an opportunity for personal enjoyment" (Barber 1992, 485)? The study found that the personalities of "active-positive" presidents such as Franklin Roosevelt and John F. Kennedy were best suited to their tasks. By contrast, those presidents who fell into the "active-negative" category, including Woodrow Wilson, Lyndon Johnson, and Richard Nixon, often met with personal frustration and professional failure.

The impact of personality on foreign policy is certainly not confined to the United States. Indeed, a measurable link between the personality traits and foreign-policy decisions of leaders in a wide range of countries can be found (see Hermann 1993; 1984). These and other cross-national findings compel us to examine the impact of presidential personality on U.S. foreign policy, especially given the president's broad powers in times of national crisis and war. A central concern in this regard is the possibility that the U.S. political system attracts "high-dominance individuals with a greater personal disposition to use force" (Etheridge 1978, 451).

To foreign-policy scholar John G. Stoessinger, U.S. presidents can be divided into two general categories: crusaders and pragmatists. *Crusaders* demonstrate a "missionary zeal to make the world better" and "tend to make decisions based on a preconceived idea rather than on the basis of experience" (1985, xiii). Among the twentieth-century presidents examined by Stoessinger, those fitting the crusader profile include Woodrow Wilson, Lyndon Johnson, Jimmy Carter, and Ronald Reagan. *Pragmatists,* in contrast, confront foreign-policy problems more flexibly. They try to make decisions based on the available evidence, weigh the pros and cons of alternative policies, and are quick to reverse themselves if those policies prove unsuccessful. Franklin Roosevelt and Harry Truman fit this category, and Richard Nixon's foreign policy was driven by the pragmatism of national security adviser Henry Kissinger. From this historical review, Stoessinger concluded that pragmatists are better equipped to manage foreign relations, which demand that presidents adapt quickly to rapidly changing circumstances.

The impact of presidential personality varies widely depending on the circumstances surrounding a given policy problem. To Greenstein (1969), the personalities of leaders can be expected to play a key role in policy outcomes when the following four conditions are present. First, the leaders occupy "strategic locations" in governments. Second, existing circumstances are ambiguous or in flux. Third, domestic and international forces are "delicately balanced" on both sides of an issue. Fourth, the problem at hand must be resolved by active effort rather than through routine procedures. Presidents probably will dominate decision making in these cases, and they will likely determine policy choices through the power of their personalities rather than through rational discourse.

Crisis behavior. A final area of political psychology concerns the behavior of pres-idents and other key decision makers in times of heightened stress or crisis. Inter-national crises are crucial because they occur at a midpoint "between peace and war" (Lebow 1981). The actions taken by political leaders in such crises often determine whether longstanding differences will be resolved peacefully or through violent conflict. Legal constraints and institutional structures play an important, but relatively indirect, role in such stressful circumstances. Of greater consequence is the psychological and behavioral orientation of decision makers.

Several factors converge in a crisis situation to shape the behavior of deci-sion makers. To Hermann (1993), these factors include an element of surprise, a strong threat to the values and interests of policy makers, and a requirement that decisions be made quickly. In this environment, normal decision-making routines are often suspended, and presidents are likely to consult only members of their inner circle of advisers. Information relating to the cause of the crisis is very lim-ited, as are precise calculations regarding the costs and benefits of possible responses. In addition, emotions run high in crisis situations, further impairing the process of rational decision making. Yet despite these impairments, some response must be made.

All these conditions applied to the September 11, 2001, terrorist attacks on the World Trade Center and Pentagon. Although government officials had long been aware that terrorism posed a danger to the nation, the attacks took the Bush administration by surprise. Further, the attacks shattered the most vital sense of national security felt not only by government leaders but by the general public. The prospects of additional attacks, affirmed by an outbreak of anthrax poison-ings from an unknown source, compelled President Bush to respond quickly by ordering a large-scale military assault on Afghanistan, whose Taliban regime "har-bored" the al Qaeda terrorists responsible for the 9-11 attacks. As Bush's advisers acknowledged, the ordeal strained the emotional capacities of all government offi-cials, who had to respond forcefully without adequate information about the source of the attacks or the viability of other policy responses.

International crises, therefore, pose the most acute challenge to the rational model of decision making. Presidents may attempt to overcome this challenge by encouraging dissent, considering a wide range of responses, and carefully antici-pating the consequences of their actions. Even their best efforts, however, cannot exclude the personal and psychological roots of foreign-policy making.

Decision Making in Groups

A final dimension of political psychology relates to group behavior, an important object of scrutiny given that much of the day-to-day formulation of U.S. foreign policy occurs in group settings. In most cases, the pressures imposed by collective decision making prevent individuals from simply demanding that their policy pref-erences be followed. Some sort of collaboration among several individuals, whose beliefs and personalities meld with those of other decision makers in the decision process, is usually involved. While cohesion rather than discord among these actors is generally preferred, dangers arise when group pressures force individuals to reach and support a consensus before they are prepared to do so.

Psychologist Irving Janis introduced the concept of **groupthink** and its resulting policy problems in the 1970s. In his view, major U.S. foreign-policy "fiascoes" such as the Pearl Harbor invasion and the Vietnam War could be attributed to the dysfunctions of collective decision making. Specifically, Janis (1982, 174–175) identified three characteristics of groupthink:

- overestimation of the group's power and morality, "inclining members to ignore the ethical or moral consequences of their decisions";

- closed-mindedness, or a collective reluctance to question basic assumptions regarding the problems at hand;

- pressures toward uniformity, or "a shared illusion of unanimity," combined with "direct pressure on any member who expresses strong sentiment against any of the group's stereotypes, illusions, or commitments."

Subsequent studies have reinforced and refined the concept of groupthink. "Structural deficiencies" in group deliberations, for example, hindered the outcome of major U.S. foreign-policy decisions (Schafer and Crichlow 2002) from 1975 to 1993. Newly formed groups appear most vulnerable to reaching premature consensus (Hart, Stern, and Sundelius 1997). Finally, the dangers of groupthink are not limited to foreign-policy crises; they apply to routine decision making as well (Hart 1994). Indeed, the problems associated with groupthink may be observed within government bodies at all levels and in private organizations.

Reports on the Bush administration's deliberations before the March 2003 invasion of Iraq offer additional evidence of persistent problems relating to groupthink. In particular are reports claiming that shortly after taking power, senior administration officials reached a consensus that Saddam Hussein should be overthrown. They then searched for an appropriate pretext in which they could make this happen (Woodward 2004). Contrary voices during this period were restrained in the name of maintaining this consensus, which was so strong that officials underestimated the dangers associated with the postwar military occupation of Iraq and the prospects for an orderly transition to democracy in the embattled country.

Conclusion

As this chapter suggests, the conduct of the United States in foreign affairs results from a variety of pressures that arise not only from overseas but also within the country's borders. The U.S. government is a large and remarkably far-flung institution that empowers public officials in multiple centers of decision making while providing private groups many venues in which to advance their interests. It is true that much of the foreign-policy process takes place out of the public's view and the daily management of U.S. foreign policy is often free of interest-group pressure. Still the bi-level pressures posed by domestic and transnational institutions greatly restrict the rational pursuit of a unitary "national interest." This *disorderly* outcome, anticipated with favor by the architects of the U.S. government in the name of restricting state power, places heavy burdens on the capacity of the nation to manage its primacy in the international system. These difficulties are magnified by a political culture that alternately welcomes and resists the immersion of the United States in the international community.

The chapters that follow examine in greater detail what occurs inside the "black box" of U.S. foreign policy. Our consideration of the president's vital role, outlined in the next chapter, demonstrates the power of the human factor located in the White House. Yet the institutional constraints on this power, based in Congress and in the various federal agencies engaged in foreign policy, guarantee that other agendas will be represented in the policy process. These agendas will be shared or resisted by external actors increasingly transnational in their composition and scope. Making "rational" decisions, always a difficult task given the limitations of human nature and political psychology, proves especially difficult in the complex institutional environment in which U.S. foreign policy is made.

Key Terms

balance of power, p. 60

belief systems, p. 84

bounded rationality, p. 83

bureaucratic-politics model, p. 77

cognitive closure, p. 85

cognitive consistency, p. 85

cognitive psychology, p. 85

congressional-dominance model, p. 77

constructivism, p. 68

elitism, p. 66

groupthink, p. 89

identity, p. 69

institutional momentum, p. 71

iron triangle, p. 67

issue networks, p. 81

liberal theory, p. 59

Marxism, p. 65

national interest, p. 60

neoliberal institutionalism, p. 62

neorealism, p. 59

norms, p. 61

operational code, p. 84

power elite, p. 66

presidential-control model, p. 77

rational actors, p. 60

realist theory, p. 59

security community, p. 62

selective perception, p. 85

sovereignty, p. 60

standard operating procedures (SOPs), p. 77

transnational advocacy networks, p. 83

transnational interdependence, p. 62

two-level game, p. 64

unitary actors, p. 60

Internet References

The **Center on Budget and Policy Priorities** (www.cbpp.org) focuses on federal and state budget priorities, including research on taxes and spending. Projects of interest include analysis of military spending, specific foreign-policy spending, and tax burdens for national security.

Hosted by Dalhousie University, the **Centre for Foreign Policy Studies** (www.dal.ca/~centre) provides useful information on conferences, seminars, publication series, and specific links to policy, government, and international institutions. The center's recent research seminars and publications analyze unilateralism and multilateralism decisions following the cold war.

Congressional Research Service's **CRS Reports** (fpc.state.gov/fpc/c4763.htm), from the research arm of Congress, provide briefings on specific policy issues that include background information, chronologies, bibliographic references, and budget statistics. Two of the larger policy domains within the CRS are "Foreign Affairs" and "Defense and Trade." CRS reports on particular topics are often updated each year. Current examples include detailed information regarding terrorism, international and free trade, foreign aid, global finance, arms trade and control, missile defense, energy policy, and bilateral reports such as U.S.-Russian and U.S.-Israeli relations.

The **Foreign Policy Research Institute** (www.fpri.org) is a research-based organization that focuses on studying U.S. national interests, the war on terrorism, security relationships, and long-term policy planning. FPRI's research is based on a multidisciplinary approach, including scholars and advisers from economics, politics, law, the media, and history. The institute publishes a quarterly journal, *ORBIS,* which consists of reports from conferences and scholars regarding U.S. and world interests (available online at www.fpri.org/orbis).

The **Institute for Foreign Policy Analysis** (www.ifpa.org) provides briefings for students interested in the costs, benefits, and planning of U.S. foreign policy. The institute covers a variety of issues but focuses on globalization, missile defense, international institutions, and grand strategies.

The **International Action Center** (www.iacenter.org) focuses on international labor, poverty, militarization, and multinational corporations from a critical standpoint. This site provides dozens of links to books, journals, and Web resources regarding antiwar and antiglobalization activities and efforts to improve the standard of living in poverty-stricken countries.

The **International Studies Association** (www.isanet.org) provides conference papers, journal articles, and relevant links to timely and scholarly research on empirical testing and analyzing issues in foreign policy and international politics in general. Included are syllabi collections, which provide additional readings and links from various professors around the globe. The Foreign Policy Analysis Section of the ISA is responsible for publishing the journal *Foreign Policy Analysis,* a multidisciplinary, peer-reviewed journal regarding the process, outputs, and empirical testing of foreign policy (available online at fpa.tamu.edu).

continues

Internet References *(continued)*

The **National Center for Policy Analysis** (www.ncpa.org) is a nonprofit and nonpartisan public policy research center that focuses on privatization alternatives to current issues. Specific topics related to U.S. foreign policy are immigration, energy, trade, and environmental issues.

The **National Center for Public Policy Research** (www.nationalcenter.org) is a conservative foundation that researches current international and national events with a free-market and individual-liberty orientation. Topics of interest for foreign-policy researchers are environmental and energy policy, national security, national sovereignty, and defense procurement.

The **Public Policy Section** of the American Political Science Association (www.fsu.edu/~spap/orgs/apsa.html) is designed by a group of scholars in that field and provides useful links to journals, think tanks, and centers for those interested in studying public policy. The site also provides links to recent conferences where papers and roundtables on public policy issues were presented; full-text downloading capabilities are available.

The **Woodrow Wilson International Center for Scholars** (wwics.si.edu) provides a research hub for scholars and students to review current events and how they relate to relevant theories of policy. In addition to specific regional coverage and research, the center has ongoing projects regarding security and peace strategies along with research in conflict prevention and international trade and finance. The center is responsible for publishing books in each area of research along with the *Wilson Quarterly* (available online at wwics.si.edu/index.cfm?fuseaction=wq.welcome).

4

Presidential Power

President George W. Bush discusses the conflict in Iraq during a cabinet meeting in the White House in December 2003. The president resisted strong international opposition to the U.S.-led preventive invasion of Iraq nine months earlier. Even the general public in the United States opposed going to war without the endorsement of the UN Security Council. Nonetheless, Bush chose to launch the attack and was able to do so given the considerable powers of the president in matters of war and peace.

Our exploration of the state sources of U.S. foreign policy begins by considering the powers of the president. The U.S. Constitution calls for the sharing of foreign-policy powers between the executive and legislative branches of government, with legal questions and occasional disputes between the White House and Congress to be resolved by the judicial branch. This central principle of **codetermination** reflects the twin fears of tyranny at home and adventurism abroad that preoccupied the early leaders of the United States.

The president of the United States operates at the "focal point, the epicenter, the hub of the American political and governmental system" (Wiarda 1996, 263). This centrality of presidential power is even stronger with regard to foreign policy, a domain in which presidents are regarded, at home and overseas, as living symbols of the United States. The concentration of White House control since World War II led one scholar (Wildavsky 1966) to conclude that **two presidencies** operate simultaneously: a constrained presidency on domestic issues, and a presidency that reigns supreme in foreign affairs.

Historically, presidential power in foreign policy has been especially strong in wartime, an important pattern given that the United States has been effectively, if not officially, at war almost continuously since it became a global superpower a century ago. The two world wars were followed by nearly half a century of cold war, a period that witnessed the concentration of foreign-policy power in the White House. In the late 1940s, the onset of a dangerous nuclear rivalry between the United States and the Soviet Union convinced congressional leaders that the president required more direct control over the instruments of national security (see Chapter 2). Furthermore, they and others agreed, domestic quarrels between the president and Congress over foreign policy could weaken the United States in the eyes of its foreign adversaries. For this reason, politics had to "stop at the water's edge."

The climate of nearly perpetual crisis did not end with the cold war. The Persian Gulf War in 1991 and the deployments of U.S. troops to Somalia, Haiti, and the former Yugoslavia in the Clinton years reinforced the president's control over matters of war and peace. The terrorist attacks of September 2001 silenced any differences between the White House and Congress over the ends and means of U.S. foreign policy. Prior to the attacks, President George W. Bush's domestic rivals openly challenged his plans for nuclear missile defense, his rejection of global environmental accords, and his shift toward a unilateral foreign policy. After the attacks, both the Senate and the House of Representatives put these differences aside, giving Bush full discretion in pursuing and punishing the attackers. Congress approved the funds requested by the president to bolster U.S. military forces, expand antiterrorism efforts within the United States, provide relief to victims, and support domestic industries hurt by the resulting economic slowdown. These and other actions gave Bush "a dominance over American government exceeding that of other post-Watergate presidents and rivaling even Franklin D. Roosevelt's command" (Milbank 2001, A1).

Although Bush claimed he did not require congressional approval to overthrow Saddam Hussein in Iraq in 2003, his desire that the invasion be considered legitimate prompted the president to seek, and receive, Capitol Hill's blessing. Members of Congress authorized Bush to "use the armed forces of the United States as he determines to be necessary and appropriate in order to defend the national security of the United States against the continuing threat posed by Iraq." To one scholar, this mandate "was so broad that it conjured memories of the 1964 Tonkin Gulf Resolution, which gave congressional imprimatur to President Lyndon Johnson's expansion of the war in Vietnam" (LeoGrande 2002, 113).

This comparison to the Vietnam War is significant. Contemporary critics of the war, such as historian Arthur M. Schlesinger Jr. (1973), argued that an **imperial presidency** had taken hold in the United States, with presidents governing foreign affairs virtually "by decree." A great many members of Congress shared these concerns; they investigated and uncovered widespread abuses of executive authority during the war. Congress has since assumed a stronger role in foreign policy, particularly with regard to gathering and assessing intelligence, approving treaties, and spending money on foreign aid and international organizations (see Chapter 5). Competition between the two branches, however, is "less than meets the eye" (Hinckley 1994) in the post-Vietnam era, with presidents maintaining the upper hand in the foreign-policy process.

An imperial presidency in the United States is of particular concern given the lack of foreign-policy experience most cold war presidents bring to the White

Point/Counterpoint
BUSH VS. KERRY

Presidents generally enjoy a substantial degree of deference from Congress in the U.S. foreign-policy process. They face direct challenges, however, from those trying to replace them in the Oval Office. Presidential campaigns often expose stark differences over foreign policy that are suppressed when control of the White House is not at stake.

The electoral importance of U.S. foreign policy varies over time. A key factor is whether the United States is at peace or war. In peaceful times, the public usually concerns itself with "pocketbook" issues and other domestic concerns and seeks a candidate who will handle them appropriately. But in wartime, voters look for the candidate that appears best equipped to defend the nation's security.

The war on terrorism, which began in George W. Bush's first year in office, was a critical campaign issue when the president sought reelection in 2004 against Sen. John Kerry, D-Mass. The differing personal experiences, worldviews, and policy preferences of the two men gave voters a real choice regarding the future course of the war on terrorism and foreign policy in general. Bush, who often referred to himself as a "war president," emphasized the need for strong national defense and unilateral action in foreign affairs, central elements of Republican Party platforms for decades. The president defended his invasions of Afghanistan and Iraq, the resulting increases in defense spending, and the rejection by the United States of many international agreements and commitments. "America will never seek a permission slip to defend the security of our country," he proclaimed in his 2004 State of the Union address.

While Bush struck themes close to the heart of his Republican base, Kerry aligned himself with positions familiar to the Democratic Party: support for the United Nations, adherence to treaties and international law, greater attention to foreign aid, and the pursuit of diplomatic, rather than military, solutions to interstate conflicts. "The new era of alliances that I propose will take different forms in different parts of the world to deal with different and urgent challenges," Kerry told the Council on Foreign Relations in December 2003. "But the overriding imperative is the same: to replace unilateral action with collective security." Kerry's reference to collective security, recalling the liberal ideals of Woodrow Wilson, was also intended to reassure the international community that the United States would pursue a more cooperative foreign policy under his watch.

Sources: George W. Bush, "State of the Union Address" (White House, January 20, 2004), www.whitehouse.gov/news/releases/2004/01/200 40120-7.html; John F. Kerry, "Making America Secure Again: Setting the Right Course for Foreign Policy" (speech, Council on Foreign Relations, New York, December 3, 2003), www.cfr.org/press /policy/video_transcripts.php?id=2003.

House. Only three presidents since World War II—Dwight Eisenhower, Richard Nixon, and George H. W. Bush—had substantial backgrounds in foreign policy. Post–cold war presidents Bill Clinton and George W. Bush were serving as governors upon their elections in 1992 and 2000, respectively. As candidates, both men emphasized domestic priorities and often described their comparative lack of experience overseas as an *asset* rather than a liability. To George W. Bush, the fact that he had not traveled overseas much during the many years his father had been immersed in foreign affairs merely demonstrated his preference for the American way of life. Such a stance may appear paradoxical given the role of presidents in leading the foremost world power, with its wide-ranging global responsibilities. Yet it is entirely consistent with the nation's ambivalent view of the "outside world," a cultural perspective that looks to foreign peoples, places, and events with a combination of intrigue and indifference, fascination and suspicion.

Whatever their backgrounds, presidents have discovered foreign affairs to be a safe haven from the withering struggles with Congress over domestic policy. Status as head of state carries with it unmatched prestige and provides an opportunity to "rise above politics" in the pursuit of national interests. For this reason, presidents "have a natural inclination to escape the frustrations and controversies of domestic policy making by seeking opportunities to strut their stuff in the realm of foreign and national security policy" (Rockman 1997, 26).

Still, presidents face a variety of constraints in conducting foreign policy. Democratic control of Congress under the Republican administrations of Ronald Reagan and George H. W. Bush led to frequent clashes over foreign policy. The Republican-led Congress of 1995–2001 waged a vigorous campaign to blunt the "neo-Wilsonian" aspects of Clinton's foreign policy. Members of Congress have skillfully attached "reservations" to international treaties that give their foreign-policy preferences the force of law and allow them to avoid the "either-or choice that is implicit in the Constitution" (Auerswald and Maltzman 2003, 1106). Although presidents remained more successful in gaining congressional support for foreign policies rather than domestic initiatives, a congressional rubber stamp in foreign policy became harder to come by between the end of the cold war and the onset of the war on terrorism (Fleisher et al. 2000).

Beyond legislative-executive relations, presidents must consider the foreign-policy preferences of multiple power centers within the executive branch (see Figure 4.1). As we saw in the previous chapter, the interests of these domestic institutions routinely conflict with one another, and coordinating their missions, overseas activities, and input in the policy process has proven very difficult. The pluralistic nature of the U.S. political system encourages societal actors, too, to play an active role in the policy process. In making foreign-policy decisions, presidents are guided by the news media and public opinion even while attempting to influence both through their actions. Just as Congress must be attentive to its constituents, so too must presidents, if they wish to be reelected or leave an enduring legacy in foreign affairs, be responsive to the demands of corporate leaders, labor unions, ethnic and religious groups, and other interest groups. Finally, presidents are engaged daily with foreign governments—whether friends or foes—along with

Figure 4.1 Influences on the President in Foreign Policy

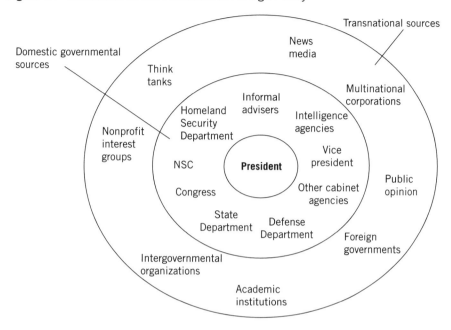

intergovernmental organizations such as the UN and NATO that have their own stakes in the U.S. foreign-policy process.

These many channels of power and influence ensure that presidents consider multiple interests in the foreign-policy process. Each participant in the process, whether government agencies or members of transnational civil society, imposes scrutiny on presidential actions and holds the president accountable for her or his foreign-policy choices, as well as their outcomes. Presidents, therefore, have much to win or lose with each decision they make, but they retain considerable freedom to make such choices as they see fit.

The Constitution's Mixed Blessing

As discussed in Chapter 2, the current U.S. political system was not clearly established immediately after the United States gained independence. Not until 1787 did widespread fears that the new country would collapse in the absence of a stronger national government lead to the Constitutional Convention. The Constitution ratified two years later abolished the system of dual sovereignty and created a system of federalism by which the national government gained greater authority over public policy. The Bill of Rights explicitly affirmed the political freedoms of the American people, and a unified legal system, to be overseen by a national judiciary, was established. Under the new system, an integrated U.S. economic market made it possible for the nation to speak with one voice in foreign trade relations.

IN THEIR OWN WORDS: THEODORE ROOSEVELT

Among twentieth century U.S. leaders, Theodore Roosevelt was one of the strongest advocates of presidential power. He believed that the president, who alone serves the nation as a whole, should be a "steward" of the people. To act as one, the president must have broad authority to exercise power without interference from Congress or the courts. According to political scientist Michael Nelson, Roosevelt's stewardship theory rests on the assumption that "the president could do anything that the Constitution or laws did not expressly forbid," a view of presidential power in sharp contrast to that held by many nineteenth-century presidents. Roosevelt explained the theory himself in his autobiography.

The most important factor in getting the right spirit in my Administration . . . was my insistence upon the theory that the executive power was limited only by specific restrictions and prohibitions appearing in the Constitution or imposed by the Congress under its Constitutional powers. My view was that every executive officer, and above all every executive officer in high position, was a steward of the people bound actively and affirmatively to do all he could for the people, and not to content himself with the negative merit of keeping his talents undamaged in a napkin. I declined to adopt the view that what was imperatively necessary for the Nation could not be done by the President unless he could find some specific authorization to do it. My belief was that it was not only his right but his duty to do anything that the needs of the Nation demanded unless such action was forbidden by the Constitution or by the laws. Under this interpretation of executive power I did and caused to be done many things not previously done by the President and the heads of the departments. I did not usurp power, but I did greatly broaden the use of executive power. In other words, I acted for the public welfare, I acted for the common well-being of all our people, whenever and in whatever manner was necessary, unless prevented by direct constitutional or legislative prohibition.

Sources: Michael Nelson, ed., Historic Documents on the Presidency, 1776–1989 *(Washington, D.C.: Congressional Quarterly, 1989), 170; Theodore Roosevelt,* An Autobiography *(New York: Macmillan, 1913), also available online at www.bartleby.com/55 (Bartleby.com, 1998).*

Much of the Constitution had less to do with the *scope* of federal authority than with its *distribution* among the branches of government. The debates that took place at the convention and in public largely concerned this issue. Alexander Hamilton believed a strong president was needed to guide the United States toward the position of global leadership that all Americans agreed was the nation's destiny. Hamilton's main antagonist in this debate was James Madison, the primary author of the Constitution, who believed a legislature must be empowered to prevent the emergence of a tyrannical head of state.[1] Madison, taking his lead from the French political philosopher Baron de Montesquieu, insisted that national powers be shared among the executive and legislative branches of government and that an independent judiciary be established to ensure that government action, as well as private behavior, complied with the rule of law.

Although the Constitution did not emphasize foreign policy, these checks and balances were intended in large part as restraints on the U.S. government in world politics. In particular, the empowerment of Congress directly curbed the president's power to plunge the country into foreign "entanglements" without popular consent. Not only would these restrictions prevent the rise of a European-style monarch, but they also would make the formulation of foreign policy so cumbersome that the United States would only rarely take aggressive action in foreign affairs. Such self-discipline seemed entirely appropriate for the new nation, whose primary concerns involved the consolidation of domestic order and state building.

Modern presidents have not questioned this constitutional design, but they have consistently resisted efforts by Congress to tie their hands. Among twentieth-century presidents, Theodore Roosevelt was the most outspoken advocate of strong presidential power in war and peace. Roosevelt's **stewardship theory** called for a dominant president in domestic and foreign policy alike. While his successors adopted a more balanced view of presidential power, they have asserted, and have generally been granted, considerable discretion, or **prerogative powers**, in managing foreign affairs (Silverstein 1997). This freedom to make independent and binding judgments extends beyond national emergencies to include day-to-day decisions that do not require the blessing of Congress or the courts. Yet the Constitution still provides the essential framework for the codetermination of foreign policy in several specific areas.

Formal Powers in Foreign Policy

The powers of Congress and the president are defined in Articles I and II of the Constitution, respectively (see Table 4.1). The language regarding foreign policy is very brief and sufficiently vague to provoke widely varying interpretations about the Framers' intent. References to foreign-policy powers are not contained in separate sections of either article, but are interspersed among references to powers in domestic policy. The president has four key areas of formal powers in foreign policy: commander in chief, negotiating and signing treaties, appointing cabinet secretaries and ambassadors, and conducting diplomacy.

Commander in chief. The rationale for the Constitution's division of labor regarding war powers is clear: sending troops to war, widely considered the most crucial

---

1. This public debate, which took the form of essays written by the two men along with John Jay, another Founder, was published anonymously in various newspapers during the ratification process. The essays, later published as the *Federalist Papers* (see Rossiter 1999), remain an eloquent statement of the logic underlying the U.S. political system.

Table 4.1 Sharing of U.S. Foreign-Policy Powers

	Executive	**Legislative**
Actors	President, cabinet, NSC, bureaucracy, and White House advisers	House of Representatives and Senate, committees and subcommittees
Advantages	Coherence, speed, secrecy, national constituency, control of information	Deliberation, compromise, openness
War powers	Commander in chief of armed forces, authority to repel attacks	Declare war, authorize ongoing deployment per War Powers Resolution
Diplomatic powers	Recognize and conduct routine relations with foreign governments	"Fact-finding" missions
Appointment powers	Nominate ambassadors and cabinet secretaries	Confirmation of nominees
Treaty powers	Negotiate and sign treaties	Ratify treaties
Administrative powers	Oversight through cabinet, bureaucracy, and staff	Appropriations, oversight of executive branch
Economic powers	Leadership of economic agencies; adoption of fiscal, monetary, and trade policies	Regulate commerce, power of the purse
Special powers	Declare national emergencies	Impeach president

decision any government can make, must be a collective, rather than an individual, undertaking. A declaration of war, therefore, must follow reasoned discussion of alternatives. Furthermore, hostilities must proceed only after most legislators determine war to be the best available option. Once war has been declared, however, the president as commander in chief must be free to direct the conflict. Given their need for prompt, unified, and decisive leadership, military conflicts require centralized command rather than legislative deliberation. In this regard, once the United States has become engaged in warfare, the governmental checks and balances deemed so essential by the Framers no longer pertain to the actions of the commander in chief.

No area of U.S. foreign policy has been as controversial with regard to presidential powers as war powers. Three factors account for this unending controversy. First, formal declarations of war are no longer standard practice in diplomacy. The United States has declared war in only five conflicts: the War of 1812, the Mexican-American War, the Spanish-American War, World War I, and World War II. Since December 1941, the U.S. government, despite its intervention in dozens of armed conflicts, including those in Korea, Vietnam, the Persian Gulf, the former Yugoslavia, and Afghanistan, has not issued such a declaration. Short of a formal war declaration, presidents can resort to military force with little concern for the preferences of Congress. Even when war declarations were customary, American presidents unilaterally deployed troops overseas when they felt national interests were at stake. Thomas Jefferson, for example, dispatched U.S. naval forces to the Mediterranean Sea without congressional authorization in a mission to repel attacks on shipping.

Second, military interventions provide a *fait accompli* for presidents. Once troops are deployed, domestic opposition not only appears unpatriotic but also may weaken the mission and threaten the lives of American servicemen and women. For this reason, members of Congress are reluctant to question presidential uses of force even when they believe their own prerogatives have been denied. President James K. Polk established this precedent in 1845 by sending U.S. troops into disputed territory along the U.S.-Mexican border. The deployment quickly provoked skirmishes between U.S. and Mexican forces that led to war between the two countries.

Third, presidents have broad discretion to conduct wars in whatever ways they deem appropriate. Although such discretion is clearly within the authority as commander in chief, critics have frequently assailed presidents whose military actions were seen as immoral or illegal. During the Civil War, for example, Abraham Lincoln suspended many constitutional freedoms for the sake of military necessity. Harry Truman did not seek congressional approval for the use of atomic bombs against Japan. Richard Nixon openly defied Congress during the Vietnam War, withholding vital information about U.S. incursions into Cambodia and Laos. In the war on terrorism, domestic critics charged the Bush administration with abusing Iraqi prisoners, violating the civil rights of Muslims in the United States, and unjustly restricting the civil liberties of all Americans (see Roth 2004).

Treaties and international agreements. The Constitution empowers both the executive and legislative branches of government to participate in the negotiation and signing of international treaties. The U.S. Senate, which has the specific power to ratify treaties signed by the president, has complied with the president's wishes in virtually every case. It is the exceptions to this rule—the Senate's rejection of the Treaty of Versailles in 1919, for example, and of the Comprehensive Test Ban Treaty (CTBT) in 1999—that illustrate how delicate the constitutional balance between branches can be.

As in the case of war powers, the terms regarding treaties reflect the general view among the Framers that such important acts of statecraft should reflect a broad national consensus. Indeed, the two-thirds "super-majority" required for treaty ratification made it clear that presidents could not take such ratification for granted. The Framers expected senators to play a role throughout the treaty-making process, and for this reason, their *advice* as well as *consent* was written into the Constitution. Effective presidents have sought the guidance of legislators in considering whether a particular treaty should be pursued, and, if so, what its terms should be. Such collaboration, of course, is helpful (and often essential) if presidents expect the smooth and successful ratification of the treaties they bring to the Senate.

A president's failure to consult with Congress can prove disastrous. After World War I, Woodrow Wilson insisted upon negotiating the Treaty of Versailles personally and took no members of Congress with him to Paris for the peace conference. The ambitious treaty, which called for a more peaceful and democratic interstate system and the creation of the League of Nations, was rejected by the Senate. In its view, the treaty would have violated U.S. sovereignty by requiring the nation to commit forces to fight overseas without the consent of Congress. Many years later, in signing the nuclear test ban in 1996, President Clinton called the multilateral accord "the longest sought, hardest fought prize in the history of arms control." He then paid little attention to the ratification process in the Senate, which proved to be a serious misjudgment three years later when the Senate rejected the CTBT. In both cases, the neglect of diplomacy at home undermined the prospect for diplomatic breakthroughs overseas.

Formal treaties, however, represent only a small fraction of the agreements reached between the United States and foreign governments. Since 1939, more than 90 percent of international agreements have been in the form of **executive agreements,** which do not require Senate ratification (Congressional Research Service 2001). While most executive agreements involve routine matters, others have had major national-security implications. These include Franklin Roosevelt's "lend-lease" agreements with U.S. European allies during World War II, the various commitments made by Roosevelt at the Yalta Conference and Truman at the Potsdam Conference, the agreement between the United States and North Vietnam ending the Vietnam War, and many agreements during the cold war granting U.S. military forces access to overseas bases.

Members of Congress became so concerned about executive agreements in the early 1950s that Sen. John Bricker, R-Ohio, proposed a constitutional amendment requiring the same two-thirds Senate majority for executive agreements as for treaties. The Bricker amendment was narrowly defeated, but tensions between the White House and Congress on this subject steadily grew. In 1972, Congress passed a more modest bill, the Case-Zablocki Act, which required the president to inform both houses of Congress of an executive agreement within sixty days of signing one with a foreign government. While the act eased the most basic Congressional concerns and allowed for opposition to be heard, "[t]he power to make such agreements remains vast and undefined, and its constitutional foundations remain uncertain" (Henkin 1996, 219).

The Case-Zabloski Act certainly did not discourage presidents from pursuing executive agreements late in the twentieth century. Ronald Reagan approved more executive agreements—2,840—than any other U.S. president, while signing just 125 treaties during his eight years in office (1981–1989). George H. W. Bush approved 1,350 executive agreements, and Bill Clinton approved another 1,870 during his two terms of office. From the Nixon through the Clinton years, the ratio of executive agreements to treaties stood at 18:1 (Congressional Research Service 2001). While this gap is hardly what the Framers had in mind when they empowered Congress to ratify treaties, it has become standard practice for presidents to make such agreements as a matter of prerogative.

Presidential appointments. As in the case of treaties, Senate approval of presidential appointees is granted in virtually every case. Observers widely agree that presidents, upon being elected, deserve to select the people they believe best equipped to promote their agendas in foreign as well as domestic policy. The rare cases in which nominations are rejected, and the circumstances surrounding them, capture the most national attention. One of the bitterest of these setbacks came in 1989, when the Senate refused to confirm Sen. John Tower, R-Tex., as George H. W. Bush's secretary of defense. To many senators, Tower's highly publicized personal problems made him unfit to lead the Pentagon.

In most cases, unpopular nominations are withdrawn before formal votes are cast. In the Clinton administration, these cases included the nominations of Anthony Lake (director of central intelligence), Robert Pastor (ambassador to Panama), and Morton Halperin (assistant secretary of state for democracy and peacekeeping). Another Clinton nominee, former Massachusetts governor William Weld, was denied the post of ambassador to Mexico in 1997 by Sen. Jesse Helms, R-N.C., the chairman of the Senate Foreign Relations Committee, who refused to allow Weld's nomination even to come before the committee. Helms, an outspoken conservative critic of President Clinton's foreign and domestic policies, rejected Weld's liberal positions on social issues such as gay rights and abortion. The personal—and highly public—dispute between the two men poisoned any chance for compromise.

Although Congress has usually deferred to the president in nominations, confirmation hearings in these uncontroversial cases still serve important functions. Nominees have a chance to outline their goals and strategies and to promote the president's agenda. For their part, committee members relish the opportunity to advance their own ideas about U.S. foreign policy and to enlist a nominee's support for their proposals.

One of the most powerful foreign-policy advisers to the president bypasses the process of Senate confirmation altogether. The special assistant for national security, more commonly known as the national security adviser (NSA), is simply appointed by the president upon taking office. When Congress created this position as part of the National Security Act of 1947, it intended that the person selected would serve primarily as coordinator of the newly established National Security Council, located inside the White House. All that changed in 1969, when Richard Nixon appointed Henry Kissinger to be his NSA. Kissinger quickly emerged as the Nixon administration's foremost architect of U.S. foreign policy. In addition, Kissinger personally negotiated arms-control treaties with the Soviet Union, engaged in "shuttle diplomacy" in the Middle East, and supervised U.S. policy in the Vietnam War.

While more recent presidents have scaled back the NSA's profile, the person who holds this position retains a vital role by working so close to the president in the White House. President George W. Bush often acknowledged that Condoleezza Rice, his NSA, was his primary source for guidance on the most vital aspects of U.S. foreign policy. Rice, also a close Bush family friend, accompanied the president and his wife to the Camp David presidential retreat on weekends and watched college football games on television with the president. Unlike Kissinger, however, Rice encouraged other senior aides, such as Secretary of Defense Donald Rumsfeld and Secretary of State Colin Powell, to brief the president and engage actively in foreign-policy deliberations. These officials also shared Rice's spotlight in press interviews and public appearances.

Conducting diplomacy. The Constitution is especially vague with regard to the day-to-day conduct of U.S. foreign policy. There is little doubt, however, that the president, as head of state, is empowered to represent the United States in foreign relations and to manage the routine functions of diplomacy. Indeed, the strongest presidential powers may be found in the conduct of these routine interactions.

Those who believe the president should dominate this process refer to the wording in Article II, Section 3, that the president "shall receive Ambassadors and other public Ministers." [2] This is considered significant because, according to international law, "the reception of an ambassador constitutes a formal recognition of the sovereignty of the state or government represented" (Adler 1996b, 133). George Washington set the precedent for U.S. recognition of newly installed foreign governments in 1793, when he invited the French envoy Edmond Charles Genêt for a state visit to Philadelphia, then the U.S. capital. Washington's invitation represented "tacit recognition" of the new revolutionary regime in Paris (Jones 1988, 34). Early in the twentieth century, Theodore Roosevelt recognized the government of Panama without first consulting Congress—even before Panama had formally freed itself from Colombian rule.

More recent presidents have generally taken it upon themselves to recognize foreign governments or deny recognition to regimes they considered illegitimate. Franklin Roosevelt's recognition of the three Baltic republics after they were annexed by the Soviet Union in 1940 became U.S. policy for the entire cold war. Richard Nixon's "opening" to the People's Republic of China in 1972 reversed the long-standing U.S. policy that denied the legitimacy of China's communist government. In the early 1990s, Bill Clinton's recognition of the breakaway Yugoslav republics of Croatia, Slovenia, and Bosnia-Herzegovina paved the way for U.S. assistance to all three governments. Clinton refused, however, to recognize the Taliban regime in Afghanistan, a position assumed by his successor, George W. Bush, as the two countries went to war in 2001.

For any president, the power of diplomatic recognition is vital to future relations between the United States and the other government—and to the president's ability to have a strong impact on U.S. foreign policy. Presidential discretion in this area extends far beyond simple recognition or nonrecognition of foreign governments. Formal recognition by the United States brings with it a wide array of potential economic, military, cultural, and political arrangements that are part of routine bilateral relationships. Nonrecognition, in contrast, is often accompanied by economic sanctions and other punitive measures. Presidents have broad control over these arrangements as well as the timing and tone of official U.S. contacts with foreign governments.

---

2. In *Federalist* No. 69, Alexander Hamilton suggested this is "more a matter of dignity than authority." He then noted the impracticality of "convening the legislature . . . upon every arrival of a foreign minister."

Legal Rulings on Presidential Powers

Debates over constitutional powers in U.S. foreign policy generally focus on the respective roles of the president and Congress. What about the judicial branch's role in tempering presidential power? The courts have assumed a relatively low profile in foreign affairs, leaving the executive and legislative branches alone so long as they did not directly violate the explicit terms of the Constitution or otherwise deny the rights of American citizens. As Louis Henkin (1996, 148), a leading scholar on the Constitution and foreign policy, noted:

> Overall, the contribution of the courts to foreign policy and their impact on foreign relations are significant but not large. The Supreme Court in particular intervenes only infrequently and its foreign affairs cases are few and haphazard. The Court does not build and refine steadily case by case, it develops no expertise or experts; the Justices have no matured or clear philosophies; the precedents are flimsy and often reflect the spirit of another day.

Although the Constitution does not make such a claim, courts have consistently dismissed issues relating to U.S. foreign policy as "political questions" and therefore beyond the scope of judicial review. In other words, struggles over the formulation and conduct of U.S. foreign policy are best waged in the political arena and should not be resolved by judges. In the case of *Marbury v. Madison* (1803), Supreme Court Chief Justice John Marshall defended the process of judicial review but argued that such review be limited. The Constitution, Marshall wrote (quoted in Smith 1989, 134), invested the president "with certain important political powers, in the exercise of which he is to use his own discretion, and is accountable only to his country . . . and to his own conscience."

Supreme Court Justice William J. Brennan Jr. restated this position in 1962. "Not only does resolution of such issues frequently turn on standards that defy judicial application," Brennan (quoted in Henkin 1996, 145) wrote, "but many such questions uniquely demand single-voiced statement of the Government's views." His view was generally shared by lower courts that felt ill-equipped to resolve matters of foreign policy. In this spirit, judges repeatedly refused to consider lawsuits that claimed U.S. presidents were waging an illegal war against Vietnam.

While the judicial branch has generally steered clear of disputes between the president and Congress, its occasional rulings have tended to support the executive branch (see Table 4.2). This tradition is traced to John Marshall (quoted in Adler 1996a, 25–26), who as a member of Congress in 1800 claimed that "the President is the sole organ of the nation in its external relations. . . . Of consequence, the demand of a foreign nation can only be made on him." Importantly, Marshall was referring to the president's exclusive role as the contact between the United States and foreign governments. His view, however, was widely construed as a rationale for broad presidential authority in foreign affairs. Marshall's language was applied much later in the landmark case of *United States v. Curtiss-Wright Export* (1936), in which the Supreme Court upheld Franklin Roosevelt's

Table 4.2 Major Supreme Court Rulings on Foreign Affairs

Year	Court Case(s)	Importance
1920	*Missouri v. Holland*	Established primacy of federal government over states in approving treaties
1936	*United States v. Curtiss-Wright Export Corporation*	Affirmed president's foreign-policy powers
1937 1942	*U.S. v. Belmont* *U.S. v. Pink*	Upheld executive agreements by the presidents
1952	*Youngstown Sheet & Tube Company v. Sawyer*	Restricted the power of the president to seize private assets in the name of national security
1971	*New York Times v. United States* (Pentagon Papers)	Ruled that First Amendment freedoms of the press outweighed presidential claims of national security
1979	*Goldwater et al. v. Carter*	Affirmed president's power to terminate treaties
1983	*INS v. Chadha*	Ruled the legislative veto was unconstitutional
1983 1985 1987 1990	*Crockett v. Reagan* *Conyers v. Reagan* *Lowry v. Reagan* *Dellums v. Bush*	Affirmed presidential war powers
2004	*Rasul v. Bush*	Upheld the right of foreign war prisoners to appeal their detentions in U.S. courts

authority to enforce an arms embargo previously authorized by Congress.[3] To Justice George Sutherland (quoted in Adler 1996a, 25), foreign policy should be considered "the very delicate, plenary, and exclusive power of the president as the sole organ of the federal government in the field of international relations."

Nevertheless, members of Congress have frequently turned to the courts to restrain presidents in foreign policy. In *Goldwater et al. v. Carter* (1979), for example, the Supreme Court supported President Carter's right to terminate the U.S. Mutual Defense Treaty with Taiwan. In the Court's view, the case was "political" since no clear violations of the Constitution had occurred. Similarly, in *Crockett v. Reagan* (1984) and *Lowry v. Reagan* (1987), the Court again dismissed as "political" congressional claims that the president had overstepped his constitutional bounds by deploying troops into conflicts overseas.

On some occasions, the courts have acted to curb presidential powers. In *Youngstown Sheet & Tube Co. v. Sawyer* (1952), for example, the Supreme Court declared unconstitutional President Truman's seizure of American steel mills to avert a national strike during the Korean War. Such authority, the Court ruled, could only be exercised with the explicit consent of Congress. Then in 1971, the Supreme Court ruled against the president in the *Pentagon Papers* case. Specifically, the Court rejected Nixon's claim that damaging information possessed by the *New York Times* regarding U.S. involvement in Vietnam should be barred

---

3. In addition, in *Curtiss-Wright*, the Court affirmed the external sovereignty of the federal government. The delegation of power from Congress to the president was appropriate in this case, the Court ruled, since the issue at hand concerned foreign, rather than domestic, policy.

from publication on the grounds of national security. The Supreme Court more recently curbed President George W. Bush's authority in the war on terrorism, ruling in June 2004 that suspected terrorists held as war prisoners have rights to legal representation in U.S. courts.

More generally, court rulings have affirmed the president's right to use his or her discretion, or prerogative, in managing U.S. foreign policy. Judgments by the Supreme Court consistently "signaled that it would not intervene unless individual rights of American citizens were threatened, or unless legislators in Congress asserted their own institutional authority" (Silverstein 1997, 84). Constitutional interpretations by the judiciary regarding foreign-policy powers have done little to temper the inherent tension between the White House and Congress. A level of mutual distrust remains between the two branches of government that is woven into the nation's institutional fabric and reinforced by historical experience.

Structures of the "Presidential Branch"

As we have seen, the Constitution and most court rulings affirm the president's preeminent role in making U.S. foreign policy. In keeping with this political reality, the White House has emerged as the institutional nucleus of the policy process (Hart 1987). This trend began before World War II, when Franklin Roosevelt convinced Congress to expand the administrative capacity of the White House and to establish "a responsible and effective chief executive as the center of energy, direction, and administrative management" (Presidential Committee on Administrative Management 1937, 2). Members of Congress, persuaded that the president required a much larger staff to reflect the arrival of the United States as a major global power, created the Executive Office of the President in 1939. This office has expanded steadily since, with eight separate divisions currently engaged in some aspect of U.S. foreign policy (see Figure 4.2).

The expansion of White House power has led to the emergence of a "presidential branch separate from the executive branch" (Polsby 1990). Institutional momentum in the White House had its greatest impact on U.S. foreign policy with the creation in 1947 of the National Security Council (NSC). The NSC, a central component of the security complex (see Chapter 6), was designed in part to *constrain* presidents by ensuring that they collaborate with other senior government officials—particularly the vice president and the secretaries of state and defense—in making major foreign-policy decisions (Hammond 1960). Presidents have consistently rejected this role for the NSC and have instead used the council and its staff as a policy-making center independent of the Pentagon, the State Department, and other cabinet agencies (Daalder and Destler 2000).[4]

---

4. The vice president's office became a major power center in the second Bush administration as Dick Cheney emerged as a major force behind the president's foreign policy (see Kengor 2004; Mayer 2004; and Lemann 2001). Cheney, who served as secretary of defense in the first Bush administration, assembled his own national-security team in the Office of the Vice President and played a key role in energy and environmental policy as well.

Figure 4.2 Councils within the Executive Office of the President

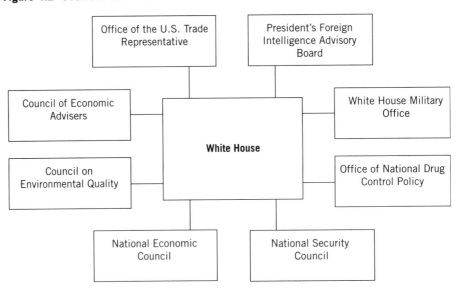

The NSC system has proven highly malleable over the years, taking on different shapes and roles in each presidential administration. In this respect, the NSC "is properly the President's creature. It must be left flexible to be molded by the President in the form most useful to him" (Tower Commission 1987, 4). Beyond meeting the needs of national security, centralized management of U.S. foreign policy produces several benefits. Presidents are better able to coordinate their objectives by working closely with officials in the White House engaged in various domains of foreign policy. Interagency disputes may be avoided by making decisions in a closer knit environment, and a coherent message is more likely to emanate from the executive branch.

The White House–centered model also has several drawbacks. First, the political appointees in these offices, including the national security adviser, are not subject to Senate confirmation. This freedom from legislative scrutiny deprives Congress of a vital constitutional power to influence the foreign-policy process. Second, decision making in the White House tends to be highly secretive, with staffers hidden from public view more than their counterparts elsewhere in the federal government. Finally, the creation and expansion of White House agencies inevitably leads to redundancy in the foreign-policy process. Their missions often overlap, covering the same functional and regional issues as those of cabinet agencies. This redundancy not only leads to inefficiencies, but also creates yet another layer of bureaucratic competition in a federal government already rife with internal rivalries. It was no secret in Washington, for example, that the White House Council on Environmental Quality, its leaders handpicked by George W. Bush in 2001, engaged in constant policy struggles with the Environmental Protection Agency as well as the State Department's specialists in this area (Jehl 2003).

Informal Powers of the President

The remaining foreign-policy powers of the president and Congress—those not explicitly written into the Constitution—are not clearly apportioned. As Supreme Court Justice Robert Jackson (quoted in Fisher 1995, 102) observed in 1952, "[T]here is a zone of twilight in which [the president] and Congress may have concurrent authority, or in which its distribution is uncertain." This is an important point since most routine actions by the U.S. government in foreign affairs fall within this zone of twilight. Our attention, therefore, should also be drawn to the *informal* powers of the president. Three of the most important are setting the agenda of U.S. foreign policy, taking the initiative, and organizing the chain of command. Effective presidents use all of them to determine the course of foreign policy. Before reviewing those informal presidential powers, it is helpful to consider the many advantages maintained by the president in the foreign-policy arena.

Balance of Power Advantages

The following five presidential advantages have the greatest impact on the legislative-executive balance of power: a national constituency, party leadership, always being "in session," role as the bureaucracy's CEO, and control of information. These five advantages have helped the presidency to strengthen its hold on foreign-policy decisions.

A national constituency. The president is the only elected official who represents a national constituency and can claim to speak for "all the people." Senators and House members represent states and congressional districts, respectively, and thus are obliged to promote the relatively narrow self-interests of their constituents in these areas even if they conflict with perceived national interests. Presidents face no such dilemma in their identification of policy preferences.

Party leader. As party leader the president can rely upon support from within her or his political party, not only in Congress but also among state and local officials. Party members who openly oppose presidents from "within the ranks" run the risk of being seen as disloyal. The president's advantage in this respect is weaker when the opposition party controls one or both houses of Congress, as President Clinton learned during his last six years in office.

Always in session. The presidency, unlike Congress, is always in session. This situation enables the president to respond to foreign-policy problems at any time and with little notice. Congress lacks this element of expediency. It is often at recess and, except for times of national emergency, operates by a legislative calendar that is comparatively slow and rigid.

The bureaucracy's CEO. The president serves as the chief executive officer of the federal bureaucracy and its employees. As discussed in Chapter 3, bureaucratic politics can be difficult to overcome. But presidents can expect that the general principles and policy goals they adopt will be supported by federal employees.

Control of information. The president's control of information is extensive and closely protected. The intelligence agencies, diplomatic corps, and armed services, all located within the executive branch, collect vital information about foreign affairs upon which the president bases decisions. In most routine areas of foreign policy, members of Congress are kept out of this loop. A further handicap for congressional members is their uncertainty about which presidential advisers have the president's ear on which issues.

Setting the Foreign-Policy Agenda

In addition to the above advantages are the president's informal powers. The most crucial relates to the president's ability to set the agenda, that is, to establish the general direction of U.S. foreign policy. Only the president can approve and articulate the grand strategy of the United States in global affairs. And only the president can make the most critical decisions regarding the *tactics* of foreign policy (whether to emphasize diplomatic bargaining, economic leverage, or military force, for example, in particular instances) derived from this chosen grand strategy.

A core element of this informal power concerns the public statements by presidents relating to the ends and means of foreign policy. Since every presidential statement is covered thoroughly in the press, the president has unmatched access to a worldwide audience on a daily basis (see Chapter 7). It is widely accepted that a president's public statements "give authoritative articulation to the nation's foreign policy" (Robinson 1996, 118). State of the Union speeches, delivered annually before an immense global audience, have a strong impact on public opinion, which in turn plays a crucial role in determining whether Congress takes the White House agenda seriously (Cohen 1995).

This presidential agenda-setting power—actively promoted through deeds as well as words—was evident throughout the cold war. Harry Truman's own doctrine became a centerpiece of the containment strategy that guided U.S. foreign policy until the Soviet Union's collapse in 1991 (see other doctrines in Table 4.3). Truman's deployment of U.S. troops to Korea in 1950 later signaled the "Asianization" of U.S. grand strategy that led to the Vietnam War. In the late 1960s, Richard Nixon adopted the *realpolitik* model of statecraft championed by national security adviser Henry Kissinger, and in the 1970s, Jimmy Carter revived the moralism of Woodrow Wilson. Following Carter, Ronald Reagan linked a series of setbacks in U.S. foreign policy to his predecessor's agenda. With a supportive Congress and favorable public opinion, Reagan had virtual free reign to implement a tougher anti-Soviet policy in the early 1980s (see Scott 1996).

Conversely, the lack of presidential vision in foreign policy can be costly. George H. W. Bush acknowledged that his failure to identify a coherent post–cold war grand strategy contributed to his unsuccessful reelection campaign in 1992. For his part, Bill Clinton remained preoccupied with domestic reforms long after

Table 4.3 Post–Cold War Presidential Doctrines

Year	Presidential Doctrine	Description
1947	Truman Doctrine	Committed U.S. support to foreign governments facing internal or external subversion
1957	Eisenhower Doctrine	Declared the Middle East a vital region to the United States
1969	Nixon Doctrine	Shifted U.S. involvement in Asia to a more limited role by encouraging allies to fight communism on their own
1985	Reagan Doctrine	Pledged U.S. support for countries fighting communism through insurgents or "freedom fighters"
1994	Clinton Doctrine	Identified global engagement and "enlargement" of democratic rule a central goal of U.S. foreign policy
2001	(George W.) Bush Doctrine	Defended preventive attacks on state terrorists, need for U.S. primacy

taking office in 1993. He finally decided on the guiding principle of his foreign policy—the "enlargement" of global democracy—but the doctrine never caught on with Congress or the public (Brinkley 1997). By the time the Republican Party captured both houses of Congress in November 1994, Clinton had largely surrendered his ability to set the foreign-policy agenda (Dumbrell 2002).

While presidents have a great deal of discretion over their foreign-policy agendas, unforeseen global events "can blow the president's foreign-policy ship into seas the president never planned to enter" (Brenner 1999, 187). The Japanese attack on Pearl Harbor in 1941, for example, shattered Franklin Roosevelt's efforts (and promises) to stay out of World War II. The same can be said for President Carter's foreign policy, which assumed a more aggressive profile after three developments abroad: the takeover of Nicaragua's government by Marxist rebels, the taking of U.S. hostages in Iran, and the Soviet Union's invasion of Afghanistan (Rosati 1987).

This pattern repeated itself with George W. Bush, for whom the terrorist attacks of September 11, 2001, provided the defining focus not only of his foreign policy, but also of his presidency.[5] The Bush Doctrine that followed, most vividly detailed in the president's 2002 National Security Strategy, contained four primary principles: the widening adoption of "universal" democratic values, the need to take preventive action against grave threats to U.S. security, the virtues of unilateral action, and the benefits of U.S. primacy not only for the United States but also for international security (Jervis 2003). These principles, which Bush had embraced prior to September 11 but did not vigorously promote, quickly gained the stature of a foreign-policy doctrine for the remainder of his presidency. Though foreign-policy analysts often disagree about the core elements of a presidential "doctrine," to the critical diplomatic historian Walter LaFeber (2002, 550), the Bush Doctrine could be summed up by the following formula: "exceptionalism plus power equals unilateralism."

---

5. In his February 2004 appearance on NBC's *Meet the Press,* Bush repeatedly said that ever since September 11, 2001, he had considered himself a "war president."

Short of formulating foreign-policy doctrines, presidents can set the U.S. foreign-policy agenda by taking a strong personal interest in particular issues. The degree of presidential interest in arms sales (Price 1996) and nuclear proliferation (Brown 1994) played a vital role in determining the outcome of U.S. policy in these areas. In some cases, presidents look for issues neglected by Congress or the news media, knowing that they can exert greater control over policy outcomes in these areas (Peake 2001). These patterns highlight the importance of personal factors in shaping the president's foreign-policy agenda.

Taking the Initiative

Beyond setting the agenda, presidents can dominate the foreign-policy process by taking the initiative, or dictating the flow of events. Presidents wield this power simply by conducting U.S. foreign policy on a day-by-day basis. They are granted considerable discretion in doing so, and they choose from many options regarding which issues to pay attention to, which foreign countries to consider friends or foes, and which actions to take to achieve their goals. Their decisions set the foreign-policy process in motion, determining the roles to be played by other government officials and forcing leaders overseas into a reactive posture.

This informal power often involves military action. The Constitution, as we have seen, permits presidents, if they believe the nation faces an imminent threat, to deploy forces without the consent of Congress. Ronald Reagan took the initiative in 1983, when he invaded the Caribbean nation of Grenada, where domestic turmoil in 1983 led to the rise of a neo-Marxist government. Reagan claimed the mission was essential to rescue U.S. medical students stranded on the island. The mission served a larger purpose, however, that of demonstrating Reagan's resolve to prevent such regimes from taking power on his watch. In overthrowing the government of Panama in 1989, George H. W. Bush showed he was serious about the "war on drugs." In 1992, Bush's relief mission to Somalia symbolized the benevolent use of U.S. military force after the cold war. For his part, Bill Clinton believed he had to act decisively to end the ethnic cleansing of Bosnia (1995) and Kosovo (1999) since Congress and the public opposed both interventions in the former Yugoslavia.

George W. Bush epitomized the imperial presidency when he seized the initiative after September 11 to change the course of U.S. foreign policy, the role and reputation of the United States overseas, and the dynamics of world politics (Gregg 2004). Even before the terrorist attacks, Bush had embraced the prevalent view among congressional Republicans, who had dominated both chambers before he arrived and through most of his first term, that the United States should disentangle itself from the international community and lead by the force of its will. He made this point clear by rejecting the Kyoto Protocol on global warming, a move that surprised even some of his close advisers. The president's aggressive action in the war on terrorism further demonstrated his penchant for taking offensive action.

The tactical consequences of such assertiveness are significant. Taking action alters the strategic landscape and changes the calculus of future foreign-policy decisions. Some options open and others close under these circumstances, with neither outcome cleanly predictable. Lyndon Johnson's decision to force the Vietnam issue through the Tonkin Gulf resolution, for example, started the United States down the slippery slope in Southeast Asia from which it could not easily extricate itself. More positively, it is likely that Reagan's announced plans for a "Star Wars" antimissile system pushed the Soviet Union beyond its limits in the arms race, thus hastening the demise of the cold war. George W. Bush's decision to invade Iraq, part of his "forward-leaning" strategy in the war on terrorism, transformed the strategic environment in the Middle East as well as in U.S. domestic politics. The health of the American economy, as well as the president's prospects for reelection in November 2004, hinged partly on this expensive decision.

Organizing the Chain of Command

A third informal power of the president in foreign policy relates to the ability to organize the chain of command. Presidents have a great deal of flexibility in determining the roles played by various government institutions in formulating and conducting U.S. foreign policy. These institutions include the National Security Council, the departments of state and defense, the intelligence agencies, and the many agencies concerned with conducting foreign economic policy (see Chapter 6 for an elaboration).

With the concentration of foreign-policy power in the executive branch after World War II, a new and more complex framework was established for the institutions of national security, which grew in number and in size during the late 1940s and early 1950s. Presidents have since assumed a crucial role in coordinating the activities of these institutions, in mediating their occasional conflicts, and, most importantly, in deciding which of them will have most influence over specific policy choices.

Much of this work is done by an **inner circle** within the White House that includes the president's staff and personal advisers along with agency heads serving on the cabinet (see Preston 2000; and Hermann and Preston 1999). These carefully chosen, highly trusted individuals see the president regularly, in some cases on a daily basis. Since many high-level foreign-policy advisers other than cabinet secretaries are appointed by the president, they do not require confirmation by the Senate. Collectively, they form **advisory networks** that regulate the flow of information regarding foreign-policy problems the president may consider (Garrison 1999). As noted by Michael Link (2000, 239–253), the structure of these networks varies widely among presidential administrations and frequently changes within single administrations (see also Rockman 1997; George 1980; and Hess 1976). What remains constant, however, is the paramount role of the president in deciding whose advice to seek and follow.

As noted above, the creation of the NSC after World War II permanently shifted the locus of foreign-policy decision making into the White House. The national security adviser, whose role was intended to be limited to coordination and gatekeeping, soon displaced the secretary of state as the primary consultant to the president on foreign-policy matters. This escalation of the NSA's role began in the Kennedy administration and peaked in the Nixon years, when Henry Kissinger overshadowed all the cabinet secretaries in shaping and personally conducting U.S. foreign policy.

Subsequent presidents have created widely varying advisory networks, depending upon their institutional preferences as well as their personal relationships with key advisers. Jimmy Carter, for example, tried unsuccessfully to strike a balance between Secretary of State Cyrus Vance and national security adviser Zbigniew Brzezinski. Ronald Reagan diminished the role of the national security adviser, rotating six through the office in eight years while leaning heavily on his secretaries of state and defense. George H. W. Bush favored a strong secretary of state, James A. Baker, although national security adviser Brent Scowcroft had considerable influence, if not a high profile. Bill Clinton relied more on ad hoc arrangements that depended on the particular foreign-policy issue under consideration at the time.

George W. Bush applied his own twist to the inner circle, granting Vice President Richard Cheney a key role in foreign, as well as domestic, policy. More broadly, Bush surrounded himself with an advisory network composed of **neo-conservatives** who shared several assumptions about U.S. foreign policy: the nation should freely utilize its immense power, it should do so on behalf of national ideals and global interests, and it should avoid multilateral engagements, particularly UN peacekeeping. Adherents to this perspective included Secretary of Defense Rumsfeld, Deputy Secretary of Defense Wolfowitz, and Richard Perle, chairman of the Defense Policy Board, the Pentagon's advisory panel.[6] Condoleezza Rice, Bush's national security adviser, did not identify herself directly with this group, although her advice to the president largely reflect its worldview. Noticeably absent from the group was Secretary of State Colin Powell, whose more moderate approach to U.S. foreign policy was rejected by Bush and his neoconservative advisers.

Management Style and Foreign Policy

Consideration of informal presidential powers relates in large measure to the *personal* aspects of *political* decision making. In short, a full understanding of U.S. foreign policy requires that we look beyond the legal and institutional factors described above and consider how policy choices commonly result from interpersonal interactions within the government. The impact of such interactions on the American presidency gained prominence in 1960 with the publication of *Presidential Power: The Politics of Leadership*. To the book's author, Richard E. Neustadt, successful presidents exploit their status and authority by effectively persuading subordinates in the executive branch, along with members of Congress, to support their policy preferences. Wrote Neustadt (1960, 34), who

---

6. This influential group, which included prominent journalists such as William Kristol and Charles Krauthammer, was also known as the "Vulcans" or "hegemonists" (see Mann 2004; and Hirsh 2003).

became an adviser to President John F. Kennedy, "The essence of a President's persuasive task is to convince [others] that what the White House wants is what they ought to do for their own sake and on their own authority."

A key factor in this regard is the **management style** of presidents, that is, the working relationship they establish among their foreign-policy advisers. This management style reflects the general worldviews and personalities of presidents and extends to all areas of policy making. The working environment within advisory networks—whether competitive or cooperative, orderly or chaotic—plays a key role in shaping policy outcomes in war (Haney 1997; Crabb and Mulcahy 1995) and peace (Best 1992). Although the management styles of presidents vary widely, three general models have been identified—the competitive, formalistic, and collegial models (Johnson 1974).

Presidents adopting the **competitive model** of management encourage open debate and conflict among advisers, often without regard to rank and formal channels of communication. To Franklin Roosevelt, an exemplar of this model, the best ideas emerged from this unfettered, occasionally chaotic competition among viewpoints. He felt comfortable presiding over such competition and choosing the policies and rationales he believed had been most persuasively argued in White House debates.

The **formalistic model** is more orderly and hierarchical. It is often associated with Harry Truman and his favorite slogan, "The buck stops here." His manage-

President Harry Truman poses at his desk, which featured a sign with the blunt message, "The buck stops here!" Although Truman came to power as a result of the death of President Franklin Roosevelt, he quickly emerged as a strong president. He took decisive action in ending World War II, including the atomic bombing of two Japanese cities in August 1945. Truman also laid the foundations for the U.S. campaign against the Soviet Union during the cold war.

ment style featured structured discussion of issues that followed well-defined procedures and communication channels. Rather than serving as a debate referee in this policy-making environment, the president receives briefings from a variety of advisers based upon their particular areas of expertise. The president then selects the best solution from among the individual presentations. This model was well suited to George W. Bush, who positioned himself at the top of a rigid hierarchy rather than at the center of a "spoke-and-wheel" policy-making system (Walcott and Hult 2004).

The management style known as the **collegial model,** most often associated with John F. Kennedy, seeks to exploit the strengths of the other two approaches while overcoming their weaknesses. The president creates informal subgroups of advisers and encourages debate within them regarding specific problems and alternative solutions. Unlike the competitive model, this model encourages consensus that reconciles the differences among advisers. Unlike the formalistic model, the collegial model encourages open debate regardless of hierarchical rank. Bill Clinton most recently adopted this management style, often encouraging open-ended policy debates that ran long into the night (Stephanopoulos 1999; and Renshon 1996).

Regardless of the management style adopted, a crucial factor in the process is the degree to which a president is actively engaged in the daily management of foreign policy. This factor, according to presidential scholar Thomas Preston (2001, 259–261), depends largely upon a president's prior experience in this area. Dwight Eisenhower, John Kennedy, and George H. W. Bush, all of whom fought in World War II, generally called their own shots in foreign policy. Other presidents, including Lyndon Johnson and Bill Clinton, were more likely to defer to their foreign-policy advisers. George W. Bush (quoted in Daalder and Lindsay 2003, 33), whose military career was limited to service in the Texas Air National Guard, summed up this position: "I may not be able to tell you exactly the nuance of the East Timorian [sic] situation, but I'll ask Condi Rice or I'll ask Paul Wolfowitz or I'll ask Dick Cheney. I'll ask the people who've had experience."

In other cases, the lack of presidential involvement has led to confusion and public struggles for power within the executive branch. Reagan's inattention to developments in Central America in the mid-1980s, for example, produced bitter disputes between the State Department and National Security Council over U.S. policy toward the region. Each agency (Krueger 1996, 1043, emphasis in original)

> believed that its own idea of what U.S. foreign policy toward Central America should be was identical to that of President Reagan. . . . [E]ach believed that the president was making faulty decisions based on inaccurate information supplied by the opposing agency. [Both] went so far as to accuse the other of working to *circumvent* U.S. policy for the region. These conflicting perceptions would have been greatly diminished had the president exerted stronger leadership and guidance within his own administration.

Such anecdotal evidence reinforces Neustadt's central thesis that the power of persuasion is crucial to successful presidential leadership. The most successful presidents have not been afraid to assert themselves in identifying key foreign-policy goals and choosing how they will be pursued. Just as important, effective presidents have not left the implementation of these policies to their subordinates. Instead, they have used the Oval Office's clout and prestige to force compliance from below. In assessing George W. Bush's management style, journalist Bob Woodward (2002, 256) observed that after September 11, 2001, the president "wanted action, solutions. Once on a course, he directed his energy at forging on, rarely looking back, scoffing—even ridiculing—doubt and anything less than 100 percent commitment. He seemed to harbor few, if any, regrets. His short declarations could seem impulsive." Despite Bush's failure to bring the culprits of September 11 to justice quickly, he received high marks for his vigorous and decisive response to the terrorist attacks.

Constraints on Presidential Power

As we have seen, the Framers of the U.S. Constitution set up a complex system of checks and balances for the formulation of U.S. foreign policy. In the modern era, however, this delicate sharing of powers has been frequently overridden in actual practice. As a global superpower, the United States has found itself in a nearly perpetual state of crisis, faced with two "hot wars" of global proportions, a protracted cold war, and more recently, a string of regional conflicts and a two-front war (domestic and overseas) against terrorism. These circumstances have produced major changes to the institutions of U.S. foreign policy, which have in turn given the president unprecedented influence in the foreign-policy process.

Despite these changes and all the other presidential advantages noted above, the president faces many constraints in managing U.S. foreign policy. In coming to grips with the possibilities for, and limitations of, presidential power, one must consider four closely related and constantly fluctuating factors.

First, current conditions within the *international system* are a large determinant of presidential power. Simply put, presidents and all other heads of state must operate within the context of an anarchic interstate system whose defining feature is the sovereignty and legal autonomy of each member state. Key factors in this respect include the balance of power among countries, the roles played by intergovernmental organizations and private groups, trends in the global economy, and the level of regional and global tensions.

Second, presidents face the nature of the *domestic political environment*. The democratic nature of the U.S. government limits the range of options available to the president, who must maintain a functional, if not always cordial, working relationship with Congress while managing a vast and fragmented bureaucracy. Whether the president's party controls one or both houses of Congress can determine the extent to which the presidential agenda will gain the necessary budget support. On the domestic side as well, presidents seeking reelection have often been forced by rival candidates to show greater "toughness" in foreign policy, even if this contradicts their previous styles of leadership or foreign-policy agendas (see Nincic 1990; and Stoll 1984).

Third, each president has *personal limitations* that constrain action. They include limitations of time, energy, perceptual biases, and personality factors. No single individual is capable of managing the massive volume of foreign-policy problems facing the United States at any given time. Choices must be made among policy priorities, and in many cases compelling problems are destined to be neglected or ignored. As noted earlier, in making these choices presidents are guided by long-standing beliefs and cognitive filters that simplify the bewildering environment of foreign-policy making. Similarly, the backgrounds, ideologies, and working relationships within the president's inner circle shape policy choices and outcomes.

Finally, the content of *foreign-policy issues* also influences a president's foreign-policy activism. Presidents have only limited control over the particular foreign-policy issues that must be confronted by the U.S. government. International crises cannot be anticipated with confidence, nor can changes within foreign governments and their consequences for U.S. bilateral relations. Each foreign-policy issue—from military intervention to trade disputes and environmental treaties—affects national interests in a distinctive way and places unique demands on the president's global agenda.

This framework for analysis highlights the central reality that the president's role in foreign policy cannot be determined without reference to the details of specific policy problems and solutions. In short, one cannot generalize about presidential powers, nor can one predict how these powers will express themselves in given situations with a high degree of certainty. The *context* of foreign policy is crucial in this respect, framing the possibilities, as well as the limitations, of presidential power.

Conclusion

Despite this ambiguity, one prediction can be made with confidence. The "invitation to struggle" written into the U.S. Constitution will remain a permanent and defining aspect of foreign-policy making. As when the United States was founded, a fundamental tension exists between two contradictory principles deeply ingrained in American political culture: a fear of overzealous and authoritarian central government, and a need for decisive leadership in the face of an often-menacing international system. Domestic debates over foreign policy, therefore, will remain contentious and ultimately irreconcilable. They will be *contentious* because the core issues at stake involve the exercise of power in what is potentially the most vital and perilous area of U.S. government: the conduct of the nation's relations in the turbulent international system. The debates will be ultimately *irreconcilable* because the precise lines of foreign-policy authority are unclear and prone to conflicting interpretations.

Politics, therefore, will never truly stop "at the water's edge" in the United States since conflicts of interest are embedded in its foreign-policy institutions. As Louis Henkin (1996, 85–86) noted, "The Executive is sometimes carried away by ready opportunity and initiative, by expertise, by responsibility, and by the security of secrecy, to invade where Congress has its claims. Congress, frustrated by separation and secrecy from the means and channels of diplomacy, distrustful of executive assertions of expertise, sensitive to domestic implications or responding to domestic 'pressures,' is sometimes tempted to tie the president's Constitutional hands."

Within the "zone of twilight" of political power, the informal and personal aspects of presidential decision making become central to the foreign-policy process. The president's character, worldview, and management style all play vital roles in determining the primary goals to be pursued by the United States and the means chosen to achieve them.

Key Terms

advisory networks, p. 113

codetermination, p. 93

collegial model, p. 116

competitive model, p. 115

executive agreements, p. 102

formalistic model, p. 115

imperial presidency, p. 94

inner circle, p. 113

management style, p. 115

neoconservatives, p. 114

prerogative powers, p. 99

stewardship theory, p. 99

two presidencies, p. 93

Internet References

The **American Presidency Project** Web site (www.presidency.ucsb.edu), maintained and researched by political scientists at the University of California, Santa Barbara, provides a wealth of data, links, statistics, and multimedia clips regarding the presidency. Included are presidential speeches, public papers, and statistics on specific policy areas. A variety of documents related to the 2000 election are also on the site.

The Web site for the **Center for Congressional and Presidential Studies** (www.american.edu/academic.depts/spa/ccps) is hosted by American University and provides access to conferences, speeches, and articles regarding the presidency. Of particular interest to the center is the relationship of the executive and legislative branches along with presidential and congressional campaigning. The center publishes a number of books and series regarding these issues as well as the peer-reviewed journal *Congress and the Presidency* (the journal's index is available online at www.american.edu/academic.depts/spa/ccps/candp.html).

The **Center for Presidential Studies, Policy, and Governance** (bush.tamu.edu/research.cpg) maintains a Web site through the George Bush School of Government and Public Service. The center is a research hub as well as an educational facility for scholars to find fellowships and programs specializing in the presidency, public affairs, and public policy. The center has a working-papers journal as well as links to specific research projects such as national security initiatives, economic policy, and presidential policy making.

continues

Internet References *(continued)*

The **Center for the Study of the Presidency** (www.thepresidency.org) provides useful links to White House documents as well as research opportunities and tips regarding studying the presidency. Along with sponsoring internship and fellowship opportunities, the center publishes *Presidential Studies Quarterly,* which studies all aspects of the presidential institution (each issue's table of contents is available on the site).

The University of Virginia's **Miller Center of Public Affairs** (millercenter.virginia.edu) provides historical biographies and recordings of the presidents. The center has a particular focus on the study of the media and the presidency. It also produces the *Miller Center Papers,* which describe presidential public policy making.

POTUS, on the Internet Public Library (www.ipl.org/div/potus), is a site hosted by the University of Michigan that provides full biographic data, timelines, and major actions of all the presidents.

The National Archives hosts a Web site on the **Presidential Libraries** (www.archives .gov/presidential_libraries/index.html), providing links to a dozen presidential libraries. Most libraries' sites contain speeches, memoirs, and research links to specific policies of the respective presidents.

Presidents of the United States of America (www.presidentsusa.net), a site hosted by CB Presidential Research Services, provides a comprehensive resource, with monthly updates, on a wide range of information regarding presidential speeches, salaries, quotes, military history, and major policies. This site also includes specific vetoes, appointments, and election data on each president.

The Web site for the **White House** (www.whitehouse.gov) provides links to presidential speeches, executive agencies and committees, and issue information released by the president and advisers. Of particular interest to foreign-policy researchers are links to the Office of the Vice President, Homeland Security, War on Terror, Iraq, and National Security.

The **White House Historical Association** (www.whitehousehistory.org) is committed to teaching citizens and providing links for scholars regarding the actual office and "hub" for presidential administrations. Included are timelines, information about administrations and first ladies, and bibliographies of every president.

5

Rep. Christopher Shays, R-Conn., observes the U.S. military occupation of Iraq during a visit to the country in April 2004. Shays, chairman of a House subcommittee involved with U.S. foreign policy, insisted on traveling the streets of Baghdad despite warnings from L. Paul Bremer, head of the Coalition Provisional Authority, to stay away from the embattled city. A gunner on top of the armored Humvee, manning a .50-caliber machine gun, protected Shays as he traveled through city streets at speeds of 100 miles per hour to avoid potential attacks.

Congress Beyond the "Water's Edge"

Alongside the president, Congress plays a vital role in the formulation and conduct of U.S. foreign policy. Despite the long-standing maxim that politics must "stop at the water's edge," the legislative branch confronts presidents on a wide variety of international issues, from military interventions to foreign aid and arms control. Even U.S. trade, long shielded from interbranch rivalry, frequently falls prey to domestic politics. While claims of an "imperial Congress" (Jones and Marini 1988) are overstated, as demonstrated by George W. Bush's virtual free reign in the war on terrorism, presidents know their global objectives cannot be realized without Capitol Hill's blessing.

As noted in the previous chapter, early U.S. leaders looked to Congress as a crucial hedge against potential abuses of executive power. Article I of the Constitution assigns "the first branch of government" more explicit grants of authority—to declare war, raise military forces, regulate commerce, and provide "advice and consent" on treaties and key appointments—than Article II does presidents. Congressional activism in foreign policy is therefore expected in a system of "separate institutions sharing power" (Neustadt 1960). Besides curbing presidential power, such activism provides opportunities for the public to be heard, encourages open deliberation, and rewards compromise on foreign-policy issues.

Legislative activism has a downside, however. Struggles between Congress and the president frequently produce policy gridlock, reversals, and public displays of disaffection that are conveyed to a worldwide audience.

Congress's refusal to pay past U.S. dues to the United Nations in the late 1990s, for example, damaged the government's stature in the world body and forced deep cutbacks in many important UN-sponsored services. Among most Americans, however, these problems are widely accepted as the necessary cost of maintaining democratic governance in the United States. The alternative—centralized and authoritarian rule by the president—would pose greater dangers to citizens and to U.S. interests overseas as well as international stability.

Congress's role has varied over time and across the many domains of foreign policy. Developments overseas—such as civil and interstate wars, regime changes, and economic crises—shape the policy options and opportunities available to congressional legislators in any given period (Henehan 2000). Domestic factors also come into play. Such pressures have led to foreign-policy "mood swings" among legislators, who historically, as discussed previously, have alternated between global engagement and detachment in reaction to U.S. public sentiment (Holmes 1985; Klingberg 1952). Significant as well is the domestic balance of power among political parties and the related shifts in the population of states and congressional districts (Rohde 1994). The mid-twentieth-century mass migration of Americans from the Rust Belt states of the Northeast to the Sun Belt states of the South and Southwest, for example, eventually transformed the partisan balance in Congress, as evidenced by the 1994 Republican takeover of both chambers (Trubowitz 1992).

The conduct of U.S. foreign policy cannot be divorced from the institutional context in which policy is made. In contrast to the president, members of Congress represent smaller constituencies whose geographic self-interests often prevail over national concerns. Congressional legislators, therefore, are often content to focus on domestic issues more closely linked to their constituents' needs than on "abstract" issues of foreign policy (Silverstein 1997; and Weissman 1995).

Members of Congress know that they rarely share the boost in popularity that president's enjoy when foreign policies are successful, and they reserve the right to criticize presidents when their initiatives overseas flounder. Still, legislators must be proactive in the foreign-policy process. Most serve states and districts that include ethnically diverse constituents, employ large numbers of workers with jobs linked to the global economy, or benefit in material ways from programs supporting national defense. In addition, because legislators are more accessible than executive branch officials to the public, citizens and interest groups know that the road to gaining policy concessions leads through Capitol Hill.

Trends in Congressional Activism

This section reviews the ebbs and flows of legislative-executive relations over foreign-policy matters since World War II.[1] As we will find, the early years of the cold war featured broad cooperation between the White House and Capitol Hill

---

1. Diplomatic histories of U.S. foreign policy rarely focus on Congress; they focus instead on the president or socioeconomic forces outside of government (Johnson 2001).

that stemmed from a consensus between the branches on the ends and means of foreign policy. The nation's failure in the Vietnam War ruptured this consensus and, along with the Watergate scandal, led Congress to become more assertive in the foreign-policy process. After the cold war, with the United States facing no direct threats from other great powers, heightened interbranch conflict continued as a Republican majority captured both houses of Congress and subsequently challenged Bill Clinton's foreign-policy agenda (McCormick and Wittkopf 1998). A brief interlude of cooperation between the branches occurred when George W. Bush took office in January 2001 with a Republican-controlled Congress—and ended again when Sen. James M. Jeffords left the GOP to become an independent in May 2001 and the Democrats gained control of the Senate. The terrorist attacks of September 2001 engendered a new bipartisanship and thus renewed congressional support for the White House. Congress supported the U.S. invasion of Afghanistan, new measures for homeland security, increases in the defense budget, and the overthrow of Saddam Hussein from Iraq.

The historical record suggests that Congress's relationship with the White House runs along a spectrum from legislative compliance at one end, through resistance and rejection, to independence at the other (see Figure 5.1). How do we account for these fluctuations? Scholarly studies suggest that the **situational context** of policy making is critical. Two sets of factors must be taken into account when considering the situational context of foreign policy: the *nature* of issues and the *timing* of decisions.

In reference to the first factor, Congress tends to play a more active role on economic issues and other issues with a strong domestic component, such as immigration, while presidents hold more sway over issues pertaining to national security. Legislators also have a greater impact on "structural" issues that determine the use of federal resources, the size and shape of government agencies, and the nature of formal U.S. agreements and arrangements with other countries (Huntington 1961).

When it comes to the timing of decisions, presidents generally enjoy freedom of action during the "honeymoon" period, the period shortly after taking office during which they have strong public and political support. Taking advantage of this support, they announce their foreign-policy agendas and expect Congress to provide the necessary resources to convert these agendas into programs. Presidents also exert more power over foreign policy during crises, such as the Japanese attack on Pearl Harbor in 1941 and the terrorist attacks on New York and Washington, D.C., in 2001. In these cases, members of Congress usually defer to the commander in chief, who can act more quickly and decisively than they can. Failed military

Figure 5.1 Spectrum of Congress's Attitude toward the White House

| Compliance | Resistance | Rejection | Independence |

SOURCE: James M. Scott and Ralph G. Carter, "Acting on the Hill: Congressional Assertiveness in U.S. Foreign Policy," *Congress and the Presidency* 29 (Autumn 2002), 151–169.

interventions and foreign-policy scandals, however, are likely to provoke congressional challenges, as the Vietnam War and the Iran-contra scandal did.

Like the situational context, **congressional diplomacy** plays a critical role in legislative-executive relations in foreign-policy matters. Congressional diplomacy concerns the degree of presidential leadership in, and attention to, the legislative process (LeLoup and Shull 2003), a vital aspect to the achievement of a president's foreign-policy goals. In short, presidents ignore members of Congress at their peril, as Bill Clinton learned. For example, by lobbying key legislators intensely, he successfully gained ratification of the North America Free Trade Agreement and of the treaty permitting NATO expansion. However, Clinton neglected Congress in the weeks before its vote on the Comprehensive Test Ban Treaty (Schmitt 1999). After discovering that he lacked the necessary votes to ratify the treaty, the president made a last-minute attempt to delay the vote but was blocked by Republican leaders.

Collaboration and Discord in the Cold War

As described in Chapter 2, the post–World War II threat posed by the Soviet Union led congressional leaders to support President Truman's efforts to put the containment doctrine into practice. The key measures approved by Congress included the Bretton Woods accords, the Marshall Plan, the Truman Doctrine, and the creation of NATO. Of greatest institutional significance was the National Security Act of 1947, which created the Department of Defense, the National Security Council, and the Central Intelligence Agency (CIA). Exploiting this support on Capitol Hill, Truman deployed U.S. troops to South Korea in 1950 without a war declaration from Congress. He justified this unilateral action on the grounds that the deployment was part of a United Nations peace-making mission. Congress did not oppose the president, and his decision to sidestep the legislative branch set a precedent for future U.S. military deployments in Vietnam, Central America, the Middle East, and other areas.

Like his predecessor, President Eisenhower encountered little resistance from Capitol Hill as he created new military alliances, expanded the U.S. nuclear arsenal, and allowed the CIA to organize and sponsor military coups in countries such as Iran and Guatemala. The foreign-policy role of Congress during this period was reduced to "the legitimizing of presidential decisions" (Bax 1977, 887–888). Such support not only reflected broad agreement regarding the containment strategy, but also stemmed from the ample benefits flowing to congressional districts in the form of military contracts, the building of military bases, and the construction of a massive interstate highway system, which was justified on national-security grounds.

The domestic consensus continued through the presidency of John F. Kennedy. Congress funded the launch of Kennedy's Alliance for Progress—a development program aimed at strengthening U.S. allies and promoting economic reforms in Latin America—and the Peace Corps—an agency of paid volunteers trained to help developing countries. On the military front, Kennedy, who had vowed during his campaign to be "tough on communism," made the fateful decision to send U.S. military advisers to Vietnam to help southern forces resist unification under communist leadership. Congress later affirmed the intervention in the1964 **Gulf of Tonkin Resolution,** which authorized Kennedy's successor, Lyndon Johnson, to "take all necessary measures" to protect U.S. forces supporting the government of South Vietnam.[2]

The protracted fighting that followed, the widespread domestic protests, the costs in U.S. lives and resources, and the eventual U.S. defeat ruptured legislative-executive consensus on foreign policy, replacing it with intense conflict. Nixon's secret invasions of Cambodia and Laos and his attempts to spy on domestic opponents further fueled the challenge by Congress. Sen. J. William Fulbright, D-Ark., chairman of the Senate Foreign Relations Committee from 1959 to 1974, expressed the legislature's confrontational mood. Once a firm supporter of executive branch power, Fulbright (quoted in Franck and Weisband 1979, 4–5) declared the United States to be under "presidential dictatorship":

> I believe that the Presidency has become a dangerously powerful office, more urgently in need of reform than any other institution in American government. . . . Whatever may be said of Congress—that it is slow, obstreperous, inefficient, or behind the times—there is one thing to be said for it: It poses no threat to the liberty of the American people.

The 1970s and 1980s saw the passage of a wide range of legislation chiefly designed to enhance the legislative branch's **oversight** role, that is, its ability to monitor the president's conduct of foreign policy. The following measures, among others, provided explicit guidelines for congressional oversight:

- The **Case-Zablocki Act** (1972), which required presidents to report all international agreements to Congress within sixty days of their entering into force

- The **War Powers Resolution** (1973), detailed below, which required presidents to inform Congress about U.S. military deployments and authorized Congress to order the troops home after sixty days if a majority of legislators opposed the deployments

- The **Nelson-Bingham Amendment** to the 1974 Foreign Assistance Act, which authorized Congress to review foreign arms sales of more than $25 million and to reject such sales through a concurrent resolution of both chambers

- The **Jackson-Vanik Amendment** to the Trade Act of 1974, which prevented presidents from granting most-favored-nation (MFN) trade status to foreign countries that restricted the emigration of their citizens[3]

---

2. The resolution, based upon Johnson's claim that two U.S. ships were attacked in the Vietnamese waterway, passed by a wide margin of 416–0 in the House and 88–2 in the Senate. Subsequent evidence raised doubts about the reported attacks (see Karnow 1983, 366–373).

3. The Soviet Union was the amendment's primary, if unstated, target.

■ The **Intelligence Oversight Act of 1980,** which empowered House and Senate committees to oversee U.S. intelligence activities and required presidents to notify Congress about covert (secret) operations in foreign countries.

Legislators found other ways to shape U.S. foreign policy after the Vietnam War. Amendments to foreign spending bills, for example, barred U.S. assistance to foreign governments that violated human rights. In 1982, the **Boland Amendment** prohibited U.S. government agencies from providing equipment, training, or other forms of support "for the purpose of overthrowing the Government of Nicaragua." The Reagan administration defied the Boland Amendment by continuing to support the *contra* rebels through secret channels established by the National Security Council. The ensuing Iran-contra scandal led to a congressional investigation that tarnished Reagan's otherwise strong record in foreign policy during the final years of the cold war.

Clinton versus the Republican Congress

The post-Vietnam animosity between Congress and the White House continued after the cold war. Despite the collapse of the nation's primary adversary and the resulting emergence of the United States as the world's "lone superpower," distrust between the branches persisted. Partisan and interbranch debates revealed deep divisions regarding the nation's grand strategy and how it should balance foreign and domestic priorities. In place of overriding security issues, **intermestic policy** (Manning 1977) concerns—the merger of international and domestic policy concerns such as trade and the environment—came to the surface following the cold war's sudden collapse in 1991. Such issues, which mobilized local- and state-level interest groups, proved of great electoral importance to Congress.

The Republican majority gained control of Congress at a time when national attention had turned from overseas concerns to domestic ones, a pattern typical in the United States in the aftermath of major wars. The leadership of Sen. Trent Lott, R-Texas, who became Senate majority leader in 1995, reflected this trend. His emphasis on domestic policy contrasted sharply with the internationalist emphasis of Sen. Robert Dole, R-Kan., who had previously led the Republican Party in the Senate. In the House, new Speaker Newt Gingrich, R-Ga., championed the GOP's Contract with America and its primary objective of significantly reducing the size and the scope of the federal government. The contract's lone reference to foreign policy called for an end to U.S. military involvement in missions overseen by the United Nations. Republican Dick Armey of Texas (quoted in Barone and Ujifusa 1999, 1583), the second most powerful House member, captured the inward-looking sentiment on Capitol Hill when he declared, "I've been to Europe once. I don't have to go again."

In the divisive years that followed, Clinton failed to gain congressional support for a string of U.S. military interventions. Congress, led by Sen. Jesse Helms, R-N.C., conservative chairman of the Senate Foreign Relations Committee, also forced cutbacks in foreign aid and State Department spending and refused to pay the nation's outstanding UN dues, which amounted to more than $1.5 billion.

Point/Counterpoint
CONGRESS VS. CLINTON

The 1994 midterm elections represented a turning point in Bill Clinton's foreign policy: for the last six of his eight years as president, Clinton was forced to contend with a Senate and House of Representatives controlled by the Republican Party. While the GOP's Contract with America focused primarily on domestic reforms, it also called for a general shift in foreign policy toward a more muscular U.S. world role serving national interests rather than global concerns.

The Republicans did not wait long to change the course of U.S. foreign policy. Legislators imposed deep cuts on the foreign-aid budget, refused to pay back dues to the UN, demanded an end to the arms embargo against Bosnia-Herzegovina, and called on Clinton to recognize Tibet as an independent country, a measure sure to shatter relations between the United States and China.

"The administration is paying a very serious price for the president's lack of decisiveness in the foreign-policy area," said Sen. Richard Lugar, R-Ind. "Much of the problem arose from the fact that the president fought his last campaign on domestic issues. He assumed that since the cold war was over, people were not interested in foreign affairs. He aided and abetted the isolationist mood in the country."

Although Clinton fought back against Congress, he allowed the aid budget to be slashed and the United States to fall into debt with the UN. "Foreign policy is playing the kind of role in national politics that it played in 1973 and 1974, in the aftermath of Vietnam and Cambodia," said Clinton spokesman Mike McCurry. "Once again, we are seeing foreign policy used as a device by the president's opponents to define themselves politically."

The president's relations with Congress only worsened in his second term in office, during which the House impeached him for his role in the Monica Lewinsky scandal. The Senate's rejection of the Comprehensive Test Ban Treaty in 1999 was as much a demonstration of Congress's control over foreign policy as a statement about the treaty's merits.

Source: Michael Dobbs, "Domestic Politics Intrudes on Foreign Policy," Washington Post *(June 26, 1995), A4.*

Futhermore, Congress denied Clinton "fast-track" authority to negotiate trade agreements, a power first granted in the mid-1970s to President Gerald Ford and then to his successors.

Helms also ensured that several of Clinton's appointments to foreign-policy posts would be rejected, including that of former Massachusetts governor William Weld, whose nomination to be ambassador to Mexico never made it past the committee stage. Other prominent casualties of the confirmation process included Morton Halperin, a liberal critic of the Vietnam War and CIA covert operations whose nomination for the new position of assistant secretary of state for democracy and peacekeeping was withdrawn by Clinton in 1994. Three years later, Congress rejected former national security adviser Anthony Lake's bid to become director of central intelligence. Finally, the Foreign Relations Committee delayed for more than a year the nomination of Richard Holbrooke, a high-level State Department diplomat, as U.S. representative to the United Nations.

Most devastating to Clinton was the Senate's rejection in 1999 of the Comprehensive Test Ban Treaty, "the international issue where partisan conflict surfaced in rawest form" (Destler 2001a, 326). The treaty, which sought to discourage nuclear proliferation by outlawing the testing of such weapons, had already been ratified by fifty foreign governments. The 48–51 vote, with all but four Republicans voting against the pact, marked the first time since the Treaty of Versailles that the Senate had defeated a major international security agreement.[4] Clinton viewed the Senate rejection as evidence of a **new isolationism** in Congress, a turning away from global engagement. Though this assessment of many legislators was correct, Clinton's failure to assume leadership in the ratification process and to resolve congressional concerns had just as much to do with the treaty's demise as isolationism did.

Rallying against Terrorism after 9-11

Republicans maintained control of both houses of Congress in the bitterly contested presidential election of November 2000 that brought George W. Bush to power. However, the narrow Republican advantage dissolved in May 2001, when Senator Jeffords of Vermont left the Republican Party and became the Senate's lone independent member. The move by Jeffords, who complained that the Bush White House did not represent his moderate views, gave the Democrats majority control of the Senate. Of particular significance to foreign policy, Sen. Joseph Biden, D-Del., became chairman of the Senate Foreign Relations Committee, ending Helms's controversial reign, and Sen. Carl Levin, D-Mich., took over the powerful Armed Services Committee. Both senators opposed Bush's foreign-policy goals in such areas as arms control and multilateral cooperation. Renewed partisan conflict appeared inevitable in the weeks following Jeffords's defection, and the president found his ability to implement his foreign-policy agenda greatly constrained (Nelson 2004).

The terrorist attacks on the World Trade Center and the Pentagon in September 2001 quickly ended the period of discord between Congress and the White House. An overwhelming majority of legislators authorized President Bush to "use all necessary and appropriate forces" in responding to the terrorist attacks against New York City and Washington, D.C. The resolution did not specify the

---

4. As noted previously, the votes of at least two-thirds of the Senate, or sixty-seven members, are needed to ratify a treaty.

targets of this military response, an omission "unprecedented in American history, with the scope of its reach yet to be determined" (Grimmett 2001, 46). In addition, Congress passed sweeping legislation, known as the **USA Patriot Act,** that increased the federal government's ability to investigate suspected terrorists in the United States (see Chapter 12). While the swift passage and broad scope of the legislation was unprecedented, the high level of congressional deference to the White House, as noted previously, was typical of periods in which the United States has faced a direct challenge from overseas.

Bush hoped for an equal level of deference from Congress in 2002 when he sought its support to wage war against Iraq. The president, whose criticism of Saddam Hussein escalated throughout 2002, insisted that military action was already sanctioned by UN resolutions passed in the wake of the 1991 Persian Gulf War. However, Bush wanted legislators to provide the legitimacy he needed to launch a preventive attack. The president hoped Congress's blessing would assure a skeptical UN Security Council that the United States was united on the need for "regime change."

With congressional elections weeks away, Republicans rallied behind the president. Fearful of being perceived as unpatriotic and hoping to neutralize Iraq as an election issue, most Democrats, too, went along with the war resolution, though it did not specify a time frame or circumstances for military action, thus giving Bush wide discretion in initiating hostilities. The House of Representatives approved the resolution by a vote of 296–133, the Senate 77–23. Neutralizing the war issue did not help Democrats in the midterm elections, however, as the Republican Party regained control of both chambers. After the United States launched its war against Iraq in March 2003, legislators approved $87 billion in additional military funding to pay for the protracted occupation of Iraq as well as other costs stemming from the war on terrorism.

During this period, criticism of the president and his policies was rarely heard on Capitol Hill, despite the concerns about the open-ended powers granted to Bush being voiced by many private citizens and groups. Criticizing a wartime president has always been considered a politically dangerous undertaking for members of Congress. Yet to scholars of American government, U.S. legislators have an obligation to speak out about questionable policies no matter what the cost is to themselves. In the opinion of Louis Fisher (2004, 120), a well-known constitutional expert, "Congress failed to discharge its constitutional duties when it passed the Iraq Resolution."

Despite the failure to locate weapons of mass destruction and the problems faced by U.S. troops during the first year of Iraqi occupation, the president remained popular with the public and continued to receive congressional support. However, as occupation wore on in 2004 and U.S. problems and troop casualties continued to mount, Sen. John Kerry, D-Mass., gained the Democratic Party's nomination for president in large part because of his outspoken criticism of Bush's foreign policy, a criticism given more weight by Kerry's military experience in Vietnam. From that point on, domestic misgivings about the Iraqi occupation and other aspects of U.S. foreign policy found expression on Capitol Hill.

Laying the Institutional Groundwork

In considering the role of Congress in the foreign-policy process, it is helpful to recall the basic features of the legislative body. Two senators, who serve six-year terms, represent each of the fifty states. Within the House of Representatives, 435 members, who serve two-year terms, represent congressional districts within each state. The number of House members a state has is based upon population. The Founders designed the bicameral (two separate chambers) Congress to create checks and balances *within* the legislative branch. More broadly, they purposefully made the writing and passage of bills difficult in order to inhibit governmental activism.

Several institutional factors also determine the extent to which Congress engages in the foreign-policy process, what form this engagement takes, and how successful its members are in gaining presidential approval for their policies and programs. Among those factors are the partisan balance of power in the House and the Senate; the congressional committee system; and the structural, legal, and political limitations Congress faces.

The Partisan Balance of Power

Congress is the U.S. government's institutional home for partisan politics, or the competition between the two dominant political parties. Since the Vietnam War, which party holds the most seats in the House and in the Senate has proven crucial because **divided government**—the control of each branch of government by different political parties—has been more common than **unified government** (see Table 5.1).[5] As policy analyst Jeffrey S. Peake (2002, 80) concluded in a recent study, this pattern is very important in regard to legislative gridlock in foreign policy: "When the two branches are controlled by opposing parties, gridlock increases. When government is divided, presidents are forced to oppose a greater number of foreign policy bills initiated by Congress."

In the 1990s, a number of factors combined to intensify partisanship in Congress. The absence of superpower tensions after the cold war "removed the ready guide for responding to events that had promoted bipartisanship" (McCormick, Wittkopf, and Danna 1997, 135). At the same time, a generational shift was rapidly diminishing the number of legislators with military experience in World War II or the Korean or Vietnam wars. The generational shift, along with a corresponding partisan shift, also produced the largest influx of new legislators since the late 1940s (Greenberger 1995/1996). These new members of Congress had no legislative experience with the politics and struggles of the cold war. The defining military

---

5. During the past several decades, Republican presidents have had to deal with opposition-controlled congressional chambers far more often than have Democratic presidents. Whereas Republican presidents have contended with Democratic majorities during twenty-eight of their last thirty-two years in the White House—about 87 percent of the time—Democratic presidents have only faced Republican majorities in eight of their last twenty-eight years in power—about 28 percent of the time (see Ornstein, Mann, and Malbin 2002).

Table 5.1 Party Control of Congress and the White House, 1961–2005

Year	Congress Session Number	House			Senate			President and Political Party	Gover- nance
		Majority	Minority	Other	Majority	Minority	Other		
1961–1963	87	D-263	R-174		D-65	R-35		Kennedy (D)	U
1963–1965	88	D-258	R-177		D-67	R-33		Kennedy (D)/ Johnson (D)	U
1965–1967	89	D-295	R-140		D-68	R-32		Johnson (D)	U
1967–1969	90	D-247	R-187		D-64	R-36		Johnson (D)	U
1969–1971	91	D-243	R-192		D-57	R-43		Nixon (R)	DG
1971–1973	92	D-254	R-180		D-54	R-44	2	Nixon (R)	DG
1973–1975	93	D-239	R-192	1	D-56	R-42	2	Nixon (R)/Ford (R)	DG
1975–1977	94	D-291	R-144		D-60	R-37	2	Ford (R)	DG
1977–1979	95	D-292	R-143		D-61	R-38	1	Carter (D)	U
1979–1981	96	D-276	R-157		D-58	R-41	1	Carter (D)	U
1981–1983	97	D-243	R-192		R-53	D-46	1	Reagan (R)	DG-H
1983–1985	98	D-269	R-165	1	R-54	D-46		Reagan (R)	DG-H
1985–1987	99	D-252	R-182	1	R-53	D-47		Reagan (R)	DG-H
1987–1989	100	D-258	R-177		D-55	R-45		Reagan (R)	DG
1989–1991	101	D-259	R-174	2	D-55	R-45		G. H. W. Bush (R)	DG
1991–1993	102	D-267	R-167	1	D-56	R-44		G. H. W. Bush (R)	DG
1993–1995	103	D-258	R-176	1	D-57	R-43		Clinton (D)	U
1995–1997	104	R-230	D-204	1	R-53	D-47		Clinton (D)	DG
1997–1999	105	R-227	D-207	1	R-55	D-45		Clinton (D)	DG
1999–2001	106	R-222	D-211	2	R-55	D-45		Clinton (D)	DG
2001–2003	107	R-221	D-211	3	R-50	D-50		G. W. Bush (R)	U
2003–2005	108	R-229	D-205	1	R-51	D-48	1	G. W. Bush (R)	U

SOURCE: David R. Tarr and Ann O'Connor, eds., *Congress A to Z*, 4th ed. (Washington, D.C.: CQ Press, 2003), 537.
NOTES: D = Democrat, R = Republican, DG = divided government, U = unified government, and DG-H = divided government, House only. Data are for the beginning of the first session of each Congress.

memory for many of them was the 1992 U.S. intervention in Somalia, a humanitarian rescue mission that degenerated the following year into bloody street fighting and attacks by Somali militias against U.S. and UN peacekeepers.

Most of the period's new congressional members came from the Republican Party, which had become dominant in the South after more than a century in which Democrats, liberal and conservative, controlled the region's politics.[6] The growing populations in southern and western states further strengthened the influence of Republicans in Congress. This partisan shift shattered the Democratic coalition of southern conservatives and northern liberals that had produced con-

---

6. This shift resulted in part from racial issues, particularly the passage of the Civil Rights Act (1964) and Voting Rights Act (1965), which especially in the South prompted "white flight" from the Democratic Party. See Jacobson (2000) for an elaboration.

sensus on U.S. foreign policy during much of the cold war. Liberal Democrats became the dominant force in their party as ideologically minded conservatives became the dominant force in the Republican Party, outnumbering the GOP's moderates. The Republican takeover of both houses of Congress in 1994 "brought an entirely new cast of committee chairmen, many of whom are the ideological opposites of their Democratic predecessors" (Rosner 1995, 2). The result was

> an unprecedented disappearance of the political center. In a political system that demands compromise and accommodation to bring about change, the center is considered vital to the moderate, bipartisan public policymaking generally preferred by the American public. Absent a political center, increased partisanship and ideological polarization are inevitable—and sure to feed public distrust and distaste for politicians and the policy process. (Binder 1996, 36)

Simply stated, Republicans in Congress had become more conservative and Democrats more liberal than they had been before the regional and political realignment (King 1997). Partisan differences between the legislative and executive branches also intensified, producing unusually bitter, and often disabling, conflicts, such as the shutdown of the federal government in 1995. The great divide affected the foreign-policy process as well. Jesse Helms demanded deep cuts in foreign aid, which he characterized as a "rat hole" of government funds, and called for the abolition of the U.S. Agency for International Development. By the end of 1995, Helms held much of U.S. foreign policy hostage as he waited for his demands to be met. Among the stalled issues were nearly 400 foreign-service promotions, thirty ambassadorial nominations, more than a dozen treaties and international agreements, and many daily functions of the State Department, including the payment of utility bills at foreign embassies and consulates.

In their attempts to meet such Republican challenges in foreign policy, Democrats have faced a central problem: the widespread public perception that they are "soft on defense." This perception has many sources, including the fact that in the previous century Democrats were more inclined than Republicans to favor diplomacy over the use of military force, to be concerned about transnational problems as opposed to narrow national interests, and to work through multilateral institutions. The Republican Party has exploited this image of Democratic "softness" ever since congressional Republicans accused President Truman of "losing China" in 1949 and Sen. Joseph McCarthy, R-Wis., accused Democrats of being communist sympathizers in the early 1950s.

Congressional action prior to the 1991 Persian Gulf War fueled the Republican fire. The first time Congress voted on war against Iraq, 42 of 44 Senate Republicans favored military action while 45 of 55 Democrats were opposed. The House of Representatives also voted largely along party lines in favoring a forceful ejection of Saddam Hussein's troops from Kuwait, although 86 of 265 Democrats voted in favor of war. A decade later, as the 2002 midterm elections approached, pollsters found that the Republicans enjoyed a 40-percentage-point advantage on the question of which party was best at keeping the United States strong. "The election was understood as a referendum on national security, and the G.O.P. swept the board" (Traub 2004).

Although the realignment of Congress has made both political parties more cohesive internally, the GOP has been more successful in maintaining unity on key votes, as the outcome of the 1991 Persian Gulf resolution demonstrates. Democrats, whose base of support includes African Americans and labor groups as well as white-collar professionals who espouse liberal causes, form a diverse—and fragile—electoral coalition. The passage of the 2002 Iraq measure, for example, was assured after Rep. Richard Gephardt, D-Mo., the minority leader in the House, broke ranks and supported the open-ended authorization of force favored by President Bush. On this and many other votes, Democrats have been more likely to cross party lines than Republicans (see Packer 2004).

Foreign Policy by Committee

Majority status within Congress brings with it great advantages, beyond the simple fact that the majority will win votes cast strictly along party lines. The majority party also receives the most seats in congressional committees and controls these committees by designating its members to chair them. The fact that Congress conducts its primary mission of drafting legislation in dozens of committees and subcommittees makes this control particularly important (see Deering and Smith 1997).

Reforms during the 1970s sought to strengthen the committee system, thereby weakening the seniority system that had previously concentrated congressional power in a few hands. The reforms opened doors to junior legislators and encouraged policy "entrepreneurs" to promote individual causes that, in turn, furthered their own political ambitions (Wawro 2000). The reforms also granted greater powers and staff to subcommittees (see Figure 5.2). As a consequence of these changes, members of Congress became knowledgeable about a wider range of policy issues, foreign and domestic. They also became more closely connected to individual constituents and interest groups in these specialized areas. Congressional influence and activism naturally increased as a result of these reforms, although the fragmented committee structure made it more difficult for legislators to identify and pursue common priorities.

Among the committees with primary concern over foreign policy are the Senate Foreign Relations Committee (FRC) and the House International Relations Committee (IRC). The FRC is especially important because its members consider treaties and presidential appointments before the full Senate votes on them. With their focus on global affairs, both committees offer members public visibility, as well as exposure to foreign leaders, intergovernmental organizations, and transnational interest groups. However, the issues the committees address rarely have material ties to constituent needs, a deficiency that has made membership less attractive to legislators in recent years. Approving a treaty, in short, is not likely to "bring home bacon" to the home state or district and thereby enhance the legislator's prospects of reelection. "Foreign Relations has been kind of a wasteland,"

Figure 5.2 Key Senate Foreign Policy Committees and Subcommittees

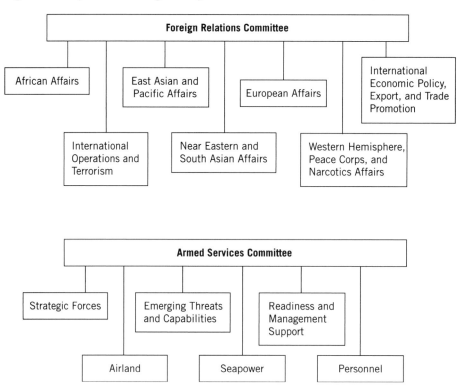

Sen. Chuck Hagel, R-Neb., said in 1998. "It is not a particularly strong committee to fundraise from" (Pomper 1998, 3203).

The Senate and House Armed Services Committees are primarily concerned with Department of Defense matters. Their jurisdictions include development of weapons systems; structure of the army, navy, and air force; benefits for active and retired military personnel; and the selective service system. The Armed Services Committees, unlike the FRC and the IRC, attract legislators as a result of the large financial stakes involved in the operations of the Pentagon. Committee members frequently represent states or districts with sizeable military bases or defense contracting firms, both of which place pressure on legislators to maintain or increase the levels of support coming from Washington. On average, legislators on these committees tend to be more conservative than their congressional colleagues, favoring strong military forces as a primary national goal.

After the Vietnam War, both congressional chambers created "select" intelligence committees, providing the legislative branch with a structural role in an area previously managed almost exclusively by the president. In addition to receiving information about conditions and developments overseas from the executive branch, these committees monitor the activities of the CIA and other intelligence-

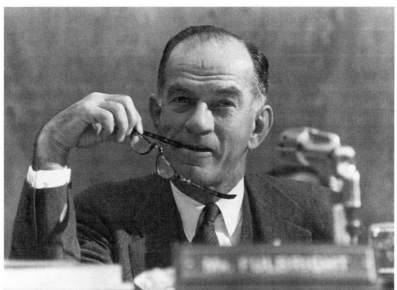

No member of Congress had more impact on U.S. foreign policy during the cold war than J. William Fulbright, D-Ark., who chaired the Senate Foreign Relations Committee from 1959 until 1974. During his long tenure on the committee, Fulbright led the legislative effort to assure U.S. entry into the United Nations and supported most presidential measures to implement the containment policy against the Soviet Union. Fulbright later became a harsh critic of U.S. involvement in Vietnam and of the "militarized economy" in the United States.

gathering agencies. Of particular concern to committee members are covert operations by the U.S. government, which occurred frequently during the cold war without congressional knowledge (see Smist 1990). After September 2001, the Senate committee conducted an investigation into the events leading up to the 9-11 attacks (U.S. Senate 2004). They concluded that the CIA and other agencies had failed to act upon mounting evidence that Islamic terrorists were planning a major attack on the United States. Congressional investigators also concluded that intelligence agencies, with prodding from the White House, later exaggerated the threat posed by Saddam Hussein to solidify domestic support for the preventive invasion of Iraq in March 2003.

Appropriations committees in each chamber designate the amount of money to be spent on individual federal programs. In foreign policy these include, among other programs, the operations of the State and Defense departments and foreign aid. Other congressional committees play roles in specific areas of U.S. foreign policy. Trade policy, for example, is primarily handled by the Senate Finance Committee and the House Ways and Means Committee.[7] Agriculture committees approve the terms of commodity exports and overseas food aid, and judiciary committees consider matters relating to international crime and terrorism. Legislation involving energy and environmental policy, agriculture programs, and military construction is also channeled through the vast network of congressional committees.

Although Congress does much of its routine work in committees and subcommittees, policy "entrepreneurs" often appeal directly to the public to gain support

---

7. At least a dozen other congressional committees and subcommittees are concerned with U.S. trade. As in other areas of U.S. foreign policy, the overlapping jurisdiction of committees in trade matters further fractures the policy-making process.

for their causes. A favored tactic is appearing on the growing number of daily talk shows, such as *Larry King Live* (CNN) and *Hardball with Chris Matthews* (MSNBC). For example, Sen. Bob Graham, D-Fla., and Rep. Christopher Shays, R-Conn., appeared on King's show in December 2003 to defend their respective positions on authorizing President Bush's use of force in Iraq. A televised discussion is sure to reach more citizens than an isolated debate in the Senate or House chambers.

For groups with competing interests in the foreign-policy process, congressional committees offer key venues for pursuing their objectives. As noted in Chapter 3, the nature of the policy issue in question largely determines the range of participants involved. Ad hoc issue networks—temporary coalitions of like-minded government officials and private actors—converge around such policy problems as aid for family-planning programs in Africa, the future of an expensive weapons system or military base, and the ratification in 1997 of the Chemical Weapons Convention (see Hersman 2000). Congress itself is commonly divided on such issues; rival members join forces with rival allies, such as the State Department, the Pentagon, interest groups, and even foreign governments that have a stake in the legislation. Once the matter at hand is resolved, one way or another, the issue network usually dissolves.

Structural, Legal, and Political Limitations

Congressional activism in foreign policy also must be viewed in the context of the legislative branch's inherent structural, legal, and political limitations. Structurally, the sheer size of Congress hinders its efforts to compete with the president, who sits alone atop the executive branch. Unity within Congress has proved a rare exception to the rule of partisan division, as Democrats and Republicans chronically disagree over the primary goals of U.S. foreign policy and the means to achieve them. In addition, given the rapid pace of developments overseas, the laborious and time-consuming nature of the legislative process places a major constraint on legislators' ability to influence the direction of foreign policy. Presidents have greater and more immediate access than Congress to information regarding these developments, and their command of the "bully pulpit" gives them an additional advantage in shaping public opinion (see Uslaner 1998). As a result, "the calculation of where the public interest lies is often passed to the Executive in matters of foreign policy" (Miller and Stokes 1963, 56).

Legally, as noted in Chapter 4, Congress has received little help from the judicial branch in foreign-policy disputes. Court rulings have consistently acknowledged the president as the "sole organ" of foreign policy or dismissed as "political" the turf battles between the White House and Congress. The Supreme Court's refusal to rule on the constitutionality of the War Powers Resolution (see below), despite repeated appeals by Congress that it do so, has encouraged presidents to dismiss the legislation.

On the political front, electoral concerns inhibit the foreign-policy role of Congress. To stay in office, legislators must serve the specific needs of their constituents, and most often these needs have more to do with local or state interests than with national or global concerns. Constituent self-interests are especially vital to House members, whose two-year terms in office force them into nearly perpetual reelection campaigns. In this pressurized environment, most members of Congress focus on domestic rather than foreign policy unless the United States faces an imminent crisis overseas. Legislators know that in any case, the president, not they, will receive credit for any breakthroughs in foreign policy. By distancing themselves from foreign policy, they also protect themselves from blame if foreign-policy initiatives undertaken by the administration fail. As congressional scholar Barbara Hinckley (1994, 13) has observed:

> This is a legislative body where time and influence must be carefully expended, where conflict must be kept within tolerable levels, and where many other policies can fulfill the goals of members better than foreign policy programs do. Seen in this light, foreign policy making by Congress should be the exception and not the rule.

All these factors limit the congressional role in making foreign policy. Recognizing their structural, legal, and political limitations in the foreign-policy arena, legislators have more incentives to focus on **constituent service,** or the material needs of the citizens in their states and districts, than on matters involving U.S. relations with foreign countries. Thus as a matter of course, domestic matters, primarily those involving the distribution of federal resources among American citizens and interest groups, take precedence on Capitol Hill. Taken together, these structural factors deprive Congress of the vital role in foreign policy the Founders designed it to play in the U.S. Constitution.

Legislating Foreign Policy

Despite these limitations, Congress has an inescapable role to play in legislating key aspects of U.S. foreign policy. In this section, we briefly review the dynamics of the legislative process, paying particular attention to different forms of legislation. We then explore the motivations underlying congressional behavior in foreign policy, particularly the calculations used by legislators in taking positions on foreign-policy issues. Finally, we consider the ongoing controversy over war powers, which the Constitution's authors explicitly reserved for Congress but presidents have dominated since World War II.

Dynamics of the Legislative Process

As students of the U.S. federal government are acutely aware, the authors of the Constitution discouraged governmental activism by putting complex procedures in place that made it very difficult for laws to be passed. These procedures, designed to protect individual freedoms, continue to constrain the legislative process today. A new piece of legislation must first be deemed worthy of consideration by both chambers; if it is, they assign the drafting of proposed language to the appropriate committees or subcommittees. If approved at this level, the two bills are introduced on the floors of the Senate and the House. Should both versions of the legislation pass, a joint conference committee must resolve any differences in the bills' provisions. The final, joint version of the legislation then goes to the White House for the president's approval. The president, however, may choose to veto, or reject, the bill. Should that happen, at least two-thirds of the membership in each chamber must vote to override the veto for the measure to become law.

Congress's role in legislating U.S. foreign policy extends beyond consideration of specific problems facing the nation at a given time. **Substantive legislation,** such as the imposition of sanctions on South Africa during its period of apartheid rule, has proven difficult to pass given the time-consuming nature and partisan realities of the legislative process. Faced with this restriction, Congress has often turned to **procedural innovations** that provide members with "a way to build their preferences into the policy-making process" (Lindsay 1994b, 282). Three of these innovations are of primary interest: creation of new agencies, imposition of reporting requirements, and enactment of law to ensure legislative participation.

First, Congress can create new federal agencies that strengthen its ability to shape U.S. policy in all areas, including foreign policy. Legislators established the General Accounting Office, for instance, to act as their investigative arm for examining the operation of federal agencies. The Congressional Research Service conducts studies for the House and the Senate on issues of foreign and domestic policy. Its annual reports on arms sales, for example, include timely data regarding global military trends of critical importance to legislators considering future sales and transfers of military assistance. Another agency, the Congressional Budget Office, analyzes trends in federal spending and tax revenues, lessening the legislature's dependence upon the executive branch's Office of Management and Budget.

Without congressional action the creation of other federal agencies is impossible. The Department of Homeland Security, for example, resulted from a joint effort by the Bush administration and Congress. Legislators can also modify the structures of—or even abolish—existing agencies. For instance, in the 1990s, Congress forced the State Department to absorb two formerly independent agencies, the U.S. Information Agency and the U.S. Arms Control and Disarmament Agency. During this same period, Sen. Jesse Helms tried to abolish the U.S. Agency for International Development. He finally agreed to allow the foreign-aid agency to survive but only under greater State Department scrutiny.

Second, Congress can impose reporting requirements on the executive branch. These reports may include special notifications to Congress on such matters as military deployments and covert operations. The executive branch may also be asked to provide one-time reports on specific issues, such as the likely impact of base closings on neighboring communities or sectors of the U.S. economy. Periodic reports, too, are required by legislators. Since 1975, for example, the Defense Department has submitted annual reports on the impact of U.S. weapons programs on global arms control. Legislators have frequently imposed such reporting requirements to gain control over federal agencies.

Finally, Congress can enact laws that ensure legislative participation in U.S. foreign relations, as it did with the Trade Act of 1974. The act required that five members of the Senate Finance Committee and House Ways and Means Committee serve as official advisers to the executive branch in international trade negotiations. Through such participation, Congress hoped to regain at least part of its constitutional power to regulate commerce, power it had surrendered to the White House decades earlier (see Chapter 11).

These procedural innovations have met with mixed success. Presidents who strongly resist such congressional interference usually prevail in keeping legislators at bay. The practical difficulties of monitoring the executive branch in highly complex and secretive areas further hinder Congress's oversight role. In investigating the U.S. government's actions prior to September 11, 2001, for example, members of the House and the Senate frequently complained that they were not granted adequate information and access to key decision makers in the White House or elsewhere in the executive branch. Bush's popularity among the public, however, combined with the Republican majority in both houses of Congress, limited the effectiveness of these appeals.

The Calculus of Voting Behavior

A central question of interest to students of Congress relates to the motivations of legislators. Why do they support some policies and programs while opposing others? What factors do they consider when determining their positions on specific issues and deciding how much time and attention to devote to these issues? In confronting these questions, one must consider four sets of factors that converge to shape voting behavior: situational, ideological, electoral, and strategic (see Figure 5.3). Each set affects decisions to varying degrees in different cases.

Situational factors. The objective details of the problem at hand and the costs and benefits of the proposed legislative solution—the **situational factors**—must be assessed. According to rational models of decision making, such relative costs and benefits can be estimated with some confidence and weighed against the status

Figure 5.3 Sources of Congressional Voting Behavior

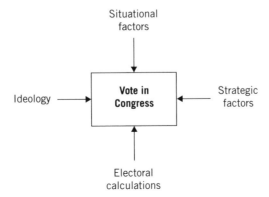

quo. In this respect, legislators approved President Bush's request for $87 billion in additional military spending in November 2003 after calculating that the benefits of providing the funds outweighed the costs.

Ideological factors. It is commonly assumed that voting behavior also reflects the **ideology** of legislators—their general principles and beliefs regarding human nature, relationships between states and society, and the nation's roles and responsibilities in world politics (see Chapter 3). From this perspective, the political activity of legislators serves as a natural extension of their deeply held worldviews. Academic studies consistently reveal a link between the ideology of legislators and their voting behavior (see Lindsay 1991; McCormick and Black 1983).

Ideology may lead legislators to vote in different ways over time. Senate conservatives, for example, voted along nationalist lines prior to the 1960s; subsequently, they favored internationalist positions on U.S. foreign policy. The votes of liberals, meanwhile, flip-flopped in the opposite direction (Cronin and Fordham 1999). Similarly, liberals in Congress reversed course in the 1990s by favoring U.S. military interventions. Conservatives, who were more likely to favor the use of force during the cold war, generally opposed the military interventions ordered by Clinton.

Electoral factors. The link between ideology and voting patterns hardly seems surprising. Citizens expect members of Congress to act upon the principles and beliefs expressed in their campaigns once they are elected to the House or the Senate. However, viewing legislative action only in terms of ideology oversimplifies the equation. Scholars today pay closer attention to the **electoral calculations** of legislators. An advocate of this perspective, David R. Mayhew (1974, 5, 16) defined legislators as "single-minded seekers of reelection" whose survival at the polls "must be achieved over and over if other ends are to be entertained." In this view, members of Congress are "strategic actors" whose choices are determined by rational calculations of political costs and benefits (see Fiorina 1989; and Kingdon 1981). These actors make their policy choices only after doing extensive research on the likely political consequences of various actions. After consulting this research, legislators take positions on issues they believe will please a majority of their constituents, who will then presumably reward the legislators with votes in the next election.

Studies of congressional voting on foreign-policy issues generally support this electoral connection. Eileen Burgin (1993), for example, interviewed dozens of House members about their foreign-policy positions in the early 1980s. She found the influence of "supportive constituents"—those who voted for the legislators in past elections and would be inclined to do so in the future—to be the decisive factor in 90 percent of these votes. A similar study of the Reagan administration found that every one-point variation in public views on the defense buildup in the 1980s was associated with a $13-billion variation in legislators' preferences for military spending programs (Bartels 1991). Electoral influences have been shown on legislation late in the cold war regarding a freeze in the nuclear arms race (Overby 1991), defense-spending increases (Carter 1989), and military base closings (Twight 1989).

In most cases, members of Congress can simultaneously satisfy their ideological preferences as well as the needs of their constituents. The reason for this is simple: the majority of voters tend to elect legislators who share their views about public policy, foreign and domestic. Representatives of liberal congressional districts, for example, will likely hold liberal positions on such issues as arms control and foreign aid, and they will be rewarded at the polls for doing so. The same can be said for conservative members of Congress, whose preferences for military over welfare spending are shared by a majority of their constituents. Unsurprisingly, members holding such views are likely to be found in districts or states with large military bases or defense-related industries. Thus, in general, legislators are not forced to "sell their souls" to maintain the support of their constituents.

Strategic factors. In deciding foreign-policy positions, congressional members also consider **strategic factors,** such as the probable consequences of individual votes for the outcome of legislation. Legislators examine the linkage between votes on different bills coming to the floor of the House and the Senate and routinely engage in **logrolling,** a practice in which they "support one measure for later support for another measure" (see Davidson and Oleszek 2004). Such behavior, combined with electorally driven voting, casts doubt on Congress's presumed capacity, as a "study and deliberative body," to play a responsible role in advancing U.S. national interests in foreign policy. Under these conditions, legislators are more inclined to advance parochial interests or interests confined to the political advancement of individual legislators. When its members succumb to pressures for reelection, Congress becomes "inordinately responsive without being responsible" (Jacobson 1987, 73).

Voting on legislation, of course, composes only part of congressional members' work. To demonstrate their service to constituents, members engage in more symbolic acts, such as making speeches and appearing on television. In addition, legislators please constituents by sponsoring bills the latter favor even if the bills never get out of committee. Constituents also expect their representatives and senators to speak out for them on issues of acute concern, such as trade protections and base closings, even when the chances that this advocacy will have any impact seem slim (see Deering 1996). Symbolic activism is particularly common in foreign policy, whose details and stakes are often remote to constituents. "On foreign policy matters, legislators can engage in activities that appeal to constituents without expending much effort, political capital, or time. They can take stands without taking action, and they can make pronouncements, hold hearings, and run investigations without having to produce results" (Zegart 1999, 32).

Ongoing Struggles over War Powers

The question of war powers is the most critical and controversial area of legislative-executive relations. As noted previously, though the Constitution explicitly bestows

·)) IN THEIR OWN WORDS: SEN. ROBERT BYRD

In October 2002, both houses of Congress approved resolutions authorizing President Bush to use force against Saddam Hussein if he did not surrender the weapons of mass destruction (WMD) the United States and others accused him of holding in large quantities. The UN Security Council then passed a similar resolution, which gave time for weapons inspectors to conduct a final round of searches. By February 2003, the United States was clearly headed toward war against Iraq. Bush was determined, even in the absence of WMD in Iraq, to go ahead with the mission of "regime change." He asked members of Congress to authorize additional funding that could be used for such an undertaking. Sen. Robert Byrd, D-W.V., chose that opportunity to express his outrage that Congress would allow the preventive attack to go forward. In his view, by doing so, Congress was surrendering its constitutional powers to decide the vital question of war over peace.

To contemplate war is to think about the most horrible of human experiences. On this February day, as this nation stands at the brink of battle, every American on some level must be contemplating the horrors of war.

Yet, this Chamber is, for the most part, silent—ominously, dreadfully silent. There is no debate, no discussion, no attempt to lay out for the nation the pros and cons of this particular war. There is nothing.

We stand passively mute in the United States Senate, paralyzed by our own uncertainty, seemingly stunned by the sheer turmoil of events. Only on the editorial pages of our newspapers is there much substantive discussion of the prudence or imprudence of engaging in this particular war.

the power to declare war upon Congress, presidents since World War II have frequently deployed troops without a congressional declaration. This apparent breach of the spirit and the letter of the Constitution led to the passage of the War Powers Resolution (WPR), over President Nixon's veto, on November 7, 1973. Congressional leaders at the time were highly critical of Nixon's conduct of the Vietnam War, particularly his secret invasions of Cambodia and Laos, his massive bombing of civilian areas, and his approval of domestic surveillance of antiwar activists. Importantly, in 1973 Congress was also in the midst of investigating the Watergate scandal, which would ultimately lead to Nixon's resignation in August 1974.

The legislators' goal in passing the resolution, as stated in its introductory section, was to "fulfill the intent of the framers of the Constitution of the United States . . . that the collective judgement of both the Congress and the President will apply to the introduction of United States Armed Forces into hostilities." To fulfill this goal, congressional members crafted a resolution with two key requirements: the president must *consult* with Congress before deploying troops into possible armed conflict in other countries and must *report* to Congress "periodically on the

And this is no small conflagration we contemplate. This is no simple attempt to defang a villain. No. This coming battle, if it materializes, represents a turning point in U.S. foreign policy and possibly a turning point in the recent history of the world.

This nation is about to embark upon the first test of a revolutionary doctrine applied in an extraordinary way at an unfortunate time. The doctrine of preemption—the idea that the United States or any other nation can legitimately attack a nation that is not imminently threatening but may be threatening in the future—is a radical new twist on the traditional idea of self defense. It appears to be in contravention of international law and the UN Charter. And it is being tested at a time of world-wide terrorism, making many countries around the globe wonder if they will soon be on our—or some other nation's—hit list. . . .

Yet this chamber is hauntingly silent. On what is possibly the eve of horrific infliction of death and destruction on the population of the nation of Iraq—a population, I might add, of which over 50% is under age 15—this chamber is silent. On what is possibly only days before we send thousands of our own citizens to face unimagined horrors of chemical and biological warfare—this chamber is silent. On the eve of what could possibly be a vicious terrorist attack in retaliation for our attack on Iraq, it is business as usual in the United States Senate.

We are truly "sleepwalking through history." In my heart of hearts I pray that this great nation and its good and trusting citizens are not in for a rudest of awakenings.

Source: Robert Byrd, "We Stand Passively Mute" (speech to the U.S. Senate, February 12, 2003), www.senate.gov/~byrd/byrd_newsroom/byrd _news_feb/news_2003_february/news_2003 _february_9.html.

status of such hostilities." Upon receiving an initial notification from the president of such a deployment (which actually may be sent up to forty-eight hours *after* the mission has been launched), Congress, through a majority vote of its members, can order that the troops be withdrawn after sixty days. The White House may extend this deadline by up to thirty days.

Presidents have dismissed the WPR as unconstitutional, claiming their powers as commanders in chief permit them to deploy troops overseas into armed conflicts without a formal declaration of war from Congress. Despite these assertions, between April 1975, the end of the Vietnam War, and October 2001, the beginning of the war on terrorism, presidents chose to comply with the resolution ninety-two times by submitting reports to Congress on U.S. troop deployments (Grimmett 2001, 53–68). President Clinton alone submitted sixty—by far the most—reflecting the greater frequency of U.S. military interventions in the aftermath of the cold war (see Table 5.2).

Only once during this period has the sixty-day "clock" actually been activated. In May 1975, President Ford cited the crucial section of the resolution,

Table 5.2 The War Powers Resolution in Practice, 1974–2003

President	Time Period	Military Interventions Reported	Unreported Interventions	Sixty-Day Clock Activated
Ford	1974–1977	4	1	1
Carter	1977–1981	1	3	0
Reagan	1981–1989	14	8	0
G. H. W. Bush	1989–1993	7	5	0
Clinton	1993–2001	60	1	0
G. W. Bush	2001–2003	20	2	0

SOURCE: Richard F. Grimmett, "Instances of Use of United States Armed Forces Abroad, 1798–2001," Congressional Research Service (February 5, 2003).

Section 4(a)(1), in ordering the rescue of the U.S. merchant ship SS *Mayaguez*, which had been seized by a Cambodian naval patrol. Under that section, presidents acknowledge the introduction of U.S. troops "into hostilities or into situations where imminent involvement in hostilities is clearly indicated by the circumstances." Since the *Mayaguez* rescue (which was actually completed by the time Ford notified Congress), no president has cited Section 4(a)(1) to trigger the time limit. In avoiding this crucial step, presidents have prevented the legislative branch from using the WPR for its primary purpose—forcing an end to military actions deemed contrary to U.S. national interests.

During the 1990s, congressional efforts to retain some measure of codetermination over military deployments consistently failed. Legislators in 1993 threatened to cut off funding for the U.S. intervention in Somalia if its mission were not completed by March 31, 1994, but U.S. troops remained in Somalia a year beyond this deadline as part of a UN mission. In 1995, the House and the Senate approved "sense-of-the-Congress" resolutions stating that U.S. combat troops should not be deployed to Bosnia-Herzegovina without congressional approval. Clinton ignored these resolutions and ordered the deployment of 32,000 troops to the former Yugoslav republic. When Clinton deployed troops to Kosovo in March 1999, several members of Congress filed suit against him to force a withdrawal. Three months later, the U.S. Court of Appeals dismissed the suit, ruling that the legislators lacked "legal standing" to sue the president. The U.S. Supreme Court upheld the ruling in October 2000. These and other legal cases affirmed the authority of presidents to send troops into combat in the absence of a declaration of war from Congress.[8]

Throughout the nation's history, presidents have claimed the authority to put U.S. forces in harm's way without a congressional declaration of war and have freely done so. In most cases, Congress has supported the commander in chief after the fact. Yet whatever the rationale invoked by presidents, whatever the ruling of the courts, whatever the subsequent position of the legislators, the unilateral exercise of war powers by a U.S. president contradicts the spirit of the U.S. Constitution, which

---

8. A number of congressional members have acknowledged the WPR's failure to support a meaningful role for Congress in this process. Their views were reflected in a House bill, narrowly defeated in June 1995, to repeal the central features of the resolution.

explicitly calls upon Congress to make this most fateful decision. In the absence of support from the judicial branch, legislators must exploit other sources of influence, including public opinion, to engage presidents in matters of war and peace.

The Power of the Purse

One of Congress's most potent weapons in foreign policy relates to its taxing and spending power, or its "power of the purse." Article I, Section 8, of the Constitution explicitly provides Congress with authority to "lay and collect taxes, duties, imposts and excises, to pay debts and provide for the common defense and general welfare of the United States." The authors of the Constitution, whose primary concern was restraining a potentially tyrannical head of state, viewed this control over government spending as a crucial hedge against excessive presidential ambition. As James Madison wrote in the *Federalist* No. 58, power over government spending is "the most complete and effectual weapon with which any constitution can arm the representatives of the people."

The power of the purse is not important simply as a matter of checks and balances. Decisions regarding the amount of money received by the government, and how that money will be spent, dictate what is possible in public policy. Those who hold the keys to the treasury, in short, establish both the opportunities and the limitations of government action. Indeed, the failure of past world powers to keep their fiscal houses in order precipitated their decline. Economic crises may result from the overwhelming commitments associated with "imperial over-stretch" (Kennedy 1987). Alternatively, in the case of modern democratic governments, the demands of domestic interest groups may drain public treasuries and deprive military forces and diplomatic services of the funds they need to maintain a strong posture in foreign affairs (Olson 1982).

Government spending has special significance in foreign policy. Foreign leaders closely watch the amount of money the United States directs toward military programs and other operations abroad, viewing it as a sign of the government's priorities and future intentions. "If budget levels are thought to affect the behavior of potential foreign threats, budget totals then become an instrument of foreign policy" (Wildavsky and Caiden 1997, 232). Similarly, the U.S. government's financial commitments to allies, whether in the form of military or development aid, often speak louder than the rhetorical statements of presidents and diplomats.

Conflicts between the legislative and executive branches over foreign policy frequently come down to matters of dollars and cents. In 1907, President Theodore Roosevelt dispatched the Great White Fleet on a symbolic cruise around the world, then dared Congress not to appropriate the funds to bring the fleet home. In the 1970s, Congress forced President Nixon to end the Vietnam War by cutting off funds for further U.S. military action. More recently, during the 1990s, the Republican-led Congress repeatedly cut the foreign-aid budget and refused to pay past U.S. dues to the United Nations.

Congressional spending authority in foreign policy comes into play in two distinct areas. First, Congress approves the *defense* budget, by far the largest single spending category in the federal budget. Second, it approves the *international affairs* budgets, including the operation of the State Department and related agencies. As part of this budget, the legislative branch also decides how much money the United States will spend on assistance to foreign governments and international financial institutions such as the World Bank and the International Monetary Fund.

Both branches of government engage in the budget process from beginning to end. At the start of a congressional session, the president submits a series of budget proposals to Congress, which then develops its own budget. Members base that budget in part on the president's proposals as well as on their own judgments about how much money the nation should spend and how that spending should be divided among the various government agencies. Finally, Congress submits its budget proposals to the president, who then has a choice of approving or vetoing the budget. Negotiations continue between the White House and Capitol Hill throughout the process, with both sides recognizing that failure to reach a final agreement may lead to a shutdown of the federal government. In most cases, this stark reality is sufficient to force the president and Congress to split their differences over federal spending.

Managing the Defense Budget

Though the share of the federal budget devoted to defense spending has dropped considerably since the mid-1950s, as has the share of U.S. economic output represented by defense spending, the government still devotes the largest share of its discretionary spending to national defense. Annual spending in this area averaged $282 billion during the first post–cold war decade (1992–2001). After the September 2001 terrorist attacks, the defense budget increased by 50 percent in three years to more than $450 billion (see Figure 5.4). The "largest organization in the free world" (Wildavsky and Caiden 1997, 219), the Department of Defense employs more than 2 million people, approximately three out of every four federal employees. More than 1 million of them serve as uniformed personnel in the armed forces; the rest are civilian employees working largely in administrative positions.

Defense spending is not only the largest component of the federal budget, but also one of its most controversial. Four factors in particular account for this controversy. First, proposed legislation for defense spending routinely provokes **guns-or-butter debates** within Congress and among the general public. In short, critics of higher defense spending argue that domestic needs are being sacrificed in the name of national defense. Generally speaking, Republicans in Congress are more likely than Democrats to support military spending over nonmilitary programs such as Medicare, education, and foreign aid.

Second, presidents and members of Congress nearly always disagree about the amount of money needed for national defense and engage in acrimonious public debates over the issue. In fiscal year 2001, for example, Republicans in Congress charged President Clinton with neglecting both the combat readiness of active U.S. troops and the living standards of veterans. The $291 billion approved for defense in that year included $5 billion in spending beyond the amount

Figure 5.4 National Defense Outlays, Fiscal Years 1995–2004

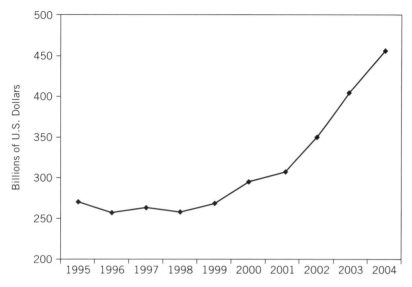

SOURCE: Office of Management and Budget, *Budget of the United States Government: Historical Tables* (Washington, D.C.: U.S. Government Printing Office, 2004), 57–58, www.whitehouse.gov/omb/budget/fy2005/pdf/hist.pdf.

proposed by Clinton. Similarly, the U.S. armed services compete with each other over the distribution of military spending. To Gen. David Jones (quoted in Wildavsky and Caiden 1997, 224), this "intramural scramble for resources" distracts the armed services from their core mission of promoting national defense.

Third, government and private studies frequently expose cases of overpriced weapons systems and wasteful spending practices in the Pentagon (see Mayer 1992; Goodwin 1985; and Gregory 1989). As noted in Chapter 3, critics charge that there exists an "iron triangle" whose three elements—Congress, the Defense Department, and military contractors—conspire to increase weapons spending beyond levels needed to maintain U.S. security. This problem is compounded when former legislators and military officials pass through a "revolving door" and become lobbyists for defense contractors with direct access to Capitol Hill. This issue gained national attention in 2003, a year that otherwise witnessed national consensus over military spending. A subsidiary of Halliburton, a major military subcontractor, admitted to overcharging the federal government for its services in Iraq. Vice President Cheney once ran the oil-services firm, which gained more than $15 billion in grants to support the U.S. occupation (Jehl 2003).

Finally, influential members of Congress are frequently able to gain spending approval for pet military projects in their states or districts. In 2000, for example, Senate Majority Leader Trent Lott, R-Miss., won approval for $460 million in spending on a helicopter carrier in Pascagoula, his hometown. Congress appropriated another $400 million that year to produce F-15 fighter jets in St. Louis, the hometown of House Minority Leader Richard Gephardt, D-Mo., and a politically vital source of support for Sen. Christopher Bond, R-Mo., a member of the Senate Appropriations Committee. Most observers view members of the Armed Services committees as "uncritical supporters of the military establishment who receive, in exchange for that support, a continuous flow of defense spending in their districts" (Deering 1993, 175).

After their party captured both houses of Congress in 1994, Republican leaders sought to boost defense spending beyond the levels proposed by President Clinton. Rep. Floyd Spence, R-S.C., chairman of the House National Security Committee, took the unusual step in 1996 of asking the four service chiefs how they would spend up to $3 billion in additional funds that Congress might give them. Not surprisingly, the chiefs quickly provided detailed proposals for new spending projects, and Congress came through with a defense budget of $267 billion, $13 billion higher than the president's requested budget (see Weiner 1996).

The September 2001 terrorist attacks transformed the domestic debate over U.S. defense spending. Congress consistently supported President Bush's calls for sharp increases in the defense budget. Outlays rose from less than $300 billion in fiscal year 2000 to more than $450 billion four years later. The boost in FY 2004 included more than $87 billion in emergency war spending, which Congress approved in November 2003 by wide margins. Democratic legislators avoided being labeled "soft on defense" by voting for the increases despite their stated misgivings about the progress of the war on terrorism and the merits of the Iraqi invasion. The increases in defense spending, combined with slow growth in the U.S. economy and stagnant tax revenues, plunged the federal budget into a deficit approaching $500 billion, by far the largest in history. The connection between soaring defense expenditures and budget deficits aptly demonstrated the economic consequences of the war on terrorism, whose costs would take years to repay.

The Price of Diplomacy

The second primary arena of congressional spending power in foreign policy involves the budget for international affairs. This budget comprises the costs of running the State Department and other nondefense agencies as well as U.S. spending on foreign aid and contributions to international organizations. Together these expenses amounted to approximately $34 billion in FY 2004—about 7 percent of the Pentagon's budget (U.S. Office of Management and Budget 2004, 58) and just 1 percent of the federal budget (see Figure 5.5).

The State Department claims only a small part of the international affairs budget—approximately $9 billion in FY 2004. These funds cover the costs of the State Department headquarters and foreign service, public-information campaigns, exchange and democratization programs, and U.S. contributions to international organizations and peacekeeping. Despite the global scope of these activities, the diplomatic service has long faced a skeptical and sometimes hostile Congress during budget deliberations, particularly since the end of the cold war.

Figure 5.5 Distribution of Federal Spending, Fiscal Year 2004

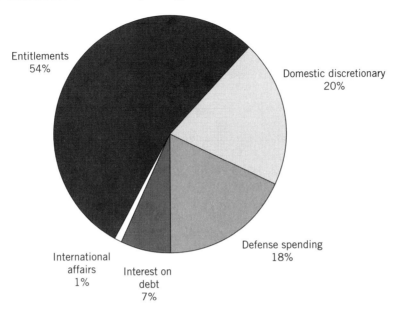

SOURCE: U.S. Office of Management and Budget, federal budget tables (2004), www.whitehouse.gov/omb/budget/fy2005/tables.html.

Congressional hostility toward the State Department stems from several sources. To legislators, the diplomatic service is poorly managed, does not make efficient use of federal resources, and resists a close working relationship with Congress. State's lack of a domestic constituency further reduces its position on the priority list of most legislators.

Congress's resistance to State Department funding has deep roots in U.S. history and political culture (see Hook 2003). Public disregard for diplomacy in general, and the State Department in particular, reflects a long-standing skepticism of traditional statecraft that extends beyond immediate circumstances or individual relations with foreign governments. As described in greater detail in Chapter 11, U.S. foreign-aid programs, the objects of deep congressional cuts in the 1990s, rank among the least popular in the federal budget. Legislators have few electoral incentives to champion the causes and costs of diplomatic engagement, so far removed from the day-to-day lives of average U.S. citizens.

As a result, the State Department is routinely neglected in each of its primary areas of responsibility: the development and articulation of foreign policy, the conduct of private and public diplomacy, and the transfer of foreign assistance. A study by the Overseas Presence Advisory Panel (1999) found U.S. embassies, consulates, and specialized missions to be "near a state of crisis." The panel reported "shockingly shabby and antiquated building conditions" in overseas missions, which were increasingly being staffed by personnel from other U.S. agencies. Despite new funding to improve security after the August 1998 bombings of the

U.S. embassies in Kenya and Tanzania, the panel reported, U.S. employees in these facilities still faced "an unacceptable risk from terrorist attacks and other threats." Since September 2001, Congress has taken a stronger interest in the State Department, recognizing the importance of diplomatic consultations and nonmilitary international programs in enhancing the "soft power" (Nye 2004) of the United States during the war on terrorism.

Conclusion

As we have seen, tensions between Congress and the White House are hot-wired into the U.S. political system and foreign-policy process. If today's national-security architecture is a relic of the early cold war, legislative-executive relations are creatures of the American Revolution and the ill-fated Articles of Confederation. Both experiences shaped the political culture of the United States in profound ways, placing individual freedoms above the orderly and efficient exercise of state power. The Framers merely codified this arrangement in the U.S. Constitution, providing enough central governance to keep the new republic intact while allowing the dynamism and centrifugal forces of civil society to freely express themselves. The fragmentation and diffusion of government power, of which legislative-executive relations compose but one element, assures the continuing prevalence of civil society in the policy process and the erratic exercise of world power by the United States.

While presidents have reigned supreme in making U.S. foreign policy, particularly in the years since the United States became a global superpower, they have learned from often bitter experience that the needs and institutional preferences of Congress must be taken into account as they plot their foreign-policy strategies. Indeed, historical experience clearly demonstrates that mutual accommodation is essential for anyone's goals to be realized, and, equally as important, for the day-to-day functions of foreign policy to take place. "In this largely informal environment," Rebecca Hersman (2000, 34) reminds us, "collaboration and negotiation are as important to the formation of foreign policy as confrontation and conflict."

Highly publicized showdowns between presidents and Congress tend to overshadow the general rule of foreign-policy collaboration. A lack of controversial new legislation may reflect general satisfaction with existing foreign-policy structures and processes or consensus regarding the appropriate direction of reform. This was certainly the case in the aftermath of the September 2001 terrorist attacks, when Congress and the public rallied behind the aggressive response adopted by President Bush. The fact that Bush's Republican Party controlled both houses of Congress ensured this harmonious response, at least until frustrations overseas and election-year politics in 2004 produced a partisan challenge to the White House.

Key Terms

Boland Amendment, p. 126

Case-Zablocki Act, p. 125

congressional diplomacy, p. 124

constituent service, p. 137

divided government, p. 130

electoral calculations, p. 140

Gulf of Tonkin Resolution, p. 125

guns-or-butter debates, p. 146

ideology, p. 140

Intelligence Oversight Act of 1980, p. 126

intermestic policy, p. 126

Jackson-Vanik Amendment, p. 125

logrolling, p. 141

Nelson-Bingham Amendment, p. 125

new isolationism, p. 128

oversight, p. 125

procedural innovations, p. 138

situational context, p. 123

situational factors, p. 139

strategic factors, p. 141

substantive legislation, p. 138

unified government, p. 130

USA Patriot Act, p. 129

War Powers Resolution, p. 125

Internet References

The **Almanac of Policy Issues** (www.policyalmanac.org) is a comprehensive site for searching policy issues passed and rejected by Congress. Research areas such as arms control, international trade, defense spending, and homeland defense are especially well covered. Government Accountability Office (GAO) and Congressional Research Service (CRS) reports are hosted on this page for each issue area.

The **Capitol.Net** (www.thecapitol.net) is a nonpartisan research group that focuses on training researchers how to network, communicate, and understand congressional policy making in Washington, D.C. Links are available to handbooks such as "How Congress Works" as well as to important directories of legislators, executive agencies, and media outlets. The site also has glossaries and dictionaries for guidance in understanding congressional politics and policy.

The **Center for Congressional and Presidential Studies** (www.american.edu/academic .depts/spa/ccps) is hosted by American University and provides access to conferences, speeches, and articles regarding the presidency. Of particular interest to the center is the relationship between the executive and legislative branches along with presidential and congressional campaigning. The center publishes a number of books and series regarding these issues, as well as the peer-reviewed journal *Congress and the Presidency*.

Organized and maintained by Indiana University, the **Center on Congress** (congress .indiana.edu) aims to provide students and researchers with the desire to become active in policy areas with a better understanding of how Congress works on a day-to-day basis. Books, radio reports, articles, and research projects are linked to the center.

Congress.org (www.congress.org) provides descriptions and analyses of the latest issues and votes on the Hill. Listed are letters sent by organizations and interest groups to congressional officials and committees.

The **Congressional Budget Office** (www.cbo.gov) provides the latest, as well as historic, data and economic forecasts on U.S. spending. Specifically, budget authorization acts

continues

Internet References (continued)

and budget forecasts relating to defense, security, and homeland security are available on this Web site.

CNN's **Inside Politics** Web site (www.cnn.com/allpolitics) integrates *Time* magazine, *Newsweek*, AP, and CNN current events and political stories. Congressional action and voting are often the topics of articles posted on this site. Video, speeches, and live coverage are added bonuses to using this site.

The **Library of Congress** (www.loc.gov) provides links to legal and policy topics along with bibliographies to support research projects. The library also provides an index of popular research topics for political and social researchers.

The direct link to the **United States Congress** (www.congress.gov), where researchers can access the House of Representatives and the Senate along with every committee and subcommittee, also provides links to each congressional member's home page and descriptions of current legislation. The site also maintains links to current and past legislation, voting records, and committee reports.

The **Weekly Political Wrap** (www.pbs.org/newshour/political_wrap/index.html), organized and maintained by PBS, provides reporting on weekly political issues in Congress. Real audio and transcribed testimony are especially helpful for researchers.

6

The Foreign-Policy Bureaucracy

Secretary of State Madeleine Albright is greeted by British Foreign Secretary Robin Cook and French Foreign Minister Hubert Vedrine in Rambouillet, France, during a 1999 meeting aimed to stop the "ethnic cleansing" in the Yugoslav province of Kosovo. Albright, the first woman to lead the State Department, was a strong advocate of U.S. intervention in Kosovo, where thousands of ethnic Albanians were being massacred or sent into exile by Serb leader Slobodan Milosevic. The military campaign that followed, which ultimately ended the conflict, was dubbed "Madeleine's War."

As we have seen in the previous two chapters, presidents and legislators share the task of *formulating* U.S. foreign policy, that is, deciding on the nation's primary goals and providing the means to achieve them. Once adopted, foreign policies must be effectively put into place and managed over time. These responsibilities fall to the agencies of the executive branch, or federal bureaucracies, that implement foreign policies on a day-to-day basis. In putting policy into practice, these agencies serve on the frontlines of the U.S. foreign-policy process.

While bureaucrats behave in similar ways across industrialized states, to truly understand how bureaucracy functions in the United States, the distinctive features of the U.S. political system must be taken into account. As noted in the previous chapters, governmental authority is highly fragmented, with powers disbursed *vertically,* among local, state, and federal agencies; *horizontally,* across the three branches of government; and *internally,* within the bureaucracies themselves. The agencies, most of which have little contact with the general public or private interest groups, represent strong power centers that can determine the success or failure of foreign-policy initiatives.

Bureaucratic managers have certain key advantages over other actors in the foreign-policy process due to a combination of three factors. The first involves **congressional deference** to the president. Whereas Congress plays a key role in creating government agencies, it generally grants the executive branch broad latitude in supervising them. Politics enters into this delegation of authority. "Legislators know that presidents take their foreign policy agencies seriously," Amy Zegart (1999, 34) has observed. "Any move to eliminate, reform, or significantly reduce the funding of these organizations without presidential approval is bound to incur executive wrath and invite inter-branch conflict—a fight that presidents almost always win."

Bureaucrats gain further advantage as a result of **presidential limitations** in controlling the vast web of foreign-policy agencies. Whereas presidents occupy the White House for a limited time, federal agencies are semipermanent structures that outlast the preferences of individual presidents. **Organizational expertise** represents the third factor that aids bureaucrats, who are specialists in the policy domains under their direction. Their command of these domains, enhanced by years of experience, gives them an upper hand among the political authorities who make foreign policy. "A consequence of delegating authority to bureaucrats is that they may become more expert about their policy responsibilities than the elected representatives who created their bureau" (McCubbins, Noll, and Weingast 1987, 247).

The agencies of U.S. foreign policy are loosely arranged within four "complexes," or bureaucratic clusters, that manage diplomacy, national security, economic affairs, and intelligence, respectively. This chapter introduces the complexes, highlighting their structural features, relationships with the White House and Congress, and impact on the overall foreign-policy process.

We turn first to the common functions and dysfunctions of foreign-policy bureaucracies, whose expansion and fragmentation since the United States became a global superpower offers a vivid example of institutional momentum. The terrorist attacks of September 2001 provided great impetus for structural change, leading to the biggest overhaul of the federal bureaucracy since the passage of the National Security Act of 1947.

As described in Chapters 3 and 4, the process of institutional momentum still leaves presidents enormous discretion in the foreign-policy process. They are the ones who create the balance of power that exists within the executive branch at a given time. A president does so by choosing which departments and agencies to bring to prominence in the pursuit of the administration's foreign-policy agenda. Even so, much of the power rests not with the president, but with the bureaucracies. A president's global ambitions cannot be realized if the bureaucracies fail to put them into practice.

Agency Functions and Dysfunctions

The United States' emergence as a global superpower after World War II gave rise to a large and far-flung foreign-affairs bureaucracy that helped sustain American primacy through the cold war. New global roles and responsibilities prompted U.S. leaders to overcome their nation's traditional distaste for standing armies, worldwide diplomatic outposts, and other permanent foreign-policy structures. In the wake of the cold war, the four U.S. foreign-policy complexes have retained much of this institutional architecture. Like their counterparts in domestic policy, each complex features "a smorgasbord of institutional types" (Seidman 1986, 249), including cabinet-level departments, subordinate bureaus, and special offices within the White House. The size, shape, and relations among these institutions shape the foreign-policy process in crucial ways.

Ideally, bureaucracies should provide "ballast," or stability, to government, lending "continuity and constancy" to legislative and executive systems that face constantly changing internal political alignments and external demands (Rockman 1997, 21). Yet as students and practitioners of bureaucratic politics (see Chapter 3) know well, such organizations often fall short of the standards of "rationality" they were designed to achieve. Rather than working as partners toward a common vision of the national interest, bureaucrats frequently compete with each other for resources and influence while resisting changes that threaten their institutional self-interests and standard operating procedures. The process of institutional momentum produces failures of interagency communication and coordination, two essential components in the conduct of foreign policy. These problems combined reinforce the paradox of world power as exercised by the United States.

Clashing goals, dominant self interests, and overlapping responsibilities contribute to the fragmentation of bureaucratic authority. Present and past examples of this problem abound. For instance, in Mexico City, the presence and competing agendas of fifty state and federal agencies in the U.S. embassy (see Table 6.1) produce bureaucratic politics "so complex, so multilayered, so conflicting, that it hamstrings, frustrates, and often paralyzes policy and makes it virtually impossible for the United States to carry out a successful foreign policy there" (Wiarda 2000, 175). According to Gen. Wesley Clark (2001, 437), supreme allied commander of U.S. forces in Europe during the 1999 Kosovo conflict, the United States nearly failed to defeat the much smaller Yugoslav army due to "deeply rooted organizational forces within the military itself." Specifically, leaders of the U.S. armed services, who opposed the intervention even after it had received President Clinton's approval, denied Clark the troops and combat options he needed to gain a prompt surrender from Serb leader Slobodan Milosevic.

The price Americans pay for agency dysfunctions can be high. Bureaucratic failures abetted the U.S. government's failure to prevent the terrorist attacks of September 2001. To Condoleezza Rice (2004), President Bush's national security adviser who testified before the 9-11 special commission, "legal and structural impediments" made it impossible for the Central Intelligence Agency (CIA) and Federal Bureau of Investigation (FBI) to effectively compare their notes regarding the growing threat of an al Qaeda attack on the United States. While the CIA limited its scope to the gathering of foreign intelligence, the FBI's counterterrorism units focused within the United States. Such a division of labor, while in keeping with the roles assigned to each agency, proved ill-suited to the task of countering a transnational threat that crossed political and organizational boundaries. Bureaucratic "groupthink" (see Chapter 3), meanwhile, was cited by congressional investigators as a cause of the intelligence breakdown preceding the U.S.-led invasion of Iraq in 2004.

Table 6.1 Anatomy of an Embassy: Selected U.S. Offices in Mexico City

Federal Agencies	U.S. State Offices
• Agency for International Development (State)	Arizona, Arkansas, California, Colorado, Connecticut, Florida, Georgia, Idaho, Illinois, Indiana, Iowa, Kentucky, Louisiana, Maryland, Massachusetts, Michigan, Missouri, New Jersey, New Mexico, New York, North Carolina, Ohio, Oklahoma, Pennsylvania, Tennessee, Texas, Utah, Virginia, Wisconsin
• Agricultural Trade Office (USDA)	
• American Battle Monuments Commission (independent)	
• Animal Plant Health Inspection Service (USDA)	
• Benjamin Franklin Library (State)	
• Bureau of Citizenship and Immigration Services (DHS)	
• Consular Affairs (State)	
• Defense Attache Office (DoD)	
• Drug Enforcement Administration (Justice)	
• Foreign Agriculture Service (USDA)	
• Internal Revenue Service (Treasury)	
• Labor Counselor (State)	
• Office of Defense Coordination (DoD)	
• Office of Economic Affairs (State)	
• Office of Environment, Science, and Technology (State/EPA)	
• Office of Public Affairs (State)	
• Personnel (State)	
• Political Affairs (State)	
• Regional Security Office (State)	
• U.S. Commercial Service (Commerce)	
• U.S. Customs and Border Protection (DHS)	
• U.S. Treasury	

SOURCE: United States Embassy in Mexico, mexico.usembassy.gov/eembdir.html (accessed May 14, 2004).

Clashing Organizational Cultures

Bureaucratic politics in the U.S. foreign-policy process are further driven by differences in **organizational culture,** or shared values, goals, and functional priorities of the members of a government agency. To James Q. Wilson (1989, 91), an expert on bureaucracy, "Culture is to an organization what personality is to an individual. Like human culture generally, it is passed from one generation to the next. It changes slowly, if at all."

The presence of many foreign-policy agencies in the U.S. government inevitably leads to clashes of organizational cultures. The tendency of foreign service officers to favor negotiated settlements over military coercion contributes to the State Department's reputation for excessive caution and timidity among members of the Defense Department. Similarly, the inherent secrecy of intelligence gathering creates a highly insular organizational culture within the

CIA and a corresponding alienation from other parts of the federal bureaucracy. Such organizational clashes sometimes extend beyond the government. The distinctive culture of military life, for instance, produces strains in **civil-military relations.** In his classic work on the subject, Samuel Huntington (1957, 345) detected "persistent peacetime tensions between military imperatives and American liberal society" long before they were fully exposed during and after the Vietnam War.

A foreign-policy institution encompassing many agencies can feature multiple, and clashing, organizational cultures. Within the Department of Defense, each of the armed services considers its own mission to be the most vital to the national interest, its forces superior to those in other services. These perceptions have led to the bestowal of unflattering nicknames on members of the other services— "jarheads" on marines, for example, and "squids" on naval forces. Thus despite constant efforts to promote unity, **interservice rivalry** remains a fact of life in the department. Beneath these rivalries lurk yet more cultural differences *within* the individual services. Sailors in the navy's surface fleet, for example, are set apart from those who operate submarines. Within the intelligence community, agents engaged in field operations share a sense of organizational mission very different from that of agents who process data from remote locations.

Such differences can energize the morale of each unit and serve as valuable recruiting tools across the foreign-policy bureaucracy. But they also can create problems by sparking public disputes over funding allocations, deployments, and the assignment of operational missions in military conflicts. In these cases, the energy expended by competing bureaucratic actors undermines the prospects for successful policy implementation.

Connecting the Dots after 9-11

Structural deficiencies, as mentioned above, contributed to the successful terrorist attacks against the United States in September 2001. Seven months before the attacks, the U.S. Commission on National Security/21st Century (2001) had found the U.S. government to be "very poorly organized to design and implement any comprehensive strategy to protect the homeland." Evidence since the attacks, including sworn statements by U.S. government leaders in office at the time, suggests that flaws in the bureaucratic network discouraged information sharing among agencies and prevented investigators from "connecting the dots" that could have led them to the plans for September 11.

This failure was not due to a lack of warning. The weeks prior to 9-11 featured a "spike" in danger signs that a large-scale terrorist attack was imminent. "Let me read you some of the chatter that was picked up in that spring and summer," Condoleezza Rice told the National Commission on Terrorist Attacks in April 2004. " 'Unbelievable news coming in weeks,' said one. 'Big event.' 'There will be a very, very, very, very big uproar.' 'There will be attacks in the near

IN THEIR OWN WORDS: CONDOLEEZZA RICE

National security adviser Condoleezza Rice, along with other Bush administration officials, testified before the 9-11 Commission in April 2004. In her testimony, Rice emphasized the institutional barriers that had prevented the U.S. government from "connecting the dots"—the numerous clues that had indicated a large-scale terrorist attack was imminent.

. . . The threat reporting that we received in the spring and summer of 2001 was not specific as to time, nor place nor manner of attack. Almost all of the reports focused on al Qaeda activities outside the United States, especially in the Middle East and in North Africa. In fact, the information that was specific enough to be actionable referred to terrorist operations overseas. Most often, though, the threat reporting was frustratingly vague.

Let me read you some of the actual chatter that was picked up in that spring and summer:

"Unbelievable news coming in weeks," said one.

"Big event . . . there will be a very, very, very, very big uproar."

"There will be attacks in the near future."

Troubling, yes. But they don't tell us when; they don't tell us where; they don't tell us who; and they don't tell us how. . . .

Throughout the period of heightened threat information, we worked hard on multiple fronts to detect, protect against and disrupt any terrorist plans or operations that might lead to an attack. For instance, the Department of Defense issued at least five urgent warnings to U.S. military forces that al Qaeda might be planning a near-term attack, and placed our military forces in certain regions on heightened alert. The State Department issued at least four urgent security advisories and public worldwide cautions on terrorist threats,

future.'" These warnings were relayed to President Bush, whose "daily brief" issued on August 6, 2001, was titled "Bin Laden Determined to Strike in U.S."[1]

The reports of a gathering threat, however, came from several disconnected sources in the U.S. government and foreign intelligence services. Considered separately, the warnings lacked sufficient detail to provoke strong action by President Bush, who spent the month of August vacationing at his Texas ranch. Instead, according to Rice, the Departments of State and Defense separately issued a series of urgent warnings to U.S. forces, government offices, and private citizens overseas. The FBI, meanwhile, issued three nationwide warnings to federal, state, and

1. According to this "President's Daily Brief" (White House 2001a), the first such memo to be made public since the Vietnam War, FBI evidence compiled since 1998 "indicates patterns of suspicious activity in this country consistent with preparations for hijackings or other types of attacks, including recent surveillance of federal buildings in New York."

enhanced security measures at certain embassies, and warned the Taliban that they would be held responsible for any al Qaeda attack on U.S. interests.

The FBI issued at least three nationwide warnings to federal, state and [sic] law enforcement agencies, and specifically stated that although the vast majority of the information indicated overseas targets, attacks against the homeland could not be ruled out. . . .

This is a brief sample of our intense activity in the high-threat period of the summer of 2001.

Yet, as your hearings have shown, there was no silver bullet that could have prevented the 9/11 attacks. In hindsight, if anything might have helped stop 9/11, it would have been better information about threats inside the United States, something made very difficult by structural and legal impediments that prevented the collection and sharing of information by our law enforcement and intelligence agencies.

So the attacks came. . . .

In looking back, I believe that the absence of light, so to speak, on what was going on inside the country, the inability to connect the dots, was really structural . . . the legal impediments and the bureaucratic impediments. But I want to emphasize the legal impediments. To keep the FBI and the CIA from functioning really as one, so that there was no seam between domestic and foreign intelligence, was probably the greatest [impediment]. . . . [W]hen it came right down to it, this country, for reasons of history and culture, and therefore, law, had an allergy to the notion of domestic intelligence, and we were organized on that basis. And it just made it very hard to have all of the pieces come together. . . .

Source: Condoleezza Rice, "Hearing of the National Commission on Terrorist Attacks Upon the United States" (April 8, 2004), www .9-11commission.gov/archive/hearing9/ 9-11Commission_Hearing_2004-04-08.pdf.

local law-enforcement agencies, and the Federal Aviation Agency issued "security information circulars" to airports regarding possible hijackings.

As noted earlier, anticipating and preventing the 9-11 attacks did not fall within the jurisdiction of any single government agency. The attacks combined domestic and international elements, including suspicious visa requests and flight training in the United States (FBI concerns) and heightened "chatter" among al Qaeda operatives in Europe and Asia (a CIA concern). Compounding this gap in jurisdiction was a reluctance by both counterterrorism units to communicate with each other. As former senator Bob Kerrey, a member of the 9-11 commission, observed to Rice during her testimony, "Everybody who does national security in this town knows the FBI and the CIA don't talk."

Reinforcing the lack of CIA-FBI contact were deep divisions between the Pentagon and State Department. Each had pursued its own institutional priorities in the first nine months of the Bush administration. While Secretary of State Colin Powell focused on improving morale and working conditions, Secretary of Defense Donald Rumsfeld sought to "transform" the military with technological innovations. For his part, the president seemed preoccupied with detaching the United States from international obligations, particularly an agreement with Russia forbidding the development of missile defenses. According to Richard Clarke (2004, Chap. 10), the National Security Council's senior counterterrorism official during this period, the entire executive branch neglected mounting evidence of impending danger that was conveyed to senior White House officials, including the president.[2]

The FBI alone faced four institutional obstacles that prevented a break-through prior to 9-11. First, counterterrorism was not a historic priority of the bureau. Second, the agency customarily investigated crimes *after* they occurred; *preventing* crimes and instituting preventive measures was not usual. The third obstacle involved legal restrictions, driven by concerns about privacy and civil liberties that limited the extent to which the FBI could meld its intelligence functions and criminal investigations. Simply put, many Americans feared the creation of a "Big Brother" in government that would violate their individual freedoms. Finally, the bureau faced chronic shortfalls in its intelligence and counterterrorism budgets; during their 16-week orientations, agents had just three days of training in the two areas. Furthermore, antiquated computer systems meant FBI agents "did not know what cases were under investigation by other agents in their own offices, much less other cities" (Johnston 2004, A1).

These characteristics of bureaucratic politics highlight the difficulties of managing U.S. foreign policy, an area in which decentralization and centrifugal forces hinder the effective implementation of policies. Recognizing the internal divisions, established routines, and resistance of government agencies, presidents and legislators tend to disregard the implementation of reforms, preferring instead to move on to new initiatives and other concerns. This problem impedes constructive change in the government and rewards business as usual (see Campbell 1991). For this and other reasons, the institutional face of U.S. foreign policy has changed little over the past half-century, despite the profound national and global changes that have occurred. It remains to be seen what lasting reforms, if any, will be implemented based on recent lessons. Because each of the four complexes in the foreign-policy bureaucracy has distinct structural features and roles in the policy process, each must be restructured separately, making any progress toward overall coordination very difficult.

The Diplomatic Complex

A central element of statecraft involves the conduct of **diplomacy,** the interactions among representatives of two or more sovereign states involving official matters

---

2. According to the White House, the FBI was conducting seventy "full-field investigations" of possible al Qaeda cells in the United States at the time of the terrorist attacks. The CIA and other foreign intelligence agencies, meanwhile, provided information regarding al Qaeda's growing threat in more than forty briefings to Bush between January 20 and September 10, 2001 (Rice 2004).

of mutual or collective concern. In particular, diplomats seek to maintain stable and functional relations with as many foreign governments as possible and to resolve interstate differences without recourse to force. The absence of tensions offers openings for constructive relations, particularly for commerce in which the citizens and governments of all parties involved may profit. Diplomats posted overseas also serve as the "eyes and ears" of their governments, providing leaders at home with timely and firsthand information about developments in host countries.

In the country's first decades, the post of chief U.S. diplomat, or secretary of state, served as a stepping-stone to the presidency. Thomas Jefferson, James Madison, James Monroe, and John Quincy Adams all became chief executives in this manner. Yet despite this impressive showing of strong secretaries, early U.S. leaders, including the nation's third president, frowned upon the routine practice of diplomacy. Jefferson (quoted in Morris 1966, 43–44), the first secretary of state, described eighteenth-century diplomacy as "the workshop in which nearly all the wars of Europe are manufactured." Rep. Benjamin Stanton of Ohio declared in 1858 that he knew of "no area of public service that is more emphatically useless than the diplomatic service—none in the world" (U.S. Department of State 1981, 9–10). In the popular imagination, the nation's early foreign-policy achievements, particularly the rapid pace of continental expansion, resulted from a *rejection*, rather than an embrace, of diplomatic relations.

Largely for this reason, the U.S. government did not create a full-scale foreign service until after World War I. American leaders agreed, however reluctantly, that the nation's arrival as a global power required it to "dirty its hands" in diplomatic activity. Even then, State Department budgets and salaries were kept at minimal levels, and the travel and schedules of diplomats were closely scrutinized. Once the United States achieved the status of a great power, other government agencies became enmeshed in the foreign-policy process. Since 1947, the U.S. government has maintained "two foreign ministries" in the State Department and National Security Council, respectively (Rockman 1981). This blurring of foreign-policy authority created problems over jurisdiction and access to the president that continue to plague the foreign service today.

The Department of State

The State Department, created in 1781 as the Department of Foreign Affairs, is the U.S. government's oldest executive agency. Officials at Foggy Bottom (the State Department's Washington, D.C., headquarters, which got its informal name from the area of the city in which it is located) manage a diplomatic complex that includes foreign-policy specialists based abroad as well as at home. As many as 60,000 federal employees from thirty agencies have been stationed in State Department offices in recent years. Duties of department employees include representing U.S. positions to foreign governments, international organizations, and private citizens, while also serving as contacts for representatives of foreign governments who wish to convey their views to the U.S. government. Beyond these diplomatic tasks, the State Department serves the following five functions:

1. advising presidents regarding the ends and means of U.S. foreign policy;
2. gathering and sharing information about recent developments overseas;
3. providing representation and services to U.S. citizens abroad;
4. regulating and managing foreign travel to the United States; and
5. investigating solutions to transnational problems such as environmental decay, large-scale poverty, and weapons proliferation (see Chapters 11 and 12).

The secretary of state, who oversees the U.S. diplomatic complex, serves as the ranking member of the president's cabinet and stands fourth in line of presidential succession. This official serves as the government's chief diplomat while also advising the president and overseeing the State Department bureaucracy. Beyond these formal duties, secretaries of state have played widely varying roles in presidential administrations, roles determined by the officeholder's relationship with the president and other top leaders, communication skills, and management style.

Further affecting the secretary of state's role is the blurring of foreign policy authority that began after World War II, as presidents chose to rely on a larger group of foreign-policy advisers. This fragmentation of authority has made life difficult for the secretary of state, who "has to use a great deal of time and energy to get anything done. He must negotiate not only with foreign countries, but also with other sectors of his own government" (Rubin 1985, 263).

The experience of Secretary of State Colin Powell illustrates this point. In the period just prior to the September 2001 terrorist attacks, Powell had such a low profile in the Bush administration that *Time* magazine asked on its cover, "Where Have you Gone, Colin Powell?" In policy deliberations, the opinions of Vice-President Dick Cheney and National Security Adviser Condoleezza Rice carried more weight than those of Powell. In addition, Bush frequently turned to Secretary of Defense Rumsfeld and his deputy, Paul Wolfowitz, whose worldviews more closely matched the president's own (see Lemann 2002). Though formally part of the president's inner circle, Powell did not play a decisive role in Bush's strategic choices in the war on terrorism and was among the last to be informed of the decision to invade Iraq (Woodward 2004).

Despite waning influence over the direction of foreign policy, the secretary of state oversees an elaborate worldwide bureaucracy organized along regional and functional lines (see Figure 6.1). In 2002, the State Department employed about 16,000 people, including about 9,000 specially trained **foreign service officers** (FSOs), who conduct day-to-day administrative and diplomatic tasks, and about 7,000 civil-service workers. A team of undersecretaries of state manage dozens of bureaus at State Department headquarters organized within six areas: political affairs; economic, business, and agricultural affairs; arms control and international security; public diplomacy and public affairs; management; and global affairs. Other officials and staffs specialize in such areas as policy planning, legislative affairs, intelligence, and counterterrorism. Two offices operate

Figure 6.1 Department of State Organization

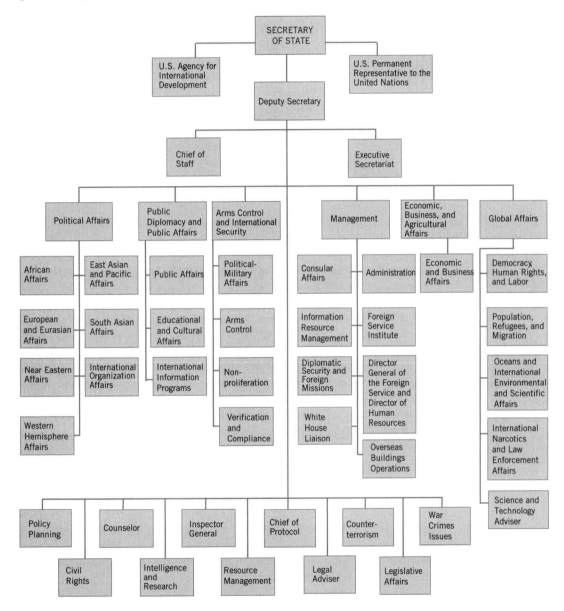

autonomously but within secretary of state's statutory authority: the U.S. Agency for International Development (AID) and the U.S. Permanent Representative to the United Nations.

Overseas, the State Department operates through a network of nearly 300 embassies (in foreign capitals), consulates (in other major cities), and other missions located in nearly every foreign country.[3] An ambassador serves as the president's official representative and the "leading protagonist, protector, and promoter" of U.S. interests within each foreign country (Kennan 1997, 207). Second in command at an embassy is the deputy chief of mission, who is responsible for the routine operation of overseas posts. This is an imposing task given that embassies include many functional sections routinely staffed by officials from other federal agencies (see Table 6.1). Military officers serve in most posts, along with aid specialists from the AID. Finally, agents from the many intelligence agencies operate out of foreign embassies and consulates, frequently under diplomatic cover.

Criticism and Reform at Foggy Bottom

For all its constitutional stature, the State Department is among the most embattled of federal agencies. Its budget has averaged about $7 billion annually in recent years, less than 2 percent of that for national defense and far less than that for intelligence and homeland security. Though its problems stem in large part from the widespread disdain for diplomacy deeply embedded in U.S. political culture, the department faces criticism for a variety of other reasons, all further limiting its prestige, influence, and budgetary support.

Three criticisms in particular continue to plague the State Department. The first relates to the perceived elitism of the foreign service. Political leaders and the general public often see diplomats as "objects of suspicion" due to "their arcane interests as well as their cosmopolitan behavior and manners" (Rubin 1985, 6). A recruitment pattern in which affluent white males from Ivy League universities have disproportionately filled the foreign service and top appointed positions has fueled this perception. In response to this criticism, Colin Powell increased the proportion of women and minorities soon after taking office as secretary in 2001. A second, related criticism involves the State Department's reputation for excessive caution. Critics often complain that FSOs resist making changes or taking chances in diplomatic relations because of their determination to maintain stable relations with foreign governments. Furthermore, critics say, FSOs frequently avoid initiatives that may not be popular among members of Congress, whose support may be needed for future initiatives.

Finally, critics accuse, foreign service officers are prone to **clientitis,** an overly close relationship to governments and citizens overseas that clouds judgment regarding U.S. global priorities. "It's a disease not unique to the Foreign Service," former secretary of state James A. Baker III (1995, 29) observed. "Some of the worst cases of clientitis I encountered involved politically appointed ambassadors who fell so thoroughly in love with their host country and its government that they sometimes lost sight of what was in the national interest." To prevent such

---

3. Among the few countries with no formal State Department offices in recent years are Cuba, Iran, and North Korea. Officials from the State Department also represent the United States in intergovernmental organizations such as the UN and NATO.

potentially compromising ties from forming, FSOs rotate every four years among overseas posts and domestic offices.[4]

Given these criticisms and cross pressures, it is not surprising that State Department morale—long a major problem—has slumped to new lows in recent years. This morale problem persisted in George W. Bush's administration despite Powell's success in increasing diversity, improving working conditions, and enhancing the compensation provided to State Department employees. The president's closer working relationship with other advisers left not only Powell in the margins, but also his assistants, whose voices could not be heard outside the diplomatic complex. As a result, attracting and keeping skilled employees has been difficult for a department already notorious for its relatively low pay, heavy and constantly shifting demands, and lack of job security.

Though the State Department has lost its predominant role as the primary source of foreign-policy guidance, it has maintained other, equally vital tasks, ones for which it remains uniquely capable. Primary among these tasks is the implementation of U.S. foreign policy through its worldwide network of embassies and consulates. More generally, the State Department can serve as an asset to presidents with its conservative approach to diplomacy. As Theodore Sorensen (1987–1988, 238), special counsel to President Kennedy, observed:

> The caution, continuity, and constant consultations for which the department is chided reflect in large part the reality of a dangerous world that does not change merely because we change presidents. The department's institutional memory, in-depth planning and orderly procedures can protect an eager president from his errors as well as his enemies. The experienced eye and pragmatic perspective of career specialists . . . are needed to balance White House pressures for quick and dramatic solutions that conform with campaign slogans or popular sentiment.

Messengers of "Public Diplomacy"

While officials generally carry out State Department work through conventional diplomatic channels, the U.S. government also resorts to **public diplomacy** to achieve its foreign-policy objectives. In effect, public diplomacy goes "over the heads" of foreign leaders by appealing directly to their countries' citizens. The messengers of public diplomacy, whose ranks have included private citizens such as scholars, artists, and journalists, are uniquely positioned to project the nation's cultural values and demonstrate the vitality of its civil society. In so doing, they can strengthen international support for the United States in ways beyond the reach of diplomats and political leaders.

The U.S. government has sponsored programs of public diplomacy for many years. The Fulbright Program, for example, provides for the international exchange of scholars, teachers, and students in many fields of study. Other

---

4. Such rotation has produced its own criticism—that FSOs lack the necessary knowledge about the countries and regions in which they work.

Point/Counterpoint

DEFENSE DEPARTMENT VS. STATE DEPARTMENT

Institutional tensions always exist between the two primary agencies of U.S. foreign policy, the Defense Department and the State Department. By the nature of their jobs, Pentagon officials focus on military solutions to foreign-policy problems while their counterparts at "Foggy Bottom" emphasize diplomatic measures.

These built-in tensions were exposed shortly after the 9-11 attacks. On September 13, Paul Wolfowitz, the deputy secretary of defense, outlined a large-scale military response. "It's not just simply a matter of capturing people and holding them accountable," Wolfowitz told reporters at a Pentagon press conference, "but [also a matter of] removing the sanctions, removing the support systems, [and] ending states who sponsor terrorism."

At a press conference soon after Wolfowitz spoke, reporters asked Secretary of State Colin Powell what he thought of "ending," or overthrowing, state sponsors of terrorism. "We're after ending *terrorism,*" Powell replied, "and if there are states and nations, regimes that support terrorism, we hope to persuade them that it is in their interest to stop doing that. I think ending terrorism is where I'd like to leave it, and let Mr. Wolfowitz speak for himself."

Powell's reference to persuasion, rather than force, typifies the State Department's mindset. As in most other interagency policy disputes during that period, however, the Defense Department gained the upper hand. President Bush, who ultimately chose the course of action to be followed, made it clear that the United States would attack not only terrorists, but their state sponsors as well. The Bush Doctrine allowed little room for diplomacy, a fact affirmed by the U.S. invasion of Afghanistan in November 2002 and the overthrow of Saddam Hussein's regime in Iraq in March 2003, the latter without the support of the UN or key U.S. allies.

Source: Public Broadcasting Service, "The War Behind Closed Doors" (Frontline documentary; February 20, 2003), www.pbs.org/wgbh/pages /frontline/shows/iraq.

programs include the Voice of America, a worldwide international radio service, joined in recent years by regional broadcasters Radio and TV Marti (to Cuba), Radio Free Europe/Radio Liberty, Radio Free Asia, and Radio Sawa (to Arab countries). As part of its public-diplomacy mission, the State Department also operates press centers in the United States and funds democracy programs in foreign countries. Overseeing these efforts is the department's Office of International Information Programs, an agency created in 1999 to replace the U.S. Information Agency (USIA).

Shortly after the September 2001 terrorist attacks, the Bush administration hired Charlotte Beers, a Madison Avenue advertising executive, to serve as undersecretary of state for public diplomacy to escalate the government's offensive in this area. Beers spent millions of dollars on a campaign of radio and television documentaries, booklets, and wall posters that portrayed a U.S. government and society open to multiple cultures and welcoming the participation of Muslims in public life. The point of these messages: the Islamic world has nothing to fear from the United States. "She got me to buy Uncle Ben's rice. There is nothing wrong with getting somebody who knows how to sell something," Secretary of State Powell (quoted in the *Economist* 2002) said of the Beers appointment. "We are selling a product. We need someone who can rebrand American foreign policy, rebrand diplomacy."

Despite its glitz, the marketing campaign failed to stem the surge of anti-American sentiment that spread across the Islamic world and other regions following the U.S.-led invasion of Iraq in March 2003. As detailed in the following chapter, public-opinion polls worldwide registered strong ill-will toward the United States, a stark contrast to the outpouring of solidarity that followed the 9-11 terrorist attacks. "America has a serious image problem," concluded an independent task force on public diplomacy sponsored by the Council on Foreign Relations (2003, 2). "World opinion of the United States has dangerously deteriorated." According to the USIA Alumni Association (2004), whose Web site (www.publicdiplomacy.org) advocated public diplomacy, "Perceptions of American unilateralism remain widespread in European and Muslim nations, and the war in Iraq has undermined America's credibility abroad."

By the time Beers resigned from her position in March 2003, citing health reasons, it had become clear that reviving the nation's image would require much more than a "rebranding" of U.S. foreign policy. Withdrawal of global support, including the support of most world leaders as well as that of mass publics in other countries, flowed predictably from a shift in American foreign policy that distanced the United States from the international community. The Bush administration defended this shift on the basis of protecting the nation's sovereignty against incursions by a variety of intergovernmental organizations and agreements (see Chapters 8 and 9). The defense fell on deaf ears. The resulting backlash, most vividly expressed in the lack of UN backing for the Iraq invasion, turned the task of public diplomacy into a steep uphill battle.

The Security Complex

In contrast to those of the diplomatic complex, the agencies of the U.S. national security complex cast an immense shadow over the entire federal government, consuming much of its discretionary funding and controlling its largest workforce. In the years following World War II, the security complex grew enormously, the framework for national defense established early on with the passage of the National Security Act of 1947 (see Chapter 2). The legislation and subsequent amendments created the National Security Council (NSC) and the National Military Establishment, which later became the Department of Defense (DoD). These institutions, which played a crucial role in waging and ultimately winning the cold war, remained intact after the Soviet Union's collapse in 1991. The terrorist attacks on the United States a decade later prompted a new expansion of the security complex with the creation of the vast Department of Homeland Security.

The National Security Council

The greatly enlarged world role of the United States after World War II, combined with the onset of the cold war, required a more centralized system of foreign-policy making. This led to the creation of the National Security Council, which since 1947 has served as the nerve center of the foreign-policy process. The council comprises four statutory members, four statutory advisers, top presidential aides, and a variety of other senior government officials who attend meetings involving their areas of expertise (see Table 6.2). Based in the White House, the NSC serves three primary functions: an agent of policy coordination, a source of *neutral* policy guidance to the president, and a forum for crisis management.

In its capacity of policy coordinator, the NSC attempts to establish an orderly working relationship among the many federal agencies involved in U.S. foreign policy, particularly the Defense and State departments and the intelligence agencies. The special assistant for national security affairs, more commonly known as the **national security adviser** (NSA), serves as a gatekeeper in the White House, controlling access to the president. Policy coordination is promoted further through an array of interagency NSC "principals" and "deputies" committees that meet regularly on foreign-policy matters.

The NSA also meets regularly with the president to review and interpret recent developments regarding U.S. national security. During these consultations, the adviser provides the president with guidance on the merits of different options, a role formerly filled by the secretary of state. The president receives additional staff support from NSC policy experts in the White House, who provide analysis in specific areas of national security. Of critical importance is the neutrality, or lack of parochial bias, underlying this guidance. The NSC presumably looks

Table 6.2 Members of the National Security Council (NSC)

Statutory Members	Statutory Advisers	Nonstatutory Members, Invited All Meetings	Nonstatutory Members, Attend as Necessary
President (chair)	National Security Adviser	President's Chief of Staff	Attorney General
Vice President	Chair of Joint Chiefs of Staff	Council to the President	Secretary of Homeland Security
Secretary of Defense	Director of Central Intelligence	Assistant to the President for Economic Policy	Director of Office of Management and Budget
Secretary of State	Secretary of the Treasury		U.S. Representative to the United Nations
			Other government officials invited by president

SOURCE: www.whitehouse.gov/nsc.

broadly toward the national interest, beyond the institutional self-interests that routinely cloud the judgment and advice of cabinet departments and agencies.

Finally, the NSC provides an organizational setting for the management of national-security crises. The breakout of the cold war and ensuing nuclear arms race created a nearly perpetual state of crisis that solidified the NSC's crisis-management role. Although recent White House occupants have preferred ad hoc meetings of selected advisers to formal NSC meetings, the council remains a useful forum for presidents.

The NSC system has proven highly malleable over the years, taking on different shapes and roles in each presidential administration. In this respect, the council "must be left flexible to be molded by the President in the form most useful to him" (Tower Commission 1987, 4). Presidents Truman and Eisenhower, for example, viewed the NSC warily, relying instead upon their secretaries of state for advice. John F. Kennedy was the first president to use his national security adviser, McGeorge Bundy, not simply as policy coordinator but as an active policy *advocate* as well. The adviser's power peaked in the Nixon administration, when NSA Henry Kissinger dominated the U.S. foreign-policy process as no one did before or has since. Kissinger actively conducted diplomatic missions and designed such policies as détente with the Soviet Union and the recognition of China. He eventually served as both NSA and secretary of state—a dual role that proved unworkable (see Hitchens 2001).

Since the Kissinger era, NSAs have generally assumed a lower profile while retaining their advantage of direct White House access to the president. Brent Scowcroft, who served as NSA under George H. W. Bush, typified this low-key demeanor, sense of bureaucratic impartiality, and command of the issues. Condoleezza Rice tried to stay behind the scenes, but she was frequently thrust into the media spotlight to defend the second President Bush's foreign-policy choices. Her ability to coordinate presidential access was put to the test due to ongoing strains between the State and Defense departments, and in the midst of an apparent breakdown in the relationship among intelligence agencies. Throughout this maelstrom, her close relationship with Bush secured her stature as an "honest broker" in the White House.

The system of the NSC, like those of other institutions of foreign-policy power, frequently has proved an object of controversy and criticism. There are three issues of primary concern. The first relates to the council's emergence as an *independent* power center within the security complex and a rival, rather than partner, of other federal agencies, most notably the State Department. Critics allege that NSC staff members have overstepped their bounds by taking formal policy positions, interacting with foreign governments, and appealing to the public through the news media (Daalder and Destler 2000, 7). This more public role reflects the growth of NSC staff to nearly 200 in the past decade, which reinforces its image as another foreign ministry in the executive branch.

A second, related concern is that Congress is left out of the NSC system, negating the checks and balances written into the U.S. Constitution. Significantly, the national security adviser and other high-level NSC staff members do not require Senate confirmation, as do cabinet secretaries and other high-level presidential appointees. Congressional leaders have sought, thus far without success, to gain this oversight power over NSC appointments, a power that seems consistent with constitutional intent.

The secretive nature of the NSC system raises the third issue of concern—potential abuses from the concentration of power within the White House. This fear was realized in the 1980s when NSC staffers conducted secret, "off-the-shelf" military operations in the Middle East and Central America, which led to the Iran-contra scandal. In this case, NSC staff members formed a **shadow government,** a secretive group operating beyond the reach of the public, Congress, the courts, or even other executive branch agencies. A more recent controversy involved Rice's reluctance to testify before the 9-11 commission regarding her actions and conversations with President Bush prior to the attacks. Rice claimed such testimony would violate the separation of powers and would discourage future NSAs from providing candid advice to the president since it might later become public. The White House finally allowed Rice to testify, but only after insisting that her appearance not be considered a precedent.

The Department of Defense

The Department of Defense is by far the largest and most expensive organization within the U.S. government. About 2.3 million men and women served in the active forces, reserves, and guard units in 2004, and nearly 700,000 civilians supported the military effort. Defense spending in the United States, averaging less than $300 billion in the first decade after the cold war, rose to more than $450 billion in fiscal years 2004 and 2005. An additional economic impact comes from the fact that the defense industry, including military contractors that provide goods and services to the DoD, employs millions of other workers. Well aware of this economic impact, the DoD promotes itself on its Web site as "America's largest company," with a payroll and "Budget/Revenue" that greatly exceed those of Wal-Mart, ExxonMobil, GM, and Ford (see www.defenselink.mil/pubs/dod101).

The DoD has a highly complex structure (see Figure 6.2). At the top of the hierarchy stands the secretary of defense, a civilian appointed by the president and confirmed by the Senate. The secretary and the secretary's deputy oversee the three armed services—the U.S. Army, the U.S. Navy, and the U.S. Air Force—which in 2003 operated out of 6,702 military installations around the world (U.S. Department of Defense 2003); (see Map 9, Nuclear Threats and U.S. Defense Installations, in the map section at the front of the book). The Pentagon oversees unified commands operating at the regional level or on the basis of specified functions.[5] The DoD maintains a global troop presence through five regional commands (see Map 7, Department of Defense Regional Commands) covering North

---

5. A fourth armed service, the U.S. Marine Corps, is based within the Department of the Navy but operates its own network of commands and agencies. The U.S. Coast Guard, formerly controlled by the U.S. Navy, is overseen by the Department of Homeland Security.

Figure 6.2 Department of Defense Organization

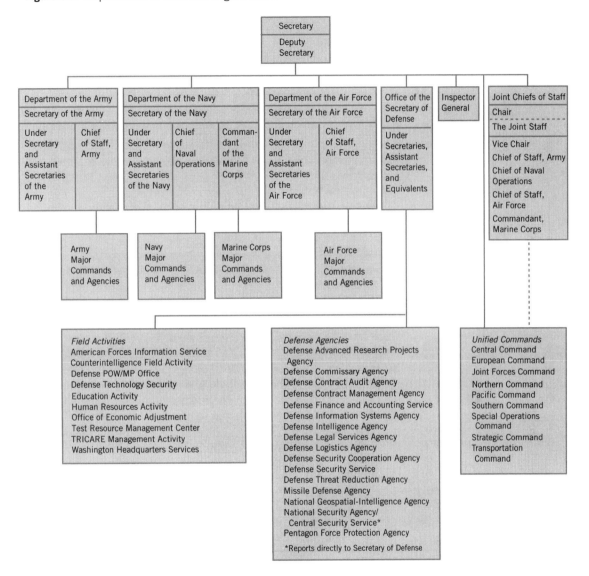

America (NORTHCOM), South America (SOUTHCOM), Southeast Asia (PACOM), eastern Africa and southwestern Asia (CENTCOM), and a broad region stretching from western Africa across Europe and Russia (EUCOM). The Joint Chiefs of Staff (JCS), composed of the leaders of all the armed services, provides guidance to the secretary of defense regarding military strategy and operations. Finally, the secretary and the secretary's deputy oversee their own staff as well as a variety of Pentagon-based agencies.

The large size, fragmented structure, and distinctive mission of the DoD give rise to a variety of tensions within the rest of the U.S. government. A primary concern is the relationship between the department's centralized civilian authorities and the military leaders who oversee the armed services themselves. This tension persists today despite a variety of changes made to the DoD's command structure since the passage of the National Security Act of 1947. Most importantly, the Defense Reorganization Act of 1986 (more commonly known as the **Goldwater-Nichols Act,** after its congressional sponsors) altered the balance of power within the Pentagon in two distinct ways. First, the act strengthened the power of the JCS chairman, who became the primary military adviser to the president and secretary of defense and was thus better able to prevent "end runs" by the individual service chiefs. Second, Goldwater-Nichols increased the power of regional commanders in chief (CINCs) who manage forces across the armed services. This measure encouraged greater "jointness" across the armed services, a central goal of all presidents since Dwight Eisenhower (quoted in Lederman 1999, 21) declared in 1958:

> Separate ground, sea, and air warfare is gone forever. Peacetime preparation and organization activity must conform to that fact. Strategic and tactical planning must be completely united, combat forces organized into unified commands, each equipped with the most efficient weapons systems that science can develop, singly led and prepared to fight as one, regardless of service.

Eisenhower's vision of a unified military establishment faced strong resistance within the armed services, which had been completely independent of each other prior to World War II. The divergent interests of the services remains a stubborn fact of military life today, with each one competing with the others for more troops, weapons, and influence over long-term strategy as well as short-term battlefield tactics. However, Goldwater-Nichols did succeed in producing greater coherence within the chain of command and a broader sense of shared mission. "The successes, and limitations, of military restructuring reflect the new patterns of conflict and coalition building that Goldwater-Nichols put in place" (Stockton 1997, 131).

The first direct beneficiary of Goldwater-Nichols was Colin Powell, chairman of the JCS under Presidents George H. W. Bush and Bill Clinton. Powell used his clout to promote a **base force proposal** that became the primary blueprint of U.S. military forces after the cold war. Foreseeing the collapse of the Soviet bloc, Powell argued that the United States had to shift from its posture of "global" defense to one based on confronting the smaller regional threats that would be more common in the future. In his view, the DoD could manage this task with a military force 25 percent smaller than that used during the cold war. If the department did not order these cuts itself, Powell warned, Congress would impose its own cuts on the Pentagon.

The plan encountered strong opposition from senior officers and legislators, but the authority granted Powell by Goldwater-Nichols, combined with his personal prestige after the Persian Gulf War, helped him overcome this resistance (see

Jaffe 1993). Based on Powell's proposals, the U.S. Army reduced its number of divisions from eighteen to ten by the mid-1990s and the U.S. Navy reduced its fleet from 551 to fewer than 400 ships. Further military cutbacks occurred under Les Aspin, Bill Clinton's first secretary of defense, whose **bottom-up review** (U.S. Department of Defense 1993) called for a leaner military force to manage the smaller-scale threats to the United States that existed after the Soviet Union's collapse. The DoD closed about 20 percent of U.S. military bases between 1998 and 2002, saving the government about $30 billion initially and $6 billion per year afterward.

The push for military restructuring continued in other areas. Congress approved the Armed Services Force Structure Act of 1996, which required the DoD to conduct a **quadrennial defense review** (QDR) outlining U.S. military strategy at the beginning of every presidential term. The first QDR, submitted in 1997 by Secretary of Defense William Cohen, quickly "devolved into a turf battle over future roles and missions" (Snodgrass 2000, 58). A similar fate seemed likely for the second QDR late in 2001, but the terrorist attacks of September 11 brought the armed services into line with the report submitted by Donald Rumsfeld (U.S. Department of Defense 2001b). In particular, Rumsfeld's call for major increases in military budgets was well received by the service chiefs and most members of Congress.

Prior to 9-11, Rumsfeld sought to "transform" U.S. military forces so they could compete more effectively on the battlefields of the future (see MacGregor 2003). He believed the DoD should exploit the **revolution in military affairs** that had changed the nature of conventional warfare (O'Hanlon 2002; Galdi 1995). Rapid changes in military technology had fueled this revolution. Automated weapons systems and surveillance, satellite-guided munitions, lighter and faster transport vehicles, and advanced networks of command and control had allowed modern militaries to increase the potency of their armed forces without making them larger or more expensive. The defense secretary, however, failed to convince the armed services that military transformation was in their interest. Knowing that deep cuts in existing forces would accompany the transformation, the service chiefs chose instead to support the status quo. By August 2001, Rumsfeld had realized he was overmatched and effectively "sued for peace" (Duffy 2001).

The September 2001 terrorist attacks provided the boost Rumsfeld needed to revive his transformation campaign. The immediate calls for higher defense spending provided something for everybody—higher pay for troops, the extension of existing weapons programs, more military sales for weapons contractors, and all the support Rumsfeld needed to accelerate the research and development of new military technologies. He gained further momentum after U.S. troops proved highly effective in Operation Enduring Freedom, overwhelming Afghanistan in 2001 with an unprecedented display of rapid deployment, tactical coordination, and concentrated firepower. Similar success followed in Operation Iraqi Freedom early in 2003. In managing the subsequent occupations of both countries, the U.S. military effort proved less successful, however, suggesting that even the most sophisticated armed forces cannot overcome intelligence failures and political breakdowns in overseas missions.

The Department of Homeland Security

The September 2001 terrorist attacks shattered the sense of invulnerability Americans had enjoyed throughout the nation's history. The United States suddenly joined dozens of other countries for which the trauma of global terrorism was a fact of life. As in the early days of the cold war, the war on terrorism's onset produced calls for new institutions to bolster the country against its enemies. In this case, the institutions were to guard against future catastrophic attacks at home while supporting rapid responses to such attacks should they occur.

One of President Bush's first actions after 9-11 was to create the Office of Homeland Security (OHS) through an executive order. Based in the White House, the OHS was to take a lead role in protecting the United States against future attacks on U.S. territory. Bush appointed Tom Ridge, former Pennsylvania governor, to the new position of homeland security adviser. The president's executive order also created the **Homeland Security Council,** which was to be responsible for "advising and assisting the President with respect to all aspects of homeland security." Along with Bush and Ridge, council members included the vice president; the secretaries of defense, transportation, the treasury, and health and human services; and the directors of central intelligence, the FBI, and the Federal Emergency Management Agency.

It soon became obvious that the U.S. government needed more than a White House office to assume the formidable burdens of homeland security. Dozens of federal agencies would have to be fused into a single department, not merely coordinated by a presidential adviser with neither legal nor budgetary authority. A large federal department would also be essential in working with the thousands of state and local governments, law-enforcement agencies, and emergency-response units involved in the effort. Furthermore, Congress, whose spending and confirmation powers would be called upon, would have to be directly involved in this process.

All these realizations prompted the creation in March 2003 of the Department of Homeland Security (DHS), which brought more than 180,000 employees from twenty-two federal agencies together under one institutional roof (see Table 6.3). These agencies included, among others, the U.S. Coast Guard, Customs Service, Secret Service, Immigration and Naturalization Service, Transportation Security Administration, and Federal Emergency Management Agency. Many programs previously run by cabinet departments, such as the Pentagon's National Bio-Weapons Defense Analysis Center, also came under DHS control. Congress and the White House approved a $37.4 billion budget for DHS in fiscal year 2004, with most of the funds coming from existing agency budgets (Relyea 2004).

The vast scope of this endeavor guaranteed that the newest federal department would face serious problems during its startup years. As noted throughout this chapter, efforts to merge federal agencies and functions often succumb to clashing organizational cultures, disputes over budgets and missions, and other forms of

Table 6.3 Department of Homeland Security

Major Division	Agency	Former Organization
Border and Trans- portation Security	U.S. Customs Service	Treasury
	Immigration and Naturalization Service	Justice
	Federal Protective Service	General Services Administration
	Transportation Security Administration	Transportation
	Federal Law Enforcement Training Center	Treasury
	Animal and Plant Health Inspection Service	Agriculture
	Office for Domestic Preparedness	Justice
Emergency Preparedness and Response	Federal Emergency Management Agency (FEMA)	FEMA
	Strategic National Stockpile and National Disaster Medical System	Health and Human Services
	Nuclear Incident Response Team	Energy
	Domestic Emergency Support Teams	Justice
	National Domestic Preparedness Office	Federal Bureau of Investigation
Science and Technology	CBRN Countermeasures Programs	Energy
	Environmental Measurements Laboratory	Energy
	National BW Defense Analysis Center	Defense
	Plum Island Animal Disease Center	Agriculture
Information Analysis and Infrastructure Protection	Critical Infrastructure Assurance Office	Commerce
	Federal Computer Incident Response Center	General Services Administration
	National Communications System	Defense
	National Infrastructure Protection Center	Federal Bureau of Investigation
	Energy Security and Assurance Program	Energy
Management		New
United States Coast Guard		Transportation, Defense
United States Secret Service		Treasury
Bureau of Citizenship and Immigration Services		Immigration and Naturalization Services
Office of State and Local Government Coordination		New
Office of Private Sector Liaison		New
Office of Inspector General		New

bureaucratic rivalry. These problems were compounded with the DHS, an unwieldy and unpredictable department that many agencies did not want to join. Officials and legislative allies of the FBI, for example, made it clear from the outset that any proposals to add the bureau to the DHS roster would be dead on arrival.

External problems, too, plagued the DHS as a series of high-profile missteps diminished public support for the new department. A color-coded national alert system, for instance, only seemed to confuse Americans, as did remarks by Ridge in 2003 that they should stock up on cellophane and duct tape to survive biochemical attacks on their neighborhoods. Long delays prevented the timely release of a terrorist "watch list" and national risk assessment. In addition, local first responders, border patrols, and federal air marshals, who had expected more federal funds for stepped-up efforts, instead suffered budget *reductions* in 2004. "Far from being greater than the sum of its parts," journalist Michael Crowley (2004, 17) observed, "DHS is a bureaucratic Frankenstein, with clumsily stitched together limbs and an inadequate, misfiring brain. . . . [E]ven allowing for inevitable transition problems, DHS has been a disaster: underfunded, under-manned, disorganized, and unforgivably slow moving."

Progress reports from other sources have also been critical. The private Markle Foundation (2003), for example, found the department's information-sharing role to be in disarray. The Gilmore Commission (2003) reported to Congress and the White House that due to "the lack of a clear articulated vision from the federal level," each of the fifty states and the five U.S. territories "has been moving to combat terrorism in its own way." Nonetheless, the DHS has become a fixture of the security complex. As with other foreign-policy bureaucracies, creation of the DHS proved far easier than the fulfillment of its great expectations.

The Intelligence Complex

Foreign-policy makers in the United States have long relied upon the gathering of accurate and timely information on conditions and developments in other countries that might affect U.S. interests. Intelligence gathering, the "first line of defense" in foreign policy, has been especially vital since World War II and the United States's arrival as a global superpower. Failures of intelligence, from the Pearl Harbor attacks of 1941 to the terrorist attacks of 9-11, have had devastating effects on the nation. In contrast, sound intelligence gathering, as during the Cuban missile crisis, has provided an invaluable service.

Many government officials and outside experts believed the Soviet Union's collapse would lessen the need for foreign intelligence. The outbreak of regional crises in the early 1990s made it clear, however, that intelligence gathering would remain a critical task (Hilsman 2000). Thus the intelligence complex has grown into an elaborate network connecting all the foreign-policy agencies, along with many other agencies concerned primarily with domestic affairs. This complex is "by any measure the largest in the free world and certainly the most complicated, bureaucratic, convoluted, and expensive system anywhere. . . . No one could have invented such a system, but because it grew in bits and pieces, it has become the complicated structure we have today" (Hulnick 1999, 191–192).

Structures and Functions of the Intelligence Complex

The intelligence complex includes fifteen federal agencies (see Table 6.4). Among them, the Central Intelligence Agency (CIA) alone is an independent agency. Of the other fourteen agencies, eight operate within the DoD, including the centralized Defense Intelligence Agency (DIA) and separate intelligence units in each of

Table 6.4 The U.S. Intelligence Community, 2004

Independent Agency	Defense Department Agencies	Nondefense Agencies
Central Intelligence Agency	Air Force Intelligence	Coast Guard Intelligence
	Army Intelligence	Department of Energy
	Defense Intelligence	Department of Homeland Security
	Marine Corps Intelligence	Department of State
	Navy Intelligence	Department of the Treasury
	National Geospatial-Intelligence Agency	Federal Bureau of Investigation
	National Reconnaissance Office	
	National Security Agency	

SOURCE: www.intelligence.gov (accessed May 13, 2004).

the four armed services. The DoD also oversees the National Security Agency, the National Reconnaissance Office, and the National Geospatial-Intelligence Agency (formerly the National Imagery and Mapping Agency), all of which gather and distribute technical intelligence. Six other intelligence agencies support the Departments of Energy, State, the Treasury, and Homeland Security, the FBI, and the U.S. Coast Guard, respectively.[6]

The chronic tensions between centralized authority and bureaucratic fragmentation that afflict other foreign-policy complexes are particularly troubling to the intelligence complex. The member agencies have long resisted a truly "central" intelligence agency, competing instead "for their own places in the postwar intelligence arena" (Zegart 1999, 164). President Truman, more determined to unify the armed services than the intelligence agencies, made the latter a low priority. Since then, the agencies have steadfastly maintained their independence to protect their sources, focus on their specialized missions, and avoid interference from other agencies. While budgets for the intelligence community are kept secret, it was revealed in 1997 and 1998 that the annual budget for both years amounted to $27 billion (Center for Defense Information 2002). One can reasonably assume that these budgets have grown significantly since the war on terrorism began.

Overseeing the intelligence complex is a director of central intelligence (DCI), who also heads the CIA. In addition, the DCI serves as the primary adviser on intelligence matters to the president and the NSC. The DCI's deputy is responsible for administering the intelligence complex. Supporting their efforts is the National Intelligence Council, composed of leading experts inside and outside the U.S. government. Through its national intelligence estimates, the council provides information on trends in international security to the DCI and other "consumers" of intelligence, including Congress.

Congress has become much more involved in the intelligence process since the Vietnam War. The Senate and the House of Representatives each created a "select" intelligence committee in 1976 to oversee the intelligence complex in general and

---

6. The DHS intelligence unit and the intelligence unit supporting the U.S. Coast Guard, which is now part of DHS, were both created in response to the September 2001 terrorist attacks.

the CIA in particular, which Sen. Frank Church, D-Idaho, charged had become a "rogue elephant." [7] Although the creation of these committees has enhanced Congress's oversight role, committee members face ongoing "problems of bureaucratic obfuscation and rigidity, of policy clashes with the agencies they are overseeing, and of obtaining information" (Holt 1995, 230). Both committees reported such problems during their investigations on the intelligence agencies' failure to prevent the 2001 terrorist attacks.[8]

Although their missions vary, the intelligence agencies are primarily involved in the process of converting **raw intelligence,** or information collected from various sources usually without their knowledge or permission, into **finished intelligence,** or information made useful to policy makers. Such information has become far more plentiful in recent years due to advances in telecommunications (Doyle 2000). In addition, the emergence of democratic governments with unrestricted news media and "transparent" record-keeping systems has further aided intelligence analysts' tasks to such an extent that information *overload,* rather than scarcity, is the foremost concern.

Each intelligence agency manages an **intelligence cycle** that includes five stages. The first of these involves *planning and direction,* which identifies what information policy makers need to have. *Collection* is the second stage in the cycle. Agents may gather information from "open sources" such as press reports and government documents. Information also comes from **human intelligence (HUMINT),** primarily foreign informants working undercover for the United States, and from **technical intelligence (TECHINT)** derived from "intercepts" of electronic transmissions, satellite photographs, and other sources.

In the third, *processing* stage of the intelligence cycle, analysts identify the most essential information available to them. They must then translate information derived from foreign-language sources, decrypt coded information, and develop film and audiotape derived in the TECHINT process. The fourth stage involves the *analysis* of intelligence, that is, the clarification and interpretation of messages so they can be understood by policy makers. This is an inherently difficult process, as raw intelligence is almost always prone to multiple interpretations. Reports of Islamic foreign nationals' taking flight lessons in the United States, for example, were only understood as truly significant after some of these students hijacked commercial jets and steered them into the World Trade Center and the Pentagon on 9-11. Finally, the *dissemination* of intelligence to the proper authorities is crucial. The failure of FBI and CIA officials to share their separate findings regarding stepped-up terrorist activity in the summer of 2001 is widely seen as a key factor in the success of the September 11 attacks.

---

7. The status of these intelligence committees as "select" rather than "standing" gives the party leadership in each chamber greater power to appoint members, a power deemed necessary given the sensitive nature of national intelligence.

8. See U.S. Senate Select Committee on Intelligence and U.S. House Permanent Select Committee on Intelligence, *Joint Inquiry into Intelligence Community Activities Before and After the Terrorist Attacks of September 11, 2001,* Senate Report No. 107-351, House Report No. 107-792 107th Congress, 2d sess., December 2002.

In addition to these standard functions, intelligence agencies engage in two other primary activities. The first involves **counterintelligence**—the "acquisition of information or activity designed to neutralize hostile intelligence services" (Richelson 1985, 3). **Covert operations,** the second type of activity, are designed to obtain information without the knowledge of foreign governments or effect changes within them that are favorable to the United States. This operational role, not originally emphasized when the intelligence complex was created, has been a prominent, and often controversial, tool of foreign policy since the Eisenhower administration in the early cold war.

The Central Intelligence Agency

As noted above, the CIA is the only independent agency in the intelligence complex. Intelligence gathered by the CIA is presumably more "neutral" than that coming from other agencies, whose findings may be swayed by bureaucratic self-interests. The CIA's role in planning and conducting covert operations, detailed below, further contributes to its distinctive position in the intelligence complex. Based in Langley, Virginia, the agency employs approximately 20,000 intelligence officers and administrative personnel. Its Intelligence Directorate is divided among eight regional and functional offices. The Operations Directorate, similarly organized along regional and functional lines, oversees covert operations abroad. Other directorates in the CIA focus on science and technology, the security of CIA agents, and administrative matters.

Running the CIA along with the rest of the intelligence complex has proven to be a formidable and often frustrating experience. Former DCI William Colby, for example, complained that he spent more time defending the intelligence agencies from domestic critics than managing them (Colby and Forbath 1978). Although ostensibly "directing" the intelligence complex, the DCI actually controls only the CIA while the military agencies are overseen by the DoD. In budget terms, this means that the director has authority over about 10 percent of the money spent by all the intelligence agencies in recent years. For this reason as well as the immense pressure placed upon the office, turnover among DCIs, with a few notable exceptions, has been rapid.[9]

By the time it turned fifty in 1997, the CIA had become "demoralized, dispirited, and bloated beyond reason" (Alterman 1997, 5). Like their counterparts in the State Department, officials in the CIA complained that they were being ignored in the foreign-policy process by members of the White House staff, particularly the national security adviser. They further complained that the CIA was fighting a losing battle for funds against the other intelligence agencies. Like Secretary of State

---

9. These exceptions include Allen Dulles, who held the DCI job throughout President Eisenhower's two terms in office, and Richard Helms, who served as DCI from 1966 to 1973. More recently, George Tenet kept his job from the Clinton into the Bush administration, resigning prior to the 2004 elections, despite the many intelligence failures surrounding the war on terrorism. Beyond those cases, the tenure of a DCI has averaged just two years.

Colin Powell, CIA director George Tenet sought to revive his agency's morale and stature by improving compensation and providing new and enhanced resources to facilitate the intelligence process.

Intelligence Failures and Scandals

The CIA and other intelligence agencies played vital roles in achieving the central goals for which they were created during the cold war: "containing" communism and contributing to the demise of the Soviet Union. In some instances, including the 1962 Cuban missile crisis, intelligence breakthroughs saved the United States from imminent threats. Accompanying this success, however, has been a variety of problems that have damaged the intelligence complex's credibility. Five problems in particular remain acute.

The first problem involves *operational failures*—intelligence analysts' failures to provide adequate warning of important developments abroad. Among other prominent examples, U.S. presidents were surprised by the strength of anti-American resistance in the 1961 Bay of Pigs crisis, by the overthrow of the shah of Iran and the Soviet invasion of Afghanistan in 1979, and by the entry of India and Pakistan into the nuclear club in 1998 (Auster and Kaplan 1998). Beginning in 2001, George Tenet's CIA suffered four failures: the 9-11 attacks, the inability to capture Osama bin Laden, miscalculation of Iraqi possession of weapons of mass destruction, and the surprisingly strong resistance to the U.S. occupation of Iraq.

The second criticism involves problems of *coordination* among the various agencies within the complex. Such problems have persisted, which may not be surprising given the intricate structure of the intelligence complex, whose separate units stubbornly maintain their independence and closely guard the information they gather. As noted earlier, the failure of intelligence agencies to "connect the dots" prior to 9-11 eliminated any chance of averting the tragedy.

Internal security is a third serious problem within the intelligence complex, particularly since the end of the cold war. Among the most troubling cases was the arrest in 1994 of Aldrich Ames, a career CIA officer who sold military secrets to the Soviet Union and Russia for more than $2 million. Ames compromised dozens of CIA missions; his leaks to Moscow led to the deaths of at least ten Soviet agents secretly working for the United States. The CIA was not alone in failing to maintain internal security. Robert Hansen, an FBI agent, passed more than 6,000 pages of highly classified documents to

A primary object of criticism in the U.S. war on terrorism from 2001 to 2004 was George Tenet, the director of central intelligence. Tenet, who was appointed to the post by President Clinton, fought an uphill battle defending the CIA's record prior to the 9-11 attacks and in gathering intelligence regarding the threat posed by Saddam Hussein's regime in Iraq. Congressional investigators concluded that faulty intelligence contributed to U.S. setbacks in the war on terrorism. Tenet resigned from his post in June 2004, citing "personal reasons."

the Soviet and Russian governments over a twenty-one-year period in return for payments exceeding $1.4 million.

Fourth, the role of intelligence agencies in sponsoring *covert operations* has always been controversial (see Prados 1996). Covert operations, not explicitly mentioned among the CIA's functions when it was created in 1947, were common during the cold war and included agency-backed overthrows of elected leaders in Guatemala, Iran, and Chile.[10] These cases led Congress to restrict covert operations in the 1970s. After September 2001, however, the Bush administration gained renewed congressional support for covert operations to penetrate and destroy terrorist cells in several countries.

Finally, the *politicization of intelligence*—the deliberate manipulation of findings about conditions overseas to promote an administration's foreign-policy preferences—creates additional problems for members of the intelligence community. A common complaint during the cold war was that the CIA and other agencies intentionally exaggerated the threat posed by the Soviet Union to generate domestic support for higher levels of U.S. military spending. The same charges were made during the Vietnam War, when investigators found that the Nixon administration had encouraged biased CIA reports of communist influence in Southeast Asia. More recently, congressional investigators concluded that the Bush administration distorted intelligence regarding the presence of weapons of mass destruction in Iraq, a charge strongly denied by the White House (see U.S. Senate 2004).

Efforts to reform the U.S. intelligence complex in response to these criticisms have made only modest progress. Although Congress imposed reporting provisions for covert operations, presidents retained their authority to launch such operations without legislative consent (see Johnson 1988). In response to the spy scandals of the early 1990s, the Brown Commission (named after its chairman, former secretary of defense Harold Brown) called for a stronger DCI but did not recommend major reforms. Thus when the terrorist attacks of September 2001 prompted new demands for reform, the intelligence complex still looked as it had for decades.

Supporters of the intelligence complex offer two central defenses. First, they claim that the record of U.S. intelligence agencies during and after the cold war has been stronger than generally believed. To former DCI Robert M. Gates (1996, 562), the fact that there were "no significant strategic surprises" late in the cold war owed much to sound intelligence reporting. Second, expectations of intelligence warnings provide a false sense of security. "Good intelligence diminishes surprise, but even the best cannot possibly prevent it altogether. Human behavior is not, and probably never will be, fully predictable" (Andrew 1995, 538).

The Economic Complex

We now turn to the fourth foreign-policy complex, the economic complex. The end of the cold war permitted the U.S. government to shift its foreign-policy

---

10. The CIA conducted more than 900 major covert operations and thousands of smaller ones between 1961 and 1974 (U.S. Senate 1976, 445).

agenda from geopolitics to **geoeconomics**—the interaction of national economies in the world economy. Among other consequences of the cold war's end was the widening support among governments for market-based economies rather than those dominated or strictly controlled by states. The U.S. model of free enterprise and open markets, in short, became a role model of sorts for the post-communist states of Eastern Europe as well as for industrialized states in East Asia, Latin America, and other areas. Economic globalization reinforced the rise of economic affairs on the U.S. foreign-policy agenda, as did the nation's commanding lead in many sectors of the globalized economy.

The heightened attention to its economy was well founded, as the United States enjoyed a spectacular burst of economic growth in the Clinton years. The nation's gross national income (GNI) grew by 50 percent between 1993 and 2000, from $6.6 trillion to $9.9 trillion. Annual economic growth averaged nearly 4 percent during this period, and unemployment was so low (averaging less than 4 percent) that firms suffered from a *shortage* of workers.[11] President Clinton succeeded in improving the competitiveness of U.S. firms as the value of exports increased from $658 billion in 1993 to more than $1.1 trillion in his final year in office. Exports composed a steadily growing share of the nation's economic output during this period, although sales to the huge domestic market continued to account for about 90 percent of GNI. For Clinton, improved fortunes overseas simply complemented his top priority as president—to improve the domestic economy and living standards (Nivola 1997; Stremlau 1994–1995).

Promoting national prosperity, of course, is a primary *intermestic* concern that has international as well as domestic components. Well-organized groups represent the interests of private actors in the federal government, which provides many points of access within the executive and legislative branches. Congress plays a stronger role in economic affairs than in national security, largely by determining the size and shape of the many executive branch departments involved in foreign economic policy. The regulatory powers approved by Congress, in such areas as labor practices, environmental standards, and product safety, affect business activity in the United States and the commercial relations of U.S. firms with their foreign counterparts. Congress also must approve major trade agreements, although it has largely deferred to the executive branch in this area for reasons fully explained in Chapter 11.

Finally, federalism is a major factor in foreign economic policy. American governors and mayors eagerly pursue foreign markets for goods and services produced by their constituents. At the same time, states and cities compete with one another for the attention of foreign-owned firms planning to set up shop in the United States. The outcome of this internal competition has long-lasting implications for American political, as well as economic, relations abroad.

Within the executive branch, various federal agencies, such as the Commerce and Treasury departments, have long engaged in different aspects of economic

---

11. The statistics cited in this section are drawn from the Bureau of Economic Analysis (www.bea.doc.gov/bea) and the U.S. Bureau of Labor Statistics (www.bls.gov).

affairs. The most important institutional change in the economic complex occurred after World War II with the creation of the World Bank and the International Monetary Fund and the signing of the General Agreement on Tariffs and Trade (now the World Trade Organization). These international financial institutions, detailed in Chapter 9, were created in large measure by American officials and thus adopted the market-friendly principles and practices of the U.S. government.

Taken together, these organizations form a highly fragmented economic complex, a structural feature shared by other parts of the federal government (Destler 1994, 132). "No one agency is 'in charge' of foreign trade policy making," Stephen Cohen, Robert Blecker, and Peter Whitney (2003, 113) observed. "Different bureaucratic actors will assume leadership roles depending on the issue at hand and the strength of personal relationships between agency heads and the president's inner circle." Beyond the array of cabinet agencies that play a role in advancing U.S. economic interests overseas (see Table 6.5), two White House-based offices merit special attention: the National Economic Council and the Office of the U.S. Trade Representative.

The National Economic Council

Among Bill Clinton's first acts as president in 1993 was the creation, through executive order, of the National Economic Council (NEC). Like the NSC, its counterpart on security matters, the NEC plays primarily a coordinating role within the White House. Its staff seeks to align the policies of all the agencies in the economic complex and to ensure that those policies are consistent with the president's

Table 6.5 Agencies of Foreign Economic Policy

Agency	Function
Council of Economic Advisers	Provides guidance to the White House regarding foreign-economic policy
Department of Agriculture	Supports efforts by farmers and agricultural firms to sell products overseas
Department of Commerce	Promotes and manages interests of firms doing business overseas
Department of State	Manages day-to-day economic relations with foreign countries
Department of the Treasury	Manages U.S. financial issues such as private investment, monetary policy, and global debt
Federal Reserve Board	Makes decisions regarding the money supply and "prime rate" of interest offered to major borrowers
National Economic Council	Plays a coordinating role with the White House to align policies of all the agencies in the economic complex
National Security Council	Integrates economic issues into its consideration of national security policy
Office of Management and Budget	Manages fiscal policy for the federal government and develops the president's budget proposals for federal spending
Office of the U.S. Trade Representative	Gains access to foreign markets by negotiating bilateral and multilateral trade agreements

goals. The NEC also oversees the implementation of U.S. foreign economic policy, a formidable task given the fragmented nature of the economic complex. Eighteen top officials serve as members of the council. These members include, among others, the president and vice president, the chair of the Council of Economic Advisers, the United States Trade Representative, the director of the Office of Management and Budget, and the secretaries of agriculture, commerce, energy, labor, transportation, and the Treasury.[12]

An assistant to the president for economic policy provides direct guidance to the president on all matters relating to economic policy, foreign and domestic. The first person to take this job, Robert Rubin, left a lucrative position as a Wall Street investment banker to head the start-up NEC. What Rubin gave up in salary he gained in political clout since he held "the keys to the issue Bill Clinton cares most about: fixing the economy" (Ifill 1993, 22). Rubin left his position in 1995 to become secretary of the treasury. His successor, Laura D. Tyson, maintained Rubin's key role as a facilitator rather than policy advocate. Like Rubin, Tyson left after just two years; she was replaced by Gene Sperling, a trusted Clinton ally. Sperling's primary goal in the president's last two years in office was coordinating a response to the economic crisis in East Asia, which quickly spread to Russia, western Europe, and Latin America before stalling the economic expansion in the United States.

After taking office in January 2001, President Bush appointed Lawrence B. Lindsey as economic policy adviser. Lindsey, who served as an aide to Bush's father and then as a governor of the Federal Reserve Board, was the primary architect of the sweeping tax cuts approved by Congress later that year. With the economy slowing and the United States plunged into the war on terrorism, Lindsey's focus shifted to devising strategies for economic recovery. Continued slow growth in 2002, however, prompted Bush in December to fire Lindsey, who was replaced by Stephen Friedman. The firing of Lindsey and Treasury Secretary Paul O'Neill were largely symbolic moves given the very limited impact either man could have had on U.S. economic growth. Nevertheless, Bush's action reassured the public, along with the economic markets, that the president was "serious" about restoring economic growth.

The Office of the U.S. Trade Representative

Concern about U.S. competitiveness in overseas trade markets has been a historical constant in the nation's history. After World War II, this concern led to the creation of an ever-widening network of executive branch agencies involved in trade promotion. As power over all facets of foreign policy became more centralized within the White House, so did the management of U.S. trade, one of the most vital and divisive areas of foreign economic policy (see Chapter 11). In 1962,

---

12. Two deputy assistants serve on the NEC as specialists on domestic and foreign economic policy, respectively. In addition, a team of "special assistants" provides guidance on such issues as agriculture, energy, and global financial markets.

Congress took a big step in this direction with creation of the Office of the United States Trade Representative (USTR), whose primary task is gaining access to foreign markets by negotiating bilateral and multilateral trade agreements.

In contrast to other agencies in the economic complex, which uphold the nation's strong devotion to open markets at home and overseas, the USTR draws much of its political support from advocates of **trade protectionism** (Dryden 1995). The trade representative, who holds the rank of ambassador and sits on the president's cabinet, promotes the interests of producers who want to see the U.S. market closed to foreign countries that discriminate against their goods. One of the most outspoken persons to hold this position, Mickey Kantor, openly complained during the Clinton years about the nation's chronic trade imbalance with Japan, whose government had long protected its domestic market from American goods while flooding the United States with Japanese exports.

Under George W. Bush, USTR Robert Zoellick adopted an even tougher trade posture. His support of higher tariffs on imported steel and massive subsidies for American farmers angered trading partners of the United States while enhancing the president's standing among influential interest groups (and voting blocs) at home. Bush subsequently fell out of favor with steel producers when he reversed his earlier protections of the steel industry, largely in response to threats of economic sanctions by the European Union and the WTO.

These developments demonstrate the highly *political* nature of foreign economic policy. For all of the rhetoric regarding the merits of private enterprise, U.S. leaders recognize the inescapable role of government. Further complicating matters is the executive branch constant engagement in a "two-level game" (Putnam 1988) that involves simultaneous bargaining with foreign governments and domestic stakeholders. The terms of foreign trade agreements, for example, must be reconciled in these talks with needs and demands of U.S. firms, workers, and consumers. More broadly, economic-policy makers must make frequent compromises between the long-term gains of economic globalization—more and larger markets engaged in market-based commerce—and the short-term costs, including the "exporting" of U.S. jobs to lower-wage production centers overseas. How these compromises are made, and how the winners and losers of economic agreements respond to them, affects not only the performance of the U.S. economy but also the fate of the political actors involved in the process.

Conclusion

As we have seen, the governing institutions of U.S. foreign policy exhibit two entrenched but contradictory patterns: the *centralization* of authority within the White House and the *fragmentation* of control across a far-flung bureaucracy. From managing military crises to negotiating trade deals, presidents and their advisers have sought, and have generally been granted, greater authority to conduct foreign policy. This authority has consequently shifted within the executive branch from the State Department and other federal agencies to the White House.

At the same time, the size, scope, and intricacy of the foreign-policy complexes described in this chapter have steadily increased since the current structure was devised after World War II. In sum, national-security concerns reinforce *centripetal forces* toward the center of power over U.S. foreign policy while institutional momentum produces *centrifugal forces* away from the center.

In implementing foreign policies, bureaucrats maintain their places on the front lines of the policy process and continue to determine, in large measure, the success or failure of policy initiatives adopted by the president and Congress. Yet while actively pursuing more personnel and greater influence, agencies have resisted the sweeping changes in their organizational structures and missions long advocated by critics inside and outside the U.S. government. Despite its name, the Central Intelligence Agency is hardly "central" to the intelligence process given the forbidding walls that separate the agency from its counterparts. The National Security Council, meanwhile, rarely meets formally as originally planned. Instead, the national security adviser's role extends beyond that of a neutral coordinator to one of policy development and public advocacy, supported by an NSC staff that has grown considerably since the end of the cold war.

Similarly, the secretary of defense continues to struggle in overcoming rivalries among the armed services and public disputes over funding, arms programs, and missions. Only the September 11 terrorist attacks and subsequent arms buildup prevented the secretary of defense from succumbing to pressure from the armed services and giving up on military transformation. A truly unified military as envisioned in the 1947 National Security Act remains a distant and remote possibility. "The conspicuous silence of defense experts on this issue at the end of the cold war can only be understood as proof of the institutionalized clout that the separate services had acquired over the previous five decades" (Stuart 2003, 305).

These tensions between centralization and fragmentation reflect the paradox of world power wielded by the United States today. The sources of these tensions—unprecedented global clout, a dynamic civil society, and a political system designed to hinder foreign-policy making—are likely to become even more pronounced in the years to come. How these tensions are reconciled, therefore, will have long-lasting implications for the coherence, consistency, and outcomes of U.S. foreign policy.

Key Terms

base force proposal, p. 172

bottom-up review, p. 173

civil-military relations,
p. 157

clientitis, p. 164

congressional deference,
p. 153

counterintelligence, p. 179

covert operations, p. 179

diplomacy, p. 160

finished intelligence, p. 178

foreign service officers,
p. 162

geoeconomics, p. 182

Goldwater-Nichols Act,
p. 172

Homeland Security
Council, p. 174

human intelligence
(HUMINT), p. 178

intelligence cycle, p. 178

interservice rivalry, p. 157

national security adviser,
p. 168

organizational culture,
p. 156

organizational expertise,
p. 154

presidential limitations,
p. 154

public diplomacy, p. 165

quadrennial defense review,
p. 173

raw intelligence, p. 178

revolution in military
affairs, p. 173

shadow government, p. 170

technical intelligence
(TECHINT), p. 178

trade protectionism, p. 185

Internet References

The **Center on Budget and Policy Priorities** (www.cbpp.org) focuses on federal and state budget priorities, including research on taxes and spending. Projects of interest deal with analysis of military spending, specific foreign-policy spending, and tax burdens for national security.

The **Central Intelligence Agency** (www.cia.gov) operates a Web site that provides detailed information about the CIA's mission as well as about global developments. The *CIA World Factbook,* available online, provides comprehensive political, economic, military, and other data regarding all nation-states.

The Congressional Research Service's **CRS Reports** (fpc.state.gov//c4763.htm; www.fas.org/irp/crs; and www.fas.org/man/crs), from the research arm of Congress, provide briefings on specific policy issues and include background information, chronologies, bibliographic references, and budget statistics. CRS reports on particular topics are often updated each year. The CRS itself does not make its reports available online, but several other sites post them, including the sites listed above. CRS reports currently posted include detailed information on terrorism, intelligence policy, international trade, foreign aid, global finance, arms trade and control, missile defense, and energy policy; bilateral reports such as those on U.S.-Russian and U.S.-Israeli relations are also posted.

The **Department of Defense** (www.defenselink.mil) is vested with military and security responsibilities for the Untied States and many countries around the globe. This site provides access to defense-related activities, specific programs, information regarding the military and its past operations, and speeches and transcripts from defense officials. Included also are links to agencies within the Defense Department as well as a list of

continues

Internet References *(continued)*

online publications such as the defense budget, *Defense Almanac,* and reports on capabilities and security measures.

The newest cabinet agency, the **Department of Homeland Security** (www.dhs.gov), provides consistent updates on the war on terrorism as well as missions to contain and combat domestic terrorism. The site also has information on immigration, border controls, and policies related to emergency actions. Speeches, documents, and research links are provided as well.

The **Department of State** (www.state.gov) is vested with many aspects of diplomacy, including foreign aid, peace building, democratization, and disease and poverty prevention, as well as other aspects of the U.S. foreign-policy process. The State Department's Web site provides speeches, policy descriptions, and issue explanations for those studying U.S. foreign policy.

The **Government Accountability Office** (www.gao.gov) evaluates and reports on congressional and presidential decision making, budgets, and policies. Included on its Web site are audits, evaluations, and policy analysis reports regarding intergovernmental relations and policy decisions. Of specific interest to researchers are published reports on long-term policy decisions such as the costs and budget information for the war on terrorism, the Iraqi war, and homeland security operations.

The **Office of Management and Budget** (www.whitehouse.gov/omb) presents budget documents and responsibilities for all federally funded departments and agencies. Information regarding particular missions for each organization, personnel statistics, and yearly funding decisions are charted and available.

The Web site for the **Office of the United States Trade Representative** (www.ustr.gov) provides links and access to bilateral and multilateral trade data and events. Information regarding NAFTA, the WTO, and Free Trade negotiations is particularly helpful for research. Speeches, testimony, trade legislation, and daily updates on international trade are also hosted on this page.

The **United States Agency for International Development** (www.usaid.gov) provides information and statistics regarding U.S. foreign and military aid to other countries. Information on humanitarian efforts and specific mission programs to other countries is included on the site. Other specific research topics are agriculture, democratization, global health, and humanitarian mission projects.

The Web site for the **United States Intelligence Community** (www.intelligence.gov) provides information on the organization of all U.S. intelligence agencies and their relationships toward each other and the government as a whole. Meetings and special report findings regarding national and international intelligence are reported and summarized on this site, the scope of which is broader than the CIA Web site described on the previous page.

7

Public Opinion and Mass Communications

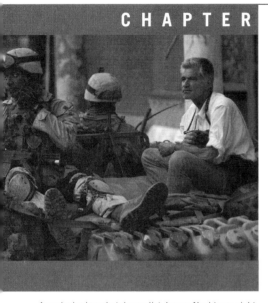

Award-winning photojournalist James Nachtwey, right, accompanies U.S. troops on a patrol through downtown Baghdad in April 2003. Hundreds of journalists were "embedded" within the U.S.-led coalition as it invaded Iraq weeks earlier. Such close proximity to the action allowed journalists to provide dramatic, instantaneous war coverage. In doing so, the "embeds" were generally positive and uncritical of the mission, which pleased the Pentagon. Nachtwey was wounded months later when the Humvee in which he was riding was struck by a grenade.

The previous section of this book focused on the key state actors engaged in the formulation and conduct of U.S. foreign policy. Our attention in this section shifts to the "outside-in" forces—private citizens, the news media, interest groups, and intergovernmental organizations—that seek to influence the foreign-policy process from many vantage points within the United States and abroad. Trends in world politics increase the importance of this outside-in dimension, which transcends common distinctions between domestic and foreign policy, public and private interaction, and national and global interests.

Like other democracies, the United States features a large and vibrant civil society composed of individual citizens, business firms, churches, news organizations, and other groups. Although their interests vary widely, they share a strong desire to shape public policy of all kinds, including foreign policy. In disbursing the powers of the federal government and otherwise constraining state powers at all levels of governance, early U.S. leaders hoped to mobilize the public as a hedge against tyranny at home and "adventurism" abroad.

Citizens and interest groups have more influence over the U.S. government than do general publics in most other countries, including many democracies. As Stephen Krasner (1978) observed, the United States features a relatively "small state" that is frequently overshadowed by a "large society." Business firms have been consulted on matters of U.S. foreign economic policy throughout the nation's history. Ethnic and religious groups have routinely pressured legislators and the

White House to provide political, economic, and often military support to their homelands. More generally, elected officials know that their careers depend upon being sensitive to the demands of public opinion. A rapidly globalizing news media, meanwhile, provides the vital linkage between Americans and the world around them.

Paradoxically, while the public is granted widespread access to the foreign-policy process, U.S. citizens tend to be poorly informed about the world around them. Although most Americans believe the nation should play an active role in world politics (Sobel 2001), they commonly focus their energies on local and state problems unless the United States is directly threatened with, or involved in, an international crisis or major military conflict. For instance, as is typical when the country is enjoying peace and prosperity, U.S. public interest in foreign affairs declined in the 1990s, after the cold war ended. The September 2001 terrorist attacks disrupted this period of complacency, which had been shared by a federal government that felt immune from threats in a "unipolar" world.

Cultural detachment from the "outside world" has a long tradition in the United States, reflecting the nation's geographic distance from other major powers as well as an "exceptional" national identity deeply rooted in U.S. political culture (see Chapter 1). Throughout their history, Americans have displayed a surprising lack of knowledge about global events that has held constant despite the United States' emergence as the world's predominant power—and despite the nation's pervasive overseas presence (see Table 7.1). The U.S. educational system has played a role in this problem. In nationwide tests conducted in 2001, less than a quarter of high school students demonstrated proficiency in history and geography, two areas consistently neglected in public schools (U.S. Department of Education 2002).

The relationship between public opinion and public policy in the United States is complex. Political leaders do not passively await the public's verdict regarding their actions. Instead, they thoroughly *gauge* citizens' attitudes in advance and base their decisions, at least in part, on the likely response. In this respect, public opinion plays the constructive role envisioned by democratic theorists—that of ensuring that policy choices reflect public preferences. Yet political leaders also *manipulate* public opinion in several ways: by focusing on particular issues in speeches and interviews, by strategically timing their actions to gain political advan-

Table 7.1 U.S. Public Knowledge about World Affairs: Nationwide Survey Results, 1942–1994

Question Topic (Survey Year)	Percentage Able to Answer
U.S. secretary of state (1958)	57%
India a British colony (1942)	51
Role of foreign aid (1958)	48
President of Russia (1994)	47
Soviet Union not in NATO (1964)	41
Purpose of NATO (1988)	40
President of France (1986)	34
Two signatories of SALT (1979)	30
Serb genocide in Bosnia (1994)	27
Location of Persian Gulf (1988)	25
U.S. national security adviser (1977)	17
Location of Common Market (1961)	13
Secretary general of UN (1953)	10
President of Mexico (1991)	3

SOURCE: Michael X. Delli Carpini and Scott Keeter, *What Americans Know about Politics and Why It Matters* (New Haven: Yale University Press, 1996), Chap. 2.

tage, and by creatively interpreting (or "spinning") developments overseas. Policy makers, well aware of the general population's lack of knowledge about most foreign-policy problems, can expect their depictions of friends and foes to be readily accepted. This tactic, a central element of constructivist theory (see Chapter 3), was used to great effect by President George W. Bush, whose portrayal of an "axis of evil" laid the moral foundation for the widening war on terrorism.

These efforts to manipulate public opinion are not unique to the current period. As Seymour M. Lipset (1966, 20) noted four decades ago, the president "makes opinion, he does not follow it. The polls tell him how good a politician he is." Such efforts have become more refined in recent years with the emergence of more sophisticated polling techniques, the use of focus groups, and new outlets of mass communication, including the Internet. A **public relations presidency** exists today as presidents "act in deliberate ways to achieve heightened popularity in the polls and in elections" (Brace and Hinckley 1993, 383). The ability of presidents to manipulate public opinion is especially strong in foreign policy given their high profile and dominant powers in this area and given Americans' general preoccupation with domestic affairs.

Political analysts generally believe that U.S. citizens, with regard to their opinions and impact on foreign policy, can be divided into three categories. The first and largest group, the **mass public,** is neither very informed nor very interested in foreign-policy issues and thus has little direct impact on the policy process. The second group, the **attentive public,** pays closer attention to foreign-policy issues and occasionally attempts to influence the government through letter-writing campaigns and support for interest groups. The smallest group, the **foreign-policy elite,** has both the interest and the means to influence U.S. foreign policy directly by holding powerful positions within the government, private industry, or interest groups. The inverse relationship between the size and the clout of each group raises questions about the democratic formulation and conduct of U.S. foreign policy, the subject of the following section.

Democracy and the Paradox of World Power

Earlier chapters of this book highlight the institutional aspects of democratic rule: constitutionalism, the separation of powers, and the dispersion of bureaucratic control. Of equal importance is the active participation of civil society in a democracy. From its origins, the U.S. government has not only expected, but also rewarded, individuals and groups who insert themselves into the policy process, expressing their wishes to policy makers. In the democratic model, elected leaders serve as servants, rather than masters, of the private citizens who allowed those leaders to take power. For this reason, "constituent service" must be viewed as an essential responsibility of elected officials.

Civil society serves many functions in the foreign-policy process, among them openness and oversight. Public engagement on foreign-policy issues enhances the openness, or transparency, of decision making. Like Congress, the news media and nongovernmental organizations (NGOs) assume oversight roles by monitoring government actions abroad and informing the public about foreign-policy issues and developments.

Fundamental tensions exist, however, between democratic governance and foreign policy. Short-term electoral pressures divert the judgment of policy makers and legislators from long-term concerns, including transnational problems that affect the "global commons" (see Chapter 12). Economic pressures also impair democratic decision making, particularly in an era of burgeoning world trade, favor-seeking corporate lobbyists, and virtually constant, media-driven political campaigns. Openness can be a liability in a secretive and competitive interstate system in which knowledge equals power. The political, economic, and social by-products of modern democracy, then, are central to the paradox of world power afflicting the foreign policies of all countries that have adopted the U.S. model of a constrained, internally fragmented state and a large, vigorous society. The paradox is magnified for the United States itself, which retains such a vast reservoir of world power that its foreign-policy decisions profoundly affect other countries and the overall climate of world politics.

Rival Views of Political Leadership

Political theorists have long disagreed about the public's ideal role in shaping policy. Two general models of political representation capture this schism in democratic governance. The **delegate model** holds that elected officials should reflect the general public's preferences on a given issue, making decisions based on the majority view. In short, officials should act as they believe their "constituents should want" (Pitkin 1967, 147) and not allow their personal preferences to enter into the equation. Abraham Lincoln (quoted in Foyle 1999, 3) expressed this position in 1848 when he declared as the "primary, the cardinal, the one great living principle of all democratic representative government—the principle that the representative is bound to carry out the known will of his constituents."

By contrast, the **trustee model** provides for greater freedom of thought and maneuver by the elected official than the delegate model. This more conservative view is most often associated with Edmund Burke, eighteenth-century British statesman and political theorist, who did not consider the mass public qualified to make informed judgments about public policy. Burke, living in an era of widespread illiteracy and ignorance, argued that representatives should follow their own, more "enlightened" beliefs regarding what is best for the *body politic*. To Burke (quoted in Hofman and Levack 1949, 115), "Your representative owes you not his industry only, but his judgment; and he betrays, instead of serving you, if he sacrifices it to your opinion."

This historic debate about the role of political leadership in democratic governance relates directly to the two primary bodies of international relations theory, realism and liberalism (see Chapter 3). Recall that realists have a pessimistic view about world politics and the prospects for peaceful cooperation. They base this pessimism, in part, on a bleak assessment of human nature, which they believe to be plagued by momentary passions, ignorance, and hostility toward others. For this reason, realists cast a skeptical eye on public opinion as a reliable guide to foreign policy. "The government is the leader of public opinion, not its slave," observed Hans Morgenthau (1967, 547–548), a prominent realist and proponent of the trustee model. "Especially when foreign policy is conducted under conditions of democratic control and is inspired by the crusading zeal of a political religion, statesmen are always tempted to sacrifice the requirements of good foreign policy to the applause of the masses."

To the realist, citizens may be competent to participate in matters of local governance, such as education, which closely concern their day-to-day lives. Most of them are not competent to do so in foreign-policy matters, however, which are more removed from daily life, as well as generally more complex, than local issues. Furthermore, foreign-policy makers rely upon classified information that by necessity gives them a more informed view about the problems being faced and alternative solutions. The need for quick and decisive action also works against a strong public role in the foreign-policy process.

Liberal theories of world politics provide a more positive view of the public's role in foreign policy. During the Enlightenment era, liberal European theorists such as Jeremy Bentham, Immanuel Kant, and John Jacques Rousseau had great confidence in the reason and judgment of the mass public, whose views of foreign as well as domestic affairs, they believed, should be followed closely by elected leaders. In modern times, Woodrow Wilson is most closely associated with the liberal view and its application to U.S. foreign policy. During World War I, Wilson (quoted in Carr 1939, 32–33) argued that private citizens, rather than political leaders, had the stronger grasp of the war's true meaning:

> It is the peculiarity of this great war that, while statesmen have seemed to cast about for definitions of their purpose and have sometimes seemed to shift their ground and their point of view, the thought of the mass of men, whom statesmen are supposed to instruct and lead, has grown more and more unclouded, more and more certain of what it is they are fighting for. National purposes have fallen more and more into the background; and the common purpose of enlightened mankind has taken their place. . . . That is why I have said that this is a people's war, not a statesman's.

This debate over the public's role in the governance of democracies continues today. In going to war against Iraq in 2003, President Bush acted contrary to public-opinion polls opposing military action in the absence of widespread support from U.S. allies and the UN Security Council. His rationale—that decisive leadership is required that may not always be popular—placed Bush squarely in the trustee camp. For those favoring the delegate model, the problems that subsequently plagued the U.S. occupation of Iraq reinforced their position that the "general will" of American citizens must be heard and heeded.

Mood Swings or Pragmatism?

The penchant of U.S. citizens to look inward is nothing new. When French sociologist Alexis de Tocqueville toured the United States in the early 1830s, he found

Americans to be far less interested in public affairs than their European counterparts. "Intent only on getting rich, they do not notice the close connection between private fortunes and the general prosperity. They find it a tiresome inconvenience to exercise political rights which distract them from industry" (de Tocqueville [1835] 1988, 540).

Scholars in the early twentieth century echoed de Tocqueville's concerns regarding the public's role in U.S. public affairs. Walter Lippmann (1922), a prominent journalist and social commentator, faulted Americans for ignoring German expansionism in Europe until it threatened their own country and forced the United States' entry into World War I. The same criticism came after World War II, when popular commentators and prominent scholars cited the U.S. public's apathy during the interwar period as a contributing factor in the rise of fascist regimes in Europe and Asia (see Almond 1950; Kriesberg 1949; and Bailey 1948).

Gabriel Almond's 1950 book, *The American People and Foreign Policy*, provided a dim view of the connection between public attitudes and U.S. foreign policy. Drawing on survey data provided by the newly founded Gallup Organization, Almond (71) complained that Americans generally felt so secure at home that "foreign policy, save in moments of grave crisis, has to labor under a handicap; it has to shout loudly to be heard even a little." Making matters worse, he argued, were the "mood swings" in public opinion that led to constantly shifting demands for global activism and withdrawal.[1]

The similarity of this view with Lippmann's produced what became known as the **Almond-Lippmann consensus** (Holsti 1992), which is based on three assumptions. First, public opinion is *volatile,* shifting erratically in response to the most recent developments. Mass beliefs early in the twentieth century were "too pacifist in peace and too bellicose in war, too neutralist or appeasing in negotiations or too intransigent" (Lippmann 1955, 20). Second, public opinion is *incoherent,* lacking an organized or consistent structure to such an extent that the views of U.S. citizens could best be described as "nonattitudes" (Converse 1964). Finally, public opinion is *irrelevant* to the policy-making process. Political leaders ignore public opinion since most Americans can neither "understand nor influence the very events upon which their lives and happiness are known to depend" (Kris and Leites 1947, 393).

More recent research challenges this gloomy assessment, detecting greater consistency and coherence in mass attitudes and greater concern among decision makers for public opinion than the early pessimists allowed. Surveys conducted since 1974 by the Chicago Council on Foreign Relations register ongoing support among the public, as well as foreign-policy elites, for active U.S. participation in foreign affairs (see Table 7.2). Interestingly, elites tend to favor multilateral cooperation, while private citizens are more likely to prefer unilateral action.[2] Although

---

1. See Holmes (1985) and Klingberg (1983) for subsequent analyses of "mood swings" in U.S. public opinion.

2. Among foreign-policy issues, those of greatest concern to the general public are the ones that concern Americans' economic fortunes, including the protection of U.S. jobs against foreign competition, the reduction of the U.S. trade deficit, and the control of immigration (Page and Barabas 2000).

some segments of the public consider themselves to be "isolationist," most favor an internationalist foreign policy. The only question among these citizens late in the cold war was whether the United States should pursue a policy of "militant" or "cooperative" internationalism (Wittkopf 1990).

Other surveys also contradict the notion of incoherent public opinion. While test scores and survey research find the public to be generally ill-informed, citizens seem to approach foreign-policy problems with deeply held principles, values, and standards of evaluation (Graber 2002). Public opposition to the Korean and Vietnam wars, for example, corresponded logically to growing U.S. casualties in each conflict (Mueller 1973; 1970). In other cases, Americans responded pragmatically to perceived excesses in presidential behavior. Whereas the "dovish" foreign policies of Jimmy Carter prompted public calls for a more aggressive response to Soviet aggression, Ronald Reagan's "hawkish" approach led to public appeals for moderation (Nincic 1988). Both presidents, it should be noted, altered their approaches to foreign policy in part because of public dissatisfaction.

From this perspective, Americans do not suffer from "mood swings" but instead react in a reasoned and predictable manner to problems facing the United States (Mayer 1992). Unless they are experts in world politics, private citizens evaluate a problem on the basis of their underlying beliefs and values (Page and Shapiro 1992). During the cold war, Americans evaluated possible military interventions on a case-by-case basis rather than supporting or opposing the use of force across the board (Jentleson 1992; see also Peffley and Hurwitz 1992).

The same can be said for public opinion since the cold war. One of the public's core beliefs—that U.S. power should be applied only to repel clear threats to vital national interests—produced support for military intervention in some cases (such as the Persian Gulf War and Afghanistan) and calls for restraint in others (such as Rwanda, the former Yugoslavia, and Iraq). Support for interventions, once underway, has hinged largely on public assessments on whether the missions would ultimately succeed or fail (Kull and Ramsay 2001). Fluctuations in public opinion thus have more to do with the *context* of foreign-policy problems than with the general population's failure to understand them.

Demographic differences within the general public regarding foreign policy should also be noted. According to Holsti (1996, Chap. 5), support for U.S. internationalism is generally strongest among affluent Americans with higher levels of education. While the "gender gap" between men and women has closed in recent years, men are still more inclined than women to favor military interventions and to downplay nonmilitary problems such as environmental decay and narcotics trafficking. Citizens in the South and western mountain states align themselves

Table 7.2 Support for Active U.S. Participation in World Affairs

	Percentage of Support	
	Public	Elites/Leaders
1974	74%	99%
1978	67	99
1982	61	99
1986	70	99
1990	69	98
1994	69	99
1998	68	97
2000	70	98

SOURCE: Chicago Council on Foreign Relations, "Worldviews 2002: American Public Opinion and Foreign Policy" (2002), www.worldviews.org/detailreports/usreport/index.htm.

Point/Counterpoint
MASTERS VS. PAWNS OF U.S. FOREIGN POLICY

A primary and enduring debate regarding public opinion and U.S. foreign policy involves the general public's fitness to guide political leaders in managing relations with other countries. To skeptics such as political scientist Gabriel Almond, Americans tend to be well informed only about immediate concerns. "But on questions of a remote nature, such as foreign policy, they tend to react in more undifferentiated ways, with formless and plastic moods which undergo frequent alteration in response to changes in events," Almond wrote in 1950. "The characteristic response to questions of foreign policy is one of indifference. A foreign policy crisis . . . may transform indifference to vague apprehension, to fatalism, to anger; but the reaction is still a mood, a superficial and fluctuating response."

According to political scientist Bruce Jentleson, more recent studies have contradicted "the traditional view of the public as boorish, overreactive, and generally the bane of those who would pursue an effective foreign policy." Citizens are not easily manipulated by presidents, these studies suggest, and citizens are able to distinguish between vital U.S. interests worth defending and nonvital interests that should not be pursued at the cost of American lives. "It is difficult to explain much of the foreign policy behavior of the United States during the mid- to late-1970s," political scientist Eugene Wittkopf has observed, "without some sense of the constraining forces of the Vietnam Syndrome that the Ford and Carter administrations must surely have perceived."

Nonetheless, the debate over public opinion continues today. Surveys conducted in 2003–2004 revealed widespread public misperceptions regarding the U.S. invasion of Iraq, including the view that Saddam Hussein had been an accomplice in the 9-11 terrorist attacks. These erroneous views proved remarkably persistent despite a steady stream of evidence to the contrary. As Almond predicted, U.S. leaders continue to exploit gaps in public attentiveness to foreign affairs and pursue their own course in foreign policy, knowing that citizens will follow their lead.

Sources: Gabriel Almond, The American People and Foreign Policy *(New York: Harcourt, Brace, 1950), 53; Bruce W. Jentleson, "The Pretty Prudent Public: Post Post-Vietnam American Opinion on the Use of Military Force,"* International Studies Quarterly *36 (March 1992), 71; and Eugene R. Wittkopf,* Faces of Internationalism: Public Opinion and U.S. Foreign Policy *(Durham, N.C.: Duke University Press, 1990), 219.*

more closely with the Republican Party on foreign-policy issues, including opposition to UN peacekeeping and support for free trade, than their northeastern and West Coast counterparts (Trubowitz 1992).

Among foreign-policy elites, recent survey findings reveal that those with military experience and those without have "systematically different opinions on whether and how to use force" (Feaver and Gelpi 2004, 184). Civilian decision makers with no service background are more inclined than their military counterparts (including veterans) to use force while also being more likely to favor *limited* uses of that force. More sensitive to the prospect of casualties in their ranks than such civilian officials, the military decision makers usually favor armed interventions only if concrete national interests are at stake and the government is committed to using overwhelming force. The Bush administration's deliberations on the U.S. invasion of Iraq illustrate these findings. Nonveterans such as Vice President Dick Cheney and Secretary of Defense Donald Rumsfeld favored the invasion more strongly than did veterans such as Secretary of State Colin Powell as well as leaders of the uniformed armed services.

Finally, the Almond-Lippmann assumption that public opinion is irrelevant in the policy process is contradicted by elected officials' vigorous efforts to gauge and manipulate that opinion in recent years. All presidents since John Kennedy have created elaborate polling operations within the White House to guide their decisions in foreign and domestic policy (see Jacobs and Shapiro 1995). In the 1990s, Bill Clinton was so concerned about public opinion that he shaped the nation's military strategy in Bosnia and Kosovo around the need to maintain support for both interventions (Stephanopoulos 1999). The growing reliance of presidents on public diplomacy, described in the previous chapter, further demonstrates the relevance of public opinion—even to "trustees" prone to override majority preferences.

Beyond the citizenry's judgments regarding specific problems, the foreign-policy behavior of U.S. leaders may be constrained by **latent public opinion** or "ingrained sets of values, criteria for judgment, attitudes, preferences, [and] dislikes" (Key 1964, 26). These unstated, but deeply held, views of private citizens narrow the options available to leaders (Stimson 1991). Potential actions "likely to generate widespread public opposition are dismissed from active consideration" (Powlick and Katz 1998, 44). Latent public opinion also has relevance because it forms the basis of citizens' judgments about specific policy problems and may be "activated" once these problems become severe. As we will explore further below, internal differences within presidential administrations, once exposed by the news media, often trigger public opposition to foreign policies that otherwise might have been avoided.

The Public Opinion Nexus

As we have seen, public opinion plays a crucial role in democratic nations, whose citizens decide through their votes who will lead them in times of war and peace. Politicians clearly recognize this central fact of democratic governance and know their survival relies upon gaining and maintaining the public's confidence. Such support provides a variety of secondary benefits as well. Aside from their improved prospects for reelection, popular presidents have generally enjoyed a more favorable partisan balance of power in Congress (Marra and Ostrom 1989). They have also been more successful in achieving the goals of their major policy initiatives (Rivers and Rose 1985).

American foreign-policy goals are no exception. Indeed, the success or failure of presidents, who alone represent "all the people," often hinges on public reactions to events overseas and how the White House manages them. For example, the failure of Woodrow Wilson to enlist public support for his activist postwar agenda led to his political downfall. Since 1945, the ebbs and flows of public support for U.S. foreign policy have determined not only the political fates of presidents but also the goals, tactics, and outcomes of their policies. Harry Truman and Lyndon Johnson watched their presidencies collapse under the weight of foreign entanglements in Korea and Vietnam, respectively, a lesson clearly apparent to George W. Bush as the Iraq occupation bogged down in 2004.

Consensus and Discord during the Cold War

After World War II, President Truman faced a major policy problem: sustaining public support for an assertive foreign policy that matched the nation's military, economic, and political predominance. With peace, Americans had demanded, and received from Congress, sharp cutbacks in military spending, which dropped from $83 billion in 1945 to less than $10 billion in 1948 (U.S. Office of Management and Budget 2002, 44).[3] Yet Truman felt the United States should be actively engaged overseas in restoring political stability and economic growth. The onset of the cold war in the late 1940s gave Truman further impetus to shake the public out of its customary shift toward postwar disengagement. The start of the Korean War solidified the containment consensus that would propel U.S. foreign policy over the next two decades (Yergin 1977).

Public support encouraged Presidents Eisenhower and Kennedy to continue Truman's military buildup and focus on anticommunism. Along with most members of Congress, the public supported Lyndon Johnson's early deployments of U.S. troops to Vietnam (Bardes 1997, 157). This support continued until the 1968 Tet offensive revealed that the United States would not, as Johnson had promised, soon win the war. Opposition mounted as Richard Nixon instituted a lottery for drafting Americans into the armed services. By May 1970, the month in which National Guard troops killed four students at Kent State University during an antiwar demonstration, a majority of the public considered their nation's involvement in Vietnam a mistake. Controversy over U.S. covert operations, revelations of CIA abuses against domestic opponents, and a prolonged economic downturn contributed further to the Vietnam syndrome, a generalized aversion to U.S. military activism (Holsti and Rosenau 1979).

In this respect, Jimmy Carter followed, rather than created, the national sentiment that identified human rights as a central pillar of U.S. foreign policy in the late 1970s. By the end of Carter's term, however, a combination of overseas devel-

---

3. Defense spending between 1945 and 1948 fell from 90 percent of overall federal spending to 31 percent.

Vietnamese children flee in terror from a napalm attack by the United States in June 1972. The nude girl in the center, nine-year-old Kim Phuc, had stripped off her burning clothes after the attack. Her brother, Phan Thanh Tam (left), lost an eye due to the effect of the napalm, a chemical defoliant used widely by the U.S. Air Force in an attempt to locate military targets. Behind the children are soldiers from the South Vietnamese army. This and other photographs fueled public opposition to the war and eventual U.S. withdrawal from Vietnam.

opments and public pressure forced the president to increase military spending and adopt a more confrontational foreign policy. The revival of cold war tensions led to the 1980 election of Ronald Reagan, who hailed the Vietnam War as a "noble effort" and promised to rid the public and the government of the Vietnam syndrome. The spiraling arms race of the early 1980s, however, spawned a new generation of public protests and a "nuclear freeze" movement in the United States and Europe. Failing to generate public or congressional support for U.S. intervention in Central America, the Reagan administration turned to covert operations that ultimately produced the Iran-contra scandal.

President George H. W. Bush, succeeding Reagan in 1989, inherited both a favorable international climate that accompanied the cold war's approaching end and the broad public approval that went with it. Bush declared the Vietnam syndrome a thing of the past at the time of the Persian Gulf War, which featured the largest deployment of U.S. troops since Vietnam. Ironically, Bush's preoccupation with foreign affairs proved his undoing after the war, when a recession at home prompted challenges in 1992 from Bill Clinton and Ross Perot, an independent candidate for president. Perot, drawing most of his votes from disillusioned Republicans, effectively handed the White House to Clinton, who received only 38 percent of the votes cast.

Public Opinion in the 1990s

The end of the cold war brought about new patterns in public opinion, ones that reflected the demise of superpower tensions and birth of U.S. predominance among the great powers. Considerable ambivalence among the public and government leaders regarding U.S. foreign policy surrounded these new dynamics. This uncertainty continued throughout the decade, as no single foreign-policy issue dominated the public's attention or played a decisive role in national elections (see Posen and Ross 1996/1997). Surveys in the early 1990s clearly demonstrated that most Americans wanted their government to pay more attention to domestic problems. By 1998, in the midst of an economic boom at home and no major perceived threats abroad, Americans generally felt little concern about foreign policy. When asked in a prominent survey what was "the biggest foreign-policy problem facing the country," the most common response was, "Don't know" (see Table 7.3).

Though public-opinion surveys revealed a low regard for his foreign policy performance, Clinton still received the highest approval ratings among the ten postwar presidents. This was due in part to his high sensitivity to the ebbs and flows of public opinion. Initially committed to completing the U.S. military intervention in Somalia, he quickly pulled the plug on the mission after U.S. troops were killed in October 1993. Similarly, he withdrew U.S. forces from Haiti after they confronted a hostile band of rebels in the nation's capital. From Clinton's perspective, such foreign-policy problems could not be allowed to interfere with his primary goal as president—reviving the nation's economic output and competitiveness in markets abroad. While Clinton identified the "enlargement" of global democracy as a top foreign-policy goal, given the limited interest of the public and Congress, he did not vigorously pursue this goal.

Recognizing a lack of public support for military intervention in the former Yugoslavia, Clinton avoided large-scale intervention in Bosnia-Herzegovina despite his stated concerns about "ethnic cleansing" in the region. In 1999, public and congressional opposition to U.S. involvement in Kosovo led the president to adopt a "zero-tolerance" policy for American casualties, which limited NATO's military role to high-altitude bombings of military targets and the Yugoslav capi-

Table 7.3 Shifting Public Concerns, 1998 and 2002

Survey Question	1998	2002
"What is the biggest foreign-policy problem facing the country today?"	Don't know: 21%	Terrorism: 33%
	Terrorism: 12%	Middle East situation: 21%
	Middle East situation: 8%	Don't know: 11%
	Foreign aid: 7%	Foreign aid: 8%
	Getting involved in affairs of other countries: 7%	Getting involved in affairs of other countries: 7%
	Immigration: 3%	Immigration: 7%

SOURCE: Chicago Council on Foreign Relations, "Worldviews 2002: American Public Opinion and Foreign Policy" (2002), www.worldviews.org/detailreports/usreport/index.htm.

tal of Belgrade. Clinton's refusal to consider deploying ground troops, further motivated by a lack of consensus among the western European allies, angered U.S. military commanders, who sought to keep all options open in order to secure a prompt and overwhelming victory (see Clark 2001; Daalder and O'Hanlon 2000).

While Americans generally resisted military intervention in the first post–cold war decade, they still favored active involvement in other areas of foreign policy. Nevertheless, the Republican-led Congress prevented Clinton from pursuing his strategy of global "engagement." Legislative leaders approved deep cuts in several areas of U.S. foreign policy, including multilateral peacekeeping, financial support of the UN, and foreign aid. In some cases, such as the government's decision not to pay its UN dues, the public did not support the cutbacks because they did not reflect its preferences for multilateral cooperation (Kull and Destler 1999). In other cases, such as foreign aid, the public did support cutbacks in aid, but its preference was based upon a misreading of current spending levels. Whereas the majority of survey respondents believed the U.S. government was spending 15–20 percent of the federal budget on foreign aid—and believed this level should be reduced to 5–10 percent—the actual level of U.S. aid spending was just 1 percent of the federal budget.

Domestic issues dominated the 2000 presidential race between George W. Bush and Vice President Al Gore. A September 2000 survey conducted by ABC News and the *Washington Post* found that, of the 17 election issues of potential concern to voters, "national defense" and "foreign affairs" ranked eleventh and thirteenth on the list, respectively. The four issues of greatest concern to the registered voters surveyed—education, the economy, social security, and health care—received the most attention in campaign advertisements and speeches. Issues regarding foreign policy were rarely brought up during the presidential debates. Despite the significant differences between the two candidates in this area—Gore favored a broad global agenda while Bush preferred a narrow focus on U.S. national interests—most voters believed the nation was sufficiently secure to make foreign policy a secondary concern.

"Rallying around the Flag" after September 11

Fears of terrorism predictably rose to the top of the public's list of concerns after the September 11 attacks (see Table 7.3), and the ensuing war on terrorism transformed Bush's presidency. Following a consistent pattern in U.S. public opinion, presidential approval rose sharply as the nation faced a major military conflict overseas. This **rally-around-the-flag effect** (Mueller 1973; 1970) is generally attributed to a patriotic sense among citizens that national unity must be maintained in times of crisis. For similar reasons, members of Congress usually avoid criticizing presidents when U.S. troops are placed in harm's way. The actual benefits from this rally effect are difficult to gauge, however, and the boost in public approval may be short lived if the missions falter (see Baker and Oneal 2001). There is little doubt, however, that presidents stand to gain politically at the onset of international crises. Some scholars have gone so far as to put forth a **diversion-**

ary theory of war, suggesting that presidents may actually *provoke* conflicts to boost their approval ratings (see Levy 1989). Republicans accused President Clinton of resorting to this tactic in 1999, when his order to intervene in Kosovo temporarily shifted public attention from his impending impeachment over the Monica Lewinsky scandal.

Bush clearly benefited from the rally-around-the-flag effect. His public-approval ratings before September 11 were lukewarm, averaging 53 percent in eight major surveys.[4] After the terrorist attacks, these ratings soared to an average of 82 percent and peaked at more than 90 percent, the highest enjoyed by any president. Bush retained his strong reservoir of public support in the following months, although his popularity sagged along with the U.S. economy and the military's failure to apprehend Osama bin Laden in 2002. Bush experienced a second rally effect in March 2003, when he ordered the invasion of Iraq. A third, but more modest and short-lived rally effect in December followed the capture of Saddam Hussein (see Figure 7.1).

Figure 7.1 George W. Bush Public Opinion and Rally Effects, February 2, 2001–April 18, 2004

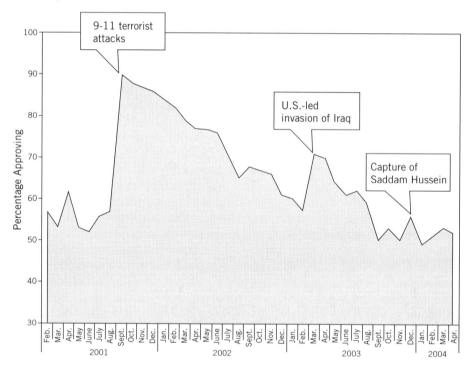

SOURCE: Gallup Organization surveys via the Roper Center for Public Opinion Research, "Presidential Approval Ratings" (2004), www.ropercenter.uconn.edu.

---

4. See www.pollingreport.com/BushJob.htm for details of these polls.

By any measure, the rally effect for Bush was enormous—three times the level experienced by Franklin Roosevelt after the Japanese attack on Pearl Harbor. This unprecedented spike in public approval prompted scholars to investigate why Bush gained so much after September 11. They found a key answer in the president's relatively low public approval prior to the terrorist attacks, which ranked third to last among postwar presidents at the com-

Table 7.4 Global Public Opinion of the United States

	Percentage Favorable	
	Summer 2002	Spring 2004
France	63%	37%
Germany	61	38
Great Britain	75	58
Jordan	25	5
Russia	61	47

SOURCE: Pew Research Center for the People and the Press, people-press.org.

parable stage of their terms. Bush had several problems in his first nine months in office, including a stagnant economy and the defection of a Republican senator that effectively gave the Democratic Party majority rule in the body. Roosevelt, by comparison, was very popular before Pearl Harbor; his public-approval rating of 72 percent gave him little room for a rally effect (see Baum 2002a).

Strong public support bolstered Bush as he ordered the invasion of Iraq in March 2003. This support was inflated, however, by widespread public misperceptions regarding Iraq and its leader, Saddam Hussein (Kull, Ramsay, and Lewis 2003–2004). Specifically, most Americans believed that (a) clear evidence had earlier linked Saddam to al Qaeda, (b) weapons of mass destruction had been found recently in Iraq, or (c) global public opinion favored U.S. military action. The strength of these misperceptions, which persisted long into the U.S. occupation of Iraq despite frequent revelations to the contrary, was closely related to the continued support of individual Americans for the war effort.

Global technological advances and growing interdependence among states heighten the importance of *transnational* public opinion to U.S. foreign policy, making the nation's stature of great importance. That stature plummeted, however, after the United States' invasion of Iraq (see Table 7.4). In a recent survey, most foreign respondents found the United States to be a less "trustworthy" world leader than before the invasion (Pew Research Center for the People and the Press 2004). Except for respondents in Great Britain, the majority of those surveyed doubted that the United States was engaged in a "sincere effort" to stop terrorism, believing the nation wanted instead to control Middle East oil, protect Israel, or "dominate the world." An earlier survey (Kennedy and Bouton 2002) found deep differences between American and European public opinion over the magnitude of global threats, the benefits of U.S. leadership, the merits of higher defense spending, and Israel's treatment of Palestinians.

Managing the News Media

A free press stands as a pillar of democratic governance, allowing citizens to follow government actions and ongoing debates about public affairs. The U.S. Constitution reflects this belief in its First Amendment, which explicitly protects freedom of the press. As Thomas Jefferson observed, "Were it left to me to decide whether we should have government without newspapers or newspapers without government, I should not hesitate for a moment to prefer the latter." The news media play an even more vital role in modern, mass-based democracies. Given the large scale of these political systems, most individuals do not participate directly in the political process. Instead, they learn about government actions primarily by following news reports in the electronic and print media. The public places even greater dependence on the news media in regard to foreign-policy issues, which commonly involve people and places never seen directly by U.S. citizens.

Print and broadcast news outlets serve three functions in the U.S. foreign-policy process. They provide public information, as described above; offer *commentaries* regarding issues of the day, some by their staff members and editorial boards, others by guest analysts; and serve as *watchdogs* overseeing government action and revealing wrongdoing. The CBS newsmagazine *60 Minutes II* served this function on April 29, 2004, when it featured horrifying photographs of Iraqi detainees at the Abu Ghraib prison, former site of brutal acts of torture under Saddam Hussein. In this case, the torture had been committed by U.S. military personnel and subcontractors. The photographs, which quickly filled newspapers, magazines, and Internet sites around the world, shattered what little goodwill the United States still enjoyed in the Islamic world. Subsequent investigative reports (for example, Hersh 2004) disclosed that U.S. military officials had known for months about the abuses in Iraq as well as others in Afghanistan, some of which led to the deaths of detainees. But the officials kept the information from Congress and the public.

The functional role of the news media in the U.S. foreign-policy process is a dynamic one in which influence runs in both directions between the news media and their partners in the information chain—the public and the government (see Figure 7.2). For government officials, the news media serve as means for explaining government policies, disseminating propaganda, and "leaking" confidential information officials want the public to know about. For the public, news organizations, as noted above, serve as vital sources of public information and as venues for governmental oversight. Citizens are also granted *voice opportunities,* or ways to express their viewpoints through letters to the editor, op-ed articles, and other means of expression. Citizens provide further feedback to the commercial news media by purchasing the goods and services they advertise.

In the absence of coverage by the print or broadcast media, there is little chance that a particular event or issue will get the public's attention (Page 1996). While TV networks, radio stations, newspapers, and magazines cannot dictate how people think about issues, they are quite capable of determining what people think about on a given day. A major story in *Time* or *Newsweek* about the AIDS virus in Africa, for example, likely will increase pressure on the U.S. government to respond. In this respect, press coverage often transforms *latent* public opinion into *mobilized* public opinion.

The relationship between journalists and the government agencies they cover is inherently fraught with tension. By their nature, reporters want to learn all they can about the actions of government, and they stand to benefit greatly when they

Figure 7.2 The News Media's Bidirectional Impact

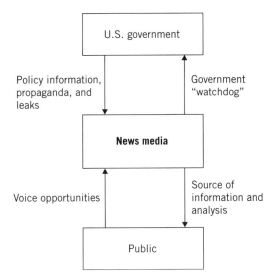

uncover evidence that government officials have acted improperly, illegally, or incompetently. This obviously makes officials hesitant to open their doors to the news media. Given the secrecy that routinely surrounds diplomatic negotiations, military maneuvers, and other aspects of foreign policy, the desire of government officials to keep journalists at arm's length is especially strong.

Despite this basic tension, the functional relationship between the media and the government can best be described as symbiotic, one based upon mutual need. Reporters rely on government sources to provide them with timely and accurate information. For all their hostility toward the press, government officials depend upon news coverage to publicize their activities and generate support among citizens. Their ability to manipulate the media to turn public opinion in their favor "becomes moot if the media do not report what [they] are saying in the first place" (Powlick and Katz 1998, 38). For example, President George W. Bush held a rare press conference in April 2004 precisely as the conflict in postwar Iraq escalated. Commentators knew that the timing of this event had everything to do with the president's acute need for public support in Iraq, where the U.S. occupation faced numerous challenges.

Trends in Foreign News Coverage

Technological innovations have historically paved the way for mass communications in all forms, allowing more people to follow, understand, and become involved in public affairs. For example, Johann Gutenberg's invention of the printing press in 1450 made written messages of all kinds available to readers, beyond the rulers who had previously monopolized the production and the consumption of information within their provinces. Martin Luther, a leader of the Protestant Reformation, seized upon this new technology in gaining popular support for his challenge to the Catholic Church in the early sixteenth century (Knutsen 1992, 46–50).

The linkages among technological advances, news coverage, and public opinion can be found throughout U.S. history. The invention of the telegraph in the nineteenth century permitted newspapers to provide immediate coverage of the Civil War. Newspaper publishers learned to rally public opinion, and greatly expand their sales, in the months preceding the Spanish-American War. Radio became an essential source of public information during World War II while newsreels shown at movie theaters and photographs featured in popular magazines provided visual images of the fighting in Europe and Asia.

The Vietnam War became the first **living-room war** (Mandelbaum 1983), bringing footage of U.S. military actions into American homes on a daily basis. Graphic scenes of carnage in Vietnamese villages incited citizens already skeptical of the war. Such coverage also provided daily reminders that U.S. victory in Vietnam was not "at hand," as had been stated repeatedly by the Johnson and Nixon administrations. Antiwar sentiment was further fueled when the *New York Times* (1971) published the **Pentagon Papers,** which detailed the administration's efforts to conceal its military activities throughout Southeast Asia.

Vietnam also represented a turning point in the news media's coverage of U.S. foreign policy. Prior to the war, reporters and editors generally had supported the government's stated goals in fighting the cold war and did not subject the tactics employed to close scrutiny. They limited their roles to conveying the government's viewpoints and describing its actions. The Vietnam War, however, and the concurrent Watergate scandal produced a generation of skeptical journalists who openly questioned the motives and judgments of national leaders. Later in the decade, President Carter could not escape saturation coverage of the Iranian hostage crisis, which began in November 1979 and continued through the rest of his presidency. The crisis gave birth to the popular ABC News program *Nightline,* originally given the provocative title *America Held Hostage.*

The advent of cable television in the early 1980s expanded the range of news providers beyond the three major networks (ABC, CBS, and NBC). Among the first cable TV operations, the Atlanta-based Cable News Network (CNN) provided around-the-clock coverage of breaking news in the United States and abroad. Its coverage of the 1984 famine in Ethiopia generated widespread sympathy for the victims and prompted a series of benefit rocks concerts, *Live Aid,* that were televised worldwide and raised tens of millions of dollars for emergency relief. Five years later, CNN transmitted live footage of the pro-democracy uprising in China that culminated in the government's killing of the protesters in Tiananmen Square, which outraged global public opinion and led to UN condemnations and economic sanctions by most industrialized states.

Globalized telecommunications from the United States and other industrialized countries also played a key role in the collapse of communist governments in Eastern Europe in 1989 and the subsequent demise of the Soviet Union. Leaders in these countries could not maintain their firm grip on information, which was increasingly being transmitted across their borders via satellite. As a result, citizens in the Soviet bloc became all too aware that their counterparts in the "first world" enjoyed political rights and living standards greater than their own. In this respect, the collapse of communism in these countries owed as much to the penetration of global telecommunications as to the foreign policies of the United States and its allies. Although the Chinese government, more distant and culturally detached from the West, suppressed the democracy movement in its country, communist leaders in the Soviet bloc succumbed to the pressures imposed by their newly enlightened and energized, if not empowered, citizens.

The end of the cold war created a "new global optic" (Grunwald 1993, 14) that included the absence of U.S.-Soviet ideological competition, the rise of regional conflicts, and accelerated economic globalization. The 1991 Persian Gulf War gave television networks their first opportunity to broadcast a major military conflict in "real time" (Bennett and Paletz 1994). Saddam Hussein reportedly tuned into CNN throughout the conflict while U.S. officials relied on the same broadcasts for battlefield information. **Rooftop journalism** became a staple of televised war coverage, with flak-jacketed CNN reporters gaining celebrity status by narrating U.S. attacks on downtown Baghdad. CNN's audience increased tenfold during the war and on some days exceeded the sizes of the broadcast networks' audiences. Twenty of the twenty-five largest U.S. newspapers experienced sharp gains in circulation during the war (Hallin and Gitlin 1994).

The rapid pace by which globalized news coverage prompts government action is often referred to as the **CNN effect.** Among the most vivid examples was Somalia's 1992 civil war and resulting famine, covered extensively by CNN and other networks. President George H. W. Bush said the images of starving Somalis so disturbed him that he felt compelled to order a humanitarian intervention by U.S. military forces. Many analysts (for example, Robinson 2001; and Strobel 1997) found a *reciprocal* relationship between press coverage and U.S. foreign policy: responses by the U.S. government to problems overseas, provoked in part by media reports, greatly increased the volume of subsequent news coverage and public interest in the areas in question.

In the 1990s, television replaced newspapers as the primary source of news for U.S. citizens. According to one survey, nearly 70 percent of Americans reported that they used television as a major source of news, followed by 43 percent for newspapers, 15 percent for radio, and 4 percent for magazines (Powlick and Katz 1998, 39). During this decade, the media repeatedly cut back coverage of international affairs despite the fact that the United States had emerged from the cold war as the undisputed world leader in terms of military power, economic wealth, and political influence. Print and broadcast news organizations closed foreign bureaus and restricted the space in their news budgets allocated to foreign news.

Foreign news predictably regained its hold on media attention after the terrorist attacks of September 2001. In accordance with the rally effect, President Bush enjoyed favorable coverage as he devised and executed his war plan against Afghanistan. News outlets provided saturation coverage of the 2003 invasion of

Table 7.5 Cable Networks and the Iraq War, Spring 2003

Network	Average Viewership	Change of Viewership Since War Started
Fox News	3.3 million	+ 236%
CNN	2.7 million	+ 313%
MSNBC	1.4 million	+ 360%

SOURCE: Nielsen Media Research, www.nielsenmedia.com.

Iraq, during which nearly 3,000 journalists armed with videophones and laptop computers received press credentials. While the "big three" broadcast networks—ABC, CBS, and NBC—recorded high ratings, cable networks such as CNN, MSNBC, and Fox News reported the largest increases in viewership (see Table 7.5). The government "embedded" reporters in U.S. forces during the twenty-one-day blitzkrieg, and the reporters provided firsthand accounts of the overthrow of Saddam's military forces and government. In approving this innovation in military journalism, the White House correctly anticipated that the **embeds** would identify with the troops and produce favorable reports of their missions (see Katovsky and Carlson 2003).

Fox News emerged from the war as the most popular cable news network—and the most supportive of the Bush administration's war effort. Launched in 1996, Fox News overtook ratings leader CNN in 2002 by appealing to the same conservative sector of U.S. society that made talk radio, and Rush Limbaugh in particular, powerful cultural forces in the 1980s. Among news consumers, Fox News viewers were the most enthusiastic about Operation Iraqi Freedom as well as the most likely to exaggerate the threat posed by Saddam Hussein's regime. A prominent survey conducted by Steven Kull, Clay Ramsay, and Evan Lewis (2003/2004, 585–586) found that among Fox viewers, "greater attention to news modestly *increased* the likelihood of misperception."

Characteristics of Foreign News Coverage

As noted earlier, the U.S. media rarely cover international news unless the United States faces a major crisis (Graber 2002). Major broadcast and print outlets curtailed their foreign coverage in the 1990s in response to viewer preferences for domestic news and increased competition from cable networks. According to one survey, foreign news coverage by the major networks dropped from more than 40 percent in the 1970s to less than 15 percent by 1995 (Dizard 2001, 173). Whereas a century ago dozens of U.S. newspapers maintained foreign news bureaus, today only major newspapers such as the *New York Times*, the *Washington Post*, the *Chicago Tribune*, and the *Los Angeles Times* employ foreign-based reporters. The others rely on wire services such as the Associated Press and Reuters. Among the top fifty magazines sold in the United States in 2001, only three—*Time* (ranked tenth), *Newsweek* (fifteenth), and *U.S. News and World Report* (thirty-third)—provide detailed coverage of international news (Magazine Publishers of America 2002).

These trends reflect the intensifying market pressures imposed on U.S. news outlets, which must respond to audience preferences to maximize market share and advertising revenue. For a decade prior to the war on terrorism, news consumers sent a clear message that they had a limited interest in foreign news.

Newspaper readers consistently ranked their interest in news coverage as follows: (1) state and local news, (2) national news, (3) foreign news involving the United States, and (4) foreign news not involving the United States (Rielly 2003). News organizations thus pay a price by focusing on foreign news in spite of the public's general preference for domestic coverage.

This does not mean that individuals with interest in foreign affairs have nowhere to turn for information. Hundreds of alternative magazines, public TV and radio stations, and foreign news services offer a greater range of foreign news than ever before. Internet sources provide an even greater variety of information about events overseas. Yet the majority of Americans find only the most urgent news about events abroad worthy of their attention. For this reason, the major outlets of news have a fleeting interest in foreign affairs, which grows only when major crises erupt that might affect the United States.

Another important characteristic of the news media is the growing concentration of media outlets (see Compaine and Gomery 2000). This trend has been hastened in recent years by media deregulation in the United States. In the name of free enterprise, government officials abolished a variety of rules designed to foster competition and diversity.[5] Conglomerates such as AOL–Time Warner, Clear Channel Communications, and the Australia-based News Corp. own most commercial TV and radio stations, as well as cable networks and major print outlets. Syndicates such as Gannett and Knight-Ridder, which own dozens of newspapers as well as broadcast outlets, increasingly draw their foreign reporting from single, centrally controlled staffs. Broadcast coverage is similarly limited to a few national networks, and two European news services—Visnews and WTN—strictly control pictorial materials from overseas.

Of concern as well are the close links between media conglomerates and concerns in other sectors of the economy. In the early 1990s, most major stockholders of ABC, CBS, and NBC were banks such as Chase Manhattan (Parenti 1993, 29). At the same time, CBS's board of directors included top executives from such large corporations (and major advertisers) as IBM, Philip Morris, AT&T, Citibank, and Metropolitan Life. Such links threaten the editorial independence of each news outlet, whose reporting is presumed to be free from economic pressure. *Political* overlaps, too, are troubling, as many media outlets are owned by corporations that provide unrelated goods and services to the government. General Electric (GE), for example, not only owns NBC, its affiliated cable news networks, and more than 200 local stations, but also serves as a primary defense contractor to the Pentagon.[6] The potential conflicts of interest in these cases are obvious.

---

5. The Bush administration encouraged this deregulation trend. Michael Powell, the son of Secretary of State Colin Powell, led the drive toward greater media concentration as chairman of the Federal Communications Commission.

6. See the Center for Public Integrity's Web site for a description of GE's role as a Pentagon contractor (www.publicintegrity.org/wow/bio.aspx?act=pro&ddlC=23) and for detailed statistics on major media conglomerates (www.publicintegrity.org/telecom/contacts.aspx?action=top).

Beyond these points, foreign news coverage in the United States can be characterized by five key factors.

From print to video. The emergence of CNN in the 1980s coincided with a long-term contraction in the newspaper industry, whose advertising revenues fell from nearly half of the national total to just 22 percent in 1998 (Compaine and Gomery 2000, 3). Most Americans rely on television as their primary source of news, with U.S. sets turned on an average of fifty hours per week. Televised news coverage, which provides dramatic, real-time visual images of events abroad, obviously has a strong advantage over the print media. Such coverage, however, naturally favors events with strong visual appeal. News executives downplay less telegenic, but equally important, events such as international summit conferences.

U.S.-centrism. News organizations have learned that foreign news, to be interesting to most Americans, must have a "peg" to the United States, such as a possible deployment of U.S. forces or an impact on trade or immigration. General news about political developments overseas usually does not concern Americans, and for this reason, news managers avoid stories that do not relate directly to this audience. This bias in news budgets produces coverage that may exaggerate the nation's importance in global affairs while leading readers and viewers to disregard important problems that affect much of the world's population but not U.S. citizens. By contrast, major foreign outlets such as the BBC provide more coverage of foreign news, including a substantial volume of news about U.S. foreign policy.

Conflict orientation. Coverage of all news, foreign and domestic, tends to emphasize conflict rather than cooperation, chaos rather than order. "If it bleeds, it leads" is a popular and widely adopted standard used by local and national news editors in deciding what is worth covering. In foreign policy, this leads to an emphasis on civil wars and international conflicts, whose dramatic images have the strongest impact on viewers and readers. Of secondary importance are nonviolent political conflicts, such as closely contested elections and struggles for power. This bias in news management distorts public understanding by leading citizens to believe the "outside world" to be more plagued by unrest and disorder than it actually is.

Superficiality. The preoccupation with visual images, conflict, and late-breaking news prevents reporters from providing in-depth coverage of their stories or paying attention to long-range problems such as global warming, economic inequalities, population growth, and weapons proliferation. News consumers thus have little *context* in which to understand day-to-day crises elsewhere and U.S. options in responding to them. Coverage of the Persian Gulf War, for example, rarely moved beyond breaking news to explore the underlying cultural and economic problems in the region that had fueled the conflict (Iyengar and Simon 1994, 79). Reporters covering the Pentagon, meanwhile, so fixate on interservice rivalries and procurement scandals that they ignore routine, but more important, stories such as the defense budget and modernization of military forces (Aubin 1998). Superficial reporting is most common on "soft news" programs such *Entertainment Tonight* and *Oprah Winfrey,* whose human-interest stories during major foreign-policy crises reach a large segment of the national news audience (Baum 2002b).

Arbitrariness. Foreign news coverage in the United States tends to be guided by immediate developments rather than long-range priorities and principles. The news media's attention to a foreign country generally lasts as long as a crisis there does, after which journalists flock en masse to other trouble spots. This was clearly the case during and after the 1989 U.S. invasion of Panama, a tiny Central American country that suddenly became a focus of media attention and then, just as abruptly, disappeared from the radar screens of U.S.-based editors (see Figure 7.3). Such coverage has given rise to **parachute journalism,** a pattern in which reporters descend on a trouble spot and then move on, never gaining a deep understanding of the problems in the areas that would have given their reporting greater substance.

As noted earlier, the U.S. military intervention in Somalia was prompted in large part by media coverage of a war-induced famine in the African nation while a similar crisis in nearby Sudan received little press or government attention. Even in areas that attract the media spotlight, however, the effects on government policy are skewed. "If you look at how humanitarian aid is delivered in Bosnia you

Figure 7.3 News Articles About Panama Before and After December 1989 U.S. Invasion

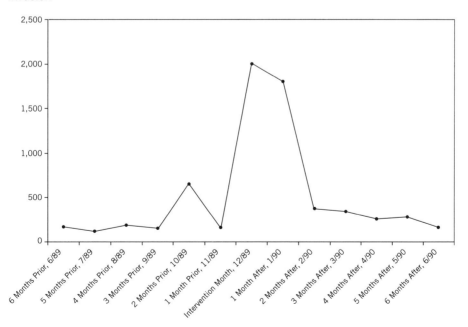

SOURCE: LexisNexis news database, www.lexisnexis.com.

see that those areas where the TV cameras are most present are the ones that are best fed, the ones that receive the most medicine," observed Mohamed Sacirbey (quoted in Seib 1997, 90), Bosnia's ambassador to the United Nations. "While on the other hand, many of our people have starved or died of disease and shelling where there are no TV cameras."

The ability of global news coverage to shape the agenda of U.S. foreign policy raises troubling questions, one that Jefferson and other early advocates of a free press could not have anticipated. First, public and government attention is drawn only to trouble spots abroad that are readily accessible to camera crews. In other war-torn areas, such as Sudan and the former Zaire in the 1990s, the lack of news coverage precludes public pressure for action and discourages a U.S. response. Second, an overreliance on news coverage leads foreign-policy makers to ignore long-term problems and to focus instead on impending disasters (Van Belle and Hook 2000). By the time ethnic conflict in Rwanda reached genocidal proportions in 1994, for example, it was too late for the United States and other governments to prevent massive death and destruction. Similarly, the lack of dramatic visual imagery related to global warming prevents the news media from alerting the public to this growing global problem (see Chapter 12). The U.S. government, which often takes its cue from the news media, thus has less incentive to confront the problem.

Most importantly, media-driven foreign policy erodes the capacity of diplomats and other public officials to pursue a clear, consistent, and coherent national strategy. As George Kennan (1996, 297) observed, "If American policy from here on out, particularly policy involving the uses of our armed forces abroad, is to be controlled by popular impulses, and particularly policy ones provoked by the commercial television industry, then there is no place—not only for myself, but for the responsible deliberative organs of government." Thus while the globalized news media have the capacity to bring citizens closer to world problems than ever before, such coverage may hinder as well as facilitate the U.S. government's effective use of world power.

Spin Control and "Framing" Reality

When it comes to the news media's coverage of its actions, the U.S. government is not a simple bystander. To the contrary, government officials actively work to shape that coverage in ways that show them in the best possible light. Their efforts at **spin control** have become an art form in recent years, a time that has witnessed both the globalization of the media and ever-more sophisticated means of using media images and messages to influence public opinion (see Kurtz 1998). The U.S. government uses three basic tactics to spin foreign news coverage in its favor.

The first and most common means by which the U.S. government controls information involves *keeping secrets*. This is especially common in foreign policy, which relies to a large extent on classified information and on necessarily private lines of communication between Washington, D.C., and foreign governments. In most cases, news outlets accept the need for secrecy, and they may even withhold from the public information they receive "off the record" from government officials. Journalists and government officials view this practice as essential, both to maintain national security and to preserve their mutually beneficial ties.

A second means of information control involves selective *leaks* of privileged information to journalists. Official leaks, such as those used by Bill Clinton regarding a new trade pact with China, serve as "trial balloons" to gauge public support for a possible policy change. In other cases, government officials attempt to punish dissenters by secretly providing embarrassing information about them to reporters. The Bush administration resorted to this tactic in 2003 by revealing to columnist Robert Novak that Joseph C. Wilson, a former ambassador and career foreign service officer, was married to a clandestine CIA agent. The leak, intended to discredit Wilson (2004) after he wrote a *New York Times* commentary disputing Bush's claims about Iraqi nuclear ambitions in Africa, ended his wife's career and placed her life in jeopardy.

Unofficial leaks, by contrast, come from anonymous critics who hope to improve government behavior by revealing a potentially harmful policy or practice, thereby sparing the government a foreign-policy embarrassment or setback. Government "whistle blowers" frequently alert reporters to cost overruns in the defense industry and failed weapons systems tests that would otherwise be unknown to the public. Government employees who find press leaks a useful way to affect policy from behind the scenes use the same tactics. "On Wall Street, passing insider information is standard operating procedure," journalist Hedrick Smith (1988, 81) noted. "In Washington, it is the regular stuff of the power game. Everyone does it, from presidents on down, when they want to change the balance of power on some issue."

Finally, by *manipulating information* the government hopes to advance its agenda and control public opinion. The media have historically been a primary instrument of **propaganda,** that is, false and misleading public information designed to enhance the stature of the government or its policies. To Jody Powell (1984, 223), Jimmy Carter's press secretary, the government "has not only the right but a positive obligation to lie" when national interests are at stake. Early in the war on terrorism, White House press secretary Ari Fleischer carried out an elaborate "system of disinformation—blunter, more aggressive, and in its own way, more impressive than spin" (Chait 2002, 20). Defense Secretary Donald Rumsfeld, meanwhile, proposed the creation of a new agency, the Office of Strategic Intelligence, that would spread information—some of it false—to audiences in the Islamic world. Rumsfeld quickly dropped his proposal amid public protests, although he retained the right of the CIA and other intelligence agencies to use false information as a strategic weapon.

News organizations generally support governmental attempts at **framing** foreign-policy problems, that is, structuring and simplifying them so they are understood by U.S. citizens in ways that favor the government's position. The Bush administration's portrayal of Saddam Hussein as "Hitler" and the war on terrorism as "good versus evil" exemplified this pattern (Norris, Kern, and Just 2003). As conceived by the White House, such a perspective "cascades" (Entman

·)) IN THEIR OWN WORDS: TED KOPPEL

For all of its assets in the struggle over information, the U.S. government, as it discovered during the Vietnam War, cannot guarantee compliance by the news media. This central reality reminds us that government policy, not spin, ultimately determines whether the nation's goals overseas will be achieved. Ted Koppel, the host of Nightline, *made this point to members of the House International Relations Committee, who brought leading media figures together in 1994 to discuss the impact of news coverage on U.S. foreign policy.*

Outside factors tend to influence the formation of foreign policy, to a greater or lesser degree, in almost direct proportion to the amount of credible information and policy direction that a government otherwise makes available.

To the degree, in other words, that U.S. foreign policy in a given region has been clearly stated and adequate, accurate information has been provided, the influence of television coverage diminishes proportionately. To state the premise in reverse, television's influence increases in those regions where an administration has (a) failed to enunciate a clear policy and/or (b) has done little or nothing to inform the American public on the dangers of intervention or failing to intervene. . . .

You ask whether television executives consider the impact of their decisions on foreign policy? Rarely. Should they? In my opinion, almost never. I realize that still sounds like a revolutionary concept, even though its foundations were laid nearly 200 years before the advent of television; but we, who report on events,

2004) through the federal government, being adopted by lower-level officials who maintain regular contact with the press. Only when internal divisions are exposed among U.S. officials—a relatively rare occurrence in foreign policy—do the news media depart from the government's "frame" and create their own images of the foreign-policy problem (Lewis and Rose 2002). Otherwise, news organizations freely grant government leaders access to audiences and adopt the government's ideology and viewpoints (see Hunt 1987).

The White House demonstrated its skill in "manufacturing consent" (Herman and Chomsky 1988; see also Hallin 1986) in preparing for the invasion of Iraq. Despite their expressed reservations about the invasion, the editorial boards of major U.S. newspapers "conditioned themselves to treat Bush's national-security argument with deference" (Mooney 2004, 29). Government officials have powerful allies in the corporations that own media outlets and spend billions of dollars on print and broadcast advertising. Radio giant Clear Channel displayed this muscle when it refused to play music in 2003 by the Dixie Chicks after band members spoke out against the invasion of Iraq. A year later, the Sinclair Broadcast Group prevented its eight ABC affiliates from airing an episode of *Nightline* that was devoted exclusively to the reciting of the names of U.S. casualties in Iraq.

should not be policy makers. We have a responsibility to be fair, accurate, and even-handed; but only in the rarest of instances (when lives, for example, are clearly and unambiguously at risk) should we be expected to take the consequences of our reporting into account. Should we, for example, have refrained from showing pictures of starving Somalis because it might lead to U.S. intervention and because that intervention could lead to the death of American personnel? What if we had not shown those pictures? Should we be prepared to take responsibility for losing the hundreds of thousands of lives that were reportedly saved by the operation? Should we refrain from showing the American public what's happening in Rwanda because that might lead to U.S. or UN intervention? Or is the argument the very reverse? Should we not have shown that Ranger's body being

dragged through the streets of Mogadishu, because now we're disinclined to intervene when perhaps we should?

With all respect, Mr. Chairman, it is our function to inform, it is your function to consider, debate, advise, consent, fund or not fund; and the function of the executive branch to make decisions and to carry out foreign policy.

If an administration has thought its own foreign policy through, and is prepared and able to argue the merits and defend the consequences of that policy, television and all its technologies can be dealt with. If, on the other hand, the foreign policy is ill-conceived and poorly explained, it does not matter much whether the news arrives by satellite or clipper ship. Eventually the policy will fail.

Source: Ted Koppel, testimony before the House International Relations Committee (April 26, 1994).

The Internet's Window on the World

Technological advances have historically fueled major changes in relations between citizens and states, in the role and impact of the press, and in the day-to-day conduct of foreign policy. This pattern certainly applies to the Internet, a vital fact of life in the "brave new wired world" of the twenty-first century (Burton 1997). This technology, barely known a generation ago, provides new outlets for government and private expression along with a nearly limitless range of information available to students, observers, and practitioners of world politics.

The Internet has altered the landscape of U.S. foreign policy in all areas. The swift and precise U.S. conquests of Afghanistan (2001) and Iraq (2003) owed much to improvements in Web-based communications—a key element of the "revolution in military affairs" (see Chapters 6 and 10).[7] Managers of U.S. foreign economic policy, meanwhile, use the nation's technical superiority to gain a greater market share of overseas investments and exports. The Internet accelerates the pace of diplomatic communications within the foreign service and between the

---

7. The Defense Department was the primary sponsor of the Internet's research and development during the 1960s and 1970s (Margolis and Resnick 2000, 25–51).

United States and foreign governments. This shift toward **digital diplomacy** marks "the most important innovation affecting diplomatic practices since the fifteenth century" (Dizard 2001, 1).

The Internet combines the immediacy and visual impact of television with the substantive depth of the print media, offering its users a vast range of information at little or no cost. E-mail, the second component of the Internet, makes the new technology *interactive*. Users gain ample opportunities to voice their opinions, ask questions, and share information among others with similar interests. This "two-way electronic street" has produced exponential growth in the volume of global communications—Internet use doubled every hundred days in the late 1990s as the number of Web sites grew from about 50 in 1993 to 5 million by the end of the decade (Nye 2002b, 42). This Internet burst includes e-mail messages between U.S. military troops overseas and their families and friends in the United States; messages between them used to take days or weeks to deliver.

The rapid growth of the Internet fueled the U.S. economic boom of the 1990s. "E-commerce" was the fastest-growing segment of the economy at the turn of the century, growing by 120 percent in 1999 alone, to $111 billion (Dizard 2001, 156). Although this growth has slowed in recent years and still represents a modest share of the nation's economic activity, the use of the Internet in the development, production, sales, and distribution of products has assumed a vital and permanent place in the U.S. economy.

For the United States, the Internet also represents a powerful source of cultural influence, or "soft power" (Nye 2004). English is the dominant language of the Web, and more than 80 percent of Web "visits" involve sites in the United States. More than 20 percent of all Internet communications involve participants in the United States (see Table 7.6), and the 5,000 U.S.-based data banks in 2000 outnumbered those in the rest of the world combined. Though this domination of the Internet will undoubtedly decline in the coming years, the United States is expected to maintain its edge as this technology continues to advance and new applications are discovered.

The Internet provides an effective vehicle for the transmission of U.S. political and cultural values. "If the United States government had tried to come up with a scheme to spread its brand of capitalism and its emphasis on political liberalism around the world, it couldn't have invented a better model than the Internet," observed Don Heath (quoted in Lohr 2000, WK-1), president of the Internet Society. The decentralized, loosely governed structure of the Internet encourages the kind of informal, uninhibited dialogue familiar to Americans. To Daniel Burton (1997, 33), former president of the Council on Competitiveness, "The Internet is a tangible expression of the world coming together. If regionalism was the intermediate step toward a true global community, the World Wide Web is its consummation."

The new age of digital diplomacy affects U.S. foreign policy in four distinct ways. First, as a fully integrated computer network is put into place, internal communications among the hundreds of U.S. diplomatic posts improves greatly. This encourages a more rapid response to problems as well as greater *coordination* in

Table 7.6 Global Online Populations, 2004

Nation	Internet Users (in Millions)	Percentage of Total World Internet Users
United States	185.90	21.5%
China	95.80	11.1
Japan	77.95	9.0
Germany	41.86	4.8
India	39.20	4.5
United Kingdom	34.11	4.0
South Korea	32.05	3.7
Italy	28.61	3.3
France	26.34	3.1
Brazil	23.05	2.7
Russia	22.30	2.6
Canada	20.45	2.4
Spain	16.65	1.9
Indonesia	15.30	1.8
Taiwan	13.20	1.5

SOURCE: ClickZ Network, "Population Explosion!" (May 10, 2004), www.clickz.com/stats/big_picture /geographics/article.php/151151. Data come from *CIA World Factbook* and *Computer Industry Almanac*.

implementing policies adopted in Washington, D.C. Second, the integration of computer networks among the State Department and other federal departments produces greater *consistency* in the day-to-day conduct of foreign policy. In short, it is more likely that information known to one foreign-policy agency will be available to others. Third, the creation of direct electronic ties between the United States and foreign governments encourages greater *responsiveness* to political problems and crises abroad. This accelerates the pace of diplomacy, which historically has been hampered by the slow movement of communications among governments.

Finally, digital diplomacy fosters greater *mobilization* of nongovernmental organizations (NGOs). Thousands of such groups—firms, religious institutions, research foundations, and public-interest groups—use the Web as their primary source of communications. The International Campaign to Ban Landmines (ICBL), for example, used the Internet to generate grassroots support for a global ban on the weapons. In the 1999 debate over Sino-American trade relations, dozens of NGOs on both sides of this issue organized their lobbying strategies through the Internet (Hook 2005). Internet campaigns were instrumental in hastening the end of apartheid in South Africa in 1994, in supporting East Timor's secession from Indonesia in 1999, in securing the arrest of Serbian leader Slobodan Milosevic in 2000, and in rallying global opinion against the U.S. mistreatment of Iraqi prisoners in 2004. With this last case, the Internet demonstrated its ability to challenge U.S. foreign policy as well as to promote U.S. actions and values abroad.

Until recently, the State Department's transition to the Internet had been sluggish, largely due to repeated cutbacks in congressional funding during the 1990s. No centralized system of electronic information existed in the State Department until 1998, and even then no common network connected Foggy Bottom with the other federal departments engaged in foreign policy. Upon taking office in 2001, Secretary of State Powell gained the resources necessary to make the State Department's Web truly "worldwide," but problems related to the war on terrorism slowed the installation of these new systems. While intelligence agencies have also used the Internet to great advantage, they remain stubbornly protective of the information they receive. As a result, the utility of the Internet in coordinating intelligence remains limited, even after the revelations of interagency communication breakdowns before and after 9-11.

A main concern involving the Internet is maintaining **information security,** or unfettered flows of online communications. Computer "hackers" frequently disrupt such communications and introduce viruses that can cripple even the most advanced computer systems in the public and private sectors. In this respect, the growing reliance of U.S. government agencies on the Internet makes **cyberterrorism** a source of vulnerability and a threat to foreign policy (Stanton 2002). Of concern as well are the ways in which knowledge gained from Internet sources may be used. The Clinton administration placed massive volumes of government documents, including the Congressional Record and key government studies, on the Web. This effort succeeded in making the U.S. government more "transparent" and accessible to citizens, thus serving a central function of democratic rule. Such transparency, however, may be equally useful to U.S. adversaries, including states and terrorist groups, who can draw upon the same sites to better "know thy enemy."

Even before the terrorist attacks of September 2001, the Bush administration had begun reversing the Clinton administration's policy of placing most government documents and records online. This effort intensified after the attacks, as officials worried that terrorist groups were exploiting their easy access to government information that could be useful in the planning and execution of future attacks. In accordance with the USA Patriot Act, signed by Congress just weeks after 9-11, the Bush administration gained greater access to e-mail messages sent by U.S. citizens as well as resident aliens living the United States (see Chapter 12). These actions further revealed the tension between democracy—including the privacy of personal communications and citizens' "right to know" about government—and maintaining national security in a competitive and dangerous world. Indeed, a key battleground in the decades to come will involve the control of information.

Conclusion

As we have seen, public opinion and mass communications play vital roles in U.S. foreign policy, in keeping with the underlying virtue of democratic governance.

These roles, however, are fraught with problems and complications. Public attention usually focuses on immediate and local concerns, which means long-term problems in other parts of the world are neglected or ignored entirely. Only when these problems reach crisis proportions do they become known to the public, whose impulsive demands for action result in hasty and ineffective responses. The news media reinforce this pattern by alternately ignoring foreign news and providing saturation coverage of crises overseas. The Internet, while greatly expanding access to public information and dialogue, creates its own challenges to U.S. security. Taken together, these problems add a public dimension to the paradox of world power, a dimension compounded by civil society's role in enhancing as well as frustrating the coherent conduct of U.S. foreign policy.

A key part of this paradox stems from a disconnect between public opinion and government behavior. As I. M. Destler (2001b, 75) reminds us, "We seem to have a rational public and an ideological ruling class. Average Americans are basically centrist, prone to balance, compromise, fair shares, reasonable resolutions. Their Congress is polarized, hyperpartisan, responsive to 'cause' activists of left and right." This argument is strengthened by several recent foreign-policy actions taken by the government that ran against prevailing public preferences: the failure to pay past UN dues, the rejection of the Comprehensive Test Ban Treaty, and the invasion of Iraq without the endorsement of the UN Security Council. While the majority of Americans did not support these initiatives, their general inattention to foreign affairs—reflected in test scores and public-opinion surveys—surely made the government's decisions to defy the popular will easier and safer politically.

National news outlets contribute to these problems by ignoring such issues as the UN backlash and treaty debate until their outcomes are assured. In terms of ratings, the biggest U.S. news story in the early 1990s was not the collapse of communism and the coming of U.S. global primacy, but the trial of O. J. Simpson. For cable news networks, the defining story of the late 1990s did not involve foreign affairs but the sex scandal involving President Clinton, whose impeachment by the House of Representatives was followed intently by the networks' viewers. To James Fallows (1997, 247), a prominent journalist and author, superficial and scandal-driven news coverage simply adds to the public's cynical view of U.S. politics and foreign policy: "The press, which in the long run cannot survive if people lose interest in politics, is acting as if its purpose is to guarantee that people are repelled by public life."

These tensions are not likely to dissipate in the near future. Widespread cutbacks in school funding will make it difficult for teachers to broaden the next generation's understanding of world history, geography, culture, and current events. The growing concentration of media ownership, meanwhile, will further discourage popular debate and dissent. In the absence of mass participation, public involvement will continue to take place within narrow interest groups and NGOs, whose members have strong views about U.S. foreign policy and express them daily to the federal government. It is to this second "outside-in" influence on the foreign-policy process, foreign-policy interest groups, that we now turn our attention.

Key Terms

Almond-Lippmann consensus, p. 194

attentive public, p. 191

CNN effect, p. 207

cyberterrorism, p. 218

delegate model, p. 192

digital diplomacy, p. 216

diversionary theory of war, p. 201

embeds, p. 208

foreign-policy elite, p. 191

framing, p. 213

information security, p. 218

latent public opinion, p. 197

living-room war, p. 206

mass public, p. 191

parachute journalism, p. 211

Pentagon Papers, p. 206

propaganda, p. 213

public relations presidency, p. 191

rally-around-the-flag effect, p. 201

rooftop journalism, p. 207

spin control, p. 212

trustee model, p. 192

Internet References

A newer media conglomerate, **Aljazeera** (english.aljazeera.net) provides in-depth coverage of worldwide events. Specifically, Aljazeera covers events relevant to the Arab World. Included on this site are polls, news reports about world events, and cultural reports on Middle Eastern countries.

Based in England, the **BBC** (news.bbc.co.uk) is a large media hub for worldwide news coverage, which includes special reports on conflicts and major world events. The BBC has regional coverage for all major areas across the globe.

The **Chicago Council on Foreign Relations** (www.ccfr.org) is one of the world's largest groups organized for studying and informing the community about world affairs. The Chicago Council is responsible for the biannual reports of worldviews of American and international public opinion on many aspects of U.S. foreign policy. It also hosts conferences and speakers and helps to sponsor public opinion studies regarding U.S. foreign policy.

CNN (www.cnn.com) is a communication hub for articles and news coverage of world issues. Included are articles from magazines such as *Time* as well as stories from the AP wire. Political coverage is both domestic and foreign, with a special focus on U.S. foreign policy.

The **Gallup Organization** (www.gallup.com) has studied public opinion and behavior for nearly a century and continues to conduct nationwide and international surveys regarding political and social issues. Surveys focus on presidential approval, current events, and conflicts.

The **Inter-University Consortium for Political and Social Research** (www.icpsr .umich.edu) is a part of the University of Michigan and hosts historical and new databases ranging from public opinion to aggregate statistics. Data are deposited from news stations as well as from colleges and universities.

In conjunction with the University of Kentucky and the University of North Carolina, the **National Network of State Polls** (survey.rgs.uky.edu/nnsp) organizes and completes

Internet References

research on public opinion, with states as the unit of analysis. More than 350 studies are stored in the free data archives of the NNSP, in which questions range from domestic to international topics.

The **National Opinion Research Center** (www.norc.uchicago.edu) is responsible for national research specializing in public opinion data and analysis. Current research projects and special reports include studies of public responses to September 11.

The **Pew Research Center for the People and the Press** (people-press.org) is an independent, nonpartisan research center focusing on studying public opinion, press and media coverage, and political issues. The Pew Center conducts a wide range of surveys and allows the databases and reports to be accessed free of charge. The five areas of study are the people and the press; the people, the press, and politics; the news interest index; the United States' place in the world; and media use. Much of the research by Pew is ongoing and conducted on current events topics.

Polling Report (www.pollingreport.com) is an independent, nonpartisan group that hosts public opinion data from a variety of sources and organizes them by research category. Of particular interest to foreign-policy researchers are topics such as national security, presidential elections, and the role of the United Nations.

Russia's largest news and media source, **Pravda** (english.pravda.ru) provides articles and news coverage of world affairs and relations with the United States. Specific focus is given to the United Nations, eastern European relations, and critical views of the war on terrorism.

The **Program on International Policy Attitudes** (www.pipa.org) is part of the School of Public Affairs at the University of Maryland and focuses on public opinion and media coverage related to U.S. foreign policy and international issues. PIPA conducts its own nationwide surveys and studies on issues such as opinions on leaders, terrorism, globalization, arms control, and regional issues. Articles and studies are posted on the Web site.

Quinnipiac University (www.quinnipiac.edu/x705.xml) provides national survey trend polls to basic foreign and domestic policy questions such as presidential approval, war on terrorism opinion, and opinions of government leaders such as the vice president and other cabinet officials.

The **Roper Center for Public Opinion Research** (www.ropercenter.uconn.edu) offers access to public opinion and polling data through a large archive of historical and current data. Included are presidential approval, General Social Survey, National Election Survey, and a variety of other polls conducted by research groups.

The *Washington Post* (www.washingtonpost.com/wp-srv/politics/polls/polls.htm) has articles related to public opinion and politics regarding policy issues. Included in the reports are data breakdowns and direct links to the *Washington Post* surveys. Specific research topics include public opinion toward the United Nations, the war on terrorism, relations with Iraq, and energy policies.

8

Members of Greenpeace stand at their mock oil derricks in the Reflecting Pool outside the U.S. Capitol during a February 2002 protest of U.S. energy policy. Greenpeace, a well-known environmental group, often resorts to high-profile acts of civil disobedience to bring attention to its causes. The protest, aided considerably by the appearance of this photo in many newspapers, contributed to the defeat in Congress of the Bush administration's energy policy. The White House later tried, without success, to strip Greenpeace of its status as a tax-exempt organization.

Interest Groups at Home and Abroad

As we learned in the previous chapter, public opinion and the news media are key external actors in the U.S. foreign-policy process. Another set of important actors is the worldwide web of nongovernmental organizations (NGOs), formally instituted private groups seeking to influence public policy in their favor. Of particular interest are *transnational* NGOs, organizations whose members are located in more than one country or, though based in a single country, nevertheless are stakeholders in the foreign-policy process. While transnational NGOs have widely differing interests and adopt a variety of tactics to achieve their disparate goals, they share two traits significant to this book: a keen interest and a potent role in U.S. foreign policy.

In this chapter, we provide an overview of the vast constellation of NGOs. First, we place the groups in theoretical context and then examine the various types engaged in the policy process. Finally, we describe the common functions of these groups and the tactics they employ to achieve their foreign-policy-related objectives. The collective involvement of private groups, their degree of interconnectedness, and their proven capacity to shape government agendas represent the "power shift" (Mathews 1997) discussed in Chapter 1, whereby sovereignty is threatened by the influence of the marketplace and international public opinion.

Private groups, or voluntary associations, have always formed a backbone of the U.S. government's democratic system. Like public opinion and the news media, private groups represent alternative centers of power that can prevent government tyranny while offering outlets for the expression of societal needs. Like economic markets, the *demand* for favorable government policies determines the *supply* of groups promoting them. "The public is not only represented in the formal political sense by a variety of elected officials," political scientist Gabriel Almond noted long ago, "but there are few groups of any size in the United States today which do not have their interests represented" (Almond 1950, 231).

Several features of the U.S. government and society favor the development and persistence of NGOs (see Risse-Kappen 1995). First, highly fragmented *governmental structures* offer many points of access into the legislative and executive branches through which private groups can affect foreign policy. Second, robust *societal structures,* a result of constitutional restraints on government power and the broad political and social freedoms granted to individuals and groups, provide a fertile environment for NGOs to recruit new members and affect policy. Finally, the existence of numerous *policy networks* allows NGOs to join with issue-related government agencies that share a basic consensus regarding the merits of U.S. government and society. Because the ideological spectrum in the United States is narrow, as compared to that found in most other countries, group activism focuses on policy reforms rather than on the fundamental strengths or deficiencies of the U.S. political system.

This is not to say that the U.S. government enjoys a harmonious relationship with the thousands of transnational NGOs that exist today. To the contrary, the United States is often a target, rather than an ally, of these groups. President Clinton faced the full wrath of certain NGOs in 1999, when antiglobalization protesters disrupted the annual meetings of the World Trade Organization (WTO) in Seattle, Washington. As the world's predominant power, with unrivaled influence over the global economy, related ecological issues, weapons proliferation, and the protection of human rights, the United States naturally attracts the most NGO attention. Recognizing the importance of these groups, Clinton reached out to them throughout his presidency as part of his strategy of "engagement." Despite his efforts, the U.S. government remained more adversary than friend to many public-interest groups, as the Seattle protests showed.

The relationship between Washington, D.C., and public-interest NGOs became even more adversarial with the coming to power of George W. Bush, who distanced his administration from these groups as well as from the many intergovernmental organizations (IGOs) that opposed key elements of his foreign policy (see Chapter 9). At the same time, however, Bush reached out to a different set of NGOs, including multinational corporations (MNCs) and Christian evangelicals who had funded his campaign and shared his policy priorities. The ideological complexion of active nonprofit NGOs shifted during this period as conservative groups, from the American Enterprise Institute to the Family Research Council, joined the NGO community once dominated by more liberal groups (Peterson 2004). A major driving force behind Bush's unilateral turn in foreign policy was the Project for the New American Century, whose executive board in the 1990s had included Dick Cheney, Donald Rumsfeld, and Paul

Wolfowitz, among other neoconservative members of the first and second Bush administrations.

This pattern demonstrates that, while private groups maintain an important presence in the U.S. foreign-policy process, the composition and objectives of these groups regularly shift in relation to the priorities and worldviews of the policy makers in power at the moment. In this respect, the balance of power among NGOs at any given time reflects the broader power balance within the U.S. government. As nonstate institutions of power, the net impact of private groups is a historical *constant* while the impact of individual groups is *variable,* dependent upon which way the political wind is blowing. Like a defeated candidate, an NGO that loses its power base assumes the role of government critic while simultaneously plotting strategies for regaining control.

Public-interest NGOs are most troublesome to conservative leaders in the United States, including members of the Republican Party, which has dominated Congress for most of the past decade. In the view of conservatives, group demands for more foreign aid, curbs on U.S. arms sales, mandatory reductions in fossil-fuel emissions, and U.S. adherence to the International Criminal Court infringe upon the government's sovereign authority to make its own policy choices. Liberals, in contrast, tend to be more sympathetic to such demands, frequently placing global concerns above national interests in pursuing their policy goals.

Although constraints on state power were precisely what the Constitution's Framers had in mind when they fostered a vigorous civil society at home, they could not have anticipated the challenges to U.S. autonomy, or freedom of choice, that transnational groups would pose two centuries later. Groups routinely entering the fray over U.S. foreign policy include not only nonprofit NGOs, but also MNCs. Corporations exert enormous influence while providing essential funds for the semipermanent campaigns of elected leaders. The "constitutional" world order (Ikenberry 2001), which U.S. leaders took the lead in creating after World War II, makes such challenges to state sovereignty inevitable. This central tension of world power affects all democratic countries that open themselves to group pressures, but especially the primary target of such pressure, the United States.

NGOs in Theory and Practice

Before assessing the impact of transnational NGOs on U.S. foreign policy, it is helpful to consider their broader roles in world politics. In some cases, certain NGOs, such as the International Red Cross (IRC), assume quasi-governmental roles when they respond to societal needs that governments cannot meet, as the IRC does in providing emergency health care. In other cases, NGOs act as global advocates for the equitable provision of **public goods,** such as clean air and water, for people in all countries, not just the citizens of a single nation (see Chapter 12). The role of most NGOs, however, is much narrower: to advocate for the specific needs of their members and stakeholders.

The number of NGOs politically active today cannot be stated with precision. No formal mechanism to license or register the vast majority of these groups exists, particularly at the transnational level on which much of their foreign-policy activism takes place. To further complicate matters, NGOs are created and dismantled constantly in response to shifting needs, unforeseen developments, and evolving stages of the policy process. However, the number of NGOs that have gained "consultative status" with the UN Economic and Social Council is known and offers a perspective on the growth of NGOs over the past decade (see Figure 8.1). In 1946, just four NGOs held this status; by 1996 the number had grown to 1,226, and by 2002 to 2,236 (Willetts 2003).

Politically active NGOs assume a wide variety of institutional forms. Some are small, focus narrowly on single issues, and disappear when their policy preferences are satisfied. Other groups have large staffs and budgets, promote policies along a broad spectrum of issues, and maintain a permanent presence in Washington, D.C., and foreign capitals. The Worldwide Fund for Nature, for instance, boasts a membership of 5 million and maintains a staff of more than 3,300. The development group CARE controls an annual budget of more than $100 million (Bond 2000).

The missions and objectives of NGOs are also diverse. Multinational corporations (MNCs) seek changes in government economic policies that increase their profits. Religious and ethnic groups demand legal protections against discrimination, while prochoice women's groups demand greater control of their reproductive rights. Public-interest groups serve a worldwide constituency and call attention to human rights, environmental preservation, the reduction of mass poverty, and arms control, all of which require cooperation and occasional sacrifices among governments.

Figure 8.1 NGOs and the UN: Members with UNESCO Consultative Status, 1990–2002

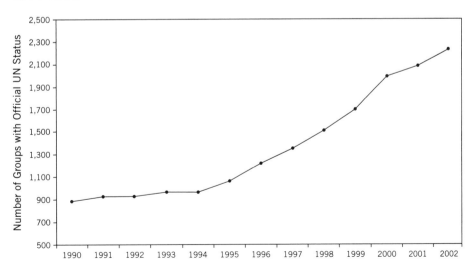

SOURCE: Peter Willetts, "The Growth in the Number of NGOs in Consultative Status with the Economic and Social Council of the United Nations" (2003), www.staff.city.ac.uk/p.willetts/NGOS/ngo-home.htm.

Normative values play a central role in the formation and growth of these groups. Individuals form public-interest NGOs upon deeply held and widely shared values, such as belief in the universality of human rights and nations' joint obligation to preserve the global environment. Such value orientations serve as catalysts for collective action and the creation of political organizations and networks that demand changes in government policy. Often, though certainly not always, effective group action does lead to the desired changes, demonstrating the importance of values and ideas in foreign policy (see Goldstein and Keohane 1993).

The Globalization of Civil Society

The ability of NGOs to adapt to a changing cultural environment is critical to the development of transnational civil society, an extension of the domestic civil societies that shape political life in the United States and other democracies. As noted in Chapter 7, public opinion increasingly matters outside national borders as foreign-policy makers appeal to citizens overseas as well as to governments for support. The news media, their impact "globalized" by the arrival of cable television and satellite technology, play a crucial role in informing the public, scrutinizing government actions, and providing arenas for policy debates. The greatest external influence, however, comes from interest groups, which channel the day-to-day participation of private citizens in the policy process at home and abroad. While these groups are not unique to the current era, never before have they been so well organized, visible, and connected with their counterparts in other countries.

The issue of land mines, for example, barely registered on government radar screens until a coalition of NGOs, the International Campaign to Ban Landmines (ICBL), called for a global ban on antipersonnel land mines in the mid-1990s. The coalition launched a well-orchestrated international campaign to raise public consciousness about these weapons, most placed in poor countries, where they maim civilians long after the end of the military conflict. By December 1997, 123 countries had signed a comprehensive ban on land mines.[1] The ban became the quickest major international agreement ever to enter into force when it took effect in March 1999. The ICBL and its coordinator, Jody Williams, received the 1997 Nobel Peace Prize "in part for helping create a fresh form of diplomacy" (Rutherford 2000, 75). Although the U.S. government refused to sign the treaty, claiming the weapons were still needed in the Korean Peninsula, this did not prevent the dismantling of land mines in most parts of the world. The United States found itself in a small minority of countries that opposed the ban, as it did with many other NGO-driven measures regarding arms control and global security.

Such antagonism exposes conflicts within the U.S. government itself, as NGOs seek out legislators and bureaucrats who support the groups' policy goals. In the legislative process over defense spending, for example, each of the four armed services maintains contacts with veterans' groups, military contractors, and

---

1. The full name of the agreement is the Ottawa Convention on the Prohibition of the Use, Stockpiling, Production and Transfer of Anti-Personnel Mines and on their Destruction.

officials in state and local governments that push for greater support for their respective services, often at the expense of the others. Similarly, development NGOs declare common cause with State Department administrators who seek higher budgets for economic aid, even if they come at the expense of other government programs such as national defense.

Thus the growing importance of NGOs will not necessarily promote a harmony of interests in the emerging era of **global governance,** which combines traditional state-to-state diplomacy with policy collaboration among private groups and intergovernmental organizations. Transnational civil society, though most often associated with liberal theories of world politics (see Chapter 3), can be better understood as "an arena of struggle" among political actors (Keck and Sikkink 1998, 33) and should not be seen as a stepping-stone to world government. Instead, "we should think of networks of governance crisscrossing and coexisting with a world divided formally into sovereign states" (Nye 2002b, 104–105). In this respect then, the empowerment of NGOs is compatible with realist theories, whose emphasis on chronic conflicts of interests may be extended beyond the anarchic interstate system.

Strengths and Weaknesses of NGOs

While NGOs are larger and more numerous than ever and their place in the U.S. foreign-policy process secure, they must not be viewed as all-powerful political actors on the verge of rendering the nation-state obsolete. To the contrary, NGOs are limited in what they can accomplish, either alone or in coalition with other groups. Each group possesses a unique set of strengths and weaknesses that affects its ability to influence government policy. Nonetheless, some generalizations can be made about the overall capabilities and limitations of NGOs, particularly nonprofit groups.

The primary strength of an NGO stems from its direct links to citizens at all levels of governance—local, state, national, and transnational. These links often prove stronger than those between states and private citizens, as U.S. citizens are more likely to participate politically through NGOs than through government programs or political parties. Furthermore, nonprofit NGOs benefit greatly from a strong sense of shared values among their members, who are determined to see these values converted into tangible goals and political action. The high levels of commitment and solidarity within a group form the glue that holds the members together over an extended period of time. Finally, the members of many NGOs have an expertise in policy areas involved, which gives them credibility and leverage when they attempt to influence government officials. Their expertise is also an asset when governments need help implementing programs or monitoring their effectiveness.

At the same time, NGOs suffer from five primary weaknesses. First, most groups have very limited resources, which forces them to rely on private donations to survive. Under these circumstances, long-term planning is difficult, and fund raising, rather than achieving stated goals, often consumes the groups' time and energy. Second, most NGOs do not maintain formal contacts with governments and must penetrate policy-making circles from the outside. Simply gaining access to key decision makers is a constant challenge, particularly for smaller groups lacking political or economic muscle. Even if it gains access, a group must still get policy makers to support its position, itself a formidable task.

A third weakness, alluded to above, is the inevitable division between NGOs with contrary or competing claims on governments. Multinational corporations and environmental groups, among other prominent examples, frequently call for government policies that are mutually exclusive. In the 1980s, U.S.-based corporations tried to prevent the imposition of U.S. sanctions against South Africa, which maintained a system of apartheid that persecuted the country's majority black population (Rogers 1993). However, African American groups, in alliance with human rights NGOs in the United States and abroad, vigorously pushed for the sanctions and ultimately succeeded in reversing the Reagan administration's antisanctions policy. In other cases, tactical differences stymie the effectiveness of like-minded groups. For instance, while some antiglobalization groups choose to work through government channels to reign in corporations, other groups call for mass boycotts and demonstrations. A common effect of clashing of interests and differing tactics is the *neutralization* of the groups' overall impact.

Fourth, NGOs frequently suffer from a **democratic deficit,** lacking the legal requirements for elected representation and openness that apply to the majority of government agencies. As a consequence, when providing information to the public, the groups tend to distort statistics and present exaggerated claims to gain support for their causes. The most established and best-endowed groups are "accountable only to themselves but often with significant financial resources, the management structure of a multinational company and a media image that governments can only envy" (Bond 2000). According to P. J. Simmons (1998, 83), these NGOs

> have the potential to do as much harm as good. Hailed as the exemplars of grassroots democracy in action, many NGOs are, in fact, decidedly undemocratic and unaccountable to the people they claim to represent. Dedicated to promoting more openness and participation in decision making, they can instead lapse into old-fashioned interest-group politics that produces gridlock on a global scale.

The final limitation facing NGOs involves their sheer mass. As noted earlier, more than 2,000 private groups currently maintain consultative status within the UN Economic and Social Committee. Each group hopes to affect the committee's work. For obvious logistical reasons, however, not all of them can take part in the deliberations. The UN committee must select which groups will participate in any given session. Similarly, private groups in the United States compete intensely for opportunities to testify before congressional committees or meet in person with top policy makers. Given the inherent limitations on the time available for such input, most NGOs get crowded out of the U.S. foreign-policy process. Under these circumstances, the best bet for a group is to appeal directly to private citizens—

through news media appearances, Internet reports, and direct-mail campaigns—and hope its message gets through to policy makers via their constituents.

Types of Transnational NGOs

In this section, we consider the various types of NGOs seeking to influence U.S. foreign policy. As the listing below reveals, a wide range of nonstate actors have a stake in the policy process. Most of these are **particularistic groups,** serving a limited number of individuals with stakes in the NGOs' missions. The rest are **cosmopolitan groups,** addressing transnational problems, such as environmental decay and weapons proliferation, affecting people in all areas. The success or failure of U.S. policy makers, who must contend with both types on a regular basis in these interactions, can depend on their ability to reconcile often conflicting group demands. Yet since a clean middle ground among NGOs is rarely found, policy makers most often must choose sides and reap whatever political costs or benefits follow.

Multinational Corporations

The largest and most powerful NGOs can be found in the business world. It is not unusual for a company to have its headquarters in one country and its other operations (such as research and development, production, marketing, and sales) in others. Profit-seeking firms with operations, subsidiaries, and markets in more than one country are known as **multinational corporations** (**MNCs**). For example, the energy and construction giant Halliburton, which had significant contracts in postwar Iraqi reconstruction, has offices in more than 120 countries. In responding to technological advances, primarily in the areas of research and development, telecommunications, and transportation, MNCs are both the by-products and the catalysts of globalization. These types of firms have grown rapidly in number, size, and global reach in the past century. The annual revenues of today's largest MNCs far exceed the economic output of most countries. Wal-Mart Stores, for instance, brought in more money in 2001 than the economy of Austria. In that same year, General Motors and Ford had higher revenues than the economies of Indonesia, Poland, Venezuela, and dozens of other countries (Kegley and Wittkopf 2004, 175).

The U.S. government, whose founding principles include a belief in the virtues of free markets and global commerce, has long been an advocate of MNCs. In 2003, four of the world's six largest multinational corporations were based in the United States (see Table 8.1). Other leading MNCs, including DaimlerChrysler, have most of their production facilities in the United States. Still others, such as the electronics firms based in Japan, derive most of their revenues from American consumers. These corporations can serve as agents of U.S. foreign policy by embracing many of the interests, values, and beliefs about political economy held by government leaders. Three areas of convergence may be identified.

Table 8.1 The World's Twenty Largest Multinational Corporations, 2003

Company	Base Country	Revenues (in Billions of U.S. Dollars)
1. Wal-Mart Stores	United States	$263
2. BP	United Kingdom	233
3. Exxon Mobil	United States	223
4. Royal Dutch Shell	Netherlands, United Kingdom	202
5. General Motors	United States	195
6. Ford Motor	United States	165
7. DaimlerChrysler	Germany	157
8. Toyota Motor	Japan	153
9. General Electric	United States	134
10. Total	France	118
11. Allianz	Germany	115
12. Chevron-Texaco	United States	113
13. Axa	France	112
14. ConocoPhillips	United States	99
15. Volkswagon	Germany	99
16. Nippon Telegraph & Telephone	Japan	98
17. ING Group	Netherlands	96
18. Citigroup	United States	95
19. International Business Machines (IBM)	United States	89
20. American International Group	United States	81

SOURCE: "Global 500," *Fortune* (July 26, 2004), 163.

First, corporate leaders and the U.S. government share interests in a world economy based upon private property and open markets. The government's bias toward free trade favors U.S.-based MNCs that are wealthier and more technologically advanced than their competitors overseas. For this reason, many foreign governments fear that open markets will intensify the domination of U.S. corporations, hasten the loss of domestic jobs and industries, and further reduce their capacity to control their economic futures. Nonetheless, political leaders in the United States continue to join corporate executives in embracing the process of economic globalization.

Second, corporations and U.S. political leaders share the belief that a free-market economy will foster political freedoms. In this view, firms will avoid doing business in countries that cannot guarantee the security of their assets, that tolerate corruption, and that repress political rights to such an extent that mass revolts pose constant dangers. Furthermore, the educated workforces required in the modern world economy are better informed and hence less likely to be manipulated or exploited by governments.

Finally, corporate and government officials agree that countries respecting economic and political freedoms most likely will engage in peaceful relations toward one another. Private investors and firms require a stable and predictable environment, impossible in areas prone to violent regional conflict. This acceptance of democratic-peace theory, described in Chapters 2 and 3, is deeply embedded in U.S. political culture.

In addition to having economic clout, MNCs are powerful *political* actors. Business groups have always been influential at all levels of U.S. politics. Their prospects for higher profits depend on favorable government policy in several areas, including corporate taxation, health and safety regulations, defense spending, and labor rights. Trade policy is of particular importance to MNCs, which want access to foreign markets along with protection from foreign competition. Corporations also stand to gain by food aid and development projects overseas, many of which require the provision of U.S.-based goods and services. Aid-funded roads, utilities, housing projects, schools, and hospitals also help MNCs in the long run by improving the prospects for future economic development and access to domestic markets. As the world economy becomes more closely knit, these corporations negotiate with many national governments at once to improve their prospects for future business.

The pervasive role of MNCs in U.S. foreign policy makes them frequent targets of criticism by other NGOs. Animosity is not limited to individuals and groups within the United States; foreign-based groups complain that multinational corporations are agents of cultural imperialism, force feeding people consumer products such as Coca-Cola and McDonald's hamburgers through aggressive marketing and advertising. Groups also "name and shame" corporations for damaging ecosystems, mistreating labor, and intimidating the political leaders of foreign countries and communities. Exposés of oppressive labor practices in overseas "sweatshops" by such companies as Nike, Wal-Mart, Walt Disney, and Gap prompted all of these corporations to establish codes of conduct for their suppliers (Gereffi, Garcia-Johnson, and Sasser 2001). Pressure from environmental NGOs such as the Rainforest Network and the Natural Resources Defense Council forced major retail stores in the United States, including Home Depot and Lowe's Home Improvement Warehouse, to certify that the lumber they sold did not come from suppliers inflicting irreversible damage to natural habitat.

The Military-Industrial Complex

Among U.S.-based corporations, those involved in the defense industry have the closest ties to the foreign-policy process. The U.S. defense industry, by far the largest of its kind in the world, has grown rapidly in recent years, after a decade of post–cold war cutbacks. Weapons production represents a large segment of the U.S. economy and is a leading source of new technologies, many of which find their way into civilian industries.[2] The defense industry currently employs more than 2 million people, about 2 percent of the civilian workforce (Center for Defense Information

---

2. For example, the U.S. Department of Defense sponsored much of the research and development of the Internet during the cold war.

2003b). As the largest discretionary category of U.S. government spending, the defense budget has a strong impact on whether the overall federal budget ends each fiscal year with a surplus or deficit. As Sen. Everett Dirksen, R-Ill., once wryly observed, "A billion here, a billion there, sooner or later it adds up to real money."

Defense spending is also a major arena of competition for federal dollars. Industry giants such as Lockheed Martin, Boeing, Raytheon, and General Dynamics have billions of dollars in government contracts for building the newest generation of high-technology fighter jets, tanks, and ships (see Table 8.2). Hundreds of smaller MNCs support the defense sector as well, providing ammunition, spare parts, uniforms, food, medical supplies, and other goods to the armed services. Deciding which military contractors receive the massive volumes of money is part of an intense and often bitter political process within Congress, its members making or breaking the fortunes of arms merchants with each defense appropriation.

The latest military buildup, focusing on high-technology weapons systems, accelerated after the terrorist attacks of September 2001. Of the nearly $400 billion

Table 8.2 Top Ten Military Contractors, 2002

Company and Headquarters	Defense Department Contracts (in Billions of U.S. Dollars)	Percentage of DoD Contracts	Major Weapons Systems (Selected)
Lockheed Martin Bethesda, Md.	$17.0	10.0%	F-16 Falcon fighter jet, AH-64 Apache helicopter, Trident missiles
Boeing St. Louis, Mo.	16.6	9.7	F-15 Eagle fighter jet, V-22 Osprey helicopter, C-17 cargo aircraft
Northrop Grumman Los Angeles, Calif.	8.7	4.8	B-2 bomber, F-15, F/A-18 Super Hornet fighter jet
Raytheon Lexington, Mass.	7.0	4.1	AMRAAM, Patriot, and Tomahawk missiles
General Dynamics Falls Church, Va.	7.0	4.1	Nuclear submarines, DDG-51 destroyers, M1A2 Abrams tank
United Technologies Hartford, Conn.	3.6	2.1	Aircraft engines, UH-60 Black Hawk helicopter
Science Applications Intl. San Diego, Calif.	2.1	1.2	Programmatic, logistical, and technical support
TRW Cleveland, Ohio	2.0	1.2	Electronic systems and support
Health Net Los Angeles, Calif.	1.7	1.0	Health care services
L-3 Communications New York, N.Y.	1.7	1.0	Underwater warfare systems
Total for top ten	*$67.4*	*39.2%*	
Total DoD contracts	*$170.8*		

SOURCE: Center for Defense Information, "Ten Largest U.S. Military Contractors, Fiscal Year 2002" (2003), www.cdi.org/news/mrp/contractors.pdf.

·))) IN THEIR OWN WORDS: DWIGHT D. EISENHOWER ((((·

Although Dwight D. Eisenhower's farewell address in 1961 was the first such event to be televised, observers registered surprise not so much at the medium of delivery as at the message sent. The man who had made his name as supreme allied commander during Word War II and then as supreme commander of NATO warned against the defense industry's unchecked influence in the halls of government. Coining the term military-industrial complex, *Eisenhower offered a cautionary tale about some of the nation's largest and most powerful foreign-policy interest groups. While many political and business leaders agreed with Eisenhower, the military-industrial complex is even stronger today. As defense budgets have soared in recent years, much of this funding has gone to private companies to build weapons and provide services that were previously provided by the U.S. government.*

A vital element in keeping the peace is our military establishment. Our arms must be mighty, ready for instant action, so that no potential aggressor may be tempted to risk his own destruction.

Our military organization today bears little relation to that known by any of my predecessors in peacetime, or indeed by the fighting men of World War II or Korea.

Until the latest of our world conflicts, the United States had no armaments industry. American makers of plowshares could, with time and as required, make swords as well. But now we can no longer risk emergency improvision of national defense; we have been compelled to create a permanent armaments industry of vast proportions. Added to this, three and a half million men and women are directly engaged in the defense establishment. We annually spend on military security more than the net income of all United States corporations.

This conjunction of an immense military establishment and a large arms industry is new in the American experience. The total influence—economic, political, even spiritual—is felt in every city, every State house, every office of the federal government. We recognize the imperative need for this development. Yet we must not fail to comprehend its grave implications. Our toil, resources, and livelihood are all involved; so is the very structure of our society.

In the councils of government, we must guard against the acquisition of unwarranted influence, whether sought or unsought, by the military-industrial complex. The potential for the disastrous rise of misplaced power exists and will persist.

We must never let the weight of this combination endanger our liberties or democratic processes. . . .

Source: Michael Nelson, ed., "Dwight D. Eisenhower's Farewell Address (1961)," Historic Documents on the Presidency: 1776–1989 (Washington, D.C.: Congressional Quarterly, 1989), 350–354.

in U.S. defense spending authorized by Congress for fiscal year 2003, $120 billion was designated for the research, development, and production of weapons (Squeo 2002, R4). Major weapons systems boosted by the Pentagon's latest modernization drive included the Joint Strike Fighter, expected to cost more than $200 billion, the F-22 Fighter ($69 billion), the Virginia Attack Submarine ($66 billion), the DDG-51 Destroyer ($56 billion), and the Commanche Helicopter ($48 billion). This massive influx of new defense funds is distributed across the armed services and among hundreds of U.S.-based corporations. Some weapons systems are cosponsored by two or more armed services and are developed by several military contractors at once. The Joint Strike Fighter, for example, will be shared by the Air Force, Navy, and Marine Corps; its primary contractors include Lockheed Martin, Northrop Grumman, BAE Systems, and Pratt & Whitney.

The large size and political clout of these MNCs have formed a central feature of U.S. society since World War II. President Eisenhower grew worried during the cold war that the "military-industrial complex" in the United States posed a danger to the economy by diverting a significant share of output from civilian production. In his view, the reliance of huge and politically influential corporations on arms manufacturing created a perverse incentive on the government's part to expand the nation's military arsenal. In such an environment, Eisenhower believed, both the arms merchants and their patrons in Congress were tempted to inflate the magnitude of foreign threats. Evidence that government officials exaggerated a "missile gap" favoring Soviet forces affirmed these concerns in the 1960s. In the 1980s, intelligence estimates of Soviet military capabilities proved inaccurate as well, raising doubts about the necessity of the huge U.S. military buildup.

Eisenhower's warning also highlighted the potential dangers iron triangles pose in the policy process (see Chapter 3). For many former military officers, who retire from active service in their forties and fifties, a logical next step in their careers is the defense industry, with its familiar products and functions. This crossing of career paths creates a strong bond between the Pentagon and defense contractors. Together, they are able to get the attention and support of powerful members of Congress, who receive campaign contributions and other forms of political support from the defense industry and its **political action committees (PACs),** the electoral arm of organized groups responsible for fund raising and distributing money to promote the election of desired candidates. The groups in the military industrial complex, as well as those in countless other areas, have proven to be highly influential in the U.S. foreign-policy process.

With such huge volumes of money involved—Lockheed Martin alone received $22 billion in new military contracts in fiscal year 2003—conflicts of interest and potential corruption inevitably exist, as documented abuses have shown. In some cases, defense contractors have bribed members of Congress in return for lucrative contracts. In other cases, former Pentagon officials who took positions as lobbyists for military contractors gained privileged access to legislators. Measures have been taken to reduce the impact of this "revolving door" in the procurement process. Former public officials must now be out of government a certain amount of time before they can accept jobs with private firms seeking government contracts. Reforms in campaign finance have also limited the potential for corruption. Yet the incentives of all concerned to maintain these ties persist within the military-industrial complex.

The case of Vice President Dick Cheney and Halliburton, the company he formerly headed, illuminates the dangers associated with the revolving door. Cheney, who earned $44 million from the military contractor during his five years as CEO, received about $150,000 annually in deferred pay between 2001 and 2005 and held another $18 million in stock options (Mayer 2004). As secretary of defense in 1992, Cheney hired the company to study ways it could support U.S. military needs after the cold war. A dozen years later, just prior to the 2003 Iraq invasion, which Cheney supported, Halliburton and its subsidiary—Kellogg Brown & Root—were the primary recipients of DoD contracts to feed the troops, maintain their bases, construct new government buildings, and rebuild Iraqi oil wells (see Baum 2003). Halliburton received nearly $4 billion in government contracts in fiscal year 2003 alone for services in Iraq and Afghanistan (U.S. Department of Defense 2004b). The administration did not advertise most of these contracts or receive competing bids on them, in part because few other firms were prepared to manage such a complex undertaking on short notice.

Not long after its Iraqi contracts received approval, Halliburton ran into trouble. In January 2004, the company announced that it would repay the U.S. government $6.3 million to cover "improper payments" two of its employees had received for their hiring of a subcontractor in Kuwait. In February, auditors found that a Halliburton subsidiary might have charged the government $16 million for meals it never served. Worse still, that same month the Pentagon launched a criminal investigation into allegations that Halliburton had overcharged U.S. taxpayers by $61 million for oil from Kuwait, oil which had exceeded market prices (Spinner 2004). Yet despite these problems, Halliburton continued to receive new government contracts after Iraq regained formal sovereignty in June 2004 and as the rebuilding and military-support costs continued to mount.

Trade Associations and Labor Unions

Private groups that represent entire sectors of the U.S. economy or the business community in general promote business interests in the United States as well. Many of these groups are active in shaping not only U.S. foreign policy, but also the policies of governments abroad. Prominent among these is the U.S. Chamber of Commerce, which seeks business access to foreign markets by pressuring policy makers in the United States and their counterparts in other countries. In 2002, the chamber, which represents more than 3 million firms and nearly 1,000 business associations, had a presence in eighty-two foreign nations. Using many of the same tactics, foreign-based MNCs and trade associations maintain full-time staffs in Washington, D.C., to pursue favorable treatment in U.S. trade policy and other legislation.

Labor unions, such as the United Auto Workers, the Teamsters Union, and the Communications Workers of America participate in this process as well, often as adversaries of the MNCs that employ their members. Keeping their workers' jobs in the United States is the major concern of these groups. The clout of this sizable voting bloc, though weakening in recent years as the number and proportion of unionized workers have declined, remains beyond question. Proponents of the steel industry, for example, persuaded President Bush in 2002 to increase tariffs on foreign-made steel to keep domestic producers in business, a decision popular in U.S. steel-producing regions of the United States that play a critical role in national elections. However, Bush's decision angered foreign political and business leaders as well as the WTO, which criticized Bush for violating his own standards regarding free trade and WTO regulations. In the face of this criticism and the threat of imminent WTO and European Union sanctions, Bush lowered the steel tariffs.

The protection of U.S. jobs is a classic intermestic issue as are other aspects of economic activity, such as environmental regulation and immigration. Policy makers in these cases play a two-level game (Putnam 1988) in which they negotiate simultaneously with representatives of foreign governments and those of U.S. interest groups with a stake in the outcome. Interests at the two levels frequently come into conflict. For example, after the U.S. government secures access to another country's domestic market, American firms are tempted to move their factories to that country to reduce labor costs, thus laying off workers in the United States. Decision makers in these cases must walk a political tightrope, trying to find areas of agreement among the interested parties at home and abroad.

Ethnic and Religious Groups

Ethnic and religious groups, too, play vital roles in the U.S. foreign-policy process (DeConde 1992). Like all particularistic interest groups, these NGOs promote the interests of segments of the population that, in their view, would otherwise be neglected by policy makers. Changes in American society, especially the trend toward a more multicultural population, encouraged the mobilization of these groups in the 1980s and 1990s (see Figure 8.2). The broader U.S. foreign-policy agenda after the cold war, and the growing political impact of ethnicity and religious identification in world politics, further propelled the formation and growth of the NGOs (Uslaner 2002). These developments clearly illustrate how race and religion serve as "a natural base for group formation and organized political action" (Goldberg 1990, 2–3).

The most successful groups form large, cohesive, and politically active organizations to advance the interests of their members. In addition, they appeal to all U.S. citizens within their ethnic or religious group to vote as a bloc for the most sympathetic political candidates. Because support from the general public can be crucial in advancing their interests, the groups also must espouse causes that apply to a broader population than their membership. Finally, such groups focus their lobbying efforts on Congress, not the White House, because of their greater access to Capitol Hill and legislators' greater responsiveness to parochial, rather than national, concerns (Haney and Vanderbush 1999, 344–345).

One of the largest and most potent of these NGOs is the American Israel Public Affairs Committee (AIPAC). With 65,000 members residing in all fifty

Figure 8.2 U.S. Population by Race and Hispanic Background, 2002

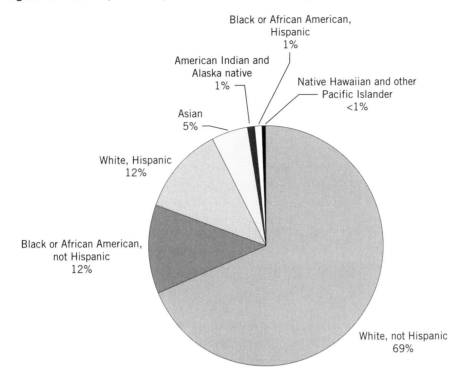

SOURCE: U.S. Census Bureau, "Hispanic Population Reaches All-Time High of 38.8 Million, New Census Bureau Estimates Show" (press release, June 18, 2003), www.census.gov/Press-Release/www/releases /archives/hispanic_origin_population/001130.html.

NOTES: The Asian, American Indian and Alaska Native, and Native Hawaiian and other Pacific Islander categories each include Hispanic and non-Hispanic populations. People who identify their origin as Hispanic or Latino may be of any race.

states, AIPAC exerts a strong and constant influence on the policy process. The organization claims credit for the passage of more than 100 pro-Israel legislative measures every year, including the annual transfer of $3 billion in foreign aid to Israel, making it by far the leading recipient of U.S. assistance. The AIPAC office is so immersed in the policy process that it provides a "Congressional Briefing Book" to legislative staffers. Chapters in the online volume include an overview of the U.S.-Israel "partnership," an analysis of regional threats to Israel, and a guide to the Middle East peace process (American Israel Public Affairs Committee 2004b).

Islamic and Arab-American groups have had far more difficulty gaining influence over U.S. foreign policy, despite their large numbers in big cities and electorally important "swing" states such as Michigan. According to Eric Uslaner (2002, 362–364), these groups are less cohesive, affluent, and politically active than the members of AIPAC. In addition, whereas AIPAC members overwhelmingly support the Democratic Party, Arab-Americans are more equally divided between Republicans and Democrats. Furthermore, the societal stature of these groups has suffered, not surprisingly, since the onset of the war on terrorism, and Arab-Americans frequently have been "profiled" and singled out for government scrutiny.

Hispanic and Latino citizens, who now compose the largest minority group in the United States, also have suffered from a lack of internal cohesion, economic power, and assimilation into mainstream U.S. society (Huntington 2004). Certain subgroups, however, have fared better. The Cuban-American National Foundation (CANF) offers an outstanding example. CANF, based in Miami, uses sophisticated promotional techniques to gain government support for Cuban exiles living in the United States. It calls upon the U.S. government to maintain harsh sanctions against Cuba's communist regime, which has remained in power since the Cuban people overthrew a U.S.-backed government in 1959. The organization successfully pushed for the creation of two government-run media outlets, Radio Marti (1985) and TV Marti (1990), which provide news and entertainment programs directly to the Cuban population. Political leaders in Florida, and even presidential candidates, routinely include CANF meetings in their campaign stops, fully aware that the group's endorsement can be vital to their chances of gaining or maintaining elected offices.

In the wake of the cold war, ethnic groups linked to the former communist countries in eastern Europe have become actively involved in U.S. foreign policy toward the region. For example, in 1998 Polish-American groups mobilized in large numbers to support the eastward expansion of NATO.[3] During the Kosovo conflict of 1999, legislators were careful to address the concerns of Greek-Americans regarding possible spillover of the conflict into northern Greece. While it would be an exaggeration to assert that these groups dictated the terms of U.S. foreign policy in these cases, their concerns undoubtedly carried enormous weight among elected officials. This will continue to be the case for transplanted ethnic groups from all regions that look to their adopted governments for support "as the independence, survival, or general welfare of [their] ethnic kin or homeland is threatened" (Ambrosio 2002, 8–9).

Less prominent ethnic and religious NGOs engage in the foreign-policy process as well. The Japanese-American Citizens League, for example, promotes the interests of its members and calls for closer relations between the United States and Japan. Among religious NGOs, the concerns of particular faiths are advanced through groups such as the American Muslim Council, the American Jewish Congress, and the Catholic League for Religious and Civil Rights. These and other groups have been most successful when their objectives align with U.S. strategic interests and when their members are politically united (Ahari 1987).

In the 2000 election, Evangelical Christian groups were of particular importance to President Bush, who received about 40 percent of his votes from this segment of the population (Bumiller 2003; see also Fineman 2003). Bush repaid these

---

3. The U.S. government paid close attention to public opinion in the former Soviet bloc in considering two rounds of NATO expansion after the cold war. See Kostadinova (2000) for an elaboration.

core supporters by vigorously pursuing their policy preferences. In foreign policy, one of Bush's first acts as president was to restore a ban on U.S. aid to foreign governments that included abortion counseling as part of their family-planning programs. Bush's frequent references to biblical scripture in his speeches affirmed his link to the 43,000 congregations composing the National Association of Evangelicals, whose continued support he needed for reelection in 2004.

Public-Interest Groups

As noted earlier, cosmopolitan NGOs seek to affect government policies in ways the participants see as conducive to the general public, either in one country or worldwide. These groups confront a large range of transnational problems ineffectively managed by national governments and intergovernmental organizations. To greatly enhance their impact, members form transnational advocacy networks (Keck and Sikkink 1998). As with domestic groups, governments are more likely to listen to large, well-organized coalitions of transnational groups that can affect the electoral fortunes of political leaders. Shared values play an especially strong role in the mobilization of the public-interest groups. The issues that have prompted the most NGO activity involve human rights, environmental protection, and international development.

Human rights. The protection of human rights is one of the most pervasive concerns of public-interest NGOs (see Welch 2001). This cause resonates strongly in the United States, where support for global human rights has historically been based upon the constitutional foundations of its own government. Attention to human rights intensified during the cold war. To American leaders, the denial of political and economic freedoms in communist countries amounted to a wholesale violation of human rights. However, U.S. support for repressive governments around the world prompted charges that the United States did not live up to its own standards of human rights.

In the 1970s and 1980s, the lapses of the U.S. government, combined with widespread abuses of human rights by communist regimes and many developing countries, inspired millions of private citizens worldwide to join NGOs focusing on the issue (see Korey 1999; and Weissbrodt 1984). Private groups in the industrialized countries formed links with their counterparts in the developing regions. Private funding for these groups, from individuals as well as other public-interest NGOs, grew rapidly during these decades. Economic support from foundations, for example, jumped from less than $1 million in the mid-1970s to more than $20 million in the early 1990s (Keck and Sikkink 1998, 99).

This growth occurred during a period—from the Vietnam War to the end of the cold war—when many human-rights groups viewed the United States with suspicion. The Reagan administration in particular maintained an adversarial relationship with these NGOs. By 1990, however, Congress was not only listening to them, but also, in some instances, using their reports as the basis for public hearings and possible sanctions. After Americas Watch, a prominent Latin American NGO, released findings in the late 1980s of widespread torture and political killings in Mexico, Congress held public hearings on the problem. The publicity generated by these hearings, combined with pressure from the U.S. government, prompted Mexican leaders to create the National Commission on Human Rights and, later, to reform their country's electoral system.

Several human-rights groups mobilized against the U.S.-led invasions and subsequent occupations of Afghanistan and Iraq. The most prominent of these groups, Amnesty International and Human Rights Watch, published dozens of critical reports on civilian casualties and the mistreatment of prisoners in both countries as well as in the U.S. detention center at its Guantanamo Bay Naval Base in Cuba. A confidential report by the International Committee of the Red Cross (ICRC), which visited detention centers across Iraq in 2003, described widespread abuses committed by U.S. and British guards and interrogators. The report, leaked to the public, heightened criticism of the United States after its own reports of mistreatment at the Abu Ghraib prison, along with graphic photographs of the abuses, were made public.[4]

Environmental protection. Another primary concern of public-interest NGOs is the global environment. As in the case of human rights, public activism in the environmental arena increased in the late twentieth century, especially following the cold war, when security concerns gave way to transnational problems previously neglected by the world powers. Prior to this time, environmental decay in the United States had been considered primarily a domestic problem to be solved by domestic measures such as the Clean Air Act and the Clean Water Act. However, mounting evidence that the effects of pollution could not be contained within political boundaries, along with scientific findings of a "greenhouse effect" and global warming, made it clear that the world needed cooperative solutions (see Chapter 12).

Membership in environmental NGOs more than doubled during this period as did financial contributions from members and private foundations. The largest of these groups, including Greenpeace, the Environmental Defense Fund, the Nature Conservancy, and the Natural Resources Defense Council, formed chapters in dozens of countries. The 1992 UN Conference on Environment and Development, more commonly known as the Earth Summit, served as a catalyst for NGO activism. More than 1,500 NGOs and government leaders from more than 170 countries officially took part in the conference, held in Brazil. At the Earth Summit, environmental groups gained unprecedented access to the policy process and were directly involved in the drafting of environmental agreements.

As with human-rights NGOs, the U.S. government is chronically at odds with environmental groups. As the world's leading source of fossil fuel emissions and solid waste and its leading consumer of finite energy resources, the United States is the foremost object of criticism among the groups. The close ties President Bush

---

4. The leaked ICRC report was entitled "Report of the International Committee of the Red Cross (ICRC) on the Treatment of Prisoners of War and Other Protected Persons by the Geneva Convention in Iraq during Arrest, Internment, and Interrogation." For the full report, see www.globalsecurity .org/military/library/report/2004/icrc_report_iraq_feb2004.htm.

and many of his senior advisers had to the oil industry, whose lobbyists called for greater oil extraction, rather than conservation, added to the criticism. Private groups as well as many governments view with skepticism, if not disdain, the common defense of U.S. officials that restrictions on private enterprise impairs economic growth while violating economic liberties. Ironically, the environmental NGOs owe much of their rapid rise and growing influence to the damaging impact of the United States on the global ecosystem and its refusal to abide by the norms of conservation espoused by these groups.

International development. Hundreds of U.S.- and foreign-based NGOs engage daily in the transfer and delivery of humanitarian assistance to people in need. The most prominent of these groups, including CARE, World Vision International, Oxfam Federation, and Doctors Without Borders, have each controlled more than $500 million of the estimated $8 billion in development aid disbursed annually to poor countries in recent years (Simmons 1998, 92). More than one-half of World Bank loans today involve NGOs in the development process.[5]

Groups based in industrialized countries routinely form partnerships with NGOs from developing countries to deliver food aid, conduct health programs, and plan long-term development projects. Government agencies in many developing countries are not equipped to manage the needs of their rapidly growing populations. In these cases, development NGOs fill a void in the public sector, drawing on resources from private sources as well as from wealthy governments that greatly exceed those available to the governments of poor states.

The United States has increasingly turned to NGOs to manage the aid programs it sponsors (see Chapter 11). The International Red Cross, for example, receives annual grants from the U.S. Agency for International Development (USAID) to immunize the citizens of developing countries against infectious diseases such as polio, measles, and malaria. The Red Cross, which has offices in more than 175 countries, provides emergency relief in the aftermath of hurricanes, earthquakes, and other natural disasters. From the U.S. government's standpoint, NGOs provide a more "neutral" vehicle for such programs than agencies affiliated with the United Nations, which many American policy makers see as politically biased and hostile to their country.

A major concern among many development NGOs in recent years has been the foreign debts of developing countries. A global coalition of private development agencies, church groups, human-rights activists, and other groups mobilized around the issue of debt relief by forming a movement called Jubilee 2000. Supported by high-profile celebrities such as Bono, the lead singer of the rock band U2, the Jubilee 2000 movement prompted wealthy countries and international financial institutions to forgive billions of dollars in foreign debt owed by the world's poorest countries. By February 2004, ten impoverished countries had received more than $12 billion in debt relief, freeing them from the withering costs

5. The World Bank, like governments, benefits by outsourcing development projects to private groups rather than managing these projects itself with permanent staff. As the largest source of World Bank funding, the U.S. government has the most to gain from these arrangements.

of debt service that had stunted economic growth in previous years.[6] Another seventeen countries, mostly in sub-Saharan Africa, were scheduled for an additional $19 billion in debt relief, pending the outcome of negotiations between the debtor governments and their creditors.

Think Tanks and Private Foundations

Public debate regarding U.S. foreign policy often originates within the dozens of "think tanks" located in Washington, D.C., and elsewhere across the country. While the news media provide the medium for debate, these private institutions supply the debaters in the form of academic specialists, former government and military officials, and outspoken figures from the private sector. The primary goal of these **idea brokers** (Smith 1991) is to influence public opinion and government policy through the dissemination of research findings and the airing of opinions on a variety of national issues. Indeed, observers sometimes refer to major think tanks as "governments in waiting," providing those out of power with an opportunity to remain active in the policy community while the rival political party controls the White House or Congress (see Figure 8.3).

Among these groups, the Council on Foreign Relations (CFR), formed in 1921, is the most influential in the U.S. foreign-policy process. The council limits

Figure 8.3 Select Foreign-Policy Think Tanks: The Ideological Spectrum

Liberal	Centrist	Conservative
Center for Defense Information	Brookings Institution	American Enterprise Institute
Center for Nonproliferation Studies	Carnegie Endowment for International Peace	Cato Institute
Federation of American Scientists	Council on Foreign Relations	Center for Strategic & International Studies
Global Policy Forum	Freedom House	Ethics and Public Policy Center
Institute for Policy Studies	Institute for International Economics	Family Research Council
Interhemispheric Resource Center	New America Foundation	Heritage Foundation
Project on Defense Alternatives	U.S. Institute of Peace	Hoover Institution
Union of Concerned Scientists		Project for the New American Century
World Policy Institute		RAND Corporation

6. These countries included Benin, Bolivia, Burkina Faso, Guyana, Mali, Mauritania, Mozambique, Nicaragua, Tanzania, and Uganda (International Monetary Fund and International Development Association 2004).

Point/Counterpoint
GLOBAL COMPETITION VS. COOPERATION

Much of the public debate regarding U.S. foreign policy occurs among think tanks, the private research NGOs that have become more sophisticated in shaping public opinion and influencing government policies. Many prominent think tanks focus on foreign policy, often drawing upon the expertise of former (and possibly future) government officials who want outlets for their viewpoints. This has particularly been the case in recent years as policy analysts have disagreed over the course of U.S. foreign policy, especially on the question of whether the United States should adopt a competitive or a cooperative posture in world politics.

The Project for the New American Century (PNAC) is one of the most outspoken advocates of a more "muscular" foreign policy. According to the PNAC statement of principles, adopted at the group's founding in 1997, "We seem to have forgotten the essential elements of the Reagan Administration's success: a military that is strong and ready to meet both present and future challenges; a foreign policy that boldly and purposefully promotes American principles abroad; and national leadership that accepts the United States' global responsibilities." From this perspective, the United States should exploit its global primacy to make the world more hospitable to U.S. values and interests.

More moderate and liberal think tanks call for a "nonoffensive" approach to U.S. foreign policy. The Project on Defense Alternatives (PDA), for example, promotes a "transitional security policy" that would curb military spending, encourage arms control, and foster "an increasing reliance on collective and global peacekeeping agencies and nonmilitary means of conflict prevention, containment, and resolution." Such cooperative measures are in keeping with Bill Clinton's grand strategy of global engagement and democratic reforms, with Jimmy Carter's emphasis on human rights, and with Woodrow Wilson's much earlier call for collective security.

The PNAC gained the upper hand in this debate in 2001 when many of its founding members, including Dick Cheney, were appointed to high-level positions in the Bush administration. Other PNAC officers, including Donald Rumsfeld and Paul Wolfowitz, took command of the Pentagon and adopted the "neoconservative" principles espoused by the group. For its part, the PDA became a vocal critic of the Bush administration's preventive-war strategy and its 2003 invasion of Iraq. The subsequent developments in that country only hardened the positions of the two think tanks, whose vocal members continued to advocate very different strategies for U.S. foreign policy.

Sources: Project for the New American Century Web site, www.newamericancentury.org; Project on Defense Alternatives Web site, www.comw.org.

membership, highly valued as a sign of prestige in the policy community, to 4,000. Attendance at CFR-sponsored policy forums, which often involve current foreign-policy makers and foreign leaders, also serves as an important status symbol. The journal *Foreign Affairs,* edited and published by the council, is a widely read source of elite opinion regarding U.S. foreign policy. Although the council considers itself nonpartisan, it espouses an activist world role that has been a centerpiece of U.S. foreign policy for the past century. The CFR and other moderate think tanks play a major part in the "revolving door" of policy elites. Richard Haass, for example, left the Brookings Institution in 2001 to become director of policy planning in the State Department, then left the Bush administration two years later to become president of the CFR.

Other think tanks, some with institutional links to universities and government agencies, participate more directly in the U.S. foreign-policy process.[7] California-based RAND (an acronym for research and development) has received billions of dollars worth of grants since 1948 to conduct research on military technology for the Department of Defense. Its scope has broadened in recent years to include health care, education, and criminal justice, among other areas of public policy. In addition to its work for the U.S. government, RAND has conducted research for the governments of China, Germany, the Netherlands, Romania, and the United Kingdom.

Finally, hundreds of private foundations in the United States provide grants for international research and programs in such areas as public health, education, environmental protection, development, and conflict resolution. The Ford Foundation, for example, has approved more than $10 billion in grants since 1950, primarily in economic development, political reform, and international cooperation. By the end of 2003, the Bill and Melinda Gates Foundation, with a $27 billion endowment from the founder and chairman of Microsoft Corp., had donated nearly $4 billion for health-care and literacy programs in the developing world. Recipients urgently needed the funds as a result of the growing income gaps between developed and less-developed countries and cutbacks in aid programs from many governments, including the United States.

The Microsoft case signals a new era in global development, with corporations stepping in to fund programs that governments are either unwilling or unable to support. In other cases, wealthy individuals have stepped in to fill the void in government funding. CNN founder Ted Turner, for example, announced in 1997 that he would donate $1 billion to the UN over ten years, in part to pay for development programs that faced cutbacks resulting from decreased contributions from the U.S. government.

Terrorist Groups and Criminal Syndicates

The September 2001 attacks literally brought home to the United States the effect of terrorist groups, which fit the broad definition of NGOs adopted in this chapter:

---

7. The U.S. Institute of Peace, though technically considered an "independent" research organization, is funded by Congress. Its board of directors is appointed by the president and confirmed by the Senate.

organized private groups devoted to changing public policies in their favor. Highly unconventional NGOs, terrorist groups have profoundly altered the scope and strategy of U.S. foreign policy. In declaring a "war on terrorism," President Bush launched a large-scale military conflict against an enemy that was not a sovereign country, a first in the history of the United States. With the exception of smaller-scale conflicts against pirates and drug smugglers, U.S. military actions had previously taken place within the confines of the Westphalian nation-state system.

Although they may maintain informal contacts with governments and receive material or moral support from them, terrorist groups are usually legally independent of any nation-state. Members of terrorist groups often feel *disenfranchised,* or left out of the conventional channels of policy making. They regularly claim that their past efforts to gain concessions peacefully were ignored, forcing them to resort to political violence.

The United States was a frequent target of terrorist attacks prior to 9-11, but rarely on its own soil. The wave of attacks by Islamic militants began in 1983 with suicide car bombings of a Marine barracks and the U.S. embassy in Beirut, Lebanon. The 1988 bombing of a commercial jet over Scotland killed 259 people, including 189 Americans. Terrorists first tried to destroy the World Trade Center in 1993 with underground explosives. Attacks on U.S. troops in Saudi Arabia produced hundreds of casualties in 1995 and 1996. Later in the decade, al Qaeda terrorists bombed U.S. embassies in Kenya and Tanzania, killing more than 300 people and injuring 5,000 others. While these attacks were linked to foreign groups, domestic terrorists have also targeted government buildings and employees. The most prominent domestic attack was the 1995 bombing of the federal building in Oklahoma City, which left 168 people dead.

Overseas terrorist groups that have targeted the United States are most often associated with Islam and are based in the Middle East and the Persian Gulf. Their leaders share a hatred of the U.S. government and resent its close ties to Israel, its support for repressive monarchs in Saudi Arabia, and its past attempts to control the oil reserves of the Persian Gulf. More generally, these radical Islamic groups reject Western culture, viewing it as decadent and contrary to Islamic values and traditions. Much of the money to support these groups comes from governments in the Middle East, in part to prevent the terrorists from challenging the officials' own claims to power. The money paid by these governments, including that of Saudi Arabia, derives in large part from the same Western oil consumers the terrorists vow to destroy. Among the most notable of these Islamic terrorist groups:[8]

- *al Qaeda* (The Base)—an offspring of the Afghan resistance to Soviet occupation from 1979 to 1989 led by Osama bin Laden; goals include removing Western influence from Islam, the destruction of Israel, and the killing of Americans; responsible for the September 11, 2001, attacks.

- *Hamas* (Islamic Resistance Movement)—based in Gaza and other occupied territories of Israel; devoted to the creation of an Islamic Palestinian

---

8. These descriptions are drawn from the U.S. Department of State (2003b), *Patterns of Global Terrorism,* and the Center for Defense Information (2004b), "Terrorism Project."

state in place of Israel; linked to multiple suicide bombings against Israelis; supported by Iran, Palestinian expatriates, and private benefactors.

- *Hezbollah* (Party of God)—based in southern Lebanon; responsible for attacks on a U.S. embassy and Marine barracks in the early 1980s and for kidnappings of Israelis in the early 1990s in South America; established role as political party; supported by Syria and Iran.

- *Islamic Jihad* (Holy Struggle)—Headquartered in Syria, but primarily active in occupied territories of Israel; proclaimed goal is to liberate Palestine "from the river to the sea"; linked to multiple suicide bombings against Israelis.

Many of these groups perform a variety of functions beyond the staging of terrorist attacks. Hezbollah, for example, operates a network of schools and hospitals in Lebanon, and al Qaeda sponsors similar institutions in Saudi Arabia, occasionally with public funds. Such activities cement the bonds between the groups and civil societies, often superceding the role of government agencies the terrorists consider corrupted by Western influence. Efforts by the United States and its allies to defeat these groups are especially difficult when they are deeply enmeshed in their communities and enjoy widespread public support.

Criminal syndicates pose another threat to the United States and its citizens. Narcotics cartels in Colombia and other South American countries have created elaborate networks for the cultivation and processing of illegal drugs and their distribution in the United States. The "war on drugs" waged by the United States for more than two decades has been fought with only limited success against these groups, which have resisted the pressure from the United States and their own governments. Other criminal syndicates are involved in illegal trading of weapons and ammunition, many of which end up in the hands of terrorists, and the piracy of intellectual property. Like terrorist groups, the syndicates have proved elusive, moving their operations regularly and concealing their assets in foreign financial institutions out of the reach of U.S. investigators.

Functions and Tactics of NGOs

Our attention in this section turns to the primary functions of NGOs and the tactics the groups' employ to influence U.S. foreign policy. These tactics vary widely, depending on the type of NGO involved, the resources at its disposal, and the foreign-policy issue it seeks to influence. Generally speaking, NGOs have become far more sophisticated as they have moved from the fringes to the mainstream of the policy process. Increasingly, they participate *within* the process, drafting legislation, serving on international commissions, and implementing government programs in areas previously monopolized by states.[9]

---

9. Permanent members of the UN Security Council, including the United States, regularly brief NGOs and seek their input on regional problems that may call for UN action. See the Web site www.globalpolicy.org, under the Security Council section, for a detailed listing of these collaborations.

Agenda Setting

Many NGOs simply want to call attention to their causes. In most cases, before a government can be expected to do something about such problems as global warming or the plight of political prisoners, large numbers of private citizens must make officials aware of these problems and forcefully call for government action. Accomplishing this goal is particularly difficult in the United States, where thousands of NGOs compete daily for attention and support in a crowded, often bewildering media environment. The continued existence of many NGOs depends upon their success in taking hold of the media spotlight, if only for a brief time.

Well-organized private groups have been instrumental in setting the agendas of states and intergovernmental organizations. The creation of the United Nations in 1945 and the UN's early emphasis on human rights and decolonization owed much to the work of churches, peace groups, and ethnic minorities. In the 1960s and 1970s, environmental groups mobilized effectively to force changes in automobile emission standards and enhance the protection of natural habitat. Peace groups in the 1980s rallied in favor of a nuclear freeze and in opposition to a new round of U.S. missile deployments. In the 1990s, private groups managed to place a global ban on land mines and a treaty restricting small arms on the international agenda.

The most effective of these groups exploit advances in communication technology, particularly the Internet, to get their messages across. Their Web sites serve as crucial sources of information about their organizations, their causes, and the strategies to achieve their objectives. These sites commonly provide links to related groups and information sources, encouraging the collaboration of NGOs and collective political action. Mass e-mailings also provide a low-cost means by which the groups communicate with their members as well as with influential policy makers. Well-orchestrated media events, such as press conferences or demonstrations, have proved useful in attracting attention as well.

Sophisticated public-relations techniques are vital to these NGOs because, in most cases, their main "product" is an idea, principle, or objective in shaping public policy, not a tangible object that can be directly observed. Normative values, which relate to how governments *should* behave, rather than how they actually do, form an NGO's core, around which the activities it sponsors and the legislation it endorses circulate. The promotion of values, therefore, is the primary mission of these groups; to do so, they rely on the same tools of public relations used by companies and political campaigns.

Like government officials, NGOs frame their adopted causes in dramatic and clearly understandable ways to gain media attention and public support. In the NGO campaign for banning land mines, for example, visual images of maimed victims proved more effective than hard numbers on the death toll produced by these weapons (Rutherford 2000). Similarly, members of Amnesty International found that the plight of political prisoners resonated more strongly among the public when individual cases were presented in graphic detail. Environmentalists gained world attention more quickly when they focused on individual victims of development rather than on the results of scientific studies regarding ecological decay.

Given that the problems of concern to NGOs tend to be ongoing, a primary function they serve is to *monitor* the extent of these problems and the U.S. government's response to them, and to *report* their findings on a regular basis to their members, policy makers, and the general public. Freedom House, a U.S.-based human-rights group, accomplishes this task by publishing an annual volume called *Freedom in the World,* which rates the conduct of all governments in respecting human rights (see Map 11, Freedom in the World, in the map section at the front of the book). Policy makers and activists from other groups watch the rating closely because Freedom House, unlike a government agency, is an independent organization that stakes its reputation on its objective assessment of government practices. In a similar fashion, periodic reports by the Council on Economic Priorities review the practices of major corporations and provide needed guidance to political and business leaders. Environmental NGOs, meanwhile, police the implementation of past agreements even as they pressure governments to sign new ones.

Political Pressure and Policy Reform

In addition to influencing government agendas, private groups directly intervene in the U.S. foreign-policy process. Their tactics include direct-mail campaigns to congressional offices and the White House that ask for support on matters of immediate concern. Representatives of NGOs also appeal in person to legislators and key executive branch officials. In the process of **lobbying,** they present these officials with "carrots," or potential rewards, for support of their preferences, as well as "sticks," or potential punishments, for nonsupport.

Carrots and sticks generally come in two forms—electoral and financial support. The first relates to the central reality that elected officials need votes to gain and stay in office and that organized groups can deliver more votes than individuals can. Politicians listen carefully to these groups, particularly large religious and ethnic NGOs, labor unions, and business groups that can mobilize multitudes of voters. In the 2000 presidential election, George W. Bush actively sought the support of Cuban Americans in southern Florida and promised to continue the economic embargo against Fidel Castro's communist regime that these voters widely supported. Florida governor Jeb Bush, who had close ties to the Cuban Americans, helped his brother win the state (however narrowly, and after intervention by the U.S. Supreme Court) largely on the basis of an overwhelming majority of votes from this closely knit ethnic group. Public-interest NGOs generally have smaller membership rolls, but their members tend to feel very strongly about their missions and tend to form solid voting blocs.

Another way NGOs influence the policy process is by providing, or withholding, contributions to political campaigns through their affiliated PACs. Despite recent reforms in campaign finance, money still speaks volumes in national politics. (See Table 8.3.) The high price of campaigning, primarily the

Table 8.3 Top Overall Political Donors, 2000 Elections

Rank	Contributor	Group Type	Total Contributions (in Millions)	Percentage to Democrats	Percentage to Republicans	Primary Support
1.	American Federation of State, County, and Municipal Employees	Labor	$8.6	99%	1%	Solidly Democrat
2.	Service Employees International Union	Labor	6.1	96	3	Solidly Democrat
3.	AT&T	Communications/ electronics	4.9	40	60	Leans Republican
4.	Carpenters and Joiners Union	Labor	4.7	94	6	Solidly Democrat
5.	Microsoft	Communications/ electronics	4.7	47	53	On the fence
6.	International Brotherhood of Electrical Workers	Labor	4.5	98	2	Solidly Democrat
7.	Goldman Sachs	Finance/insurance/ real estate	4.3	64	36	Leans Democrat
8.	Citigroup	Finance/insurance/ real estate	4.1	54	46	On the fence
9.	National Association of Realtors	Finance/insurance/ real estate	3.9	42	58	Leans Republican
10.	United Food and Commercial Workers	Labor	3.9	99	1	Solidly Democrat
11.	Communications Workers of America	Labor	3.9	99	0	Solidly Democrat
12.	Philip Morris	Agribusiness	3.8	18	81	Strongly Republican
13.	SBC Communications	Communications/ electronics	3.8	45	55	On the fence
14.	Association of Trial Lawyers of America	Lawyers	3.7	90	10	Strongly Democrat
15.	MBNA	Finance/insurance/ real estate	3.6	14	86	Strongly Republican
16.	Verizon Communications	Communications/ electronics	3.5	36	63	Leans Republican
17.	American Federation of Teachers	Labor/education	3.3	99	1	Solidly Democrat
18.	Laborers Union	Labor	3.1	93	7	Solidly Democrat
19.	National Rifle Association	Issue group	3.1	8	92	Solidly Republican
20.	Teamsters Union	Labor	2.9	93	6	Solidly Democrat

SOURCE: Center for Responsive Politics, "Who Gives—Industries," www.opensecrets.org/industries/index.asp.

Employees from Halliburton, a U.S.-based energy company, inspect an oil and gas facility in Iraq in February 2004. Halliburton, which was led by Dick Cheney prior to his becoming vice president in 2001, gained billions of dollars in Pentagon contracts to rebuild the Iraqi oil industry after years of decline under Saddam Hussein and the subsequent U.S.-led invasion in 2003. Critics alleged that Cheney's close ties to Halliburton symbolized the overly close relations between the U.S. government and major corporations.

costs of producing and airing television commercials, forces candidates to rely heavily on financial contributions. Private groups needing help from the government—as almost all groups do—gain favor among political leaders by contributing money to their campaigns. In return for these funds, candidates assure the groups that their concerns will be taken into account.

Multinational corporations influence U.S. foreign policy by setting up PACs to contribute to political campaigns. This applies to MNCs based in the United States as well as to those with headquarters elsewhere. The Netherlands-based KKMG International, for example, spent nearly $2 million on U.S. congressional campaigns in 2002. The accounting firm supported candidates in nearly half of all Senate and House races, primarily Republicans. The German-based DaimlerChrysler Corp., with large subsidiaries in the United States, proved more evenhanded, supporting twenty-three Republicans and twenty-two incumbents from the Democratic Party for reelection to the U.S. Senate in 2002 and 2004.[10]

The reliance of presidential candidates on MNC campaign contributions casts doubt upon their ability to govern on the basis of national interests rather than the interests of their financial backers. As noted earlier, Vice President Cheney spent five years heading Halliburton before taking office, then endorsed billions of dollars in military contracts to the firm to provide logistical support for the U.S. invasion and occupation of Iraq. Between 1999 and 2002, the company spent more than $700,000 on campaign contributions, including $17,677 to the Bush-Cheney campaign in 2000. Taken together, the six U.S. firms that gained the largest contracts to rebuild Iraq contributed $3.6 million to political campaigns, of which two-thirds went to Republican candidates (Center for Responsive Politics 2003a).

---

10. Among U.S.-based MNCs, the largest contributors to congressional campaigns in recent years have included AT&T, Microsoft Corp., Goldman Sachs, Citigroup, and Philip Morris (U.S. Federal Election Commission 2004). In terms of economic sectors, the largest amount of campaign contributions in 2000, nearly $115 million, came from legal firms. Other top donors have included securities and investment firms, realtors, medical groups, and insurance companies.

Like MNCs, labor unions seek political advantage by contributing generously to political campaigns. In 2000, five of the top ten donors to congressional campaigns were labor unions. These included the American Federation of State, County, and Municipal Employees ($8.6 million); the Service Employees International Union ($6.1 million); the Carpenters and Joiners Union ($4.7 million); the International Brotherhood of Electrical Workers ($4.5 million); and the United Food and Commercial Workers Union ($3.9 million). Whereas most campaign contributions from MNCs supported Republican candidates during this period, labor unions overwhelmingly favored Democrats. In return for their financial support, labor groups expect officials to promote trade policies beneficial to their members.

As NGOs become more engaged in the policy process, moving from open confrontation to a more cooperative stance toward governments, they often participate in the drafting of international treaties and conventions. Examples of this legislative role include the ban on land mines, the creation of the International Criminal Court, and the Chemical Weapons Convention. In the latter case, scientists from chemical and pharmaceutical companies identified toxic substances likely to be used for military purposes, methods used in their production, their likely effects, and ways they could be restricted from public circulation. Similarly, the World Bank and the WTO invite environmental NGOs to advise them on the likely ecological effects of development projects and trade agreements (Weinstein and Charnovitz 2001).

Policy and Program Implementation

A rapidly growing arena of NGO activity is implementation of policies and programs approved by national governments. In these instances, which require shared preferences between the government and groups, NGOs serve as functional extensions of the governments they serve and as instruments of their policy ambitions. Development NGOs, for example, manage the shipment and delivery of U.S. foreign aid to governments in need. Human-rights NGOs conduct voter-registration drives sponsored by the State Department and monitor elections in countries undergoing democratic transitions.

Government contracting, the "public financing of private provision" (Berrios 2000, 23), is attractive to all parties concerned. The NGOs acquire material resources as well as legitimacy in advancing their agendas. And the federal government, by far the largest customer of such contracted services in the United States, can pursue its foreign-policy goals, such as economic development and political reform, without adding to its permanent workforce. More broadly, the practice of contracting services is consistent with the nation's ideological basis in favor of limited government and free enterprise. **Public-choice theory,** which argues that competitive private firms can supply goods and services more efficiently than government agencies can (see Buchanan 1977), reinforces this bias.

Recent evidence demonstrates that the U.S. government takes these NGOs seriously in its conduct of foreign policy. After the Kosovo conflict in 1999, the State Department disbursed more than $10 million in grants among NGOs so they could help refugees return to their homes and rebuild their communities. In January 2001, Secretary of State Madeleine Albright announced nearly $4 million in grants to NGOs so they could monitor working conditions in overseas sweatshops. Early in 2002, the Bush administration asked more than twenty NGOs to identify the most deserving recipients of $5 billion in new foreign-aid projects proposed by the president.

As noted above, the outsourcing of U.S. foreign-policy functions has become common in the military sector. Of particular interest are **corporate warriors,** private companies that "trade in professional services linked to warfare" (Singer 2003, 8). Dozens of private military firms (PMFs) provide a wide range of military functions once reserved for the government, from food services to maintaining the grounds on U.S. bases. The U.S. government has embraced this practice largely for economic reasons, stating that private contractors can supply services more efficiently and cheaply than can government workers. Other countries have turned to these companies for assistance, including combat forces that are in some instances better trained and equipped than their own troops (see Adams 1999; Shearer 1998; and Isenberg 1997).

The use of corporate warriors during Operation Iraqi Freedom, combined with new innovations in military technology, allowed the Pentagon to mobilize less than half the number of troops it had had to deploy twelve years earlier in Operation Desert Storm. These contractors, many of them military veterans, directly supported the mission of securing military bases and civilian sites in Iraq. Other contractors included private workers who built schools and hospitals, installed telephone and satellite systems, and advised Iraqi officials regarding effective means of political and economic reform.

The benefits of outsourcing defense, however, come at considerable costs, ones extending beyond the potential for corruption revealed by the Halliburton scandals. By their nature, private firms are more secretive and less accountable than public agencies, which must adhere to provisions for legislative oversight and public scrutiny. Controlling corporate warriors can also be difficult, as the U.S. government learned in the 2004 prison-abuse scandals in Iraq. Only after the media reported the story did Congress and U.S. citizens learn that private contractors serving as prison interrogators had resorted to brutal tactics that violated the Geneva Conventions. Private contractors in Iraq, better paid than their military counterparts, provoked widespread resentment among U.S. troops during the conflict. Finally, contractors from the United States and other coalition forces became frequent targets of kidnappings in Iraq. Some of the most publicized U.S. casualties during the Iraq occupation, including the beheading of businessman Nicholas Berg, involved private contractors.

Civil Disobedience

When private groups feel their voices are not being heard through conventional channels of political discourse, they frequently resort to civil disobedience to get attention. For example, as noted earlier, in 1999 a loosely knit alliance of environmentalists, human-rights advocates, anarchists, and labor unions staged street demonstrations, some of which turned violent, during the annual meetings of the WTO in Seattle, Washington. Their antiglobalization protests stole the spotlight from the WTO delegates and altered the agenda and outcome of the meetings. Several months later, protesters in Davos, Switzerland, disrupted the annual meetings of the World Economic Forum, a prominent business NGO that brought corporate and government leaders together for discussions about global commerce and politics. In response to this pressure, and to the damaging publicity it suffered from this unrest, the forum invited fifteen NGOs to the 2000 annual meeting. By 2002, more than 100 private groups had joined the discussions, although they remained excluded from many events.

According to Howard Zinn (1968, 119), civil disobedience involves "the deliberate, discriminate violation of law for a vital social purpose. It becomes not only justifiable but necessary when a fundamental human right is at stake, and when legal channels are inadequate for securing that right." The tactics of civil disobedience are considered most significant for their symbolic value. While a protester's arrest may have little immediate consequence for the policy process, protesters expect public attention to the arrest, and the sympathies it provokes, to build pressure for reform. Civil disobedience has long been an important tactic of transnational NGOs. Greenpeace, for example, gained the world's attention by sending boats into restricted areas of the South Pacific where the French government was planning to conduct nuclear tests.[11]

In the United States, critics of the Vietnam War frequently resorted to civil disobedience to express their displeasure with the government's war effort. The Students for Democratic Society (SDS), created by campus activists in several major universities, conducted "sit-ins," peaceful occupations of public spaces to express opposition through the assertion of their physical presence. Some SDS members burned their draft cards; others staged hunger strikes to raise public consciousness. Demonstrations against the war, while generally peaceful, sometimes led to violent clashes with police and mass arrests. In the 1980s, organized groups protested the escalation of the arms race and called for a nuclear freeze, much to the dismay of the Reagan administration.

Relations between Greenpeace and the U.S. government, strained since the group's inception in 1971, reached new lows in 2003. The Justice Department charged Greenpeace with criminal conspiracy after its members illegally boarded a cargo ship, the *APL Jade,* that had brought contraband mahogany from Brazil to the port of Miami. The group, which unfurled a banner on the ship that read "Stop Illegal Logging," was charged under an obscure 1872 law, last cited in 1890, that had more to do with piracy than civil disobedience. Attorney General John Ashcroft supported the strong measures, which threatened Greenpeace's existence as a tax-exempt nonprofit organization. Two other NGOs, the American Civil Liberties Union and the People for the American Way Foundation,

---

11. Membership in Greenpeace soared in 1985 after the French Secret Services sunk the Greenpeace vessel *Rainbow Warrior* off the coast of New Zealand.

helped defend Greenpeace in federal court, claiming that the prosecution "amounts to nothing more than an act of intimidation by the government, apparently directed at silencing political speech" (quoted in Huus 2003).[12]

Conclusion

This chapter has identified the many functions served by transnational interest groups in the U.S. foreign-policy process. As we have found, the ends and means of these groups vary widely as does their current stature in the eyes of policy makers. Some NGOs "have reputations and credibility that give them impressive domestic as well as international political clout," observed Joseph S. Nye, Jr. (2004, 94), a Harvard University professor and former official in the State and Defense departments. "Others may lack credibility among moderate citizens, but have organizational and communication skills that allow them to mobilize demonstrations that governments cannot ignore. Few international meetings can be planned today without consideration of the prospect of demonstrations."

Taken together, NGOs have led a "quiet revolution" (Welch 2001, 262) in world politics and U.S. foreign policy. The critical role of interest groups in democratic societies is now frequently on display at the global level, where transnational interest groups have identified common concerns and forms of collaboration. In so doing, they have discovered links across issue areas—from economic development to family planning, human rights to environmental protection—that offer even more opportunities to exploit their strengths in numbers.

As with domestic interest groups in the United States, however, the harnessing of transnational NGOs has more often been a force for societal fragmentation than for unity. Most of these groups are not concerned with public interests in general but with the particular needs of their own members. In this respect, NGO networks serve as microcosms of broader balances of power within U.S. society, which feature wide disparities in economic wealth and direct links between wealth and political influence. The U.S. government must contend with the full range of private groups, at home and abroad, whose proven capacity to disrupt, as well as to exploit, the status quo makes them inescapable players in the foreign-policy process.

Key Terms

corporate warriors, p. 252

cosmopolitan groups, p. 229

democratic deficit, p. 228

global governance, p. 227

idea brokers, p. 242

lobbying, p. 248

multinational corporations (MNCs), p. 229

particularistic groups, p. 229

political action committees (PACs), p. 234

public goods, p. 224

public-choice theory, p. 251

---

12. The case was thrown out in June 2004 on technical grounds: the ship was docked six miles from downtown Miami and was not "about to arrive," a requirement of the 1872 law.

Internet References

The **Brookings Institution** (www.brook.edu) is a think tank that provides scholarly reports and in-depth research on domestic and international sources affecting U.S. foreign policy. Specific attention is given to the role of private companies in defense, trade, environment, and energy policy.

The **Center for Defense Information** (www.cdi.org) publishes reports and statistics on defense and security policies, which include information on interest groups and private companies involved in U.S. foreign policy. In particular, the center focuses on U.S. arms sales/trade, missile defense, defense projects and budgets, and nuclear issues.

The **Center for Responsive Politics** (www.opensecrets.org) is a nonpartisan, nonprofit research center focusing on researching the connection between campaign donations and elections. The center compiles donor and recipient financial statistics, which can be used to support research on specific candidates, industries, sectors, parties, and elections.

The **directory of think tanks** (www.lib.umich.edu/govdocs/frames/psthinfr.html), a University of Michigan Web site, offers links to think tanks and working-papers journals inside the United States and around the globe. The links are organized both alphabetically and by political ideology.

The **directory of U.S. lobbyists** (www.csuchico.edu/~kcfount) provided by California State University, Chico, has links to a variety of issue advocacy groups. Of particular interest to U.S. foreign policy are links for peace and war, the environment, international affairs, and political parties.

The **Federal Election Commission** (www.fec.gov) Web site provides election laws, statistics on donations, and election trends. Historical data and state-by-state breakdowns for recent elections are a helpful resource for researchers.

Foreign Policy in Focus (www.fpif.org) is a "think tank without walls," which explores citizen-based foreign-policy issues. Researchers compose short policy briefs on U.S. foreign-policy issues and global involvement such as trade, energy, environment, security, human rights, and labor. The site focuses on the connection between private actors and the government.

The **Global Policy Forum** (www.globalpolicy.org) is a center that integrates information and research on globalization, security issues, and the United Nations. The Global Policy Forum is an NGO itself and focuses on UN and state accountability along with the promotion of international peace and justice.

The **Moving Ideas Network** (www.movingideas.org) seeks to clarify policies and issues for citizens looking to understand complex policy areas and mobilize. Included are issue briefs, congressional reports, and data sources about most current policy initiatives.

The **NGO Global Network** (www.ngo.org) tracks and analyzes NGOs with UN consultative status. This site has links for NGOs around the globe, organized by their mission and category of operation.

continues

Internet References *(continued)*

Published and recorded by the U.S. State Department, **"Patterns of Global Terrorism"** (www.state.gov/s/ct/rls/pgtrpt) is a yearly report on terrorist incidents that affect U.S. citizens and interests around the globe. Included are regional reports, chronologies of events, U.S. programs and policies of counterterrorism, and background information on state-sponsored and transnational terrorist groups.

The **Progressive Policy Institute** (www.ppionline.org) is a think tank that examines technological innovation, rather than ideology, as it relates to government policy. Of particular interest are research projects on national defense and homeland security, foreign policy, trade and global markets, and energy and the environment.

Project Vote Smart (www.vote-smart.org) is a nonpartisan group focusing on connecting democratic values with complete information about candidates, interest groups, and political parties. Project Vote Smart offers information on voting records, interest groups, issue positions, and biographical information of elected officials.

9

The Strength of Intergovernmental Organizations

An armored United Nations security convoy patrols the streets of Sarajevo, the capital of Bosnia-Herzegovina. The UN peacekeepers in this 1993 photograph sought to restore security in "Sniper Alley," an area that faced daily attacks by government-led Serb forces. The peacekeeping effort in the former Yugoslav province finally gave way to intervention by the North Atlantic Treaty Organization (NATO) and to a settlement mediated by the United States. Frustrations associated with several UN peacekeeping missions after the cold war prompted the U.S. government to steer clear of such missions.

Like public opinion and the news media, the nonstate actors discussed in the previous chapter have a proven capacity to shape the U.S. government's global ambitions and the means to achieve them. In this chapter, we examine the network of **intergovernmental organizations (IGOs)**, formal political bodies that represent two or more national governments. These organizations permit their members to pursue goals beyond their individual reach and to solve shared problems. Although the United States, as the world's predominant power, bears the largest costs of most IGOs in which it is active, it also benefits greatly from the organizations, which provide outlets for the projection of U.S. power and influence.

The United States is currently represented in nearly eighty IGOs, a large majority of the worldwide total (U.S. CIA 2004). While most Americans might recognize the prominent ones, such as the United Nations (UN), they likely would not recognize the greater part of these organizations, such as the Universal Postal Union, the World Meteorological Organization, the Nuclear Energy Agency, and Interpol, a global police agency. The nation's involvement in certain IGOs might even come as a surprise. For example, the United States serves as a "regional partner" in the Association of Southeast Asian Nations, an "observer" of the European Organization for Nuclear Research, and most curiously, a "guest" of the Non-Alignment Movement, created during the cold war to *restrain* the United States.

The United States took the lead in creating the IGO network after World War II. **Multilateralism,** the collaborative foreign-policy making of several countries, further acknowledges the collective and overlapping national interests of states. For the U.S. government, IGOs offer an alternative to going it alone through *unilateral* action, or to working with individual governments through *bilateral* channels. The United States employs all three strategies in its daily conduct of foreign policy. The strategy chosen in each case is determined by the issue of concern, the strategic interests of the United States, and the capabilities and goals of other countries.

The role of the United States in IGOs has sparked intense controversy in recent years. Critics of *assertive multilateralism,* a term coined by the Clinton administration, believe the United States is becoming a captive, instead of being the master, of the IGOs it played a lead role in creating. From this perspective, multilateralism means "submerging American will in a mush of collective decision-making—you have sentenced yourself to reacting to events or passing the buck to multilingual committees with fancy acronyms" (Krauthammer 2001). To Pat Buchanan (1998, 107), a conservative commentator and former presidential candidate, these organizations weaken, rather than strengthen, the United States:

> Like a shipwrecked Gulliver on the beach of Lilliput, America is to be tied down with threads, strand by strand, until it cannot move when it awakens. Piece by piece, our sovereignty is being surrendered. . . . America has ensnared itself in a web that restricts its freedom of action, diminishes its liberty, and siphons off its wealth.

Critics most often direct this accusation at the UN, which they claim is overly large, inefficient, and unduly hostile to the United States, its primary benefactor. The U.S. government first turned against the UN in the 1980s, under President Reagan, and then again after the cold war. In the 1990s, Congress refused to pay nearly $1.5 billion in U.S. dues to the world body, exploiting its power of the purse to force the world body to make budgetary changes. These and similar actions by the U.S. government prompted UN Secretary General Kofi Annan to ask rhetorically, "Is Washington's will to lead diminishing even as many around the world look to it for leadership? Is it no longer convinced of the myriad benefits to be had from multilateral cooperation?"

The domestic backlash against multilateralism found an ally in George W. Bush, who took office in January 2001. The new president and his advisers believed the unilateral assertion of U.S. power would better serve the nation than continued enmeshment in IGOs. A unilateral turn in U.S. foreign policy, they argued, would liberate the United States from an array of global commitments that reduced its ability to exploit its global primacy. Condoleezza Rice (2000, 47), Bush's national security adviser, made this case publicly during the campaign:

> [M]any in the United States are (and have always been) uncomfortable with the notions of power politics, great powers, and power balances. In an extreme form, this discomfort leads to a reflexive appeal instead to notions of international law and

norms, and the belief that the support of many states—or even better, of institutions like the United Nations—is essential to the legitimate exercise of power. . . . To be sure, there is nothing wrong with doing something that benefits all humanity, but that, in a sense, is a second-order effect. America's pursuit of the national interest will create conditions that promote freedom, markets, and peace.

Bush put these principles into practice by reversing Clinton's support for the International Criminal Court (ICC), abrogating the Anti-Ballistic Missile Treaty with Russia, and rejecting a variety of other international agreements (see Foot, McFarlane, and Mastanduno 2003). These included the Kyoto Protocol, which sought to reduce the worldwide emission of greenhouse gases associated with global warming. Bush's dismissal of the treaty as "fatally flawed" was especially crippling to this environmental goal, the United States being by far the world's foremost consumer of fossil fuels (see Chapter 12). The U.S. turn against IGOs reached a new and ominous level in 2003, when the president spurned the UN Security Council by launching a preventive invasion of Iraq over UN objections.

Despite these tensions, the United States remains engaged in a world of multilateral diplomacy (see Figure 9.1). As noted in Part I, the process of institutional momentum that has fragmented U.S. foreign policy also has played a role in the growth and proliferation of IGOs. The United Nations, its clashes with the United States notwithstanding, has broadened its agenda considerably since the cold war. The European Union (EU) now encompasses nearly the entire continent, wields sovereign powers in many policy areas, and has inspired the formation of similar organizations elsewhere, such as the African Union. In addition, the network of cold war alliances remains in place even though the Soviet Union has collapsed.

Figure 9.1 Multilateral Treaties in Force for the United States

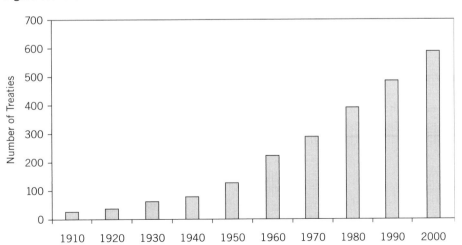

SOURCES: 1910–1990 data: Stewart Patrick and Shepard Forman, eds., *Multilateralism and U.S. Foreign Policy: Ambivalent Engagement* (Boulder, Colo.: Lynne Rienner, 2000); 2000 data: U.S. Department of State, "Treaties in Force," www.state.gov/s/l/c8455.htm.

The North Atlantic Treaty Organization (NATO) has not only steadily increased in size, but also extended its military operations beyond Europe. Outside the channels of these organizations, wealthy countries have been meeting annually since 1975 as members of the **Group of 8 (G-8),** an informal body that includes Canada, France, Germany, Italy, Japan, the United Kingdom, the United States, and the newest member, Russia. Finally, international financial institutions have assumed greater responsibilities in the globalizing economy.

All these organizations interact with U.S. governmental institutions and play vital, if often contentious, roles in the foreign-policy process. The White House frequently disagrees with congressional leaders over the missions and policies of IGOs, with legislators generally more skeptical than presidents that constituents will benefit from multilateral engagement. Within the executive branch, the State Department frequently finds itself battling other federal agencies over U.S. relations with the UN and other IGOs. These organizations are also the objects of competition among private interest groups, as in the case of trade associations and labor unions that clash over U.S. foreign investment (Lyman 2002).

The shift of the United States from assertive to ambivalent multilateralism (Patrick and Forman 2002) is paradoxical given the nation's lead role in creating the worldwide web of IGOs half a century ago. Many Americans now see the system of multilateral diplomacy, once viewed as a springboard for U.S. foreign-policy goals, as a stumbling block. However, like it or not, U.S. foreign-policy makers must navigate this institutional landscape on a daily basis. As demonstrated in the cases of the Kyoto Protocol and the ICC, other governments will press on with these agreements and institutional arrangements with or without the United States.

Foundations of the Multilateral Order

Unlike the dominant world powers of the past, the United States extended its overseas presence after World War II with substantial support from the foreign nations that fell within its growing sphere of influence. In this sense, the United States was in a position to create an "empire by invitation" (Lundestad 1999). At the time, only the United States possessed the necessary resources to provide the public goods, such as economic stability and military security, that stretch across political boundaries and affect all countries (see Chapters 10–12). Furthermore, the would-be IGO partners shared the U.S. government's stated ambition—to create a more democratic, peaceful, and prosperous world order. The presence of a rival political and economic system in the form of Soviet-led communism cemented these bonds.

The calamity of World War II taught American leaders two crucial lessons. First, as the world's preeminent power, the United States could not ignore the pressures for global engagement. A return to isolationism would only invite new challenges for regional supremacy and regression to the crippling economic warfare that brought on the Great Depression. Second, the United States had to manage its primacy in a way that *reassured* other powers rather than frightening them. A cooperative form of engagement would enhance the "hard" assets of the United States, such as military forces and economic resources, while complementing the nation's soft power, or the legitimacy and transnational appeal that stemmed from its democratic government and vibrant civil society (Nye 2004, 102–103).

The strategy U.S. leaders chose to apply to both lessons was multilateralism. They placed the United States at the hub of a global network of IGOs and international agreements that reinforced the nation's strengths while providing greater security and material resources for its allies (see Figure 9.2). Although the United States had to pay the lion's share of funds for these organizations, it and the other nations involved would all reap much from the investment. Ultimately, the IGOs would produce a greater pooling of resources and stimulate a stronger sense of common purpose than would have resulted from each state's acting independently. Thus the interstate system would be better able to manage the growing **interdependence** of all governments and societies in the more tightly knit, heavily populated world of the late twentieth century.

Multilateralism also appealed to U.S. leaders on cultural grounds. As a nation founded on political principles rather than on a common ethnic identity, the United States drew its population from many parts of the world and thus immersed itself in a transnational community that extended far beyond its borders. "A multilateral world order vision is singularly compatible with America's own collective self-concept," John G. Ruggie (1994, 564) observed. "Indeed the vision taps into the very idea of America itself."

These factors formed the basis of an **institutional bargain** between the United States and its partners by which "the leading state agrees to restrain its

Figure 9.2 Hub and Spokes: The U.S. Model of Multilateral Engagement after World War II

own potential for domination or abandonment in exchange for the long-term institutionalized cooperation of subordinate states" (Ikenberry 2001). While such cooperation may "conform more to the preferences of the powerful than of the weak, [it] provides a degree of predictability and stability that may be especially valuable for less powerful and poorer states" (Martin 1999, 94). In short, strong and weak states alike have something to gain through organized cooperation. This central claim of neoliberal institutionalism (see Chapter 3), that such cooperation stems from self-interests "rightly understood" rather than altruism, makes the approach appealing to many realists who otherwise see little reason or hope for global cooperation (see Keohane and Martin 1995; and Keohane 1984).

The newly enlarged European Union demonstrates the potential **spillover effects** of institutional cooperation (Mitrany 1943). Members of these organizations have a stake in their long-term successes and thus have incentives to "play by the rules" of acceptable behavior. Successful cooperation in one area, such as trade, encourages cooperation in more troublesome areas, such as arms control and the resolution of territorial disputes. This prospect for "spillover" cooperation played a key role in the creation and incremental expansion of the EU, which now shares many sovereign powers with its member states and has emerged as a potent independent center of world power.

The United States encouraged this strategy of regional cooperation in Europe, making it a precondition for the delivery of Marshall Plan funds in the late 1940s. Indeed, the U.S. government proved to be a catalyst of European **integration,** or the creation of *supranational* institutions that claimed sovereign powers above those maintained by member states.[1] Four decades later, amid the demise of the cold war, the "new world order" proclaimed by George H. W. Bush placed global IGOs at center stage. To Bush's secretary of state, James A. Baker (1995, 605–606), the success enjoyed by President Truman and Dean Acheson, his secretary of state, in building a multilateral order after World War II offered compelling reasons to maintain this order after the cold war:

> Men like Truman and Acheson were above all, though we sometimes like to forget it, institution builders. They created NATO and the other security organizations that eventually won the cold war. They fostered the economic institutions . . . that brought unparalleled prosperity. . . . At a time of similar opportunity and risk, I believed we should take a leaf from their book.

Bill Clinton's adoption of assertive multilateralism continued this tradition in U.S. foreign policy through the end of the twentieth century. The new millennium, however, brought a unilateral turn by the United States as described in this chapter. This turn away from the international community dismayed other governments

---

1. Some clarification on these terms may be helpful. Whereas *international* relations are generally considered to take place among nation-states through diplomacy, *supranational* institutions assume state powers and functions in specified areas, as with trade policy in the case of the WTO or the prosecution of war crimes by the ICC. Finally, *transnational* relations refer to the mix of interactions of states, IGOs, and private groups, including the news media.

that had become accustomed to the institutional bargain. Nowhere has this discord been more visible than in the UN, where the love-hate relationship between the U.S. government and the international community reveals itself most dramatically.

The United Nations

The U.S. government's most visible, complex, and controversial multilateral relationship involves the UN, the world's only general-purpose, universal-membership IGO. Although the U.S. Senate had rejected the League of Nations in 1919 and 1920, the catastrophic depression and revival of world war that followed compelled national leaders to maintain their quest for such an organization. Following World War II, many analysts came to view the United States' absence from the League as directly contributing to the unraveling of world order during the interwar period and the onset of World War II.

When the United States and other countries drew up plans for a new world body, they knew it had to be significantly different from the League—in its structure, scope, and legal authority—to survive. Thus the great powers would have far more control over the UN, which would have no pretensions of collective security and a legislative branch with no binding powers. There would be no confusing the UN, whose General Assembly met for the first time in January 1946, with an aspiring world government, a widespread perception in Congress that had doomed the League.

Agreement over the UN's architecture came before World War II ended, at the 1944 Dumbarton Oaks conference. Representatives of the United States, the Soviet Union, China, and Great Britain settled upon the powers and limitations of the UN at these meetings, held in a Washington, D.C., mansion. At the final conference in San Francisco in June 1945, representatives of fifty countries signed the UN Charter, and a month later, the U.S. Senate ratified it by an 89–2 vote. President Franklin Roosevelt had ensured bipartisan support for the UN by including members of Congress in the negotiations and making it clear that the new organization would not impair U.S. sovereignty or supercede Congress's constitutional powers. The limitations of the UN thus proved to be its greatest strength in ensuring U.S. support.

UN Goals and Structures

Members of the newly formed UN agreed that the organization would adopt the principle of **sovereign equality,** the shared legal rights of all internationally recognized nation-states. The UN would be open to all "peace-loving" states and provide a forum for resolving international problems. Specifically, the charter identified four key goals for the United Nations: to save the world from the "scourge of war," to promote human rights and democracy, to facilitate peaceful conflict resolution, and to enhance social progress and global living standards.[2]

---

2. See www.un.org/aboutun/charter/index.html for the full text of the UN Charter.

Importantly, the principle designers of the UN preserved their rights to self-defense through "regional arrangements," or military alliances. This central feature of the UN Charter, specified in Article 52, satisfied the demands of the great powers that the UN not usurp their authority over national security. Beyond this important provision, most of the UN Charter outlined the structural features of the organization, which comprises six key units: Security Council, General Assembly, Secretariat, Economic and Social Council, International Court of Justice, and Trusteeship Council. The first three units, described below, are the core institutions.

The Security Council is the UN's principal agent of international conflict resolution and the center of overall decision-making power within the world body. The council consists of fifteen members, including five *permanent* members and ten *rotating* members selected by the General Assembly for two-year terms.[3] The permanent members—China, France, Great Britain, Russia, and the United States—exercise veto power in the council and can prevent the UN from taking actions they oppose.

The council's foremost goal is to seek peaceful conflict resolution through mediation, arbitration, or the imposition of economic sanctions. If these measures fail, the council may call for the use of UN military force in one of two ways. First, *peacemaking* forces may be deployed into active combat to reverse an act of aggression, as they were in the Korean War (1950–1953) and the Persian Gulf War (1990–1991). More commonly, the Security Council deploys *peacekeeping* troops, civilian police forces, and military observers to separate adversaries, enforce cease-fires, and facilitate negotiated settlements. Many of these missions, undertaken years ago, continue today (see Table 9.1). As of July 2004, the United States contributed troops to six of the sixteen peacekeeping missions, including the operation in Kosovo formally managed by the North Atlantic Treaty Organization.

The General Assembly carries out the UN's limited legislative functions. Every member state has an equal voice in the assembly under the principle of "one country, one vote." As in the U.S. Congress, legislation in the General Assembly is drafted within committees organized along functional lines, such as economic development, health, and security. Unlike acts of Congress, most UN resolutions do not carry the force of law but instead express the majority opinion of the organization's members. Any measures involving the UN budget, a large category that includes day-to-day functions and programs, must be approved by the Security Council. Nevertheless, the General Assembly's power of *exhortation* can be significant in conveying "world opinion" and moral authority, particularly in cases in which the Security Council is divided.

Finally, the UN Secretariat provides for the administrative functions of the world body. The secretary-general, or chief administrative officer, assumes a highly visible position in shaping the agenda and speaking out on international issues. For this reason, all the great powers have a large stake in the occupant of

---

3. These ten nonpermanent members are elected along regional lines, allocated as follows: Africa (three seats), Asia (two), Latin America (two), western Europe (two), and eastern Europe (one).

Table 9.1 Ongoing UN Peacekeeping Missions

Mission Name	Mission Location	Starting Date	Military Presence (July 2004)
UN Truce Supervision Organization (UNTSO)	Egypt, Israel, Lebanon, and Syria	May 1948	154 observers
UN Military Observer Group in India and Pakistan (UNMOGIP)	Ceasefire line between India and Pakistan	January 1949	44 observers
UN Peacekeeping Force in Cyprus (UNFICYP)	Cyprus	March 1964	1,202 troops
UN Disengagement Observer Force (UNDOF)	Syrian Golan Heights	June 1974	1,042 troops 80 observers
UN Interim Force in Lebanon (UNIFIL)	Southern Lebanon	March 1978	1,998 troops 50 observers
UN Mission for the Referendum in Western Sahara (MINURSO)	Western Sahara	April 1991	27 troops 194 observers
UN Observer Mission in Georgia (UNOMIG)	Abkhazia (Georgia)	August 1993	121 observers 11 civilian police
UN Interim Administration Mission in Kosovo (UNMIK)	Kosovo	June 1999	18,000 troops (approx.)[a] 4,377 civilian police
UN Mission in Sierra Leone (UNAMSIL)	Sierra Leone	October 1999	15,255 troops 256 observers 52 civilian police
UN Organization Mission in the Democratic Republic of the Congo (MONUC)	Democratic Republic of the Congo and the subregion	November 1999	9,925 troops 568 observers 139 civilian police
UN Mission in Ethiopia and Eritrea (UNMEE)	Ethiopia and Eritrea	July 2000	3,681 troops 215 observers
UN Mission of Support in East Timor (UNMISET)	The Democratic Republic of Timor-Leste	May 2002	428 troops 42 observers 129 civilian police
UN Mission in Liberia (UNMIL)	Liberia	September 2003	13,375 troops 192 observers 1,049 civilian police
UN Operation in Côte d'Ivoire (UNOCI)	Côte d'Ivoire	April 2004	3,360 troops 134 observers 85 civilian police
UN Operation in Burundi (ONUB)	Burundi	May 2004	2,415 troops 57 observers
UN Stability Mission in Haiti (MINUSTAH)	Haiti	June 2004	2,081 troops 67 civilian police

SOURCE: United Nations, "UN Peacekeeping Missions," www.un.org/Depts/dpko/dpko/index.asp.

[a] Military troops in Kosovo overseen by NATO Kosovo Force (KFOR).

this office. In 1996, the United States stood alone in opposing a second term for UN Secretary General Boutros Boutros-Ghali. As a veto-wielding member of the Security Council, the United States was able to force Boutros-Ghali's replacement by Kofi Annan, another African, whom U.S. officials considered to be more supportive of their calls for bureaucratic reform. Annan, however, emerged as a vocal and eloquent critic of U.S. unilateralism during the Bush administration.

Growing Pains in U.S.-UN Relations

Throughout its history, the United Nations has maintained a love-hate relationship with its most powerful member, the United States. The world body maintains its headquarters in New York City and looks to the U.S. government for the largest share of the organization's income. More broadly, upon its founding, the UN espoused the same values of political and economic freedom, human rights, and world peace long promoted by the United States.

Yet differences have always existed between the United Nations and its primary benefactor. These differences were inevitable from the start, given the gaps between the affluent and militarily powerful United States and most UN member states, which are smaller, lacking in wealth, and more limited in their military capabilities. These gaps, which have widened in recent years, have led the United States and the majority of UN members to adopt different foreign-policy preferences, primarily on economic issues such as foreign aid and the sharing of natural resources. The United States has also found itself in a minority of countries that support Israel in its ongoing conflict with the Palestinians.

Economic disparities between rich and poor countries, a central reality in world politics throughout modern history, are defining elements of UN politics. During the cold war, these disparities led developing nations to align with the Soviet Union, whose stated concern for economic equality struck a chord in impoverished societies recently freed from colonial rule. The **Group of 77 (G-77)**, a coalition of poor countries created in the 1970s, represented most of the world's population and wielded majority status in the General Assembly. The G-77, whose membership now exceeds 130, caused frustration for the United States, commonly viewed as the primary obstacle to global economic equality. Responding to this anti-American sentiment, President Reagan in 1984 withdrew the United States from the UN Economic, Social, and Cultural Organization (UNESCO), a primary UN outlet for challenging U.S. policies in these areas.

During the cold war, when nearly every UN issue was linked to the struggle, U.S. and Soviet vetoes—whether threatened or actually employed—ensured chronic stalemate within the Security Council. At first, the Soviet Union cast the most vetoes as the United States retained its greater hold over the world body. Then, as the growing number of newly independent developing countries came to support Soviet positions, the United States became the primary source of General Assembly vetoes. By the mid-1980s, Latin American governments were sharing U.S. positions on less than 22 percent of UN resolutions, and African states were casting the same votes as the United States less than 14 percent of the time (Kegley and Hook 1991).

The cold war's end at first produced greater harmony in the UN, which suggested that the world body might yet realize its historic ambitions. The widespread support of UN members for multilateral action against Iraq in 1991 encouraged this wave of euphoria and solidarity. But in the mid-1990s, new splits emerged, preventing the United Nations from acting in several areas, including the former Yugoslavia and sub-Saharan Africa. Meanwhile, developing countries realized

Point/Counterpoint
UN ADVOCATES VS. UN SKEPTICS

As the world's only multipurpose, universal-membership IGO, the United Nations naturally attracts the most attention—and controversy—in the U.S. foreign-policy process. While its advocates promote the world body as an extension of U.S. democratic values, critics of the UN claim the organization hinders, rather than helps, the United States achieve its goals in global politics. This debate was dampened by the end of the cold war and the momentary sense that a harmonious "new world order" had arrived. But the frustrations associated with UN peacekeeping missions in Somalia and the former Yugoslavia revived criticism of the world body.

Outside of Congress, whose Republican majority approved deep cutbacks in U.S. funding to the UN, prominent private citizens mounted a campaign to distance the United States from the organization. Among the most outspoken of these critics was John Bolton, senior vice president of the American Enterprise Institute, a conservative think tank. In a 1997 article, Bolton argued that the United Nations "has been associated with major policy failures that have made it an unattractive vehicle through which to conduct American foreign policy." He complained about the "abuse heaped upon" Americans during the cold war. He also predicted that a "deep philosophical disjunction between the prevailing ethos of the United Nations and the fundamental American approach to governance is not something that will change in the foreseeable future."

President Clinton resisted these attacks on the UN, although he could not prevent Congress from withholding payment of past U.S. dues to the world body. "The men and women of the United Nations have expertise across the entire range of humanitarian and development activities. Every day they are making a difference," Clinton told the UN General Assembly later in 1997. "The United States was a founder of the UN. We are proud to be its host. We believe in its ideals. We continue to be, as we have been, it largest contributor. We are committed to seeing the United Nations succeed in the 21st century."

This debate grew more bitter after Bill Clinton was succeeded by George W. Bush, who counted himself among the UN skeptics. The new president ensured that this perspective would be well represented in the State Department when he nominated Bolton to become undersecretary for arms control and international security. Other UN critics filled high-level positions in the Bush administration, whose decision to invade Iraq early in 2003 without the UN's endorsement marked a low point in post–cold war U.S.-UN relations.

Sources: John Bolton, "America's Skepticism about the United Nations," U.S. Foreign Policy Agenda 2 (May 1997), usinfo.state.gov/journals /itps/0597/ijpe/pj2bolt.htm; Bill Clinton, "Remarks by the President to the 52nd Session of the United Nations General Assembly" (New York, September 22, 1997), www.lib.umich.edu /govdocs/text/clin52.txt.

they would not receive their expected "peace dividend," or economic aid made available by reductions in military spending. In addition, the UN confronted a formidable set of problems: a spreading AIDS epidemic, widening civil wars in Africa, frequent acts of international terrorism, unchecked weapons proliferation, stunted democratic reforms, and a stagnant world economy (see Stedman 2002).

The primary political rift within the UN during the cold war had been between the United States and the Soviet Union. In recent years, the most acute tensions have involved the United States and the UN *itself*. Relations between the world body and its most powerful member improved markedly as the superpower struggle gave way to a "new world order" in 1991. This harmony soon gave way, however, to skepticism and hostility in the U.S. government. Conservative leaders accused the United Nations of seeking to become the very world government Congress had rejected decades earlier. In 1996, Sen. Jesse Helms (1996, 4), chairman of the Senate Foreign Relations Committee, charged,

> The United Nations has moved from facilitating diplomacy among nation-states to supplanting them altogether. The international elites running the United Nations look at the idea of the nation-state with disdain. . . . In their view, the interests of nation-states are parochial and should give way to global interests. Nation-states, they believe, should recognize the primacy of these global interests and accede to the United Nations' sovereignty to pursue them.

Beyond general concerns about the UN's scope, two specific issues produce continuing tensions between the United States and the United Nations. The first involves UN-sponsored peacekeeping missions, which were rarely conducted during the cold war due to chronic superpower differences but became common in 1990s. Between 1991 and 1993 alone, the UN launched "security operations" in thirteen countries.[4] Of the sixteen UN peacekeeping operations under way on January 1, 2000, all but five had been launched during the 1990s (Weiss, Forsythe, and Coate 2001, 67–68, 85). Peacekeeping missions typically involve the deployment of military personnel from various UN states to separate combatants, enforce ceasefires, and assist with implementation of peace agreements. These forces are politically "neutral," lightly armed, and under orders to fire only in self-defense (see Durch 1993).

The U.S. government favored the expansion of UN peacekeeping in the early 1990s. This enthusiasm waned, however, after a series of failed UN interventions in the former Yugoslavia, Somalia, Haiti, and other countries. Recognizing growing public and congressional concern over these failures, Clinton (1994) issued an executive order in May 1994 limiting U.S. involvement in future UN-sponsored peacekeeping missions. According to Presidential Decision Directive 25, the United States would henceforth make "disciplined and coherent choices about which peace operations to support," and the UN had to be "selective and more

---

4. These included, in 1991, Kuwait, Angola, El Salvador, and Western Sahara; in 1992, Cambodia, Yugoslavia, Somalia, and Mozambique; and in 1993, Uganda-Rwanda (a joint mission), Georgia, Haiti, and Liberia.

effective" in undertaking these missions. Among other stipulations, the United States would only join such missions under the following conditions:

- a demonstrable threat to U.S. interests posed by the conflict

- a threat to or breach of international peace and security

- international consensus favoring UN peacekeeping

- clear objectives regarding the proposed mission

- adequate available means to accomplish the mission

- unacceptable humanitarian consequences in the absence of UN intervention

- "realistic criteria" for completing the mission

The harder U.S. line went beyond presidential rhetoric. The United States refused to intervene in the genocidal warfare plaguing Rwanda and Burundi in the spring of 1994. Clinton turned to NATO to end ethnic violence in Bosnia-Herzegovina and Kosovo after UN peacekeepers proved impotent in the former conflict. The command and control of UN troops remained a contentious issue, along with rising costs of such deployments, for which the United States bore the largest burden. Yet since June 1999, U.S. leaders have contributed troops to UN peacekeeping missions in Eritria, Ethiopia, Haiti, and Liberia while expecting other countries—particularly regional powers—to handle peacekeeping in other UN-sponsored operations.[5]

The second UN-related issue of particular concern to the United States involves funding the 191-member world body. As it has since the UN's creation, the United States annually provides the largest share of the UN's budget. This contribution amounted to $363 million in 2004, or just under one-quarter of the UN's budget of $1.49 billion in 2004 (see Figure 9.3). To many, the United States pays too much for an organization that routinely opposes U.S. foreign-policy preferences. In addition, these critics claim, the United Nations is badly managed and wastes much of its budget on "bloated" headquarters in New York City and Geneva, Switzerland. These concerns are not new. In 1984, they had prompted Congress to pass the Kassebaum-Soloman Amendment, which reduced U.S. funding to the UN by 20 percent until the world body instituted cost-cutting budget reforms.

Much like Congress uses its "power of the purse" to force changes in U.S. foreign policy, the U.S. government found its manipulation of UN finances useful. Since U.S. contributions had amounted to a quarter of the annual UN budget, the world body suffered severe financial difficulties. The cutbacks forced the United Nations to curtail many of its services, trim its bureaucratic staff, and borrow money from other member states to cover its expenses. The United States, meanwhile, was amassing massive debts, or *arrears,* to the UN for unpaid dues. The

---

5. The U.S. government also contributed civilian police forces to many UN operations. These included the mission in Kosovo, where UN-sponsored civilian police worked alongside NATO-sponsored military forces in keeping the fragile peace in the war-torn province of the former Yugoslavia.

Figure 9.3 Funding the United Nations: 2004 Budget Assessments

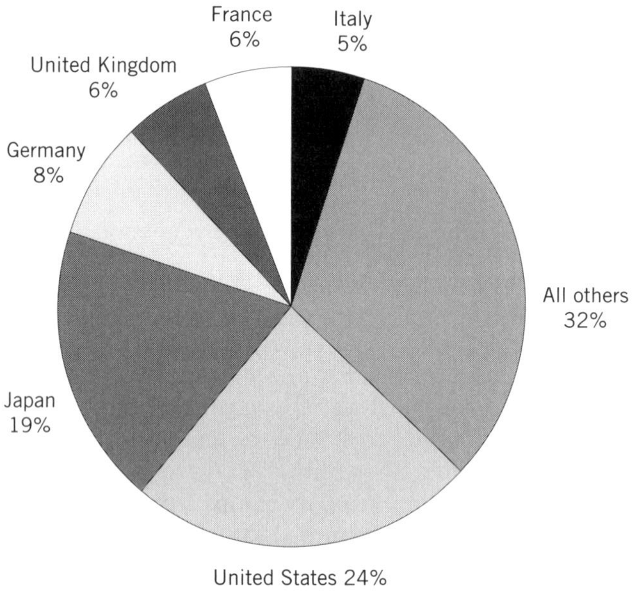

France
6%

Italy
5%

United Kingdom
6%

Germany
8%

All others
32%

Japan
19%

United States 24%

SOURCE: Global Policy Forum, "UN Finance: Tables and Charts" (2004), www.globalpolicy.org/finance/tables/reg-budget/large04.htm.

U.S. government allowed its arrears to surpass $1.5 billion, exceeding the combined debt of all other member states.

The funding impasse was broken in December 1999. Congress approved the **Helms-Biden Act,** which called for the payment of $926 million in unpaid U.S. dues to the UN, approximately two-thirds of the estimated U.S. debt, over the next three years. The measure contained a wide range of conditions for U.S. repayment: a reduced permanent share of U.S. funding to 22 percent, a "no-growth" budget, and bans on international conferences, a UN standing army, and UN taxing authority. Finally, the United States insisted that it would no longer pay more than 25 percent of the costs associated with UN-sponsored peacekeeping missions. The UN had no choice but to accept the lower rates of U.S. funding.

This budget dispute worsened the already negative image of the United States within the UN (see Karns and Mingst 2002). By the turn of the century, relations between the U.S. government and the world body were "in a shambles, dominated by finger pointing, recriminations, and mutual mistrust" (Luck 1999, 1). Still, the resolution of the funding stalemate provided a glimmer of hope that U.S.-UN relations might not be beyond repair. The terrorist attacks of September 11 prompted Bush to approve the final installment of unpaid dues to the UN. The following year, the United States rejoined UNESCO after an absence of nearly two decades.

Despite these tensions, American citizens have consistently approved of the world body and favored an active U.S. role in UN activities (see Rielly 2003; and Kull 2002). To most Americans, the United Nations continues to serve an important function in advancing U.S. interests and in solving problems not confined within political boundaries. Those who oppose the UN frequently overstate U.S. financial contributions to the organization, as they do foreign aid in general (Kull and Destler 1999, 56). This reservoir of public support, however, did not prevent the United States from heading down a collision course with the UN in 2002 and 2003.

The Rupture over Iraq

As noted previously, President Bush came to office vowing to liberate the United States from the IGOs and international agreements that, in his view, were collectively tying the hands of the world's preeminent power. The United Nations was of particular concern to the president and his conservative allies in Congress, who resented the anti-American rhetoric coming out of the General Assembly. Yet in the aftermath of the September 11 terrorist attacks, it appeared the United States and UN had found sufficient common cause to overcome their mutual hostilities.

This feeling of solidarity did not last. Bush's decision to invade Iraq preventively and without the Security Council's blessing struck a blow not only to U.S.-UN relations but also to central tenets of international law. In recruiting a "coalition of the willing" rather than a UN-sanctioned force, the United States demonstrated that in matters of war and peace, it considered the world body dispensable (see Table 9.2). Bush decided to make Iraq the second target of the U.S. counteroffensive in November 2001, while his first target, the Taliban regime of Afghanistan, was still being routed (Clarke 2004). In the case of Iraq, U.S. action would take place in the context of a previous war, fought a decade earlier over Kuwait, and a long series of UN-sponsored resolutions, weapons inspections, and economic sanctions against Saddam Hussein's oppressive regime. The Bush administration would claim that a "regime change" in Iraq was authorized by previous UN resolutions demanding that Saddam relinquish his weapons of mass destruction (WMD). The collapse of the UN-led inspections process in 1998 had left it unclear whether the chemical weapons used previously by Iraq had been destroyed, as Saddam insisted they had.

Table 9.2 A "Coalition of the Willing:" Operation Iraqi Freedom, March 2003

Member Countries	
Afghanistan	Macedonia
Albania	Marshall Islands
Angola	Micronesia
Australia	Mongolia
Azerbaijan	Netherlands
Bulgaria	Nicaragua
Colombia	Palau
Costa Rica	Panama
Czech Republic	Philippines
Denmark	Poland
Dominican Republic	Portugal
El Salvador	Romania
Eritrea	Rwanda
Estonia	Singapore
Ethiopia	Slovakia
Georgia	Solomon Islands
Honduras	South Korea
Hungary	Spain
Iceland	Turkey
Italy	Uganda
Japan	Ukraine
Kuwait	United Kingdom
Latvia	United States
Lithuania	Uzbekistan

SOURCE: The White House, "Operation Iraqi Freedom, Coalition Members" (March 21, 2003), www.whitehouse.gov /news/releases/2003/03/20030321-4.html

IN THEIR OWN WORDS: GEORGE W. BUSH

Relations between the United States and the United Nations reached an all-time low in 2002 as President George W. Bush challenged the world body to support the U.S.-led invasion of Iraq. Bush came into power determined to detach the United States from many intergovernmental organizations, and the UN was at the top of his list. The president agreed, however, to give UN members a chance to support his plan for regime change in Iraq. In keeping with custom, he appeared before the General Assembly on September 12, 2002. During his appearance, which was closely followed by a worldwide audience, Bush made it clear that the United States was determined to pursue its objectives in Iraq—with or without the world body's blessing.

Delegates to the General Assembly, we have been more than patient. We've tried sanctions. We've tried the carrot of oil for food, and the stick of coalition military strikes. But Saddam Hussein has defied all these efforts and continues to develop weapons of mass destruction. The first time we may be completely certain he has nuclear weapons is when, God forbid, he uses one. We owe it to all our citizens to do everything in our power to prevent that day from coming.

The conduct of the Iraqi regime is a threat to the authority of the United Nations and a threat to world peace. Iraq has answered a decade of UN demands with a decade of defiance. All the world now faces a test, and the United Nations a difficult and defining moment. Are Security Council resolutions to be honored and enforced, or cast aside without consequence? Will the United Nations serve the purpose of its founding, or will it be irrelevant?

The United States helped found the United Nations. We want the United Nations to be effective, and respectful, and successful. We want the resolutions of the world's most important multilateral body to be enforced. And right now those resolutions are being unilaterally subverted by the Iraqi regime. Our partnership of nations can meet the test before us, by making clear what we now expect of the Iraqi regime.

Source: White House, "President's Remarks at the United Nations General Assembly" (New York, September 12, 2002), www.whitehouse.gov/news /releases/2002/09/20020912-1.html.

Some U.S. officials, such as Secretary of State Powell, believed the road to Baghdad, unlike that to Kabul, should pass through the Security Council. Powell persuaded Bush to take his case for preventive war to the UN. The president's speech on September 12, 2002, challenged the world body to enforce its will against Saddam or otherwise become "irrelevant." The Security Council responded in November by approving Resolution 1441, which called for a new round of WMD inspections by the UN and the International Atomic Energy Agency. Bush, who had previously gained authority from Congress to use military force against Saddam if necessary, agreed to delay military action until these inspections had run their course. But the subsequent failure of weapons inspectors to find WMD stockpiles merely confirmed to Bush that Iraq still had something to hide. Turning aside UN appeals for more inspections, the president decided to launch an attack against Iraq in March 2003 without the Security Council's approval.

Lacking the legitimacy that would have accompanied a Security Council endorsement, the United States faced predictable difficulties in gaining UN support for the subsequent U.S. occupation of Iraq. This proved especially true as the mission bogged down, coalition forces came under daily attack and global outrage spread following the May 2004 revelation of U.S. mistreatment of Iraqi detainees at the Abu Ghraib prison. The UN, whose small-scale support mission in Iraq was previously cut short by a terrorist attack on its headquarters, still offered to broker a settlement restoring sovereignty to the country by the scheduled date of June 30. Although the United States formally turned over sovereignty to an interim Iraqi government by that date, the future control over Iraq remained highly uncertain. What was clear, however, was that the most serious rupture in U.S.-UN relations would take years to overcome.

Military Alliances

Among other intergovernmental organizations of importance to U.S. foreign policy are **military alliances,** formal collaborations between two countries or more on security matters of mutual concern. Alliances have taken various forms throughout history—large or small in size, long or short term in duration, and offensive or defensive in intent. Some alliances entail elaborate joint training exercises and the pooling of weapons procurement; others simply call for pledges of assistance should a crisis erupt.

For all their variety, alliances share several defining features: an explicit intergovernmental agreement, a focus on military collaboration, and a set of commitments to achieve shared goals. Although these commitments are not legally binding and, when push comes to shove, are frequently broken (see Sabrosky 1980), they provide a measure of security lacking in the anarchic international system described in Chapter 3. To Hans Morgenthau (1959, 186), "An alliance adds precision . . . to an existing community of interests and to the general policies and concrete measures serving them."

As noted previously, the U.S. government's avoidance of "entangling alliances" formed a central pillar of its early foreign policy. American leaders worried that such arrangements would distract the nation from domestic priorities, create unhealthy ties to corrupt foreign governments, and drag the United States into regional conflicts overseas of little relevance to its national interests. These fears were overcome during the world wars, when the benefits of alliances—enhanced power projection, increased protection from enemies, and the sharing of military expenses and responsibilities—clearly outweighed the possible costs. After World War II, the traditional U.S. aversion to military alliances in peacetime gave way to a wave of "pactomania" that swept the United States into open-ended alliance relationships with dozens of countries in nearly every region of the world (Osgood 1968).

The alliance network that exists today is a product of this pactomania, though some cold war alliances have disbanded (see U.S. Department of State, Bureau of Public Affairs 2003).[6] No new alliances have been formed since the early cold war. The U.S. government and its continuing alliance partners have identified new missions, of which fighting terrorism has become most prominent since September 2001. In waging the war on terrorism, the United States has also established cooperative relationships with several other governments, including the Philippines and Pakistan, which face their own challenges from terrorist groups. These relationships, while lacking the formal and long-term commitments written into military alliances, nonetheless enhance the strategic positions and options of both sides.

As in the past, the United States serves as a leader and primary benefactor of the alliances to which it belongs. Although the arrangements generally call for mutual or collective defense, the United States holds a **security umbrella** over its allies. In this respect, the alliances in which the United States participates are "asymmetric" in nature, based upon an unequal distribution of power among partners and an unequal sharing of burdens. Nevertheless, the United States benefits by extending its political influence, economic wealth, and military muscle far beyond its borders.

The North Atlantic Treaty Organization

Growing cold war concerns prompted the United States to join forces with its Western European allies in 1949 through the creation of NATO. Five of these allies—Belgium, France, Great Britain, Luxembourg, and the Netherlands—had earlier formed the Western European Union to establish a united front against Soviet intimidation. Subsequent developments, such as Moscow's blockade of Berlin in 1948, sufficiently alarmed the United States into allying itself with these governments and six others: Canada, Denmark, Iceland, Italy, Norway, and Portugal (see Map 8, NATO Expansion, in the front of the book). According to Article 5 of the North Atlantic Treaty, "[A]n armed attack on one or more countries in Europe or North America shall be considered an attack against them all." [7]

The United States had never before made such a commitment in peacetime, but the rationales for this exception were compelling. Lord Hastings Ismay, NATO's first secretary general, succinctly captured the alliance's threefold mission: "NATO was designed to keep the Americans in, the Russians out, and the Germans down" (quoted in Yost 1998, 52). Regarding the first of these rationales, the new alliance complemented ongoing U.S. efforts to strengthen its European

6. Two defunct multilateral treaties are the Central Treaty Organization and the Southeast Asia Treaty Organization, both of which outlived their usefulness as agents of anticommunist containment during the cold war.

7. See www.nato.int/docu/basictxt/treaty.htm for the complete text of the North Atlantic Treaty.

allies through the Marshall Plan and Truman Doctrine aid programs (see Chapter 2). More broadly, NATO advanced the process of **regional integration** in Europe, that is, closer economic and political cooperation that offered a remedy for the chronic wars that had ravaged the continent throughout history. Such collaboration was clearly a national interest of the United States, which had twice been called upon to save Europe from its self-destructive rivalries. The close cultural and economic ties between the Old World and the United States cemented this security link.

By staying "in" Europe through NATO, the United States ensured that a Soviet advance across the Iron Curtain would be met with an overwhelming collective response. As for West Germany, created after World War II along with East Germany, a Soviet ally, NATO provided an opportunity for its government to join the "community of nations" while placing its military forces under the alliance's control. West Germany's membership further allowed this portion of the German nation to regain its economic strength without alarming its neighbors, and to play a key role in the process of European integration.

Although formally an agent of collective security, NATO has always been dominated by the United States. To one scholar, David Calleo (1970, 27–28), any semblance of equality among NATO members during the cold war was an "Atlantic fantasy." This imbalance of power resulted in frequent disputes between the United Sates and other alliance members. In 1966, the French government withdrew from NATO's military structure and established an independent nuclear force that remains today. For its part, the U.S. government routinely complained about a lack of "burden sharing" among NATO members, which spent far less of their government budgets on mutual defense spending than the United States.

The persistence of NATO after the cold war poses a central challenge to alliance theory, which holds that alliances naturally dissolve when their stated adversaries are defeated (see Walt 1987, 26–27). NATO has not only endured since 1991, but has steadily grown larger as well (see Asmus 2002). The first round of NATO "enlargement" added the Czech Republic, Hungary, and Poland in 1999. Seven other eastern European countries—Bulgaria, Estonia, Latvia, Lithuania, Romania, Slovakia, and Slovenia—joined the alliance in 2004. Another twenty countries currently participate in the **Partnership for Peace (PfP)**, a NATO auxiliary that provides for mutual consultations, the sharing of resources, and possible future NATO membership among its members.[8]

The "enlargement" process unfolds as NATO members identify new roles for the alliance long after the accomplishment of its original primary mission—containing Soviet expansion. While keeping the Russians "out" is no longer an acknowledged goal, Russia's massive nuclear arsenal, vast geographic reach, and chronic internal problems still concern its western neighbors. Russia and NATO maintain vital and potentially conflicting interests in central and southern Europe and in the post-Soviet states, all of which have at times been considered within

8. Members of PfP currently include Albania, Armenia, Austria, Azerbaijan, Belarus, Croatia, Finland, Georgia, Ireland, Kazakhstan, the Kyrgyz Republic, Macedonia, Moldova, Russia, Sweden, Switzerland, Tajikistan, Turkmenistan, Ukraine, and Uzbekistan.

Moscow's sphere of influence. NATO members recognized Russia's enduring influence in Eurasia in May 2002, when they and Russian officials created the NATO-Russia Council to give Russia "a voice, but not a veto" in NATO deliberations.

Despite recent strains in transatlantic relations, keeping the Americans in Europe remains a central function of NATO. The United States can not only ensure the ongoing security of the European states, but also suppress historic tensions among them, tensions that have erupted in world wars. As during the cold war, the United States continues to "buffer, dampen, and thereby keep within defined bounds the inevitable tensions that will continue to arise" across Europe (Art 1996, 38). In this important respect, NATO serves as an agent of *regional* collective security, an arrangement by which "member states are concurrently committed to maintaining adequate defense against external threats, specified and unspecified, and to promoting internal stability and cohesion through a process of self-regulation" (Hook and Robyn 1999, 86).

The third NATO objective cited by Lord Ismay—keeping the Germans "down"—also remains relevant though not acknowledged openly due to political sensitivity. As during the cold war, the subordination of Berlin's military forces within NATO reassures its neighbors. With a now reunited Germany embedded in NATO as well as the European Union, there is little prospect for the "renationalization" of German foreign policy. Advocates of NATO enlargement have cited the German case as evidence of the alliance's "socializing" effects. To former secretary of state Madeleine Albright, "[A] larger NATO will make us safer by expanding the area in Europe where wars simply do not happen," (1998, 58).

One new mission for NATO is the resolution of **out-of-area conflicts.** "Because many threats to the NATO members come from outside of Europe," President Bush observed, "NATO forces must be organized to operate outside of Europe." The first of these interventions occurred in the former Yugoslav province of Bosnia-Herzegovina, where NATO deployed an implementation force in 1996 following years of civil war. The alliance intervened in Kosovo three years later, ending years of ethnic cleansing and preventing the conflict from spreading across southern Europe. A NATO-led Kosovo force remains in place long after the war, with assistance from the UN and the Organization for Security Cooperation in Europe, another regional IGO looking for a post–cold war mission.

The September 2001 terrorist attacks prompted NATO members to take the unprecedented step of invoking Article 5 of its charter. Although the United States, with help from Great Britain, invaded Afghanistan without formal NATO involvement, the alliance later deployed a peacekeeping force to maintain order in the country and prevent the return of the Taliban regime. This protracted out-of-area conflict, the first outside of Europe, offered new opportunities for the alliance to refine its complicated system of command and control, a system of "war by committee" that hampered the military effort in Kosovo (see Clark 2001; and Daalder and O'Hanlon 2000). Of particular concern to U.S. leaders during that conflict was the requirement that all bombing targets be unanimously approved by NATO members.

The United States faces an ongoing dilemma in its relationship with NATO. By continuing to dominate the alliance with its disproportionate military spending and armed forces (see Table 9.3), the United States frequently provokes resentment among smaller powers. If it loosens control over NATO, however, the United States risks losing influence in Europe and encouraging the emergence of a stronger and more independent European "pole" in the global balance of power. This dilemma is hardly new to the alliance, in which the United States has always acted "as Atlas, with much of the structure on his shoulders" (Yost 1998, 287).

Table 9.3 Troop Strength of NATO Forces: Major Powers, 2003

Country	Armed Forces (in Thousands)
United States	1,496
Turkey	823
France	356
Italy	325
Germany	285
UK	214
Greece	203
Poland	150
Spain	135
Total (including all member states)	4,334

SOURCE: NATO, "Financial and Economic Data Relating to NATO Defense" (2003), www.globalsecurity.org/military/library/news/2003/12/mil-031201-nato05.htm.

The U.S.-led invasion of Iraq caused the "near-death" of the transatlantic alliance (Pond 2004), making this balancing act far more difficult. Opposition by France and Germany prompted Secretary of Defense Donald Rumsfeld to dismiss the two strongest continental powers as "old Europe." Rumsfeld turned instead to Great Britain and smaller NATO states to join the "coalition of the willing." These included eastern European countries such as Poland and Hungary whose governments and citizens were grateful for U.S. actions on their behalf in the cold war and depended on U.S. military and economic assistance. Spain also joined the coalition as an enthusiastic founding member but withdrew in 2004 after terrorist attacks in Madrid led citizens and a newly elected government to turn against the Iraq mission.

Anti-American sentiment in European public opinion (see Chapter 7) also renders the task of holding NATO together more difficult. At the same time, the transatlantic chasm encourages leaders of the European Union, whose own membership has expanded steadily over the past few years, to pursue a "common foreign and security policy" that would exclude the United States. Bullying by the U.S. government, a common complaint throughout the NATO era but especially in recent years, reflected a "mistaken assumption that might makes right and that [European] allies would fall in line behind a simple assertion of U.S. power" (Asmus 2003). To an even more critical observer, the historian Gabriel Kolko (2003, 294), "Washington has decided that its allies must now accept its objectives and work solely on its terms, and it has no intention whatsoever of discussing the merits of its actions in NATO conferences."

The Rio Treaty

While Europe served on the frontline of the cold war, the Western Hemisphere has been of greater geopolitical concern to the United States throughout its history. The Monroe Doctrine of 1823 rendered the entire region a U.S. sphere of influence, and since then the United States has freely used or threatened force to protect its interests in the region and to discourage other great powers from challenging U.S. hegemony. After World War II, U.S. leaders worried that the region would be vulnerable to communist revolutions and the rise of regimes hostile to the United States. This concern was shared by many Latin American leaders, who joined with the United States in signing the Inter-American Treaty of Reciprocal Assistance on September 2, 1947.

The Rio Treaty, as it became known, represented the first postwar regional defense alliance and as such set a precedent for the subsequent creation of NATO. The treaty further affirmed Washington's longstanding commitment to protect the Western Hemisphere. As in the case of Europe, this protection allowed the Rio Pact members to focus on economic, rather than military, concerns. The alliance, which formalized U.S. military domination of the hemisphere, allowed the United States to focus its cold war energies in Western Europe and Asia. Only the coming to power of Cuba's Fidel Castro in 1959 and the rise of revolutionary movements in Central America in the 1980s disrupted unity within the alliance. The Rio Treaty has been invoked numerous times during its history, including in September 2001, following the terrorist attacks on the United States.

The governments of Latin America and the Caribbean regions that joined the Rio Treaty had expectations that went beyond military protection. They hoped to benefit from their own Marshall Plan to relieve their nations' chronic poverty. Although the United States did not provide substantial economic aid to the region during these years, it joined twenty other regional governments in 1948 in creating the Organization of American States (OAS). Based in Washington, D.C., the OAS offers a forum for discussion of regional problems and collective decision making. As in the case of NATO, the predominance of the United States in the OAS, which now includes thirty-five countries, allows U.S. leaders to set the agenda for the organization and determine its primary functions, which thus far have been modest.

The ANZUS Treaty

The United States also built alliances in East Asia. Most of these took the form of bilateral pacts with countries such as Japan and South Korea that were strategically vital to the United States but antagonistic toward one another. In 1951, Australia, New Zealand, and the United States (ANZUS) signed a treaty that brought them together in a mutual-defense pact. Each member of the ANZUS Treaty recognized "that an armed attack in the Pacific Area on any of the parties would be dangerous to its own peace and safety." This alliance, a forerunner to the larger Southeast Asia Treaty Organization (SEATO), sought to discourage communist expansionism in the region, particularly in Southeast Asia during the Vietnam War (see Nuechterlein 1997; and Pugh 1989).

The ANZUS alliance suffered a serious blow in 1985, when New Zealand refused to allow U.S. ships capable of carrying nuclear weapons to use its ports. The government of New Zealand, concerned about the revival of superpower tensions and a nuclear arms race, hoped to create a nuclear-free zone in the Oceania region. The Reagan administration responded by suspending all forms of military cooperation with New Zealand, including any deliberations on regional security through ANZUS. Since 1986, the alliance has effectively been a bilateral one involving the United States and Australia, although New Zealand has not formally withdrawn from the alliance. The Australian prime minister John Howard became an enthusiastic supporter of the war on terrorism after the September 2001 attacks. His loyalty to the United States was rewarded in May 2004, when the two countries signed a free-trade agreement.

Bilateral Military Alliances

The nations of Western Europe and Latin America made for cordial alliance partners with the United States during the cold war due to their shared political cultures and regional proximity to the United States, respectively. Neither was the case for the three East Asian states that the U.S. government considered strategically vital: Japan, South Korea, and the Philippines.[9] In place of a multilateral alliance linking the United States to these states, U.S. officials created bilateral pacts with each of them. While these were primarily directed toward containing communism, they paved the way for large-scale U.S. economic support and access to the U.S. consumer market.

Japan. The primary obstacle to a regionwide accord in East Asia after World War II was Japan, whose prewar imperial conquests had made it a regional pariah. However, Japan was crucial to East Asia's long-term recovery and to the global balance of power. When the United States ended its postwar occupation in 1951, it signed a security treaty with Japan that affirmed the latter's vital link in the containment "belt" around the Soviet Union and China. Japan, whose new constitution prohibited large-scale military rearmament, agreed not to establish alliances with other countries. The two nations reaffirmed their alliance in 1996 and in 2001 pledged mutual support for the war on terrorism. Japan sent troops to Iraq in 2004 as part of Operation Iraqi Freedom, the first time it had deployed troops abroad since World War II. Tensions between the United States and Japan exist, however, particularly regarding the huge U.S. troop presence in Okinawa, home to several U.S. military bases.

The Philippines. Nine days before signing its treaty with Japan, the United States approved a similar bilateral alliance with the Philippines. The vast archipelago, freed from U.S. colonization in 1946, further extended the anticommunist bloc in the Pacific region. The U.S.-Philippines Bilateral Defense Agreement, signed on

---

9. The United States suspended a fourth bilateral pact in the region, with Taiwan, in 1980, after recognizing the People's Republic of China as a legitimate government on the mainland. The United States continues to support Taiwan unofficially and would likely defend its regime, which seeks independence, if it were attacked by the central government.

August 30, 1951, provided a U.S. security guarantee to the Philippines, which reciprocated by giving the United States access to Filipino military bases. The alliance persisted after the cold war even as the United States withdrew, under domestic Filipino pressure, from the military bases in the Philippines. The bilateral pact achieved new importance after September 2001 as the Philippines' struggle against Islamic separatists led President Bush to declare the nation a "major non-NATO ally." [10] A planned deployment of U.S. military advisers, announced early in 2003, was later cancelled due to opposition within the Filipino government.

South Korea. The third U.S. bilateral alliance is with South Korea, another Pacific Rim state whose strategic importance to Washington survived the demise of the alliance's founding threats, the Soviet Union and China. An October 1953 defense agreement established a virtual U.S. protectorate of South Korea following the Korean War. As with Japan and the Philippines, tensions have recently grown between the United States and South Korea, particularly over the handling of North Korea's announced plans to become a nuclear power. While the Bush administration refused to negotiate directly with North Korea, which reneged on an earlier promise not to build nuclear weapons, South Korea favored a more cooperative approach. Despite these strains, South Korea has much to gain by remaining under the U.S. security umbrella and maintaining cordial, and highly profitable, trade relations with the United States.

International Financial Institutions

The United States also relies upon IGOs to pursue its economic interests overseas. Global economic relations become more vital to states as technological advances, particularly in communications and transportation, produce a more integrated world economy. For the United States, the process of globalization—the melding of national and regional markets into a single world market with limited political barriers to commerce—has long been a foreign-policy goal. The United States has therefore encouraged, and benefited greatly from, globalization.

Yet for all of the advances in the global economy, much of the world's population remains in poverty, and the gaps between the richest and poorest nations continue to widen. Simply adopting the free-market principles of Adam Smith, the eighteenth-century father of capitalism, cannot resolve the immediate problems of acute poverty in most countries of the world. Long-term development lies beyond the reach of these countries, which lack resources to build roads, utilities, schools, hospitals, and other public resources necessary for economic growth. Wealthy governments, meanwhile, routinely manipulate financial markets, subsidize their domestic industries, and seek advantages in global trade in ways that violate the rules of a "stateless" world economy.

---

10. Other major non-NATO allies, which are eligible for an array of economic and security benefits, included in 2004 Argentina, Australia, Bahrain, Egypt, Israel, Jordan, Kuwait, New Zealand, South Korea, Taiwan, and Thailand.

Both sets of problems call for solutions unachievable by individual states acting alone. As a result, **international financial institutions (IFIs),** formal associations of nation-states designed to regulate and promote the global market economy, serve as vital agents of U.S. foreign policy. The most important of these—the World Bank, the International Monetary Fund (IMF), and the World Trade Organization (WTO)—play separate, but overlapping, roles in promoting a world economy founded upon free-market principles.

The U.S. government took the lead in the creation of all three IFIs. As noted in Chapter 2, the World Bank and the IMF are the products of the 1944 Bretton Woods conference, which "enshrined U.S. views of how the world economy should be organized" (Woods 2000, 133). The WTO, created fifty years later as the institutional spin-off of the General Agreement on Tariffs and Trade, promotes open markets in international trade, a central objective of U.S. foreign-economic policy since the nation's founding. Taken together, these organizations serve four distinct functions in U.S. foreign policy.

First, IFIs serve as an extension of U.S. **market democracy,** a domestic political economy that combines free enterprise and constitutional, representative government. The World Bank, the IMF, and the WTO advocate economic principles central to U.S. foreign-economic policy: respect for private property, the encouragement of private investment and enterprise, and limited government intervention in economic matters. These principles relate closely to the protection of individual freedoms and civil society from the state and to the connection between democratic rule and pacific foreign relations.

Second, IFIs provide economies of scale. By pooling their resources through IFIs, nations can achieve goals in the world economy outside their individual capabilities. The whole, in short, is greater than the sum of its parts. The World Bank and the IMF grant loans that cannot be found at comparable rates on private markets. They also provide a forum for economic planning and coordination among states. The resulting codes of conduct reflect a consensus, primarily among the industrialized states, that cannot be attained through bilateral foreign-policy channels (see Abbott and Snidal 1998). For its part, the WTO provides an institutional foundation for open markets that otherwise would be threatened by the protectionist, "beggar-thy-neighbor" trade policies of individual governments.

Third, IFIs offer political "cover" for creditors and debtors. It is hardly a secret that the United States is the largest contributor and most influential decision maker in these institutions. Nevertheless, these IFIs allow the United States to share the political and administrative responsibility for its favored programs and policies among other states. The same benefit applies to nations in economic distress, which prefer financial aid from global organizations to assistance coming directly from an individual country (Ascher 1992).

Finally, there are domestic political benefits to being involved in IFIs. Foreign-policy makers in the executive branch find these organizations useful in enhancing their domestic political powers. Officials in the State, Treasury, Commerce, and other cabinet departments enjoy extensive freedom of action within these institutions. Despite Congress's constitutional power to "regulate commerce," legislators generally leave the World Bank and the IMF to their own devices. Congressional members may limit the amount of funding available to these organizations, but they defer to the White House in approving most individual aid packages and policy initiatives (see James 1996). The same can be said for the majority of trade issues, as will be elaborated in Chapter 11.

With these benefits come problems for the United States. The World Bank and the IMF are expensive and volatile, exposing U.S. taxpayers to financial risks and possible large-scale defaults on foreign debts. Politically, IFIs have proved highly controversial. Antiglobalization protesters and NGOs routinely target the annual meetings of all three institutions, which the protesters view as agents of economic imperialism, political repression, social inequality, and environmental destruction. Protest groups often single out the United States; their disruption of the 1999 annual meetings of the WTO in Seattle delivered a devastating blow to President Clinton's globalization agenda.

Such upheavals were of particular interest to Joseph E. Stiglitz, who chaired Clinton's Council of Economic Advisers and later served as chief economist for the World Bank. Stiglitz, who left these positions highly critical of the IFIs, believes they serve the needs of powerful financial and commercial interests while neglecting the plight of the world's poor. The domination by wealthy nations and firms over the World Bank, the IMF, and the WTO, he argues, makes them unresponsive to the majority of the global population they are designed to serve. To Stiglitz (2002, 251–252), "Development is not about helping a few people get rich or creating a handful of pointless protected industries that only benefit the country's elite."

Below we provide a brief overview of each of these institutions. We begin by describing the World Bank, whose primary mission is to foster economic development in the world's impoverished regions. We then examine the IMF, which supports global financial markets by ensuring a stable supply of foreign exchange among trading states and by preventing fiscal and monetary crises in one country from spreading beyond its borders. Finally, we review the WTO's role in encouraging its members to open their markets to the goods, services, and investments of other states.

The World Bank

The World Bank offers low-interest loans, grants, and technical assistance to struggling economies for long-term development projects. Its 184 member states and more than $100 billion in outstanding loans make the bank the largest source of multilateral economic assistance in the world and a powerful player in North-South economic relations. Funds for the World Bank are derived in large measure from the issuance of bonds, whose AAA credit rating makes them attractive to investors. The bank, which must satisfy lenders at the same time it serves the needs of creditors, "relies on a delicate balancing of political forces in order to maintain itself. Above all, it must pay attention to its most powerful member—the United States" (Woods 2000, 133).

World Bank President James Wolfensohn, right, speaks in July 2002 to a group of former combatants in Rwanda about possible reconstruction projects in the war-torn African country. The World Bank pledged more than $1 billion in grants and low-interest loans in the decade following the genocidal conflict in Rwanda and neighboring Burundi early in 1994. Wolfensohn frequently traveled to the sites of World Bank-sponsored programs, as well as to industrialized countries whose governments were needed to finance such efforts. The World Bank, part of the Bretton Woods system, is based in Washington, D.C.

Two agencies form the core of the World Bank Group, which has provided about $500 billion in low-interest loans since World War II (World Bank 2004a). The largest of these programs is the International Bank for Reconstruction and Development (IBRD), created in 1946 to manage the distribution of Marshall Plan loans to U.S. allies, primarily in Western Europe. The bank's focus moved on to developing nations, many newly freed from colonial rule. More recent IBRD loans have funded economic and political reforms in the former Soviet bloc as well as modernization projects in Latin America and East Asia. World Bank loans, provided to ninety-six projects in forty countries, amounted to $11.5 billion in 2002.

The second key agency, the International Development Association (IDA), helps the world's poorest countries address more immediate problems, such as malnutrition and the HIV/AIDS epidemic. Recipients of IDA loans pay little or no interest and have up to forty years to repay the loans. The value of these loans, which amounted to $8.1 billion in 2002, was disbursed among 133 projects in sixty-two countries. The rest of the World Bank Group consists of the International Finance Corporation, the Multilateral Guaranty Agency, and the International Center for Settlement of Investment Disputes.

All World Bank presidents have been U.S. citizens appointed by the federal government, which located the bank's headquarters near the U.S. Treasury for

•))) IN THEIR OWN WORDS: JAMES D. WOLFENSOHN (((•

As a key agent of economic globalization, the World Bank is closely linked to the problems, as well as the benefits, resulting from this trend. Nonetheless, World Bank officials stress that globalization has deep roots that reach beyond economics to include social and cultural forces increasingly transnational in scope. To James D. Wolfensohn, the bank's president, coming to grips with all these dimensions of globalization is vital to the prospects for world peace and prosperity in the twenty-first century.

[T]he first thing about globalization is that if you have terror somewhere today, it's really terror everywhere. If you have poverty somewhere today, the impact of poverty somewhere is really everywhere. This is something that is not broadly or fully understood. It's not fully reflected in domestic politics, but from our experience and from what we've seen about the outgrowth of not only terror but other things that link us in the world, crime, health, environment, trade, finance, and migration, these are issues which we're all starting to come to terms with but about which the press, the media, the politicians rarely have yet reached a level of understanding where intuitively they recognize that the wall is not there. The fact is the wall is not there.

The wall is not there for trade, environment, crime, drugs, medicine, disease, terror. But most people of my age and of above a certain age still think of it as two worlds, when in fact it isn't. It's not that we are just there at this point in time with five billion out of six billion people, but in the next 25 years the world becomes eight billion, of which then seven billion will be in developing countries. And by the year 2050, which is not all that far away, it will be eight billion out of nine. . . .

This is the fundamental reality. This is not science fiction. It is not something—new brilliant insight. But that is the demographics. Within those demographics you have a whole series of other global movements which are not visible in terms of a bomb going off immediately, or a headline, but which are nonetheless real and nonetheless important. . . .

We talk about globalization without really knowing what it is. For most people globalization is multinational companies taking jobs from one place to another and screwing everything up. That is not globalization. It is an aspect of globalization. The aspect of globalization that I'm talking about is the interdependence of the planet which now exists in which poverty has a huge role, and which inequity is a huge issue, and which if it is allowed to continue cannot lead to a stable planet.

Source: James D. Wolfensohn, "Keynote Address at Visions, Voices, Visibility Symposium for Broadcasters on International Development" (Washington, D.C., June 14, 2004).

more than symbolic reasons. The United States, whose contributions to the bank's budget (17 percent) is more than twice that of the second-largest member, Japan, casts a long shadow over the organization. Voting shares in the bank are proportionate to the financial contributions of member states. This effectively gives the United States veto power over bank policies and loans, which must be supported by at least an 85 percent share of votes cast. For this reason, Washington's informal consent is customarily sought before potential development loans are brought before the bank.

World Bank presidents such as Robert McNamara, the former secretary of defense and president of Ford Motor Co., have sought to make the organization more independent of the U.S. government. The close association persists, however, and remains an object of criticism. The bank has also been criticized for "subsidizing" repressive governments and for supporting projects, such as a large dam in India, that displace large numbers of citizens and disrupt natural habitats. The bank has also been criticized for sponsoring a development program in China that would resettle Chinese citizens on traditionally Tibetan lands.

Of additional concern is the bank's record of funding flawed development projects, then providing even more funds to rescue the states that caused the failures in the first place. To critics, the World Bank fosters a "culture of loan approval" and throws good money after bad. "By its very nature, the World Bank's only answer to the growing economic difficulties of its most indebted client countries is to loan more money" (Rich 2002, 28). Similar criticism followed the World Bank's agreement in 2004 to provide a $1.5-billion loan to Russia, where market reforms had succumbed for more than a decade to political corruption and the creation of industrial monopolies.

The International Monetary Fund

A central lesson of the Great Depression was that trading states must have confidence in the currencies, fiscal policies, and long-term political stability of their trading partners. States quickly lose this confidence when countries accumulate large deficits in their budgets and balance of payments and cannot pay for routine government programs. Much like consumers who spend more than they earn, countries facing this plight turn to commercial banks for loans, which may be denied if repayment appears doubtful. The consequences that follow in the case of national governments—deep cuts in public services, defaults on foreign debts, political disarray, and social unrest—extend far beyond the individual debtors and creditors to include the world economy as a whole. To bolster confidence, the IMF serves three primary functions:

- supervising the monetary policies of its member states
- coordinating the current system of floating exchange rates among national currencies
- providing emergency loans to governments in economic crisis

The third IMF function receives the most attention and is subject to the greatest controversy (see Bird 2003; and Blustein 2001). Once a country joins the IMF, it contributes a specified sum of money to the fund based upon its size and the health of its economy. IMF loans, which draw from this pool of resources, are designed to control the damage resulting from financial crises and pave the way for long-term recovery. About $107 billion worth of such loans, granted to eighty-seven countries, were outstanding in 2004 (IMF 2004b).

In the late 1990s, governments in East Asia received the largest share of IMF loans. Support for Indonesia alone equaled the amount lent to thirty-six other low-income countries (Bird 2003, 12). Overall, the IMF provided economic support to sixty-two countries during this period, about one-third of the fund's member states. While most borrowers were poor, others represented "transition" economies in the midst of large-scale economic reforms. A prominent example in this regard is Russia, whose transition to market economics and democracy could not, from the IMF's perspective, be "allowed to fail." Critics of the IMF believe such commitments simply reward corruption and **crony capitalism,** the favorable treatment government officials give to private-sector associates, often in exchange for illicit financial rewards.

As in the case of the World Bank, the United States is the largest contributor to the IMF and its most influential member. None of the major IMF bailouts approved in its history would have occurred without support from U.S. leaders. Their clout is so strong that conditions placed upon IMF loans—restricted government spending, privatized industries, openness to foreign trade and investments—stem from a **Washington consensus** regarding appropriate economic behavior (Williamson 1990). The key elements of this consensus collectively limit the role of governments in economic affairs, relying instead upon "the magic of the market."

Borrowers resent these intrusions into their economic sovereignty and the stringent conditions on loans, which have made the IMF "a poster child for the evils of globalization" (Willett 2001, 594). According to its critics, the IMF is responsible for most of the economic calamities of the post–cold war period, including the collapse of economic reform in Russia, the East Asian economic crisis, and the revival of social unrest in Latin America. A U.S.-sponsored study found that IMF interventions "have not been associated, on average, with any clear gains to recipient countries" (Meltzer Commission 2000, 40). Defenders of the organization counter that a lack of fiscal and monetary "discipline" brought these countries to the brink of financial ruin, not the conditions imposed by the IMF (see Rogoff 2003; and Eichengreen 2002).

The World Trade Organization

Another lesson of the Great Depression was that the world economy required a trading system unhampered by protectionist barriers. As more and more countries built walls around their domestic markets in the 1920s, protecting their firms from foreign competition, the world economy became less and less prosperous and stable. The ensuing financial collapse in Europe and the United States fueled challenges to market economies, including communism on the left end of the political spectrum and fascism on the right end. The association of both with repressive governments, and of the latter with territorial conquest across Europe and Asia, compelled the United States and its allies to create a system for regulating free trade.

The United States and other governments first sought to create the International Trade Organization (ITO), designed not only to promote trade but also to regulate foreign investments and general business practices. The ITO, however, went too far for many members of Congress. Fearing the loss of U.S. economic sovereignty and wanting to retain many domestic trade protections, the Senate refused to ratify the Havana Charter, the ITO's founding document. Instead, in 1947, the U.S. government supported the more modest General Agreement on Tariffs and Trade (GATT), which affirmed the consensus favoring open markets while allowing member states more autonomy and flexibility in protecting their industries. After GATT's creation, several rounds, or negotiations, further opened the domestic markets of these states to foreign competition. The Uruguay round of GATT talks, which ended in 1994, created the World Trade Organization and empowered the new agency not simply to devise the rules of the game but to enforce them as well (see Krueger 1998).

The WTO, based in Geneva, Switzerland, monitors the trade policies of its member states while providing a forum for negotiating multilateral trade agreements and resolving disputes among trading partners. More than 130 countries, accounting for more than 90 percent of world trade, operate in a "nondiscriminatory" system that prevents trade wars from breaking out among them. The presence of the WTO has not eliminated the role of governments in world trade. To the contrary, tariffs and nontariff barriers are still common in every country, including the United States. Nevertheless, in pursuing systemwide goals that cannot be achieved by individual states or bilateral agreements, the WTO fills the same void in global trade that the World Bank fills in economic development and the IMF fills in financial management.

As with the World Bank and the IMF, the United States enjoys an "unspoken veto" over the leadership of the WTO. The **structural power** of the United States, or the leverage it gains from the unparalleled size of its economy, permits U.S. leaders to set the terms of WTO debates and decide which countries will be considered for membership (Strange 1988). As the world's largest importer (see Chapter 11) and the primary trading partner of dozens of countries, the United States has correctly been described as an "engine of growth" in the world economy. With this distinction comes unrivaled clout over the trade policies of other states.

Nonetheless, the WTO often maintains a contentious relationship with the United States, which itself has run afoul of the organization's standards in recent years. Increased tariffs on foreign steel prompted the WTO to rule against the Bush administration in a complaint filed by the European Union, which threatened to impose more than $2 billion in import sanctions against the United States. Bush reversed himself on these tariffs, which pleased the EU as well as steel consumers in the United States (particularly the automobile industry) while disappointing the domestic steel producers and workers Bush had earlier courted. In exchange for such heightened scrutiny of its trade policies, the United States generally benefits from WTO rulings. This tradeoff, recognition of mutual interests and reciprocal obligations, is typical of the institutional bargain the United States has struck in other areas of multilateral foreign policy.

The WTO suffered a major blow with the collapse of trade talks in Cancun, Mexico, in September 2003. At the meetings, part of the Doha round of trade negotiations, the United States and the EU confronted a defiant group of developing countries led by Brazil, China, and India. Their leaders complained that the wealthy nations imposed a double standard on poorer countries, demanding that they open their markets to foreign competition while the wealthy nations protected their own farmers and industries. By walking out of the meetings in dramatic fashion, the developing countries demonstrated that their strength in numbers, if not wealth, can be a formidable weapon in the globalized economy. Aside from the WTO, the United States has found regional trading blocs a useful means of promoting commerce with other nations. The North American Free Trade Agreement (NAFTA), created in 1993 with Canada and Mexico, reduced trade barriers within the region and allowed for expanded cooperation among the three countries in other areas. The volume of U.S. trade within NAFTA jumped from $81 billion in 1993 to $232 billion a decade later, a nearly threefold increase due in part to the reduced barriers to trade resulting from the agreement (Griswold 2002). The success of NAFTA prompted five Central American nations—Costa Rica, El Salvador, Guatemala, Honduras, and Nicaragua—to join with the United States in 2004 in signing the Central America Free Trade Agreement.

Regional problems persist, however, among the economies of the Western Hemisphere. Opponents of these agreements, particularly government leaders in South American nations such as Brazil and Venezuela, argue that these agreements neglect environmental concerns and the rights of workers. Furthermore, these critics charge, open markets are fine for the United States, with its huge corporations, technological superiority, and economies of scale but perilous for their own countries. *Globalization,* in this view, is a code word for *Americanization.* This critique has denied the U.S. government its foremost goal in the region: a "Free Trade Area of the Americas" that would include nearly the entire Western Hemisphere.

Another regional bloc, Asia-Pacific Economic Cooperation (APEC), has led to closer economic ties between the United States and its trading partners throughout that region. Like Latin America, the United States is a primary trading partner with the newly industrialized countries of East Asia, whose economic boom in the 1970s and 1980s was followed by an economic crisis in the late 1990s that slowed economic growth throughout the world. In addition to promoting the recovery of the twenty-one APEC countries, the United States uses the regional grouping as a vehicle for gaining greater access to the region's vast internal market, including China's 1.3 billion potential consumers of American goods. Annual APEC meetings also offer important opportunities for regional leaders to confer on political and security issues of common concern as well as on economic collaborations.

Finally, the U.S. government seeks to improve its economic prospects further by signing free-trade agreements with single countries. As of mid-2004, these included Chile, Israel, Jordan, Israel, and Singapore. Similar agreements had been signed earlier that year with Australia, the Dominican Republic, and Morocco, and negotiations were under way with the governments of Bahrain, Colombia, Ecuador, Panama, Peru, Thailand, and the five member countries of the Southern African Customs Union (Botswana, Lesotho, Namibia, South Africa, and Swaziland). In each deal, both sides hoped to benefit. The United States would gain access to more export markets overseas. Its trading partners would gain more private investment from the United States, privileged access to U.S. consumers, and the prospect of economic and military aid and other favors.

All of these trade pacts seek to replicate the gains achieved by the EU, whose member states have profited, quite literally, from the opening of their vast internal market. As in the case of U.S. states, the free movement of workers, products, and capital across the national borders of Europe greatly enhances efficiency and the prospects for economic growth. Cooperation in the economic realm can also be expected to spill over into other areas, such as environmental protection, democratic reforms, and regional security, all major EU priorities. The United States, for example, is keenly aware that regional solidarity resulting from NAFTA and APEC can enhance its prospects for support among their member countries in the war on terrorism and other security matters.

Conclusion

This chapter has highlighted the growing profile of intergovernmental organizations in the U.S. foreign-policy process. These IGOs offer a variety of benefits to the United States and other members: sources of information, venues for collaboration, codes of appropriate conduct, mechanisms for compliance and enforcement. At the same time, IGOs have become increasingly bothersome to the United States. Once viewed as an outgrowth of U.S. exceptionalism, these bodies have assumed their own momentum and agendas, which, on many occasions, challenge U.S. values and foreign-policy goals. The Bush administration's rejection of the "international community," a concept it considered fictitious, represented the high-water mark of this backlash against multilateralism.

In this respect, IGOs create yet another arena for power politics, a concept central to realist theories of world politics (see Chapter 2). While IGOs tend to reflect the preferences of their most powerful members (see Mearsheimer 1994–1995), they develop institutional self-interests while providing opportunities for weaker, but more numerous, members to counterbalance the stronger states. Much like domestic agencies in the United States, global agencies such as the World Health Organization, once created, have a compelling interest to expand their missions and increase their resources. For liberals, the fact that national governments so often find IGOs useful in solving shared problems and resolving their grievances toward one another proves they lessen the "anarchy" of world politics.

The world of multilateral cooperation envisioned by liberals, therefore, has roots in the power balances emphasized by realists. "It is precisely the asymmetry of power between a strong state and weaker partners that creates the potential for mutually beneficial exchange," explains G. John Ikenberry (2002, 136). "The United States has an incentive to take advantage of its dominant position to lock in a favorable set of international relationships—that is, to institutionalize its pre-eminence. The subordinate states are willing to lock themselves in, at least to some point, if it means that the leading state will be more manageable as a dominant power."

With all of its clout, the United States has the proven capability and the luxury either to dominate IGOs, as in the case of NATO and the World Bank, or to defect from them entirely, as in the case of UNESCO and the International Criminal Court. The U.S. government also holds the paradoxical distinction of being the strongest force in multilateral diplomacy and its most frequent target. In most cases, the United States plays the role of 800-pound gorilla, whose overwhelming mass and potential to create havoc demands constant attention, and vigilance, among others in the vicinity.

The primacy of the United States does not mean that it can "go it alone" in world politics (see Nye 2002b). The war on terrorism in general, and the U.S. invasion and subsequent occupation of Iraq in particular, offer compelling evidence of the benefits of collaboration and the high costs of "aggressive unilateralism" (Malone 2003, 90). Nor does multilateralism require that the United States surrender its sovereignty to IGOs, whose growth and expanded powers in recent years have only been possible on terms acceptable to their member states, especially those with the most resources to offer. Thus the institutional bargain struck more than half a century ago, when the United States emerged as the world's predominant state and linked its primacy to a multilateral world order, will endure long into the future despite the frequent displeasure voiced by parties on both sides of the bargain.

Key Terms

crony capitalism, p. 286

Group of 8 (G-8), p. 260

Group of 77 (G-77), p. 266

Helms-Biden Act, p. 270

institutional bargain, p. 261

integration, p. 262

interdependence, p. 261

intergovernmental organizations (IGOs), p. 257

international financial institutions (IFIs), p. 281

market democracy, p. 281

military alliances, p. 273

multilateralism, p. 258

out-of-area conflicts, p. 276

Partnership for Peace (PfP), p. 275

regional integration, p. 275

security umbrella, p. 274

sovereign equality, p. 263

spillover effects, p. 262

structural power, p. 287

Washington consensus, p. 286

Internet References

The *CIA World Factbook* (www.cia.gov/cia/publications/factbook/index.html), recorded and published by the U.S. Central Intelligence Agency, provides recent data and background information on every country. Statistics on population, wealth, military capabilities, and government types are included.

Europa (europa.eu.int), the main Web site for the European Union, offers information on the integration of twenty-five European countries. Links to maps, historic documents, and institutions such as the parliament and central bank are provided.

The **Foreign and International Law Library** (www.washlaw.edu/forint/forintmain.html), maintained by Washburn University School of Law Library, allows access to international and foreign law topics and journals. The Web site is organized alphabetically and by subject for quick reference.

Sovereignty International's Web page on **Global Governance** (www.sovereignty .net/p/gov) offers links and text regarding global governance and country cooperation. Included are commission reports, speeches, and treaty descriptions of policy areas such as the International Criminal Court, United Nations bureaus, and environmental regimes.

The **Globalization Website** (www.emory.edu/SOC/globalization), maintained by Emory University, has links to international organizations, NGOs, and globalization sources. Included are data links, newsletters, quick reference guides, and glossaries, and debates concerning international governance and globalization.

The list of **International Affairs Resources** (www.etown.edu/vl/research.html) from the World Wide Web Virtual Library provides links to research think tanks, international organizations, and NGOs for issues such as international law, global governance, human rights, peacekeeping, and international economic affairs. The site is organized by data, journal, and electronic resources, with full descriptions of each link.

The **International Monetary Fund** (www.imf.org) promotes a more stable global economy by promoting monetary cooperation and aiding countries in distress. The IMF's Web site provides details on its financial programs along with country-by-country economic data and reports on current issues such as globalization, rural poverty, financial regulation, and debt relief.

The **North American Institute** (www.northamericaninstitute.org) is a nonprofit, private institute that focuses on transnational policy issues concerning Canada, Mexico, and the United States. Immigration, trade, and environmental issues are at the forefront of the resources offered by the institute.

The **North Atlantic Treaty Organization's** Web site (www.nato.int) provides information and speeches concerning the world's largest international defense organization. Included are platforms and data regarding country contributions, combating terrorism, and NATO historical data.

The **Organisation for Economic Co-operation and Development** (www.oecd.org) is an international organization of thirty member countries who share a commitment to

continues

Internet References *(continued)*

democracy and free economic markets. Included on this Web site are data links concerning national wealth, foreign aid and investment, and development regimes.

The **United Nations** (www.un.org) is the largest intergovernmental organization in the world. The UN Web site provides links to its missions, councils, bureaus, and governing resources. Data resources concerning member countries and missions are also included.

The **World Bank** (www.worldbank.org) is an intergovernmental organization that focuses on economic development and growth. Its Web site has speeches, project summaries, regional analysis, and data resources for all countries.

The **World Health Organization** (www.who.int), based in Geneva, Switzerland, is a major UN agency that seeks the "attainment by all peoples of the highest possible level of health." The WHO's Web site offers links describing health issues in each member country as well as detailed summaries of health-care topics and problems concerning all countries.

The **World Trade Organization** (www.wto.org) is an intergovernmental organization that provides rules and norms for trade and currency dealings between countries. Its Web site offers data on international trade, investment, and economic growth.

10

National Security and Defense Policy

A Chinook helicopter prepares to pick up U.S. forces in the Tora Bora region of Afghanistan, where Osama bin Laden and other al Qaeda leaders were known to operate in 2002. American military supremacy allowed the United States to swiftly displace Afghanistan's Taliban regime. But achieving the Bush administration's political goals—including the capture and prosecution of bin Laden for the September 2001 terrorist attacks on the United States—proved far more elusive. The same dilemma faced U.S. forces in Iraq, where a second "asymmetrical" war dragged on long after the U.S. overthrow of Saddam Hussein in March 2003.

The final three chapters of this book examine the primary domains of U.S. foreign policy, the substantive issue-areas that affect the nation's relations with governments and citizens overseas. Our objective in this section is to highlight the problems posed within these policy domains and to consider how the many state and non-state actors in the U.S. foreign-policy process interact to achieve their objectives. The three domains—national security, global economic relations, and transnational issues—capture the diversity of foreign-policy problems facing the United States today. It must be noted, however, that the problems of one domain frequently intersect those of another and thus solutions cannot be considered in isolation. The specific issues described in this section, of course, do not exhaust the full range of issues confronted daily by foreign-policy makers.

We begin by considering the foreign-policy problems that relate to **national security,** the freedom a nation-state enjoys from threats to its sovereignty, territory, and political autonomy. This term is inherently controversial given the tendency of political leaders to justify their actions on security grounds. Dwight Eisenhower, for example, created the interstate highway system on the basis of national security, and Richard Nixon used the same rationale to defend his secret bombings of Cambodia during the Vietnam War. Yet despite the ambiguity and manipulations surrounding it, national security "has come into such broad usage since World War II that, like a boomerang, we cannot throw it away" (Jordan, Taylor, and Mazarr 1999, 3).

The security that states and their citizens experience derives from a variety of sources. To the Canadian scholar Barry Buzan (1991, 19–20), five elements combine to create a sense of national security:

- military security—the strength and effectiveness of the armed forces

- economic security—the productive use of natural and human resources, financial assets, technological advancements, and foreign markets

- political security—the stability and legitimacy of government institutions

- societal security—the vitality of civil society, including interest groups, mass culture, and the news media

- environmental security—the degree to which natural resources are protected and human activity takes place on an ecologically sustainable basis.

This chapter focuses on the first of these elements, military security, and its contribution to U.S. national security through **defense policy,** or the organization and strategic deployment of armed forces to protect a state against foreign threats. Maintaining national defense is an essential responsibility of all governments. In the United States, determining which strategies to pursue is complicated by the highly fragmented security complex in which defense policy is managed. This security complex, as previously discussed in Chapter 6, includes the White House–based National Security Council (NSC) and the four armed services overseen by the Department of Defense.

For nearly half a century after World War II, concerns over communist expansion drove U.S. defense policy. The cold war's abrupt conclusion forced a policy reappraisal. The Soviet Union's collapse ended fears of a head-on collision between the two superpowers and reduced the danger that U.S. intervention in regional conflicts would escalate into a third world war. The United States emerged from the cold war as the world's "lone superpower," a status that provided U.S. leaders considerable freedom of action.

This same global primacy, however, made the reappraisal of U.S. defense policy difficult. Given its far superior military power, what should the United States consider an actionable threat? Did the ethnic conflicts, struggles over natural resources, and humanitarian crises in "failed states" occurring in eastern Europe and Africa as the millennium approached represent serious threats to the nation? If so, the dangers were less clear-cut than those once posed by the Soviet Union's nuclear missiles and huge armies (see Blacker 1994). The conflicts of the post–cold war era were mostly fought *within* countries and thus did not directly threaten U.S. sovereignty, territory, or political autonomy. Many officials therefore believed the United States should allow such conflicts to run their courses, especially since resolving them would require more than just brute force. Any country trying to do so would need a high degree of patience, an understanding of regional and national cultures, and a substantial commitment of public resources. Other foreign-policy makers felt U.S. primacy compelled action, whether to remedy the problems in these areas or simply to satisfy the "imperial temptations" for U.S. global engagement (Tucker and Hendrick-son 1992).

These same questions continue to confront American leaders, although the range of regional problems and security threats has taken on a new complexion in the war on terrorism. The current balance of military power among the world's nations offers a useful starting point in any analysis of U.S. defense policy (see Table 10.1). In most measures of military strength, the United States maintains a wide lead over other great powers. Its defense spending of nearly $500 billion in FY 2004, including the costs of the Afghanistan and Iraq occupations, exceeded that of all other countries combined (Center for Defense Information 2003a). While other nations lead in some categories of military power—China in armed forces, for example, and Russia in tanks—only the United States maintains a worldwide military presence that carves the globe into five separate regional commands, and has military installations in nearly forty countries.[1] (See Map 7, Department of Defense Regional Commands, and Map 9, Nuclear Threats and U.S. Defense Installations, in the map section at the front of the book.) Through this pervasive reach, the United States dominates the "commons" of air, sea, and space (Posen 2003). Advances in U.S. military technology, clearly on display in Kuwait, Kosovo, Afghanistan, and Iraq, significantly widen this gap in military power.

Table 10.1 Global Military Balance of Power

	Military Spending 2003 (in Billions)	Military Spending as Percentage of GDP, 2003	Armed Forces, 2001 (in Thousands)	Jet Fighters, 2001	Naval Combat Ships, 2001	Tanks, 2001	Nuclear Warheads 2002
United States	$405	3.7%	1,367	4,900	280	7,620	18,656
Russia	65	5.0 (est.)	977	2,636	320	21,820	10,000
China	60	3.5–5.0	2,310	1,966	590	7,010	400
France	45	2.6	273	473	125	809	350
Japan	43	1.0	239	280	125	1,040	0
United Kingdom	43	2.4	211	427	110	636	185
Germany	35	1.5	308	434	80	2,521	0
India	14	2.4	1,298	701	110	2,798	60

SOURCES: International Institute for Strategic Studies, *The Military Balance* (London: International Institute for Strategic Studies, 2003); Christopher Hellman, "Last of the Big Time Spenders: U.S. Military Budget Is the World's Largest, and Still Growing," Center for Arms Control and Non-Proliferation, 64.177.207.201/static /budget/annual/fy05/world.htm; Central Intelligence Agency, *The World Factbook,* www.odci.gov/cia/publications /factbook/index.html; and Anthony H. Cordesman, with the assistance of Eric E. Fillinger, "The Global Nuclear Balance: A Quantitative and Arms Control Analysis" (Washington, D.C.: Center for Strategic and International Studies, 2002).

NOTES: Military spending figures are mostly for 2003; figures for Russia and China military spending represent 2002 funding.

---

1. In addition to the 702 overseas U.S. military installations, the United States maintained 6,000 installations at home in FY 2003. For a complete listing of U.S. domestic and overseas military installations, see U.S. Department of Defense (2003).

These indicators highlight the importance of military strength in the global balance of power. To Hans Morgenthau (1967, 26), who equated *world* politics with *power* politics, "[A]rmed strength as a threat or a potentiality is the most important material factor making for the political power of a nation." In this regard, power represents more than a tangible resource, the identifiable and measurable sum of a country's military assets. It also represents an intangible capability to "effect the outcomes you want, and if necessary, to change the behavior of others to make this happen" (Nye 2002b, 4).

Throughout its history, the United States has frequently employed its military forces to achieve a wide variety of foreign-policy goals. A 2002 study by the Congressional Research Service identified 299 instances of overt military force between 1798 and 2002, an average of about 1.5 military actions per year (Grimmett 2002). Of this total, 168 occurred through 1945, an average of 1.14 per year. This rate slowed modestly during the cold war, when the United States used military force "for other than normal peacetime purposes" 53 times between 1945 and 1991. The pace of U.S. military involvement accelerated after the cold war. Between 1992 and 2001, seventy-eight such instances were recorded, an average of nearly eight per year.

Real and potential military challenges confront U.S. leaders along a **spectrum of armed conflict** (Hays, Vallance, and Van Tassel 1997) in which the chance of each type of conflict occurring is *inversely proportionate* to its destructiveness (see Figure 10.1). Nuclear war is the most lethal, yet least likely, form of warfare. Conversely, "military operations other than war" are less destructive but more

Figure 10.1 Spectrum of Armed Conflict

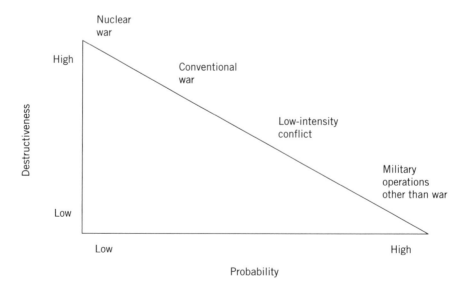

SOURCE: Peter L. Hays, Brenda J. Vallance, and Alan R. Van Tassel, eds., *American Defense Policy,* 7th ed. (Baltimore: Johns Hopkins University Press, 1997), 8. © The Johns Hopkins University Press. Reprinted by permission.

common. Conventional wars, such as those fought in Korea and Vietnam, fall in the middle of this spectrum. Military planners and their political masters must carefully gauge these ratios in considering the use of force.

The nature of U.S. military interventions varies widely. In some cases, as in World War II, U.S. forces fight **wars of necessity,** conflicts resulting from direct challenges to the nation's security. More commonly, as in Panama in 1989 and Kosovo in 1999, the United States fights **wars of choice,** conflicts concerning non-vital interests.[2] Most frequently, U.S. power and influence are employed through **peaceful coercion,** that is, without the use of large-scale violence, to compel foreign leaders to reverse acts of aggression, respect the human rights of their citizens, or protect U.S. citizens and assets from harm. The nation's overwhelming military strength never lies far from the surface in negotiations with its adversaries, even on nonmilitary issues.

The Foundation of Strategy

Conflicts of interest, real and potential, are central realities of world politics and must be confronted and overcome on a regular basis. In facing such conflicts, political leaders devise a **grand strategy,** a statement of the nation's essential objectives in world politics and the means to achieve those objectives. A clear statement of grand strategy "sets priorities and focuses available resources—money, time, political capital, and military power—on the main effort" (Posen 2001–2002, 42). Effective grand strategy is derived from the articulation of global objectives, as seen through the lens of the state's perceived threats and an assessment of its available resources (see Figure 10.2). Once applied strictly to military affairs, the scope of grand strategy has broadened over time to include "*all* the resources at the

Figure 10.2 The Strategic Matrix

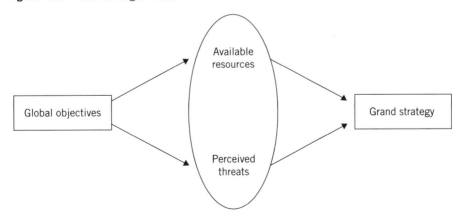

---

2. In many instances, including the 2003 Iraq war, supporters and opponents of the U.S. interventions have disagreed about whether a conflict was necessary or a matter of choice.

disposal of the nation [and] attempts to array them effectively to achieve security in both peace and war" (Rosecrance and Stein 1993, 4, emphasis in original).

In the absence of grand strategy, states approach international conflicts without a sense of purpose, and their military tactics bear little relation to the political stakes at hand in the conflict (Liddell Hart 1967). To Carl von Clausewitz, who nearly two centuries after his death remains the most influential military strategist in history, nations sever the link between politics and war at their peril. "Under all circumstances War is to be regarded not as an independent thing, but as a political instrument," wrote Clausewitz ([1832] 1982, 121), a Prussian general and veteran of the Napoleonic Wars. "This view shows us how Wars must differ in character according to the nature of the motives and circumstances from which they proceed."

Elements of Strategic Thought

A state derives the elements of its grand strategy from a variety of external and internal sources. Among external sources, the **strategic environment** provides the context in which strategy must be applied. This term incorporates trends in global and regional balances of power and the degree to which a state considers other powerful nations and politically mobilized private groups friends or foes. Key developments in world politics, particularly those that challenge the state's vital security assets—its sovereignty, territorial integrity, and political autonomy—also compose the strategic environment and require immediate as well as long-term accommodation. The terrorist attacks of September 2001, for example, altered the strategic environment for the United States and called for a recasting of its foreign-policy priorities and diplomatic relations. Of novel strategic significance in this case was the elevation of nonstate actors, in the form of Islamic terrorist groups, as proven threats to U.S. security, and the tactical challenges posed by terrorism as a form of warfare.

In addition to these external sources of grand strategy, several internal factors must be taken into account for a full understanding of strategic thought. These domestic factors include geopolitical assets, strategic culture, state-society relations, and structural arrangements.

Geopolitical assets. **Geopolitical assets** pertain to a nation's available physical and human resources and their utility in foreign policy. The most basic of these—the size, location, and natural resources of the state—establish its possibilities, limitations, and strategic options. The young United States' considerable distance from the great powers of Europe and Asia made the nation's early grand strategy of strategic detachment possible. Other, more changeable, factors include the size, structure, and growth of the national economy; the degree of technological progress; the health and education of the population; and such elements of "soft power" as political legitimacy and cultural influence (see Nye 2004). Related to population, the worldwide deployment of U.S. troops reflects the nation's military predominance, a vital geopolitical asset (see Table 10.2).

Global power balances and statistical measures of capabilities do not fully explain the grand strategies adopted by states or the outcomes of international conflicts. If they did, perhaps the U.S. government would have anticipated and deterred the Japanese attack on Pearl Harbor in 1941 and North Korea's attack on South Korea in 1950. The United States also might not have lost the Vietnam War or been forced out of Somalia by a mob of irregular forces in 1993. Thus a variety of domestic factors involving a nation's capacity to extract and mobilize public resources for the attainment of proclaimed goals enter into the equation. One must therefore consider the impact of strategic culture, state-society relations, and structural arrangements.

Table 10.2 Selected Deployment of U.S. Troops, 2003

Country Where Based	Number of Troops
United States and territories	1 million (approx.)
Germany	74,796
South Korea	41,145
Japan	40,519
Italy	13,152
United Kingdom	11,616
Afloat	150,000 (approx.)

SOURCE: Department of Defense, "Worldwide Manpower Distribution by Geographical Area 2003," web1.whs.osd.mil/mmid/M05/m05sep03.pdf.

NOTE: Figures based on deployments as of September 30, 2003.

Strategic culture. **Strategic culture** reflects widely shared normative beliefs, attitudes, and policy preferences as they pertain to a country's foreign relations (see Snow 2004, Chap. 3). As noted in Chapter 1, the United States has exhibited several distinct characteristics of strategic culture throughout its history. These include a sense of *exceptionalism,* or standing apart from "ordinary" nation-states; a related sense of *moralism,* or a conception of world politics as a struggle between good and evil; and an *ambivalence* regarding the nature and extent of U.S. global engagement (see Hook and Spanier 2004). These characteristics help explain the nation's erratic approach to foreign affairs—at times ignorant of and indifferent toward events abroad, at other times committed passionately to reforming foreign governments and international order, whatever the costs.

Two important aspects of strategic culture deserve emphasis. First, states do not passively absorb cultural values and act as neutral channels for their expression. To the contrary, leaders play a powerful independent role in promoting values widely shared within the government and with favored segments of the public (see Wendt 1999). In this respect, militarized states adopt a "culture of national security" (see Katzenstein 1996) that guides their calculations of grand strategy. President Bush's 2002 statement of U.S. grand strategy, founded upon the preservation of U.S. primacy and the need for *offensive* as well as *defensive* action against foreign threats, served this purpose. The Bush Doctrine cast this action in the context of moral and political ideals, a tactic familiar to students of constructivism in foreign-policy making (see Chapter 3).

A second and related point is that ideas, not simply material interests, play an integral role in this process (Goldstein and Keohane 1993). This becomes particularly important when adversaries differ ideologically, that is, over fundamental issues of the proper functions of states and their relationships with their citizens and civil societies. The cold war resulted not merely from material differences between the superpowers, but also from their vastly different models of an ideal society. "It is entirely possible that the United States and a liberal Moscow regime would have adopted grand strategies that entailed joining with Britain and other important democracies to form a consortium to deal jointly with world problems, particularly those involving issues of war and peace" (Mueller 1993, 52). Similarly, the U.S. government's current conflict with Islamic terrorists is ideological in nature—with a strong religious component—although the conflict is intimately related to competing claims for political power and economic resources.

State-society relations. Grand strategy stems, too, from **state-society relations,** or the interaction of government and private actors in matters of foreign policy. As described earlier, the United States maintains a vibrant civil society, including private interest groups and a pervasive mass media that exert great influence over the foreign-policy process. A prominent example in the 1990s was the Clinton administration's zero-tolerance policy regarding combat fatalities after the Somalia mission in 1993, a mission cut short by mounting attacks on U.S. troops. Lukewarm public support for the NATO intervention in Kosovo greatly limited Clinton's military options, strengthening the hand of Serb leader Slobodan Milosevic and provoking a massive exodus of refugees. "Especially in a democracy," Arthur A. Stein (1993, 122) noted, "politics can create a disjuncture between commitments and capabilities." [3]

Structural arrangements. Finally, a country's **structural arrangements,** or the governing bodies and legal system within which policy making takes place, shape grand strategy as well. Constitutional provisions constrain the actions of political leaders in the United States. Shared powers by the executive and legislative branches extend beyond legal authority to include the appropriation of resources by Congress that may be required by a president's adopted grand strategy. Of consequence, too, are the roles and resources granted to the state's diplomatic corps, defense forces, and intelligence services, all of which must be aligned with the government's foreign-policy objectives. The U.S. government's huge financial commitment to military forces relative to diplomacy and foreign assistance provide a structural constraint on the strategic choice of incoming presidents, whose ability to change course is also limited by standard operating procedures, ongoing commitments, and other forms of institutional inertia.

The Evolution of U.S. Grand Strategy

Debates over U.S. grand strategy occur along two dimensions. The first dimension relates to the *degree* of U.S. involvement in foreign affairs. Should the United

---

3. A useful comparison can be made between the United States and most western European governments, whose citizens expect more generous state services than their U.S. counterparts. This reliance on domestic social-welfare spending limits the European governments' defense spending, a fact that causes ongoing tension with the U.S. government and within NATO.

States impose its will on other states through an activist foreign policy? Or is the nation sufficiently secure to permit a more restrained posture, allowing most troubles abroad to work themselves out? The second dimension relates to the *nature* of U.S. involvement. Should the United States be primarily concerned with attaining its own national interests? Or does it have a greater responsibility to pursue transnational interests, some with little or no direct effect on the security or prosperity of American citizens?

As noted in Chapter 2, the geopolitical good fortune of the newly founded United States provided a basis for its initial grand strategy of **strategic detachment.** Facing no large-scale military threat at home and protected at sea through a tacit naval alliance with Great Britain, the U.S. government did not have to build a large, permanent military force nor even to establish and deploy a substantial diplomatic corps. American strategic thought in the late nineteenth century was profoundly influenced by the "closing" of the continental frontier and the end of direct U.S. territorial expansion in the Western Hemisphere. Westward expansion did continue, however, by sea, into the Eastern Hemisphere. The principle figure behind this maritime strategy was Capt. Alfred T. Mahan (1897), who called for a rapid increase of U.S. naval forces and the creation of a network of U.S. bases on the Pacific Ocean.

Foreign events drove the nation's grand strategy during the world wars. When the European powers descended into mass violence, the United States altered its grand strategy, basing the new stratagem upon the geopolitical premise that Americans would only be secure if no single power dominated Europe. Germany's launch of its continental conquests in 1914 made the possibility of such domination all too real. The United States entered the war in 1917 and helped to end the threat. Between the world wars, the United States relapsed into strategic detachment, which lasted until Germany overran Europe once again and U.S. forces became targets of submarine attacks on the Atlantic. The direct impetus for U.S. entry into World War II—Japan's attack on Pearl Harbor—extended this strategic logic to East Asia, which, as with Europe, the United States considered hospitable to its foreign policy only so long as a balance of power existed among the region's major countries.

The arrival of the United States as the world's strongest power after World War II and the onset of the cold war demanded a new U.S. grand strategy. The government adopted a strategy of **sustained primacy,** the preservation of the nation's military and economic predominance in the interstate system. American officials devised two tactics—global engagement and communist containment—to serve this strategy. First, the U.S. government would solidify its primacy by maintaining military activism, pursuing market-led economic expansion, and fostering the creation of multilateral organizations in which the United States would play a lead role. By doing so, the nation would preserve its advantages in relative power while reassuring allies through promises of economic aid, military protection, and the pursuit of shared social and political goals. Second, the United States would use George Kennan's containment doctrine as the tactical blueprint for waging the cold war. This doctrine would help the nation avoid the pitfalls of renewed strategic detachment, on the one hand, and a potentially cataclysmic "hot war," on the other. The United States effectively used both tactics during the next forty-five years, sustaining its primacy through the support of allies and the eventual dismemberment of the Soviet bloc.

The concept of hegemony, introduced earlier, is central to the effort to sustain U.S. primacy. Hegemonic powers can dominate the affairs of weaker states without denying them sovereignty or assuming formal political control of them. The Monroe Doctrine established U.S. hegemonic control over Latin America early in the nineteenth century. Its hegemony in the Western Hemisphere, extended to western Europe and other regions after World War II, was *benign* in nature as the subordinates within the U.S. sphere of influence found "special avenues of access and convenience in the postwar order that made American power more useful and predictable" (Ikenberry 2001, 205). Through this benign form of hegemony, the United States found a way to sustain its primacy and ultimately subdue the only threat to that primacy, the Soviet Union.

While the cold war's collapse brought an end to the communist threat, the U.S. government was determined to maintain the unipolar world that defined the new era. To the Pentagon's Joint Chiefs of Staff (1992, 4), the major challenge facing the United States was "instability and being unprepared to handle a crisis or war that no one predicted or expected." Under President George H. W. Bush, the United States renewed its commitment to the grand strategy of sustained primacy with little fanfare (*New York Times* 1992). The government pledged continued support for the UN and other multilateral organizations, including NATO, that served U.S. interests in the absence of the Soviet threat. Although unstated, the strategy of sustained primacy embraced key elements of **hegemonic stability theory,** which became prominent during the cold war (see Gilpin 1981). In this view, a stable and commercially dynamic interstate system is only possible when a dominant power assumes the public costs of military security and economic coordination.

The terrorist attacks of September 2001 again altered the strategic environment while leaving intact the U.S. grand strategy of sustained primacy. According to the NSC's *National Security Strategy* (White House 2002b, 21), "Our forces will be strong enough to dissuade potential adversaries from pursuing a military build-up in hopes of surpassing, or equaling, the power of the United States." The huge budget increases awarded to the Pentagon accelerated the modernization of military technology and the trend toward smaller, but more lethal and mobile force structures. In confronting terrorists and their state sponsors, Secretary of Defense Rumsfeld argued, U.S. forces must be "forward leaning" and not allow their enemies to take the offensive. Rumsfeld's hawkish view was shared by most other advisers, including national security adviser Condoleezza Rice and Vice President Dick Cheney. This consensus led directly to Bush's decision to overthrow Saddam Hussein in Iraq even as the United States conducted its war in Afghanistan (see Woodward 2004).

Promoting democracy has served as a consistent and central element of U.S. grand strategy throughout the period of the nation's primacy (see Chapter 12). Foreign-policy makers concluded long ago that the United States could not thrive as a "democratic island in a totalitarian sea." American leaders advanced their cause of global democratization by first defeating the fascist powers in World War II, then overwhelming the Soviet Union in the cold war. When this conflict ended, President George H. W. Bush pledged support for democratic reforms across the former Soviet bloc, including Eastern Europe. Bill Clinton, who placed the "enlargement" of the democratic world at the center of his national-security strategy, pursued new gains in East Asia and across Africa.

Among U.S. efforts to promote democracy, the most ambitious was George W. Bush's attempt to democratize the heart of Islam through military force. The region had no tradition of democratic rule in the Western sense, and its people were bitterly divided into political, economic, and religious factions. Making matters worse, many Muslims did not see the United States as a role model for democracy or anything else. They reviled the United States for its materialism, secularism, and history of dominating the oil fields of the Persian Gulf. Islamic leaders also charged the United States with maintaining a double standard by insisting on democracy in Iraq while supporting authoritarian, but pro-American governments in Saudi Arabia, Pakistan, and other countries in the region. Nevertheless, Bush insisted that only a democratic regime in Iraq would respect the territorial integrity of its neighbors along with the political rights of its own people. His political initiative in Iraq was based upon a calculation that the three major groups in Iraq—Islamic Shiites and Sunnis, along with ethnic Kurds in the north—would agree that the benefits of a democratic central government outweighed the costs of pursuing their rivalries against one another.

From Strategy to Tactics

The fate of nations is often decided on the battlefield. Grand strategy, therefore, is only effective if it provides direction to military strategy. The organization of armed services, in terms of size as well as tactical capabilities, must be compatible with the nation's strategic goals. This force structure, in turn, must deter external challenges to these goals, or if deterrence fails, to overcome those challenges with superior military force. "To neglect strategy in defense planning or the conduct of war would be like trying to play chess without kings on the board; there would be no point" (Gray 1999, 44). Similarly, military strategy must lead deductively to effective **tactics,** the translation of political ends into military means. In short, strategists *plan* and tacticians *do*. A functional relationship therefore exists among all these elements of security policy. Only when grand strategy, military strategy, force structure, and tactics are aligned can the United States or any other country pursue a sound defense policy.

These functional relationships direct our attention to the ways in which the United States wages war. Modern warfare is fought in three domains—on the ground, at sea, and in the air—the relative significance of which varies over time, largely in response to technological developments. For the United States, military strategy during its first century was based upon adequate ground forces to defend its territory and consolidate new acquisitions. Naval power, traditionally associated with the *projection* of power, became vital to the United States late in the nineteenth century. Air power emerged as a critical instrument of power projection during the world wars. Continued advances in aerial technology, particularly involving the accuracy and potency of strategic bombing, reinforce the predominance of air power, which is also favored *politically* when it reduces the need for large-scale ground troops. This proves especially true when the troops engage in conflicts the public does not deem vital to U.S. national security.

Recent U.S. wartime experiences illustrate both the strengths and the weaknesses of air power in military strategy. More broadly, this experience reveals the problems that result when military strategy and political objectives clash with one another. The 1991 Persian Gulf War against Iraq, for example, featured an overwhelming demonstration of U.S. air power. Five weeks of intense bombing first decimated Iraq's military and industrial assets, then pummeled elite Republic Guard divisions in Kuwait. The subsequent ground offensive by the UN-sponsored coalition met little resistance as it gained control of Kuwait City four days later. However, this overwhelming military victory did not establish a stable political order in the Persian Gulf. Since a forced removal from power exceeded the UN's mandate, Saddam Hussein remained as Iraq's leader. His subsequent defiance of the UN produced a political breakdown within the UN coalition that overshadowed the military success of Operation Desert Storm.

The Balkan wars in Bosnia (1995) and Kosovo (1999) further revealed the limitations of military supremacy. In the first instance, few doubted that the combined resources of the NATO countries could crush the Serb forces led by Milosevic. Yet the United States' lack of resolve, combined with the mixed allegiances and internal preoccupations of the European powers, produced a tepid show of military force that encouraged Milosevic to escalate "ethnic cleansing" of Muslims. Beyond the problems regarding Kosovo noted earlier, the high-altitude NATO bombing raids were not always precise. Hundreds of Kosovar civilians died from errant bombs; other civilians, including Chinese, died when the United States mistakenly targeted the Chinese embassy in Belgrade. Although the missions in Bosnia and Kosovo ultimately achieved their key goals of ending the bloody civil war in the former Yugoslavia, the victors and their overseas patrons were hardly in a mood to celebrate.

This pattern repeated itself in the war on terrorism. The swift U.S. overthrow of Afghanistan's Taliban regime was made possible by a new generation of munitions, including laser-guided "smart bombs" and "bunker busters." Such lethal firepower, however, failed to bring down al Qaeda leader Osama bin Laden, who eluded the U.S.-backed forces in the treacherous terrain along the 1,500-mile Afghan-Pakistani border (see Moore 2003). The military victory also proved of limited *political* value as the United States and its NATO allies still struggled to establish a new Afghan government and maintain control of the provinces long after their initial victory (see Katzman 2003).

Similarly, the "shock-and-awe" blitzkrieg of Operation Iraqi Freedom achieved its immediate objective, the overthrow of Saddam's government, but the low-tech mission of occupying a hostile population in the heart of Islam diminished the initial success. The tactics of the 2003 Iraq invasion departed from the Persian Gulf War by featuring *simultaneous* air and ground offensives. Gen. Tommy Franks, the military commander, abandoned his original war plan to delay the ground invasion until bombing raids "softened" Iraqi defenses. While British ground forces raced to the oil-rich northeast region near Basra to prevent Saddam from setting fire to his oil fields, U.S. tank divisions sped toward Baghdad from Kuwait. The coalition controlled all the major Iraqi cities by April 15, and on May 1 President Bush declared an end to combat.

At first it seemed there might be some harmony between political strategy and the military success, but it soon turned into discord as Bush's declaration proved premature. Hostile Iraqi forces, joined by volunteers from other countries, mounted a low-intensity guerilla war against the occupying powers. The struggle coincided with the U.S. government's failed effort to uncover weapons of mass destruction, the alleged presence of which constituted Bush's primary *casus belli,* or cause of war, in the preventive invasion. The resulting political conflict within the U.S. government complicated the president's effort to reconcile with other UN members, whose help the United States needed in the reconstruction effort. Once again, a disconnect between politics and military strategy undermined the benefits gained by overwhelming military victory. These and other cases remind us that, while the "hard power" of military supremacy is necessary, it is not sufficient for gaining the upper hand politically. Such an outcome also requires the effective use of "soft power" (Nye 2004), or ideas and ideals that provide legitimacy to military action and encourage cooperation from other states.

Justifying the Use of Force

The most crucial decision facing the leader of any country is whether to send military forces into combat (see Art and Waltz 2004). The outcome of armed conflicts is never certain and unintended consequences—sneak attacks by the enemy, economic sabotage, third-party interventions, domestic uprisings, the introduction of weapons of mass destruction—immerse rational military strategy and tactics in the "fog of war" (see Betts 2002). In contrast to this ambiguity, leaders on the brink of war face the near certainty of casualties, widespread physical destruction, and economic liabilities. The choices they make at these critical junctures "between peace and war" (Lebow 1981) determine the fate of their nations for decades to come. The acceptable rationales for using force have changed dramatically over time, making these decisions even more difficult (Finnemore 2003; and Weisburd 1997).

Questions regarding the use of military force have become especially vital today due to the overwhelming military predominance of the United States. Despite its clout, however, the nation remains ambivalent and divided about the use of force. These divisions, as well as the physical, political, and moral limitations of U.S. military policy, were exposed during the Vietnam War. The divisions deepened following the cold war as national politics, particularly in Congress, became more polarized, and as the United States plunged ever more deeply into the war on terrorism. The controversies surrounding the U.S.-led invasion of Iraq in 2003 raised troubling new questions about the use of military force when other options have not been exhausted, evidence of a clear and present danger is mixed, and an international consensus supporting war is lacking.

Considerations of War over Peace

The greatly expanded institutions of U.S. power after World War II—including the newly created Department of Defense, National Security Council, and Central Intelligence Agency—assured a pervasive U.S. global military presence for decades to come. Less clear, however, was under what circumstances that power should be harnessed to protect the nation's worldwide interests. The containment doctrine set forth a singular rationale for U.S. intervention—an attempted expansion of the communist sphere of influence—that most Americans found acceptable, although some considered it too passive (see Lippmann 1947). In the 1950s, domestic debates about the use of force were shaped by Eisenhower's doctrine of **massive retaliation,** whose threat of nuclear annihilation understandably encouraged caution among would-be adversaries as well as U.S. foreign-policy makers.

The Soviet Union's achievement of nuclear parity in the 1960s, combined with the frustrations associated with the Vietnam War, ruptured any prospects for national consensus in the late 1960s and 1970s. Successive U.S. presidents tried, but failed, to outline a coherent rationale for the U.S. intervention in Vietnam, and the military strategies they devised ultimately made for a slow and debilitating defeat. Public protests, many of which turned violent, further assured a lengthy period of introspection regarding the future course of U.S. defense policy.

Recognizing the persistent uncertainty regarding the use of force, Caspar Weinberger, Ronald Reagan's secretary of defense, outlined the conditions for military intervention. The **Weinberger Doctrine** called for the avoidance of "hot" wars while the United States was preoccupied with the Soviet Union and the cold war, and it demanded that interventions be thoroughly planned, with all contingencies covered, before any offense action is initiated (see In Their Own Words box). The doctrine enjoyed widespread support in the executive branch.

The end of the cold war profoundly altered the calculations of defense-policy makers regarding the use of force. Whereas the Soviet Union's collapse clearly enhanced U.S. security, the shifting sands of global, regional, and subregional power balances created new fears and uncertainties not easily shunted aside. As chairman of the Joint Chiefs of Staff in the George H. W. Bush and Clinton administrations, Colin Powell (1992–1993) expressed doubts that a "fixed set of rules" could provide a definitive guide to military intervention. Nonetheless, Powell identified seven questions for U.S. leaders to consider in making their decisions:

> Is the political objective we seek to achieve important, clearly defined and understood? Have all other nonviolent policy means failed? Will military force achieve the objective? At what cost? Have the gains and risks been analyzed? How might the situation that we seek to alter, once it is altered by force, develop further and what might be the consequences?

·))) IN THEIR OWN WORDS: CASPAR WEINBERGER (((·

In 1984, Caspar Weinberger, Ronald Reagan's secretary of defense, made the first systematic attempt by a U.S. military leader to identify the criteria for post-Vietnam U.S. military intervention. He identified six "major tests" that all proposed interventions would have to pass before troops could be placed in harm's way. At the time Weinberger enunciated these points, the United States was preoccupied with its primary rival, the Soviet Union, in the cold war. The Weinberger Doctrine received wide support within the Reagan administration, whose defense priorities focused on military rearmament and the modernization of nuclear forces.

Under what circumstances, and by what means, does a great democracy such as ours reach the painful decision that the use of military force is necessary to protect our interests or to carry out our national policy? . . .

First, the United States should not commit forces to combat overseas unless the particular engagement or occasion is deemed vital to our national interest or that of our allies. . . .

Second, if we decide it is necessary to put combat troops into a given situation, we should do so wholeheartedly, and with the clear intention of winning. . . .

Third, if we do decide to commit forces to combat overseas, we should have clearly defined political and military objectives. . . .

Fourth, the relationship between our objectives, and the forces we have committed—their size, composition and disposition—must be continually reassessed and adjusted if necessary. . . .

Fifth, before the U.S. commits combat forces abroad, there must be some reasonable assurance we will have the support of the American people and their elected representatives in Congress. . . .

Finally, the commitment of U.S. forces to combat should be a last resort.

Source: Caspar Weinberger, "The Uses of Military Power" (speech delivered before the National Press Club, Washington, D.C., November 28, 1984), www.pbs.org/wgbh/pages/frontline/shows /military/force/weinberger.html.

Powell (1992) insisted that the United States, once it committed to using force in a military conflict, must prevail *decisively*. As an architect of the 1991 Persian Gulf War, he argued that sufficient U.S. forces should be deployed to the region to ensure that the Iraqi military would be quickly overwhelmed. He further insisted that an **exit strategy,** a plan to conclude fighting and remove the country's presence, be adopted prior to the intervention so that U.S. troops would not be mired in a long-term, open-ended foreign occupation. These stipulations of the **Powell Doctrine,** like those identified by Weinberger, reflected the lessons of Vietnam, a war in which U.S. troops were deployed incrementally over many years, supported a vague political objective, lacked popular support, and could not score a quick victory and complete their mission. Powell and Weinberger also shared an aversion to **mission creep,** the tendency of limited deployments to take on new tasks and open-ended commitments.

Powell's strict conditions for the use of U.S. force, while finding favor within the uniformed ranks, prompted criticism by civilians within the Defense Department and other parts of the executive branch. Clinton's first secretary of defense, Les Aspin (1992), rejected Powell's "all-or-nothing" approach. Madeleine Albright, U.S. ambassador to the UN, criticized the Powell Doctrine's implicit resistance to using U.S. force, asking Powell at one point, "What's the point of having this superb military that you're always talking about if we can't use it?" [4] Albright and Aspin favored the "limited-objectives" school of thought that recognized the need for smaller-scale military engagements. Anticipating future interventions in Yugoslavia, Aspin noted that advances in air power made it possible for the United States to cause "unacceptable" damage to its adversaries without risking large-scale U.S. casualties. Clinton supported this view, although the setback in Somalia forced him to restrict future U.S. humanitarian interventions.

President George W. Bush came to power in 2001 favoring the more restrictive conditions of the Weinberger Doctrine. His only modification to the doctrine—that military interventions first and foremost serve U.S. national interests—signaled a turn away from the humanitarian and UN-sponsored peacekeeping missions of the Clinton administration. Bush viewed the September 2001 terrorist attacks as a challenge to the nation's vital interests and declared an open-ended "war on terrorism" in which U.S. military forces would play a central role. The president's decision to wage preventive war against Iraq was ultimately supported by Powell, then secretary of state, despite the inconclusive results of UN weapons inspections and strong opposition from most U.S. allies. The protracted U.S. occupation of Iraq that followed resembled the type of "state-building" missions Bush had earlier rejected as military officials searched for a face-saving exit strategy.

Threats and Coercive Diplomacy

Short of actually resorting to military force, U.S. officials often pursue their foreign-policy goals through **coercive diplomacy,** the threat to use force to reverse an adversary's offensive action. "The attractiveness of coercive diplomacy as a tool of foreign policy is quite clear," Alexander George (2000, 80) observed. "It offers the possibility of achieving one's objective economically, with little bloodshed, fewer political and psychological costs, and often with much less risk of escalation than does resort to military action to reverse an adversary's encroachment." The Cuban missile crisis, which ended peacefully in 1962 largely on U.S. terms, is widely viewed as a textbook example of effective coercive diplomacy. The

---

4. Responding to this and similar comments, Powell (1995, 576) noted in his memoir, "I thought I would have an aneurysm. American GI's were not toy soldiers to be moved around on some kind of global game board."

Kennedy administration skillfully combined five elements of this tactic to prevent the crisis from leading to a nuclear holocaust (George 2000, 84–85):

- Clear demands: The U.S. government issued clear demands with specific deadlines and penalties if the Soviet Union refused to remove its newly installed nuclear missiles from Cuba.

- Severe penalty: The penalty identified by President Kennedy—that the missiles would be forcefully removed and the Cuban government overthrown by U.S. forces—would clearly have "hurt" the Soviet Union and its leader, Nikita Khrushchev.

- Credible demands: The U.S. demands were credible. The presence of the nuclear warheads in Cuba clearly threatened U.S. security, and Kennedy had the political support and military capability to make good on his threat.

- Coherent plan: The United States had a clear plan of action to remove the missiles if Kennedy's threats were ignored, a fact made known to the Soviet leader.

- Flexible application: Kennedy offered Khrushchev a "carrot" as well as the "stick" of military retaliation. By offering to remove U.S. nuclear missiles from Turkey, an action already decided privately by the U.S. government, Kennedy provided the Soviet leader a face-saving exit from the crisis.

Not all adversaries respond so well to coercive diplomacy. In fact, the United States has failed to resolve conflicts through coercive diplomacy more often than it has succeeded. Foreign leaders, even those of very weak states, commonly resist such threats, vowing instead to withstand U.S. pressure and hoping to "call the bluff" of their American counterparts. In so doing, adversaries present a threat of their own—a blow to the credibility of the United States should its threats be successfully defied. "There is a generation of political leaders throughout the world whose basic perception of U.S. military power and political will is one of weakness, who enter any situation with a fundamental belief that the United States can be defeated or driven away" (Blechman and Wittes 1999, 5).

The obstacles to coercive diplomacy come from several sources. Foreign leaders may conclude that succumbing to U.S. threats will prove more dangerous than resisting such pressure, even if this resistance leads to a military showdown against superior U.S. forces. Capitulation may invite political challenges at home, or even physical retribution. In addition, after succumbing to threats, a leader may be apprehended by the U.S. government or face criminal prosecution by international courts. To aid them in their efforts to defy U.S. demands, foreign leaders may hope to exploit lukewarm public or congressional support in the United States for the government's actions. Although presidents consistently sidestep the Senate's constitutional power to declare war, they still rely on Congress for the budgetary resources necessary to sustain military interventions in the event coercive diplomacy fails. Such support may not be forthcoming, however, thus exposing the president's threats as empty.

Since the Vietnam War, foreign leaders have consistently defied the tactics of coercive diplomacy, forcing the United States to take costly military action against them. In 1989, for example, Manuel Noriega of Panama ignored U.S. demands to step down; ousting him required a large-scale invasion of the country (see Buckley 1991). Four years later, U.S. threats against Somalian warlords merely sparked more violent attacks on U.S. forces. The deaths of eighteen soldiers in Mogadishu, which sharpened domestic opposition to the mission, prompted President Clinton to withdraw from Somalia, thereby suffering a humiliating defeat.[5]

This pattern of U.S. threats, foreign resistance, and subsequent U.S. military interventions continued in Haiti (1994) and in the former Yugoslavia (1993–1995, 1999). In the first case, Haitian rebels exploited the "Somalia syndrome," calculating—wrongly—that Clinton would not risk a second military humiliation. In the Yugoslav conflicts, Milosevic gambled that domestic opposition in the United States and Europe would undermine Clinton's effort to stop the "ethnic cleansing" against Muslims. Milosevic was finally defeated, but only after his country suffered large-scale bloodletting, physical devastation, and the displacement of millions of civilians.

Coercive diplomacy also failed to prevent the two U.S.-led wars against Saddam Hussein's Iraq in 1991 and 2003. In both cases, Saddam refused to meet the full range of U.S. demands, then suffered overwhelming military defeats and, ultimately, his overthrow from power. While speculation persists regarding his rationales for inviting such calamities, Saddam's fateful strategic choices demonstrated the limitations of coercive diplomacy and the inevitability of military conflict when threats are not sufficient to resolve fundamental differences.

Preventive War: The Iraq Precedent

Countries engage in interstate war for many reasons. In cases of offensive war, they disrupt the status quo to gain resources, tangible or intangible, unavailable through peaceful or legal means. States act on the defensive in the face of external aggression. In cases of outright attack, they face the grim choice of responding with armed resistance to the attack or submitting to the demands of the attackers.

Not all cases of defensive war, however, are a response to outright, clear-cut attacks (see Walzer 1977, 74–85). Foreign intelligence may signal that an external attack is imminent, perhaps only days away, tempting leaders to strike first against the would-be invader. This recourse to **preemptive war,** rare in modern history, formed a key element of the Bush administration's *National Security Strategy* released in September 2002.[6] More commonly, an emerging challenger may be perceived by a

---

5. "We have studied Vietnam and Lebanon and know how to get rid of Americans, by killing them so that public opinion will put an end to things," stated Somali warlord Mohamed Farah Aideed (quoted in Blechman and Wittes 1999, 6), the primary target of Operation Restore Hope.

6. To Dan Reiter (1995), only three armed conflicts of the modern era qualify as preemptive wars: the start of World War I, China's 1950 intervention in the Korean War, and Israel's attack on Egypt in 1967.

more powerful rival as presenting a long-term threat to the security of that nation or the security of its allies, tempting the stronger state to launch a **preventive war** to eliminate the threat before it materializes (see Levy 1987). Although not using the term explicitly, the Bush administration launched preventive war against Iraq, which at the time did not present an imminent threat to the United States or its allies.

Prior to the Iraqi invasion, the United States, like most other governments, had long renounced preventive war as a strategic option. "We do not believe in aggressive or preventive war," Harry Truman (quoted in Jordan, Taylor, and Mazarr 1999, 57) proclaimed. "Such war is the weapon of dictators, not of free democratic societies." Although well aware of Japan's growing challenge in the Pacific Ocean, Franklin Roosevelt did not anticipate an immediate threat that would require the United States to strike first. The United States also refrained from initiating a military confrontation against its cold war rival, the Soviet Union, despite that nation's rapidly growing nuclear arsenal, declared hostility toward the United States and its Western allies, and capacity to influence the outcome of numerous regional conflicts.

In contrast to preemptive wars, which can frequently be justified, preventive wars are highly controversial. It is very difficult to predict with confidence what kind of military threat a foreign country may pose many years in the future. It is even more difficult to anticipate where that threat will be directed and what form it will take. For this reason, most nations generally consider taking military action against such a hypothetical threat illegitimate, especially given the ample time available to seek a peaceful resolution of the conflict (see Betts 2003). For even preemptive war to be justifiable, four conditions must be met (Crawford 2003):

- the initiator of force must be clearly acting in *self-defense*

- *compelling evidence* must exist of imminent danger to the state taking action

- the potential aggressor must have a clear *capability and intention* to attack

- military force must be used as a *last resort*, after all other options have failed.

In justifying the 2003 invasion of Iraq, U.S. leaders characterized Saddam Hussein's regime as both an immediate and a long-term threat to Iraq's neighbors and the United States. Saddam's secret arsenal of biochemical weapons, Bush claimed, could be unleashed at any time. He also cited U.S. and British intelligence findings of a secret nuclear-weapons program in Iraq that could make it a regional and global menace in the years to come. The invasion thus could be justified either as preemptive or preventive. In both cases, national security adviser Condoleezza Rice argued, the United States could not afford to wait until a "mushroom cloud" awakened the United States to Saddam's menace. She further argued that the U.S. government could not wait for help from the UN, whose members often expressed disdain for the United States and seemed willing to appease the Iraqi regime.

Critics countered that the U.S. action against Iraq fell short on all four grounds (see Clarke 2004; and Schlesinger 2002). First, the United States appeared to have interests, particularly in Iraqi oil, that went beyond matters of self-defense. Second, U.S. officials produced no compelling evidence of Iraqi weapons of mass destruction; nor did they demonstrate strong links between Iraq and al Qaeda terrorists. Third, Iraq was exhausted by a decade of sanctions and exhibited neither a capability nor an intention to threaten the United States, a point made earlier by Secretary of State Powell. Finally, the United States did not exhaust all other options before deciding to overthrow Saddam by force. This debate between defenders and critics of the U.S. invasion of Iraq will continue long into the future and, like that regarding the Vietnam War, will never be settled conclusively. It is clear, however, that the United States established a dangerous precedent by initiating war against Iraq without compelling evidence that a clear and present danger existed that could not be overcome in another way.

The Nuclear Shadow

A central task of U.S. security policy involves managing the nation's nuclear arsenal, by far the largest in the world. Nuclear weapons are *strategic* forces that play a vital role in military strategy that fundamentally departs from that played by nonnuclear, or *conventional,* forces. Since their first and only wartime use, by the United States against Japan in August 1945, nuclear weapons have remained unused but "absolute weapons" (Brodie 1946), capable of obliterating foreign enemies—and possibly the entire global population—in one swift blow. The Soviet Union's successful test of a nuclear bomb in 1949 transformed the cold war balance of power into a "delicate balance of terror" (Wohlstetter 1959).

Despite the peaceful ending of the U.S.-Soviet arms race, the perils posed by nuclear weapons are more acute than ever. By 2004, a record *nine* countries had the materials and means to deliver nuclear weapons (see Table 10.3 and Map 9, Nuclear Threats and U.S. Defense Installations, in the map section at the front of the book). These countries included India and Pakistan, bitter rivals in South Asia, and North Korea, an impoverished dictatorship with an affinity for ballistic-missile exports and nuclear blackmail. Israel also maintained a nuclear arsenal, although its government refused to confirm or deny this fact. Russia's vast nuclear stockpile, although still formidable, has degraded since the Soviet Union's collapse.[7] Private terrorist groups, meanwhile, covet fissionable materials and ballistic missiles on transnational black markets (see Stern 1999).

The enduring menace posed by nuclear weapons, a standard feature of twenty-first-century world politics, was not inevitable. Just after World War II, the United States proposed placing all the world's nuclear materials, including its own, under the control of a UN-sponsored international authority. The Soviet Union

---

7. The deteriorating condition and questionable security of Russia's nuclear arsenal required a major relief effort by the U.S. government in the 1990s. For more on this "cooperative threat-reduction program," see Michael Krepon (2003).

Table 10.3 Nuclear Balance of Power, 2004 Estimates

Country	Total Nuclear Warheads	Strategic Warheads	Non-Strategic Warheads
Russia	8,250	4,850	3,400
United States	7,000	5,880	1,120
China	400	280	120
France	350	350	0
Israel	200	100–200	Unknown
United Kingdom	180	180	0
India	60	60	0
Pakistan	24–48	24–48	0

SOURCE: Ali Chaudhry and Andrew George, "The World's Nuclear Arsenals," Center for Defense Information (July 9, 2004), www.cdi.org/program/index.cfm?programid=32.

NOTES: North Korea is believed to have a small nuclear arsenal but details are unknown. "Non-strategic" warheads are designed for use against short-range military targets. The United States and Russia possess thousands of additional warheads "in reserve" under the terms of the Treaty of Moscow (2002).

opposed the **Baruch Plan,** however, because it allowed the U.S. government to maintain its monopoly of nuclear-weapons technology. By the 1970s, Soviet nuclear as well as conventional forces had reached "parity" with those maintained by the United States. The U.S. nuclear arsenal, though, was more accurate and better protected within its "triad" of delivery systems—underground silos, strategic bombers, and nuclear submarines. Clearly, the nuclear arms race, which included Great Britain, France, and China by the late 1960s, had progressed beyond the point of no return.

Efforts to restrain this arms race quickly became a key foreign-policy priority. The SALT and START treaties beginning in the early 1970s placed limits on U.S. and Soviet stockpiles and delivery systems, then provided for deep cuts after the cold war. The Treaty of Moscow signed by the United States and Russia in 2002 called for ten-year reductions in *active* nuclear stockpiles to between 1,700 and 2,200 warheads on each side.[8] As for multilateral accords, the United States signed the Non-Proliferation Treaty that came into force in 1970 and had gained the signatures of 187 governments by 2002. Earlier, the U.S. government had signed the 1963 Limited Test Ban Treaty, which prohibited nuclear tests in the atmosphere, under water, and in outer space. However, Congress's rejection in 1998 of a ban on *all* nuclear testing, as called for in the Comprehensive Test Ban Treaty, signaled a U.S. turn away from multilateral cooperation in nuclear arms control.

Deterrence in Theory and Practice

Since the 1945 bombing of Hiroshima and Nagasaki, nuclear weapons have had a unique functional distinction among military weapons—they are not meant to

---

8. The treaty allowed both sides to store thousands of inactive warheads, which could quickly be reactivated in a crisis.

be used. Such use would not only invite nuclear retaliation from the target government or its nuclear-equipped allies, but also threaten the habitat of the entire world population (see Sagan 1983–1984). The primary goal of nuclear strategy, therefore, is to gain concessions from an adversary through the threatened use of nuclear weapons without the actual use of them in a conflict. Maintaining **nuclear deterrence,** the prevention of hostilities through the threat of using nuclear weapons, is vital to securing a nuclear power's interests while preventing an apocalypse (see Snyder 1961). Both cold war superpowers refined the concept of nuclear deterrence by building massive nuclear arsenals and ensuring that the victim of a first strike would survive to hit back, having "second-strike capabilities." The United States and Soviet Union also engaged in **extended deterrence** by vowing nuclear retaliation against attacks not only on their territory, but on the territory of their allies.

Successful nuclear deterrence, the first line of defense in U.S. nuclear policy, depends on two key factors. The first involves the unquestionable *ability* of the deterring state to make good on its threats. The second, more ambiguous, factor relates to the *credibility* of the threatened response. Will the deterring state actually launch a nuclear attack if its threat is ignored? There can be no certain answer to this question in advance. In this respect, the effect of nuclear weapons is psychological rather than physical. "The threat of retaliation does not have to be 100 percent certain," nuclear strategist Bernard Brodie (1946, 74) wrote at the dawn of the nuclear age. "It is sufficient if there is a good chance of it, or if there is belief that there is a good chance of it. The prediction is more important than the fact."

American leaders believed a promise of massive retaliation was sufficient to deter challenges to the United States as long as it maintained nuclear superiority. When the Soviet nuclear arsenal "caught up" with the United States, however, the new era of **mutual assured destruction (MAD)** meant both superpowers had to be effectively "self-deterred." In the MAD world, the compelling prospect of nuclear Armageddon made foreign-policy makers more cautious, reducing the danger of a head-on collision between the two countries. Some U.S. officials complained, however, that their military options had become unduly constrained by this all-or-nothing strategic stalemate. President Kennedy approved a strategy of **flexible response,** meant to resolve this problem by condoning U.S. involvement in "limited wars," such as that in Vietnam, which could be fought below the nuclear threshold.[9]

The strategy of flexible response survived into the post–cold war era as U.S. military forces repeatedly intervened in regional conflicts without threatening to use nuclear weapons or risking nuclear attack by its adversaries (Daalder 1991). The logic of MAD, however, still lurks today in the background of U.S.-Russian relations, and would-be aggressors still face the prospect of massive retaliation by

---

9. For prominent studies of nuclear strategy during this critical period, see Henry Kissinger (1957), Robert Osgood (1957), Thomas Schelling (1960), and Morton Halperin (1963). Lawrence Freedman (2003) provides a useful review of cold war nuclear strategies.

U.S. nuclear forces if the nation's survival is at stake. The war on terrorism raises the open question about the extent to which some adversaries, particularly religious extremists without allegiances to any country, are actually "deterrable." Unclear as well is the utility of nuclear deterrence in a world of proliferating nuclear powers, the growing number of which complicates the vital calculations upon which the "balance of terror" rests.

Still other questions regarding U.S. nuclear policy have yet to be resolved. In 2002, the Defense Department revived the notion, raised in the Reagan years, of using lower-yield "tactical" nuclear weapons. The Pentagon's *Nuclear Posture Review* called for threatening the use of such weapons on future battlefields to maintain **full-spectrum deterrence,** discouraging challenges in a wide array of military scenarios, not simply a showdown with another nuclear power. To the Defense Department (2002, 7), "Nuclear attack options that vary in scale, scope, and purpose will complement other military capabilities." By lowering the threshold between conventional and nuclear war, however, tactical nuclear weapons may make a large-scale nuclear war more likely.

The Missile Defense Controversy

Among other paradoxes of nuclear strategy, the success of deterrence requires that states be defenseless against nuclear attacks. "Shielded" nations would be free to inflict overwhelming harm on their enemies without fear of retaliation. Recognizing this paradox, the United States and Soviet Union signed the **Anti-Ballistic Missile (ABM) Treaty** in 1972, which kept both superpowers vulnerable to nuclear attack beyond the cold war's end. In the United States, critics of the ABM Treaty longed for the day they would no longer be held hostage to threats of nuclear annihilation. Among these critics was President Reagan, whose 1983 **Strategic Defense Initiative (SDI),** better known as "Star Wars," called for space-based "interceptors" that would destroy long-range nuclear missiles in midflight. Congress approved $26 billion for the development of SDI, which Reagan promised to share with other nuclear powers once the system became operational.

Reagan's Star Wars program marked the beginning of the end of the ABM Treaty. The antimissile technology advanced slowly, but by the 1990s the United States had established a program for national missile defense that, if deployed, would violate the treaty's core provisions. This research continued in the 1990s under President Clinton, then accelerated in 2001 under George W. Bush. The United States officially withdrew from the ABM Treaty in 2002, the first U.S. renunciation of an arms-control treaty in the nuclear era. Bush authorized the newly created Missile Defense Agency to develop a ballistic missile defense system that would be "layered" to intercept missiles in all phases of their flight, from liftoff through reentry into the lower atmosphere. The president ordered the first deployment of missile defenses, in Alaska and California, by September 2004 despite the poor track record and high costs of previous ABM tests (see David 2002).

President Bush based his decision to scuttle the ABM on three key assumptions. First, even in the absence of nuclear tensions with Russia and China, the risk of an *accidental* launch of those nations' intercontinental ballistic missiles (ICBMs) could not be ignored. Second, "rogue states" and their allied terrorist groups could not reliably be deterred from launching surprise attacks on the United States. Religious extremists viewed suicide, even mass suicide, as a form of spiritual or national salvation and thus lacked the capacity for "rational" decision making that nuclear deterrence presumes. Finally, U.S. missile-defense research had advanced sufficiently to warrant reliance on such a system.

The case for missile defense gained momentum after the September 11 terrorist attacks. With little debate, Congress approved the funds Bush requested for missile-defense research and development. This funding, which grew from $8 billion in FY 2003 to more than $9 billion the following year, is expected to total $50 billion by 2010. Officials estimate that a fully deployed system, which at the earliest would be operational by 2020, will cost at least $200 billion.

Opponents of missile defense, including many legislators, strategic analysts in think tanks and universities, and peace groups, challenged the president's arguments for missile defense with three arguments of their own. The first argument challenges the presumed reliability of missile defenses, a presumption that leaves no margin for error. Experimental tests, critics point out, have thus far produced, at best, mixed results. The General Accounting Office (GAO), for example, reported evidence of "immature technology and limited testing" of missile-defense systems. A rush to deploy these systems, the GAO warned, "places the Missile Defense Agency in danger of getting off track early and impairing the effort over the long term" (General Accounting Office 2003).

Second, critics warn, even a "perfect" ABM system would leave the United States vulnerable to nuclear attacks not delivered by missile. So-called suitcase bombs made in the United States or smuggled into its territory can prove just as deadly. Finally, it is not clear how other governments will react if the United States comes close to having *both* a massive nuclear arsenal and the certainty of nuclear defense. Such a combination in the hands of any other government would surely be viewed in Washington as an invitation to nuclear blackmail. Would other leaders feel the same way about the United States, despite its professed good intentions, especially given the anti-American climate in the wake of the 2003 Iraqi invasion?

Beyond these concerns about nuclear defense, longstanding questions remain about the morality of nuclear deterrence, which seeks to preserve world peace through the promise of mass death and destruction (see Hook and Clark 1991). The perverse nature of this strategy has vexed strategic theorists and produced agonizing appraisals by religious leaders. Gregory Kavka (1987, 12) aptly summarized this dilemma: "An official nuclear policy of retaliating only in a morally proper way might not be an effective deterrent. This means that a sufficiently reliable policy of nuclear deterrence might require making threats to retaliate immorally." A report by the National Conference of Catholic Bishops (1983) condemned the use of nuclear weapons but reluctantly condoned nuclear deterrence until a way out of the dilemma could be found (see Point/Counterpoint box).

Point/Counterpoint

NUCLEAR DETERRENCE VS. "JUST WAR"

One of the central dilemmas facing U.S. military strategists involves the potential use of nuclear weapons in defending vital national interests. Given their immense lethality, nuclear weapons are not designed to be *used,* but to *deter* attacks on their owners by assuring the destruction of enemies.

Yet the mere prospect of actually employing nuclear weapons raises serious moral questions that continue to confront military strategists today. Such use would violate two key elements of just-war doctrine. The first element, *proportionality,* insists that the harm done by a military retaliation be proportionate, or roughly equal, to the damage inflicted by the initial attack. The first use of nuclear weapons would, by its very nature, be disproportionate to any attack using conventional weapons.

The second key element of the just-war doctrine, *discrimination,* insists that military attacks spare the lives of non-combatants to the fullest extent possible. Nuclear weapons, however, inevitably target civilians and military personnel alike, particularly as the ecological damage caused by such weapons would remain for decades, if not centuries, to come.

These considerations did not discourage U.S. strategists during the cold war from giving nuclear weapons a central place in the nation's military arsenal. To Henry Kissinger, whose 1957 book, *Nuclear Weapons and Foreign Policy,* caught the attention of then vice president Richard Nixon, nuclear weapons provide great advantages to the states that possess them. The more likely the use of these weapons appears to the enemies of nuclear states, Kissinger argued, the less likely they will be to resort to aggressive behavior. The moral "end" of nuclear deterrence, in this view, justifies the immoral "means" of threatening mass annihilation.

Such views prompted a challenge as nuclear tensions rose in the early 1980s. The National Conference of Catholic Bishops published a pastoral letter in 1983 that rejected notions of a protracted nuclear stalemate. In the following year, Jonathan Schell declared in *The Abolition* that nuclear weapons were an "evil obsession" that must be eliminated if any hopes of world peace could be sustained.

Although the prospect of large-scale nuclear war appears remote today, the United States and other nuclear powers continue to rely on the logic of nuclear deterrence in protecting themselves and their allies. A new concern—that nuclear terrorists will not follow the same "rational" logic of deterrence—adds to the uncertainty concerning these ultimate weapons of mass destruction.

Sources: Henry Kissinger, Nuclear Weapons and Foreign Policy *(New York: Harper & Row, 1957); National Conference of Catholic Bishops,* Challenge and Peace: God's Promise and Our Response *(Washington, D.C.: United States Catholic Conference, 1983); and Jonathan Schell* The Abolition *(New York: Knopf, 1984).*

Waging War on Terrorism

Since September 2001, U.S. foreign-policy makers have elevated terrorism to the top of the U.S. security agenda. President Bush declared such attacks to be acts of war, not incidents to be turned over to criminal investigators and courts. In response to the president's declaration and its subsequent affirmation by Congress, the government granted the Pentagon wide latitude to pursue the terrorists and their state sponsors. Rather than taking on a conventional, sovereign nation-state, the U.S. counteroffensive faced a shadowy, loosely connected network of private groups whose members shared an intense hatred of the United States and a determination to resist its political, economic, and cultural influence by any means, including large-scale violence.

National Security Adviser Condoleezza Rice testifies to the independent 9-11 commission in April 2004. President Bush had earlier refused to allow Rice to testify to the panel but later relented. Rice enjoyed strong influence over U.S. foreign policy in the Bush administration, more so than Colin Powell, the secretary of state. With her office in the White House and her own staff in the National Security Council, Rice had close contact with President Bush and was considered a family friend. She also served as an effective White House "gatekeeper," controlling access to the president among other foreign-policy advisers.

Bush's war declaration had profound and long-lasting implications. Citing "terrorism" as the target, rather than the militant Islamic groups linked to September 11 and other attacks against U.S. interests in the Middle East, made the ensuing conflict especially open-ended. Terrorism, it should be recalled, is a *tactic* of political violence, not a tangible enemy that can be identified, located, and defeated. Nonetheless, the trauma of 9-11, public demands for decisive action, and his own perception of the emerging clash as one between "good" and "evil" compelled Bush to strike back on a grand scale.

Foreign terrorists had previously spared the U.S. homeland from large-scale attacks. When they did strike, the terrorists generally chose targets overseas. This was the case with the June 1996 attacks on U.S. military troops in Saudi Arabia, the 1998 bombings of U.S. embassies in Kenya and Tanzania, and the 2000 attacks on the USS *Cole* off the coast of Yemen. The most prominent exception to this rule, a failed initial attempt by Islamic militants to topple the World Trade Center with an underground detonation in February 1993, left 6 people dead and more than 1,000 injured.

While these attacks alarmed U.S. government officials and dominated news coverage for a few days, other concerns soon recaptured the attention of the White House, the Pentagon, and Congress. This complacency was partly encouraged by a general *decline* in the number of international terrorist attacks since the mid-1980s (see Figure 10.3), even though the casualties from such attacks spiked

Figure 10.3 International Terrorist Attacks, 1981–2003

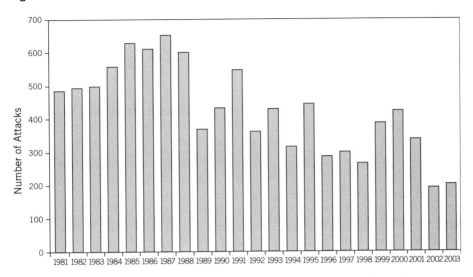

SOURCE: U.S. Department of State, "Patterns of Global Terrorism 2003" (updated June 22, 2004), www.state
.gov/s/ct/rls/pgtrpt.

every few years. In 2001, the year in which the September 11 attacks ended U.S.
complacency, terrorist attacks worldwide claimed 5,799 victims.

As noted in Chapter 1, the terrorist attacks elevated the concept of asymmetric warfare, that is, wars between adversaries of highly uneven material strength, in U.S. defense policy. Asymmetric threats "work around, offset, and negate" their targets' relative strengths as measured by standard calculations of military power (Gray 2002, 6). The advantages of even the most muscle-bound states, including the United States, may be undercut by asymmetric threats, such as terrorist attacks, which exploit the weaknesses of those nations. The very openness of the United States, combined with the fragmentation and limitations placed upon governmental power, are traditional strengths that can become sources of vulnerability (see Barnett 2003).

The rise of nonstate actors, like tactical innovations and advances in military technology, has contributed to the transformation of modern warfare (Van Creveld 1991). Private groups such as al Qaeda may possess sufficient economic, political, and military resources to threaten vital U.S. interests. Like the guerilla warriors in Vietnam, terrorist groups blur the line between civilians and military personnel. In so doing, they confound war plans and diplomatic practices based upon enemies with fixed territory and political sovereignty. As is also the case in guerilla warfare, terrorists gain the upper hand by determining the time, place, and means for violent attacks. This places their enemies on the defensive, unable to respond decisively. Whereas overpowering retaliation "tends to be unduly heavy-handed, if not plainly irrelevant," an attempt at a negotiated settlement "all too easily can be ensnared in a lengthy political process that inhibits real action" (Gray 2002, 6).

The Nature of Terrorism

Terrorism, as we have seen, poses acute challenges to U.S. foreign policy. Simply defining the term has proven difficult as one person's "terrorist" may be another's "freedom fighter" (see Combs 2003). In its definition of *terrorism,* the U.S. government identifies the essential elements: terrorism involves "premeditated, politically motivated violence perpetrated against noncombatant targets by subnational groups or clandestine agents, usually intended to influence an audience." [10]

The *psychological effect* of terrorism is crucial to this type of warfare. To the perpetrators of seemingly random acts of violence, the raising of public anxieties and doubts about the government's ability to protect its citizens represents a victory in and of itself (Wardlaw 1989). Another distinctive aspect of terrorism is its use of a single violent act to send a symbolic message. In Greece and Peru, for example, antiglobalization groups have bombed McDonalds, Pizza Hut, and other restaurant chains seen as the embodiment of U.S. economic and cultural imperialism. Osama bin Laden (quoted in Esposito 2002, 22) acknowledged the symbolic function of terrorism when he stated that the September 11 attacks "were not targeted at women and children. The real targets were America's icons of military and economic power."

Although terrorism is usually associated with nonstate actors, **state terrorism,** too, has been practiced throughout history. Roman and Greek emperors publicly tortured their rivals to scare off further opposition. During the "reign of terror" following the French Revolution, Robespierre found the guillotine a convenient device to pacify his enemies. Another useful distinction can be made between domestic and international terrorism. Whereas the deadliest terrorist attack in U.S. history, September 11, came from overseas, the second deadliest came from within. The American Christian Patriots revealed the dangers posed by **domestic terrorism** in 1995, when they destroyed the Murrah Federal Building in Oklahoma City, killing 168 people and injuring hundreds more.

The Oklahoma City attacks also revealed the growing role of religion in motivating terrorist activity. This perverse relationship dates back to the first and second centuries AD, when Jewish *zealots* and Islamic *assassins* used terror tactics to advance their spiritual ideals. Terrorism in the nineteenth and early twentieth centuries focused more on secular causes, as anarchists and Marxist revolutionaries attempted to overthrow governments through assassinations and other acts of violence. The revival of "sacred terror" (Benjamin and Simon 2002; see also Lacquer 2003) came late in the twentieth century as ideological conflicts associated with the cold war gave way to heightened tensions between the proponents of different world religions. To Bruce Hoffman (1998, 87), a leading expert on terrorism, "The religious imperative for terrorism is the most important defining characteristic of terrorist activity today." Militant Islamic groups such as al Qaeda openly embrace armed struggle as a matter of self-defense against encroachments by Western "infidels." To bin Laden (quoted in Esposito 2002, 24),

---

10. See United States Code, Title 22, Section 2656f (d), 2000.

We are carrying out the mission of the prophet, Mohammad (peace be upon him). The mission is to spread the word of God, not to indulge in massacring people. We ourselves are the target of killings, destruction, and atrocities. We are only defending ourselves. . . . [Western powers] rob us of our wealth and resources and of our oil. Our religion is under attack. They kill and murder our brothers. They compromise our honor and our dignity and dare we utter a single word of protest against the injustice, we are called terrorists.

Bin Laden's statement reflects the image of terrorists as standing apart from conventional statecraft. This status is reflected in **just-war doctrine,** a moral code of conduct in war that originated in the Middle Ages and is widely accepted by states and international law in theory, though often violated in practice (see Johnson 1981). A central condition of "just" wars is that they must be declared by *proper authorities,* a term that applies exclusively to sovereign states. Terrorist attacks conducted by private groups such as al Qaeda clearly violate this condition. They also violate another element of just-war doctrine, the one prohibiting the targeting of civilians. Terrorists believe, however, that attacks on civilian targets are essential to demonstrating the gravity of their concerns.

Elements of U.S. Counterterrorism

The increasing destructiveness and sophistication, as well as the religious character, of international terrorism make it very difficult to contain and virtually impossible to eliminate (see Lesser et al. 1999). In cutting across political jurisdictions and state-societal boundaries, terrorists hinder their enemies' efforts to identify, pursue, apprehend, and prosecute suspects. In this respect, the United States faces great difficulties and chronic uncertainties in the war on terrorism. Two things have become clear. First, the war will be a long one, with success coming from "attrition, not a blitzkrieg" (Posen 2001–2002, 42). Second, the U.S. response will be multifaceted, involving many elements of counterterrorism: military combat, law enforcement, diplomacy, intelligence, foreign aid and arms sales, and homeland security.

Military combat. In declaring "war" on terrorism after September 11, the White House granted the nation's military forces a lead role in the counteroffensive. The invasions of Afghanistan and Iraq involved large-scale deployments of U.S. and allied troops, complex tactical alliances with supportive indigenous forces, and long-term military occupations in hostile environments. The initial military offensives effectively routed the state sponsors of terrorism (Afghanistan) and the state terrorists themselves (the ruling Baath Party in Iraq). By engaging in asymmetric warfare, however, the terrorists and their supporters prevented occupying forces from gaining full control of both countries. Their hit-and-run attacks in Iraq heightened public anxieties in the United States and pressure for withdrawal. Nevertheless, the Bush administration insisted that U.S. military forces would remain in Iraq indefinitely, even after the country regained its sovereignty in June 2004.

Law enforcement. The U.S. government employed its domestic law-enforcement agencies at all levels—federal, state, and local—to support the counterterrorism effort. Most prominently, the FBI assumed substantial authority to investigate terrorist attacks in the United States and abroad. The government encouraged cooperation between the FBI and local law-enforcement agencies, previously limited, to create a more united front against domestic terrorist cells. On another front, Attorney General John Ashcroft expanded domestic surveillance, the "profiling" of potential terrorists, and other measures authorized by the USA Patriot Act, signed by Congress shortly after the 9-11 terrorist attacks (see Chapter 12). The act expanded some government agencies' power beyond terrorism. The Justice Department used its new powers "to investigate suspected drug traffickers, white-collar criminals, blackmailers, child pornographers, money launderers, spies, and even corrupt foreign leaders" (Lichtblau 2003).

Diplomacy. Conventional diplomacy has little value in resolving differences directly with terrorist groups, which, as noted earlier, stand apart from the standard channels of statecraft. National governments may benefit, however, by cooperating with each other in counterterrorist efforts and engaging in public diplomacy (see Chapter 6) that isolates the terrorists politically. The experience of the United States clearly demonstrates the need for effective diplomacy. As noted, widespread global support for the U.S. government after 9-11 crumbled when Bush chose Iraq as the next major front in the war on terrorism. The diplomatic rupture, which was most pronounced in the UN, left the United States virtually isolated at a time it needed help from other governments, as well as the world body, in bringing its enemies to justice and reconstructing war-torn Iraq.

Intelligence. As with conventional wars, a central goal of counterterrorism is to "know thy enemy." This is especially difficult with terrorists, who rely upon stealth and deception to protect themselves. High-tech electronic intelligence may prevent al Qaeda operatives from communicating by phone or computer, but only human intelligence can penetrate terrorist cells and expose them to retaliation by the U.S. government. This reality prompted U.S. intelligence agencies to step up recruiting of foreign agents and to offer large rewards for information leading to the capture of key suspects, a tactic that produced mixed results. As described in Chapter 6, the tangle of U.S. intelligence agencies, and their traditional reluctance to compare notes with one another, greatly hinders the potential role of intelligence in fighting terrorism. The selective use of intelligence for political purposes creates another problem, as documented by a congressional committee in its 2004 report on prewar intelligence on Iraq (see In Their Own Words box).

Foreign aid and arms sales. It is widely presumed that distressed living conditions create hotbeds of discontent, rebellion, and international terrorism. While the

IN THEIR OWN WORDS: PAT ROBERTS

When the Senate Select Committee on Intelligence reported in July 2004 that the Bush administration's rationales for invading Iraq were exaggerated, the committee's cochair, Sen. Pat Roberts, R-Kan., blamed the lapse on a problem familiar to foreign-policy analysts. He cited the problem of groupthink, that is, excessive peer pressure to conform to a widely held point of view (see Chapter 3). Roberts's reference to groupthink, a term first coined by political psychologist Irving Janis in 1972, included specific details of the consequences of this breakdown in foreign-policy making.

[T]he committee concluded that the intelligence community was suffering from what we call a collective groupthink, which led analysts and collectors and managers to presume that Iraq had active and growing WMD programs. This groupthink caused the community to interpret ambiguous evidence, such as the procurement of dual-use technology, as conclusive evidence of the existence of WMD programs.

While we did not specifically address it in our report, it is clear that this groupthink also extended to our allies and to the United Nations and several other nations as well, all of whom did believe [that] Saddam Hussein had active WMD programs. This was a global intelligence failure. . . .

[T]he committee [also] concluded there was a failure by intelligence community managers to adequately encourage analysts to challenge their assumptions, to fully consider alternative arguments, to accurately characterize intelligence reporting, and to counsel analysts who had lost their objectivity.

Source: Pat Roberts, with John D. Rockefeller (news conference, Washington, D.C., July 9, 2004), www.cq.com.

evidence for this is mixed—many terrorists such as Osama bin Laden come from affluent backgrounds—there is no doubt that al Qaeda and other groups exploit the turmoil in "failed states" to expand their operations. Thus the U.S. and other governments have increased their economic aid to many developing countries, citing the prospect of terrorism as a motivating force. The United States has also expanded its military-aid programs and arms sales to "frontline" states, such as Pakistan and Tajikistan, for the same reasons (see Chapter 12). Bolstering these governments, officials believe, will allow them to support U.S. efforts while better preparing them for terrorist attacks on their own soil.

Homeland security. The September 2001 attacks proved especially traumatic for Americans because they demonstrated, once and for all, that U.S. geographical separation from other world power centers no longer guaranteed the nation's security. The resulting sense of vulnerability required "new vigilance in the most fragile corners of the transportation, energy, power, and communications systems and closer attention to the security of government buildings" (Posen 2001–2002, 45). In addition to patrolling borders and protecting "high-value" targets in the United States, homeland security involves the pursuit of domestic terrorist cells and preparing "first responders" for future attacks (see O'Hanlon et al. 2002). The U.S. government's push for homeland security linked dozens of federal agencies into a new cabinet department (see Chapter 6) while coordinating federal efforts with thousands of state and local government agencies. Despite these efforts, the U.S. government continues to warn agencies and citizens that new attacks are possible at any given time or place.

Obstacles to U.S. Victory

By their nature, terrorist groups are extremely skillful at avoiding capture. Their members are highly motivated and unswervingly loyal toward one another. They conceal themselves in remote, inaccessible terrain or within the political and social chaos of failed states. They also limit their internal communications to prevent detection. Terrorist groups form clandestine alliances with governments that share their political agendas and provide safe havens and logistical support. The groups also form ad hoc alliances with like-minded terrorists and political movements. Their widely disbursed membership and "flat" organizational structures make terrorists especially elusive (see Arquilla, Ronfeldt, and Zanini 1999).

All governments share the challenges posed by these terrorist characteristics; the United States faces several distinctive obstacles as well in combating terrorism. A key obstacle is the very global primacy that served as a cornerstone of the NSC's 2002 *National Security Strategy.* Such claims to dominance naturally fuel resentment within foreign countries, particularly among frustrated societal groups in the developing world that link their impoverished living standards to U.S. wealth and power. Such groups may mobilize against all forms of U.S. primacy—military, economic, and cultural—and resort to terrorism whenever they feel other avenues of protest are closed to them. A second and related obstacle facing the United States stems from the nation's high profile overseas, which creates its own vulnerabilities to terrorism. As Paul Pillar (2001, 59) noted before the war on terrorism:

> The official U.S. presence overseas includes diplomatic representation in 162 countries. In addition to embassies, there are dozens of separate consulates, delegations to international organizations, and other missions, for a total of 290 diplomatic posts overseas as of late 2000. More than thirty U.S. government agencies operate overseas, employing more than 14,000 Americans and about 30,000 foreign nationals. Added to the civilian population is a substantial overseas military presence. As of the end of fiscal year 1998, out of 1.4 million U.S. military personnel on active duty, about 260,000 were serving outside the United States and its territories. Added to the official presence . . . is the enormous overseas commercial presence of U.S. business, as well as individual Americans traveling for business or pleasure.

Finally, the liberal nature of the U.S. government and civil society makes it difficult for the United States to gain the upper hand against terrorists. The fragmented U.S. political system—its checks and balances, federalism, and loosely connected bureaucracies—prevents effective planning and coordination. Interest groups, including those bent on harming the government and its citizens, have considerable freedom to organize, express their views, and recruit new members. Even after new restrictions were imposed, these groups retained ample access to government facilities. Further obstacles are posed by the general public, which has viewed even modest preventive measures such as restrictions on curbside baggage check-in at airports to be undue inconveniences.

These domestic obstacles hinder a coherent and aggressive U.S. response to the terrorist challenge. Overreaction poses a greater danger to the counterterrorism effort, however. A common tactic of asymmetric warfare is to transform the *victim* of attack into the *aggressor* and to bait the victim into violent backlashes that damage its credibility and presumed moral authority. "The temptation to do something, for the sake of being seen to be doing something—even something strategically stupid—can be politically irresistible" (Gray 2002, 12). Prudence is essential in responding to terrorism, something that does not come easy for a global superpower that often relies upon overwhelming military force to achieve its foreign-policy goals.

Conclusion

Like other countries, the U.S. government considers the protection of national security to be its essential function, one that makes other policy goals at home and abroad attainable. This chapter has focused on the ends and means of security and defense policy and its relationship to the nation's evolving grand strategy. As we have seen, for more than half a century, this strategy has focused on sustaining U.S. primacy in the interstate system. A combination of hard-power assets, including vast natural resources, a productive population, and cutting-edge military power, made this primacy possible after World War II. These resources and the nation's soft-power assets—the legitimacy of governmental institutions, economic freedoms, and a dynamic civil society—propelled U.S. primacy into the new millennium.

But many warning signs that U.S. primacy may not be indefinite have recently appeared. To historian Paul Kennedy (2003; 1987), the United States is exhibiting the same symptoms of "imperial overstretch"—rising budget and trade deficits and foreign debts, expanding military commitments and occupations—that brought down the empires of the second millennium. While few observers question the fact that the United States retains its lead in hard power, the erosion of U.S. moral authority within the international community, a key element of soft power, suggests difficulties lie ahead. In particular, the government's 2002 national-security strategy "may prove more radically disruptive of world order than anything the terrorists of September 11, 2001, could have hoped to achieve on their own. Through its actions, the United States seems determined to bring about precisely the threats that is says it is trying to prevent" (Johnson 2004, 287).

Expectations of U.S. decline have been commonplace from the very start of the *pax Americana,* which began after the world wars. Indeed, the previous wave of "declinism" in the mid-1980s was abruptly swamped by the U.S. victory in the cold war and its ensuing economic boom. Nevertheless, the problems facing the United States today are substantial. They have multiple roots in the paradox of world power, which highlights the cultural, institutional, and transnational constraints on the effective management of U.S. foreign policy that come with its global primacy. As Henry Kissinger (2001, 18) observed before the war on terrorism began,

> The result is that the country's preeminence is coupled with the serious potential of becoming irrelevant to many of the currents affecting and ultimately transforming the global order. The international scene exhibits a strange mixture of respect for— and submission to—America's power, accompanied by occasional exasperation with its prescriptions and confusion as to its long-term purposes.

Maintaining U.S. military security will be especially difficult given the variety of armed conflicts likely to engage U.S. forces in the future, from conventional wars to the lower-level "operations other than war" that have been common since the cold war. It is also clear that the dominance of U.S. military technology will be of little value in resolving the long-term political, economic, and cultural tensions that exist in U.S. foreign relations, tensions that make winning the war on terrorism so elusive. The "revolution in military affairs" did not lead to the prompt apprehension of Osama bin Laden nor did it offer the United States a compelling exit strategy in the Iraq war. Indeed, the primitive swords used by terrorists in beheading foreign captives in Iraq proved more effective weapons than advanced fighter jets in affecting the course of the U.S. occupation of that country in 2003 and 2004.

All of this suggests that preserving U.S. national security in the future will depend upon learning the lessons of the past that provided foreign-policy makers with both the blessings and burdens of world power. As noted earlier, military security makes other national priorities possible, including the profitable conduct of foreign-economic policy, the subject of our next chapter.

Key Terms

Anti-Ballistic Missile (ABM) Treaty, p. 315

Baruch Plan, p. 313

coercive diplomacy, p. 308

defense policy, p. 294

domestic terrorism, p. 320

exit strategy, p. 307

extended deterrence, p. 314

flexible response, p. 314

full-spectrum deterrence, p. 315

geopolitical assets, p. 298

grand strategy, p. 297

hegemonic stability theory, p. 302

just-war doctrine, p. 321

massive retaliation, p. 306

mission creep, p. 308

mutual assured destruction (MAD), p. 314

national security, p. 293

nuclear deterrence, p. 314

peaceful coercion, p. 297

Powell Doctrine, p. 307

preemptive war, p. 310

preventive war, p. 311

spectrum of armed conflict, p. 296

state-society relations, p. 300

state terrorism, p. 320

strategic culture, p. 299

Strategic Defense Initiative (SDI), p. 315

strategic detachment, p. 301

strategic environment, p. 298

structural arrangements, p. 300

sustained primacy, p. 301

tactics, p. 303

wars of choice, p. 297

wars of necessity, p. 297

Weinberger Doctrine, p. 306

Internet References

The **Center for Defense Information** (www.cdi.org) publishes reports and statistics on defense and security policies, which include information on interest groups and private companies involved in U.S. foreign policy. Among other topics, the center's work focuses specifically on U.S. arms sales and trade, missile defense, defense projects and budgets, and nuclear issues.

The **Center for Strategic and International Studies** (www.csis.org) is a nonprofit and nonpartisan organization focused on international defense and security issues, in particular policy analysis, policy recommendations, and geographic analysis. The center publishes the *Washington Quarterly* (online at www.twq.com), which analyzes global changes and foreign policies with an emphasis on the U.S. role in the world, defense procurement, terrorism and counterterrorism, and regional issues.

The **Congressional Research Service (CRS)** (www.loc.gov/crsinfo/whatscrs.html) provides briefings to Congress on specific policy issues. Though there is no single repository for all CRS reports, several Web sites archive a large selection, including the U.S. embassy in Italy (www.usembassy.it/policy/crs.htm), the State Department (fpc.state.gov//c4763.htm), the Federation of American Scientists (www.fas.org/man/crs/index.html), and the National Library for the Environment (www.ncseonline.org/NLE/CRS).

The **Department of Defense** (www.defenselink.mil) is vested with military and security responsibilities for the United States and many countries around the globe. The depart-

continues

ment's Web site provides access to defense-related activities, specific programs, information regarding the military and past operations, and speeches and transcripts from defense officials. Included as well are links to agencies within the Defense Department and a list of online publications such as the defense budget, *Defense Almanac*, and reports on capabilities and security measures.

The newest cabinet agency, the **Department of Homeland Security** (www.dhs.gov) offers consistent updates on the war on terrorism as well as missions to contain and combat domestic terrorism. Its Web site also provides information regarding immigration, border controls, and policies related to emergency actions in the form of speeches, documents, and research links.

The **Federation of American Scientists** (www.fas.org) is a nonprofit organization committed to researching causes and tactics of war. Areas of research include nuclear arms, terrorism, intelligence gathering and reporting, small arms trade, and the connection between technology and weaponry. In addition to providing facts and figures on these areas, FAS also publishes a newsletter, *Arms Sales Monitor* (www.fas.org/asmp/library /armsmonitor.html), and a journal, *Public Interest Report* (www.fas.org/faspir/index .html), along with short books on each research topic.

The **International Institute for Strategic Studies** (www.iiss.org) is a London-based leading research organization on political and military conflict. The institute focuses its research agenda on grand strategy, armed forces, technological and military equipment, and programs on regional relations.

"Patterns of Global Terrorism" (www.state.gov/s/ct/rls/pgtrpt), published and recorded by the State Department, is a yearly report on terrorist incidents that affect U.S. citizens and interests around the globe. It includes regional reports, chronologies of events, U.S. programs and policies of counterterrorism, and background information on state-sponsored and transnational terrorist groups.

The **RAND Corporation** (www.rand.org) is a private research group focusing on international affairs, homeland security, terrorism, and U.S. national security issues. It also produces reports on individual countries that have close ties to the United States. RAND is responsible for producing the *RAND Review* (www.rand.org/publications/randreview), a magazine about current security and defense issues.

The Web site for the **United States Intelligence Community** (www.intelligence.gov) offers information regarding the organization of all U.S. intelligence agencies and their relationships toward each other and the government as a whole. Meetings and special report findings regarding national and international intelligence are reported and summarized on the site.

The **World Policy Institute** (www.worldpolicy.org/wpi/index.html) is a research organization focused on the connection between domestic and international factors that drive foreign policy. Its research topics include counterterrorism, arms trade, U.S. grand strategy, cultural relations, and relationships between military superpowers.

11

Tractor trailers line up for miles at a customs station along the Mexican-American border in 1998. This traffic jam remains a daily occurrence more than ten years after the signing of the North American Free Trade Agreement (NAFTA), which fostered free trade among Mexico, the United States, and Canada. The U.S. government considers the agreement a prototype for larger, more ambitious pacts. But antiglobalization groups, along with many developing countries, resist free trade and instead promote "fair trade" that would protect smaller economies from U.S. domination.

Economic Statecraft

While the protection of military security is the primary concern of U.S. foreign policy, *economic* security is vital to the nation as well. American leaders, like their counterparts overseas, consider national prosperity essential to achieving broader strategic goals. The military preponderance currently enjoyed by the United States would not be possible in the absence of a productive population, vast natural resources, advanced technology, and commercial links to other markets. Economic strength is also a source of the nation's "soft power" (Nye 2004), wielded by private citizens and expressed, in part, by their material well-being.

Beyond the functional benefits of a vibrant U.S. economy, the day-to-day conduct of foreign-economic policy is regarded as a worthy end in itself. Productive foreign-economic relations tend to moderate the behavior of U.S. trading partners, which are more stable and reliable if they rule justly and "play by the rules" of interstate relations. At home, commercial activity harnesses the energies of private citizens, whose pursuit of material self-interests contributes to the realization of national goals. In this respect, the domain of foreign-economic policy is more democratic than security policy, which often takes place beyond the view or reach of civil society (Zegart 1999).

The notion that "the business of America is business" is deeply engrained in the nation's cultural identity. Americans have long been regarded abroad as highly *materialistic*, or driven by the acquisition of wealth. Alexis de Tocqueville ([1835] 1988, 534, 536), a Frenchman who toured the United States in 1831 and 1832, captured this materialistic spirit in his classic cultural study, *Democracy in America*:

> [T]he desire to acquire the good things of this world is the dominant passion among Americans. . . . It is odd to watch with what feverish ardor the Americans pursue prosperity and how they are ever tormented by the shadowy suspicion that they may not have chosen the shortest route to get it. Americans cleave to the things of this world as if assured that they will never die, and yet are in such a rush to snatch any that come within their reach, as if expecting to stop living before they have relished them. They clutch everything but hold nothing fast, and so lose grip as they hurry after some new delight.

In this chapter, we explore the key aspects of U.S. foreign economic policy. We first describe the primary models of **political economy,** an arena of public life located at the crossroads of states and markets. The chapter then reviews the current strengths of the United States in the world economy as well as its weaknesses and vulnerabilities. Two central elements of the nation's foreign-economic policy—trade and foreign aid—are then examined in detail. Finally, the chapter explores the controversial role of economic sanctions in promoting U.S. foreign-policy goals.

As we will discover, the United States confronts growing challenges in the market-driven world economy that are, to a considerable degree, products of the nation's own commercial dynamism and clout. By its nature, economic globalization leads to the diffusion of wealth, technology, and production from the centers of economic activity to peripheral areas that seek to exploit their own competitive advantages, such as lower wage rates and cheap raw materials. Emerging economic powers in East Asia, for example, succeeded by protecting their own firms from foreign competition and "importing" modern manufacturing technologies developed elsewhere. In so doing, they met their citizens' material needs while offering high-quality goods on trade markets at bargain prices. More recently, the economy of India has advanced at a faster pace due in large part to the hiring of computer specialists in the country to serve U.S. firms and their customers half a world away.

The flow of private capital across national borders, a crucial part of globalization, further hinders the U.S. government's economic autonomy, or ability to control its fortunes in the global marketplace. Foreign investments, which reached record levels in the 1990s before falling dramatically during the recent global recession, are difficult to control and impossible to predict. Further, as U.S.-based multinational corporations (MNCs) expand into new markets and join forces with firms from other countries, they are less likely to align themselves automatically with U.S. foreign-policy goals.

In some cases, global economic pressures may impair U.S. national security. Heightened competition in the arms industry, for example, has prompted U.S. leaders to ease restrictions on weapons exports in recent years even though their actions created a more militarized and potentially threatening international system (Hook and Rothstein 2005; Keller and Nolan 2001). And while globalization has allowed for wealth and technology to be disbursed more widely, its impact is highly uneven. Wide gaps remain between the world's richest and poorest nations as well as *within* most countries. As the U.S. government has acknowledged, socioeconomic distress and perceived inequities fuel political resentments that breed terrorist movements and attacks.

Regulating commerce is a highly *political* enterprise given the routine interaction of public and private actors in the U.S. economic complex (see Chapter 6). The makeup of Congress is determined in large part by the economic interests of constituents (Fordham and McKeown 2003), and presidential candidates know that "pocketbook" issues typically concern voters more than any others. Political intervention in private markets is inevitable because the economic affairs of Americans, widely diffused regionally and across business sectors, routinely come into conflict and cannot be fully reconciled. Amid the cross-pressures imposed by competing, self-interested investors, firms, and workers, the U.S. government must act as the final arbiter of these conflicts of interest (see Ikenberry, Lake, and Mastanduno 1988).

American leaders, however, rarely speak with one voice in foreign-economic policy. Members of Congress routinely differ with the White House, as well as each other, on potential trade agreements and aid packages. At the same time, nearly every cabinet agency has a stake in foreign commerce, with no single agency having full jurisdiction of this foreign-policy domain (see Cohen, Blecker, and Whitney 2003). Agency disputes reflect institutional biases and contrary ideas regarding the best ways to maximize national prosperity while meeting the needs of diverse societal groups (Goldstein 1993). While some presidents, such as Franklin D. Roosevelt, called for active state intervention in the name of social stability and equity, others, such as Ronald Reagan, extolled the "magic of the market" and the cause of economic liberty.

As in the case of security policy, institutional arrangements play a key role in shaping the foreign-economic policies of all countries. In the United States, corporations enjoy a privileged place in the policy process, while workers in Great Britain and Germany have greater political influence over trade and foreign investment than their American counterparts. The central governments of Japan and France, meanwhile, are better equipped to overcome pressure from either of these societal groups (Hart 1992). These comparisons reveal the extent to which foreign economic relations reflect the bargains struck daily among contending actors in domestic society.

Models of Political Economy

As noted earlier, regulating commerce is inherently a political process given the state's role in deciding which economic system will be in place at any particular time, what the rules of the system will be, and how its costs and benefits will be distributed across society. These questions become matters of foreign-economic policy when they involve the government's commercial, financial, and regulatory ties with other countries. The **international political economy** is the arena in which governments engage with an array of private actors—firms, workers, investors, public-interest groups—as well as with foreign governments and intergovernmental organizations such as the World Bank and the WTO. This engagement is partly competitive, as each nation seeks benefits for itself at the expense of others; but there is also a need for cooperation if the global economy is to function in the orderly manner required by financial managers.

An essential function of all governments is to organize economic activity within their societies and establish the relationships among economic actors in the public and private sectors. In doing so, political leaders adopt different models of political economy that feature distinctive trade-offs between labor and capital, political liberty and economic equality, and the power of states versus civil society. The model of political economy chosen by each nation determines the role it will play in the global economy and the broader relations it will maintain with other governments. Three models of political economy have been adopted in modern times: economic liberalism, socialism, and economic nationalism.[1] In managing economic affairs, governments commonly draw upon the elements of more than one model.

The United States is widely considered the primary proponent of **economic liberalism,** a system of free enterprise that protects private property and commercial activity from government intervention. To Adam Smith ([1776] 2000), a leading proponent of this model during the Enlightenment, free markets offer an ideal environment for entrepreneurs to take risks, introduce technological innovations, and expand production, all of which improves societal living standards beyond what governments can provide. In this view, a natural "harmony of interests" exists between states and markets, and among the producers and consumers of goods and services. This model became known as *capitalism,* a term reflecting the importance of private wealth (capital) in driving economic activity.

The second model of political economy, **socialism,** rejects the liberal notion of a harmony of interests and argues instead that free markets inevitably produce disparities in wealth and the exploitation of workers by business owners and managers. This critique, identified with Karl Marx and often referred to today as neo-Marxism (see Chapter 3), considers the political leaders of liberal states to be co-conspirators with business firms in the exploitation of workers. A socialist system seeks to ensure economic equality through social-welfare programs and government ownership of vital enterprises, while also allowing citizens to own private property and operate firms. The Soviet Union adopted a stronger version of this model, *communism,* by assuming ownership of all economic activity and dominating political control. While this model failed to improve living standards, the neo-Marxist critique of liberal economics persists and modified versions of socialism exist in many parts of the world.[2]

---

1. See Robert Gilpin (1987) for a similar breakdown of political-economic models.

2. Several countries in Europe manage economies that resemble the socialist model, although they have moved toward liberalism under pressure from the European Union's central bank. Still, governments such as Austria, Hungary, and Italy spent more than 40 percent of national output on public programs in 2002; the United States spent less than 20 percent (World Bank 2004b, 222–224).

Finally, **economic nationalism** considers commercial activity fruitful only if it serves the interests of the state, whose power depends upon the accumulation of wealth. Political actors adopting this model, also known as *mercantilism,* view the world economy as a "zero-sum game" in which the losses suffered by one country offset the gains enjoyed by another. During the Renaissance era, the maritime empires of Europe adopted this model by accumulating vast amounts of *specie,* or mineral wealth, which they used to enhance their military defenses and domestic political power. The revival of economic nationalism in the 1920s led to the closing of world trade markets, a severe global depression, and the onset of World War II. More recently, Japan and other East Asian countries have been accused of "neo-mercantilism," flooding global export markets with their goods while protecting their domestic producers from foreign competition.

The United States first adopted a mercantile approach to foreign-economic policy while simultaneously preaching the gospel of open markets. This behavior changed as the nation emerged from World War I as the world's economic powerhouse. Woodrow Wilson, who included free trade as one of his "fourteen points" for restoring global stability, pledged to dismantle U.S. trade barriers and encouraged others to follow his lead. The trade wars of the interwar period, however, delayed this transition to market liberalism. The calamity of the Great Depression and second world war prompted Franklin Roosevelt's secretary of state, Cordell Hull (quoted in Gardner 1980, 9), to later observe, "Unhampered trade dovetailed with peace; high tariffs, trade barriers, and unfair competition with war. If we could get a freer flow of trade—freer in the sense of few discriminations and obstructions . . . we might have a reasonable chance of lasting peace."

This spirit of free trade animated the U.S. government's foreign-economic policy after World War II and continues to do so today. Yet traces of economic nationalism remain, as evidenced by President Bush's raising of steel tariffs in 2002 and the country's highly subsidized agricultural sector, which also exhibits the characteristics of socialism. Contradicting the liberal rhetoric of government leaders, such practices expose the United States to charges of hypocrisy. Critics of globalization also point out that the U.S. government's exalting of free markets can actually be construed as a tactic of economic nationalism. After all, U.S. economic primacy would grow even stronger if U.S. firms, with their superior technology, huge marketing budgets, and economies of scale, swamp their challengers on open trade markets, a prospect that prompts aggressive counter-measures by trading states overseas.

The Balance of Economic Power

The United States has managed the world's largest economy for nearly a century. Its output eclipsed that of Great Britain and other economic rivals early in the twentieth century, and the lead widened with the decimation of U.S. competitors in the two world wars. By 1945 and the start of the cold war, U.S. firms produced roughly as much economic output as the rest of the world combined. Although this percentage predictably fell as other economies recovered, the U.S. share of world output, which leveled off at between one-quarter and one-third, remains unsurpassed today.

Record levels of foreign investment contributed greatly to the rapid pace of U.S. economic growth in the 1990s, which averaged nearly 4 percent annually. The economic boom, aided further by the creation of new capitalist states in the former Soviet bloc, put to rest (temporarily at least) widespread expectations of U.S. decline. The economies of the nation's most serious challengers—the newly industrialized countries of East Asia—peaked in the mid-1990s and then suffered a dramatic fall at the turn of the century (see Clifford and Engardio 2000). This reversal of fortunes coincided with a boom in the high-tech sectors of the U.S. economy and unprecedented growth in stock prices.

By 2002, the **gross national income** (GNI) of the United States amounted to $10.2 trillion, a level nearly one-third the global total of $31.5 trillion (World Bank 2004b).[3] This proportion is especially striking given that the U.S. population of 290 million represented less than 5 percent of the global population of 6.3 billion. Japan, which managed the world's second largest national economy in that year, produced about 42 percent of U.S. economic output; other leading economies produced less than 20 percent of the U.S. total. The volume of U.S. output in 2002 exceeded the *combined* totals of more than 150 low- and middle-income countries. As for Russia, the geopolitical rival of the United States in the cold war, a decade of turbulent economic and political reforms cut its output to less than 4 percent of U.S. output (see Freeland 2000).

Other statistics illustrate the magnitude of U.S. economic abundance. The per-capita income of the United States, the nation's economic output divided by its population, amounted to $35,060 in 2002. Only Norway and Switzerland exceeded this level of affluence. The average life expectancy of Americans reached seventy-eight in 2001, significantly higher than the world average of sixty-seven years (World Bank 2004b, 114). Americans today can be expected to live twice as long on average as citizens in several African countries, including Malawi (38), Sierra Leone (37), and Zambia (37). The contrast in living standards could not be more striking: while more than 1 billion citizens of low-income countries live in absolute poverty, earning less than $2 a day, American consumers are increasingly drawn to extravagant "trophy homes" and sport-utility vehicles.

The momentum in U.S. economic growth that started in the early 1990s, however, has slowed since the turn of the century. Several factors contributed to this downturn. First, the East Asian economic crisis that erupted in 1997 eventually spread around the world, suppressing demand for U.S. goods and reducing foreign investment. Second, the United States experienced a wave of accounting scandals that resulted in billions of dollars in losses for such corporations as Enron and Worldcom (see Krugman 2003, Chap. 4). The scandals, which weighed heavily on the corporations' investors, pensioners, and workers, further suppressed the optimism that had fueled steady rises in stock prices. Finally, the terrorist attacks

---

3. GNI represents the total of goods and services produced by residents of a country in a single year, plus receipts of private income and foreign aid from abroad.

of September 2001 dealt a major blow to the U.S. and global economies, which rely upon political stability and confident expectations about the future.

Global trade, which had expanded by 12.5 percent in 2000, grew by just 0.1 percent in 2001 and 3.1 percent in 2002 (IMF 2004a). The volume of U.S. exports fell by nearly 8 percent in those two years. Imports to the United States, which had grown by nearly 50 percent between 1997 and 2000, *decreased* in volume by 2.6 percent in 2001. Volumes of foreign investment across all national borders also plummeted from their record levels of 2000. The primary victim of this downward spiral was the United States. Its inflow of **foreign direct investment** (**FDI**) fell by $278 billion over a two-year period, from $308 billion in 2000 to $131 billion in 2001 to $30 billion in 2002 (OECD 2003). By then, the United States had dropped from first to fourth in FDI receipts, behind France, Germany, and Luxembourg.

Despite these setbacks, the United States has maintained its status as the leading world trader (see Table 11.1). American firms exported more than $1 trillion worth of goods and commercial services in 2003, more than 17 percent more than Germany, its chief competitor (WTO 2004b). The United States remains the world's foremost importer as well. The volume of U.S. imports nearly doubled that of Germany, the second largest import market in 2003.

For the first four decades after World War II, the United States maintained a **balance of trade,** an equilibrium between imports and exports. But in the 1980s, the nation began buying more goods from foreign countries than it was selling to them (see Figure 11.1). The U.S. trade deficit grew steadily during the boom years of the 1990s and then soared in the new millennium. By 2003, the trade deficit approached half a trillion dollars. China alone exported $124 billion more to the United States than the latter imported from all other sources during that year. Consumer spending represented the largest category of import growth as Americans rushed to buy the lowest-cost goods they could find, regardless of national origin.

Table 11.1 Leading World Merchandise Traders, 2003

Exporter	Volume (in Billions of U.S. dollars)	Importer	Volume (in Billions of U.S. dollars)
1. United States	$1,007	1. United States	$1,523
2. Germany	860	2. Germany	769
3. Japan	542	3. United Kingdom	500
4. China	483	4. Japan	493
5. France	483	5. France	470
6. United Kingdom	434	6. China	467
7. Italy	363	7. Italy	363
8. Netherlands	357	8. Netherlands	327
9. Canada	311	9. Canada	294
10. Belgium	297	10. Belgium	275

SOURCE: World Trade Organization, "Stronger than Expected Growth Spurs Modest Trade Recovery" (April 5, 2004), www.wto.org/english/news_e/pres04_e/pr373_e.htm.

Figure 11.1 U.S. Balance of Trade, 1964–2003

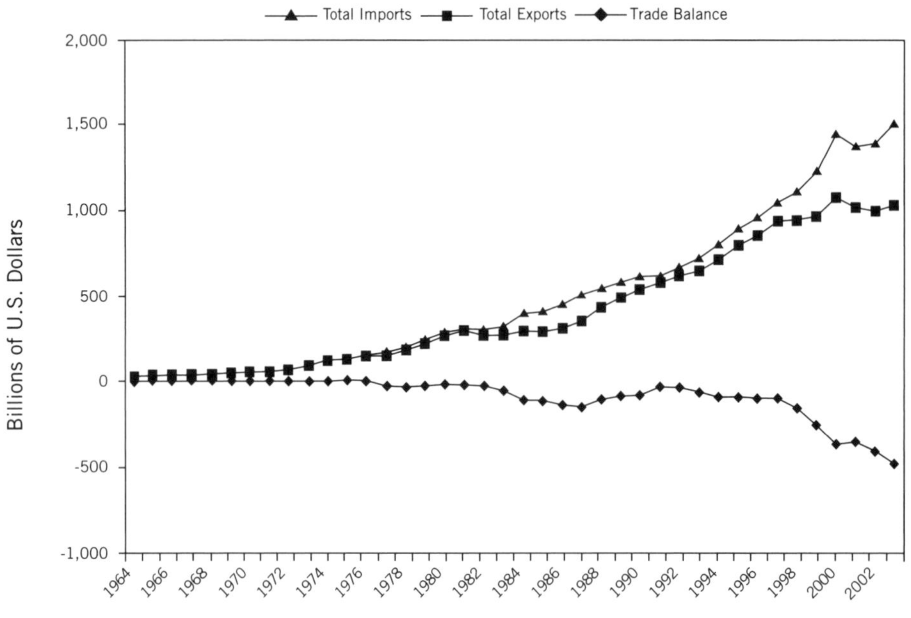

SOURCE: International Trade Administration, "TradeStats Express," tse.export.gov.

Meanwhile, the U.S. government posted record budget deficits, which approached $500 billion in 2003 and were expected to total nearly $1.2 trillion between fiscal years 2005 and 2008 (Congressional Budget Office 2004). The rise in these deficits followed a major tax cut President Bush proposed in 2001 and Congress quickly approved. The growing federal deficit was also due to the costs of the war on terrorism and particularly the military operation in Iraq, estimated at nearly $4 billion per month in 2004. The Bush administration argued that the deficits, although troubling, could still be overcome given the large scale and resilience of the U.S. economy. Still, paying off the national debt, which exceeded $7 trillion by this time, would impede economic growth for many years.

An examination of U.S. bilateral trade flows reveals the importance of the nation's North American neighbors, Canada and Mexico, as export markets as well as sources of imported goods and services. Total trade between the United States and these NAFTA partners amounted to $630 billion in 2003 (U.S. International Trade Administration 2004b). In 2003, exports from the United States to Canada alone, valued at $170 billion, exceeded the value of all U.S. exports to the European Union. The $97 billion in U.S. exports to Mexico, meanwhile, exceeded the combined total of U.S. exports to Japan and China, the top Asian export destinations. Imports from Canada and Mexico, valued at $362 billion, exceeded the value of imports from all European countries and the combined imports from Japan and China (see Table 11.2 and Map 10, U.S. Foreign Economic Relations, in the map section at the front of the book).

Table 11.2 Top U.S. Trading Partners, 2003

Source of Imports	Volume (in Billions of U.S. dollars)	Export Market	Volume (in Billions of U.S. dollars)
1. Canada	$224	1. Canada	$170
2. China	152	2. Mexico	97
3. Mexico	138	3. Japan	52
4. Japan	118	4. United Kingdom	34
5. Germany	68	5. Germany	29
6. United Kingdom	43	6. China	28
7. South Korea	37	7. South Korea	24
8. Taiwan	32	8. Netherlands	21
9. France	29	9. Taiwan	17
10. Ireland	26	10. France	17

SOURCE: U.S. International Trade Administration, "U.S. Foreign Aggregate Trade Data," *Office of Trade and Economic Analysis* (June 6, 2004), www.ita.doc.gov/td/industry/otea/usfth/tabcon.html.

While Canada and Mexico posted large trade surpluses with the United States, the two countries' dependence on this trade relationship created vulnerabilities for them. Canadian exports to the United States in 2002 represented nearly 88 percent of Canada's global exports. For Mexico, the corresponding figure was 83 percent. Other Latin American countries depended on the United States as their primary trading partners, but to a far lesser extent than the NAFTA states.[4] Among the Asian economic powers, 29 percent of Japan's exports and 22 percent of China's exports were bound for the United States. The European states were far less dependent on U.S. trade, as demonstrated by the shares of U.S.-bound exports posted by the "big three" economies, Great Britain (16 percent), Germany (10 percent), and France (8 percent).

The Politics of U.S. Trade

By far the most important aspect of U.S. foreign-economic policy involves trade with other countries. As we have seen, Americans have robust appetites for foreign goods, even those that come at the cost of shuttered factories in U.S. cities. While the United States is no longer the world's dominant exporter, the nation enjoys a commanding lead in many sectors of foreign trade, particularly services, military equipment, and high-technology goods associated with the computer industry. Whereas trade accounted for about 10 percent of U.S. economic output in 1960, about one-fourth of the goods and services produced today are destined for foreign customers.

---

4. The two NAFTA partners also *imported* a predominant share of goods and services from the United States. For Canada, the percentage of U.S.-based imports stood at 63 percent in 2002, and for Mexico, 70 percent.

The conduct of trade policy offers a prime example of a "two-level game" (Putnam 1988). In this game, officials in the executive branch negotiate simultaneously with foreign leaders and domestic stakeholders, including business firms, labor unions, and members of Congress. The terms of prospective trade agreements must be acceptable to parties at both levels if those agreements are to be approved and ratified, so negotiators must be sure to resolve everyone's concerns to the largest extent possible. At the same time, the foreign governments and domestic actors involved recognize the benefits of expanded trade and know compromises and trade-offs have to be made.

Global Trade Politics

As the walls between domestic, regional, and world markets have broken down, the global politics of trade have become increasingly vital to the security of the United States. Cooperative trade relations foster goodwill between the United States and other nations while creating incentives for stable political ties and the coordination of security policies. The interdependence resulting from economic ties, while creating occasional tensions, enhances the prospects for broader bilateral cooperation. Likewise, forming military alliances and more informal security agreements paves the way for trade and foreign investments. Concessions in one area improve the prospects for agreement in the other, encouraging foreign-policy makers to use trade concessions as a "carrot," and trade sanctions as a "stick," in the conduct of security policy.

The United States holds the upper hand in most trade negotiations. With the world's largest economy, the U.S. government naturally favors open markets because its industries are in a strong position to compete with smaller, less-advanced competitors in other countries (see Lake 1988; and Grieco 1990). Through their disproportionate effects on supply, U.S.-based producers in many sectors of the global economy can affect prices of goods that are produced everywhere. Corporate farmers, for example, have overwhelmed competitors in smaller countries by flooding world trade markets and lowering the "unit costs" of commodities (Prestowitz 2003, Chap. 3). Lacking these economies of scale, small farmers in developing countries cannot make a profit. Well aware of the advantage enjoyed by the United States, its trading partners commonly restrict access to their markets— just as the United States did when it was an up-and-coming regional power.

Other factors shape the global context of U.S. trade politics. Economic interdependence allows disruptions in one region to spread more easily to other regions, as happened with the 1997 East Asian economic crisis that continues to suppress global demand today. Increases in foreign tariffs evoke strong reactions in other countries, making trade wars a constant possibility (A. Krueger 1996). The United States and the European Union, representing the two largest centers of world trade, engage in a contentious trade rivalry even while cooperating on most matters of international security.

The management of foreign-economic relations became a top foreign-policy priority after the United States established itself as a formidable agricultural and

Point/Counterpoint
FREE TRADE VS. FAIR TRADE

A major fault line in U.S. foreign-economic policy separates two opposing points of view: free trade versus fair trade. The two approaches have conflicted since the United States emerged as a major trading power. But historical experience has hardly resolved these differences, which remain stronger than ever in the globalized economy of the twenty-first century.

To advocates of free trade, the United States should promote a world economy of goods and services moving freely across national boundaries. "Wherever globalization has taken hold, there has been a measurable improvement in incomes and working conditions," claims the Center for Trade Policy Studies, an offshoot of the CATO Institute. "The historical record is very clear that free trade bestows many benefits to the average person. . . . While there are inevitable short-term transition costs in some sectors of the economy, the long-term benefits of free trade for all far outweigh such costs."

Opponents of free trade argue that open markets are not "fair" because they benefit the United States and other major industrialized nations at the expense of less-developed countries. The U.S. Green Party believes that trade rules "must always comply with higher laws of human rights, as well as economic and labor rights established by the Universal Declaration of Human Rights. . . . In a Fair Trade regime . . . the United States would acknowledge the protection of human rights, ecological systems, and local cultures, as an essential first principle."

The CATO Institute, a conservative think tank, believes that while fair trade "sounds good in theory, in practice, the term is really code for protectionism. Fair trade, as the term is now used, usually means government intervention to direct, control, or restrict trade." The Green Party and other fair-trade proponents agree that trade must be "restricted" in many cases—against countries that abuse human rights and exploit workers, for example. They also agree that U.S. trade should be "protectionist" if this means protecting the economic rights and living conditions of workers in the United States and abroad.

The U.S. government generally upholds the principle of free trade, reflecting the nation's political culture, which favors private property over government regulation. This position creates tensions on the international level, however, as the U.S. system draws in citizens of other countries through closer economic ties. As a result, trade policy in the United States has consequences throughout the world.

Sources: Center for Trade Policy Studies, "Free Trade FAQs," www.freetrade.org/faqs/faqs.html; Green Party of the United States, "International Resolution of the Green Party of the United States, Calling for Fair Trade and Opposing 'FTAA'—Free Trade of the Americas" (November 2003), www.gp.org/committees/intl/ftaa _declaration.htm.

industrial power early in the twentieth century. The nation's population had recently surpassed 100 million, due in large part to a wave of European immigration at the turn of the century, which brought a much-needed influx of workers to support the country's rapid industrial expansion. By the early 1920s, the United States was producing more steel, oil, and automobiles than the rest of the world combined.

The decimation of other major economies in World War II allowed the United States to assume a decisive role in creating the market-driven world economy that exists today. American banks financed much of Europe's reconstruction in the postwar period. The emerging threat of Soviet-style communism reinforced Washington's drive to promote capitalism and open trade markets. In 1947, industrialized states met in Havana, Cuba, and created the International Trade Organization (ITO) to encourage and regulate world trade. As with the League of Nations in 1919, however, the U.S. Senate found this organization too threatening to U.S. sovereignty and refused to ratify its founding treaty. As a fallback position, the United States supported the General Agreement on Tariffs and Trade (GATT), which later served as the primary vehicle of market reforms and the forerunner of the World Trade Organization (WTO). The GATT negotiations, or "rounds," were based upon the principle of **most-favored-nation,** the provision of equal market access and terms of trade to all states participating in the GATT system.

As described in Chapter 9, the United States assumed primary responsibility for managing global monetary and development policies through the International Monetary Fund (IMF) and the World Bank, respectively. After World War II, the United States ensured foreign currencies by basing their values on the U.S. dollar, which the nation backed up with its gold reserves. Then in 1971, rising inflation, along with the high costs of the Vietnam War, prompted President Richard Nixon to abandon this **gold standard.** In its absence, a system of **floating exchange rates** came into being which determined the value of one country's currency based upon the value of other currencies on foreign-exchange markets. Nonetheless, the U.S. government still provided the largest share of IMF and World Bank funds and maintained the greatest influence over their policies.

The postwar period also witnessed a protracted economic rivalry between the capitalist and communist blocs. The Export Control Act of 1949 allowed the president to restrict U.S. exports even in the absence of a national emergency. In the 1950s and 1960s the U.S. government insisted upon an embargo, or cessation of exports, against the Soviet Union, China, and their allies. At the same time, the United States refused to purchase goods from the communist states, whose own economic doctrine called for independence from the capitalist world.

Nuclear tensions and the high costs of the arms race in the 1970s brought a period of détente between the communist world and the United States. Among other conciliatory measures, President Nixon eased trade sanctions against Moscow, which at the time badly needed U.S. agricultural products to feed its population. The Western European allies also established modest, but growing, economic ties across the Iron Curtain during this thaw in superpower tensions, which occurred as the United States severed the gold standard and sought a face-saving withdrawal from the Vietnam War.

In 1973, the Nixon administration confronted an economic challenge posed by the Organization of Petroleum Exporting Countries (OPEC), the cartel whose embargo on oil exports sparked high inflation and a protracted economic recession across the industrialized world states for the next decade (see Chapter 9). As the largest oil importer, the United States was especially hard hit by the OPEC embargo, which was directed toward all supporters of Israel in its latest military conflict against neighboring Arab countries. The dependence of the United States on Middle East oil led President Jimmy Carter, in the late 1970s, to accelerate the development of new sources of supply, reward energy conservation, and promote the development of renewable energy, such as solar power. To Carter, the energy crisis was "the moral equivalent of war" (see Rothgeb 2001, Chap. 7).

Subsequent strains on the U.S. economy in the 1980s chipped away at the nation's commitment to free trade. The United States became a victim of its own success during this period as newly industrialized countries took advantage of open U.S. markets to hasten their own economic growth. As noted earlier, newly industrialized countries in East Asia kept their markets largely closed to foreign competition while flooding export markets with low-cost, highly subsidized goods. The result was a rapidly growing trade deficit in the United States, whose industries stagnated in several key sectors such as steel, textiles, and consumer electronics. Although the U.S. automobile industry retained its sales edge with the help of federal assistance (see Nelson 1996), Japan enjoyed a steadily growing market share by selling smaller and more fuel-efficient vehicles than those sold by the "big three" U.S. automakers, Chrysler, Ford, and General Motors.

The refusal of trading partners to open their markets to U.S. exports was not limited to East Asia. Members of the European Community (now the EU) continued to protect its farmers through a "Common Agricultural Policy" that strictly limited access by foreign producers, especially the United States (see Cohen, Blecker, and Whitney 2003, Chap. 11). The end of the cold war in 1991 prompted President Clinton to base U.S. foreign policy on geoeconomics, the global production and distribution of economic output as a national priority. In 1992, Clinton secured Senate ratification of the NAFTA agreement. He succeeded again a year later in gaining legislative approval of sweeping tariff reductions in the **Uruguay Round** of GATT negotiations, which also led to the creation of the WTO early in 1995 (see Preeg 1995). Clinton numbered among his later accomplishments a landmark 2000 trade pact with China, which led to that's country's entry into the WTO the following year.

This revived push for free trade produced its own counter-reaction in the form of the anti-globalization movement. Led by public-interest NGOs such as Public Citizen, opponents of trade "liberalization" in 1997 successfully derailed the Multilateral Agreement on Investments that would have encouraged higher volumes of private investment across national borders (see Kobrin 1998). By taking to the streets during the 1999 WTO meetings in Seattle, anti-globalization protesters drew considerable public support from workers, environmentalists, human-rights advocates, and other transnational interest groups. The collapse in September 2003 of WTO talks in Cancun, Mexico, due to the collective resistance of many developing countries, posed a direct challenge to continued globalization.

As noted in Chapter 9, the U.S. government under President George W. Bush sought to overcome these deadlocks by negotiating separate free-trade agreements with individual countries or all countries in a particular region. Negotiating these pacts is easier for the United States than forging global agreements because it can more easily modify its demands and concessions in keeping with the preferences of its trading partners. However, trade "regionalism" can prove counterproductive, as history suggests that "trade blocs in one region simply beget trade blocs in other regions" (Gordon 2003, 112).

Domestic Trade Politics

Trade policy is also contested domestically within all levels of U.S. government and across civil society. President Bush made this clear in March 2002 when he raised tariffs on foreign-made steel to satisfy the demands of domestic producers who had complained about low-cost steel from overseas. While Bush gained political support in Pennsylvania, a "battleground state" he needed for reelection, he alienated automakers in Michigan, another battleground state, as the higher tariffs forced them to pay more for steel. When the president reversed his decision and lowered the tariffs in 2003, he experienced equal, but opposite gains and losses politically. Domestic politics are also at play when individual states compete with each other to lure foreign firms and the jobs their ventures would create.

Early in the history of the United States, two opposing views of trade policy vied for government support. Economic nationalists believed the nation should protect its domestic market from foreign competition and seek to become economically self-sufficient. Alexander Hamilton, the first U.S. treasury secretary and a strong proponent of this view, felt the United States required a strong industrial base that could be used for military purposes in case of a challenge from abroad.

Economic liberals such as Benjamin Franklin and Thomas Jefferson favored a free-trade policy more in keeping with the nation's distrust of an activist federal government, especially in economic affairs. They believed a foreign policy based on economic relations would encourage peaceful cooperation with other states. Franklin and Jefferson shared Adam Smith's contention that living standards everywhere would be enhanced by the creation of a global division of labor in which each country's producers would contribute in areas drawing upon their unique strengths. David Ricardo and other early advocates of economic globalization later refined this notion of **comparative advantage** (see Heilbroner 1999).

While early U.S. leaders embraced Jefferson's view in principle, Hamilton prevailed in practice. The government subsidized and protected "infant industries" from foreign competition while encouraging large-scale agricultural production that would make Americans self-sufficient in this crucial economic sector. These policies remained in place as the United States expanded its territory throughout the nineteenth century and completed the transition to an industrialized society. By the early twentieth century, the United States had become a formidable economic power that was capable of tipping the balance of two world wars in its favor.

Since the United States became an economic giant, Congress, despite its constitutional power to "regulate commerce," has largely deferred to the executive branch. This deference stemmed from a painful chapter in U.S. economic history in the 1920s, when trade wars broke out among the major industrial powers. Members of Congress jumped into the fray in 1930 by passing the **Smoot-Hawley Tariff Act,** which dramatically increased tariffs on goods coming into the country.[5] The act, designed to strengthen domestic firms and bolster the nation's economic strength, instead reduced the volume of U.S. trade by nearly 70 percent and helped plunge the U.S. and world economies into the Great Depression.

Two lessons emerged from the Smoot-Hawley debacle. First, members of Congress learned that the United States bore the primary responsibility for promoting and sustaining global economic growth. As the "locomotive" of the world economy, the United States could not engage in the trade wars that commonly occurred among smaller economic powers. Second, legislators recognized that constituent pressure for trade protections prevented them from living up to this global responsibility. While protecting domestic firms from overseas competition made political sense, such actions stunted global commerce and economic growth.

This second lesson led Congress to pass the Reciprocal Trade Agreement of 1934, which shifted responsibility for trade agreements to the executive branch. The legislation presumed that presidents, in representing the "national interest," could better withstand the parochial pressures than legislators, with their closer contact to constituents. In the decades that followed, the occupants of the White House became the chief advocates of a liberal trade regime in which all countries were encouraged to open their markets to foreign goods and services.

Support for this position among Republicans and Democrats changed drastically in the previous half-century. During the late nineteenth century, Republicans generally favored government intervention in the economy while Democrats believed the "invisible hand" of market forces should dictate foreign-economic relations. The parties reversed roles as the United States emerged as an industrialized society early in the twentieth century. Millions of factory workers, many of them European immigrants, identified with the Democratic Party. They became a force to be reckoned with by joining labor unions and demanding protections against foreign competition. Republicans, increasingly drawing their strength from affluent white-collar workers and corporations, adopted the cause of free markets and globalization.

---

5. This measure raised the average tax on imports from 39 to 53 percent of their value. Other countries retaliated with higher tariffs of their own, prompting the volume of global exports to plummet from $5.2 billion in 1929 to $1.6 billion in 1932. Unemployment in the United States soared, peaking at 32 percent in 1932, or affecting nearly one in every three workers (Rothgeb 2001, 38–39).

These alignments solidified late in the twentieth century with the expansion of the Republican power base across the southern and interior western states. Republicans also established voting blocs in the sprawling suburban areas surrounding major cities. The political power of Democrats was concentrated in the Northeast and Pacific Coast states and in the inner cities. Unfortunately for the Democratic Party, the clout of labor unions began to fade as factories closed in large numbers, either moving to nonunionized southern states, exporting their jobs to low-cost labor markets abroad, or shutting down entirely.

Free marketers remained dominant in the executive branch until economic growth stagnated in the 1970s. Japan's rapid rise as the second largest world economy during this period was fueled by neo-mercantilist government policies, including high tariffs and nontariff barriers (NTBs) such as industry subsidies, import quotas, and health and safety regulations that effectively shut out foreign products. Japanese car manufacturers such as Toyota and Honda captured much of the U.S. market share by producing fuel-efficient, reliable, and relatively inexpensive vehicles that were in high demand as gasoline prices soared. Despite this challenge, automakers in the United States continued to produce larger, gas-guzzling vehicles.

Heightened trade competition in the 1970s prompted Congress to provide **fast-track authority** to presidents negotiating trade agreements with foreign governments. Congress first granted President Gerald R. Ford this authority with the Trade Reform Act of 1974; legislators renewed this fast-track authority on five occasions during the next three decades. Under these provisions, the relevant committees were given no more than forty-five days to review trade agreements once the president submitted them. The House and Senate then had fifteen days to approve or reject the deals without amendments. In granting this authority, legislators acknowledged once again that the president could better resist interest-group pressures for trade restrictions (Destler 1995; and O'Halloran 1993).

The 1974 trade legislation also elevated the role of the U.S. trade representative (USTR), who gained cabinet rank and permanent legal standing (Dryden 1995). While acting on behalf of national interests, the USTR remains sensitive to congressional concerns, well aware that the legislative branch retains the ultimate power to reject trade agreements (Zoellick 1999–2000). The 1974 trade act created the International Trade Commission as well, a quasi-judicial federal agency charged with handling grievances by domestic firms claiming to be harmed by unfair foreign trade competition.

While strengthening the U.S. government's hand in trade policy, these measures did not slow the pace of U.S. imports from Japan, which increased by more than 500 percent between 1970 and 1980 (Lincoln 1990). Japanese leaders during this period refined the art of **industrial policy,** which combined the protectionist tactics described above with a close working relationship between government agencies, corporate boards, and financial institutions (see Johnson 1982). Japanese industrial workers and their employers established a high degree of solidarity as workers were allowed more input into production methods and greater job security than American factory workers.

As plants closed across the United States, eliminating the jobs of millions of U.S. workers, the free-trade consensus quickly gave way to "a recurring suspicion that free trade is not necessarily desirable at all costs" (Gibson 2000, 114). Appeals for relief were directed largely to Congress, which responded in the 1980s and 1990s by passing several bills designed to stabilize the U.S. trade balance. The Omnibus Trade and Competitiveness Act of 1988 required presidents to identify the most serious violators of free trade and propose steps to retaliate against them. Under pressure from Congress, U.S. trade negotiators sought—and frequently gained—concessions from foreign countries to lower barriers to trade. These trading partners agreed to **voluntary export restraints** that satisfied American demands for market access without forcing the U.S. government to impose formal trade sanctions or jeopardize cordial relations in other areas.

The polarized politics of the Clinton years extended to the trade realm, rupturing the division of labor between the executive and legislative branches that had been in place for two decades. Republicans in Congress, having gained majority power in both chambers in 1994, joined with labor-backed Democrats in denying Clinton the fast-track authority granted his predecessors. The two groups did so for very different reasons. Democrats were concerned that the president would not protect U.S. jobs in his pursuit of economic globalization. Some Republicans feared that Clinton would surrender too much power over U.S. trade to the WTO; others simply wanted to embarrass the president by tying his hands on the foreign-policy issue most important to him.

As we have seen, trade policy is a key battleground in the ongoing tug of war between Congress and presidents over U.S. foreign policy. The free-trade consensus that prevailed during the cold war has given way to the partisan rivalries that have infused other areas of U.S. foreign policy. In this environment, the balance of power between the parties in Congress, as well as that between the White House and Capitol Hill, will significantly affect U.S. foreign-economic policy in the future (see Shoch 2001). The shape of these policies will further reflect the growing pressures facing the United States from the European Union, East Asian states, and the developing countries that have formed a defiant bloc within the WTO.

National Interests and Foreign Aid

Another major component of U.S. foreign-economic policy involves **foreign aid,** or economic resources provided by affluent governments to less-developed countries (LDCs) on terms unavailable to the recipients on commercial markets. The United States provides funds to LDCs directly, in the form of bilateral aid, or through multilateral channels such as the World Bank.

Foreign aid is a common element of world politics today, as nearly every country serves either as an aid donor or recipient. The high levels of poverty that continue to inflict much of the world make this global aid network a necessity. As of 2002, more than 80 percent of the people in the world lived in low- or middle-income countries, where they produced less than 20 percent of global wealth (World Bank 2004b). While many parts of the world experienced unprecedented prosperity during the globalization boom of the 1990s, the gap between the richest and poorest peoples widened as the new millennium began.

The United States, which provided the largest volume of foreign assistance during the cold war, continues to maintain that status today. Its $13.3-billion contribution of development aid in 2002 was nearly 50 percent larger than the contribution of Japan, the second largest aid donor, a gap that continues today (OECD 2004). The United States, however, ranks at the bottom of industrialized countries in terms of the proportion of U.S. national output being devoted to foreign aid (see Figure 11.2). As a result, the world's most prolific aid donor is also widely considered its biggest *miser.*

Although foreign aid represents less than 1 percent of the U.S. federal budget, this highly controversial program generates strong opposition from many political leaders and private citizens. As John D. Montgomery (1962, 197) observed more than four decades ago, "In few areas of American public life is there so little national consensus on purposes as in foreign aid." This public disdain for foreign assistance continued through the end of the cold war. As legislators knew then and still realize, "It is the program their constituents most want to see cut" (Obey and Lancaster 1988, 146).

Critics of foreign aid make three central arguments: domestic needs should be taken care of first, aid funds only reward incompetence and corruption abroad,

Figure 11.2 Levels of Sacrifice among Major Aid Donors, 2002

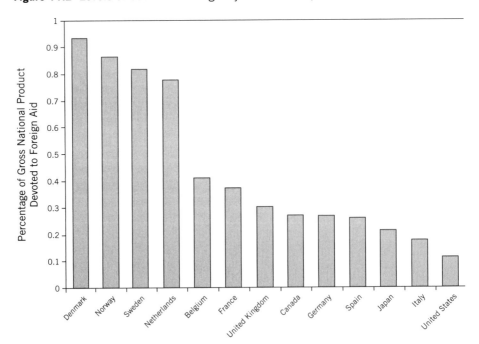

SOURCE: World Bank, *World Development Indicators* (New York: Oxford University Press, 2004).
NOTE: Figures limited to donors of at least $1 billion in development assistance.

and past programs have not prevented the developing world from slipping further into poverty and social distress. A fourth, related, argument is that the private agencies delivering most aid-funded programs place their institutional interests above the interests of the starving and war-torn societies they serve (Maren 1997). Trade, not aid, should be the developing countries' vehicle for economic growth in this view. Supporters of foreign aid, while acknowledging the failure of past aid programs to stem the poverty of LDCs, believe more effective and well-coordinated programs can create the conditions for long-term growth throughout the world. A world without foreign aid, they further argue, would leave much of the world without hope of economic progress.

Motivations for U.S. Aid

Tensions have always existed between the humanitarian and self-serving functions of U.S. foreign aid. At one level, generosity by the United States toward impoverished peoples is consistent with its historic self-image as a messianic "city on the hill." At another level, U.S. aid contradicts the self-help principles of many Americans as reflected in their historic distrust of government and their skepticism toward social-welfare programs. To garner support for foreign aid from a skeptical public, the U.S. government has consistently identified national interests as a primary rationale for aid programs. After the cold war, the U.S. Agency for International Development (USAID 1992, 1) issued a report entitled *Why Foreign Aid?* The agency answered this question bluntly: "Because it is in the United States' own interest."

As a reluctant but leading contributor of foreign aid on an absolute level, the United States closely ties its aid contributions to the pursuit of its own prosperity and military security. This linkage between self-interests and the needs of aid recipients is not unique to the United States. Japan, for example, has routinely used foreign aid as an instrument to expand its trade ties across East Asia, while France and Great Britain have used aid as means to retain influence within their former African colonies (Hook 1995). All aid donors, meanwhile, expect a certain degree of political allegiance from their recipients. These patterns were evident four decades ago to the political economist David Baldwin (1966, 3), who observed,

> [F]oreign aid is first and foremost a technique of statecraft. It is, in other words, a means by which one nation tries to get other nations to act in desired ways. . . . Thus, foreign aid policy is foreign policy, and as such it is a subject of controversy in both the international and the domestic political arenas.

Prior to the cold war, U.S. foreign aid generally "consisted of admonition and was consequently neither expensive nor effective" (O'Leary 1967, 5). Examples of early U.S. initiatives included security assistance to Greece in the 1820s and disaster aid for victims of Ireland's famine in the 1840s. In the early stages of World War II, U.S. military hardware to Great Britain bolstered the allied defense against Nazi Germany. Not until after the war did the U.S. aid program assume global proportions. Through the Marshall Plan, the United States helped rebuild decimated states in Western Europe and Asia.[6] And through the military aid programs derived from the Truman Doctrine, the United States utilized a second form of foreign assistance in the pursuit of its foreign-policy goals.

Two motivations propelled U.S. foreign aid during this period. First, aid flows were designed to strengthen anticommunist regimes throughout the world and ultimately to tip the balance of world power in favor of the capitalist states. Second, the United States sought to help emerging nation-states it hoped would become allies. The cold war coincided with the decolonization of Africa and the creation of new nation-states in other developing regions, such as India in South Asia and the Philippines and Indonesia in the Pacific region. These new states faced many obstacles on the path to political and economic development, obstacles they could not overcome without external assistance.

In this respect, the East-West struggle of the cold war intersected with emerging North-South tensions, or those between wealthy, industrialized countries (primarily located in the Northern Hemisphere) and the poor nations of the developing world (primarily in the Southern Hemisphere). The United States had strong interests along *both* dimensions: in defeating the communist powers, in the first case; and in creating allies and potential trading partners among the LDCs, in the second. Through foreign aid, the United States supported almost every country outside of the Soviet Union's sphere of influence. By 1990, the U.S. government had transferred $374 billion in loans and grants to more than 100 LDCs, $233 billion in the form of economic assistance (USAID 1992).

Whereas early U.S. aid efforts in the post–World War II period focused on the reconstruction of industrialized states and the establishment of a global alliance of anticommunist states, beginning in the 1960s U.S. economic assistance emphasized the social and economic aspects of decolonization and "state-building" as well (see Packenham 1973). President John Kennedy redirected U.S. aid toward broader developmental goals. He supported the Foreign Assistance Act of 1961, the Alliance for Progress, the Peace Corps, and other initiatives aimed at promoting political and socioeconomic development in LDCs, particularly in Latin America. However, the United States largely discarded these goals as it became mired in the Vietnam War, which claimed nearly one-half of all U.S. aid flows until the mid-1970s.

President Carter hoped to revive the humanitarian elements of U.S. foreign aid, but other strategic concerns overtook his aid plans. The Camp David Accords involving Israel and Egypt, although a major foreign-policy achievement, came at a huge price tag: about $5 billion annually in foreign aid to the two countries. These commitments overwhelmed the U.S. aid budget, reducing funds available

---

6. The Marshall Plan is widely regarded as one of the most successful efforts in the history of U.S. foreign policy. To Samuel P. Huntington (1970–1971) this was because the Marshall Plan was "(a) directed to specific and well-defined goals; (b) limited to a geographic area of vital concern to the U.S.; and (c) designed for a limited period of time."

IN THEIR OWN WORDS: JESSE HELMS

When Sen. Jesse Helms, R-N.C., retired from the Senate in 2003, Congress lost its most vocal critic of U.S. foreign aid. Helms, who chaired the Foreign Relations Committee for six years, frequently ridiculed foreign aid as a "rathole" of wasted government spending. He sought, without success, to abolish the U.S. Agency for International Development, the government's primary aid agency. Before his retirement, Helms proposed that U.S. foreign aid be provided not to governments abroad, but to private, "faith-based" organizations that would deliver aid to poor people. Helms laid out his proposal in a January 2001 speech to the American Enterprise Institute, a conservative think tank based in Washington, D.C.

Too often . . . faith-based charities are dismissed by the U.S. foreign aid bureaucracy. The bureaucrats treat them as if the efforts of these faith-based charities are quaint but unworthy of government support. . . .

We must—I repeat, we *must*—reform the way America helps those in need (not only at home but abroad as well). We must *replace* the bureaucracy-laden U.S. Agency for International Development with something new.

I intend to work with the Bush administration to replace AID with a *new* International Development Foundation whose mandate is to deliver "block grants" to support the work of private relief agencies and faith-based institutions such as Samaritan's Purse, Catholic Relief Services, and countless others like them.

We will reduce the size of America's bloated foreign aid bureaucracy—then take the money saved and use *every penny* of it to empower these "armies of compassion" to help the world's neediest people.

Those who know me are aware that I have long opposed foreign aid programs that have lined the pockets of corrupt dictators, while funding the salaries of a growing, bloated bureaucracy. And I remain adamantly opposed to waste, fraud and abuse in foreign aid.

Source: Jesse Helms, chairman, Senate Foreign Relations Committee, "Towards a Compassionate Conservative Foreign Policy" (speech, American Enterprise Institute, Washington, D.C., January 11, 2001), www.aei.org/news/newsID.17927/news _detail.asp.

for other regions and development priorities. Strategic concerns prevailed during the 1980s as well. The Reagan administration used foreign aid, along with steep increases in defense spending, to support anticommunist regimes and thus increase pressure on the Soviet Union in the revived cold war.

The demise of the cold war deprived many bilateral aid programs—and U.S. foreign policy in general—of their previously stated rationales. The absence of the containment of communism as the guiding principle behind U.S. policy raised new doubts about many established programs while the needs of the former Soviet

Union and its Eastern European clients imposed new demands on limited aid funds. Bill Clinton's efforts to direct funds toward "sustainable development" and democracy in the developing world fell victim to deep cuts imposed by Congress. Not until after the September 2001 terrorist attacks did the government revive its aid program as President Bush sought to reward allies in the war on terrorism with economic and military assistance and to reward LDCs that followed the U.S. model of economic and political development.

Recent Patterns in Aid Flows

Like his predecessors, President Bush came into office with his own agenda for U.S. foreign aid. Skeptical of past programs, Bush demanded that future recipients be "accountable" for the money received from Washington. Aid recipients, in his view, should establish democratic governments and market economies freed from government intervention at home and barriers to foreign trade. After the terrorist attacks, Bush identified international development as one of the three "pillars" of his national-security strategy, along with diplomacy and defense. A policy paper released by USAID (2004, 14) called for "far-reaching reforms . . . that [would] enable a country to sustain further economic and social progress without depending on foreign aid."

Funding the reconstruction of Iraq quickly emerged as the primary U.S. foreign aid expenditure in 2004.[7] In that year alone, a U.S.-occupied Iraq received $18.4 billion in aid, far more than the $2.6 billion provided to the second largest recipient, Israel. The emergence of Iraq as a top aid recipient in 2003 demonstrated how aid flows follow the foreign-policy priorities of different administrations. A comparison of the top ten recipients over the past three decades illustrates this linkage between U.S. national interests and its foreign-aid program (see Table 11.3). Despite the differences in aid distributions over these years, one pattern has remained consistent: significant U.S. aid to the Middle East and southern Asia. This pattern reveals the enduring importance of these regions to the United States, in stark contrast to the more impoverished but less strategically vital states of sub-Saharan Africa.

During the first years of the new millennium, the U.S. government provided some form of foreign aid to about 150 governments, nearly three-fourths of all countries in the world. The $21 billion in 2004 overall aid spending (including programs beyond economic development) represented a major increase from past years. Yet the share of U.S. economic output devoted to foreign aid remained at the lowest level of all industrialized countries. As a percentage of the U.S. government's discretionary budget authority, the 2004 level of 2.4 percent was the second lowest ever. Thus the United States, while remaining the world's biggest aid spender in absolute terms, also remained among the stingiest spenders when the degree of national sacrifice is taken into account.

---

7. The statistics used in this section are derived from Curt Tarnoff and Larry Nowels (2004).

Table 11.3 Top Recipients of U.S. Economic Aid, 1981–2002

1981–1982	1991–1992	2001–2002
1. Egypt	1. Egypt	1. Egypt
2. Israel	2. Israel	2. Pakistan
3. Turkey	3. Nicaragua	3. Serbia and Montenegro
4. India	4. Jamaica	4. Colombia
5. Bangladesh	5. Bolivia	5. Jordan
6. Northern Marianas	6. Honduras	6. Peru
7. El Salvador	7. Bangladesh	7. Afghanistan
8. Pakistan	8. Philippines	8. Indonesia
9. Indonesia	9. El Salvador	9. Honduras
10. Sudan	10. Iraq	10. India

SOURCE: Organization for Economic Cooperation and Development, *Development Co-Operation Report: Efforts and Policies of the Members of the Development Assistance Committee* (Paris: OECD, 2004), 216.

The U.S. government's spending on foreign aid falls into five functional categories:

- development assistance, or state-to-state transfers designed to hasten recipients' long-term economic growth ($6.2 billion in FY 2004)

- economic-support assistance, or financial aid to countries of political and security interest ($5.4 billion)

- military assistance, including military supplies and training ($4.8 billion)

- humanitarian relief, to nations under acute stress ($2.6 billion)

- multilateral aid, to UN agencies, the World Bank, and similar international organizations ($1.7 billion).

Other donors, whose aid programs are coordinated by the Organisation for Economic Co-operation and Development (OECD), closely monitor the U.S. government's aid policies. During the 1970s, the OECD, based in Paris, set a standard for aid contributions, suggesting that all donors should devote at least 0.7 percent of national output to official development assistance (ODA). Only five countries—Denmark, Luxembourg, the Netherlands, Norway, and Sweden—reached this level in 2002 (OECD 2004). Yet it is the failure of the United States to meet that standard—its level bottomed out at 0.1 percent in 2000 before reaching 0.13 percent in 2003—that has proved a chronic source of discord within the OECD. As noted earlier, the U.S. government defends its record on several grounds: the United States spends the most on an *absolute* level, its large military budget provides an indirect source of assistance to U.S. allies, and the United States has no peer in promoting global economic growth through the consumption of goods and services from other countries.

The Millennium Challenge Account

A central element of President Bush's foreign-aid policy involved a new program, the Millennium Challenge Account (MCA), designed to reward developing countries that adopted the U.S. government's model of market democracy. In 2002, the president pledged $10 billion in foreign aid by 2006 to a limited number of countries, which would presumably serve as role models for other impoverished states to follow. Sixteen countries were identified in 2004 as the first recipients of MCA funds.[8] According to the White House, the governments of all these countries had fulfilled the three requirements of the new program: the protection of economic freedom, "good governance," and sound investments in the health and education of their citizens.

Despite the White House's high expectations for the MCA, members of Congress proved less than enthusiastic during the appropriations process. The funding originally approved for the program's first year amounted to $650 million, well below the administration's request of $1.7 billion. The Bush administration increased the available funding to $1 billion by shifting money to the MCA from other international programs. The resistance from Congress raised doubts that White House requests for $2.5 and $5 billion in the following two years would be approved at these levels. Similar concerns were raised about the Bush administration's five-year, $15-billion HIV/AIDS initiative, whose approved funding of $1.4 billion in 2004 was less than half the amount needed annually to reach the president's target (Tarnoff and Nowels 2004, 10).

A central critique of the MCA is that it targets only a small portion of the developing world (Radelet 2003). Resources are primarily concentrated among Honduras (population 7 million in 2002), Mongolia (2 million), and Cape Verde (458,000) while none are directed toward the widespread poverty found among India's 1 billion inhabitants. More broadly, the heated debates over these programs and resistance from Congress reflect foreign aid's uncertain status as a tool of U.S. foreign-economic policy. The greatest challenge to foreign aid, however, stems from a generally held belief that the United States can best stimulate economic growth in developing areas not by government programs, but by allowing the global marketplace to thrive.

The Foreign Investment Fix

The 1990s witnessed a turning point in capital flows from rich to poor countries. While the volume of foreign aid declined during this period, *private* capital flows grew rapidly and exceeded government transfers. In 1990, private investments, either in new enterprises or in the stocks and bonds of existing firms, accounted for about one-third of all capital flows to developing countries. By the late 1990s, these investments composed three-fourths of the cash flows from North to South

---

8. The group of sixteen comprised Armenia, Benin, Bolivia, Cape Verde, Georgia, Ghana, Honduras, Lesotho, Madagascar, Mali, Mongolia, Mozambique, Nicaragua, Senegal, Sri Lanka, and Vanatu.

(OECD 1998). As Ajay Chhibber and Monsoor Dailami (1990, 1) of the World Bank observed, "It is now widely accepted that expansion of private investment should be the main impetus for economic growth, allowing public investment resources gradually to focus on social areas, including alleviation of poverty and the upgrading of social capital and resources."

Private investments are more volatile than most foreign-aid flows and more prone to abrupt swings that affect the economic growth of individual states and the global market (see Kahler 1998). Whereas the rapid expansion in FDI flows in the mid-1990s fueled the worldwide economic boom, equally abrupt cutbacks in them contributed to the slump in the global economy at the turn of the century. The net flow of private capital to developing countries, which averaged $30 billion in 1991–1992, reached $116 billion in 1999 before plummeting to less than $19 billion by 2002 (OECD 2004, 136–137).

This reversal of fortunes was particularly acute in East Asia, whose economic "miracle" in the 1990s was "largely due to superior accumulation of physical and human capital" (World Bank 1993, 5). East Asia, which accounted for about half of all FDI inflows during the decade, suffered from **capital flight,** the large-scale withdrawal of private funds from domestic industries and stock markets. The sudden outflow of foreign investment prompted the IMF to provide more than $100 billion in relief to Indonesia, South Korea, and Thailand in 1997. The IMF's effort to prevent "contagion" effects from damaging the world economy proved unsuccessful; the regional crisis spurred a global recession that lasted for several years.

Rapid swings in global investments make long-term economic planning difficult. This proves especially true in the developing world, which is highly dependent upon external funding whether in the form of private investment or foreign aid. Although FDI provides new opportunities for poor countries to escape from their plight, there are no guarantees the money will last beyond the next financial setback. This reality makes skeptics of FDI long for the days before the pattern of smaller, but more stable capital flows was replaced by "a private non-system driven by roller-coaster shifts in focus and manias of the collective herd of global financial investors" (Solomon 1995).

As for the United States, long the primary *destination* of FDI, the volatility of private-investment flows has had adverse effects on its economy, too. As noted earlier, inflows of private investment fell by more than 90 percent between 2000 and 2002 (OECD 2003). The United States became a net "exporter" of investment capital in 2002, reinforcing complaints by trade unions that American jobs were being exported abroad. Financial analysts attributed the drop in private investments to the "unsettled international political and security environment" resulting from the war on terrorism (OECD 2003, 1).

Economic Sanctions as a Policy Tool

The final element of foreign-economic policy explored in this chapter involves **economic sanctions**—material penalties imposed on target countries that involve trade, aid, investments, or other aspects of foreign economic relations. Presidents may impose sanctions by executive order, or sanctions may originate in congressional legislation. The U.S. government seeks to use its economic leverage in these cases to modify the behavior of foreign countries in ways consistent with U.S. foreign-policy objectives.

Economic sanctions are an attractive foreign-policy tool because they provide the United States with a means to exert pressure on foreign governments without resorting to war against them. In this sense, sanctions "send a signal" to their targets that the U.S. government is serious about the dispute in question. Sanctions play a strategic role when they are backed up by promises of military action in the event the sanctions do not produce the necessary changes in behavior. More generally, sanctions serve a symbolic function by identifying the target state and establishing the moral supremacy of the "sanctioning community" (Addis 2003).

Forms and Functions of Sanctions

Economic sanctions can assume several forms and governments often use them in combination with one another (see Table 11.4). The most common types of sanctions include trade embargoes and boycotts, increases in export quotas, withdrawal of most-favored-nation status, and other measures that restrict bilateral trade. While all these measures are *negative* in nature, involving the "stick" of economic penalties, the United States can also employ the "carrot" of *positive* sanctions, such as potential increases in foreign aid or trade, to modify the behavior of other governments (Baldwin 1985, 40–44).

Economic sanctions vary in other ways. In some instances, the United States joins with other countries or intergovernmental organizations or both to impose *multilateral* sanctions. This was the case with the former Yugoslavia and Iraq in the 1990s; sanctions imposed by the United Nations globally isolated their economies. Otherwise the United States acts alone in imposing *unilateral* sanctions. Though other countries may act independently to impose their own sanc-

Table 11.4 Types and Examples of U.S. Economic Sanctions

Type	Description	Historical Example
Boycott	Restriction on the import of another country's goods or services	Ban on diamond imports from Sierra Leone, used to finance domestic insurrection (2001)
Divestment	Withdrawal of assets from a foreign country, ban on future investments	Ban on investments in South Africa to penalize its apartheid policy of minority rule (1986)
Embargo	Refusal to provide one's own goods and services to a potential customer abroad	Grain embargo against the Soviet Union following its invasion of Afghanistan (1979)
Freezing of assets	Impoundment of domestically held financial assets owned by government or citizens of target country	Freezing of Iraqi assets in the United States following Iraq's invasion of Kuwait (1990)
Suspension of foreign aid	Refusal to honor previous commitments to provide economic or military assistance	Aid to Pakistan suspended due to concerns about its nuclear ambitions (1977)

tions against the offending state, there is no concerted effort to do so in these cases. Finally, sanctions may have very specific demands—that a country withdraw from a country it recently invaded, for example. Or the sanctions may involve broader demands, as when the imposing state insists on a change in the policies, or even the regime type, of the offending state.

This latter case applied to the cold war, during which economic sanctions served as one of the most potent weapons used by the United States against the Soviet Union. American officials imposed strict restrictions on commercial relations with Moscow, and they expected their allies to do the same. As the cold war thawed, these allies resumed trade across the Iron Curtain, though at a lower level than before the conflict began. The United States itself had temporarily eased sanctions against Moscow as part of the Nixon administration's **linkage strategy,** which tied a promise of future economic concessions to improved Soviet behavior on human rights and key foreign-policy issues.

Prominent Cases of U.S. Sanctions

The Soviet Union hardly stood alone as a target of U.S. economic sanctions during the cold war, as the examples noted in Table 11.4 demonstrate. After the cold war, the common use of sanctions continued, often preceding U.S. military actions against a nation, such as Iraq and the former Yugoslavia. In many other instances, such as that involving Pakistan, threats of sanctions became a routine part of bilateral diplomacy both during and after the cold war.

Cuba. Fidel Castro's rise to power in 1959 and his creation of a communist government in Cuba, formerly a close U.S. economic and military ally, prompted sweeping economic sanctions by the United States. The Trading with the Enemy Act of 1963 prohibited nearly all trade with the Castro regime. The penalties for breaking these laws were substantial: up to ten years in prison, $1 million in corporate fines, and $250,000 in individual fines. The **Helms-Burton Act,** passed by Congress in the 1990s, imposed even stronger penalties. The act targeted foreign countries benefiting economically from confiscated U.S. property in Cuba. These measures, politically popular in Congress and the White House, still incited criticism that they had done little to weaken Castro's hold on power after nearly half a century. In addition, countries accused the United States of maintaining a double standard, isolating Cuba while economically "engaging" China, another communist state.

Pakistan. The case of Pakistan reveals that, in some instances, the U.S. government must be careful not to alienate less affluent but strategically vital LDCs (see Kux 1998). Fears of nuclear proliferation in South Asia prompted the Carter administration to suspend aid deliveries to Pakistan in 1977. The Soviet invasion of Afghanistan later that year, however, changed the strategic calculus and prompted Ronald Reagan to renew aid to Pakistan in 1981. This aid stopped once the Soviets withdrew from Afghanistan in 1989. Pakistan's explosion of a nuclear device in

1998 prompted the United States and other UN members to impose additional sanctions against Pakistan as well as against India, whose nuclear-weapons test provoked the Pakistani response. The terrorist attacks of September 2001 elevated Pakistan once again to the status of a U.S. "strategic partner." The Bush administration lifted the sanctions shortly after 9-11 while providing millions of dollars worth of military equipment and training to President Pervez Musharraf.

Iraq. The UN-sponsored sanctions against Iraq, which were imposed from Saddam Hussein's invasion of Kuwait in 1990 until the U.S.-led invasion of Iraq in 2003, remain the subject of bitter controversy. President George H. W. Bush first acted by declaring a national emergency and issuing an executive order forbidding future trade with Iraq. To later critics, these sanctions against Iraq became "one of the decade's great crimes" (Rieff 2003, 41). The denial of aid eventually led to the deaths of hundreds of thousands of Iraqi civilians from malnutrition and disease. Critics of the sanctions found the scope of these casualties especially troubling because Saddam Hussein and his advisers continued to enjoy lavish lifestyles, clearly undisturbed by the sanctions. The UN's Oil-for-Food Program, established in April 1995, eased the crisis somewhat but failed to dislodge Saddam from power or gain concessions from him.

Libyan leader Muammar Qaddafi, attending an Arab League summit in 2004, overcame hostile relations with the United States earlier in the year by renouncing plans to develop weapons of mass destruction in his North African country. In easing U.S. economic sanctions against Libya, President Bush viewed the friendlier bilateral relationship as evidence that the war on terrorism was gaining ground. The eased sanctions permitted closer ties between U.S. oil firms and Libya, a possible new source of U.S. oil imports. Qaddafi was earlier considered a leading global terrorist and enemy of the United States.

Libya. While *lifting* economic sanctions attracts less attention than imposing them, both steps are equally significant to U.S. foreign policy. This was the case in April 2004, when the Bush administration lifted many of the sanctions against Libya that had been in effect for nearly a decade. The White House praised Muammar Qaddafi, Libya's leader, for dismantling the nation's WMD facilities and renouncing terrorism. The move represented a major reversal for the United States. It had previously linked Qaddafi to a variety of terrorist attacks, including the December 1988 bombing of Pan Am Flight 103 over Lockerbie, Scotland, that killed 259 people. President Bush cited the transformation of Qaddafi from state terrorist to trading partner as evidence that the U.S. war on terrorism was bearing fruit. In making its concessions to U.S. demands, including financial restitution to the families of the Lockerbie victims, Libya was also freed from UN sanctions.

Taken together, these and other instances of economic sanctions provide four key lessons regarding the utility of these measures as instruments of U.S. foreign policy. First, economic sanctions rarely have the immediate impact their advocates desire—the collapse of Cuba's communist government, for example, or Saddam Hussein's withdrawal from Kuwait. Second, the leaders of targeted states rarely suffer directly from sanctions, which instead tend to victimize citizens with little political power. Even **smart sanctions,** designed to punish elites rather than their most vulnerable citizens, have limited effect (Tostensen and Bull 2002; Cortright and Lopez 2002; and Heine-Ellison 2001).

Third, multilateral sanctions have a greater probability of succeeding than unilateral measures. When the United States acts alone, its targets can readily turn to other trading partners to fill the gap (see Haass 1998). Finally, the costs and benefits of economic sanctions are notoriously difficult to measure. They cannot be simply calculated with reference to reductions in trade and investment volumes (the "costs") or to the response by targeted states to the demands posed by sanctioning states (the "benefits"). A complete assessment must take into account indirect costs and benefits, including the symbolic value of placing offending states on notice, as well as the relative value of alternative foreign-policy tactics that would be employed in the absence of sanctions (Baldwin 1999–2000).

Conclusion

As this chapter has shown, the U.S. government pursues commerce abroad with the same vigor it promotes economic development within its borders. American leaders have always looked forward to a world whose people and governments will be intimately connected to one another by the bonds of trade and foreign investments. They have envisioned the United States as a catalyst of global commerce by producing an abundance of goods for export while craving goods from abroad and stimulating foreign economies. This vision appeared to be realized with the victory of the United States in the cold war and the triumph of capitalism over communism as the superior form of political economy.

The globalization boom of the 1990s encouraged this sense of euphoria. Yet the process left much of the world behind, and the "contagion" effects of the East Asian economic crisis revealed the darker sides of globalization (see Broad 2002). Stunted economic growth in the former Soviet bloc and Latin America eventually prompted government officials in both regions to turn away from liberal reforms. The creation of regional trading blocs, meanwhile, stimulated greater commerce within the blocs while ensuring trade rivalries between them.

The United States itself has suffered the side effects of globalization as millions of manufacturing jobs have moved to overseas countries with lower wage rates. The chronic trade deficits still being experienced today provide further evidence that globalization is a mixed blessing for the United States. Another cause for concern are the nation's budget deficits, a result, in part, of the security costs borne by the United States to keep the peace globally and oil flowing to other industrialized countries.

For now, the United States retains its status as the "engine" of global economic activity. This status, however, relies upon the seemingly limitless appetite of American consumers for goods and services produced in other countries. Their desire for products at the lowest possible price, epitomized by the emergence of Wal-Mart as the world's largest company in terms of revenue, is entirely consistent with the borderless logic of capitalism. Nevertheless, the reality persists that jobs must be found for American workers to replace those exported every year. As laid-off factory workers well know, service-industry jobs at Blockbuster and Starbucks do not pay nearly as well as those on the assembly line. Unfortunately, such jobs in heavy industries are not likely to return in large numbers, and government support for retraining and college educations has become less available due to cutbacks in state and federal budgets.

In considering the future course of U.S. foreign-economic policy, one must consider the constantly shifting balances of global and domestic power. New centers of production will sustain the momentum toward a multipolar world economy, with the United States, the EU, East Asian states, and emerging markets such as India claiming significant shares of global output. Technological advances, including Internet connections that now extend to all corners of the world, will reinforce this trend toward the diffusion of wealth and production.

Growing challenges from overseas, however consistent with the transnational logic of capitalism, may ignite pressures at home to resurrect trade barriers in order to prevent the further hemorrhaging of American jobs. Political leaders know their careers depend on economic growth that benefits a broad cross-section of the U.S. population, not simply corporate leaders and stockholders. Despite a decline of union membership in the United States, from its high of 20 percent of the U.S. workforce in 1983 to less than 13 percent in 2003, "big labor" still provides a strong voice for economic nationalism (U.S. Department of Labor 2004).

Avoiding a return to protectionism and trade wars requires effective restructuring of the U.S. economy and the revival of worldwide demand in such vital areas as East Asia, Russia, and Latin America. As globalization inevitably spreads, the U.S. government loses the considerable leverage it enjoyed during its peak years of economic hegemony just after World War II. The nation must now contend with other states, as well as foreign-based corporations, on a more equal footing. In short, the United States must contend with the globalized world economy it strenuously worked to create. As in the past, the outcome of the ongoing economic struggles over U.S. foreign-economic policy will be decided in the political arena, at home and abroad.

Key Terms

balance of trade, p. 335

capital flight, p. 353

comparative advantage, p. 342

economic liberalism, p. 332

economic nationalism, p. 333

economic sanctions, p. 353

fast-track authority, p. 344

floating exchange rates, p. 340

foreign aid, p. 345

foreign direct investment (FDI), p. 335

gold standard, p. 340

gross national income, p. 334

Helms-Burton Act, p. 355

industrial policy, p. 344

international political economy, p. 331

linkage strategy, p. 355

most-favored-nation trading status, p. 340

political economy, p. 330

smart sanctions, p. 357

Smoot-Hawley Tariff Act, p. 343

socialism, p. 332

Uruguay Round, p. 341

voluntary export restraints, p. 345

Internet References

The **Economic Policy Institute** (www.epinet.org) conducts research on global trade, globalization, NAFTA, and China-U.S. relations, among other economic and budgetary policies. The EPI's Web site provides statistics and policy reports on research topics including free trade, U.S. agricultural/commercial relations, fast-track powers, and other trade and globalization issues.

The **Institute for International Economics** (www.iie.com) is a nonprofit, nonpartisan research center focused on international economic policy. In addition to providing statistics and information regarding globalization, U.S. economic policy, debt, international trade, and international investment, IIE's Web site includes policy briefs, speeches, working papers, information on its books, and links to similar topics.

The **International Monetary Fund** (www.imf.org) is a 184-member international organization focusing on international monetary cooperation, financial stability, and temporary financial assistance to needy countries. The IMF's Web site provides fact sheets on lending, country statistics, helpful glossaries of financial terms, and links to other banks and international organizations.

The **International Political Economy Network** (www.isanet.org/sections/ipe/) is hosted through the IPE section of the International Studies Association, a professional organization for political scientists focusing on issues related to global politics. This Web site, which includes links to journals, books, think tanks, organizations, book reviews, and announcements, is a helpful research tool for those interested in studying international political economy.

The **International Trade Administration** (www.ita.doc.gov) is a government agency committed to providing U.S. export and import data. The ITA's Web site includes data on export growth and market expansion and information on national and state trade levels, balances, sectors, and regions.

continues

Internet References *(continued)*

The home page of the **Office of the United States Trade Representative** (www.ustr.gov) provides links and access to bilateral and multilateral trade data and events. Information on the site regarding NAFTA, the WTO, and free-trade negotiations, in addition to speeches, testimony, trade legislation, and daily updates regarding international trade, are particularly helpful for research.

The **Organisation for Economic Co-operation and Development** (www.oecd.org) is an international body that promotes stability and growth—economic, democratic, and social—around the globe. The primary mission of the OECD is to promote capital markets and democratic growth by focusing on trade and aid development issues. OECD's Web site includes extensive statistical data on trade, aid, and economic growth, as well as publications discussing specific foreign economic missions.

The **United States Agency for International Development** (www.usaid.gov) provides information and statistics regarding U.S. foreign and military aid to other countries. USAID's Web site includes detailed information regarding humanitarian efforts and specific mission programs to other countries. Other research topics on the site are agriculture, democratization, global health, and humanitarian mission projects. A full database of U.S. foreign aid is available for all years of allocation.

The mission of the **World Bank** (www.worldbank.org) is to reduce poverty and economic disparities by providing loans and financial assistance to countries around the globe. The World Bank site discusses the bank's specific projects and missions as well as providing statistics on trade, aid, poverty, and other demographic issues.

The **World Trade Organization** (www.wto.org) is an international organization that promotes open trade relations among countries. The WTO Web site includes information regarding trade regulations, industry and business sector descriptions, currency and trade statistics, and annual growth reports.

12

Transnational Policy Problems

Members of the Yanomami tribe in Brazil gather in their hut after burning and clearing a part of the Amazon rain forest to make way for a farm. Much of the rain forest, which is larger than Western Europe and is critical to the global environment, has been destroyed in recent years. The United States, along with other countries, is likely to suffer the consequences of massive deforestation in Brazil and elsewhere. But solving the problems that confront the "global commons" is impossible without cooperation and shared sacrifice among governments, including the United States.

The United States manages a variety of foreign-policy problems that extend beyond national defense and the pursuit of gains in the global economy. Transnational policy problems, which do not respect political boundaries and cannot be solved in isolation from other states, also confront U.S. leaders. This chapter examines the U.S. government's response to three sets of transnational problems: environmental decay, weapons proliferation, and restrictions on human rights and democratic freedoms. Although a matter of domestic governance, the third problem is also transnational given the connection between political moderation at home and foreign-policy behavior.

As we will find, the United States has a mixed record in managing transnational problems that conflict with other policy priorities. While American officials rhetorically support cooperative problem solving in these areas, domestic self-interests often stand in the way. This has proved especially true when the solutions require sacrifices by influential domestic groups or reelection-minded politicians. Cooperating with transnational civil society—including states and international organizations (public and private)—has increasingly become viewed as threatening to the sovereignty of the United States, which paradoxically played a major role in the development of these transnational actors. We explore these tensions in greater detail in this chapter, then conclude with a general assessment of the paradox of world power as the United States wields it today and will likely do so far into the future.

Public Goods and Collective Action

World peace and economic growth can be considered **global public goods,** resources that enhance living conditions of all persons and can benefit individuals without diminishing the goods' availability to others (see Kaul, Grunberg, and Stern 1999). The same applies to the resolution of transnational problems such as global warming, whose victims are not confined to a particular region of the world. A *functioning* habitat, sustaining human life, is the most essential of global public goods, but a *secure* environment is vital to the quality of life. Providing such security requires transnational cooperation.

Public goods also exist at the domestic level. As a matter of routine public administration, local and state governments manage parks, schools, police forces, and roads that serve all their citizens. These collective resources, funded by tax revenue, differ fundamentally from private goods, such as real estate, motor vehicles, and country club memberships, all of which are made available on market terms to a restricted pool of consumers able to afford them.

The provision of global public goods, unlike their domestic counterparts, cannot be taken for granted. In the anarchic interstate system, there exists no central authority responsible for serving the collective interests of the world's population. Individual countries may sign international agreements to limit their air and water pollution, protect their forests and wildlife, control their military arsenals, or respect the human rights of their citizens. Sovereign states, however, are under no obligation to contribute to these causes, whose beneficiaries live also in other countries. Furthermore, national governments cannot be stopped from violating or nullifying treaties as they see fit. The incentive for individual actors to shirk such burdens forms a central element of the collective-action problem that inhibits cooperation in all areas of societal organization, including world politics (see Olson 1965).

Given its immense resources, the United States is in a unique position to foster the provision of global public goods. During the cold war, the nation assumed leadership in providing for the defense of its allies around the periphery of the communist bloc and across Latin America. The United States further bore the greatest burden in maintaining a market-friendly global economy. "While this responsibility of the largest often lets others become 'free riders,' the alternative is that the collective bus does not move at all" (Nye 2002a, 240). The problem of **free riders,** actors who benefit from cooperative efforts without sharing their costs, is especially pronounced when a wide gulf exists between the capabilities of one actor—the United States in the current balance of world power—and others.

The fact that the United States is a primary contributor to the first two problems described in this chapter, pollution and weapons proliferation, while resisting multilateral measures to limit both, makes the country appear to be a free rider in these areas. While other governments have pushed ahead with multilateral pacts to solve these problems, the absence of the United States weakens the prospects for success and gives other states a ready excuse to "defect." The U.S. government has also adopted an inconsistent approach toward human rights and democratization, which American leaders tend to support only if political reforms do not conflict with other foreign-policy goals (see Mertus 2004).

Managing the Global Commons

The first transnational problem to be examined in this chapter involves the **global commons,** the earth's fragile ecosystem that sustains animal and plant life. Soaring world population, the depletion of finite natural resources, rampant deforestation, and the fouling of air and water have forced countries to confront environmental decay as a major foreign-policy issue. These problems are inherently *transnational* in scope in that pollution, as well as the loss of habitat and nonrenewable resources, ultimately affects the entire human population, not just a single nation. The rapid destruction of the Amazon rainforest, for example, removes a vast area of vegetation necessary to absorb toxic gases in the atmosphere.

The bleak future of the Amazon rainforest provides a stark lesson in the **tragedy of the commons,** a situation in which a group of people stand to lose a common resource due to overuse unless some limiting measures are taken (see In Their Own Words box). The pace of deforestation has accelerated in this South American region, where between 1995 and 2000 nearly 5 million acres of land were destroyed annually (Laurance, Albernaz, and Da Costa 2001). A new government program, Advance Brazil, calls for a nationwide network of highways and rail lines that would open the surviving 40 percent of the rain forest to logging, housing and industrial development, and hydroelectric projects. The demise of the rainforest has grave implications for the global climate. Yet Brazil's decision to put its own urgent and immediate needs for economic growth before long-term global concerns can be seen as rational politically. Its behavior is also consistent with the actions of the world's affluent countries, including the United States, during and after their periods of industrialization.

In the United States, the movement for environmental protection started at the grass roots in the 1960s and 1970s. Citizens demanded that environmental quality be considered a government priority. Rapid industrial growth earlier in the century left urban areas shrouded in smog and many waterways so contaminated they could not sustain marine life. Landmark legislation, including the Clean Air Act and the Clean Water Act, improved the quality of both public goods after passage in the early 1970s. The Environmental Protection Agency (EPA) came into being during this period, as did similar state and local agencies.

The United States, however, has been less assertive in seeking global remedies. Political leaders resist global environmental agreements, which they feel threaten the nation's sovereignty as well as its economic well-being. At the 1992 **Earth Summit,** held in Brazil, which brought together the largest number of heads of state in history, President George H. W. Bush was a reluctant participant, knowing the United States, as the world's richest country and chief source of pollution, would be a lightning rod. His hesitation proved well founded, as delegates singled out the United States as a primary obstacle to environmental protection. More recent U.S. actions have lent credence to the accusation. For example, the

IN THEIR OWN WORDS: GARRETT HARDIN

Global environmental decay emerged as a central U.S. foreign-policy issue in the 1960s and 1970s. In his 1968 article in Science, *Garrett Hardin, a scientist devoted to the study of bioethics, clearly captured the dilemma facing governments in coming to grips with such decay. Hardin revealed the many obstacles that stand in the way of preserving the environment, a global public good that will continue to decay without cooperation and shared sacrifice among all countries.*

The tragedy of the commons develops in this way. Picture a pasture open to all. It is to be expected that each herdsman will try to keep as many cattle as possible on the commons. Such an arrangement may work reasonably satisfactorily for centuries because tribal wars, poaching, and disease keep the number of both man and beast well below the carrying capacity of the land. Finally, however, comes the day of reckoning, that is, the day when the long-desired goal of social stability becomes a reality. At this point, the inherent logic of the commons remorselessly generates tragedy.

As a rational being, each herdsman seeks to maximize his gain. Explicitly or implicitly, more or less consciously, he asks, "What is the utility to me of adding one more animal to my herd?" This utility has one negative and one positive component.

1) The positive component is a function of the increment of one animal. Since the herdsman receives all the proceeds from the sale of the additional animal, the positive utility is nearly +1.

2) The negative component is a function of the additional overgrazing created by one more animal. Since, however, the effects of overgrazing are shared by all the herdsmen, the negative utility for any particular decision-making herdsman is only a fraction of −1.

Adding together the component partial utilities, the rational herdsman concludes that the only sensible course for him to pursue is to add another animal to his herd. And another; and another. . . . But this is the conclusion reached by each and every rational herdsman sharing a commons. Therein is the tragedy. Each man is locked into a system that compels him to increase his herd without limit—in a world that is limited. Ruin is the destination toward which all men rush, each pursuing his own best interest in a society that believes in the freedom of the commons. Freedom in a commons brings ruin to all.

Source: Garrett Hardin, "Tragedy of the Commons," Science 162, no. 3859 (December 13, 1968), 1243–1248. Copyright 1968 AAAS. Excerpted by permission.

United States has opposed the Convention on Biological Diversity, which by July 2004 had been approved by 188 other governments.[1]

---

1. For more information on the provisions and membership of the Convention on Biological Diversity, see the convention's Web site at www.biodiv.org.

Gridlock has characterized recent environmental policy in the United States (Kraft 2003). The polarization that has made consensus so elusive in other policy areas also prevents concerted action on the environment. President Clinton was unable to achieve his goal of strengthening many environmental protections in the face of congressional opposition and pressure by industrial interest groups. The same domestic forces led President George W. Bush to oppose global environmental treaties while easing restrictions on industrial pollution, mining and timber cutting on federal lands, and the protection of wetlands. Members of Congress opposed Bush's proposals to cut the EPA's budget but did little to pass "green" legislation, knowing it would face a veto in the White House. While public opinion generally favored stronger environmental protections, the stronger *intensity* of preferences among those favoring weaker restrictions captured the president's attention and swayed his policy choices.

Population Control and Family Planning

One of the most critical problems facing the global commons today concerns the increase in the world's population, which during the past century has grown in size from fewer than 2 billion inhabitants to more than 6 billion. Global population is expected to increase by another 50 percent by 2050 before leveling off at between 11 and 13 billion by the century's end (Population Reference Bureau 2004). The population explosion raises questions about the world's **carrying capacity,** the limits to which existing natural resources can meet the demands and withstand the strains imposed upon them by human development (see S. B. Cohen 2003).

The most rapid rates of population growth are concentrated in the world's poorest regions (see Table 12.1). Growth rates in less-developed countries (LDCs) averaged 2.1 percent annually between 1980 and 2002, as compared with 1.3 percent in middle-income countries and 0.7 percent in high-income countries (World Bank 2004b, 40, 98). The rate of growth in the United States during this period was 1.1 percent, with the most rapid growth occurring in economically depressed areas. Fertility rates, or average numbers of births per woman, were twice as large in poor countries (3.5) as in affluent countries (1.7). These trends illustrate the effects of the **demographic transition** that societies experience as their birth rates fall and life expectancies rise during the process of industrialization.[2]

The UN and other international organizations also recognize the link between population growth and economic development. The first UN-sponsored global conference on family planning was held in 1974 and subsequent meetings in 1984 and 1994 placed the issue squarely in the context of development. Hundreds of nonprofit NGOs offer family-planning services in the developing world, focusing their efforts on the distribution of contraceptives and the education of

---

2. All countries are generally considered LDCs except Australia, Canada, Japan, New Zealand, the United States, and those in Europe. See Ronald Lee (2003), David Bloom, David Canning, and Jaypee Sevilla (2003), and Hans Fehr, Sabine Jokisch, and Laurence Kotlikoff (2003) for recent assessments of demographic transitions.

Table 12.1 Twentieth-Century Population Explosion

	Population (in Millions)			Percentage Change, 1900–2000
	1900	1950	2000	
World	1,650	2,519	6,071	268%
Industrialized countries	539	813	1,194	121
Less-developed countries	1,111	1,706	4,877	339

SOURCE: UN Population Division, "World Population Prospects: The 2002 Revision" (February 26, 2003).

women regarding their reproductive rights and choices. Among aid donors, the U.S. government has provided the largest share of family-planning assistance in the past few years. Although funding levels fell in the mid-1990s, they have grown in recent years, amounting to $432 million in fiscal year 2004 (Nowels 2004).

While a broad consensus exists in the United States regarding the merits of family planning, the funding of programs that include abortion counseling and services is highly controversial. Opposition to abortion in many segments of U.S. society has not subsided since the Supreme Court's *Roe v. Wade* decision of 1973, which ruled that in most cases abortion was constitutional. This opposition to abortion has been well represented in Congress and the White House since *Roe,* and has emerged as a key foreign-policy, as well as domestic, issue.

The Reagan administration first took the offensive against abortion funding overseas at the 1984 UN International Conference on Population, held in Mexico City. The administration announced that the United States would no longer provide aid to agencies that endorsed or performed abortions "as a method of family planning." The policy also suspended grants to private hospitals and clinics, women's groups, and health-research centers that engaged in political lobbying to decriminalize or legalize abortions. Reagan's decision, known as the **Mexico City policy,** was significant given the lead role played by the United States in providing family-planning funds and the centrality of abortions in the population policies of many developing countries (see Cincotta and Crane 2001).

Although family-planning agencies protested the decision, most decided to accept the restrictions. The Mexico City policy remained in place throughout the Reagan and George H. W. Bush administrations. Among President Clinton's first acts upon taking office in January 1993 was the restoration of funding for these programs. George W. Bush was just as prompt in reinstating the restrictions (U.S. Department of State 2001).

The Mexico City policy is now a fixture of partisan politics in the United States, with most Republicans supporting, and most Democrats opposing, the policy. While Republican leaders gain favor among conservative Christians and other "pro-life" groups by doing so, Democrats gain support from women's groups, other supporters of reproductive rights, and civil libertarians who condemn government intrusions into private matters. Critics charge that the Mexico City policy is tantamount to a global "gag rule" on health-care professionals. The International Planned Parenthood Federation (2004, 1) claims the policy "has, and will have, a devastating effect on all our members and those that we support." Pregnant women are unlikely to forego abortions, the group claims; they will instead turn to unregulated clinics to perform the service—at greater risk to their health. Furthermore, the restrictions will impede the developing world's progress toward population control, prolonging its economic plight.

The abortion issue has led as well to curbs on U.S. contributions to the UN Population Fund, the world body's primary agency for supporting family-planning programs. The United States has refused to support the agency's efforts in China, whose reduced growth rates in recent years were due in part to mandated abortions. American officials have also condemned the forced sterilization of Chinese women. The ongoing restrictions imposed by the U.S. government provoke angry reactions from Chinese officials, who accuse the United States of "meddling" in their internal affairs. In this and other bilateral relations, abortion politics enter into the calculations of U.S. foreign policy.

The Global Warming Debate

Another controversial aspect of U.S. environmental policy concerns the effects of fossil-fuel emissions on the global climate. Scientific evidence suggests that these emissions, in addition to creating health problems and habitat loss in industrialized areas, contribute to **global warming.** Increasing temperatures in the Northern Hemisphere during the twentieth century were "likely to have been the largest of any century during the past 1,000 years," reported the Intergovernmental Panel on Climate Change (Houghton et al. 2001, 2). The panel, a consortium of scientific organizations, found the 1990s to be the warmest decade on record and 1998 the warmest year ever. "There is new and stronger evidence that most of the warming observed over the last 50 years is attributable to human activities," the panel concluded (10).

The effects of global warming, which the panel predicted would raise average world temperatures between 1.4 and 5.8 degrees by 2100, are difficult to ascertain (Schneider 2003). It is generally expected that weather patterns will become more volatile. Higher surface temperatures are expected to increase the frequency of "extreme weather events," such as hurricanes, tornadoes, and droughts, throughout the world (see Firor and Jacobson 2002; and Luterbacher and Sprinz 2001). In the United States, southern coastal cities such as New Orleans, Miami, and Charleston will be threatened by rising water levels.

Earlier evidence of global warming prompted delegates at the 1992 Earth Summit to ratify the UN Framework Convention on Climate Change. The agreement, supported by the U.S. government, called upon industrialized countries to reduce their emissions of greenhouse gases on a voluntary basis.[3] These governments met again in Kyoto, Japan, in 1997 to strengthen the earlier agreement with

---

3. These greenhouse gases include carbon dioxide, methane, nitrous oxide, hydrofluorocarbons, perfluorocarbons, and sulfur hexafluoride. The primary sources of these gases include gasoline-powered vehicles, coal-burning electric utilities, and large factories. The gases raise the earth's surface temperature by trapping the sun's heat and preventing it from returning to space, similar to the process that occurs in a greenhouse.

legally binding standards and timetables for emission cutbacks. The **Kyoto Protocol,** signed by eighty-four governments in 1998 and 1999, required industrialized nations to reduce these emissions to 5 percent below their 1990 levels by 2012.

The United States signed the Kyoto Protocol in December 1998. The nation's support for the measure was crucial given the status of the United States as the leading source of greenhouse gases (see Figure 12.1). Not only does the United States produce the largest volume of these gases, its per-capita emissions are among the highest in the world. The hopes of all countries for coming to grips with global warming hinged upon U.S. actions (Athanasiou 2001).

Although President Clinton supported the treaty, it faced strong opposition in the Senate, which had earlier passed a nonbinding resolution by a vote of 95–0 rejecting the Kyoto Protocol if it would harm the U.S. economy. Lawmakers also refused to ratify the agreement if it exempted major LDCs, including China and India, from the required cutbacks. These nations were allowed to waive the Kyoto restrictions on the grounds that the industrialized countries, including the United States, had not faced such barriers during their periods of "dirty" industrialization. With these exemptions written into the protocol, Clinton knew the treaty would be defeated and did not submit it to the Senate.

As a presidential candidate, George W. Bush expressed concern about global warming and pledged to seek reductions in carbon dioxide (CO_2) emissions, which most scientific studies linked to global warming. After taking office, however, Bush announced, in March 2001, that he would not seek to reduce CO_2

Figure 12.1 Carbon Dioxide Emissions by Country of Origin, 2000

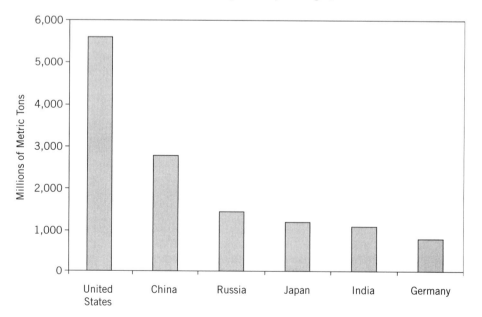

SOURCE: World Bank, *World Development Indicators* (New York: Oxford University Press, 2004), 144.

emissions. The White House later declared the Kyoto Protocol to be so "fatally flawed" that the United States would no longer participate in climate-change negotiations. The president restated the objections widely held in Congress, questioning the scientific evidence that included CO_2 among greenhouse gases and disputing the dire forecasts of climatologists. Bush's position was supported by an industry NGO, the Global Climate Coalition, which claimed that adherence to the treaty would reduce U.S. economic output by 1 to 2 percent and cause widespread layoffs of industrial workers.

Bush proposed a series of alternative measures to manage fossil-fuel emissions. First, he called for voluntary efforts that would reduce U.S. emissions as a percentage of U.S. economic output rather than in absolute terms. Under Bush's plan, the volume of U.S. greenhouse-gas emissions in 2010 would be about 28 percent *higher* than their levels in 1990, though lower as a percentage of the nation's output (Gallagher 2002). The president also proposed a "Clear Skies Initiative" that would limit emissions from electric power plants, the largest industrial source of air pollution, and allow them to trade "pollution credits" for the overall level of air pollution in the United States to decline. Finally, Bush called for the development of hydrogen-powered "Freedom Cars," which would rid U.S. motorists of their dependence on foreign oil by 2020, the target date for widespread sales of these cars.

While the voluntary program sought to recruit hundreds of companies to participate, few chose to do so in the program's first years. "Many of the companies with the worst pollution records have shunned the voluntary program because even a voluntary commitment would necessitate costly cleanups or possibly set the stage for future government regulation" (Gugliotta and Pianin 2004, A1). Environmental NGOs criticized the Clear Skies Initiative because it did not include CO_2 emissions and weakened many health protections already required by federal law (Natural Resources Defense Council 2004). As for the Freedom Cars, critics complained that little would be done to reduce the pollution caused by the 17 million passenger vehicles expected to roll off U.S. assembly lines every year until 2020 (see *New York Times* 2003).

Despite the U.S. government's withdrawal, the Kyoto Protocol gained new signatories and approached the point at which it would come into force. The Japanese government ratified the agreement in March 2004, and Russian president Vladimir Putin signaled in May that his government would follow suit if Russia were allowed to join the World Trade Organization. A total of 122 countries, which collectively produced 44 percent of greenhouse gases, had ratified the Kyoto Protocol by the middle of 2004. Russia's entry would raise that percentage above the 55-percent level needed to make the agreement legally binding.

The global-warming debate was overshadowed by the war on terrorism as a U.S. foreign-policy issue despite the fact that 2002 and 2003 tied for the second-hottest years on record (U.S. National Oceanic and Atmospheric Administration 2004). Public-opinion polls consistently registered strong popular support for emission cutbacks. A poll by Zogby International (2003), for example, found nearly 80 percent of respondents favoring such cutbacks and nearly 70 percent believing they could be made without harming the U.S. economy. Similar results emerged from a June 2004 poll by the Program on International Policy Attitudes (Kull 2004). In 2003, mayors from 155 U.S. cities called on President Bush to reduce the threat of global warming. And in May 2004, the president received the same message from a coalition of religious groups, including the National Association of Evangelicals that otherwise served as a political ally of the president. Yet this domestic pressure, combined with harsh criticism of the United States from overseas, still failed to force concessions from the White House.

Support for Bush's policies came largely from the energy and automobile industries that benefited from the nation's reliance on fossil fuels. Farmers also opposed the agreement on the grounds that higher energy prices, which they feared would result from increased gasoline taxes to discourage consumption, would make their goods less competitive on foreign markets. Efforts by Congress to pass legislation that would require emission cutbacks independent of the Kyoto process succumbed to these pressures. The Climate Stewardship Act of 2004, cosponsored by Sens. John McCain, R-Ariz., and Joseph Lieberman, D-Conn., was defeated in the Senate in October 2003 by a vote of 55-43. The two senators, along with like-minded legislators in the House of Representatives, vowed to continue to bring up the measure until it passed (see Climate Action Network 2004).

Stalemate over Energy Policy

To understand the positions taken by U.S. foreign-policy makers on environmental issues, the debate over global warming and the Kyoto Protocol must be considered in the context of U.S. energy policy. The United States has generally enjoyed a steady and relatively inexpensive energy supply, due in large part to low taxes on gasoline and friendly relations with major oil exporters in the Middle East (see Yergin 1991). But when "oil shocks" occur, as in the 2004 surge in gasoline prices to more than $2 a gallon, they keenly demonstrate the vulnerability of the United States to fluctuations in the global energy market. American motorists are especially vulnerable since the nation's ratio of 779 motor vehicles for every 1,000 citizens is the largest in the world (World Bank 2004b, 160–162).

The first oil shock occurred in 1973, when the OPEC cartel embargoed oil exports to the United States and other allies of Israel, then greatly increased the wholesale price of crude oil. That experience inspired the first nationwide push for energy efficiency and conservation along with growing interest in alternative energy sources such as solar, geothermal, and wind power, as well as synthetic and alcohol-based fuels. The 1975 Energy Policy and Conservation Act mandated minimum levels of fuel efficiency with a goal of increasing the average efficiency of passenger cars from 13 miles per gallon (mpg) in 1974 to 27.5 mpg by 1985.

A second oil shock occurred in 1979–1980, when the revolution in Iran led to another disruption in OPEC supplies. Conservation efforts in the United States, combined with greatly increased imports of fuel-efficient automobiles, allowed the nation to withstand this second shock. A decline in fuel prices during the 1980s, however, encouraged U.S. leaders to put off major reforms in energy policy. The

Reagan administration cut federal funding for conservation by 70 percent; federal support for the research and development of new energy sources was cut by nearly two-thirds (Prestowitz 2003). While Iraq's invasion of Kuwait in 1990 caused yet another spike in fuel prices, from $16 to $36 a barrel, the OPEC states maintained full production and prices fell again in 1991. The low energy prices and stable supplies of the 1990s literally fueled the sustained U. S. economic boom that took place under President Clinton.

This boom allowed conservation efforts to lag (Joskow 2002). The efficiency of new U.S.-made cars peaked at 26.2 mpg in 1987, then fell to 24 mpg by 2002. Congress prohibited any changes to fuel-efficiency as sport-utility vehicles (SUVs) became the passenger vehicles of choice by the turn of the century. These SUVs were exempt from the efficiency standards for passenger cars because they were regarded as "trucks" by the federal government, a regulatory loophole that pleased automakers. Energy consumption grew rapidly into the new millennium, both in absolute terms and on a per-capita basis. The production of electricity kept up with this growth, nearly doubling between 1980 and 2002.

Despite its prosperity, the United States remains vulnerable to disruptions in energy supplies. This became clear to citizens of California, whose electricity prices doubled in 2001 and 2002. State officials ordered "rolling blackouts" across the state and passed emergency legislation allowing the state government to secure electrical power for their citizens. Political turmoil in Venezuela, another OPEC member, sent prices of crude oil soaring again in January 2003. The upward spiral continued in spring 2004, pushed by rising demand in India and China and security concerns in the Middle East, as crude oil prices exceeded $41 a barrel.

These developments revealed the close links between events abroad and U.S. "energy security." President Bush recognized these links shortly after taking office by creating a National Energy Policy Development Group to devise a strategy for making the United States less vulnerable to oil shocks and other threats to energy supplies. Vice President Dick Cheney chaired the task force (White House 2001b, 5), whose report in May declared that

> a fundamental imbalance between supply and demand defines our nation's energy crisis. . . . If energy production increases at the same rate as during the last decade our projected energy needs will far outstrip expected levels of production. This imbalance, if allowed to continue, will inevitably undermine our economy, our standards of living, and our national security.

The work of this task force proved controversial for two reasons. First, Cheney did not reveal which private citizens and groups had influenced the task force's report, which called for accelerated domestic oil and gas production and the construction of more than 1,300 power plants. The General Accounting Office (GAO) filed a suit against Cheney in February 2002 to gain this information, but the Supreme Court rejected the suit in June 2004. Nonetheless, the GAO (2003, 5) learned that Cheney's task force had sought and received input from "nonfederal energy stakeholders, principally petroleum, coal, nuclear, natural gas, and electricity representatives and lobbyists." The task force turned to non-profit environmental groups and private citizens "to a more limited degree."

The second criticism of the task force concerned its emphasis on *production,* rather than *conservation,* as means to increase the nation's energy independence. By presuming higher levels of energy consumption, government reports dismissed the possibility that Americans could be encouraged to conserve energy by modifying their lifestyles or turning to renewable sources of energy such as solar or wind power. The United States ranks among the least aggressive industrialized countries in seeking new ways to generate electricity from renewable sources (U.S. Public Interest Research Group 2002). While its use of coal as a source of energy is much higher than world averages, its use of hydroelectric power is much lower.

A related concern about domestic oil production concerns Alaska's Arctic National Wildlife Refuge (ANWR). The energy task force called for oil and gas drilling in the remote, but pristine, area, arguing that new drilling technology would pose only minimal risks to it. But environmental groups charged that the potential gains were slight and that significant ecological damage would result in the form of lost habitat and the likelihood of accidental spills in extracting or transporting oil (Bamberger 2003, 8–9). Drilling in the ANWR region has become a recurring controversy in the United States, one that symbolizes the tensions between economic and environmental priorities.

The Alaska issue also raises the broader question of U.S. reliance on foreign oil. The nation in 2002 imported about 62 percent of its crude oil from foreign sources, a level expected to rise above 77 percent by 2025 (U.S. Department of Energy 2004a, 133). Saudi Arabia has served as the chief supplier of oil in recent years, along with Canada, Mexico, Venezuela, and Nigeria (see Table 12.2). The U.S. invasion of Iraq was motivated in part by a desire to increase future imports from that country. The U.S. government is actively seeking new sources of supplies in the Caspian Sea region of central Asia, western Africa, and Latin America. With domestic reserves not expected to increase and demand remaining high, access to foreign oil will remain a primary concern of U.S. foreign policy. "Not only must officials ensure access to these overseas suppliers," Michael Klare (2002, 100) observed, "they must also take steps to make certain that foreign oil deliveries to the United States are not impeded by war, revolution, or civil disorder." Heightened competition among producers in the face of unchecked global demand for energy may threaten domestic and regional stability in areas of vital concern to the United States, including Russia and the Middle East.

Table 12.2 Sources of U.S. Crude Oil, 2000–2003

Exporting Country	Value of Exports (in Billions of U.S. Dollars)
Saudi Arabia	54
Canada	48
Mexico	47
Venezuela	46
Nigeria	34
Iraq	21
United Kingdom	14
Angola	13
Norway	13
Colombia	11

SOURCE: International Trade Association, "TradeStats Express" (2004), tse.export.gov.

Political disputes over energy made it impossible for the Bush administration and Congress to enact a national energy policy. The Energy Policy Act of 2003, reflecting the views of the task force and White House, was defeated in November of that year, after weeks of bitter debate. Opponents of the bill, including most Democrats along with some Republicans, objected to its large subsidies to energy industries, potential impact on ecologically sensitive areas, and neglect of conservation measures. Democrats also complained about being shut out of the process of drafting the bill and participating on the Cheney task force. As in the case of population control and global warming, the domestic politics of energy reveal deep political and ideological divisions within the U.S. government and the government's susceptibility to outside pressures that prevent the nation from taking a lead role on global energy security.

The Dangers of Weapons Proliferation

Another transnational problem facing all governments today involves the proliferation of weapons, from small arms to weapons of mass destruction. The spread of these weapons, whose accuracy and destructive power increases each year, aggravates internal and regional power balances while diverting scarce economic resources from productive uses. A more militarized world poses clear risks to the United States, a primary target of resentment among many foreign governments and terrorist groups.

The prospect of nuclear proliferation is a paramount global concern, and preventing "rogue states" and terrorist groups from gaining access to such weapons is a central goal of U.S. foreign policy. As described in Chapter 10, the number of acknowledged nuclear powers reached seven in 1998, when India and Pakistan conducted underground tests. Most observers believe that Israel and North Korea possess nuclear weapons along with the means to use them. Iran has also threatened to join the "nuclear club," alarming U.S. leaders acutely aware of Iran's links to Islamic terrorists and animosity toward Washington. While U.S. officials have declared nuclear proliferation in North Korea and Iran—both parts of Bush's "axis of evil"—to be unacceptable, they have tolerated Israel's nuclear arsenal. This conspicuous gap in U.S. nuclear policy angers Arab nations that would be likely targets of an Israeli nuclear attack.

The United States supports multilateral efforts to prevent the spread of these weapons through the Nuclear Non-Proliferation Treaty, signed by 187 countries by 2000. In recent years, would-be nuclear powers have shunned these weapons. These states include major regional powers in South America and Africa that feel more secure in "nuclear-free zones." Yet the prospect that nuclear materials in Russia may be sold to the highest bidder on black markets, or that China may export ballistic-missile technology to nuclear terrorists, worries U.S. leaders. As noted in Chapter 10, fears of a long-range nuclear attack prompted the Bush administration to scrap the Anti-Ballistic Missile (ABM) treaty and deploy a National Missile Defense (NMD) system.

The United States also supports efforts to prevent the development of chemical and biological weapons, although its record in this area is not strong. The

United States had once maintained a large stockpile of chemical weapons, used toxic defoliants in Vietnam, and shared chemical agents with Saddam Hussein in the 1980s. Citing potential intrusions on private U.S. companies by on-site inspectors, the U.S. government has resisted multilateral measures to enforce the Biological Weapons Convention, which was ratified by Congress in 1975. While the Senate ratified the Chemical Weapons Convention in 1997, senators and Bush administration officials complained that the ban would be difficult to enforce.

Alongside the danger posed by weapons of mass destruction, the spread of conventional weapons, either through government contracts or on the black market, also poses serious risks to regional and global security. Small arms, costing between $200 and $400, are the most commonly used weapons in civil wars. With nearly 500 million such weapons currently in circulation (Prestowitz 2003, 149), restricting the flow of small arms across national borders is a priority of most governments and arms-control NGOs. As in other areas of multilateral cooperation, the United States has been among the few dissenters on this issue. John Bolton (2001), undersecretary of state for arms control and international security, rejected the view that "all small arms and light weapons are the same or that they are all problematic." He reminded UN delegates at a 2002 UN conference that the right to bear arms is a constitutional right in the United States and that the use of sport rifles and pistols poses no security risks. The State Department's refusal to discuss binding restrictions on small arms stymied multilateral talks on such an agreement.

The U.S. "Arms Bazaar"

Official arms transfers from country to country raise their own set of concerns (see Hook and Rothstein 2005). Regional arms races, primarily those in the developing world, divert public resources while inflaming rivalries and making military conflicts between them potentially deadlier. The problem of conventional weapons proliferation worsens as recipients gain the expertise and materials necessary to manufacture the weapons themselves. Regulating this market is enormously difficult given the overlapping public and private actors involved, the prevalence of black-market weapons sales, and the need for concerted efforts by all governments to bring the flow of these weapons under control.

Arms transfers first played a vital role in U.S. foreign policy in the early days of World War II with the provision of military equipment to Great Britain under the Lend-Lease program. Military aid in the cold war, first authorized by the Truman Doctrine, figured prominently in the U.S. containment strategy (see Klare 1984). The Nixon Doctrine, proclaimed late in the Vietnam War, called for replacing U.S. troops with security assistance, thereby forcing U.S. allies to "take responsibility" for their own defense. After a lull during the Carter administration, the levels of arms exports soared in the 1980s. Increasing exports during the Reagan years reflected three strategic priorities: revived cold war competition with the Soviet Union; new obligations to Israel and Egypt under the Camp David accords; and growing obligations to nations such as Turkey, Spain, and the Philippines that opened their military bases to U.S. forces.

After the Soviet Union's collapse in 1991, overcapacity in the defense industry fueled the push for weapons exports to sustain the nation's military-industrial base. Bill Clinton oversaw a consolidation of U.S. defense firms and expanded federal subsidies for the surviving giants, Boeing, General Dynamics, Lockheed Martin, Northrop Grumman, and Raytheon (see Markusen and Costigan 1999). George W. Bush favored the easing of restrictions on U.S. arms exports, a response to appeals by these manufacturers. While the outbreak of the war on terrorism in 2001 did not produce an immediate upturn in the global arms market, the value of U.S. export agreements rose from $12.1 billion to $13.3 billion between 2001 and 2002 (Grimmett 2003). The United States captured nearly one-half of the global market share (see Figure 12.2), with two-thirds of arms exports destined for developing countries, mostly in the Middle East.

The United States has several advantages in the global arms market. The nation's technological superiority in most weapons systems makes U.S.-made arms attractive to potential buyers. The sheer size of the U.S. military-industrial complex provides economies of scale to arms makers, or relatively lower costs per unit. Finally, the United States can better afford security assistance, or weapons provided on a grant or low-interest basis, than other suppliers. Creative financing arrangements allow many foreign governments to afford weapons systems from the United States that otherwise would be beyond their reach.

Figure 12.2 Sources of Arms Exports, 1994–2002

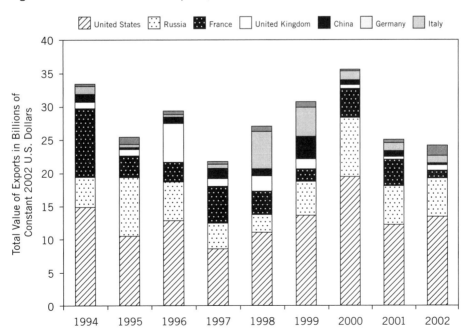

SOURCE: Richard F. Grimmett, "Conventional Arms Transfers to Developing Nations, 1995–2002," *Congressional Research Service* (September 22, 2003), 73.

The U.S. government manages four programs that facilitate arms exports (U.S. Defense Security Cooperation Agency 2004). The largest of these is the *foreign military sales* program, which administered more than $125 billion in sales between 1992 and 2002. Second, the United States promotes *direct commercial sales* that are negotiated by individual weapons manufactures before export licenses are reviewed by the State Department. Third, the U.S. government provides *foreign military financing* to developing countries, or low-interest loans for arms sales. Finally, the United States trains thousands of foreign defense forces through the *International Military Education and Training* (IMET) program.

Upward pressure on U.S. arms exports derives from a variety of international and domestic factors. At the global level, tensions arising from the war on terrorism have increased demand for military equipment from many nations after an extended period in the 1990s when the arms market was "saturated" by cold war-era weapons. Foreign competition is another motivating factor. Rival exporters in the European Union, China, and Russia look to arms exports as a means to improve their trade balances. As William Keller and Janne Nolan (2001, 178) observed, "[T]he arms business is rapidly becoming an adjunct of private enterprise." While multilateral measures such as the Missile Technology Control Regime try to restrain transfer of delivery systems, such measures are widely disputed and rarely enforced.

The issue of U.S. arms exports is rarely a subject of political debate in Congress or the executive branch. For its part, the public displays little interest in the issue. In this void, arms sales are driven by interest groups with a tangible stake in the manufacture and export of weapons. Defense firms, which maintain cordial relations with the government through Pentagon contracts for domestic procurement, aggressively compete for weapons exports. The clout of these contractors is strengthened when retired military leaders pass through the "revolving door" and become lobbyists for the arms industry (see Chapter 3).

It is now customary for U.S. leaders to use economic rationales in promoting arms exports. Among the reasons commonly cited for export licenses and military-aid packages are the gains they bring to domestic producers, manufacturing employment, and the U.S. balance of trade, which suffers chronic deficits in most other sectors (see Chapter 11). Weapons exports offer other benefits to the United States. These include:

- serving as extensions of U.S. military power by strengthening friends and allies

- allowing weapons systems to be "tested" in combat situations that may be instructive to U.S. military commanders

- preserving military capacity in peacetime for use in possible future military conflicts

- reducing "unit costs" for the procurement of the same weapons by the U.S. government

- providing an economic stimulus to the U.S. economy that is immune from cycles in national or global economic growth

- stimulating U.S. economic growth by introducing technological innovations with "spin-off" applications in civilian sectors.

As in other foreign-policy areas, the president has a variety of advantages in governing arms exports: direct ties to foreign governments, an ability to set the agenda, and a presumed disposition to speak for the national interest rather than parochial concerns. Within the executive branch, the State Department negotiates military-aid packages with foreign governments and reviews export-license applications. The Department of Defense oversees weapons production and conducts military-training programs, while the Commerce Department promotes commercial arms sales. The power of the purse gives Congress considerable leverage in shaping the direction, volume, and terms of U.S. security assistance. Although the Arms Export Control Act of 1976 authorized Congress to review major arms deals, the rejection of arms exports has been rare.

Dangers of Unrestricted Arms Transfers

While the U.S. government finds arms exports attractive for many reasons, attention must be paid to the dangers of these transfers. Some problems apply to exports from all countries. Arms exports increase the risk of large-scale political violence in volatile regions. In the Iran-Iraq war during the 1980s, for example, vast stockpiles of weapons deliveries from the United States and other suppliers to both countries greatly increased the scale of death and destruction. The large volume of military exports to the developing world presents another problem, as these countries are least able to afford such weapons and most in need of development rather than military assistance.

Arms transfers from the United States, whether in the form of security assistance or commercial sales, raise a set of distinctive concerns. The first involves the potential for **backfire,** the unexpected use of U.S. weapons exports against the United States or its allies. The U.S. government experienced this type of backfire twice in 1979—in Iran after Shah Mohammad Reza Pahlavi's overthrow, and in Nicaragua following the Sandinista revolution. In subsequent military interventions in Panama (1989), Somalia (1992–1993), and Haiti (1994), U.S. troops confronted adversaries largely equipped with U.S.-made weapons.

Given recent developments in Iraq, the backfire of U.S. arms transfers to that country has been the most serious to date. Iraq imported a wide variety of conventional weapons from the United States and other suppliers during the 1980s, ranking first among arms importers around the world. (Iran held that distinction in the 1970s.) Among other military equipment, Saddam Hussein received materials from the United States he used to develop chemical and biological weapons (see Jentleson 1994). These same weapons of mass destruction, used against Iran and Saddam's own citizens, first posed a danger to the United States in the Persian Gulf War. Thus exported weapons changed from an *extension* of U.S. power to a *threat* to that power.

Point/Counterpoint
ARMS SALES VS. ARMS CONTROL

The issue of U.S. arms sales raises a number of questions about the nation's foreign policy: Should the United States be primarily concerned with its own interests or with global concerns? To what extent should economic factors influence decisions regarding national security? Are U.S. arms sales a help or a hindrance to the cause of international stability?

As the world's leader in arms sales, the U.S. government argues that such sales promote national, as well as global, interests. Government officials, therefore, have been highly sympathetic to complaints from arms contractors that their exports are hindered by bureaucratic obstacles at home and growing competition from abroad. "From an industry perspective, the current U.S. defense trade regulations are complex and restrictive, seriously inhibiting cooperation with this nation's closest allies," observed *National Defense,* an industry magazine. "Current defense trade laws and policies must be revised to balance rational national security concerns and strategies with the need to enhance both the international competitiveness of the U.S. defense industry and the military effectiveness of U.S.-led international coalitions."

Critics of U.S. arms sales, however, dispute this claim, asserting instead that exports suffer from too *few* regulations and controls. To Rachael Stohl of the Center for Defense Information, "The lack of controls on the global arms trade is fueling conflict, poverty and human rights violations worldwide. Every government around the world is responsible in stopping these horrors and abuses. In some cases, arms are being transferred to illegal groups that are terrorizing governments and civilians. The United States, as the world's largest exporter, has a special duty to lead the world in pushing for stronger arms controls."

Source: Dennis Kennelly and Ben Stone, "Bush Team Reviewing Defense Trade Policy," National Defense (May 2003), www.nationalde-fensemagazine.org/article.cfm?Id=1086; Rachael Stohl, "Control Arms Campaign" (2003) Center for Defense Information, www.cdi.org/friendlyver-sion/printversion.cfm?documentID=1765.

By exporting weapons systems in such large volumes, the United States also risks losing its edge in military technology. Arms importers increasingly demand concessions from their suppliers, including licensed production in their own factories. While such arrangements may be justified in isolation, they threaten to erode U.S. technological superiority in the long term. This is particularly true as arms buyers demand access to more sophisticated weapons systems and play exporters off each other in making deals. Of concern as well is the iron triangle of military contractors, government officials, and influential legislators described in Chapter 3 (see Hartung 1994). As military exports are encouraged in Washington as a matter of economic as well as security policy, weapons producers gain unprecedented access to decision makers and receive favorable treatment in the form of subsidies and tax breaks. This pattern of behavior creates obvious problems for democratic governance.

Finally, arms transfers from the United States are problematic when they are shipped to repressive regimes. This pattern could be seen throughout the cold war, as dictators such as the shah of Iran and Ferdinand Marcos of the Philippines received massive volumes of security assistance in return for their pledges to assist the United States in containing communism. This system of weapons-for-allegiance continues today in the war on terrorism. Countries such as Armenia and Azerbaijan were denied U.S. arms from 1993 to 2002 due to human-rights concerns but became eligible for U.S. weapons when they became frontline states in the war. The repressive states of Tajikistan and Uzbekistan also received U.S. security assistance despite that fact that the U.S. Department of State (2003a) reported systematic persecution of the inhabitants of both countries. The government of Egypt, meanwhile, continues to receive more than $1 billion in U.S. military aid annually despite its routine violations of human rights.

Promoting Human Rights and Democracy

While the proliferation of weapons threatens U.S. security, policy makers consider the spread of democracy also to be vital to the national interest. For this reason, promoting democratic reforms, or **democratization,** has long been a central objective of U.S. foreign policy. American leaders have historically believed that the nation could not be secure as a democratic island in a sea of despotic regimes. The twin victories of the United States during the twentieth century, first against the fascist powers of World War II and then against Soviet communism in the cold war, reinforced the consensus among U.S. foreign-policy makers that domestic repression at home leads to adventurism abroad. Since then, the "most consistent tradition in American foreign policy . . . has been the belief that the nation's security is best protected by the expansion of democracy worldwide" (Smith 1994, 9).

This formula received new validation with the terrorist attacks of September 2001—with a significant twist. The attackers on that day were not government agents, but Islamic terrorists who harbored intense hostility toward the U.S. government and Western society in general. Most of the al Qaeda terrorists came from Saudi Arabia, whose ruling monarchy had long excluded rival groups from power while maintaining cordial relations with the United States, the primary destination of its petroleum exports and the primary source of the royal family's extravagant wealth (Yergin 1991). Thus the attacks on the United States were linked, however indirectly, to a dictatorial regime overseas. Oppression in Saudi Arabia spawned the dissidents that chose to gain vengeance against the monarchy's perceived accomplices in New York City and Washington, D.C.

More generally, the terrorist attacks originated from the region of the world that has most resisted the global trend toward democratic rule. In 2003, more countries than ever provided a "broad scope for open political competition, a climate of respect for civil liberties, significant independent civic life, and independent media" (Freedom House 2000–2004, 4). That year saw a record number of "free" countries in the world (89 of 192) and share of the world's population (44 percent) living in free countries, as defined by Freedom House, a nongovernmental organization devoted to human rights (see Figure 12.3). The NGO's 2003 survey noted political reforms in eastern Europe, where the governments of Bulgaria and Slovenia had sought membership in the EU. Other reforms were recorded in Latin America, where Brazil, Chile, Mexico, and Venezuela took important democratic steps such as strengthening the rule of law, tolerating press criticism, holding free elections, or improving civil-military relationships.

Most countries in the Middle East and other nations with majority Muslim populations, however, missed out on this democratic trend. Freedom House (2000–2004, 12) attributed this pattern to the numerous military regimes in the region and "the persistence of monarchies that have resisted the devolution of power to democratically accountable governments." Democratic transitions, meanwhile, stalled in other regions, including Russia and other former Soviet states. Although these countries held elections and embraced limited reforms, entrenched elites continue to maintain their grip on power as they had during the cold war. Russian president Vladimir Putin won reelection for a four-year term in March 2004 largely by thwarting the news media and preventing alternative parties from challenging his rule.

Figure 12.3 Freedom in the World, 1973–2003

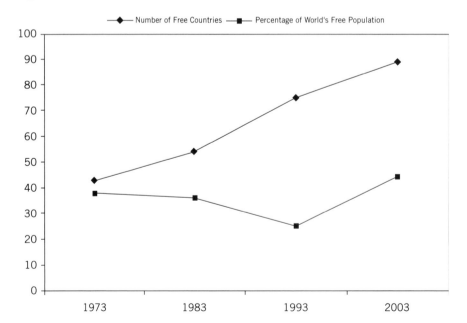

SOURCE: Freedom House, *Freedom in the World* (New York: Freedom House, 2003), 8–9.

The uncertainties surrounding these autocratic regimes as well as "failed states" in the developing world, whose governments cannot control events within their borders, make democracy promotion a compelling objective of U.S. foreign-policy makers. Their efforts in this area have broadened historically along with political freedoms in the United States itself. John F. Kennedy approved major increases in foreign aid, much of it designed to enhance democratic rule in recipient nations, at the same time he pressed Congress to approve civil-rights legislation that would empower African Americans. The lack of universal suffrage in the nation's early history and subsequent denials of minority rights "contributed to the prevalence of restricted democracy, and the achievement of full democracy comparatively later than most West European and Commonwealth liberal democracies" (Gonzalez and King 2004, 195).

According to democratic-peace theory, the more democratic world of the early twenty-first century will be a more peaceful one. Governments that uphold political freedoms and empower their civil societies are more likely to cooperate with one another. These countries are also likely to engage in productive trade relations. This prospect of a stabler international order makes the promotion of democracy a U.S. act not of altruism, but of enlightened self-interest.

A Distinctive View of Human Rights

These linkages between regime type, economic productivity, and foreign-policy behavior reinforce a historic tendency of American leaders to promote the respect of human rights beyond its shores. Yet the United States maintains a conception of human rights that differs from that adopted by most other countries. To the U.S. government, human rights apply primarily to *political* and *civil* rights. Of primary concern in the United States is that government power must be tightly constrained for individuals to enjoy the "inalienable" freedoms of "life, liberty, and the pursuit of happiness." The more widely accepted view of human rights is broader, encompassing *social* and *economic* rights as well as political freedoms. From this perspective, citizens cannot be truly free if many of them suffer from deep economic inequalities and the societal disadvantages that stem from gaps in material welfare.

Stated another way, while the U.S. conception of human rights focuses on *liberty*, the conception favored by most other governments emphasizes *equality* as well as liberty. This more inclusive perspective was written into the Universal Declaration of Human Rights, adopted by UN members in 1948. Its thirty articles include political rights familiar to Americans, such as freedoms of thought, assembly, and the ownership of private property. The declaration also comprises social and economic rights, such as the right to equal pay for equal work, an "adequate" standard of living, assistance for child care, and sufficient opportunities for "rest and leisure."

Distancing itself from the language of the UN declaration during the cold war, the United States seized upon communism, in both its Soviet and Chinese forms, as a primary threat to human rights. Communist leaders claimed that their system better protected their citizens' human rights by assuring them jobs, housing, educations, and medical care, if not the political freedoms of utmost value to Americans. Most European governments as well as developing countries adopted the broader conception of human rights, leaving the United States virtually alone in the UN General Assembly.

Further complicating matters, the U.S. government anxiously sought allies in the bipolar balance of power, few of whom had strong democratic credentials. American leaders resolved this dilemma by choosing the lesser of evils—"authoritarian" states that oppressed their people while providing some political and economic openings as opposed to "totalitarian" communist regimes that dominated all aspects of public life (see Kirkpatrick 1982). Military dictators across Latin America, Africa, and Asia maintained cordial relations with the United States, which provided enough military aid to protect the rulers against their domestic enemies.

Congress took the initiative in the late 1970s to raise the profile of human rights as a foreign-policy priority. Foreign aid funds were suspended to countries that engaged in "gross violations" of human rights. Congress created the Office of Humanitarian Affairs, which required the secretary of state to submit annual reports on the human-rights behavior of all foreign governments. Jimmy Carter embraced this emphasis on human rights. "Because we are free we can never be indifferent to the fate of nations elsewhere," Carter (quoted in Schlesinger 1978, 514) stated in his 1977 inaugural address. "Our commitment to human rights must be absolute." But even Carter could not avoid double standards. His support for the despotic shah of Iran not only contradicted the president's moral standards but also led to the shah's overthrow and replacement by an Islamic theocracy hostile toward the United States.

While the collapse of Soviet communism represented a moral, as well as geopolitical, victory for the United States, the nation remains vastly outnumbered by foreign countries that oppose its narrow conception of human rights. If anything, those nations' focus on socioeconomic equality strengthened as globalization pressures sparked new tensions between the world's rich and poor. President George W. Bush, remaining true to the traditional stance of the United States, substituted the term *human rights* in his speeches with *human dignity,* a term that emphasized individual freedoms *from* state interference rather than an obligation *by* the state to provide for the material welfare of its citizens (Mertus 2003).

The United States today remains caught between "two worlds" that can never be reconciled (Forsythe 1995). The first world relates to the liberal tradition of U.S. moral exceptionalism and to the nation's self-image as an inspiring "city upon a hill." Beyond serving as the exemplar of human rights, the United States in this view should commit its vast resources to the cause of global reform. George W. Bush (2001b) captured this crusading spirit in his inaugural address by referring to Biblical scripture: "When we see that wounded traveler on the road to Jericho, we will not pass to the other side."

The second world corresponds to the bleak vision of realism that foresees endless conflicts among states and the primacy of national defense above other foreign-policy goals, including the promotion of human rights (see Chapter 3). The United States must make moral compromises in this darker world, allying itself with dictators and foreign monarchs whose interests align with those of U.S. defense and security policy. American forces abroad must play by the ruthless rules of this world, even if those rules compel close trade relations with the chronic human-rights violators in China and Saudi Arabia, as well as the torture and humiliation of Iraqi war prisoners.

The United States inhabits both of these worlds at once. Moral appeals to human rights, which have contributed to democratic reforms in many countries, are as central to the nation's political culture as its resort to the law of the geopolitical jungle. As noted in Chapter 3, while the stated *principles* of U.S. foreign policy are consistent with liberalism, its *practice* is more often compatible with realism. This dilemma cannot be easily overcome. The United States appears destined to be plagued by the mismatch between its words and deeds. All of this contributes to the paradox of U.S. world power, itself a by-product of the competing demands of global ambitions and national self-interests.

Prospects for "Exporting" Democracy

The U.S. government does not merely proclaim the benefits of human rights, American style. It actively supports political reforms in other countries. The longevity of the United States' own democratic system, however strained by internal contradictions and double standards, provides a powerful basis and temptation for the "export" of its system (Muravchik 1991). This proactive effort, a key element of U.S. foreign policy for three decades, stands in contrast to the more passive approach adopted earlier, when the United States sought to inspire democratic revolutions *by example* alone. As Secretary of State John Quincy Adams (quoted in Merrill and Paterson 2000, 167) declared in 1821:

> Where the standard of freedom and independence has been unfurled, there will her heart, her benedictions and her prayers be. But she goes not abroad, in search of monsters to destroy. She is the well-wisher to the freedom and independence of all. She is the champion and vindicator only of her own.

More than a century later, President Franklin Roosevelt framed the growing U.S. involvement in World War II in the context of a global conflict between tyranny and democracy. He identified "four freedoms"—freedom of expression, freedom of religion, freedom from want, and freedom from fear—that would be essential to a lasting peace following the conflict. Rather than relying solely on the power of the nation's democratic example, Roosevelt proposed that the United States offer its like-minded allies material support. The postwar Marshall Plan and other aid programs heralded the arrival of a new era in which the U.S. government shaped the domestic political institutions of foreign governments.

This effort, overshadowed in the 1950s by the security imperatives of the first years of the cold war, took on a new urgency in the early 1960s with the

·))) IN THEIR OWN WORDS: FRANKLIN D. ROOSEVELT (((·

American presidents have historically cast U.S. military interventions in the context of the nation's moral ideals. Franklin D. Roosevelt, while avoiding the sweeping rhetoric of Woodrow Wilson, told Congress in January 1941 that the United States would strive to ensure that "four freedoms" were protected by all governments after World War II. Although the United States had not yet entered the conflict directly, Roosevelt needed legislative and public support for aid packages to its European and Asian allies. In seeking this support, the president made it clear that the United States would pursue outcomes in the war that extended beyond national self-interests. Indeed, Roosevelt's desired world order pertained equally to the outcome of the cold war.

In the future days which we seek to make secure, we look forward to a world founded upon four essential human freedoms.

The first is freedom of speech and expression—everywhere in the world.

The second is freedom of every person to worship God in his own way—everywhere in the world.

The third is freedom from want, which, translated into world terms, means economic understanding which will secure to every nation a healthy peacetime life for its inhabitants—everywhere in the world.

The fourth is freedom from fear, which, translated into world terms means a worldwide reduction of armaments to such a point and in such a thorough fashion that no nation will be in a position to commit an act of physical aggression against any neighbor—anywhere in the world.

That is no vision of a distant millennium. It is a definite basis for a kind of world attainable in our own time and gen-

eration. That kind of world is the very antithesis of the so-called "new order" of tyranny which the dictators seek to create with the crash of a bomb.

To that new order we oppose the greater conception—the moral order. A good society is able to face schemes of world domination and foreign revolutions alike without fear.

Since the beginning of our American history we have been engaged in change, in a perpetual, peaceful revolution, a revolution which goes on steadily, quietly, adjusting itself to changing conditions without the concentration camp or the quicklime in the ditch. The world order which we seek is the cooperation of free countries, working together in a friendly, civilized society.

Source: Michael Nelson, ed., Historic Documents on the Presidency, 1776–1989 *(Washington, D.C.: Congressional Quarterly, 1989), 283–284.*

decolonization of Africa and growing concerns about poverty in Latin America. John F. Kennedy's Peace Corps, Alliance for Progress, and foreign-aid programs supported political reform as well as economic development in these areas. Once again, however, the focus of U.S. foreign policy shifted to cold war concerns, this time in Vietnam, which consumed most of the foreign-aid budget. Jimmy Carter revived the State Department's democracy programs in the late 1970s, and in 1983, the Reagan administration created the National Endowment for Democracy, a nonprofit NGO designed to fund political reforms abroad, primarily in the developing world.

After the cold war ended, Bill Clinton (quoted in Brinkley 1997, 119) sought to "enlarge the circle of nations that live under . . . free institutions" as a central element of his grand strategy. The U.S. Agency for International Development's budget for democracy assistance jumped from $165 million in FY 1991 to $637 million eight years later, with the largest share of these funds designated for the former communist states of eastern Europe (Carothers 1999, 50–51). Most of this funding supported independent news media, interest groups, labor unions, and other elements of civil society.

Aside from foreign aid, U.S. leaders often feel compelled to impose "democracy by force" (von Hippel 2000). Iraq was only the latest in a long project of **state building,** the creation of political institutions that facilitate the orderly and democratic conduct of governance (see Fukuyama 2004). Whereas **nation building** refers to the development of a harmonious civil society, state building involves the brick and mortar of public administration. In both cases, major world powers have consistently endeavored to reform the governments of small countries that do not have adequate resources to manage the task themselves.

The U.S. occupations of the western portion of Germany and Japan after World War II are still regarded as the most successful state-building enterprises to date. The United States built new governments virtually from scratch in these countries, writing constitutions that separated powers, produced independent judiciaries, and protected freedoms of speech, press, and religion. Foreign-aid funds were then used for the construction of government buildings and the training of civil servants, military and police officers, journalists, and trade unionists. The German and Japanese efforts became role models for subsequent state-building missions, although none would compare in scope or in the significance of their outcomes. Until Iraq, the states being "rebuilt" maintained their sovereignty and were not occupied by U.S. troops. Yet the hegemony of the United States, that is, its ability to shape the behavior of other countries in the absence of formal political authority over them, allowed for dozens of state-building missions after World War II.

The shape of these missions varied widely. In many cases, particularly in Latin America during the 1960s, the combination of U.S. economic support and political persuasion was sufficient to open the doors to U.S. state builders. When foreign leaders objected, as in the case of Panama in 1989 and Haiti in 1994, the United States applied economic coercion and then military force when the nonviolent measures proved inadequate. The end of the cold war produced additional opportunities for state building. The 1992 U.S. intervention in Somalia, while successful in providing emergency relief to thousands of starving victims of a war-induced famine, fell apart after U.S. and UN peacekeeping forces tried in vain to create a viable government that would prevent a recurrence of humanitarian crises after they left.

A hooded Iraqi prisoner, standing on a box and strapped to electrical wires, is subjected to torture by U.S. interrogators at the Abu Ghraib prison in 2003. This photograph, along with many others, undermined the credibility of the United States as it attempted to bring democracy to Iraq after Saddam Hussein's overthrow. The United States has long promoted democratic reforms in foreign countries, so its repressive behavior naturally sparked charges of hypocrisy. Maintaining global primacy, a stated goal of the U.S. government since World War II, is made more difficult when the United States violates its own moral principles.

Military interventions in the former Yugoslavia were more successful in ending political violence and erecting new political institutions that kept the peace. Karin von Hippel (2000), a civil affairs officer at the UN mission in Kosovo, identified four factors that most state-building missions had in common: large refugee flows, widespread media attention to humanitarian suffering, failed efforts to impose economic sanctions, and defiance by rulers. The latter three factors applied to the Iraqi crisis in 2003 and 2004, but U.S. state builders faced a far more difficult task given the intense hostilities between the two countries since Saddam Hussein's invasion of Kuwait more than a decade earlier. The United States also lacked the legitimacy it would have gained by an endorsement of its actions by the UN Security Council. The credibility of the U.S. state-building effort was further battered by the Abu Ghraib prisoner-abuse scandal in 2004.

Several lessons emerge from these attempts by the U.S. government to export democracy. First, state-building efforts are unlikely to succeed without public support. Clinton's effort to "enlarge" global democracy occurred during a time when the public had little interest in foreign-policy activism. Thus it was predictable that when Clinton intervened in Haiti in 1994 to restore an elected regime, the initiative received little public support and later failed to restore democratic order.

Second, free and fair elections do not ensure the coming to power of democratic leaders or the conduct of government policy that respects domestic freedoms or international norms. Elections may instead produce an **illiberal democracy** (Zakaria 1997) in which elected leaders such as Russia's Vladimir Putin suppress the political rights of their citizens.

Third, security concerns almost always override concerns about democratic governance in the allocation of U.S. foreign aid. The government of Egypt, whose recognition of Israel is a linchpin of the Arab-Israeli peace process, remains a primary aid recipient despite its repressive government (see Hook 1998).

Finally, external support is most helpful to governments that have already initiated their democratic transitions. In countries where attempted transitions "are stagnating or slipping backward, democracy aid has few chances of reversing this trend" (Carothers 1999, 306). The prospects for jump starting reforms in countries with no experience with democratic rule are even remoter.

This final lesson offers a crucial reminder that democracy must ultimately originate *within* countries, not from outside persuasion or coercion. Domestic political leaders and citizens must have the will to undertake these difficult transitions. While external support can increase the chances that democratic reforms will succeed, no amount of foreign aid can transform a repressive state into a viable democracy without the support and engagement of that state's own people.

The International Criminal Court

The trend toward global democratization features new efforts to punish the most egregious crimes committed by governments in the name of political causes. The notion of **global jurisprudence,** or legal standards and restrictions above the nation-state level, was first raised at the Hague conferences of 1899 and 1907. Legal precedents for the International Criminal Court (ICC) go back to the Nuremberg and Tokyo tribunals after World War II (see D. Jones 2002). Efforts by the newly formed UN to create a permanent court succumbed to cold war pressures, as both superpowers vowed to veto any measures that violated their political agendas. International support for such a court was revived in the mid-1990s as ad hoc tribunals were established for the former Yugoslavia and Rwanda, scenes of large-scale ethnic warfare that left more than 1 million dead, almost all civilians.

These tribunals fueled the momentum for an international court that would hold other governments accountable for atrocities against their citizens or neighboring states (Schabas 2004). A 1998 conference in Italy produced an agreement known as the **Rome Statute,** which identified four categories of crimes to be handled by the proposed ICC (see Schmitt and Richards 2000). The first crime, *genocide,* includes mass attacks "with intent to destroy, in whole or part, a national ethnic, racial, or religious group." A second category, *crimes against humanity,* covers systematic violence against citizens, including murder, enslavement, torture, rape, and other inhumane acts. The ICC would also punish *war crimes,* the use of indiscriminate violence against civilians in pursuit of military goals, as well as unlawful acts of *foreign aggression.*

Negotiators of the ICC agreed that the court would consider only those cases that governments were unable or unwilling to handle on their own, thus upholding the vital principle of national jurisdiction. More than ninety countries ratified the Rome Statute and are now parties to the ICC, which came into force with the ratification of sixty governments. A panel of ICC judges will determine which cases will be referred to the court, and in some instances the UN Security Council will have influence over the selection of cases. A central presumption in creating the court was that its mere presence would encourage governments to strengthen their own legal protections and court systems so that outside intervention would not be necessary (Mayerfield 2003).

The United States reversed its stance from a strong supporter of the court to its primary opponent and critic. In opposing the Rome Statute, which passed by a vote of 120–7, the United States was joined by China, Iraq, Libya, Israel, Qatar, and Yemen.[4] Still, President Clinton signed the conference's final act on his last day in office so the United States could participate in negotiations on the structure of the court and the scope of its authority. Although the delegates in Rome made many concessions demanded by the United States, the concessions did not go far enough to prevent President Bush from "unsigning" Clinton's commitment and pulling out of future ICC negotiations.

The U.S. resistance to the ICC is rooted in the nation's global primacy. Beyond its unrivaled military power and economic productivity, the United States has been called upon to give greater contributions to UN peacekeeping forces than other countries. American primacy, as noted previously, creates inevitable resentments elsewhere. The deployment of U.S. troops in numerous regional conflicts, many under the UN flag, provides opportunities for adversaries to target the United States with charges of war crimes and foreign aggression. It is this fear of being singled out by the many countries hostile toward it that has kept the United States out of the ICC.

Even as the Clinton administration was considering the Rome Statute, critics of U.S. foreign policy suggested that Henry Kissinger, the former national security adviser and secretary of state, be indicted for his role in the Vietnam War and the 1973 coup in Chile (see Hitchens 2001). Errant bombings by the United States in the 1999 Kosovo intervention, which killed dozens of civilians, have also been identified as possible war crimes, as were the more recent prisoner abuses by U.S. forces in Iraq. In anticipating these charges, U.S. officials argue, the United States would be reluctant in the future to participate in any military interventions, even those widely supported by other countries and intergovernmental organizations.

Bush solidified U.S. opposition to the ICC in August 2002 by signing the American Service Members' Protection Act, which had passed in Congress by wide margins. The legislation banned U.S. financial assistance to the ICC and prohibited investigations by the court on U.S. soil. The act also limited U.S. involvement in peace-keeping missions to those in which the host nations guaranteed that U.S. forces would not be prosecuted for war crimes. In addition, it barred U.S. military aid to ICC members not part of NATO. Once the ICC's creation became inevitable, the U.S. government began making deals with individual countries not to prosecute the United States in future multilateral military operations.

The U.S. government's rejection of the ICC, along with the Kyoto Protocol and a variety of arms-control measures, has compounded the isolation of the United States within the international community. "The principle is one of national sovereignty at all costs over any binding form of international accountability," legal analyst Jean Galbraith (2003, 702) observed. "The image of America brandishing the human rights flag around the world has suffered a heavy blow," Claire Trean (2002, 2) wrote in the French newspaper *Le Monde*. As a country

---

4. Another twenty-one countries abstained on the vote for the Rome Statute.

relegated to observer status in ICC deliberations, the United States lost power over the court, including its budget, definition of crimes, and judicial nominations. Regaining such influence may serve as an incentive for the United States to join the ICC despite its many objections to the court.

Threats to Democracy at Home

The September 2001 terrorist attacks caused a seismic shift in how Americans perceived threats to the nation. Among these changes was a greater willingness to grant the federal government more powers in combating terrorism within the nation's borders. This support gained strength after investigations revealed that the hijackers had spent months in the United States preparing for the attacks. Many Americans felt that government officials at all levels should be granted heightened powers to prevent a reoccurrence of 9-11 even if the new measures encroached upon individual freedoms and civil rights.

In construing the terrorist attacks as acts of war, the Bush administration pursued and eagerly accepted this strengthening of federal powers. The primary missions of the Department of Justice and FBI abruptly turned to fighting terrorism. Attorney General John Ashcroft (2001) testified before Congress that the "wartime reorganization" of the Justice Department was necessary for federal agents to conduct "the largest, most comprehensive criminal investigation in history."

Reflecting this shift in the national mood, Congress quickly and overwhelmingly passed the USA Patriot Act in October 2001.[5] The measure, an acronym for "Uniting and Strengthening America by Providing Appropriate Tools Required to Intercept and Obstruct Terrorism," expanded federal powers of surveillance, detention, and search and seizure. More than 300 pages in length, the act broke down the "walls" that separated domestic intelligence gathering and law enforcement. Recognizing the potential threats to liberties and legal challenges posed by the act, Congress imposed "sunset provisions" on many measures, provisions that required their expiration of the measures by the end of 2005 unless renewed by subsequent legislation.

Among the Patriot Act's most contested provisions is Section 215, which expands the kinds of records the federal government can search in investigating suspected terrorists. The FBI previously had to demonstrate "probable cause" when requesting search warrants against such suspects, and the domains of FBI searches were limited largely to hotels, airlines, storage lockers, and car rentals. The Patriot Act expanded the list of searchable items to include "any tangible thing," including financial statements, library records, travel receipts, telephone logs, medical information, and memberships in religious institutions. Rather than making the case for probable cause, the act required that FBI agents only assert

---

5. Considering its vast scope, the rapid passage of the Patriot Act was unprecedented. The act was introduced in the House of Representatives on October 23, 2001, and passed the next day by a vote of 357–66. On October 26, the Senate approved the bill without amendment by a vote of 98–1. President Bush signed the bill later that day.

that the requested search would protect the United States against terrorism. The object of the search does not have to be an actual suspect, but anyone who might have information relating to terrorism.

Another of the Patriot Act's controversial provisions is the so-called sneak-and-peak measure. Before passage of the act, federal agents had to inform the targets of search warrants of the government's activities prior to the searches or soon afterward. The new measure held that search targets need be told only "within a reasonable period" as long as they are not charged with any violations of U.S. law. The act also provided more money for border security, broadened the definition of terrorism to include most violent acts against public officials and property, and expanded the grounds for denying foreign citizens entry into the United States. Harboring terrorists became a federal crime under the act, which allowed the Justice Department to detain suspects indefinitely and conduct "roving wiretaps" on the phone lines of suspected terrorists.

Despite being passed by huge margins in Congress in the wake of the 9-11 attacks, the Patriot Act has drawn fire from civil libertarians (see Dadge 2004; Brown 2003; and Leone and Anrig 2003). The American Civil Liberties Union sued the federal government, charging that many stipulations of the Patriot Act violated constitutional guarantees to privacy and equal protection under the law. The American Library Association, meanwhile, protested federal inspections of library records. Writing in the *American University Law Review,* John W. Whitehead and Steven H. Aden (2002, 1087) claimed that the nation's most cherished political liberties were under assault.

> The Act is only the phalanx of a broad new set of operating procedures adopted by federal law enforcement agencies, procedures which demonstrate a reassessment by the Bush administration—and perhaps the public itself—of the political expediency of maintaining a commitment to certain established civil and constitutional rights. . . . Regardless of the manner of execution, it is clear that all of these measures will have a significant impact on the American views of civil liberties enshrined in the Constitution and the traditional functioning of government.

A common complaint among critics concerns the "profiling" of suspected terrorists by the federal government (see Cole 2003). Expanded monitoring of immigration applications and passports did not apply equally to all foreign citizens. Instead they applied primarily to males from the Middle East and other areas with large Islamic populations. U.S. officials frequently singled out resident aliens—those permitted to reside in the country without gaining U.S. citizenship—for scrutiny and often detained them for lengthy periods. Further troubling to civil libertarians was the Justice Department's refusal to provide the public with information regarding the department's ongoing counterterrorism activities, including domestic surveillance on U.S. citizens.

This is not the first time in U.S. history that domestic political rights have been curbed in response to perceived threats from abroad (see Parenti 2003). The Alien and Sedition Acts of 1798, passed by Congress in anticipation of a war with France, made it illegal to "print, utter, or publish" criticisms of government policies. During

World War II, the U.S. government placed Japanese-Americans in detention camps, solely on the grounds of their heritage. Richard Nixon's efforts to suppress criticism during the Vietnam War provoked Supreme Court intervention on behalf of press freedoms in the *Pentagon Papers* case (see Chapter 4).

A key problem in the war on terrorism involves the open-ended nature of the conflict. The lack of clarity regarding the source of the terrorist threat and its impact within the United States provides cover for overzealous federal officials seeking to restrict political rights in the name of maintaining order. Highly uncertain as well are the circumstances that would allow the United States to declare "victory" in the conflict. This suggests that the war on terrorism, along with many provisions of the Patriot Act, will remain troubling facts of life far into the future. If political freedoms in the United States become casualties of the war, terrorists will have achieved a measure of success against their primary adversary, and U.S. leaders will face charges of hypocrisy as they promote greater respect for democracy by other governments.

Conclusion

The transnational problems highlighted in this chapter do not lend themselves to simple solutions. Barring a reversal of relentless historical patterns or a rethinking of scientific evidence, ecological threats to the global commons will intensify as the developing world undergoes its own industrial revolution. Given trends in the global arms market, the proliferation of weapons will also pose a continuing threat to international security. Differences over the meaning of human rights, the dilemmas stemming from "illiberal democracies," and tensions between promoting democracy and maintaining order will remain difficult to reconcile. Finally, problems related to the USA Patriot Act aptly demonstrate the dangers posed by open-ended global conflicts to democratic freedoms at home.

The United States has long been a catalyst for the two most vital forces in modern world politics: democratization and economic globalization. The first of these forces empowers citizens and civil societies, inviting them to serve as counterweights to the power of the state. The second of these forces provides the technological means for these private actors to connect with each other, both within their polities and increasingly across national borders. While enabling mass movements to gather momentum, globalization also encourages the pooling of financial resources and the dissemination of weaponry and techniques of political violence. Paradoxically, the pivot of world power shifts from the nation that most effectively *stimulated* these forces to transnational actors who consider that country to be the primary *obstacle* to their political aspirations. Thus the greatest threat to continued U.S. primacy comes from the very political and economic forces the United States inspired and actively supported.

Amid these changes in the structure and scope of transnational institutions, the United States maintains a system of governing institutions largely unchanged from the days of its founding. Here as well the objective is to fragment and fracture state power to deter tyranny, ensuring that societal pressures can penetrate the policy process and shape the course of government action within the United States and elsewhere. Since all interest groups are not created equal, however, their influence is skewed. Corporate influence over U.S. foreign policy, always considerable, has been particularly visible in the government's resistance to energy conservation, in its push for arms exports, and in its calculations behind the invasion and rebuilding of Iraq.

The diffusion of policy-making authority across a widening array of federal agencies, an inevitable by-product of efficient large-scale bureaucracy, further inhibits the government from advancing a singular, coherent set of principles and priorities. Little guidance can be expected from public opinion in the foreign-policy process given the inattention to world politics of many Americans, products of an educational system that has long neglected world history and geography. While the news media provide more information than ever regarding developments overseas, coverage of the Iraq invasion demonstrated the government's considerable power to manipulate journalists and discourage dissenting views. The concentration of media ownership, affecting television networks, radio stations, and newspaper chains, reduces the diversity of voices being heard.

The nation's political culture produces another recurring pattern of behavior: a chronic ambivalence regarding the global roles and responsibilities of the United States. As in the nation's early years, the U.S. government alternately seeks to detach itself from the outside world and to transform that world in its own image. Both impulses may coexist, as in George W. Bush's simultaneous retreat from the international community and his effort to lead a balance of power "that favors human freedom." A middle ground between the two, cooperating with other states on the basis of sovereign equality, seems to be ruled out by an ingrained sense of American exceptionalism.

The United States finds itself at a crucial point in its historical evolution. Despite its military and economic preponderance, the nation faces a world that stubbornly resists U.S. foreign-policy ambitions. Although pretensions of manifest destiny may have rationalized the extension of U.S. hegemony across the Western Hemisphere two centuries ago, they cannot so easily secure hegemonic control on a global scale today. Americans cannot assume that allies will "bandwagon" with the United States. Doubts about U.S. world power are especially strong at a time when the nation faces mounting budgetary constraints, trade deficits, and the tactical limitations of its military supremacy. Most disabling is the erosion of the country's moral authority, which stems from its recent actions overseas. Other countries see these actions as impetuous, arrogant, and contrary to the international community's widely adopted norms.

No single foreign government appears capable of upending the current unipolar world order. China, Russia, and Japan will likely remain preoccupied with internal concerns, and the European Union will focus primarily on absorbing new members and easing the strains that come with "dual sovereignty." Domestic problems will also preoccupy second-tier powers such as Brazil, India, Indonesia, and Nigeria, still recovering from a decade of economic stagnation and internal unrest. Nonetheless, a coalition of states supported by mobilized segments of global civil society can effectively resist the United States if its behavior appears more menacing than reassuring to them. All of this will render the task of U.S. foreign policy makers especially difficult in the years to come and the stakes enormously high for the security of the United States and of the international system.

Given the absence of other major powers that can match the U.S. government's economic, military, and political assets, the United States will likely retain its predominant status in the generation to come. American leaders will wield the greatest capacity to promote resolutions of the Arab-Israeli conflict, the standoff on the Korean peninsula, political turmoil in Russia, and humanitarian crises in Africa. The United States will also be best equipped to confront the transnational policy problems outlined in this chapter and to encourage the preservation of global public goods.

Whether or not the United States overcomes the paradox of its own world power will determine its fate in successive generations. The nation's success will depend upon its management of a world order largely of its own making—a turbulent order that is at once more closely interconnected and more disjointed than ever before. Such contradictions, integral elements of the United States' own political system and society during the nation's rise to global primacy, should be familiar to foreign-policy makers. The ability of past leaders to embrace these contradictory forces offers a fitting lesson for the future navigation of U.S. foreign policy.

Key Terms

backfire, p. 377

carrying capacity, p. 365

democratization, p. 379

demographic transition, p. 365

Earth Summit, p. 363

free riders, p. 362

global commons, p. 363

global jurisprudence, p. 387

global public goods, p. 362

global warming, p. 367

illiberal democracy, p. 386

Kyoto Protocol, p. 368

Mexico City policy, p. 366

nation building, p. 385

Rome Statute, p. 387

state building, p. 385

tragedy of the commons, p. 363

Internet References

The **Carnegie Council on Ethics and International Affairs** (www.carnegiecouncil.org) focuses on human rights, military conflict, environmental issues, economic disparities, and political reconciliation in war-torn areas. Scholars at the Carnegie Council produce research briefs and books regarding current topics that analyze the ethics of international relations and the U.S. role in these policy issues. The Carnegie Council produces a number of publications, including the journal *Ethics and International Affairs,* much of which is available online through the link to "publications" on its home page.

The **Carnegie Endowment for International Peace** (www.ceip.org) is a private, non-profit, and nonpartisan organization that focuses on global change by examining international organizations, bilateral relations, and political-economic forces in the world. The organization devotes specific attention to U.S.-Russian relationships as well as the geopolitics of the United States and other countries. The Carnegie Endowment for International Peace is also responsible for publishing *Foreign Policy* (www.foreignpolicy .com), one of the leading magazines for discussing world politics and foreign policy.

Foreign Policy in Focus (www.fpif.org) is a "think tank without walls" that emphasizes citizen-based foreign-policy issues. FPIF researchers compose short policy briefs on U.S. foreign-policy issues and global involvement such as trade, energy, environment, security, human rights, and labor. Much of the focus in their work is on the connection between private actors and the government.

Freedom House (www.freedomhouse.org) is a nonprofit, nonpartisan research organization committed to promoting and understanding civil and political freedoms around the world. The organization conducts research at the national, regional, and global levels of analysis. Many of its publications, including *Freedom in the World*, which uses an ordinal scale to measure civil and political freedoms, are available on the Freedom House Web site.

The **Global Policy Forum** (www.globalpolicy.org) integrates information and research on globalization, security issues, and the United Nations. Resources on the GPF Web site focus on UN and state accountability, issues of sovereignty, questions of empire, and the crisis in Iraq.

The **Institute for Global Communications** (www.igc.org) is a network for NGOs to discuss, promote, and influence transnational policies. Subject areas on the IGC Web site include human rights, peace promotion, environmental protection, women's rights, and workers' rights, found through the portals of four central networks: PeaceNet, AntiRacismNet, WomensNet, and EcoNet.

The **NGO Global Network** (www.ngo.org) tracks and analyzes NGOs with consultative status with the United Nations. The organization's Web site has links to NGOs around the globe organized by their missions and categories of operation.

U.S. Public Interest Research Group (www.uspirg.org) is a nonpartisan research group that serves state PIRGs by lobbying and researching large-scale policy issues. Areas of focus on the group's Web site include environment, energy, democratic governance, and health care. Research reviews and policy reports as well as congressional and presidential "score-cards" on multiple issues are also provided.

U.S. Administrations since World War II

President	Secretary of State	Secretary of Defense	National Security Adviser
Harry Truman 1945–1953	Edward Stettinius James Byrnes George Marshall Dean Acheson	James Forrestal Louis Johnson George Marshall Robert Lovett	
Dwight Eisenhower 1953–1961	John Dulles Christian Herter	Charles Wilson Neil McElroy Thomas Gates	Robert Cutler Dillon Anderson Robert Cutler Gordon Gray
John F. Kennedy 1961–1963	Dean Rusk	Robert McNamara	McGeorge Bundy
Lyndon Johnson 1963–1969	Dean Rusk	Robert McNamara Clark Clifford	McGeorge Bundy Walt Rostow
Richard Nixon 1969–1974	William Rogers Henry Kissinger	Melvin Laird Elliot Richardson James Schlesinger	Henry Kissinger
Gerald Ford 1974–1977	Henry Kissinger	James Schlesinger Donald Rumsfeld	Henry Kissinger Brent Scowcroft
Jimmy Carter 1977–1981	Cyrus Vance Edmund Muskie	Harold Brown	Zbigniew Brzezinski
Ronald Reagan 1981–1989	Alexander Haig George Shultz	Caspar Weinberger Frank Carlucci	Richard Allen William Clark Robert McFarlane John Poindexter Frank Carlucci Colin Powell
George Bush 1989–1993	James Baker Lawrence Eagleburger	Richard Cheney	Brent Scowcroft
Bill Clinton 1993–2001	Warren Christopher Madeleine Albright	Les Aspin William Perry William Cohen	Anthony Lake Samuel Berger
George W. Bush 2001–	Colin Powell	Donald Rumsfeld	Condoleezza Rice

The War Powers Resolution of 1973

JOINT RESOLUTION CONCERNING THE WAR POWERS OF CONGRESS AND THE PRESIDENT

Resolved by the Senate and House of Representatives of the United States of America in Congress assembled,

Short Title

SECTION 1. This joint resolution may be cited as the "War Powers Resolution."

Purpose and Policy

SEC. 2. (a) It is the purpose of this joint resolution to fulfill the intent of the framers of the Constitution of the United States and insure that the collective judgment of both the Congress and the President will apply to the introduction of the United States Armed Forces into hostilities, or into situations where imminent involvement in hostilities is clearly indicated by the circumstances, and to the continued use of such forces in hostilities or in such situations.

(b) Under article I, section 8, of the Constitution, it is specifically provided that the Congress shall have the power to make all laws necessary and proper for carrying into execution, not only its own powers but also all other powers vested by the Constitution in the Government of the United States, or in any department or officer thereof.

(c) The constitutional powers of the President as Commander-in-Chief to introduce United States Armed Forces into hostilities, or into situations where imminent involvement in hostilities is clearly indicated by the circumstances, are exercised only pursuant to (1) a declaration of war, (2) specific statutory authorization, or (3) a national emergency created by attack upon the United States, its territories or possessions, or its armed forces.

Consultation

SEC. 3. The President in every possible instance shall consult with Congress before introducing United States Armed Forces into hostilities or into situations where imminent involvement in hostilities is clearly indicated by the circumstances, and after every such introduction shall consult regularly with the Congress until United States Armed Forces are no longer engaged in hostilities or have been removed from such situations.

Reporting

SEC. 4. (a) In the absence of a declaration of war, in any case in which United States Armed Forces are introduced—

(1) into hostilities or into situations where imminent involvement in hostilities is clearly indicated by circumstances;

(2) into the territory, airspace or waters of a foreign nation, while equipped for combat, except for deployment which relate solely to supply, replacement, repair, or training of such forces; or

(3) in numbers which substantially enlarge United States Armed Forces equipped for combat already located in a foreign nation; the President shall submit within 48 hours to the Speaker of the House of Representatives and to the President pro tempore of the Senate a report, in writing, setting forth—

(A) the circumstances necessitating the introduction of United States Armed Forces;

(B) the constitutional and legislative authority under which such introduction took place; and

(C) the estimated scope and duration of the hostilities or involvement.

(b) The President shall provide such other information as the Congress may request in the fulfillment of its constitutional responsibilities with respect to committing the Nation to war and to the use of United States Armed Forces abroad.

(c) Whenever United States Armed Forces are introduced into hostilities or into any situation described in subsection (a) of this section, the President shall, so long as such armed forces continue to be engaged in such hostilities or situation, report to the Congress periodically on the status of such hostilities or situation as well as on the scope and duration of such hostilities or situation, but in no event shall he report to the Congress less often than once every six months.

Congressional Action

SEC. 5. (a) Each report submitted pursuant to section 4 (a) (1) shall be transmitted to the Speaker of the House of Representatives and to the President pro tempore of the Senate on the same calendar day. Each report so transmitted shall be referred to the Committee on Foreign Affairs of the House of Representatives and to the Committee on Foreign Relations of the Senate for appropriate action. If, when the report is transmitted, the Congress has adjourned sine die or has adjourned for any period in excess of three calendar days, the Speaker of the House of Representatives and the President pro tempore of the Senate, if they deem it advisable (or if petitioned by at least 30 percent of the membership of their respective Houses) shall jointly request the President to convene Congress in order that it may consider the report and take appropriate action pursuant to this section.

(b) Within sixty calendar days after a report is submitted or is required to be submitted pursuant to section 4 (a) (1), whichever is earlier, the President shall terminate any use of United States Armed Forces with respect to which such report was submitted (or required to be submitted), unless the Congress (1) has declared war or has enacted a specific authorization for such use of United States Armed Forces, (2) has extended by law such sixty-day period, or (3) is physically unable to meet as a result of an armed attack upon the United States. Such sixty-day period shall be extended for not more than an additional thirty days if the President determines and certifies to the Congress in writing that unavoidable military necessity respecting the safety of United States Armed Forces requires the continued use of such armed forces in the course of bringing about a prompt removal of such forces.

(c) Notwithstanding subsection (b), at any time that United States Armed Forces are engaged in hostilities outside the territory of the United States, its possessions and territories without a declaration of war or specific statutory authorization, such forces shall be removed by the president if the Congress so directs by concurrent resolution.

Congressional Priority Procedures for Joint Resolution or Bill

SEC. 6. (a) Any joint resolution or bill introduced pursuant to section 5(b) at least thirty calendar days before the expiration of the sixty-day period specified in such section shall be referred to the Committee on Foreign Affairs of the House of Representatives or the Committee on Foreign Relations of the Senate, as the case may be, and such committee shall report one such joint resolution or bill, together with its recommendations, not later than twenty-four calendar days before the expiration of the sixty-day period specified in such section, unless such House shall otherwise determine by the yeas and nays.

(b) Any joint resolution or bill so reported shall become the pending business of the House in question (in the case of the Senate the time for debate shall be equally divided between the proponents and the opponents), and shall be voted on within three calendar days thereafter, unless such House shall otherwise determine by yeas and nays.

(c) Such a joint resolution or bill passed by one House shall be referred to the committee of the other House named in subsection (a) and shall be reported out not later than fourteen calendar days before the expiration of the sixty-day period specified in section 5 (b). The joint resolution or bill so reported shall become the pending business of the House in question and shall be voted on within three calendar days after it has been reported, unless such House shall otherwise determine by yeas and nays.

(d) In the case of any disagreement between the two Houses of Congress with respect to a joint resolution or bill passed by both Houses, conferees shall be promptly appointed and the committee of conference shall make and file a report with respect to such resolution or bill not later than four calendar days before the expiration of the sixty-day period specified in section 5 (b). In the event the conferees are unable to agree within 48 hours, they shall report back to their respective Houses in disagreement. Notwithstanding any rule in either House concerning the printing of conference reports in the Record or concerning the printing of conference reports in the Record or concerning any delay in the consideration of such reports, such reports shall be acted on by both Houses not later than the expiration of such sixty-day period.

Congressional Priority Procedures for Concurrent Resolution

SEC. 7 (a) Any concurrent resolution introduced pursuant to section 5 (c) shall be referred to the Committee on Foreign Affairs of the House of Representatives or the Committee on Foreign Relations of the Senate, as the case may be, and one such concurrent resolution shall be reported out by such committee together with its recommendations within fifteen calendar days, unless such House shall otherwise determine by the yeas and nays.

(b) Any concurrent resolution so reported shall become the pending business of the House in question (in the case of the Senate the time for debate shall be equally divided between the proponents and the opponents) and shall be voted on within three calendar days thereafter, unless such House shall otherwise determine by yeas and nays.

(c) Such a concurrent resolution passed by one House shall be referred to the committee of the other House named in subsection (a) and shall be reported out by such committee together with its recommendations within fifteen calendar days and shall thereupon become the pending business of such House and shall be voted upon within three calendar days, unless such House shall otherwise determine by yeas and nays.

(d) In the case of any disagreement between the two Houses of Congress with respect to a concurrent resolution passed by both Houses, conferees shall be promptly appointed and the committee of conference shall make and file a report with respect to such concurrent resolution within six calendar days after the legislation is referred to the committee of conference. Notwithstanding any rule in either House concerning the printing of conference reports in the Record or concerning any delay in the consideration of such reports, such report shall be acted on by both Houses not later than six calendar days after the conference report is filed. In the event the conferees are unable to agree within 48 hours, they shall report back to their respective Houses in disagreement.

Interpretation of Joint Resolution

SEC. 8. (a) Authority to introduce United States Armed Forces into hostilities or into situations of wherein involvement in hostilities is clearly indicated by the circumstances shall not be inferred—

(1) from any provision of law (whether or not in effect before the date of the enactment of this joint resolution), including any provision contained in any appropriation Act, unless

such provision specifically authorizes the introduction of United States Armed Forces into hostilities or into such situations and states that it is intended to constitute specific statutory authorization within the meaning of this joint resolution; or

(2) from any treaty heretofore or hereafter ratified unless such treaty is implemented by legislation specifically authorizing the introduction of United States Armed Forces into hostilities or into such situations and stating that it is intended to constitute specific statutory authorization within the meaning of this joint resolution.

(b) Nothing in this joint resolution shall be construed to require any further specific statutory authorization to permit members of United States Armed Forces to participate jointly with members of the armed forces of one or more foreign countries in the headquarters operations of high-level military commands which were established prior to the date of enactment of this joint resolution and pursuant to the United Nations Charter or any treaty ratified by the United States prior to such date.

(c) For purposes of this joint resolution, the term introduction of United States Armed Forces includes the assignment of members of such armed forces to command, coordinate, participate in the movement of, or accompany the regular or irregular military forces of any foreign country or government when such military forces are engaged, or there exists an imminent threat that such forces will become engaged, in hostilities.

(d) Nothing in this joint resolution—

(1) is intended to alter the constitutional authority of the Congress or the President, or the provisions of existing treaties; or

(2) shall be construed as granting any authority to the President with respect to the introduction of United States Armed Forces into hostilities or into situations wherein involvement in hostilities is clearly indicated by the circumstances which authority he would not have had in the absence of this joint resolution.

Separability Clause

SEC. 9. If any provision of this joint resolution or the application thereof to any person or circumstance is held invalid, the remainder of the joint resolution and the application of such provision to any other person or circumstance shall not be affected thereby.

Effective Date

SEC. 10. This joint resolution shall take effect on the date of its enactment.

SOURCE: *Statutes at Large,* 93d Cong., 1st session, Nov. 7, 1973, 555–560.

Glossary

advisory networks   Issue-based groups of presidential advisers who have direct influence over policy decisions in their issue areas *(p. 113)*.

Almond-Lippmann consensus   A widespread, negative view jointly articulated by Gabriel Almond and Walter Lippmann that U.S. public opinion is volatile, incoherent, and irrelevant to the policy-making process *(p. 194)*.

Anti-Ballistic Missile (ABM) Treaty   A 1972 agreement between the United States and Soviet Union restricting each side's deployment of antimissile systems. Designed to enhance deterrence by keeping both superpowers vulnerable to nuclear attack. Nullified by the United States in 2002 *(p. 315)*.

asymmetric warfare   A tactic of armed conflict between two sides of unequal strength characterized by the weaker side exploiting the vulnerabilities of the stronger *(p. 10)*.

attentive public   The small segment of the U.S. general public that pays close attention to foreign-policy issues but has little influence in the government's policy making *(p. 191)*.

backfire   The unexpected use of U.S. weapons exports against the United States or its allies *(p. 377)*.

balance of power   The distribution of resources and capabilities among nation-states. Also, in realist theory, a belief that global stability can be maintained when the strongest nation-states have roughly equal levels of power *(p. 60)*.

balance of trade   The relationship between the value of a state's imports and exports. A surplus indicates a higher level of exports, whereas a deficit indicates a higher level of imports *(p. 335)*.

Baruch Plan   Proposal by the United States in 1946 to outlaw nuclear weapons and create common stocks of fissile material for development of peaceful nuclear programs. The terms of the plan were later rejected by the Soviet Union *(p. 313)*.

base force proposal   A blueprint of U.S. military forces after the cold war calling for the United States to shift from its posture of global defense to one based on confronting regional threats to the United States and its allies *(p. 172)*.

belief systems   Individual worldviews, formed early in life, that directly influence decision makers' foreign-policy goals and strategies as well as their responses to specific problems *(p. 84)*.

bipolar balance of power   A global power structure in which two countries maintain a predominant share of resources and form rival blocs to offset each other's advantages *(p. 37)*.

Boland Amendment   A congressional ban on U.S. financial aid "for the purpose of overthrowing the Government of Nicaragua" in the 1980s. Violations by the Reagan administration prompted the Iran-contra scandal *(p. 126)*.

bottom-up review   A plan developed by President Bill Clinton's secretary of defense, Les Aspin, calling for a leaner military force to manage the smaller-scale threats to the United States after the collapse of the Soviet Union *(p. 173)*.

bounded rationality   A decision-making environment characterized by an influx of more information than can be managed effectively, leading to policy decisions that do not fully conform to standards of rationality *(p. 83)*.

Bretton Woods agreements   A series of agreements approved by the United States and other market economies in 1944 that led to the creation of the World Bank and International Monetary Fund *(p. 42)*.

bureaucratic-politics model   A model of policy making that emphasizes inherent conflicts of interest among government agencies. The state is perceived as an arena of bureaucratic struggle rather than a "unitary actor" *(p. 77)*.

capital flight   The abrupt and large-scale withdrawal of private investments from a nation's domestic industries and stock markets, usually in response to a political or economic crisis *(p. 353)*.

carrying capacity   The physical limit of the earth's ecosystem to sustain human life threatened by population growth, resource depletion, and environmental degradation *(p. 365)*.

Case-Zablocki Act   Congressional bill passed in 1972 requiring presidents to report all international agreements to Congress within sixty days of their entering into force *(p. 125)*.

civil-military relations   The uneasy coexistence of civilian and military "cultures" in the United States that may hinder cohesion and effective security policy *(p. 157)*.

clientitis   State Department employees' overly close relationships with foreign governments and citizens that may cloud their judgment regarding U.S. global priorities *(p. 164)*.

CNN effect   A pattern in which globalized news coverage of a crisis abroad prompts government action in U.S. foreign policy *(p. 207)*.

codetermination   A principle expressed in the U.S. Constitution calling for the sharing of foreign-policy powers between the executive and legislative branches of government *(p. 93)*.

coercive diplomacy   The threat to use force to reverse an adversary's offensive action. Often used by stronger powers to achieve foreign-policy goals without violence *(p. 308)*.

cognitive closure   The adoption of a solution to a problem before all the available information has been fully examined and alternative strategies have been considered *(p. 85)*.

cognitive consistency   The common, subconscious tendency of individuals to perceive political actions as consistent with their preexisting belief systems *(p. 85)*.

cognitive psychology   The process by which individuals obtain and process information about the world around them *(p. 85)*.

collective security   A system of preventing interstate conflict in which world leaders renounce war as an instrument of statecraft, then pledge to defend each other in the case of aggression. A hallmark of the League of Nations *(p. 32)*.

collegial model   A management style that encourages open dialogue among presidential advisers in order to gain consensus *(p. 116)*.

comparative advantage   A global division of labor in which each country's producers contribute to the world economy in areas that draw on their unique strengths. According to Ricardian economics, this would lead to a prosperous global market economy *(p. 342)*.

competitive model   A management style that encourages open debate among advisers, often without regard to rank, allowing the president to select the policy that is defended most persuasively *(p. 115)*.

congressional deference   A tendency among legislators to grant the executive branch substantial autonomy in managing federal agencies created by Congress *(p. 153)*.

congressional diplomacy   Efforts by the president to consult members of Congress at various stages of the foreign-policy process. Seen as crucial to achieving White House goals in foreign policy *(p. 124)*.

congressional-dominance model   A model of policy making that views legislators in Congress as masters of the federal bureaucracy, capable of ensuring that their policy preferences are carried out in the policy process *(p. 77)*.

constituent service   Legislators' primary attention to the needs of citizens in their states and districts as opposed to more general national concerns *(p. 137)*.

constructivism   A critical body of social and political thought which argues that public problems, including those involving foreign policy, do not have fixed or "objective" properties but rather are socially constructed, primarily through public discourse *(p. 68)*.

containment   The U.S. strategy devised by George Kennan at the start of the cold war to prevent Soviet expansion. A mid-range alternative to the extremes of U.S. withdrawal from global activism and direct military conflict with the Soviet Union *(p. 37)*.

corporate warriors   Private contractors engaged in the provision of military services, from cooking meals to interrogating prisoners, in theaters of armed conflict. Increasingly utilized by the United States and some smaller governments *(p. 252)*.

cosmopolitan groups   Nongovernmental organizations that seek to influence transnational problems in world politics, such as environmental decay and weapons proliferation, which affect people in all areas *(p. 229)*.

counterintelligence   Efforts by intelligence agents to counter and obstruct attempts by foreign agents to infiltrate a country's political process or compromise its national interests *(p. 179)*.

covert operations   Secret efforts by U.S. intelligence agencies to effect changes that are favorable to the United States within foreign governments *(p. 179)*.

crony capitalism   The favorable treatment government officials give to private business interests, often in exchange for illicit financial rewards *(p. 286)*.

cyberterrorism   Form of nonmilitary political conflict by which an adversarial state or private group gains access to and disrupts a government's computer system *(p. 218)*.

defense policy   The organization and strategic deployment of armed forces to protect a state against foreign military threats *(p. 294)*.

delegate model   One of two models of political representation (the other is the trustee model). Holds that elected officials should act on the general public's preferences on a given policy issue *(p. 192)*.

democratic deficit   The lack of legal requirements for openness and elected representation in nongovernmental organizations *(p. 228)*.

democratic peace   A theory of international relations arguing that a world of democracies would be more cooperative and less prone to interstate violence *(p. 50)*.

democratization   The process by which states adopt and implement democratic reforms. Also a foreign government's promotion of democratic reforms in other states, often through the use of foreign aid or moral suasion *(p. 379)*.

demographic transition   The process by which societies experience falling rates of population growth and rising life expectancies as they undergo the transition from agricultural to industrial economies *(p. 365)*.

détente   A policy devised by Henry Kissinger, national security adviser and secretary of state under presidents Richard Nixon and Gerald Ford, to ease tensions between the United States and the Soviet Union *(p. 46)*.

digital diplomacy   Increased contact among governments made possible by advances in telecommunications technology *(p. 216)*.

diplomacy   The negotiations among representatives of two or more sovereign states involving official matters of mutual or collective concern *(p. 160)*.

diversionary theory of war   A possible cause of war in which political leaders provoke armed conflicts to divert public attention from domestic problems or to boost their public-approval ratings *(p. 201)*.

divided government   A political deadlock that results when Congress and the White House are controlled by different political parties *(p. 130)*.

domestic terrorism   Acts of terrorism in which the perpetrators and their targets are located within the same nation-state *(p. 320)*.

domino theory   Widespread view within the U.S. government early in the cold war that a communist victory in one country would lead to a succession of additional victories in neighboring states *(p. 45)*.

Earth Summit   A major UN-sponsored environmental conference in 1992 held in Brazil, which identified "sustainable development" as a central objective in the post–cold war era *(p. 363)*.

economic liberalism   A political-economic system that protects private property and commercial activity from government intervention. Identified with Adam Smith, an Enlightenment theorist *(p. 332)*.

economic nationalism   A political-economic system that considers commercial activity fruitful to the extent that it serves the interests of the state, whose power depends on the accumulation of wealth and its use for military armament *(p. 333)*.

economic sanctions   Material penalties imposed by states or intergovernmental organizations on foreign countries involving trade, aid, foreign investments, or other aspects of economic relations. Imposed to force adherence to political demands *(p. 353)*.

electoral calculations   The strategic voting choices of members of Congress focused on getting reelected. Determined by rational calculations of political costs and benefits *(p. 140)*.

elitism   A challenge to pluralist theory that argues that political power even in democratic systems is highly concentrated among a few government leaders and the wealthiest citizens *(p. 66)*.

embeds   Reporters "embedded" with U.S. military troops during the 2003 invasion of Iraq to provide firsthand accounts. Accurately anticipated by government leaders to produce more favorable coverage *(p. 208)*.

engagement and enlargement   President Bill Clinton's national security policy emphasizing U.S. global activism and the promotion of political reforms abroad that would "enlarge" the sphere of democratic rule *(p. 51)*.

exceptionalism   A widely held sense of national distinctiveness or superiority, exemplified by Americans' traditional view of their nation as a "city upon a hill" *(p. 13)*.

executive agreements   Formal agreements with foreign governments negotiated by the executive branch that do not require Senate ratification. Often serve as an alternative to treaties *(p. 102)*.

exit strategy   A coherent plan that is adopted to conclude military hostilities and remove a country's presence from a theater of conflict in a way that preserves the country's political and military interests in the conflict *(p. 307)*.

extended deterrence   Avowed nuclear retaliation against attacks not only on a country's territory, but also on the territory of its allies *(p. 314)*.

failed states   National governments that are incapable of maintaining order or providing even minimal services to their citizens *(p. 53)*.

fast-track authority   An arrangement in which Congress expedites the review and possible approval of trade agreements reached by U.S. presidents and foreign governments *(p. 344)*.

finished intelligence   Information about foreign countries or developments abroad that is processed and interpreted by intelligence agencies so it is useful to policy makers *(p. 178)*.

flexible response   A security strategy adopted by the U.S. government during the cold war that allowed for a range of military actions—nuclear and conventional—in response to offensive threats posed to the United States and its allies *(p. 314)*.

floating exchange rates   A system in which the value of a country's currency is determined by market forces rather than government intervention, based largely on the relative value of other currencies *(p. 340)*.

foreign aid   Economic resources provided by affluent governments to less-developed countries on terms unavailable to the recipients through commercial markets. May take the form of development or security assistance *(p. 345)*.

foreign direct investment (FDI)   Private capital used to secure commercial assets in one country by residents or corporations in another country *(p. 335)*.

foreign service officers   Members of the State Department who conduct administrative and diplomatic tasks in foreign embassies and consulates *(p. 162)*.

foreign-policy elite   The small segment (less than five percent) of the U.S. population that has both the interest and the means to influence U.S. foreign policy *(p. 191)*.

formalistic model   A presidential management style characterized as orderly and hierarchical, featuring structured discussion of issues following well-defined procedures and communication channels *(p. 115)*.

framing   Governmental attempts at structuring and simplifying foreign-policy problems so they are understood by citizens in ways that favor the government's position. Generally supported by news organizations *(p. 213)*.

free riders   Individuals or groups that benefit from the sacrifices of others without making sacrifices of their own on matters of shared concern. Central to the collective-action problem in the management of public goods *(p. 362)*.

full-spectrum deterrence   A security strategy intended to discourage challenges to the United States in a wide array of military scenarios, not simply to prevent a showdown with another nuclear power *(p. 315)*.

geoeconomics   The interaction of national economies in the world economy. Also the global production and distribution of economic output as a national priority *(p. 182)*.

geopolitical assets   A nation's available physical and human resources, such as its size, location, and natural resources, and their utility in foreign policy *(p. 298)*.

geopolitics   The impact of geographical factors on the distribution of global power and the foreign policies of states *(p. 32)*.

glasnost   Political reforms adopted by Soviet President Mikhail Gorbachev in the late 1980s that called for greater openness in the political system and a loosening of control by the Communist Party *(p. 48)*.

global commons   The earth's fragile ecosystem that sustains animal and plant life. Generally involves physical resources shared by all inhabitants *(p. 363)*.

global governance   Combines traditional state-to-state diplomacy with policy collaboration among private groups and intergovernmental organizations *(p. 227)*.

global jurisprudence   Legal standards and restrictions that are applied above the nation-state level *(p. 387)*.

global public goods   Collective resources that are shared by inhabitants in more than one region of the world *(p. 362)*.

global warming   Rising average temperatures on the earth's surface due to population growth, industrialization, and the resulting fossil-fuel emissions *(p. 367)*.

globalization   The melding of national and regional markets into a single world market with limited political barriers to commerce *(p. 8)*.

gold standard   A system of "fixed" exchange rates in which the values of national currencies are based on the value of gold. An alternative to "floating" exchange rates that currently define currency values *(p. 340)*.

Goldwater-Nichols Act   Legislative measure approved in 1986 that altered the balance of power within the Pentagon by strengthening the power of the Joint Chiefs of Staff chairman and increasing the power of regional commanders in chief who manage forces across the armed services *(p. 172)*.

grand strategy   A statement of a nation's essential objectives in world politics and the means to achieve those objectives *(p. 297)*.

gross national income   Measure of economic output that represents the total value of goods and services produced by residents of a country in a single year, plus receipts of private income and foreign aid from abroad *(p. 334)*.

Group of 8 (G-8)   An informal body of wealthy countries that meets annually to coordinate economic and, in some cases, political and security policies. Comprises Canada, France, Germany, Italy, Japan, the United Kingdom, the United States, and Russia (the most recent member) *(p. 260)*.

Group of 77 (G-77)   A coalition of developing countries created in the 1970s that represents most of the world's population and wields majority status in the UN General Assembly. Designed to gain benefits from wealthy states *(p. 266)*.

groupthink   Dysfunctional collective decision making characterized by a strong sense of a group's moral righteousness, closed-mindedness, and pressures toward conformity *(p. 89)*.

Gulf of Tonkin Resolution   Congress's 1964 authorization for President Lyndon Johnson to "take all necessary measures" to protect U.S. forces supporting the government of South Vietnam *(p. 125)*.

gunboat diplomacy   The use of deployed military forces as a means of political intimidation in order to achieve a nation's foreign-policy preferences without actually resorting to violence *(p. 29)*.

guns-or-butter debates   Ongoing tensions regarding federal spending for defense versus social programs and domestic needs *(p. 146)*.

hegemonic stability theory   A model of world politics in which a stable and commercially dynamic interstate system is only possible when a dominant power assumes the public costs of military security and economic coordination *(p. 302)*.

hegemony   Controlling influence by one nation-state over other countries and societies that falls short of formal political authority *(p. 6)*.

Helms-Biden Act   Congressional legislation passed in 1999 calling for the partial payment of unpaid U.S. dues to the United Nations in return for a variety of UN reforms *(p. 270)*.

Helms-Burton Act   Congressional legislation passed in 1996 imposing penalties on foreign countries that benefit economically from confiscated U.S. property in Cuba *(p. 355)*.

Homeland Security Council   A body of advisers created by executive order after the 9-11 attacks to consult with the president on all matters related to homeland security *(p. 174)*.

human intelligence (HUMINT)   Information gained by intelligence agencies from foreign informants working undercover *(p. 178)*.

idea brokers   Nongovernmental actors in policy debates who attempt to influence public opinion and government action through the dissemination of research findings and the airing of opinions on a variety of issues *(p. 242)*.

identity   The definition and widely held conception of an individual or group as considered apart from others. A component of constructivist theory *(p. 69)*.

ideology   A person's general principles and normative beliefs regarding human nature, the relationships between state and society, and the nation's roles and responsibilities in world politics *(p. 140)*.

illiberal democracy   Form of government in which an elected governmental regime adopts policies that repress political freedoms and human rights *(p. 386)*.

imperial presidency   A critique of the U.S. political system advanced in the 1970s by historian Arthur M. Schlesinger, who described the president as governing virtually "by decree" *(p. 94)*.

industrial policy   An outgrowth of economic nationalism that combines protectionist trade measures with a close working relationship among government agencies, corporate boards, and financial institutions *(p. 344)*.

information security   Unfettered communication flows protected from disruption by computer hackers, particularly within governmental agencies *(p. 218)*.

inner circle   A small group of presidential advisers, including agency heads and personal advisers, who have direct influence over the president's policy choices *(p. 113)*.

institutional bargain   An arrangement by which the dominant state in the interstate system provides economic and other benefits to smaller powers in return for their compliance with its policy preferences *(p. 261)*.

institutional momentum   The proliferation and expanding roles of organized political actors in the foreign-policy process at home and abroad *(p. 71)*.

integration   The creation of supranational political institutions that claim sovereign powers above those maintained by member states. More generally, the process by which nation-states become more functionally interconnected through intergovernmental organizations *(p. 262)*.

intelligence cycle   The five-stage intelligence process moving from planning and direction to collection, processing, analysis, and finally dissemination to policy makers *(p. 178)*.

Intelligence Oversight Act of 1980   Legislative measure empowering House and Senate committees to oversee U.S. intelligence activities and requiring presidents to notify Congress about covert operations in foreign countries *(p. 126)*.

interdependence   The concept that nation-states are increasingly dependent on conditions and events that extend beyond their borders and must cooperate with one another in response to such factors *(p. 261)*.

intergovernmental organizations (IGOs)   Formal political bodies, representing two or more national governments, that permit their members to pursue goals beyond their individual reach and to solve shared problems *(p. 257)*.

intermestic policy   The merger of international and domestic policy concerns, such as trade and the environment *(p. 126)*.

international financial institutions (IFIs)   Formal associations of nation-states designed to regulate and promote the global market economy. The most prominent examples include the World Bank, International Monetary Fund, and World Trade Organization *(p. 281)*.

international political economy   The domain of political economy in which governments seek to manage economic activity beyond their borders in ways that advance their policy goals and principles *(p. 331)*.

interservice rivalry   The clashing institutional interests, resource requirements, missions, and organizational cultures of different U.S. armed services *(p. 157)*.

iron curtain   A term coined by British Prime Minister Winston Churchill in 1946 to describe the metaphorical line separating communist countries under Soviet control from the capitalist countries of western Europe supported by the United States. Remained intact throughout the cold war *(p. 37)*.

iron triangle   The alliance of influential interest groups, congressional committees, and corresponding executive-branch agencies to carry out policies of mutual concern to the exclusion of other policy actors or outside interests *(p. 67)*.

issue networks   A model of decision making that involves more actors and is more open to competing viewpoints than the iron-triangle model. Brings together interested governmental and private actors with shared expertise in a given area of public policy *(p. 81)*.

Jackson-Vanik Amendment   Legislative measure, approved in 1974, preventing presidents from granting most-favored-nation trade status to foreign countries that restricted the emigration of their citizens *(p. 125)*.

just-war doctrine   A code of conduct that originated in the Middle Ages establishing moral and ethical standards regarding the use of military force *(p. 321)*.

Kyoto Protocol   An intergovernmental agreement approved in 1997 calling on signatories to reduce greenhouse-gas emissions linked to global warming. Not approved by the United States *(p. 368)*.

latent public opinion   Ingrained, generalized values and beliefs regarding public life that are dormant until they are "activated" by the emergence of specific, related issues on the policy agenda or in public debates *(p. 197)*.

liberal internationalism   A key aspect of President Jimmy Carter's foreign policy that called for active U.S. global involvement that was consistent with its moral principles and political ideals *(p. 47)*.

liberal theory   A prevalent political theory of the Enlightenment era emphasizing the importance of political and economic freedom versus the power of the state *(p. 59)*.

linkage strategy   The Nixon administration's policy toward the Soviet Union that tied U.S. economic concessions to improved Soviet behavior on human rights and key foreign-policy issues *(p. 355)*.

living-room war   A term that originated during the Vietnam War to describe a U.S. military conflict brought to American homes graphically and daily through extensive television coverage *(p. 206)*.

lobbying   A tactic of appealing directly to government officials for support of policy preferences. Commonly employed by interest groups *(p. 248)*.

logrolling   The practice of "trading" legislative votes in which a member of Congress supports one measure with the expectation of garnering support from other legislators for a separate measure *(p. 141)*.

management style   The working relationship a president establishes among his advisers that reflects the president's worldview and personality *(p. 115)*.

manifest destiny   A belief popular in the early history of the United States that the nation had God's blessing to expand and assume political control of a wider population *(p. 28)*.

market democracy   A model of political economy that combines free enterprise and constitutional, representative government *(p. 281)*.

Marshall Plan   Named after President Harry Truman's secretary of state, George Marshall, a U.S. foreign-policy initiative approved in 1947 that provided U.S. allies with economic aid to hasten their recovery after World War II *(p. 42)*.

Marxism   A set of theories developed by Karl Marx (1818–1883) that is critical of capitalism and the exploitation of workers by wealthy property owners and their governmental patrons. Today it is an explanation for the persistent gaps between the world's richest and poorest peoples and a model for a new political and economic order that removes the uncertainties of market economics *(p. 65)*.

mass public   The large segment of the U.S. population that is neither well informed nor strongly interested in most foreign-policy issues and thus has little direct impact on the policy process *(p. 191)*.

massive retaliation   A security strategy based on the promise of the nuclear annihilation of the sponsor of an attack on the vital interests of the state that adopts the strategy *(p. 306)*.

Mexico City policy   A policy first approved by the Reagan administration prohibiting U.S. economic assistance to foreign family-planning agencies that offer abortion counseling or services *(p. 366)*.

military alliances   Formal collaborations between two or more countries on security matters of mutual concern *(p. 273)*.

mission creep   The tendency of limited military deployments to take on new tasks and open-ended commitments *(p. 308)*.

Monroe Doctrine   Proclamation by President James Monroe in 1823 that politically separated the United States from Europe and declared future colonization in the Western Hemisphere a threat to U.S. national security *(p. 27)*.

most-favored-nation trading status   The provision of equal market access and terms of trade to all states participating in the General Agreement on Tariffs and Trade (GATT) system *(p. 340)*.

multilateralism   The collaborative foreign-policy making of several countries, which acknowledges the collective and overlapping interests of states *(p. 258)*.

multinational corporations (MNCs)   Profit-seeking firms with operations, subsidiaries, and markets in more than one country. The largest and arguably most politically powerful type of nongovernmental organization *(p. 229)*.

mutual assured destruction (MAD)   A nuclear stalemate that occurs when two nuclear-equipped adversaries credibly promise massive retaliation against each other in the event of an attack *(p. 314)*.

nation building   The process by which an external government, intergovernmental organization, or nongovernmental organization attempts to create the conditions necessary for a nation to gain internal cohesion and solidarity *(p. 385)*.

national interest   A self-justifying rationale for foreign-policy actions that presumes an inherent "interest" maintained by the state that overrides parochial interests of government bureaucracies or societal groups *(p. 60)*.

national security   The freedom a nation-state enjoys from threats to its sovereignty, territory, and political autonomy *(p. 293)*.

national security adviser   Technically known as the special assistant for national security affairs. A top aide who consults the president on a regular basis and coordinates the input of other foreign-policy advisers *(p. 168)*.

national security state   A political system in which the institutions of national defense overshadow the nonmilitary agencies of the government *(p. 39)*.

national style   The expression of cultural influences that have historically shaped a country's identity and approach to international relations *(p. 12)*.

Nelson-Bingham Amendment   Legislative measure approved in 1974 authorizing Congress to review foreign arms sales of more than $25 million and to reject such sales through a concurrent resolution of both chambers *(p. 125)*.

neoconservatives   Adherents to a U.S. foreign-policy perspective that believes the nation should freely use its immense power to change the world order in ways that reflect U.S. economic and political principles *(p. 114)*.

neoliberal institutionalism   A view of international cooperation that emphasizes reciprocal gestures of trust and goodwill, leading to a pattern of rewards on both sides that discourages future acts of coercion or aggression *(p. 62)*.

neorealism   A variant of realist theory focusing on the anarchic nature of the international system as the ultimate and inevitable cause of interstate conflicts *(p. 59)*.

new isolationism   Congressional trend in the late 1990s marked by a turning away from U.S. global engagement *(p. 128)*.

New Look   President Dwight Eisenhower's shift in security strategy that enlarged the role of nuclear weapons and created new military alliances to contain the Soviet Union and China *(p. 44)*.

new unilateralism   A shift in U.S. foreign policy in the late 1990s characterized by a hostile stance toward multilateral agreements and intergovernmental bodies, particularly the United Nations and its agencies *(p. 53)*.

new world order   President George H. W. Bush's characterization of the emerging post–cold war international system, emphasizing democratization, economic globalization, and multilateral cooperation *(p. 50)*.

norms   Widely agreed-upon normative principles and standards of appropriate conduct in political life, including foreign policy. A central element of liberal theory *(p. 61)*.

NSC-68   A secret 1950 National Security Council study calling for a massive U.S. military buildup around the world to prevent Soviet expansion *(p. 43)*.

nuclear deterrence   The prevention of hostilities through the threat of using nuclear weapons *(p. 314)*.

open-door policy   A policy adopted by the U.S. government in 1899 that called for free trade access to China and discouraged other trading states from dividing China into spheres of influence *(p. 30)*.

Operation Desert Storm   The name of the U.S.-led counteroffensive against Iraq to eject its forces from Kuwait in 1991 *(p. 52)*.

operational code   An individual's integrated set of conceptions about political life that informs his or her calculations of appropriate and effective policy *(p. 84)*.

organizational culture   The set of shared values, goals, and functional priorities of the members of a government agency *(p. 156)*.

organizational expertise   The specialized knowledge federal bureaucrats gain in the policy domains under their direction *(p. 154)*.

out-of-area conflicts   Armed conflicts that occur outside the territory of a military alliance. More specifically, the potential conflicts NATO members used to justify maintaining the alliance after the cold war *(p. 276)*.

oversight   Congress's ability, enhanced in the 1970s and 1980s, to monitor the president's conduct of foreign policy *(p. 125)*.

parachute journalism   A pattern of news coverage in which reporters descend on a trouble spot and then move on, never gaining a deep understanding of the problems in the areas that would have given their reporting greater substance *(p. 211)*.

particularistic groups   Nongovernmental organizations seeking to influence U.S. foreign policy that serve a limited number of individuals with stakes in the groups' missions. An alternative to cosmopolitan groups *(p. 229)*.

Partnership for Peace (PfP)   A NATO auxiliary that provides for mutual consultations and the sharing of resources among its members, as well as possible future NATO membership *(p. 275)*.

peaceful coercion   A tactic employed by a superior military power of exercising influence across national borders and gaining foreign-policy preferences without the use of violence *(p. 297)*.

Pentagon Papers   The detailed reports published in 1971 by the *New York Times* on the Nixon administration's efforts to conceal its military activities in Southeast Asia. Publication of these reports, which Nixon tried to block, was affirmed by the U.S. Supreme Court on constitutional grounds *(p. 206)*.

perestroika   Political reforms adopted by Soviet President Mikhail Gorbachev in the late 1980s that called for the restructuring of the Soviet economy to spur innovation and efficiency *(p. 48)*.

pluralist theory   A body of democratic political thought that claims that diverse interest groups are vital to political outcomes and compete with one another for influence on a generally equal basis *(p. 19)*.

political action committees (PACs)   The electoral arms of organized groups that are responsible for fund-raising and distributing money to promote the election of desired candidates *(p. 234)*.

political economy   An arena of public life, located at the crossroads of states and markets, in which governments seek to organize domestic economic activity in ways that advance their policy goals and principles *(p. 330)*.

Powell Doctrine   Policy articulated in the early 1990s by Colin Powell when he was chairman of the Joint Chiefs of Staff. Calls for the United States to prevail decisively in military conflicts and to have a clear exit strategy *(p. 307)*.

power elite   A term used to describe the small number of government officials, business leaders, and top figures in civil society who, according to elite theorists, control U.S. foreign and domestic policies *(p. 66)*.

preemptive war   A military attack initiated by one country whose leaders believe an attack from another country is imminent *(p. 310)*.

prerogative powers   A president's freedom to make independent and binding judgments, extending beyond national emergencies to include day-to-day decisions, that do not require the blessing of Congress or the courts *(p. 99)*.

presidential limitations   The restrictions presidents face, because of their limited time in office and need to focus on a wide variety of policy matters simultaneously, that provide advantages to "semipermanent" bureaucratic specialists *(p. 154)*.

presidential-control model   A model of policy making that views presidents as caretakers of the national interest who can rise above domestic politics, particularly in cases where U.S. security interests are at stake *(p. 77)*.

preventive war   A military attack initiated by one country whose leaders believe an emerging challenger presents a long-term threat, thereby eliminating the threat before it materializes *(p. 311)*.

primacy   A country's predominant stature in the hierarchy of global power *(p. 2)*.

procedural innovations   Structural and institutional reforms that enhance congressional impact on the policy-making process. Often of greater political value and easier to pass than substantive legislation *(p. 138)*.

propaganda   False or misleading public information designed to enhance the stature of the originating government or its policies *(p. 213)*.

public diplomacy   Efforts by the U.S. government, often through the mobilization of private citizens and groups, to appeal directly to foreign citizens and strengthen international support for the United States *(p. 165)*.

public good   Collective resources, such as clean air and water, that benefit individuals without diminishing their availability to others *(p. 224)*.

public relations presidency   A governing style in which the U.S. president is primarily guided by public opinion in making policy decisions *(p. 191)*.

public-choice theory   A model of public policy arguing that competitive private firms supply goods and services more efficiently than government agencies *(p. 251)*.

quadrennial defense review   A congressionally mandated report on U.S. military forces and strategy to be compiled and submitted by the Defense Department at the beginning of each presidential term *(p. 173)*.

rally-around-the-flag effect   The sharp increase in a president's public approval rating that occurs when the nation faces a military crisis. Generally attributed to a patriotic sense among citizens that national unity must be maintained in times of crisis *(p. 201)*.

rational actors   Foreign-policy makers who, in the view of realist theory, weigh their options based on common understandings of key problems and clear calculations of the costs and benefits of possible solutions *(p. 60)*.

raw intelligence   Unprocessed information about foreign governments and developments abroad collected by intelligence agents from various sources and later shared with policy makers after it has been processed *(p. 178)*.

realist theory   A pessimistic theory of world politics that emphasizes irreversible flaws in human nature and the resulting conflicts that occur at all levels of societal interaction, including interstate relations *(p. 59)*.

regional integration   The process by which close economic and political cooperation among states in a particular region offers a remedy for chronic military conflicts. Most often applied to the evolution of the European Union *(p. 275)*.

revolution in military affairs   Rapid changes in military technology that allow governments to increase the potency of their armed forces without making them larger or more expensive *(p. 173)*.

Rome Statute   An intergovernmental agreement approved in 1998 in which signatories identified a variety of crimes—genocide, crimes against humanity, war crimes, and foreign aggression—that would fall under the jurisdiction of the proposed International Criminal Court *(p. 387)*.

rooftop journalism   Style of war reporting in which journalists provide accounts of military conflicts from nearby vantage points, often the top of buildings. Became a staple of televised war coverage during the 1991 Persian Gulf War *(p. 207)*.

Roosevelt Corollary   President Theodore Roosevelt's 1904 expansion of the Monroe Doctrine proclaiming that the United States had authority to act as an "international police power" outside its borders in order to maintain stability in the Western Hemisphere *(p. 30)*.

security community   A region of the world in which governments form close political, economic, and military ties to such an extent that war among them becomes unthinkable. Often associated with the European Union *(p. 62)*.

security umbrella   A metaphorical term to describe the military protection that members of an alliance receive from the dominant state or states in the alliance *(p. 274)*.

selective perception   The process by which people tend to seek out information that reinforces their worldviews while ignoring or dismissing contradictory information. *(p. 85)*.

shadow government   A governing group operating beyond the reach of the public, Congress, the courts, or other executive branch agencies. Often used to describe the secretive National Security Council staff linked to the Iran-contra scandal *(p. 170)*.

situational context   The importance of idiosyncratic factors, including the nature and timing of issues before Congress, that influence the degree of cooperation between the legislative and executive branches *(p. 123)*.

situational factors   The objective details of a given problem facing Congress and the calculated costs and benefits of proposed legislative solutions *(p. 139)*.

smart sanctions   Economic penalties designed to punish government elites rather than the most vulnerable citizens in the target state *(p. 357)*.

Smoot-Hawley Tariff Act   Congressional measure passed in 1930 and signed by President Herbert Hoover that dramatically increased tariffs on goods coming into the United States. A key factor in the onset of the Great Depression *(p. 343)*.

socialism   A political-economy model that seeks to ensure economic equality through social-welfare programs and government ownership of vital enterprises, while also allowing citizens to own private property and operate firms *(p. 332)*.

soft power   The attractiveness of a nation's political and cultural values to other states and societies that enhances the nation's ability to gain support from other governments for its policy goals *(p. 4)*.

sovereign equality   The shared legal rights of all internationally recognized nation-states *(p. 263)*.

sovereignty   The highest level of political authority that is maintained by secular nation-states. Affirmed in the 1648 Treaty of Westphalia, which rejected political control by religious authorities and the divine right of kings *(p. 60)*.

spectrum of armed conflict   The variety of real and potential military challenges a country confronts in which the chance that each type of conflict will occur is inversely proportionate to its destructiveness *(p. 296)*.

spillover effects   A pattern in which successful cooperation between governments in one area, such as trade, encourages cooperation in more troublesome areas, such as arms control and the resolution of territorial disputes *(p. 262)*.

spin control   Action by government officials to shape news coverage in ways that show them in the best possible light *(p. 212)*.

standard operating procedures (SOPs)   Consistent, routine measures for addressing commonly encountered problems in public policy. Stress continuity over change and a high level of internal order *(p. 77)*.

state building   The process by which an external government, intergovernmental organization, or nongovernmental organization attempts to create the conditions necessary for a state to establish a stable and democratic government *(p. 385)*.

state terrorism   Acts of terrorism committed by sovereign governments, either against their own people or people in other states *(p. 320)*.

state-society relations   The interaction of government and private actors in matters of public policy. Often featuring tensions or mutual animosity in the case of U.S. security policy *(p. 300)*.

stewardship theory   A view of the presidency articulated by President Theodore Roosevelt, who called for a dominant president constrained only by formal restrictions identified in the U.S. Constitution *(p. 99)*.

strategic culture   Widely shared normative beliefs, attitudes, and policy preferences as they pertain to a country's foreign relations *(p. 299)*.

Strategic Defense Initiative (SDI)   President Ronald Reagan's 1983 plan to use space-based interceptors to destroy long-range nuclear weapons in mid-flight. Also known as "Star Wars" *(p. 315)*.

strategic detachment   An early grand strategy adopted by the United States based on the nation's self-reliance and avoidance of binding commitments to other countries *(p. 301)*.

strategic environment   The context in which security policy is devised. Reflects trends in global and regional balances of power and the degree to which a state considers other powerful nations and mobilized private groups friends or foes *(p. 298)*.

strategic factors   Political and electoral considerations weighed by legislators along with the substantive merits of bills coming up for a vote *(p. 141)*.

structural arrangements   The governing bodies and legal system within which policy making takes place and that shape grand strategy *(p. 300)*.

structural power   The leverage a nation-state gains from the size of its economy. Permits dominant economies to set the terms for debates regarding international financial institutions *(p. 287)*.

substantive legislation   Congressional measures that focus on specific issues, such as economic sanctions against South Africa in the 1980s, rather than on procedural innovations, such as enhanced oversight of the president, affecting legislative powers *(p. 138)*.

sustained primacy   A grand strategy adopted by the United States after World War II based on the preservation of the nation's predominance in the interstate system. Adopted explicitly by the George W. Bush administration in 2002 *(p. 301)*.

tactics   In the context of security strategy, the translation of proclaimed political ends into military means *(p. 303)*.

technical intelligence (TECHINT)   Information derived from "intercepts" of electronic transmissions, satellite photographs, and other nonhuman data sources *(p. 178)*.

terrorism   A tactic of gaining the upper hand in a political struggle through the use, by states or private actors, of political violence designed to raise mass fears *(p. 10)*.

trade protectionism   Efforts by national governments to restrict the entry of foreign goods and services in order to strengthen domestic industries *(p. 185)*.

tragedy of the commons   A situation in which a group of people stand to lose a common resource due to overuse unless some limiting measures are taken. A "tragedy" given the many constraints on undertaking collective action and the stark consequences of inaction *(p. 363)*.

transnational advocacy networks   Large, well-organized coalitions of groups from two or more countries that apply political pressure on several governments at once to achieve their policy preferences *(p. 83)*.

transnational civil society   Societal forces that extend beyond the political boundaries of a nation-state, including interest groups, public opinion, the news media, and intergovernmental organizations *(p. 17)*.

transnational interdependence   The mutual reliance between two or more countries that stems from shared problems and interests and results in closer cooperation *(p. 62)*.

Truman Doctrine   President Harry Truman's pledge to provide military aid to Greece and Turkey to help overcome internal communist revolts and, more broadly, to support "free peoples who are resisting attempted subjugation by armed minorities or by outside pressures" *(p. 41)*.

trustee model   One of two general models of political representation. Based on a political leader's presumed superior judgment. Provides for greater freedom of thought and autonomous decision making by elected officials than the delegate model *(p. 192)*.

two presidencies   A model of U.S. government developed by political scientist Aaron Wildavsky that describes the president as constrained on domestic issues while reigning supreme in foreign affairs *(p. 93)*.

two-level game   A situation in which foreign-policy makers simultaneously negotiate with their foreign counterparts and domestic actors (public and private) who have a stake in the policy process *(p. 64)*.

unified government   A partisan alignment that occurs when the executive and legislative branches of government are controlled by the same political party *(p. 130)*.

unilateralism   The pursuit of foreign-policy objectives without the collaboration or assistance of other governments *(p. 25)*.

unipolar balance of power   Global power structure in which one nation-state maintains a predominant share of the economic, military, and other resources needed to advance its interests in the interstate system *(p. 3)*.

unitary actors   A model of national decision making that assumes that foreign-policy makers act in a united fashion to make decisions in the name of the "national interest." A central tenet of realist theory *(p. 60)*.

Uruguay Round A series of trade negotiations among members of the General Agreement on Tariffs and Trade (GATT) that led to the creation of the World Trade Organization as well as other initiatives *(p. 341)*.

USA Patriot Act Sweeping legislation passed after the 9-11 attacks that increased the federal government's ability to investigate suspected terrorists in the United States. An acronym for Uniting and Strengthening America by Providing Appropriate Tools Required to Intercept and Obstruct Terrorism *(p. 129)*.

Vietnam Syndrome National self-doubts in the United States in the late 1960s and 1970s as the nation's involvement and defeat in the Vietnam War led to a weakened sense of U.S. primacy and moral superiority *(p. 46)*.

voluntary export restraints Concessions made by trading partners that limit their exports to another state without increased tariffs imposed by the importing government or reduced cooperation in other foreign-policy domains *(p. 345)*.

War Powers Resolution A legislative measure approved by Congress in 1973 requiring presidents to inform Congress about imminent U.S. military deployments and authorizing Congress to order the troops home after sixty days if a majority of legislators oppose the deployments. Rarely invoked and routinely dismissed by presidents as unconstitutional *(p. 125)*.

wars of choice Military conflicts concerning nonvital national interests *(p. 297)*.

wars of necessity Military conflicts resulting from direct challenges to a nation's vital interests *(p. 297)*.

Washington consensus A shared understanding among major industrialized countries regarding the development strategies of smaller economies emphasizing the developing nations' need to promote private enterprise and open markets while restricting state intervention *(p. 286)*.

Weinberger Doctrine Policy developed in the 1980s by Caspar Weinberger, secretary of defense under Ronald Reagan, requiring that U.S. military interventions be thoroughly planned and the costs and benefits be calculated before offensive action is taken *(p. 306)*.

References

Abbott, Kenneth, and Duncan Snidal. 1998. "Why States Act through Formal International Organizations." *Journal of Conflict Resolution* 42 (February): 3–32.

Abramson, Mark A., and Paul R. Lawrence, eds. 2001. *Transforming Organizations.* Lanham, Md.: Rowman and Littlefield.

Adams, Thomas. 1999. "The New Mercenaries and the Privatization of Conflict." *Parameters* 29 (Summer): 103–116.

Addis, Adeno. 2003. "Economic Sanctions and the Problem of Evil." *Human Rights Quarterly* 25 (August): 573–623.

Adler, David Gray. 1996a. "Court, Constitution, and Foreign Affairs." In *The Constitution and the Conduct of American Foreign Policy,* ed. David Gray Adler and Larry N. George, 19–56. Lawrence: University Press of Kansas.

_____. 1996b. "The President's Recognition Power." In *The Constitution and the Conduct of American Foreign Policy,* ed. David Gray Adler and Larry N. George, 133–157. Lawrence: University Press of Kansas.

Ahari, Mohammed E., ed. 1987. *Ethnic Groups and Foreign Policy.* New York: Greenwood Press.

Albright, Madeleine. 1997. Statement before the Senate Foreign Relations Committee on NATO Enlargement. October 7. Washington, D.C.: U.S. Department of State.

_____. 1998. "Should the U.S. Senate Ratify the NATO Expansion Treaty?" *Retired Officer Magazine* (January): 56–63.

Allison, Graham T. 1969. "Conceptual Models and the Cuban Missile Crisis." *American Political Science Review* 63 (September): 689–718.

_____. 1971. *Essence of Decision: Explaining the Cuban Missile Crisis.* Boston: Little, Brown.

Allison, Graham T., and Peter Szanton. 1976. *Remaking Foreign Policy: The Organizational Connection.* New York: Basic Books.

Allison, Graham T., and Philip Zelikow. 1999. *Essence of Decision: Explaining the Cuban Missile Crisis.* 2d ed. New York: Longman.

Almond, Gabriel. 1950. *The American People and Foreign Policy.* New York: Harcourt, Brace.

Alterman, Eric. 1997. "The CIA's Fifty Candles." *Nation,* October 6, 5–6.

Ambrose, Stephen E. 1988. *Rise to Globalism: American Foreign Policy since 1938.* 5th rev. ed. New York: Penguin Books.

Ambrosio, Thomas, ed. 2002. *Ethnic Identity Groups and U.S. Foreign Policy.* Westport, Conn.: Praeger.

American Israel Public Affairs Committee. 2004a. "Congressional Briefing Book." www.aipac.org/briefbook.html.

———. 2004b. *Near East Report.* www.aipac.org/neareastreport.cfm.

Andrew, Christopher. 1995. *For the President's Eyes Only: Secret Intelligence and the American Presidency from Washington to Bush.* New York: HarperCollins.

Arquilla, John, David Ronfeldt, and Michele Zanini. 1999. "Networks, Netwar, and Information-Age Terrorism." In *Countering the New Terrorism,* ed. Ian O. Lesser, Bruce Hoffman, John Arquilla, David Ronfeldt, and Michele Zanini, 39–84. Santa Monica, Calif.: RAND.

Art, Robert J. 1973. "Bureaucratic Politics and American Foreign Policy: A Critique." *Policy Sciences* 4 (December): 467–490.

———. 1996. "Why Western Europe Needs the United States and NATO." *Political Science Quarterly* 111 (Spring): 1–39.

Art, Robert J., and Kenneth N. Waltz, eds. 2004. *The Use of Force: Military Power and International Politics.* 6th ed. Lanham, Md.: Rowman and Littlefield.

Ascher, William. 1992. "The World Bank and U.S. Control." In *The United States and Multilateral Institutions: Patterns of Changing Instrumentality and Influence,* ed. Margaret Karns and Karen Mingst, 115–140. London: Routledge.

Ashcroft, John. 2001. "DOJ Oversight: Preserving our Freedoms While Defending Against Terrorism." Statement to the Senate Judiciary Committee. December 6. www.senate.gov/%7Ejudiciary/print_testimony.cfm?id=121&wit_id=42.

Asmus, Ronald D. 2002. *Opening NATO's Door: How the Alliance Remade Itself for a New Era.* New York: Columbia University Press.

———. 2003. "Rebuilding the Atlantic Alliance." *Foreign Affairs* 82 (September–October): 20–31.

Aspin, Les. 1992. "The Use and Usefulness of Military Forces in the Post–Cold War, Post–Soviet World." Remarks to the Jewish Institute for National Security Affairs. September 21.

Athanasiou, Tom. 2001. "Raise a Glass to Kyoto." *Foreign Policy in Focus,* June. www.fpif.org/commentary/2001/0106kyoto_body.html.

Aubin, Stephen P. 1998. *Distorting Defense: Network News and National Security.* Westport, Conn.: Praeger.

Auerswald, David, and Forrest Maltzman. 2003. "Policymaking through Advice and Consent: Treaty Consideration by the United States Senate." *The Journal of Politics* 65 (November): 1097–1110.

Auster, Bruce B., and David E. Kaplan. 1998. "What's Really Gone Wrong with the CIA?" *U.S. News and World Report,* June 1, 27.

Bailey, Thomas A. 1948. *The Man in the Street: The Impact of American Public Opinion on Foreign Policy.* New York: Macmillan.

———. 1980. *A Diplomatic History of the American People.* 10th ed. Englewood Cliffs, N.J.: Prentice Hall.

Baker, James A., III, with Thomas M. DeFrank. 1995. *The Politics of Diplomacy: Revolution, War and Peace, 1989–1992.* New York: Putnam.

Baker, William D., and John R. Oneal. 2001. "Patriotism or Opinion Leadership? The Nature and Origins of the 'Rally around the Flag' Effect." *Journal of Conflict Resolution* 45 (October): 661–687.

Baldwin, David A. 1966. *Foreign Aid and American Foreign Policy.* New York: Praeger.

———. 1985. *Economic Statecraft.* Princeton: Princeton University Press.

———. 1999–2000. "The Sanctions Debate and the Logic of Choice." *International Security* 24 (Winter): 80–107.

Bamberger, Robert. 2003. "Energy Policy: Historical Overview, Conceptual Framework, and Continuing Issues." CRS Report for Congress, January 30. Washington, D.C.: Congressional Research Service.

Barber, James D. 1992. *The Presidential Character: Predicting Performance in the White House.* 4th ed. Englewood Cliffs, N.J.: Prentice Hall.

Bardes, Barbara. 1997. "Public Opinion and Foreign Policy: How Does the Public Think About America's Role in the World?" In *Understanding Public Opinion,* ed. Barbara Norrander and Clyde Wilcox, 150–169. Washington, D.C.: CQ Press.

Barnett, Roger W. 2003. *Asymmetrical Warfare: Today's Challenge to U.S. Military Power.* Washington, D.C.: Brassey's.

Barone, Michael, and Grant Ujifusa. 1999. *The Almanac of American Politics, 2000.* Washington, D.C.: The National Journal Group.

Bartels, Larry M. 1991. "Constituency Opinion and Congressional Policy Making: The Reagan Defense Buildup." *American Political Science Review* 85 (June): 457–474.

Baum, Dan. 1997. *Smoke and Mirrors: The War on Drugs and the Politics of Failure.* Boston: Back Bay Books.

———. 2003. "Nation Builders for Hire." *New York Times Magazine,* June 22, 32–37.

Baum, Matthew A. 2002a. "The Constituent Foundations of the Rally-Round-the-Flag Phenomenon." *International Studies Quarterly* 46 (June): 263–298.

———. 2002b. "Sex, Lies, and War: How Soft News Brings Foreign Policy to the Inattentive Public." *American Political Science Review* 96 (March): 91–109.

Bax, Frank R. 1977. "The Legislative-Executive Relationship in Foreign Policy: New Partnership or New Competition?" *Orbis* 20 (Winter): 881–904.

Bendor, Jonathon, and Thomas H. Hammond. 1992. "Rethinking Allison's Models." *American Political Science Review* 86 (June): 301–322.

Benjamin, Daniel, and Steven Simon. 2002. *The Age of Sacred Terror.* New York: Random House.

Bennett, W. Lance, and David L. Paletz, eds. 1994. *Taken by Storm: The Media, Public Opinion, and U.S. Foreign Policy in the Gulf War.* Chicago: University of Chicago Press.

Berke, Richard L., and David E. Sanger. 2002. "Some in Administration Grumble as Aide's Role Seems to Expand." *New York Times,* May 13, A1.

Berrios, Ruben. 2000. *Contracting for Development: The Role of For-Profit Contractors in U.S. Foreign Development Assistance.* Westport, Conn.: Praeger.

Best, James R. 1992. "Who Talked with President Kennedy? An Interaction Analysis." *Presidential Studies Quarterly* 22 (Spring): 351–369.

Betts, Richard K. 2002. *Conflict After the Cold War: Arguments on Causes of War and Peace.* 2d ed. New York: Longman.

———. 2003. "Striking First: A History of Thankfully Lost Opportunities." *Ethics and International Affairs* 17 (Spring): 17–24.

Binder, Sarah A. 1996. "The Disappearing Political Center: Congress and the Incredible Shrinking Middle." *Brookings Review* 14 (Fall): 36–39.

Bird, Graham. 2003. *The IMF and the Future: Issues and Options Facing the Fund.* New York: Routledge.

Blacker, Coit D. 1994. "A Typology of Post–Cold War Conflicts." In *U.S. Intervention Policy for the Post–Cold War World: New Challenges and Responses,* ed. Arnold Kanter and Linton Brooks, 42–63. New York: Norton.

Blechman, Barry M., and Tamara C. Wittes. 1999. "Defining Moment: The Threat and Use of Force in American Foreign Policy." *Political Science Quarterly* 114 (1): 1–30.

Bloom, David E., David Canning, and Jaypee Sevilla. 2003. *The Demographic Dividend: A New Perspective on the Economic Consequences of Population Change.* Santa Monica, Calif.: RAND.

Blustein, Paul. 2001. *The Chastening: Inside the Crisis that Rocked the Global Financial System and Humbled the IMF.* New York: Public Affairs.

Bolton, John R. 2001. "Plenary Address to the UN Conference on the Illicit Trade in Small Arms and Light Weapons." July 9. Washington, D.C.: U.S. Department of State. www.state.gov/t/us/rm/janjuly/4038.htm.

Bond, Michael. 2000. "The Backlash Against NGOs." *Prospect,* April. www.globalpolicy.org/ngos/backlash.htm.

Brace, Paul, and Barbara Hinckley. 1993. *Follow the Leader: Opinion Polls and the Modern Presidents.* New York: Basic Books.

Brehm, John, and Scott Gates. 1997. *Working, Shirking, and Sabotage: Bureaucratic Responses to a Democratic Public.* Ann Arbor: University of Michigan Press.

Brenner, Carl N. 1999. "Modeling the President's Security Agenda." *Congress and the Presidency* 26 (Fall): 171–191.

Brinkley, Douglas. 1997. "Democratic Enlargement: The Clinton Doctrine." *Foreign Policy* 106 (Spring): 110–127.

Broad, Robin, ed. 2002. *Global Backlash: Citizen Initiatives for a Just World Economy.* Lanham, Md.: Rowman and Littlefield.

Brodie, Bernard, ed. 1946. *The Absolute Weapon: Atomic Power and World Order.* New York: Harcourt, Brace.

Brown, Cynthia, ed. 2003. *Lost Liberties: Ashcroft and the Assault on Personal Freedom.* New York: New Press.

Brown, Walton L. 1994. "Presidential Leadership and U.S. Nonproliferation Policy." *Presidential Studies Quarterly* 24 (Summer): 563–575.

Brzezinski, Zbigniew. 1997. *The Grand Chessboard: American Primacy and Its Geostrategic Imperatives.* New York: Basic Books.

Buchanan, James M. 1977. "Why Does Government Grow?" In *Budgets and Bureaucrats: The Sources of Government Growth,* ed. Thomas Bocherding. Durham, N.C.: Duke University Press.

Buchanan, Patrick. 1998. *The Great Betrayal: How American Sovereignty and Social Justice Are Being Sacrificed to the Gods of the Global Economy.* Boston: Little, Brown.

Buckley, Kevin. 1991. *Panama: The Whole Story.* New York: Simon and Schuster.

Bumiller, Elizabeth. 2003. "Evangelicals Sway White House on Human Rights Issues Abroad." *New York Times,* October 26, 1A.

Burgin, Eileen. 1991. "Representatives' Decisions on Participation in Foreign Policy Issues." *Legislative Studies Quarterly* 16 (November): 521–546.

———. 1993. "The Influence of Constituents: Congressional Decision-Making on Issues of Foreign and Domestic Policy." In *Congress Resurgent: Foreign and Defense Policy on Capitol Hill,* ed. Randall B. Ripley and James M. Lindsay, 67–88. Ann Arbor: University of Michigan Press.

Burton, Daniel F., Jr. 1997. "The Brave New Wired World." *Foreign Policy* 106 (Spring): 22–37.

Bush, George W. 2001a. *Executive Order Establishing the Office of Homeland Security.* October 8. Washington, D.C.: White House, Office of the Press Secretary.

———. 2001b. Inaugural Address. January 20. www.whitehouse.gov/news/print/inaugural-address.html.

Buzan, Barry. 1991. "New Patterns of Global Security in the Twenty-First Century." *International Affairs* 67 (July): 431–451.

Calleo, David. 1970. *The Atlantic Fantasy: The United States, NATO, and Europe.* Baltimore: Johns Hopkins University Press.

Campbell, David. 1992. *Writing Security: United States Foreign Policy and the Politics of Identity.* Minneapolis: University of Minnesota Press.

Campbell, Kurt M. 1991. "All Rise for Chairman Powell." *The National Interest* 23 (Spring): 51–60.

Carothers, Thomas. 1999. *Aiding Democracy Abroad: The Learning Curve.* Washington, D.C.: Carnegie Endowment for International Peace.

Carr, Edward H. 1939. *The Twenty Years Crisis: 1919–1939.* London: Macmillan.

Carter, Ashton B., William J. Perry, and John D. Steinbruner. 1992. *A New Concept of Cooperative Security.* Washington, D.C.: Brookings Institution Press.

Carter, Ralph G. 1989. "Senate Defense Budgeting, 1981–1988: The Impacts of Ideology, Party, and Constituency Benefit on the Decision to Support the President." *American Politics Quarterly* 17 (July): 332–347.

———. 1999. "Congressional Trade Politics, 1985–1995." *Congress and the Presidency* 26 (Spring): 61–76.

Castro, Fidel. 1960. "Speech to the United Nations on September 26, 1960." lanic .utexas.edu/project/castro/1960.

Center for Defense Information. 2002. *Military Almanac: 2000–2001.* www.cdi.org /products/almanac0102.pdf.

———. 2003a. "Last of the Big Time Spenders: U.S. Military Budget Still the World's Largest, and Growing." www.cdi.org/program/issue/index.cfm?ProgramID=15& issueid=34.

———. 2003b. "Ten Largest U.S. Military Contractors, Fiscal Year 2002." www.cdi .org/news/mrp/contractors.pdf.

———. 2004a. "Arms Transfer Project." www.cdi.org/program/index.cfm?programid =73.

———. 2004b. "Terrorism Project." www.cdi.org/program/index.cfm?programid=39.

Center for Public Integrity. 2004. www.publicintegrity.org/default.aspx.

Center for Responsive Politics. 2003a. "Soft Money to National Parties: 2002 Cycle Top Donors." www.opensecrets.org/softmoney/softtop.asp?txtCycle=2002&txtSort=amnt.

———. 2003b. "Who Gives—Industries." www.opensecrets.org/industries/index.asp.

———. 2004. "Rebuilding Iraq—The Contractors." www.opensecrets.org/news/rebuilding_iraq/index.asp.

Chait, Jonathan. 2002. "Defense Secretary: The Peculiar Duplicity of Ari Fleischer." *New Republic,* June 10, 20–23.

Chhibber, Ajay, and Mansoor Dailami. 1990. *Fiscal Policy and Private Investment in Developing Countries.* Washington, D.C.: The World Bank.

Chicago Council on Foreign Relations. 2002. "Worldviews 2002: American Public Opinion and Foreign Policy." www.worldviews.org/detailreports/usreport/index.htm.

Chomsky, Noam. 2002. *Media Control: The Spectacular Achievements of Propaganda.* New York: Seven Stories Press.

———. 2003. *Hegemony or Survival: America's Quest for Global Dominance.* New York: Metropolitan Books.

Cincotta, Richard P., and Barbara B. Crane. 2001. "The Mexico City Policy and U.S. Family Planning Assistance." *Science,* October 19, 525–526.

Cities for Peace Campaign. 2004. "City and County Council and Related Resolutions Opposing Preemptive/Unilateral War in Iraq." www.ips-D.C.org/citiesforpeace/resolutions.htm.

Clark, Wesley K. 2001. *Waging Modern War: Bosnia, Kosovo, and the Future of Combat.* New York: Public Affairs.

Clarke, Richard A. 2004. *Against All Enemies: Inside America's War on Terror.* New York: Free Press.

ClickZ Network. 2004. "Population Explosion!" www.clickz.com/stats/big_picture/geographics/article.php/151151.

Clifford, Mark L., and Pete Engardio. 2000. *Meltdown: Asia's Boom, Bust, and Beyond.* Paramus, N.J.: Prentice Hall.

Climate Action Network. 2004. "The Climate Stewardship Act." www.climatenetwork.org/csa.htm.

Clinton, Bill. 1994. "Presidential Directive 25: Clinton Administration Policy on Reforming Multilateral Peacekeeping Operations." May 5. Washington, D.C.: White House.

———. 1996. *A National Security Strategy of Engagement and Enlargement.* Washington, D.C.: White House.

Cohen, Bernard C. 1963. *The Press and Foreign Policy.* Princeton: Princeton University Press.

———. 1973. *The Public's Impact on Foreign Policy.* Boston: Little, Brown.

Cohen, Jeffrey E. 1995. "Presidential Rhetoric and the Public Agenda." *American Journal of Political Science* 39 (February): 87–107.

Cohen, Joel E. 2003. "The Future of Population." In *What the Future Holds: Insights from Social Science,* ed. Richard N. Cooper and Richard Layard, 29–75. Cambridge: MIT Press.

Cohen, Saul B. 2003. *Geopolitics of the World System.* Lanham, Md.: Rowman and Littlefield.

Cohen, Stephen D., Robert A. Blecker, and Peter D. Whitney. 2003. *Fundamentals of U.S. Foreign Trade Policy.* 2d ed. Boulder, Colo.: Westview Press.

Colby, William, and Peter Forbath. 1978. *Honorable Men: My Life in the CIA.* New York: Simon and Schuster.

Cole, David. 2003. *Enemy Aliens: Double Standards and Constitutional Freedoms in the War on Terrorism.* New York: New Press.

Combs, Cindy C. 2003. *Terrorism in the 21st Century.* 3d ed. Upper Saddle River, N.J.: Prentice Hall.

Compaine, Benjamin M., and Douglas Gomery. 2000. *Who Owns the Media? Competition and Concentration in the Mass Media Industry.* 3d ed. Mahwah, N.J.: L. Earlbaum Associates.

Congressional Budget Office. 2004. "CBO's Current Budget Projections." March 8. www.cbo.gov/showdoc.cfm?index=1944&sequence=0.

Congressional Research Service. 2001. "Treaties and Other International Agreements: The Role of the U.S. Senate." Washington, D.C.: Library of Congress.

Convention on Biological Diversity. 2004. www.biodiv.org/default.aspx.

Converse, Philip. 1964. "The Nature of Belief Systems in Mass Publics." In *Ideology and Discontent,* ed. David Apter, 206–261. New York: Free Press.

Cooper, Mary H. 1994. "U.S.-China Trade." *CQ Researcher Online.* April 15. library.cqpress.com/cqresearcher.

Cordesman, Anthony H., with Eric E. Fillinger. 2002. "The Global Nuclear Balance: A Quantitative and Arms Control Analysis." January 22. Washington, D.C.: Center for Strategic and International Studies. www.csis.org/burke/mb/global_Nuc_bal020122.pdf.

Cortright, David, and George A. Lopez, eds. 2002. *Smart Sanctions: Targeting Economic Statecraft.* Lanham, Md.: Roman and Littlefield.

Corwin, Edward S. 1957. *The President: Office and Powers, 1787–1957: History and Analysis of Practice and Opinion.* 4th ed. New York: New York University Press.

Council on Foreign Relations. 2003. *Finding America's Voice: A Strategy for Reinvigo-rating U.S. Public Diplomacy*. New York: Council on Foreign Relations. www.cfr .org/pdf/public_diplomacy.pdf.

Crabb, Cecil V., Jr., and Kevin V. Mulcahy. 1995. "George Bush's Management Style and Operation Desert Storm." *Presidential Studies Quarterly* 25 (Spring): 251–265.

Crawford, Neta C. 2003. "The Slippery Slope to Preventive War." *Ethics and International Affairs* 17 (Spring): 30–36.

Cronin, Patrick, and Benjamin O. Fordham. 1999. "Timeless Principles or Today's Fashion? Testing the Stability of the Linkage between Ideology and Foreign Policy in the Senate." *Journal of Politics* 61 (November): 967–998.

Crowley, Michael. 2004. "Playing Defense: Bush's Disastrous Homeland Security Department." *New Republic,* March 16, 17–21.

Daalder, Ivo H. 1991. *The Nature and Practice of Flexible Response: NATO Strategy and Theater Nuclear Forces since 1967*. New York: Columbia University Press.

Daalder, Ivo H., and I. M. Destler. 2000. *A New NSC for a New Administration,* Policy Brief 68. Washington, D.C.: Brookings.

Daalder, Ivo H., and James M. Lindsay, eds. 2003. *America Unbound: The Bush Revolution in Foreign Policy*. Washington, D.C.: Brookings.

Daalder, Ivo H., and Michael E. O'Hanlon. 2000. *Winning Ugly: NATO's War to Save Kosovo*. Washington, D.C.: Brookings.

Dadge, David. 2004. *Casualty of War: The Bush Administration's Assault on a Free Press*. Amherst, N.Y.: Prometheus Press.

Dahl, Robert A. 1967. *Pluralist Democracy in the United States: Conflict and Consent*. Chicago: Rand McNally.

D'Amico, Francine, and Peter R. Beckman, eds. 1995. *Women in World Politics: An Introduction*. Westport, Conn.: Bergin and Garvey.

David, Leonard. 2002. "U.S. Establishes Missile Defense Agency." January 7. www.space.com/missionlaunches/missile_defense_020107.html.

Davidson, Roger H., and Walter J. Oleszek, eds. 2004. *Congress and Its Members*. 9th ed. Washington, D.C.: CQ Press.

DeConde, Alexander. 1992. *Ethnicity, Race, and American Foreign Policy*. Boston: Northeastern University Press.

De Rivera, Joseph H. 1968. *The Psychological Dimension of Foreign Policy*. Columbus, Ohio: Merrill.

de Tocqueville, Alexis. [1835] 1988. *Democracy in America*. Edited by J. P. Mayer. New York: Perennial Library.

de Wijk, Rob. 2002. "The Limits of Military Power." *Washington Quarterly* 25 (Winter): 75–92.

Deering, Christopher J. 1993. "Decision Making in the Armed Services Committees." In *Congress Resurgent: Foreign and Defense Policy on Capitol Hill,* ed. Randall B. Ripley and James M. Lindsay, 155–182. Ann Arbor: University of Michigan Press.

———. 1996. "Congress, the President, and Automatic Government: The Case of Military Base Closures." In *Rivals for Power: Presidential-Congressional Relations,* ed. James A. Thurber, 153–169. Washington, D.C.: CQ Press.

Deering, Christopher J., and Steven S. Smith. 1997. *Committees in Congress*. 3d ed. Washington, D.C.: CQ Press.

Defense Security Cooperation Agency. 2004. *Background on Weapons Systems*. www.dsca.osd.mil/background.htm.

Delli Carpini, Michael X., and Scott Keeter. 1996. *What Americans Know About Politics and Why It Matters*. New Haven: Yale University Press.

Destler, I. M. 1980. "A Job That Doesn't Work." *Foreign Policy* 38 (Spring): 80–88.

———. 1994. "A Government Divided: The Security Complex and the Economic Complex." In *The New Politics of American Foreign Policy*, ed. David A. Deese, 132–147. New York: St. Martin's.

———. 1995. *American Trade Politics: System Under Stress*. 3d ed. Washington, D.C.: Institute for International Economics.

———. 2001a. "Congress and Foreign Policy at Century's End: Requiem or Cooperation?" In *Congress Reconsidered*, 7th ed., ed. Lawrence C. Dodd and Bruce I. Oppenheimer, 315–333. Washington, D.C.: CQ Press.

———. 2001b. "The Reasonable Public and the Polarized Policy Process." In *The Real and the Ideal: Essays in International Relations in Honor of Richard H. Ullman*, ed. Anthony Lake and David Ochmanek, 75–90. Lanham, Md.: Rowman and Littlefield.

Destler, I. M., Leslie H. Gelb, and Anthony Lake. 1984. *Our Own Worst Enemy: The Unmaking of American Foreign Policy*. New York: Touchstone.

Deutsch, Karl W., S. A. Burrell, R. A. Kann, M. Lee Jr., M. Lichterman, R. E. Lindgern, F. L. Loewenheim, and R. W. Van Wagenen. 1957. *Political Community and the North Atlantic Area: International Organization in the Light of Historical Experience*. Princeton: Princeton University Press.

Dizard, Wilson, Jr. 2001. *Digital Diplomacy: U.S. Foreign Policy in the Information Age*. Westport, Conn.: Praeger.

Domhoff, William G. 2002. *Who Rules America? Power and Politics*. 4th ed. Boston: McGraw-Hill.

Doyle, Kate. 2000. "The End of Secrecy: U.S. National Security and the New Openness Movement." In *National Insecurity: U.S. Intelligence After the Cold War*, ed. Craig Eisendrath, 92–117. Philadelphia: Temple University Press.

Doyle, Michael W. 1986. "Liberalism and World Politics." *American Political Science Review* 80 (December): 1151–1169.

Drezner, Daniel W. 2000. "Ideas, Bureaucratic Politics, and the Crafting of Foreign Policy." *American Journal of Political Science* 44 (October): 733–749.

Dryden, Steve. 1995. *Trade Warriors: USTR and the American Crusade for Free Trade*. New York: Oxford University Press.

Duffy, Michael. 2001. "Rumsfeld Older, But Wiser?" *Time,* August 27, 22–26.

Dumbrell, John. 2002. "Was There a Clinton Doctrine? President Clinton's Foreign Policy Reconsidered." *Diplomacy and Statecraft* 13 (June): 43–56.

Durch, William J., ed. 1993. *The Evolution of UN Peacekeeping: Case Studies and Comparative Analyses*. New York: St. Martin's.

Earle, Edward Mead, ed. 1937. *The Federalist*. Washington, D.C.: National Home Library.

Eckholm, Erik. 2004. "Auditors Testify About Waste in Iraq Contracts." *New York Times,* June 16, A13.

Economist. 1994. "Who Makes Policy?" January 8, 25.

———. 2002. "From Uncle Ben's to Uncle Sam." February 21. www.economist.com /business/printer-friendly.crf?story_ID=998594.

Edwards, Michael, and John Gaventa, eds. 2001. *Global Citizen Action*. Boulder, Colo.: Lynne Rienner.

Eichengreen, Barry. 2002. "The Globalization Wars." *Foreign Affairs* 81 (July–August): 157–164.

Engelbrecht, H. C. 1934. *Merchants of Death: A Study of the International Armament Industry*. New York: Dodd, Mead.

Entman, Robert M. 2004. *Projections of Power: Framing News, Public Opinion, and U.S. Foreign Policy*. Chicago: University of Chicago Press.

Esposito, John L. 2002. *Unholy War: Terror in the Name of Islam*. New York: Oxford University Press.

Etheridge, Lloyd. 1978. "Personality Effects on American Foreign Policy, 1898–1968: A Test of Interpersonal Generalization Theory." *American Political Science Review* 72 (June): 434–451.

Fallows, James M. 1997. *Breaking the News: How the Media Undermine American Democracy*. New York: Vintage.

———. 2002. "The Military-Industrial Complex." *Foreign Policy* 133 (November–December): 46–48.

Feaver, Peter D., and Christopher Gelpi. 2004. *Choosing Your Battles: American Civil-Military Relations and the Use of Force*. Princeton: Princeton University Press.

Federation of American Scientists. 2004. "Arms Sales Monitoring Project." www.fas.org/main/content.jsp?formAction=325&projectId=3.

Fehr, Hans, Sabine Jokisch, and Laurence Kotlikoff. 2003. *The Developed World's Demographic Transition: The Roles of Capital Flows, Immigration, and Policy*. Cambridge: National Bureau of Economic Research.

Ferrell, Robert H. 1988. *American Diplomacy: The Twentieth Century*. New York: Norton.

Fineman, Howard. 2003. "Bush and God. A Higher Calling." *Newsweek*, March 10, 22–30.

Finnemore, Martha. 1996. *National Interests in International Society*. Ithaca: Cornell University Press.

———. 2003. *The Purpose of Intervention: Changing Beliefs about the Use of Force*. Ithaca: Cornell University Press.

Fiorina, Morris. 1989. *Congress: Keystone of the Washington Establishment*. 2d ed. New Haven: Yale University Press.

Firor, John, and Judith E. Jacobson. 2002. *The Crowded Greenhouse: Population, Climate Change, and Creating a Sustainable World*. New Haven: Yale University Press.

Fisher, Louis. 1995. *Presidential War Powers*. Lawrence: University Press of Kansas.

———. 2004. "The Way We Go to War: The Iraq Resolution." In *Considering the Bush Presidency*, ed. Gary L. Gregg II and Mark J. Rozell, 107–124. New York: Oxford University Press.

Fleisher, Richard, Jon R. Bond, Glen S. Krutz, and Stephen Hanna. 2000. "The Demise of the Two Presidencies." *American Politics Quarterly* 28 (January): 3–25.

Foot, Rosemary, S. Neil McFarlane, and Michael Mastanduno, eds. 2003. *U.S. Hegemony and International Organizations: The United States and Multilateral Institutions*. New York: Oxford University Press.

Fordham, Benjamin O., and Timothy McKeown. 2003. "Selection and Influence: Interest Groups and Congressional Voting on Trade Policy." *International Organization* 57 (Summer): 519–549.

Forsythe, David P. 1995. "Human Rights and U.S. Foreign Policy: Two Levels, Two Worlds." *Political Studies* 43 (4): 111–130.

Fortune. 2003. *The 2003 Global 500*. www.fortune.com/fortune/global500.

Foyle, Douglas C. 1999. *Counting the Public In: Presidents, Public Opinion, and Foreign Policy*. New York: Columbia University Press.

Franck, Thomas M., and Edward Weisband. 1979. *Foreign Policy by Congress*. New York: Oxford University Press.

Freedman, Lawrence. 2003. *The Evolution of Nuclear Strategy*. 3d ed. New York: Palgrave Macmillan.

Freedom House. 2000–2004. *Freedom in the World*. New York: Freedom House.

Freeland, Chrystia. 2000. *Sale of the Century: Russia's Wild Ride from Communism to Capitalism.* New York: Crown Business.

Friedberg, Aaron L. 2000. *In the Shadow of the Garrison State: America's Anti-Statism and Its Cold War Grand Strategy.* Princeton: Princeton University Press.

Fry, Earl H. 1998. *The Expanding Role of State and Local Governments in U.S. Foreign Affairs.* New York: Council on Foreign Relations.

Fukuyama, Francis. 1989. "The End of History?" *National Interest* 16 (Summer): 3–18.

———. 2004. *State-Building: Governance and World Order in the 21st Century.* Ithaca: Cornell University Press.

Galbraith, Jean. 2003. "The Bush Administration's Response to the International Criminal Court." *Berkeley Journal of International Law* 21 (3): 683–702.

Galdi, Theodor W. 1995. "Revolution in Military Affairs? Competing Concepts, Organizational Responses, Outstanding Issues." December 11. Washington, D.C.: Congressional Research Service.

Gallagher, Kelly Sims. 2002. "Bush's Hot Air Plan." *Foreign Policy in Focus,* February 19. www.fpif.org/commentary/2002/0202greenhouse_body.html.

Gardner, Richard N. 1980. *Sterling-Dollar Diplomacy in Current Perspectives: The Origins and Prospects of Our International Economic Order.* Expanded ed. New York: Columbia University Press.

Garrison, Jean. 1999. *Games Advisers Play: Foreign Policy in the Nixon and Carter Administrations.* College Station: Texas A&M University Press.

Gates, Robert M. 1996. *From the Shadows: The Ultimate Insider's Story of Five Presidents and How They Won the Cold War.* New York: Simon and Schuster.

Gaubatz, Kurt T. 1991. "Election Cycles and War." *Journal of Conflict Resolution* 35 (June): 212–244.

General Accounting Office (GAO). 1998. *Military Bases: Status of Prior Base Realignment and Closure Rounds.* Washington, D.C.: General Accounting Office.

———. 2003. *Energy Task Force: Process Used to Develop the National Energy Policy.* Washington, D.C.: GAO.

George, Alexander L. 1980. *Presidential Decision-Making in Foreign Policy: The Effective Use of Information and Advice.* Boulder, Colo.: Westview Press.

———. 1989. "The 'Operational Code': A Neglected Approach to the Study of Political Leaders and Decision Making." In *American Foreign Policy: Theoretical Essays,* ed. G. John Ikenberry, 483–506. New York: HarperCollins.

———. 2000. "The Role of Force in Diplomacy: A Continuing Dilemma for U.S. Foreign Policy." In *The Use of Force After the Cold War,* ed. H. W. Brands, 59–92. College Station: Texas A&M University Press.

George, Alexander L., and Juliette L. George. 1956. *Woodrow Wilson and Colonel House: A Personality Study.* New York: J. Day Co.

Gereffi, Gary, Ronie Garcia-Johnson, and Erika Sasser. 2001. "The NGO-Industrial Complex." *Foreign Policy* 125 (July–August): 56–65.

Gibson, Martha L. 2000. *Conflict and Consensus in American Trade Policy.* Washington, D.C.: Georgetown University Press.

Gilmore Commission. 2003. *Forging America's New Normalcy: Securing Our Homeland, Protecting Our Liberty.* Task force report available at www.rand.org/nsrd/terrpanel.

Gilpin, Robert. 1981. *War and Change in World Politics.* New York: Cambridge University Press.

———. 1986. "The Richness of the Tradition of Political Realism." In *Neorealism and Its Critics,* ed. Robert O. Keohane, 301–321. New York: Columbia University Press.

_____. 1987. *The Political Economy of International Relations.* Princeton: Princeton University Press.

Glad, Betty. 1983. "Black-and-White Thinking: Ronald Reagan's Approach to Foreign Policy." *Political Psychology* 4 (March): 33–76.

Global Policy Forum. 2004. "The Security Counsel." www.globalpolicy.org/security /index.htm.

Goldberg, D. H. 1990. *Foreign Policy and Ethnic Interest Groups: American and Canadian Jews Lobby for Israel.* New York: Greenwood Press.

Goldstein, Judith. 1993. *Ideas, Interests, and American Trade Policy.* Ithaca: Cornell University Press.

Goldstein, Judith, and Robert O. Keohane. 1993. "Ideas and Foreign Policy: An Analytical Framework." In *Ideas and Foreign Policy: Beliefs, Institutions, and Political Change,* ed. Judith Goldstein and Robert O. Keohane, 3–30. Ithaca: Cornell University Press.

Gonzalez, Franciso E., and Desmond King. 2004. "The State and Democratization: The United States in Comparative Perspective." *British Journal of Political Science* 34 (April): 193–211.

Goodwin, Jacob. 1985. *Brotherhood of Arms: General Dynamics and the Business of Defending America.* New York: Times Books.

Gordon, Bernard K. 2003. "A High-Risk Trade Policy." *Foreign Affairs* 82 (July–August): 105–118.

Gormley, William T. Jr., and Steven J. Balla. 2004. *Bureaucracy and Democracy.* Washington, D.C.: CQ Press.

Gourevitch, Peter. 2002. "Domestic Politics and International Relations." In *Handbook of International Relations,* ed. Walter Carlsnaes, Thomas Risse, and Beth A. Simmons, 309–328. Thousand Oaks, Calif.: Sage.

Graber, Doris A. 2002. *Mass Media and American Politics.* 6th ed. Washington, D.C.: CQ Press.

Graebner, Norman A., ed. 1964. *Ideas and Diplomacy: Readings in the Intellectual Tradition of American Foreign Policy.* New York: Oxford University Press.

Gray, Colin S. 1999. *Modern Strategy.* New York: Oxford University Press.

_____. 2002. "Thinking Asymmetrically in Times of Terror." *Parameters* 32 (Spring): 5–14.

Greenberger, Robert S. 1995–1996. "Dateline Capitol Hill: The New Majority's Foreign Policy." *Foreign Policy* 101 (Winter): 159–169.

Greenstein, Fred I. 1969. *Personality and Politics: Problems of Evidence, Inference, and Conceptualization.* Chicago: Markham.

Gregg, Gary L., II. 2004. "Dignified Authenticity: George W. Bush and the Symbolic Presidency." In *Considering the Bush Presidency,* ed. Gary L. Gregg II and Mark J. Rozell, 88–106. New York: Oxford University Press.

Gregory, William H. 1989. *The Defense Procurement Mess.* Lexington, Mass.: Lexington Books.

Grieco, Joseph M. 1990. *Cooperation among Nations: Europe, America, and Non-Tariff Barriers to Trade.* Ithaca: Cornell University Press.

Grimmett, Richard F. 2001. "The War Powers Resolution after 28 Years." November 15. Washington, D.C.: Congressional Research Service.

_____. 2002. "Instances of Use of United States Armed Forces Abroad, 1798–2001." February 5. Washington, D.C.: Congressional Research Service.

_____. 2003. "Conventional Arms Transfers to Developing Nations, 1995–2002." September 22, 1–84. Washington, D.C.: Congressional Research Service.

Griswold, Daniel T. 2002. "NAFTA at 10: An Economic and Foreign Policy Success." *Free Trade Bulletin,* December. www.freetrade.org.

Grunwald, Henry A. 1993. "The Post–Cold War Press." *Foreign Affairs* 72 (Summer): 12–16.

Gugliotta, Guy, and Eric Pianin. 2004. "Bush Plans on Global Warming Alter Little: Voluntary Programs Attract Few Firms." *Washington Post,* January 1, A1.

Haass, Richard N., ed. 1998. *Economic Sanctions and American Diplomacy.* New York: Council on Foreign Relations.

Hallin, Daniel C. 1986. *The 'Uncensored War': The Media and Vietnam.* New York: Oxford University Press.

Hallin, Daniel C., and Todd Gitlin. 1994. "The Gulf War as Popular Culture and Television Drama." In *Taken by Storm: The Media, Public Opinion, and U.S. Foreign Policy in the Gulf War,* ed. Lance W. Bennett and David L. Paletz, 149–163. Chicago: University of Chicago Press.

Halperin, Morton H. 1963. *Limited War in a Nuclear Age.* New York: Wiley.

———. 1974. *Bureaucratic Politics and Foreign Policy.* Washington, D.C.: Brookings.

———. 1997. "What Should the National Security Act of 1998 Look Like?" In *U.S. National Security: Beyond the Cold War,* ed. David Jablonsky, 28–36. Carlisle, Pa.: U.S. Army War College.

Hammond, Paul. 1960. "The National Security Council as a Device for Interdepartmental Coordination: An Interpretation and Appraisal." In *American Political Science Review* 54 (December): 899–910.

Haney, Patrick J. 1997. *Organizing for Foreign Policy Crises: Presidents, Advisers, and the Management of Decision Making.* Ann Arbor: University of Michigan Press.

Haney, Patrick J., and Walt Vanderbush. 1999. "The Role of Ethnic Interest Groups in U.S. Foreign Policy: The Case of the Cuban American National Foundation." *International Studies Quarterly* 43 (June): 341–361.

Hantz, Charles A. 1996. "Ideology, Pragmatism, and Ronald Reagan's World View: Full of Sound and Fury, Signifying . . . ?" *Presidential Studies Quarterly* 26 (Fall): 942–949.

Hardin, Garrett. 1968. "The Tragedy of the Commons." *Science* 162 (December 16): 1243–1248.

Hart, Jeffrey A. 1992. *Rival Capitalists: International Competitiveness in the United States, Japan, and Western Europe.* Ithaca: Cornell University Press.

Hart, John. 1987. *The Presidential Branch.* New York: Pergamon Press.

Hart, Paul 't. 1994. *Groupthink in Government.* Baltimore: Johns Hopkins University Press.

Hart, Paul 't., and Uriel Rosenthal. 1998. "Reappraising Bureaucratic Politics." *Mershon International Studies Review* 42 (November): 233–240.

Hart, Paul 't., Eric Stern, and Bengt Sundelius, eds. 1997. *Beyond Groupthink: Political Group Dynamics and Foreign Policymaking.* Ann Arbor: University of Michigan Press.

Hartung, William D. 1994. *And Weapons for All.* New York: HarperCollins.

Hartz, Louis. 1955. *The Liberal Tradition in America.* New York: Harcourt, Brace.

Haslam, Jonathan. 2002. *No Virtue Like Necessity: Realist Thought in International Relations since Machiavelli.* New Haven: Yale University Press.

Hays, Peter L., Brenda J. Vallance, and Alan R. Van Tassel, eds. 1997. *American Defense Policy.* 7th ed. Baltimore: Johns Hopkins University Press.

Heclo, Hugh. 1978. "Issue Networks and the Executive Establishment." In *The New American Political System,* ed. Anthony King, 87–124. Washington, D.C.: American Enterprise Institute.

Heilbroner, Robert L. 1999. *The Worldly Philosophers: The Lives, Times, and Ideas of the Great Economic Thinkers.* 7th rev. ed. New York: Simon and Schuster.

Heine-Ellison, Sofia. 2001. "The Impact and Effectiveness of Multilateral Economic Sanctions: A Comparative Study." *International Journal of Human Rights* 5 (Spring): 81–113.

Hellman, Christopher. 2003. "Last of the Big Time Spenders: U.S. Military Budget Still the World's Largest, and Growing." Center for Defense Information. March 19. www.cdi.org/friendlyversion/printversion.cfm?documentID=1040.

Helms, Jesse. 1996. "Saving the UN: A Challenge to the Next Secretary-General." *Foreign Affairs* 75 (September–October): 2–7.

Henehan, Marie T. 2000. *Foreign Policy and Congress: An International Relations Perspective.* Ann Arbor: University of Michigan Press.

Henkin, Louis. 1987/1988. "Foreign Affairs and the Constitution." *Foreign Affairs* 66 (Winter): 284–310.

———. 1996. *Foreign Affairs and the Constitution.* 2d ed. New York: Oxford University Press.

Herman, Edward, and Noam Chomsky. 1988. *Manufacturing Consent: The Political Economy of the Mass Media.* New York: Pantheon.

Hermann, Margaret G. 1984. "Personality and Foreign Policy Decision Making: A Study of 53 Heads of Government." In *Foreign Policy Decision Making: Perception, Cognition, and Artificial Intelligence,* ed. Donald A. Sylvan and Steve Chan, 53–80. New York: Praeger.

———. 1993. "Leaders and Foreign Policy Decision-Making." In *Diplomacy, Force, and Leadership: Essays in Honor of Alexander George.* ed. Dan Caldwell and Timothy J. McKeown, 77–94. Boulder, Colo.: Westview Press.

Hermann, Margaret G., and Thomas Preston. 1999. "Presidents, Leadership Style, and the Advisory Process." In *The Domestic Sources of American Foreign Policy,* 3d ed., ed. Eugene Wittkopf and James M. McCormick, 351–367. Lanham, Md.: Rowman and Littlefield.

Herrmann, Richard K. 1984. "Perceptions and Foreign Policy Analysis." In *Foreign Policy Decision Making: Perception, Cognition, and Artificial Intelligence,* ed. Donald A. Sylvan and Steve Chan, 25–52. New York: Praeger.

Hersh, Seymour M. 2004. "Torture at Abu Ghraib." *New Yorker,* May 10. www.newyorker.com/printable/?fact/040510fa_fact.

Hersman, Rebecca. 2000. *Friends and Foes: How Congress and the President Really Make Foreign Policy.* Washington, D.C.: Brookings Institution Press.

Hess, Stephen. 1976. *Organizing the Presidency.* Washington, D.C.: Brookings Institution Press.

Hill, Christopher. 2003. *The Changing Politics of Foreign Policy.* New York: Palgrave Macmillan.

Hilsman, Roger. 2000. "After the Cold War: The Need for Intelligence." In *National Insecurity: U.S. Intelligence After the Cold War,* ed. Craig Eisendrath, 8–22. Philadelphia: Temple University Press.

Hinckley, Barbara. 1994. *Less than Meets the Eye: Foreign Policy Making and the Myth of the Assertive Congress.* Chicago: University of Chicago Press.

Hirsh, Michael. 2003. *At War with Ourselves: Why America Is Squandering Its Chance to Build a Better World.* New York: Oxford University Press.

Hitchens, Christopher. 2001. *The Trial of Henry Kissinger.* New York: Verso.

Hobbes, Thomas. [1651] 1983. *Leviathan.* London: Dent.

Hobbs, Heidi H. 1994. *City Hall Goes Abroad: The Foreign Policy of Local Politics.* Thousand Oaks, Calif.: Sage.

Hoffman, Bruce. 1998. *Inside Terrorism.* New York: Columbia University Press.

Hofman, Ross, and Paul Levack, eds. 1949. *Burke's Politics.* New York: Knopf.

Holmes, Jack. 1985. *The Mood/Interest Theory of American Foreign Policy.* Lexington: University of Kentucky Press.

Holsti, Ole R. 1962. "The Belief System and National Images: A Case Study." *Journal of Conflict Resolution* 6 (September): 244–252.

———. 1992. "Public Opinion and Foreign Policy: Challenges to the Almond-Lippmann Consensus." *International Studies Quarterly* 36 (December): 439–466.

———. 1996. *Public Opinion and American Foreign Policy.* Ann Arbor: University of Michigan Press.

Holsti, Ole R., and James M. Rosenau. 1979. "Vietnam, Consensus, and the Belief Systems of American Leaders." *World Politics* 32 (October): 1–56.

Holt, Pat M. 1995. *Secret Intelligence and Public Policy: A Dilemma of Democracy.* Washington, D.C.: CQ Press.

———. 2000. "Who's Watching the Store? Executive-Branch and Congressional Surveillance." In *National Insecurity: U.S. Intelligence After the Cold War,* ed. Craig Eisendrath, 190–211. Philadelphia: Temple University Press.

Hook, Steven W. 1995. *National Interest and Foreign Aid.* Boulder, Colo.: Lynne Rienner.

———. 1997. "Mission Without a Mandate: U.S. Foreign Aid after the Cold War." Pew Case Studies in International Affairs. Washington, D.C.: Georgetown University.

———. 1998. "Building Democracy through Foreign Aid: The Limitations of United States Political Conditionalities, 1992–1996." *Democratization* 5 (Autumn): 156–180.

———. 2003. "Domestic Obstacles to International Affairs: The State Department Under Fire." *PS: Political Science and Politics* 36 (January): 23–29.

———. 2005. "Sino-American Trade Relations: Privatizing Foreign Policy." In *Contemporary Cases in Foreign Policy: From Terrorism to Trade,* 2d ed., ed. Ralph G. Carter. Washington, D.C.: CQ Press.

Hook, Steven W., and William A. Clark. 1991. "On the Scholarly Study of Nuclear Deterrence: Historical Roots of the New Discourse." In *After the Cold War: Questioning the Morality of Nuclear Deterrence,* ed. Charles W. Kegley Jr. and Kenneth L. Schwab, 195–221. Boulder: Westview Press.

Hook, Steven W., and Richard Robyn. 1999. "Regional Collective Security in Europe: Past Patterns and Future Prospects." *European Security* 8 (Autumn): 82–100.

Hook, Steven W., and David Rothstein. 2005. "The Global Arms Market After September 11th: New Rationales and Old Concerns about U.S. Export Policy." In *Guns and Butter: The Political Economy of International Security,* ed. Peter J. Dombrowski. Boulder, Colo.: Lynne Rienner.

Hook, Steven W., and John Spanier. 2004. *American Foreign Policy since World War II.* 16th ed. Washington, D.C.: CQ Press.

Houghton, J. T., Y. Ding, D. J. Griggs, M. Noguer, P. J. van der Linden, and D. Xiaosu, eds. 2001. *Climate Change 2001: The Scientific Basis.* New York: Cambridge University Press.

Hulnick, Arthur S. 1999. *Fixing the Spy Machine: Preparing American Intelligence for the Twenty-First Century.* Westport, Conn.: Praeger.

Hunt, Michael. 1987. *Ideology and U.S. Foreign Policy.* New Haven: Yale University Press.

Huntington, Samuel P. 1957. *The Soldier and the State: The Theory and Politics of Civil-Military Relations.* Cambridge, Mass.: Belknap Press.

———. 1961. *The Common Defense: Strategic Programs in National Politics.* New York: Columbia University Press.

———. 1970–1971. "Foreign Aid for What and for Whom." *Foreign Policy* 1 (Winter): 161–189.

_____. 1982. "American Ideals versus American Institutions." *Political Science Quarterly* 97 (Spring): 1–37.

_____. 2004. "The Hispanic Challenge." *Foreign Policy* 141 (March–April): 30–45.

Huus, Kari. 2003. "U.S. Takes Hard Line on Greenpeace: Bush Critics Say Use of Obscure Law Smacks of Retribution." MSNBC. November 14. www.msnbc.msn.com.

Ifill, Gwen. 1993. "The Economic Czar Behind the Economic Czars." *New York Times,* March 7, A22.

Ikenberry, G. John. 1993. "Creating Yesterday's New World Order: Keynesian 'New Thinking' and the Anglo-American Postwar Settlement." In *Ideas and Foreign Policy: Beliefs, Institutions, and Political Change,* ed. Judith Goldstein and Robert O. Keohane, 57–86. Ithaca: Cornell University Press.

_____. 2001. *After Victory: Institutions, Strategic Restraint, and the Rebuilding of Order After Major Wars.* Princeton: Princeton University Press.

_____. 2002. "Multilateralism and U.S. Grand Strategy." In *Multilateralism and U.S. Foreign Policy: Ambivalent Engagement,* ed. Stewart Patrick and Shepard Forman, 121–140. Boulder, Colo.: Lynne Rienner.

Ikenberry, G. John, David A. Lake, and Michael Mastanduno, eds. 1988. *The State and American Foreign Economic Policy.* Ithaca: Cornell University Press.

Immelman, Aubrey. 2002. "The Political Personality of U.S. President George W. Bush." In *Political Leadership for the New Century: Personality and Behaviors among American Leaders,* ed. Linda O. Valenty and Ofer Feldman, 81–103. Westport, Conn.: Praeger.

International Institute for Strategic Studies. 2002. *The Military Balance.* London, England: International Institute for Strategic Studies.

International Monetary Fund. 2004a. *World Economic Outlook.* www.imf.org/external/pubs/ft/weo/2004/01/.

International Monetary Fund. 2004b. "IMF at a Glance." imf.org/external/np/exr/facts/glance.htm.

International Monetary Fund and International Development Association. 2004. "The Impact of Debt Reduction under the Hawaii PC Initiative on External Debt Service and Social Expenditures." www.worldbank.org/hipc/hipc-review/Impact_of_Debt_Reduction.pdf.

International Planned Parenthood Foundation. 2004. "Held to Ransom: What Is the Gag Rule?" www.heldtoransom.org/gag.asp.

Isenberg, David. 1997. *Soldiers of Fortune, Ltd.: A Profile of Today's Private Sector Corporate Mercenary Firms.* Washington, D.C.: Center for Defense Information.

Iyengar, Shanto, and Adam Simon. 1994. "News Coverage of the Gulf Crisis and Public Opinion: A Study of Agenda-Setting, Priming, and Framing." In *Taken by Storm: The Media, Public Opinion, and U.S. Foreign Policy in the Gulf War,* ed. Lance W. Bennett and David L. Paletz. Chicago: University of Chicago Press.

Jacobs, Lawrence R., and Robert Y. Shapiro. 1995. "The Rise of Presidential Polling: The Nixon White House in Historical Perspective." *Public Opinion Quarterly* 59 (Summer): 163–195.

Jacobson, Gary C. 1987. "Running Scared: Elections and Congressional Politics in the 1980s." In *Congress: Structure and Policy,* ed. Matthew McCubbins and Terry Sullivan, 34–81. New York: Cambridge University Press.

_____. 2000. "Party Polarization in National Politics: The Electoral Connection." In *Polarized Politics: Congress and the President in a Partisan Era,* ed. Jon R. Bond and Richard Fleisher, 9–30. Washington, D.C.: CQ Press.

Jaffe, Lorna S. 1993. *The Development of the Base Force, 1989–1992.* Washington, D.C.: Office of the Chairman of the Joint Chiefs of Staff.

James, Harold. 1996. *International Monetary Cooperation since Bretton Woods.* New York: Oxford University Press.

Janis, Irving L. 1982. *Groupthink: Psychological Studies of Policy Decisions and Fiascoes.* 2d ed. rev. Boston: Houghton Mifflin.

Jehl, Douglas. 2003. "On Rules for Environment, Bush Sees a Balance, Critics a Threat." *New York Times.* February 23, 1A.

Jentleson, Bruce W. 1992. "The Pretty Prudent Public: Post Post–Vietnam American Opinion on the Use of Military Force." *International Studies Quarterly* 36 (March): 49–73.

_____. Bruce W. 1994. *With Friends Like These: Reagan, Bush, and Saddam, 1982–1990.* New York: Norton.

Jervis, Robert. 1976. *Perception and Misperception in International Politics.* Princeton: Princeton University Press.

_____. 2003. "Understanding the Bush Doctrine." *Political Science Quarterly* 118 (September): 365–388.

Johnson, Chalmers. 1982. *MITI and the Japanese Miracle: The Growth of Industrial Policy, 1925–1975.* Stanford: Stanford University Press.

_____. 2000. *Blowback: The Costs and Consequences of American Empire.* New York: Metropolitan Books.

_____. 2004. *The Sorrows of Empire: Militarism, Secrecy, and the End of the Republic.* New York: Metropolitan Books.

Johnson, James T. 1981. *Just War Tradition and the Restraint of War.* Princeton: Princeton University Press.

Johnson, Loch. 1988. *A Season of Inquiry: Congress and Intelligence.* Chicago: Dorsey Press.

Johnson, Richard T. 1974. *Managing the White House.* New York: Harper and Row.

Johnson, Robert D. 2001. "Congress and the Cold War." *Journal of Cold War Studies* 3 (Spring): 76–100.

Johnston, David. 2004. "Panel's Reports Describe an Agency Institutionally Unable to Handle a Terrorist Threat." *New York Times,* April 14, A16.

Joint Chiefs of Staff. 2002. *National Military Strategy.* Washington, D.C.: Department of Defense.

Jones, Dorothy. 2002. *Toward a Just World: The Critical Years in the Search for International Justice.* Chicago: University of Chicago Press.

Jones, Gordon S., and John A. Marini, eds. 1988. *The Imperial Congress: Crisis in the Separation of Powers.* New York: Pharos Books.

Jones, Howard. 1988. *The Course of American Diplomacy: From the Revolution to the Present.* Chicago: Dorsey Press.

_____. 2002. *Crucible of Power: A History of American Foreign Relations to 1913.* Wilmington, Del.: SR Books.

Jordan, Amos A., William J. Taylor Jr., and Michael J. Mazarr. 1999. *American National Security.* 5th ed. Baltimore: Johns Hopkins University Press.

Joskow, Paul L. 2002. "United States Energy Policy during the 1990s." *Current History* 101 (March): 105–125.

Kaarbo, Juliet. 1998. "Power Politics in Foreign Policy: The Influence of Bureaucratic Minorities." *European Journal of International Relations* 4 (Spring): 67–97.

Kahler, Miles, ed. 1998. *Capital Flows and Financial Crises.* Ithaca: Cornell University Press.

Kant, Immanuel. [1795] 1914. *Eternal Peace and Other International Essays.* Boston: World Peace Foundation.

Karnow, Stanley. 1983. *Vietnam: A History.* New York: Viking.

Karns, Margaret P., and Karen A. Mingst. 2002. "The United States as 'Deadbeat'? U.S. Policy and the UN Financial Crisis." In *Multilateralism and U.S. Foreign Policy: Ambivalent Engagement,* ed. Stewart Patrick and Shepard Forman, 267–294. Boulder, Colo.: Lynne Rienner.

Katovsky, Bill, and Timothy Carlson, eds. 2003. *Embedded: The Media at War in Iraq.* Guilford, Conn.: Lyons Press.

Kattenburg, Paul M. 1980. *The Vietnam Trauma in American Foreign Policy, 1945–1975.* New Brunswick: Transaction Books.

Katzenstein, Peter J. 1996. *The Culture of National Security: Norms and Identity in World Politics.* New York: Columbia University Press.

Katzman, Kenneth. 2003. "Afghanistan: Current Issues and U.S. Policy." August 1. Washington, D.C.: Congressional Research Service.

Kaul, Inge, Isabelle Grunberg, and Marc A. Stern, eds. 1999. *Global Public Goods: International Cooperation in the 21st Century.* New York: Oxford University Press.

Kavka, Gregory S. 1987. *Moral Paradoxes of Nuclear Deterrence.* New York: Cambridge University Press.

Keck, Margaret E., and Kathryn Sikkink. 1998. *Activists beyond Borders: Advocacy Networks in International Politics.* Ithaca: Cornell University Press.

Kegley, Charles W., Jr., and Steven W. Hook. 1991. "U.S. Foreign Aid and UN Voting: Did Reagan's Linkage Strategy Buy Deference or Defiance?" *International Studies Quarterly* 35 (September): 295–312.

Kegley, Charles W., Jr., and Eugene R. Wittkopf. 2004. *World Politics: Trend and Transformation.* 9th ed. Belmont, Calif.: Thomson/Wadsworth.

Keller, William W., and Janne E. Nolan. 2001. "Mortgaging Security for Economic Gain: U.S. Arms Policy in an Insecure World." *International Studies Perspectives* 2 (May): 177–193.

Kengor, Paul. 2004. "Cheney and Vice Presidential Power." In *Considering the Bush Presidency,* ed. Gary L. Gregg II and Mark J. Rozell, 177–200. New York: Oxford University Press.

Kennan, George F. 1947. "The Sources of Soviet Conduct." *Foreign Affairs* 25 (July): 566–582.

———. 1951. *American Diplomacy, 1900–1950.* Chicago: University of Chicago Press.

———. 1996. *At a Century's End: Reflections 1982–1995.* New York: Norton.

———. 1997. "Diplomacy without Diplomats?" *Foreign Affairs* 76 (September–October): 198–212.

Kennedy, Craig, and Marshall M. Bouton. 2002. "The Real Trans-Atlantic Gap." *Foreign Policy* 133 (November–December): 66–74.

Kennedy, Paul. 1987. *The Rise and Fall of the Great Powers: Economic Change and Military Conflict from 1500 to 2000.* New York: Random House.

———. 2003. "The Perils of Empire: This Looks Like America's Moment. History Should Give Us Pause." *Washington Post,* April 20, B1.

Keohane, Robert O. 1984. *After Hegemony: Cooperation and Discord in the World Political Economy.* Princeton: Princeton University Press.

———. 1989. *International Institutions and State Power.* Boulder, Colo.: Westview Press.

———. 2002. "Institutional Theory in International Relations." *Millennial Reflections on International Studies,* ed. Michael Brecher and Frank P. Harvey, 160–164. Ann Arbor: University of Michigan Press.

Keohane, Robert O., and Lisa L. Martin. 1995. "The Promise of Institutionalist Theory." *International Security* 20 (Summer): 39–51.

Keohane, Robert O., and Joseph S. Nye Jr. 2001. *Power and Interdependence.* 3d ed. New York: Longman.

Kernell, Samuel, and Gary C. Jacobson. 2003. *The Logic of American Politics.* 2d ed. Washington, D.C.: CQ Press.

Key, V. O. 1961. *Public Opinion and American Democracy.* New York: Knopf.

King, David C. 1997. "The Polarization of American Parties." In *Why People Don't Trust Government* ed. Joseph S. Nye Jr., Philip D. Zelikow, and David C. King, 155–178. Cambridge: Harvard University Press.

Kingdon, John W. 1981. *Congressmen's Voting Decisions.* New York: Harper and Row.

Kirkpatrick, Jeane J. 1982. *Dictatorships and Double Standards: Rationalism and Reason in Politics.* New York: Simon and Schuster.

Kissinger, Henry. 1957. *Nuclear Weapons and Foreign Policy.* New York: Harper.

———. 2001. *Does America Need a Foreign Policy? Toward a Diplomacy for the 21st Century.* New York: Simon and Schuster.

Kitfield, James. 1999–2000. "The Folk Who Live on the Hill." *National Interest* 58 (Winter): 48–55.

Klare, Michael. 1984. *American Arms Supermarket.* Austin: University of Texas Press.

———. 2002. "Global Petro-Politics: The Foreign Policy Implications of the Bush Administration's Energy Plan." *Current History* 101 (March): 99–104.

Klingberg, Frank L. 1952. "The Historical Alternation of Moods in American Foreign Policy." *World Politics* 4 (January): 239–273.

———. 1983. *Cyclical Trends in American Foreign Policy Moods: The Unfolding of America's World Role.* New York: University Press of America.

Knutsen, Torbjörn L. 1992. *A History of International Relations Theory.* New York: Manchester University Press.

Kobrin, Stephen J. 1998. "The MAI and the Clash of Globalizations." *Foreign Policy* 111 (Fall): 97–109.

Kolko, Gabriel. 1962. *Wealth and Power in America: An Analysis of Social Class and Income.* New York: Praeger.

———. 2003. "Iraq, the United States, and the End of the European Coalition." *Journal of Contemporary Asia* 33 (3): 291–298.

Korey, William. 1999. "Human Rights NGOs: The Power of Persuasion." *Ethics and International Affairs* 13 (Winter): 151–174.

Kostadinova, Tatiana. 2000. "East European Public Support for NATO Membership: Fears and Aspirations." *Journal of Peace Research* 37 (March): 235–249.

Kraft, Michael E. 2003. "Environmental Policy in Congress: From Consensus to Gridlock." In *Environmental Policy: New Directions for the Twenty-First Century.* 5th ed. Norman J. Vig and Michael E. Kraft, 127–150. Washington, D.C.: CQ Press.

Krasner, Stephen D. 1972 "Are Bureaucracies Important? (Or Allison Wonderland)." *Foreign Policy* 7 (Summer): 159–179.

———. 1978. *Defending the National Interest: Raw Materials Investments and U.S. Foreign Policy.* Princeton: Princeton University Press.

Kratochwil, Friedrich. 1989. *Rules, Norms, and Decisions: On the Conditions of Practical and Legal Reasoning in International Relations and Domestic Affairs.* New York: Cambridge University Press.

Krauthammer, Charles. 1990–1991. "The Unipolar Moment." *Foreign Affairs* 70 (Winter): 23–33.

———. 2001. "The New Unilateralism." *Washington Post,* June 8, A29.

Krepon, Michael. 2003. *Cooperative Threat Reduction, Missile Defense, and the Nuclear Future.* New York: Palgrave.

Kriesberg, Martin. 1949. "Dark Areas of Ignorance." In *Public Opinion and Foreign Policy,* ed. Lester Markel, 49–64. New York: Harper.

Kris, Ernst, and Nathan Leites. 1947. "Trends in Twentieth Century Propaganda." In *Psychoanalysis and the Social Sciences,* ed. Géza Róheim, 393–409. New York: International University Press.

Krueger, Anne O. 1996. "Conclusions." In *The Political Economy of American Trade Policy,* ed. Anne O. Krueger, 423–443. Chicago: University of Chicago Press.

———. 1998. *The WTO as an International Organization.* Chicago: University of Chicago Press.

Krueger, Kimbra. 1996. "Internal Struggle over U.S. Foreign Policy Toward Central America: An Analysis of the Reagan Era." *Presidential Studies Quarterly* 26 (Fall): 1034–1046.

Krugman, Paul. 2003. *The Great Unraveling: Losing Our Way in the New Century.* New York: Norton.

Kukla, Jon. 2003. *A Wilderness So Immense: The Louisiana Purchase and the Destiny of America.* New York: Knopf.

Kull, Steven. 1988. *Minds at War: Nuclear Reality and the Inner Conflicts of Defense Policymakers.* New York: Basic Books.

———. 2002. "Public Attitudes toward Multilateralism." In *Multilateralism and U.S. Foreign Policy: Ambivalent Engagement,* ed. Stewart Patrick and Shepard Forman, 99–120. Boulder, Colo.: Lynne Rienner.

———. 2004. "Americans on Climate Change." PIPA/Knowledge Networks Study. June 25. College Park, Md.: Program on International Policy Attitudes.

Kull, Steven, and I. M. Destler. 1999. *Misreading the Public: The Myth of a New Isolationism.* Washington, D.C.: Brookings Institution Press.

Kull, Steven, and Clay Ramsay. 2001. "The Myth of the Reactive Public: American Public Attitudes on Military Fatalities in the Post–Cold War Period." In *Public Opinion and the International Use of Force,* ed. Philip Everts and Pierangelo Isernia, 205–228. New York: Routledge.

Kull, Steven, Clay Ramsay, and Evan Lewis. 2003–2004. "Misperceptions, the Media, and the Iraq War." *Political Science Quarterly* 118 (Winter): 569–598.

Kurtz, Howard. 1998. *Spin Cycle: How the White House and the Media Manipulate the News.* New York: Simon and Schuster.

Kux, Dennis. 1998. "Pakistan." In *Economic Sanctions and American Diplomacy,* ed. Richard N. Haass, 157–176. New York: Council on Foreign Relations.

LaFeber, Walter. 1989. *The American Age.* New York: Norton.

———. 2002. "The Bush Doctrine." *Diplomatic History* 26 (Fall): 543–558.

———. 2004. *America, Russia, and the Cold War, 1945–2002.* 9th ed. Boston: McGraw-Hill.

Lake, Anthony. 1993. "From Containment to Enlargement." *U.S. Department of State Dispatch* 4 (39): 658–665.

Lake, David A. 1988. *Power, Protection, and Free Trade: International Sources of U.S. Commercial Strategy.* Ithaca: Cornell University Press.

Laqueur, Walter. 1999. *The New Terrorism: Fanaticism and the Arms of Mass Destruction.* New York: Oxford University Press.

———. 2003. *No End to War: Terrorism in the Twenty-First Century.* New York: Continuum.

Larson, Deborah W. 1985. *Origins of Containment: A Psychological Explanation.* Princeton: Princeton University Press.

Laurance, William F., Ana K. M. Albernaz, and Carlos Da Costa. 2001. "Is Deforestation Accelerating in the Brazilian Amazon?" *Environmental Conservation* 28 (4): 305–311.

Lebow, Richard Ned. 1981. *Between Peace and War: The Nature of International Crisis.* Baltimore: Johns Hopkins University Press.

Lederman, Gordan N. 1999. *Reorganizing the Joint Chiefs of Staff: The Goldwater-Nichols Act of 1986.* Westport, Conn.: Greenwood Press.

Lee, Ronald. 2003. "The Demographic Transition: Three Centuries of Fundamental Change." *Journal of Economic Perspectives* 17 (4): 167–190.

Leffler, Melvyn P. 1992. *A Preponderance of Power: National Security, the Truman Administration, and the Cold War.* Stanford: Stanford University Press.

Legal Information Institute. 2004. Cornell University. "The Supreme Court Collection." supct.law.cornell.edu/supct.

LeLoup, Lance T., and Steven A. Shull. 2003. *The President and Congress: Collaboration and Combat in National Policymaking.* 2d ed. New York: Longman.

Lemann, Nicholas. 2001. "The Quiet Man: Dick Cheney's Discreet Rise to Unprecedented Power." *New Yorker,* May 7, 56–71.

———. 2002. "The Next World Order: The Bush Administration May Have a Brand-New Doctrine of Power." *New Yorker,* April 1, 42–48.

LeoGrande, William M. 2002. "Tug of War: How Real Is the Rivalry between Congress and the President over Foreign Policy?" *Congress and the Presidency* 29 (Autumn): 113–118.

Leone, Richard C., and Greg Anrig Jr., eds. 2003. *The War on Our Freedoms: Civil Liberties in an Age of Terrorism.* New York: Public Affairs.

Lesser, Ian O., Bruce Hoffman, John Arquilla, David Ronfeldt, and Michele Zanini, eds. 1999. *Countering the New Terrorism.* Santa Monica, Calif.: RAND.

Levering, Ralph B. 1978. *The Public and American Foreign Policy, 1918–1978.* New York: William Morrow.

Levy, Jack. 1987. "Declining Power and the Preventive Motivation for War." *World Politics* 40 (October): 82–107.

———. 1989. "The Diversionary Theory of War: A Critique." In *Handbook of War Studies,* ed. Manus Midlarsky, 259–288. London: Unwin Hyman.

Lewis, David A., and Roger P. Rose. 2002. "The President, the Press, and the War-Making Power: An Analysis of Media Coverage Prior to the Persian Gulf War." *Presidential Studies Quarterly* 32 (September): 559–571.

Lichtblau, Eric. 2003. "U.S. Uses Terror Law to Pursue Crimes from Drugs to Swindling." *New York Times,* September 28, A1.

Liddell Hart, B. H. 1967. *Strategy.* 2d rev. ed. New York: Praeger.

Lincoln, Edward J. 1990. *Japan's Unequal Trade.* Washington, D.C.: Brookings Institution Press.

Lindsay, James M. 1991. "Testing the Parochial Hypothesis: Congress and the Strategic Defense Initiative." *Journal of Politics* 53 (August): 860–876.

———. 1994a. *Congress and the Politics of U.S. Foreign Policy.* Baltimore: Johns Hopkins University Press.

———. 1994b. "Congress, Foreign Policy, and the New Institutionalism." *International Studies Quarterly* 38 (June): 281–304.

Lindsay, James M., and Randall B. Ripley. 1997. "U.S. Foreign Policy in a Changing World." In *U.S. Foreign Policy After the Cold War,* ed. Randall B. Ripley and James M. Lindsay, 3–17. Pittsburgh: University of Pittsburgh Press.

Link, Michael W. 2000. "The Presidential Kaleidoscope: Advisory Networks in Action." In *Presidential Power,* 11th ed., ed. Robert C. Shapiro, Martha Joint Kumar, and Lawrence R. Jacobs, 235–265. New York: Columbia University Press.

Lippmann, Walter. 1914. "Timid Neutrality." *New Republic,* November 14.

_____. 1922. *Public Opinion.* New York: Macmillan.

_____. 1947. *The Cold War: A Study in U.S. Foreign Policy.* New York: Harper.

_____. 1955. *Essays in the Public Philosophy.* Boston: Little, Brown.

Lipset, Seymour M. 1963. *The First New Nation: The United States in Historical and Comparative Perspective.* New York: Basic Books.

_____. 1966. "The President, the Polls, and Vietnam." *Trans-Action* 3 (6): 20–22.

Lohr, Steve. 2000. "Welcome to the Internet, the First Global Colony." January 9. www.crab.rutgers.edu/~goertzel/globalcolony.htm.

Lowenthal, Mark M. 2003. *Intelligence: From Secrets to Policy.* Washington, D.C.: CQ Press.

Lowi, Theodore J. 1979. *The End of Liberalism: The Second Republic of the United States.* 2d ed. New York: Norton.

_____. 1985. *The Personal President: Power Invested, Promise Unfulfilled.* Ithaca: Cornell University Press.

Luck, Edward C. 1999. *Mixed Messages: American Politics and International Organization, 1919–1999.* Washington, D.C.: Brookings Institution Press.

Lundestad, Geir. 1999. " 'Empire by Invitation' in the American Century." *Diplomatic History* 23 (Spring): 189–217.

Luterbacher, Urs, and Detlef F. Sprinz. 2001. *International Relations and Global Climate Change.* Cambridge: MIT Press.

Lyman, Princeton. 2002. "The Growing Influence of Domestic Factors." In *Multilateralism and U.S. Foreign Policy: Ambivalent Engagement,* ed. Stewart Patrick and Shepard Forman, 75–97. Boulder, Colo.: Lynne Rienner.

Macgregor, Douglas A. 2003. *Transformation Under Fire: Revolutionizing How America Fights.* Westport, Conn.: Praeger.

Machiavelli, Niccolò. [1532] 1985. *The Prince.* Translated by Harvey C. Mansfield Jr. Chicago: University of Chicago Press.

Mackinder, Halford J. 1942. *Democratic Ideals and Reality.* New York: Norton.

Magazine Publishers of America. 2002. "Fact Sheet: Average Circulation for Top 100 ABC Magazines 2001." www.magazine.org.

Mahan, Alfred Thayer. 1897. *The Interest of America in Sea Power.* Boston: Little, Brown.

Malone, David. 2003. "U.S.-UN Relations in the UN Security Council in the Post–Cold War Era." In *U.S. Hegemony and International Organizations: The United States and Multilateral Institutions,* ed. Rosemary Foot, S. Neil McFarlane, and Michael Mastanduno, 73–91. New York: Oxford University Press.

Mandelbaum, Michael. 1983. "Vietnam: The Television War." *Parameters* 13 (March): 89–97.

Mann, James. 2004. *Rise of the Vulcans: The History of Bush's War Cabinet.* New York: Viking.

Manning, Bayless. 1977. "The Congress, the Executive, and Intermestic Affairs: Three Proposals." *Foreign Affairs* 55 (January): 306–324.

Maren, Michael. 1997. *The Road to Hell: The Ravaging Effects of Foreign Aid and International Charity.* New York: Free Press.

Margolis, Michael, and David Resnick. 2000. *Politics as Usual: The Cyberspace "Revolution."* Thousand Oaks, Calif.: Sage.

Markle Foundation. 2003. *National Security in the Information Age.* Task force report. www.markletaskforce.org.

Markusen, Ann R., and Sean S. Costigan, eds. 1999. *Arming the Future: A Defense Industry for the 21st Century.* New York: Council on Foreign Relations.

Marra, Robin F., and Charles W. Ostrom Jr. 1989. "Explaining Seat Changes in the U.S. House of Representatives, 1950–1986." *American Journal of Political Science* 33 (August): 541–569.

Martin, Lisa L. 1999. "An Institutionalist View: International Institutions and State Strategies." In *International Order and the Future of World Politics,* ed. T. V. Paul and John A. Hall, 78–98. New York: Cambridge University Press.

Marx, Karl, and Frederick Engels. [1848] 2002. *The Communist Manifesto.* New York: Penguin Books.

Masci, David. 1997. "China After Deng." *CQ Researcher Online,* June 13. library .cqpress.com/cqresearcher.

Mathews, Jessica T. 1997. "Power Shift." *Foreign Affairs* 76 (January–February): 50–66.

May, Ernest R. 1961. *Imperial Democracy: The Emergence of America as a Great Power.* New York: Harcourt Brace and World.

———. 1993. *American Cold War Strategy: Interpreting NSC 68.* New York: Bedford.

Mayer, Jane. 2004. "Contract Sport: What Did the Vice-President Do for Halliburton?" *New Yorker,* February 16 and 23, 80–91.

Mayer, William G. 1992. *The Changing American Mind: How and Why American Public Opinion Changed between 1960 and 1988.* Ann Arbor: University of Michigan Press.

Mayerfield, Jamie. 2003. "Who Shall Be Judge? The United States, the International Criminal Court, and the Global Enforcement of Human Rights." *Human Rights Quarterly* 25 (February): 93–129.

Mayhew, David R. 1974. *Congress: The Electoral Connection.* New Haven: Yale University Press.

McConnell, Grant. 1966. *Private Power and American Democracy.* New York: Knopf.

McCormick, James M., and James M. Black. 1983. "Ideology and Voting on the Panama Canal Treaties." *Legislative Studies Quarterly* 8 (February): 45–63.

McCormick, James M., and Eugene R. Wittkopf. 1998. "Congress, the President, and the End of the Cold War: Has Anything Changed?" *Journal of Conflict Resolution* 42 (August): 440–467.

McCormick, James M., Eugene R. Wittkopf, and David M. Danna. 1997. "Politics and Bipartisanship at the Water's Edge: A Note on Bush and Clinton." *Polity* 30 (Fall): 133–149.

McCormick, Thomas J. 1995. *America's Half Century: United States Foreign Policy in the Cold War and After.* 2d ed. Baltimore: Johns Hopkins University Press.

McCubbins, Mathew, Roger Noll, and Barry R. Weingast. 1987. "Administrative Procedures as Instruments of Political Control." *Journal of Law, Economics, and Organization* 3 (Fall): 243–277.

McDougall, Walter A. 1997. *Promised Land, Crusader State: The American Encounter with the World Since 1776.* Boston: Houghton Mifflin.

McNamara, Robert S. 1995. *In Retrospect: The Tragedies and Lessons of Vietnam.* New York: Times Books.

Mearsheimer, John. 1994–1995. "The False Promise of International Institutions." *International Security* 19 (Winter): 5–49.

———. 2001. *The Tragedy of Great Power Politics.* New York: Norton.

Meltzer Commission. 2000. "The Meltzer Commission Report." www.house.gov /jec/imf/meltzer.pdf.

Merrill, Dennis, and Thomas G. Paterson, eds. 2000. *Major Problems in American Foreign Relations.* 5th ed. Boston: Houghton Mifflin.

Mertus, Julie. 2003. "The New U.S. Human Rights Policy: A Radical Departure." *International Studies Perspectives* 4 (November): 371–384.

_____. 2004. *Bait and Switch: Human Rights and U.S. Foreign Policy*. New York: Routledge.

Milbank, Dana. 2001. "In War, It's Power to the President." *Washington Post,* November 20, A1.

Miller, Warren E., and Donald E. Stokes. 1963. "Constituency Influence in Congress." *American Political Science Review* 57 (March): 45–56.

Mills, C. Wright. 1956. *The Power Elite*. New York: Oxford University Press.

Mitrany, David. 1943. *A Working Peace System*. London: Royal Institute of International Affairs.

Moe, Terry M. 1989. "The Politics of Bureaucratic Structure." In *Can the Government Govern?* ed. John E. Chubb and Paul E. Peterson, 267–330. Washington, D.C.: Brookings Institution Press.

Montgomery, John D. 1962. *The Politics of Foreign Aid: American Experience in Southeast Asia*. New York: Council on Foreign Relations by Praeger.

Mooney, Chris. 2004. "The Editorial Pages and the Case for War: Did Our Leading Newspapers Set Too Low a Bar for a Preemptive Attack?" *Columbia Journalism Review* 42 (March–April): 28–34.

Moore, Robin. 2003. *The Hunt for Bin Laden: Task Force Dagger*. New York: Random House.

Moravcsik, Andrew. 1997. "Taking Preferences Seriously: A Liberal Theory of International Politics." *International Organization* 51 (Autumn): 513–553.

Morgenthau, Hans J. 1959. "Alliances in Theory and Practice." In *Alliance Policy in the Cold War,* ed. Arnold Wolfers, 184–212. Baltimore: Johns Hopkins University Press.

_____. 1967. *Politics among Nations: The Struggle for Power and Peace*. 4th ed. New York: Knopf.

Morris, Edmund. 2001. *The Rise of Theodore Roosevelt*. New York: Modern Library.

Morris, Richard. 1966. *Great Presidential Decisions*. Greenwich, Conn.: Fawcett.

Mowle, Thomas S. 2003. "Worldviews in Foreign Policy: Realism, Liberalism, and External Conflict." *Political Psychology* 24 (September): 561–592.

Mueller, John. 1970. "Presidential Popularity from Truman to Johnson." *American Political Science Review* 64 (March): 18–33.

_____. 1973. *War, Presidents, and Public Opinion*. New York: Wiley.

_____. 1989. *Retreat from Doomsday: The Obsolescence of Major War*. New York: Basic Books.

_____. 1993. "The Impact of Ideas on Grand Strategy." In *The Domestic Bases of Grand Strategy,* ed. Richard Rosecrance and Arthur A. Stein, 48–62. Ithaca: Cornell University Press.

_____. 1994. *Policy and Opinion in the Gulf War*. Chicago: University of Chicago Press.

Multilateral Investment Guarantee Agency. 1998. Annual Report. Washington, D.C.: MIGA.

Muravchik, Joshua. 1991. *Exporting Democracy: Fulfilling America's Destiny*. Washington, D.C.: American Enterprise Institute Press.

National Conference of Catholic Bishops. 1983. *Challenge and Peace: God's Promise and Our Response*. Washington, D.C.: United States Catholic Conference.

National Defense Panel. 1997. *Transforming Defense: National Security in the 21st Century*. Arlington, Va.: National Defense Panel.

National Election Studies. 2002. *National Election Guide to Public Opinion and Electoral Behavior*. Ann Arbor: Center for Political Studies.

National Intelligence Council. 2000. *Global Trends 2015: A Dialogue About the Future With Nongovernmental Experts*. Washington, D.C.: National Intelligence Council.

National Resources Defense Council. 2004. "The Bush Administration's Air Pollution Plan." www.nrD.C.org/air/pollution/qbushplan.asp.

National Security Act of 1947, Public Laws, 80th Cong., 1st sess. 495.

National Security Strategy of the United States of America. 2002. Washington, D.C.: White House. www.whitehouse.gov/nsc/nss.pdf.

Nelson, Douglas R. 1996. "The Political Economy of U.S. Automobile Protection." In *The Political Economy of American Trade Policy,* ed. Anne O. Krueger, 133–190. Chicago: University of Chicago Press.

Nelson, Keith L., and Spencer C. Olin Jr. 1979. *Why War? Ideology, Theory and History.* Berkeley: University of California Press.

Nelson, Michael. 2004. "George W. Bush and Congress: The Electoral Connection." In *Considering the Bush Presidency,* ed. Gary L. Gregg II and Mark J. Rozell, 141–160. New York: Oxford University Press.

Neustadt, Richard E. 1960. *Presidential Power.* New York: Wiley.

New York Times. 1954. "Transcript of President Eisenhower's Press Conference, with Comment on Indo-China." April 8, A18.

———. 1971. *The Pentagon Papers.* New York: Bantam Books.

———. 1992. "Excerpts from Pentagon's Plan: Prevent the Re-Emergence of a New Rival." March 8, A14.

———. 2003. "Empty Promises." January 31, A28.

Nincic, Miroslav. 1988. "The United States, the Soviet Union, and the Politics of Opposites." *World Politics* 40 (July): 452–475.

———. 1990. "U.S.-Soviet Policy and the Electoral Connection." *World Politics* 42 (April): 370–396.

Nivola, Pietro S. 1997. "Commercializing Foreign Affairs? American Trade Policy After the Cold War." In *U.S. Foreign Policy After the Cold War,* ed. Randall B. Ripley and James M. Lindsay, 235–256. Pittsburgh: University of Pittsburgh Press.

Norris, Pippa, Montague Kern, and Marion Just, eds. 2003. *Framing Terrorism: The News Media, the Government, and the Public.* New York: Routledge.

North Atlantic Treaty Organization (NATO). 2004a. "Financial and Economic Data Relating to NATO Defense." www.globalsecurity.org/military/library/news/2003/12/mil-031201–nato05.htm.

———. 2004b. *The North Atlantic Treaty.* www.nato.int/docu/basictxt/treaty.htm.

Nowels, Larry. 2004. "Population Assistance and Family Planning Programs: Issues for Congress." March 24. Washington, D.C.: Congressional Research Service.

Nuechterlein, Donald E. 1997. *A Cold War Odyssey.* Lexington: University Press of Kentucky.

Nye, Joseph S., Jr. 1990. *Bound to Lead: The Changing Nature of American Power.* New York: Basic Books.

———. 2002a. "The American National Interest and Global Public Goods." *International Affairs* 78 (April): 233–244.

———. 2002b. *The Paradox of American Power: Why the World's Only Superpower Can't Go It Alone.* New York: Oxford University Press.

———. 2004. *Soft Power: The Means to Success in World Politics.* New York: Public Affairs.

O'Halloran, Sharyn. 1993. "Congress and Foreign Trade Policy." In *Congress Resurgent: Foreign and Defense Policy on Capitol Hill,* ed. Randall B. Ripley and James M. Lindsay, 283–304. Ann Arbor: University of Michigan Press.

O'Hanlon, Michael E. 2002. *Defense Policy Choices for the Bush Administration.* 2d ed. Washington, D.C.: Brookings Institution Press.

O'Hanlon, Michael E., Peter R. Orszag, Ivo H. Daalder, I. M. Destler, David Gunter, Robert E. Litan, and James Steinberg. 2002. *Protecting the American Homeland: One Year On.* Washington, D.C.: Brookings Institution Press.

O'Leary, Michael K. 1967. *The Politics of American Foreign Aid.* New York: Atherton Press.

Obey, David, and Carol Lancaster. 1988. "Funding Foreign Aid." *Foreign Policy* 71 (Summer): 141–156.

Olson, Mancur. 1965. *The Logic of Collective Action: Public Goods and the Theory of Groups.* Cambridge: Harvard University Press.

_____. 1982. *The Rise and Decline of Nations.* New Haven: Yale University Press.

Onuf, Nicholas G. 1989. *World of Our Making: Rules and Rule in Social Theory and International Relations.* Columbia: University of South Carolina Press.

Organisation for Economic Co-operation and Development (OECD). 2003. "Trends and Recent Developments in Foreign Direct Investment." Paris: OECD, Directorate for Financial, Fiscal, and Enterprise Affairs.

_____. Various years. *Development Co-Operation Report: Efforts and Policies of the Members of the Development Assistance Committee.* Paris: OECD.

Ornstein, Norman J., Thomas E. Mann, and Michael J. Malbin. 2002. *Vital Statistics on Congress, 2001–2002.* Washington, D.C.: American Enterprise Institute Press.

Osgood, Robert E. 1957. *Limited War.* Chicago: University of Chicago Press.

_____. 1968. *Alliances and American Foreign Policy.* Baltimore: Johns Hopkins University Press.

Overby, L. Marvin. 1991. "Assessing Constituency Influence: Congressional Voting on the Nuclear Freeze, 1982–1983." *Legislative Studies Quarterly* 16 (May): 297–312.

Overseas Presence Advisory Panel. 1999. *America's Overseas Presence in the 21st Century.* Washington, D.C.: GPO.

Oye, Kenneth, ed. 1986. *Cooperation under Anarchy.* Princeton: Princeton University Press.

Packenham, Robert A. 1973. *Liberal America and the Third World.* Princeton: Princeton University Press.

Packer, George. 2004. "A Democratic World: Can Liberals Take Foreign Policy Back from the Republicans?" *New Yorker,* February 16 and 23, 100–108.

Page, Benjamin I. 1996. *Who Deliberates? Mass Media in Modern Democracy.* Chicago: University of Chicago Press.

Page, Benjamin I., and Jason Barabas. 2000. "Foreign Policy Gaps Between Citizens and Leaders." *International Studies Quarterly* 44 (September): 339–364.

Page, Benjamin I., and Robert Y. Shapiro. 1992. *The Rational Public: Fifty Years of Trends in Americans' Policy Preferences.* Chicago: University of Chicago Press.

Parenti, Christian. 2003. *The Soft Cage: Surveillance in America from Slavery to the War on Terror.* New York: Basic Books.

Parenti, Michael. 1993. *Inventing Reality: The Politics of News Media.* 2d ed. New York: St. Martin's.

_____. 2002. *Democracy for the Few.* 7th ed. Boston: Bedford-St. Martin's.

Paterson, Thomas G., J. Garry Clifford, and Kenneth J. Hagan. 2000. *American Foreign Relations: A History Since 1895.* Vol. 2, 5th ed. Boston: Houghton Mifflin.

Patrick, Stewart. 2002. "Multilateralism and Its Discontents: The Causes and Consequences of U.S. Ambivalence." In *Multilateralism and U.S. Foreign Policy: Ambivalent Engagement,* ed. Stewart Patrick and Shepard Forman, 1–46. Boulder, Colo.: Lynne Rienner.

Patrick, Stewart, and Shepard Forman, eds. 2002. *Multilateralism and U.S. Foreign Policy: Ambivalent Engagement.* Boulder, Colo.: Lynne Rienner.

Peake, Jeffrey S. 2001. "Presidential Agenda Setting in Foreign Policy." *Political Research Quarterly* 54 (March): 69–86.

———. 2002. "Coalition Building and Overcoming Legislative Gridlock in Foreign Policy." *Presidential Studies Quarterly* 32 (March): 67–83.

Peffley, Mark, and Jon Hurwitz. 1992. "International Events and Foreign Policy Beliefs: Public Response to Changing Soviet-American Relations." *American Journal of Political Science* 36 (May): 431–461.

Peterson, Mark A. 2004. "Bush and Interest Groups: A Government of Chums." In *The George W. Bush Presidency: Appraisals and Prospects,* ed. Colin Campbell and Bert A. Rockman, 226–264. Washington, D.C.: CQ Press.

Pew Global Attitudes Project. 2004. "Mistrust of America in Europe Ever Higher, Muslim Anger Persists." March 16. Washington, D.C.: Pew Research Center for the People and the Press. people-press.org/reports/pdf/206.pdf.

Pew Research Center for the People and the Press. 2004. people-press.org.

Pillar, Paul R. 2001. *Terrorism and U.S. Foreign Policy.* Washington, D.C.: Brookings Institution Press.

Pitkin, Hanna F. 1967. *The Concept of Representation.* Berkeley: University of California Press.

Polsby, Nelson W. 1990. "Congress, National Security, and the Rise of the 'Presidential Branch.'" In *The Constitution and National Security: A Bicentennial View,* ed. Howard E. Shuman and Walter R. Thomas, 201–210. Washington, D.C.: National Defense University Press.

Pomper, Miles. 1998. "The New Faces of Foreign Policy." *CQ Weekly,* November 28, 3203–3208.

Pond, Elizabeth. 2004. *Friendly Fire: The Near-Death of the Transatlantic Alliance.* Washington, D.C.: Brookings Institution Press.

Population Reference Bureau. 2004. "Transitions in World Population." *Population Bulletin* 59 (1): 3–40. www.prb.org/pdf04/TransitionsinWorldPop.pdf.

Posen, Barry R. 2001–2002. "The Struggle Against Terrorism: Grand Strategy, Strategy, and Tactics." *International Security* 26 (Winter): 39–55.

———. 2003. "Command of the Commons: The Military Foundation of U.S. Hegemony." *International Security* 28 (Summer): 5–46.

Posen, Barry R., and Andrew Ross. 1996–1997. "Competing Visions for U.S. Grand Strategy." *International Security* 21 (Winter): 5–53.

Powell, Colin. 1992. "Why Generals Get Nervous." *New York Times,* October 8, A35.

———. 1992–1993. "U.S. Forces: Challenges Ahead." *Foreign Affairs* 71 (Winter): 32–45.

Powell, Colin, with Joseph E. Persico. 1995. *My American Journey.* New York: Random House.

Powell, Jody. 1984. *The Other Side of the Story.* New York: Morrow.

Powlick, Philip J., and Andrew Z. Katz. 1998. "Defining the Public Opinion/Foreign Policy Nexus." *Mershon International Studies Review* 42 (May): 29–61.

Prados, John. 1996. *Presidents' Secret Wars: CIA and Pentagon Covert Operations from World War II through the Persian Gulf War.* Rev. ed. Chicago: I. R. Dee.

Pratt, Julius. 1927. "The Origin of Manifest Destiny." *American Historical Review* 32 (July): 795–798.

Preeg, Ernest H. 1995. *Traders in a Brave New World: The Uruguay Round and the Future of the International Trading System.* Chicago: University of Chicago Press.

Presidential Committee on Administrative Management. 1937. *Administrative Management in the Government of the United States.* Washington, D.C.: GPO.

Preston, Thomas. 2000. "The President's Inner-Circle: Personality and Leadership Style in Foreign-Policy Decision-making." In *Presidential Power: Forging the Presidency for the Twenty-First Century*, ed. Robert Y. Shapiro, Martha Joynt Kumar, and Lawrence R. Jacobs, 105–155. New York: Columbia University Press.

_____. 2001. *The President and his Inner Circle: Leadership Style and the Advisory Process in Foreign Affairs*. New York: Columbia University Press.

Prestowitz, Clyde V. 2003. *Rogue Nation: American Unilateralism and the Failure of Good Intentions*. New York: Basic Books.

Price, Daniel E. 1996. "Presidential Power as a Domestic Constraint on Foreign Policy: Case Studies Examining Arms Sales to Saudi Arabia." *Presidential Studies Quarterly* 26 (Fall): 1099–1113.

Program on International Policy Attitudes. 2001. *Americans and the World Public Opinion on International Affairs*. www.americans-world.org.

Pugh, Michael C. 1989. *The ANZUS Crisis, Nuclear Visiting and Deterrence*. New York: Cambridge University Press.

Putnam, Robert. 1988. "Diplomacy and Domestic Politics: The Logic of Two-Level Games." *International Organization* 42 (Summer): 427–460.

Radelet, Steven. 2003. "Bush and Foreign Aid." *Foreign Affairs* 82 (September–October): 104–117.

Ray, James Lee. 1995. *Democracy and International Conflict: An Evaluation of the Democratic Peace Proposition*. Columbia: University of South Carolina Press.

Reiter, Dan. 1995. "Exploding the Powder Keg Myth: Preemptive Wars Almost Never Happen." *International Security* 20 (Fall): 5–34.

Relyea, Harold C. 2004. "Homeland Security: Department Organization and Management Implementation Phase." May 27. Washington, D.C.: Congressional Research Service.

Renshon, Stanley. 1996. *High Hopes: The Clinton Presidency and the Politics of Ambition*. New York: New York University Press.

Renshon, Stanley, and Deborah W. Larson, eds. 2003. *Good Judgment in Foreign Policy: Theory and Application*. Lanham, Md.: Rowman and Littlefield.

Rice, Condoleezza. 2000. "Promoting the National Interest." *Foreign Affairs* 79 (January–February): 45–62.

_____. 2004. "Testimony of Condoleezza Rice Before 9/11 Commission." *New York Times*, April 8, A6. www.nytimes.com/2004/04/08/politics/08RICE-TEXT.html.

Rich, Bruce. 2002. "The World Bank under James Wolfensohn." In *Reinventing the World Bank*, ed. Jonathan R. Pincus and Jeffrey A. Winters, 26–53. Ithaca: Cornell University Press.

Richelson, Jeffrey T. 1985. *The U.S. Intelligence Community*. Cambridge: Ballinger.

Rieff, David. 2003a. "Blueprint for a Mess: How the Bush Administration's Prewar Planners Bungled Postwar Iraq." *New York Times Magazine*, November 2, 28–78.

_____. 2003b. "Were Sanctions Right?" *New York Times Magazine*, July 27, 41–46.

Rielly, John E. 1999. "Americans and the World: A Survey at Century's End." *Foreign Policy* 114 (Spring): 97–114.

_____, ed. 2003. *American Public Opinion and U.S. Foreign Policy 2002*. Chicago: Chicago Council on Foreign Relations.

Risse-Kappen, Thomas. 1995a. *Bringing Transnational Relations Back In: Non-State Actors, Domestic Structures, and International Institutions*. New York: Cambridge University Press.

_____. 1995b. *Cooperation Among Democracies: The European Influence on U.S. Foreign Policy*. Princeton: Princeton University Press.

_____. 1996. "Collective Identity in a Democratic Community: The Case of NATO." In *The Culture of National Security: Norms and Identity in World Politics,* ed. Peter J. Katzenstein, 357–399. New York: Columbia University Press.

Rivers, Douglas, and Nancy Rose. 1985. "Passing the President's Program." *American Journal of Political Science* 29 (May): 183–196.

Robinson, Donald L. 1996. "Presidential Prerogative and the Spirit of American Constitutionalism." In *The Constitution and the Conduct of American Foreign Policy,* ed. David Gray Alder and Larry N. George, 114–132. Lawrence: University Press of Kansas.

Robinson, Piers. 2001. "Operation Restore Hope and the Illusion of a News Media Driven Intervention." *Political Studies* 49 (December): 941–956.

Rockman, Bert. 1981. "America's Department of State: Irregular and Regular Syndromes of Policy Making." *American Political Science Review* 75 (December): 911–927.

_____. 1997. "The Presidency and Bureaucratic Change after the Cold War." In *U.S. Foreign Policy After the Cold War,* ed. Randall B. Ripley and James M. Lindsay, 21–41. Pittsburgh: University of Pittsburgh Press.

Rogers, Elizabeth S. 1993. "The Conflicting Roles of American Ethnic and Business Interests in the U.S. Economic Sanctions Policy: The Case of South Africa." In *The Limits of State Autonomy,* ed. David Skidmore and Valerie M. Hudson, 185–204. Boulder, Colo.: Westview Press.

Rogoff, Kenneth. 2003. "The IMF Strikes Back." *Foreign Policy* 134 (January–February): 38–46.

Rohde, David W. 1994. "Partisanship, Leadership, and Congressional Assertiveness in Foreign and Defense Policy." In *The New Politics of American Foreign Policy,* ed. David E. Deese, 76–101. New York: St. Martin's.

Roosevelt, Theodore. 1913. *An Autobiography.* New York: Macmillan.

Roper Center for Public Opinion Research. 2004. "Presidential Approval Ratings." www.ropercenter.uconn.edu/.

Rosati, Jerel. 1987. *The Carter Administration's Quest for Global Community.* Columbia: University of South Carolina Press.

Rosato, Sebastian. 2003. "The Flawed Logic of Democratic Peace Theory." *American Political Science Review* 97 (November): 603–620.

Rose, Gideon. 2000–2001. "Democracy Promotion and American Foreign Policy." *International Security* 25 (Winter): 186–203.

Rosecrance, Richard, and Arthur A. Stein, ed. 1993. *The Domestic Bases of Grand Strategy.* Ithaca: Cornell University Press.

Rosner, Jeremy D. 1995. *The New Tug-of-War: Congress, the Executive, and National Security.* Washington, D.C.: Carnegie Endowment for International Peace.

Rossiter, Clinton, ed. 1999. *The Federalist Papers.* New York: Mentor.

Roth, Kenneth. 2004. "The Law of War in the War on Terror." *Foreign Affairs* 83 (January–February): 2–7.

Rothgeb, John M., Jr. 2001. *U.S. Trade Policy: Balancing Economic Dreams and Political Realities.* Washington, D.C.: CQ Press.

Rubin, Barry. 1985. *Secrets of State: The State Department and the Struggle over U.S. Foreign Policy.* New York: Oxford University Press.

Ruggie, John G. 1993. "The Anatomy of an Institution." In *Multilateralism Matters: The Theory and Praxis of an Institutional Form,* ed. John G. Ruggie, 3–47. New York: Columbia University Press.

_____. 1994. "Third Try at World Order? America and Multilateralism after the Cold War." *Political Science Quarterly* 109 (Fall): 553–570.

_____. 1996. *Winning the Peace: America and World Order in the New Era.* New York: Columbia University Press.

Russett, Bruce. 1993. *Grasping the Democratic Peace: Principles for a Post–Cold War World.* Princeton: Princeton University Press.

Rutherford, Kenneth R. 2000. "The Evolving Arms Control Agenda: Implications of the Role of NGOs in Banning Antipersonnel Landmines." *World Politics* 53 (October): 74–114.

Sabrosky, Alan. 1980. "Interstate Alliances: Their Reliability and the Expansion of War." *The Correlates of War II: Testing Some Realpolitik Models,* ed. J. David Singer, 287–295. New York: Free Press.

Sagan, Carl. 1983–1984. "Nuclear War and Climatic Catastrophe: Some Policy Implications." *Foreign Affairs* 62 (Winter): 257–292.

Schabas, William. 2004. *An Introduction to the International Criminal Court.* 2d ed. New York: Cambridge University Press.

Schafer, Mark, and Scott Crichlow. 2002. "The Process-Outcome Connection in Foreign Policy Decision Making: A Quantitative Study Building on Groupthink." *International Studies Quarterly* 46 (March): 45–68.

Schattschneider, E. E. 1960. *The Semisovereign People: A Realist's View of Democracy in America.* New York: Holt, Rinehart, and Winston.

Schelling, Thomas. 1960. *The Strategy of Conflict.* Cambridge: Harvard University Press.

Schlesinger, Arthur M., Jr. 1973. *The Imperial Presidency.* Boston: Houghton Mifflin.

_____. 1978. "Human Rights and the American Tradition." *Foreign Affairs* 57 (May–June): 503–526.

_____. 1989. "The Legislative-Executive Balance in International Affairs: The Intention of the Framers." *Washington Quarterly* 12 (Winter): 99–107.

_____. 2002. "The Immorality of Preemptive War." *New Perspectives Quarterly* 19 (Fall): 41–43.

Schmitt, Eric. 1999. "Senate Kills Test Ban Treaty." *New York Times,* October 14, A1.

Schmitt, Michael N., and Peter J. Richards. 2000. "Into Uncharted Waters: The International Criminal Court." *NWC Review* 53 (Winter): 93–136.

Schneider, Stephen H. 2003. "Modeling Climate Change Impacts and Their Related Uncertainties." In *What the Future Holds: Insights from Social Science,* ed. Richard N. Cooper and Richard Layard, 123–155. Cambridge: MIT Press.

Schulzinger, Robert D. 1994. *American Diplomacy in the Twentieth Century.* 3d ed. New York: Oxford University Press.

Sciolino, Elaine. 1995. "Awaiting Call, Helms Puts Foreign Policy on Hold." *New York Times,* September 24, A1.

Scott, James M. 1996. "Reagan's Doctrine? The Formulation of an American Foreign Policy Strategy." *Presidential Studies Quarterly* 26 (Fall): 1047–1061.

Scott, James M., and Ralph G. Carter. 2002. "Acting on the Hill: Congressional Assertiveness in U.S. Foreign Policy." *Congress and the Presidency* 29 (Autumn): 151–170.

Seib, Philip. 1997. *Headline Diplomacy: How News Coverage Affects Foreign Policy.* Westport, Conn.: Praeger.

Seidman, Harold R. 1986. *Politics, Position, and Power: From the Positive to the Regulatory State.* New York: Oxford University Press.

Shearer, David. 1998. "Private Armies and Military Intervention." *Adelphi Papers* 316. London: International Institute for Strategic Studies.

Shepsle, Kenneth A. 1979. "Institutional Arrangements and Equilibrium in Multidimensional Voting Models." *American Journal of Political Science* 23 (February): 27–59.

Shoch, James. 2001. *Trading Blows: Party Competition and U.S. Trade Policy in a Globalizing Era.* Chapel Hill: University of North Carolina Press.

Shuman, Michael H. 1992. "Dateline Main Street: Courts v. Local Foreign Policies." *Foreign Policy* 86 (Spring): 158–177.

Sicker, Martin. 2002. *The Geopolitics of Security in the Americas: Hemispheric Denial from Monroe to Clinton.* Westport, Conn.: Praeger.

Silverstein, Gordon. 1997. *Imbalance of Powers: Constitutional Interpretation and the Making of American Foreign Policy.* New York: Oxford University Press.

Simmons, P. J. 1998. "Learning to Live with NGOs." *Foreign Policy* 112 (Fall): 82–96.

Simon, Herbert. 1957. *Administrative Behavior.* New York: Macmillan.

_____. 1985. "Human Nature in Politics: The Dialogue of Psychology with Political Science." *American Political Science Review* 79 (June): 293–304.

Singer, P. W. 2003. *Corporate Warriors: The Rise of the Privatized Military Industry.* Ithaca: Cornell University Press.

Sloan, Stanley R. 1991. "The U.S. Role in a New World Order: Prospects for George Bush's Global Vision." March 28. Washington, D.C.: Congressional Research Service.

Smist, Frank J. 1990. *Congress Oversees the United States Intelligence Community, 1947–1989.* Knoxville, Tenn: University of Tennessee Press.

Smith, Adam. [1776] 2000. *Inquiry into the Nature and Causes of the Wealth of Nations.* New York: Modern Library.

Smith, Hedrick. 1988. *The Power Game.* New York: Random House.

Smith, James A. 1991. *The Idea Brokers: Think Tanks and the Rise of the New Policy Elite.* New York: Free Press.

Smith, Jean E. 1989. *The Constitution and American Foreign Policy.* St. Paul, Minn.: West.

Smith, Tony. 1994. *America's Mission: The United States and the Worldwide Struggle for Democracy in the Twentieth Century.* Princeton: Princeton University Press.

_____. 2000. "National Security Liberalism and American Foreign Policy." In *American Democracy Promotion: Impulses, Strategies, and Impacts,* ed. Michael Cox, G. John Ikenberry, and Takashi Inoguchi, 85–102. New York: Oxford University Press.

Snodgrass, David E. 2000. "The QDR: Improve the Process to Improve the Product." *Parameters* 30 (Spring): 57–68.

Snow, Donald M. 2004. *National Security for a New Era: Globalization and Geopolitics.* New York: Pearson Longman.

Snyder, Glenn H. 1961. *Deterrence and Defense: Toward a Theory of National Security.* Princeton: Princeton University Press.

Snyder, Richard C., Henry W. Bruck, and Burton Sapin. 2002. *Foreign Policy Decision Making: An Approach to the Study of International Politics.* 2d ed. rev. New York: Palgrave Macmillan.

Sobel, Richard. 2001. *The Impact of Public Opinion on U.S. Foreign Policy Since Vietnam.* New York: Oxford University Press.

Solomon, Steven. 1995. *The Confidence Game: How Unelected Central Bankers Are Governing the Global Economy.* New York: Simon and Schuster.

Sorensen, Theodore. 1987–1988. "The President and the Secretary of State." *Foreign Affairs* 66 (Winter): 231–248.

Spinner, Jackie. 2004. "Halliburton Reviews Food Service Bill." *Washington Post,* February 3, A2.

Spykman, Nicholas J. 1942. *America's Strategy in World Politics: The United States and the Balance of Power.* New York: Harcourt, Brace.

Squeo, Anne Marie. 2002. "Dollars for the Defense: Military Contractors Are Likely to Get a Big Boost from the War on Terrorism." *Wall Street Journal Europe,* October 18–20, R4.

Stanton, John J. 2002. "Terror in Cyberspace: Terrorists Will Exploit and Widen the Gap Between Governing Structures and the Public." *American Behavioral Scientist* 45 (February): 1017–1032.

Stedman, Stephen J. 2002. "Making and Keeping the Peace." In *A Global Agenda: Issues Before the 56th General Assembly of the United Nations,* ed. Diana Ayton-Shenker and John Tessitore, 1–59. Lanham, Md.: Rowman and Littlefield.

Steele, Ian K. 1994. *Warpaths: Invasions of North America.* New York: Oxford University Press.

Stein, Arthur A. 1990. *Why Nations Cooperate.* Ithaca: Cornell University Press.

_____. 1993. "Domestic Constraints, Extended Deterrence, and the Incoherence of Grand Strategy: The United States, 1938–1950." In *The Domestic Bases of Grand Strategy,* ed. Richard Rosecrance and Arthur A. Stein, 96–123. Ithaca: Cornell University Press.

Stephanopoulos, George. 1999. *All Too Human: A Political Education.* Boston: Little, Brown.

Stern, Jessica. 1999. *The Ultimate Terrorists.* Cambridge: Harvard University Press.

Stiglitz, Joseph E. 2002. *Globalization and Its Discontents.* New York: Norton.

Stimson, James A. 1991. *Public Opinion in America: Moods, Cycles, and Swings.* Boulder, Colo.: Westview Press.

Stockton, Paul. 1997. "When the Bear Leaves the Woods: Department of Defense Reorganization in the Post–Cold War Era." In *U.S. Foreign Policy After the Cold War,* ed. Randall B. Ripley and James M. Lindsay, 106–131. Pittsburgh: University of Pittsburgh Press.

Stoessinger, John. 1985. *Crusaders and Pragmatists: Movers of Modern American Foreign Policy.* New York: Norton.

Stohl, Rachel. 2003. "Post–Sept. 11 Arms Sales and Military Aid Demonstrate Dangerous Trend." Center for Defense Information. www.cdi.org/friendlyversion/printversion.cfm?documentID=844.

Stoll, Richard J. 1984. "The Guns of November: Presidential Reelections and the Use of Force, 1947–1982." *Journal of Conflict Resolution* 28 (June): 231–246.

Strange, Susan. 1988. *States and Markets.* 2d ed. London: Pinter.

Strobel, Warren P. 1997. *Late-Breaking Foreign Policy: The News Media's Influence on Peace Operations.* Washington, D.C.: U.S. Institute of Peace Press.

Stuart, Douglas T. 1997. "Introduction." In *U.S. National Security: Beyond the Cold War,* ed. David Jablonsky, ii–vii. Carlisle, Pa.: U.S. Army War College.

_____. 2002. "Ministry for Fear: The Evolving Debate over Reform of the U.S. National Security Bureaucracy." Conference paper presented to the International Studies Association. March 24.

_____. 2003. "Ministry of Fear: The 1947 National Security Act in the Historical and Institutional Context." *International Studies Perspectives* 4 (August): 293–313.

Sylvan, Donald A., and James F. Voss, eds. 1998. *Problem Representation in Foreign Policy Decision Making.* New York: Cambridge University Press.

Tarnoff, Curt, and Larry Nowels. 2001. "Foreign Aid: An Introductory Overview of U.S. Programs and Policy." January 16. Washington, D.C.: Congressional Research Service.

_____. 2004. "Foreign Aid: An Introductory Overview of U.S. Programs and Policy." April 15. Washington, D.C.: Congressional Research Service.

Tarr, David R. and Ann O'Connor, eds. 2003. *Congress A to Z.* 4th ed. Washington, D.C.: CQ Press.

Tostensen, Arne, and Beate Bull. 2002. "Are Smart Sanctions Feasible?" *World Politics* 54 (April): 373–403.

Tower Commission. 1987. *The Tower Commission Report.* New York: Bantam/Times Books.

Traub, James. 2004. "The Things They Carry." *New York Times Magazine,* January 4: 28–36.

Trean, Claire. 2002. "Washington versus International Justice." *Le Monde,* July 2. www.globalpolicy.org/intljustice/icc/crisis/0702wash.htm.

Trubowitz, Peter. 1992. "Sectionalism and American Foreign Policy: The Political Geography of Consensus and Conflict." *International Studies Quarterly* 36 (March): 173–190.

Truman, David B. 1951. *The Governmental Process: Political Interests and Public Opinion.* New York: Knopf.

Tuchman, Barbara W. 1962. *The Guns of August.* New York: Macmillan.

Tucker, Robert W., and David C. Hendrickson. 1992. *Imperial Temptations: The New World Order and America's Purpose.* New York: Council on Foreign Relations.

Turchin, Peter. 2003. *Historical Dynamics: Why States Rise and Fall.* Princeton: Princeton University Press.

Turner, Frederick Jackson. 1920. *The Frontier in American History.* New York: Holt.

Twight, Charlotte. 1989. "Institutional Underpinnings of Parochialism: The Case of Military Base Closures." *Cato Journal* 9 (Spring/Summer): 73–105.

United Nations. 2004a. *Charter of the United Nations.* www.un.org/aboutun/charter /index.html.

———. 2004b. *Economic and Social Development.* www.un.org/esa.

———. 2004c. "UN Peacekeeping Missions." www.un.org/Depts/dpko/dpko/home.s html.

United Nations Department of Peacekeeping Operations. "United Nations Peacekeeping: In the Service of Peace." www.un.org/Depts/dpko/dpko/home.shtml.

U.S. Agency for International Development. 1992. Bureau for Legislative Affairs. *Why Foreign Aid? The Benefit of Foreign Assistance to the United States.* Washington, D.C.: USAID.

———. 2004. *U.S. Foreign Aid: Meeting the Challenges of the Twenty-First Century.* Washington, D.C.: USAID.

U.S. Bureau of Economic Analysis. Various years. www.bea.doc.gov/bea.

U.S. Bureau of Labor Statistics. Various years. www.bls.gov.

U.S. Bureau of the Census. 1976. *The Statistical History of the United States: From Colonial Times to the Present.* New York: Basic Books.

———. 2004a. "Foreign Trade Statistics." www.census.gov/feriegh-trade/www.

———. 2004b. "U.S. International Trade in Goods and Services Highlights: Goods and Services Deficit Increases in March 2004." May 12.

U.S. Central Command. 2003. "Operation Enduring Freedom." www.centcom.mil.

U.S. Central Intelligence Agency. 2003. *The World Factbook.* www.cia.gov/cia/publications/factbook/index.html.

———. 2004. *The World Factbook.* www.cia.gov/cia/publications/factbook/index.html.

U.S. Commission on National Security/21st Century. 2001. *Roadmap for National Security: Imperatives for Change.* www.nssg.gov/Reports.html.

U.S. Congress, House Committee on Armed Services. 1992. *Defense for a New Era: Lessons of the Persian Gulf War.* Washington, D.C.: GPO.

U.S. Defense Security Cooperation Agency. 2003. *DSCA Facts Book 2003.* www.dsca.osd.mil/programs/biz-ops/facts_book_2003.pdf.

_____. 2004. *Background on Weapons Systems.* www.dsca.osd.mil/background.htm.

U.S. Department of Commerce. 2004. *Statistical Abstract of the United States.* www.census.gov/statab/www.

U.S. Department of Defense. 1993. *Report on the Bottom-Up Review.* Washington, D.C.: Office of the Secretary of Defense.

_____. 1998. *The Report of the Department of Defense on Base Realignment and Closure.* Washington, D.C.: Department of Defense.

_____. 2001a. *Annual Report to the President and Congress.* Washington, D.C.: GPO.

_____. 2001b. *Quadrennial Defense Review Report.* Washington, D.C.: Department of Defense.

_____. 2002. *The Nuclear Posture Review.* Washington, D.C.: Department of Defense.

_____. 2003. *Base Structure Report: Fiscal Year 2003 Baseline.* Washington, D.C.: Department of Defense. www.defenselink.mil/pubs/almanac/almanac/Graphics/BSR_03.pdf.

_____. 2004a. *Defense Almanac.* www.defenselink.mil/pubs/dod101.

_____. 2004b. "Procurement Statistics: Directorate for Information Operations and Reports." web1.whs.osd.mil/peidhome/procstat/procstat.htm.

U.S. Department of Education. 2002. *The Nation's Report Card, 2001.* Washington, D.C.: Office of Educational Research and Improvement.

U.S. Department of Energy. 2004a. *Annual Energy Outlook 2004 with Projections to 2025.* www.eia.doe.gov/oiaf/aeo/pdf/appa.pdf.

_____. 2004b. "International Total Primary Energy and Related Information." www.eia.doe.gov/emeu/international/total.html.

U.S. Department of Homeland Security. 2004. "DHS Organization." www.dhs.gov/dhspublic/display?theme=9&content=2973.

U.S. Department of Labor. 2004. Bureau of Labor Statistics. "Union Members Summary." January 21. www.bls.gov/news.release/union2.nr0.htm.

U.S. Department of State. 1981. Bureau of Public Affairs. *A Short History of the U.S. Department of State, 1781–1981.* Washington, D.C.: GPO.

_____. 1993. Bureau of Public Affairs. *State 2000: A New Model for Managing Foreign Affairs.* Washington, D.C.: U.S. Department of State Publication 10029.

_____. 2000. Bureau of Public Affairs. *World Military Expenditures and Arms Transfers, 1998.* Washington, D.C.: GPO.

_____. 2001. "Restoration of the Mexico City Policy Concerning Family Planning." January 22. www.usaid.gov/bush_pro_new.html.

_____. 2003a. "Country Reports on Human Rights Practices, 2002." www.state.gov/g/drl/rls/hrrpt/2002.

_____. 2003b. "Patterns of Global Terrorism 2003." Updated June 22, 2004. www.state.gov/s/ct/rls/pgtrpt.

_____. 2003c. Bureau of Public Affairs. *United States Collective Defense Arrangements.* Special Report 81. Washington, D.C.: State Department.

_____. 2004a. "Department of State Organizational Chart." www.state.gov/r/pa/ei/rls/dos/7926.htm.

_____. 2004b. "Patterns of Global Terrorism 2004." www.state.gov/s/ct/rls/pgtrpt.

_____. 2004c. *Treaties in Force.* www.state.gov/s/l/c8455.htm.

U.S. Embassy in Mexico. 2004. "Sections in the U.S. Embassy." mexico.usembassy.gov/eembdir.html.

U.S. Federal Election Commission. 2004. *Campaign Finance Reports and Data.* www.fec.gov/finance_reports.html.

U.S. Information Agency Alumni Association. 2004. www.publicdiplomacy.org.

U.S. Intelligence Community. 2004. www.intelligence.gov.

U.S. International Trade Administration. 1993. *The East Asian Economic Miracle.* New York: Oxford University Press.

———. 1997. *Private Capital Flows to Developing Countries: The Road to Financial Integration.* New York: Oxford University Press.

———. 2004a. Office of Trade and Economic Analysis database. www.ita.doc.gov/td /industry/otea/usfth/tabcon.html.

———. 2004b. "TradeStats Express." tse.export.gov.

———. 2004c. "U.S. Foreign Aggregate Trade Data." Office of Trade and Economic Analysis. June 6. www.ita.doc.gov/td/industry/otea/usfth/tabcon.html.

U.S. National Oceanic and Atmospheric Administration. 2004. *Climate of 2003 Annual Review.* www.ncdcnoaa.gov/oa/climate/research/2003/ann/global.html#Gtemp.

U.S. Office of Management and Budget. 2002. *Budget of the United States Government: Historical Tables.* Washington, D.C.: GPO.

———. 2004. *The Budget of the United States Government, Fiscal Year 2005.* www.whitehouse.gov/omb/budget/fy2005/.

———. Various years. *The Budget of the United States Government: Historical Tables.* Washington, D.C.: GPO.

U.S. Public Interest Research Group. 2002. "U.S. Lags Behind in Development of Renewable Energy." March 12. *uspirg.org/uspirg.asp?id2=5958&id3=USPIRG&.*

U.S. Senate. 1976. Select Committee to Study Governmental Operations with Respect to Intelligence Activities of the United States. *Final Report.* 94th Cong., 2d sess. April 26.

U.S. Senate. 2002. Select Committee on Intelligence and U.S. House Permanent Select Committee on Intelligence. *Joint Inquiry into Intelligence Community Activities Before and After the Terrorist Attacks of September 11, 2001.* 107th Cong., 2d sess. S. Rep. 107–351. H. Rep. 107–792.

U.S. Senate. 2004. Select Committee on Intelligence. *Report on the U.S. Intelligence Community's Prewar Intelligence Assessments on Iraq.* 108th Cong., 2d sess. July 7.

Uslaner, Eric M. 1998. "All in the Family? Interest Groups and Foreign Policy." In *Interest Group Politics,* 5th ed., ed. Allan J. Cigler and Burdett A. Loomis, 365–388. Washington, D.C.: CQ Press.

———. 2002. "Cracks in the Armor? Interest Groups and Foreign Policy." In *Interest Group Politics,* 6th ed., ed. Allan J. Cigler and Burdett A. Loomis, 355–377. Washington, D.C.: CQ Press.

Van Alstyne, Richard W. 1965. *Empire and Independence: The International History of the American Revolution.* New York: Wiley.

Van Belle, Douglas A., and Steven W. Hook. 2000. "Greasing the Squeaky Wheel: News Media Coverage and U.S. Development Aid, 1977–1992." *International Interactions* 26 (July-September): 321–346.

Van Creveld, Martin L. 1991. *The Transformation of War.* New York: Free Press.

Verba, Sidney. 1961. "Assumptions of Rationality and Non-Rationality in Models of the International System." In *The International System,* ed. Klaus Knorr and Sidney Verba, 93–117. Princeton: Princeton University Press.

Vertzberger, Yaacov. 1990. *The World in Their Minds: Information Processing, Cognition, and Perception in Foreign Policy Decisionmaking.* Stanford: Stanford University Press.

von Clausewitz, Carl. [1832] 1982. *On War.* New York: Penguin Books.

von Hippel, Karin. 2000. "Democracy by Force: A Renewed Commitment to Nation Building." *Washington Quarterly* 23 (Winter): 95–112.

Walcott, Charles E., and Karen M. Hult. 2004. "The Bush Staff and Cabinet System." In *Considering the Bush Presidency,* ed. Gary L. Gregg II, and Mark J. Rozell, 52–68. New York: Oxford University Press.

Waldron, Beth. 2003. "All Politics Should *Not* Be Local." *Christian Science Monitor,* May 22, 11.

Walker, Stephen G. 1977. "The Interface between Beliefs and Behavior: Henry Kissinger's Operational Code and the Vietnam War." *Journal of Conflict Resolution* 21 (March): 129–168.

Walker, Stephen G., Mark Shafer, and Michael D. Young. 1998. "Systematic Procedures for Operational Code Analysis: Measuring and Modeling Jimmy Carter's Operational Code." *International Studies Quarterly* 42 (March): 175–190.

Walt, Stephen M. 1987. *The Origin of Alliances.* Ithaca: Cornell University Press.

Waltz, Kenneth N. 1959. *Man, the State, and War: A Theoretical Analysis.* New York: Columbia University Press.

_____. 1979. *Theory of International Relations.* Reading, Mass.: Addison-Wesley.

_____. 1997. "Evaluating Theories." *American Political Science Review* 91 (December): 913–917.

Walzer, Michael. 1977. *Just and Unjust Wars: A Moral Argument with Historical Illustrations.* 2d ed. New York: Basic Books.

Wardlaw, Grant. 1989. *Political Terrorism: Theory, Tactics, and Counter-Measures.* 2d ed. rev. New York: Cambridge University Press.

Warshaw, Shirley A. 1996. *Powersharing: White House-Cabinet Relations in the Modern Presidency.* Albany: State University of New York Press.

Washington Council on International Trade. 1997. "Issue Brief: China's MFN Status." Updated April 11, 1997. www.wcit.org/resources/publications/issue_briefs/ib_china_mfn_status.htm.

Wawro, Gregory. 2000. *Legislative Entrepreneurship in the U.S. House of Representatives.* Ann Arbor: University of Michigan Press.

Weber, Max. 1946. *From Max Weber: Essays in Sociology.* New York: Oxford University Press.

Weinberger, Caspar. 1984. "The Uses of Military Power." Speech delivered before the National Press Club in Washington, D.C. www.pbs.org/wgbh/pages/frontline/shows/military/force/weinberger.html.

Weiner, Tim. 1996. "Military Chiefs Trying to Gain Extra Billions." *New York Times,* April 10, A10.

Weingast, Barry R. 1984. "The Congressional-Bureaucratic System: A Principal-Agent Perspective with Applications to the SEC." *Public Choice* 44 (1): 147–191.

Weinstein, Michael M., and Steve Charnovitz. 2001. "The Greening of the WTO." *Foreign Affairs* 80 (November–December): 147–156.

Weisburd, A. Mark. 1997. *The Use of Force: The Practice of States Since World War II.* University Park: Pennsylvania State University Press.

Weiss, Thomas G., David P. Forsythe, and Roger A. Coate. 2001. *The United Nations and Changing World Politics.* 3d ed. Boulder, Colo.: Westview Press.

Weissbrodt, David. 1984. "The Contribution of International Nongovernmental Organizations to the Protection of Human Rights." In *Human Rights in International Law: Legal and Policy Issues,* ed. Theodor Meron, 403–448. Oxford: Clarendon Press.

Weissman, Stephen R. 1995. *A Culture of Deference: Congress's Failure of Leadership in Foreign Policy.* New York: Basic Books.

Welch, Claude E., Jr. 2001. "Conclusion." In *NGOs and Human Rights: Promise and Performance,* ed. Claude E. Welch Jr., 261–280. Philadelphia: University of Pennsylvania Press.

Welch, David A. 1992. "The Organizational Process and Bureaucratic Politics Paradigms: Retrospect and Prospect." *International Security* 17 (Fall): 112–146.

Weldes, Jutta. 1999. *Constructing National Interests: The United States and the Cuban Missile Crisis*. Minneapolis: University of Minnesota Press.

Wendt, Alexander. 1992. "Anarchy Is What States Make of It: The Social Construction of World Politics." *International Organization* 46 (Spring): 391–425.

———. 1999. *Social Theory of International Politics*. New York: Cambridge University Press.

White House. 2001a. *The President's Daily Briefing*. August 6. www.washingtonpost .com/wp-dyn/ articles/A2285–2004Apr10.html.

———. 2001b. *Reliable, Affordable, and Environmentally Sound Energy for America's Future: Report of the National Energy Policy Development Group*. Washington, D.C.: White House.

———. 2002a. "Remarks by the President at 2002 Graduation Exercise of the United States Military Academy at Westpoint, New York." June 1. www.whitehouse.gov /news/releases/2002/06/20020601–3.html.

———. 2002b. "The National Security Strategy of the United States of America." September. www.whitehouse.gov/nsc/nss.pdf.

Whitehead, John W., and Steven H. Aden. 2002. "Forfeiting 'Enduring Freedom' for Homeland Security: A Constitutional Analysis of the USA Patriot Act and the Justice Department's Antiterrorism Initiatives." *American University Law Review* 51 (August): 1081–1095.

Wiarda, Howard J. 1996. *American Foreign Policy: Actors and Process*. York, Pa.: HarperCollins.

———. 2000. "Beyond the Pale: The Bureaucratic Politics of United States Policy in Mexico." *World Affairs* 162 (Spring): 174–190.

Wildavsky, Aaron. 1966. "The Two Presidencies." *Trans-Action* 4 (December): 7–14.

Wildavsky, Aaron, and Naomi Caiden. 1997. *The New Politics of the Budgetary Process*. 3d ed. New York: Longman.

Willett, Thomas D. 2001. "Understanding the IMF Debate." *Independent Review* 5 (Spring): 593–610.

Willetts, Peter. 2003. "The Growth in the Number of NGOs in Consultative Status with the Economic and Social Council of the United Nations." www.staff.city.ac.uk/p.wil-letts/NGOS/ngo-home.htm.

Williams, Cindy. 2001. "Introduction." In *Holding the Line: U.S. Defense Alternatives for the Early 21st Century,* ed. Cindy Williams, 1–33. Cambridge: MIT Press.

Williams, William A. 1959. *The Tragedy of American Diplomacy*. Cleveland: World Publishing.

Williamson, John. 1990. *Latin American Adjustment: How Much Has Happened?* Washington, D.C.: Institute for International Economics.

Wilson, James Q. 1989. *Bureaucracy: What Government Agencies Do and Why They Do It*. New York: Basic Books.

Wilson, Joseph C. 2004. *The Politics of Truth: Inside the Lies that Led to War and Betrayed My Wife's CIA Identity: A Diplomat's Memoir*. New York: Carroll and Graf.

Wilson, Woodrow. 1927. "Speech at the Coliseum, St. Louis, Missouri." In *War and Peace: Presidential Messages, Addresses, and Public Papers, 1917–1924*. Vol. 1. New York: Harper and Brothers.

Wittkopf, Eugene R. 1990. *Faces of Internationalism: Public Opinion and U.S. Foreign Policy*. Durham: Duke University Press.

Wohlstetter, Albert. 1959. "The Delicate Balance of Terror." *Foreign Affairs* 37 (January): 211–234.

Wolfers, Arnold. 1962. *Discord and Collaboration: Essays on International Politics*. Baltimore: Johns Hopkins University Press.

Woods, Ngaire. 2000. "The Challenges of Multilateralism and Governance." In *The World Bank: Structure and Policies,* ed. Chris Gilbert and David Vines, 132–158. New York: Cambridge University Press.

Woodward, Bob. 2002. *Bush at War.* New York: Simon and Schuster.

———. 2004. *Plan of Attack.* New York: Simon and Schuster.

World Bank. 1993. *The East Asian Economic Miracle.* New York: Oxford University Press.

———. 2003a. "About Us: What Is the World Bank?" www.worldbank.org.

———. 2003b. *World Development Report.* New York: Oxford University Press.

———. 2004a. *Debt Initiative for Heavily Indebted Poor Countries.* www.worldbank.org/hipc.

———. 2004b. *World Development Indicators.* New York: Oxford University Press.

World Commission on Environment and Development. 1987. *Our Common Future.* New York: Oxford University Press.

World Trade Organization (WTO). 2004a. "Stronger than Expected Growth Spurs Modest Trade Recovery." *WTO News,* April 5. www.wto.org/english/news_e/pres04_e/pr373_e.htm.

———. 2004b. "International Trade Statistics." www.wto.org/english/res_e/statis_e/statis_e.htm.

Yergin, Daniel. 1977. *Shattered Peace: The Origins of the Cold War.* New York: Penguin Books.

———. 1991. *The Prize: The Epic Quest for Oil, Money, and Power.* New York: Simon and Schuster.

Yost, David S. 1998. *NATO Transformed: The Alliance's New Roles in International Security.* Washington, D.C.: U.S. Institute of Peace Press.

Zakaria, Fareed. 1997. "The Rise of Illiberal Democracy." *Foreign Affairs* 76 (November–December): 22–43.

Zegart, Amy B. 1999. *Flawed by Design: The Evolution of the CIA, JCS, and NSC.* Stanford: Stanford University Press.

Zinn, Howard. 1968. *Disobedience and Democracy: Nine Fallacies on Law and Order.* New York: Random House/Vintage.

Zoellick, Robert B. 1999–2000. "Congress and the Making of U.S. Foreign Policy." *Survival* 41 (Winter): 20–41.

Zogby International. 2003. "Results from Zogby International Poll." October 21. www.climatenetwork.org/uscanweb/csadocs/zogby.pdf.

Map Credits

All maps (see color map section at the front of the book) by International Mapping Associates, adapted from, or based on data from, the following sources:

Map 1 Nineteenth-Century European Empires and U.S. Continental Expansion

Thomas M. Magstadt, *An Empire If You Can Keep It: Power and Principle in American Foreign Policy* (Washington, D.C.: CQ Press, 2004), xviii, xix.

Map 2 Cold War Division of Europe

Bruce Bueno de Mesquita, *Principles of International Politics: People's Power, Preferences, and Perceptions,* 2d ed. (Washington, D.C.: CQ Press, 2003), 197; Steven W. Hook and John Spanier, *American Foreign Policy Since World War II,* 16th ed. (Washington, D.C.: CQ Press, 2004), 33.

Map 3 Cold War Alliances with the United States

Organization of American States, www.oas.org; North Atlantic Treaty Organisation, www.nato.int; Steven W. Hook and John Spanier, *American Foreign Policy Since World War II,* 16th ed. (Washington, D.C.: CQ Press, 2004), 78.

Map 4 Post–Cold War U.S. Military Operations

Richard F. Grimmett, *The War Powers Resolution: After Thirty Years*, CRS Report RL32267 (Washington, D.C.: Congressional Research Service, March 11, 2004).

Map 5 Major Ongoing Conflicts in the Middle East and South Asia

In part, from consultation with Robert J. Lieber, professor of government and foreign service at Georgetown University.

Map 7 Department of Defense Regional Commands

U.S. Department of Defense, www.defenselink.mil/specials/unifiedcommand.

Map 8 NATO Expansion

Wikipedia: The Free Encyclopedia, s.v. "NATO," en.wikipedia.org/wiki/NATO.

Map 9 Nuclear Threats and U.S. Defense Installations

"Department of Defense Base Structure Report: A Summary of DoD's Real Property Inventory" (Washington, D.C.: Office of the Deputy Under Secretary of Defense, Installations and Environment, fiscal year 2003 baseline), www.defenselink.mil/pubs/almanac/almanac/Graphics/BSR_03.pdf.

Map 10 U.S. Foreign Economic Relations

U.S. Department of the Treasury, Office of Foreign Assets Control, www.ustreas.gov/offices/eotffc/ofac/sanctions/index.html; International Trade Administration, www.ita.doc.gov/td/industry/otea/usfth/tabcon.html, Table 9; United States Agency for International Development, U.S. Overseas Loans and Grants ("The Greenbook"), qesdb.cdie.org/gbk/home.html.

Map 11 Freedom in the World, 2004

"Freedom in the World, 2004: Global Freedom Gains Amid Terror, Uncertainty" (Washington, D.C.: Freedom House, 2004), www.freedomhouse.org/research/freeworld/2004/table2004.pdf.

Photo Credits

Author Citations Index

Note: Tables, figures, and notes are indicated by *t, f,* and *n,* respectively.

Subject Index

Note: Tables, figures, photos, and notes are indicated by *t, f, p,* and *n,* respectively.